FORGOTTEN CIVILIZATION

———

"Schoch is a true scientist, following the data wherever it leads, heedless of political pressures or worn-out paradigms. His redating of the Sphinx in 1991 launched the New Archaeology. *Forgotten Civilization* distills all that has happened since into a simple conclusion: that solar activity ended the last cycle of high culture and may destroy ours in turn. Schoch is no scaremonger, no hawker of a pet theory. What we do with this knowledge is up to us, but once digested, it changes everything."

JOSCELYN GODWIN, AUTHOR OF
ATLANTIS AND THE CYCLES OF TIME

FORGOTTEN CIVILIZATION

NEW DISCOVERIES ON THE SOLAR-INDUCED DARK AGE

Revised and Expanded Edition

Robert M. Schoch, Ph.D.,
with Catherine Ulissey

Inner Traditions
Rochester, Vermont

Inner Traditions
One Park Street
Rochester, Vermont 05767
www.InnerTraditions.com

Cataloging-in-Publication Data for this title is available from the Library of Congress

ISBN 978-1-64411-292-2 (print)
ISBN 978-1-64411-293-9 (ebook)

Printed and bound in China by Reliance Printing Co., Ltd.

10 9 8 7 6 5 4 3

Photo insert layout by Catherine Ulissey
Text design by Jack Nichols and layout by Debbie Glogover

This book was typeset in Garamond Premier Pro with ITC Avant Garde Gothic
Std, Gill Sans MT Pro, Optima LT Std, and Copperplate Gothic Std used as
display typefaces

To send correspondence to the author of this book, mail a first-class letter to the
author c/o Inner Traditions • Bear & Company, One Park Street, Rochester, VT
05767, and we will forward the communication, or contact the author directly
through his website **www.robertschoch.com**.

A Note on the Authorship of the Revised and Expanded Edition of This Book

The actual text was penned by me, Robert M. Schoch, and the first edition carried only my name on the title page. However, during our years together, Katie and I have been (and remain) close collaborators regarding the material contained within this book. This has been all the more so since the first edition was published in 2012. Therefore, I believe it is only fitting that she be given credit for all that she has contributed, as this book is truly a product of our joint efforts. Thus, the title page now carries the authorship of "Robert M. Schoch, Ph.D., with Catherine Ulissey" at my insistence. However, I have maintained the first person throughout, and I want to keep the dedication that I included in the first edition, which reads:

I dedicate this book to my beloved wife,
Catherine (Katie) Ulissey.
She has truly been the inspiration and driving force
behind it. As is evident in the pages that follow, this book
could not have been written without her.

ACKNOWLEDGMENTS

A special thanks goes to Grzegorz Popławski, who invited me to participate in a conference in Warsaw, Poland, on May 29, 2011, which he organized. The first edition of this book was a direct outgrowth of my presentation there.

I thank Wendell Davis, who has become a cherished friend to Katie and me, for his unwavering encouragement and support. In many ways, and on a personal level, he helped to make this revised edition possible.

C. Alicia Schoch (née Goetz), my mother, was touched by the manuscript of the first edition, which she read in its entirety before she unexpectedly passed away on April 2, 2012. While I was undertaking the revision of this book, my father, Milton R. Schoch, passed away due to COVID-19 on May 14, 2020. Here I want to acknowledge all of the love and support that both of my parents gave me. It is because they provided me with the opportunities that they did when I was a young child, and instilled in me a love of reading, history, and seeking out knowledge, that I pursued the paths that I have, leading to the writing of this book. I also want to acknowledge a few other close family members: my sister, Marguerita (Rita) Schoch; my sons, Nicholas Schoch and Edward Schoch; and my late grandmother, Adriana M. Goetz (née den Turk), who in my youth encouraged my fascination with ancient cultures.

I appreciate the care Inner Traditions put into the publication of this book, and in particular I thank Mindy Branstetter, Manzanita Carpenter Sanz, Jon Graham, John Hays, Eliza Homick, Jeanie Levitan, Erica Robinson, and Patricia Rydle.

Since the first edition of this book was published in 2012, my longtime colleague and friend, John Anthony West (1932–2018) passed away. It was J.A.W. who first introduced me to the issue of the true age and origins of the Great Sphinx in the late 1980s. That

Milton R. Schoch (*left*, 1931–2020) and C. Alicia Schoch (*right*, 1932–2012), parents of Robert M. Schoch; photograph taken in December 2010. (Photograph courtesy of R. Schoch and C. Ulissey.)

introduction to a geological mystery (How could the Sphinx have been so severely weathered and eroded by rain and water if it dates back to only circa 2500 BCE, long after arid Sahara conditions had become established in the vicinity of the Sphinx?) changed the course of my life.

> I can think of no major valid scientific or scholarly theory in place today that has not undergone a long process of development involving correction, winnowing, refinement and revision. The quest to redate the Sphinx is no different.
>
> JOHN ANTHONY WEST
> SERPENT IN THE SKY (1993 EDITION, PAGE 225)

Finally, and it may seem silly to some, but there are a few other living entities I wish to acknowledge, for I carry them with me in my heart. "Mighty" was a tree in our local neighborhood that was cut down, literally, by the authorities in its prime. With its roots continuously endeavoring to regrow, Mighty always was and continues to be an inspiration for Katie and me. And I thank a few exceptional cats, all of whom have passed away but were there for me in companionship during different periods of my life: Tinkerbell, Thomas the Cat, Rowan, Tabby, and Daryl. Their souls were precious, loving, and unique.

CONTENTS

PREFACE TO THE REVISED AND EXPANDED EDITION

Initially, I was hesitant to produce a revised edition of *Forgotten Civilization*. For me, it is in some ways easier to start fresh and write a new book (and I have several in mind). However, *Forgotten Civilization* has found a wide audience, and I feel that at this point, nearly a decade since its original publication, readers deserve an updated version while keeping the tenor and feel of the original edition (first published in 2012). With this in mind, the original text (chapters 1 through 14 and appendices 1 through 5) has been kept intact. I have incorporated selected updates in these chapters, but none of these chapters has been fully rewritten.

The major addition to this revised and expanded edition of the book is chapter 15. In this new chapter, I discuss various developments that have taken place, evidence that has come forward, which supplement and reinforce the major themes of *Forgotten Civilization*. Now more than ever, I stand by the data and analyses that I present below. True civilization existed at the end of the last ice age but was decimated by the natural catastrophes—namely, solar outbursts—that brought the last ice age to a sudden end, circa 9700 BCE. Today it is imperative that we learn from the past, as our active and sometimes unstable Sun is posed to unleash another major solar outburst, the likes of which we have never experienced in modern times. (The Carrington Event, discussed in chapter 12, is a minor herald of what the future will bring.)

While going through this revised and expanded version of *Forgotten Civilization,* I continue to be impressed by how much we do not know, how much we do not understand, and thus how much there is still to learn. Relative to some of the material in chapter 14 in particular, I think of the early scientists working with electricity in the seventeenth and eighteenth centuries. They knew of electricity primarily in such forms as static electricity, spontaneous sparking, and lightning. How many people in circa 1740 could have imagined how we would tame, control, and use electricity for everything from cooking and heating to communicating through the internet and smartphones? In the future, how much better might we understand some of the topics discussed in this book? Topics that are highly controversial today, or even dismissed entirely by conventional mainstream status quo thinking, may be accepted as common knowledge in the future. And I wonder how much ancient people may have understood, what knowledge and insights they may have possessed, that have since been forgotten.

As I currently work on the revised and expanded edition of this book, COVID-19 (an illness caused by the 2019 novel coronavirus, also known as 2019-nCoV) is spreading around the globe. Here in Boston, Massachusetts, voluntary curfews, "stay at home" orders, and other measures have been put into place. Working on this revision, the following quotation came to mind.

> Here was a way to compensate for current unhappiness, by research into relics of the remote past, by exploring the remains of antiquity. (Wandrei 1948, 125)

And "by exploring the remains of antiquity" I believe we can improve our situation today.

ROBERT M. SCHOCH
BOSTON, MASSACHUSETTS, USA

A Note Regarding Dates

A number of different systems are currently in use for dating years; for instance, AD 2021 = 2021 CE.

AD (A.D.) refers to *Anno Domini,* "in [the] year of [the] Lord" where the "Lord" commonly refers to the figure Jesus Christ of Christianity.

CE typically refers to "Common Era" or "Current Era," removing the explicitly religious aspects of the date.

BC (B.C.) is commonly held to be an abbreviation for "Before Christ."

BCE refers to "Before the Common Era" or "Before the Current Era." Thus, for example, 9700 BC = 9700 BCE.

In this book I have used the nonreligious CE for Common Era and BCE for Before the Common Era, except in quoted material.

PREFACE TO THE
FIRST EDITION

Forgotten Civilization. A few notes on the title, which was the brain-child of my wife, Katie, are in order.

To place things in context, when I was a youngster, the British art historian Kenneth Clark (1903–1983) wrote and produced an influential thirteen-part television documentary series (first aired in 1969 by the British Broadcasting Corporation) and accompanying book, both of which were titled *Civilisation: A Personal View.* We were enthralled by the TV series and digested every word of the book, falling under the spell of this uncommon arbiter of taste and excellence, accepting his pronouncements without question. Clark codified for a generation the common concept of what civilization (being British, Clark spelled it as "civilisation") was all about, and his views endure among much of the public (or at least the Western European and American public) to this day. For his contributions, Clark received the title Lord Clark of Saltwood (Saltwood is a castle in Kent that Clark purchased in 1955).

In actuality, Clark had a rather narrow view of what exactly constituted civilization. His book and series concentrated on Western European Christian civilization from the period of about 1100 CE through the nineteenth century and had a decidedly English slant to it. About the concept of civilization more generally, leading up to the apparent height of civilization as he viewed it, Clark wrote:

There have been times in the history of man when the earth seems suddenly to have grown warmer or more radio-active. . . . I don't put that forward as a scientific proposition, but the fact remains that three or four times in history man has made a leap forward that would have been unthinkable under ordinary evolutionary conditions. One such time was about the year 3000 BC, when quite suddenly civilisation appeared, not only in Egypt and Mesopotamia but in the Indus valley; another was in the late sixth century BC, when there was not only the miracle of Ionia and Greece—philosophy, science, art, poetry, all reaching a point that wasn't reached again for 2000 years—but also in India a spiritual enlightenment that has perhaps never been equalled. Another was round about the year 1100. It seems to have affected the whole world; but its strongest and most dramatic effect was in Western Europe—where it was most needed. It was like a Russian spring. In every branch of life—action, philosophy, organization, technology—there was an extraordinary outpouring of energy, an intensification of existence. (Clark 1969, 33; ellipses in the original)

My contention, as I will develop in this book, is that the sudden appearance of civilization circa 3000 BCE of which Clark speaks is not the first appearance of civilization. Rather it is the reemergence of civilization after some six thousand or more years. True, unambiguous civilization is evident during the period of circa 10,000 BCE, thousands of years earlier than the dynastic Egyptians and their contemporaries in Mesopotamia and the Indus Valley. This earlier flowering of civilization has been generally forgotten by humanity, although allusions to it are still to be found in sacred scriptures, traditional legends, and ancient texts; the Garden of Eden, tales of a golden age, and Plato's recounting of Atlantis may all be referencing this primordial civilization. Now it is time to recognize its legacy.

. . . the Day of the Lord is going to come like a thief in the night. It is when people are saying, "How quiet and peaceful it is" that the worst suddenly happens, as suddenly as labour pains come on a pregnant woman; and there will be no way for anybody to evade it.

THE JERUSALEM BIBLE,
1 THESSALONIANS 5:2–3

The fourth angel emptied his bowl over the sun and it was made to scorch people with its flames. . . .

THE JERUSALEM BIBLE,
REVELATION 16:8

1

A WHIRLWIND TRIP

How could I say no? Here was an invitation to join a short expedition to one of the most remote locations on Earth. The Chilean ambassador to the United Arab Emirates, Jean-Paul Tarud-Kuborn, who befriended us when I spoke at the first International Conference on Ancient Studies in Dubai (UAE), November 29 and 30, 2008, had invited Katie (Catherine E. Ulissey, my fiancée at the time) and me to not only visit him and his family in Santiago but also to join him on a short expedition to Easter Island (which has been Chilean territory since its annexation in 1888). Honestly, I experienced some trepidation when initially considering the trip. On the one hand, this little speck of land is virtually synonymous with ancient mysteries, which for the last twenty years I had devoted much of my life to exploring around the globe, from Egypt to Peru to Japan. Easter Island was a definite on my list of "must see" destinations. On the other hand, it was a long way to travel for such a short excursion; the plan was to spend just seventy-three hours on the island. What could I accomplish in such a short period of time? But Katie convinced me we should take advantage of the opportunity. So it was a go. In hindsight, those seventy-three hours on Easter Island changed my life in more than one way!

Something that attracted me personally to Easter Island was its remoteness, for here I reasoned might be preserved ancient traditions that elsewhere were lost or transformed by contact and conquest. Apparently isolated from the rest of the world for centuries or millennia—located in the South Pacific over two thousand kilometers from the nearest inhabited island—this tiny triangular piece of real estate (just 24.6 kilometers long and 12.3 kilometers at its widest point), was unknown to Westerners until Dutch explorers under the command of Jacob Roggeveen spotted it on Easter Sunday 1722. Easter Island is the home of hundreds of gigantic stone heads and torsos, known as *moai,* that adorn the island. It is also the source of mysterious glyphs inscribed on pieces of wood; known as the *rongorongo* script, just over two dozen original tablets and objects (such as an inscribed wooden staff) have been preserved and are now scattered among museums around the world. So far undeciphered, although as I will discuss later in this book various gallant attempts have been made, they have been one of the great enigmas of linguistics. Might the moai and the rongorongo texts, I wondered, preserve some kind of legacy, some kind of message, from remote antiquity?

On the evening of December 28, 2009, Katie and I boarded a flight to Miami, and from Miami we flew to Santiago, Chile. Upon our arrival in Santiago the next morning, the ambassador and his wife, Valentina Troni, met us at the airport. Initially, we were to stay with them and their family, and indeed we visited extensively, but because other family members were also in town, we were graciously accommodated at a friend's house, even as they profusely apologized for the inconvenience to us. This turned out to be a most fortunate inconvenience, as the friend (who quickly became our friend too) was a native Easter Island (Rapanui) artist living in Santiago, and furthermore his father (who just happened to be visiting him at the time and, initially unbeknownst to us, would travel with us to Easter Island) was a former governor of the island. (Rapa Nui and Easter Island are used somewhat interchangeably for the name of the island; the term Rapanui is used for the people and their culture.)

We spent several days dividing our time between hiking in the Andes Mountains on the outskirts of Santiago and absorbing Easter Island lore. Katie and I had already prepared ourselves over the preceding months by poring through and digesting all the books and literature about the island we could lay our hands on; we were determined to maximize our experience. Especially exciting to me was the collection of hundreds of old photos that our host shared with us, showing many of the moai and other ancient stone structures on the island before their modern restorations. Also included with the photos were numerous vignettes of life on the island in an earlier time. From a scientific point of view, such documentation is invaluable.

On New Year's Eve, Katie and I participated in a fantastic costume ball hosted by the ambassador's mother (who joined the expedition to Easter Island, along with various other friends and family). New Year's Day was a time to relax and invigorate ourselves for the days to come. Early on the morning of Saturday, January 2, we headed for the Santiago airport to catch our flight. Traveling over five hours across the majestic Pacific, we touched down on Easter Island at about 1:00 p.m. local time.

The next three-plus days were wild, crazy, and wonderful. A magic carpet ride, as Katie likes to say. Reviewing in my mind or looking at the thousands of photos we shot, I am not sure how we fit so much in. We toured the island from end to end, using a small private bus under the guidance of another former governor, who also happened to be an extremely prominent Rapanui archaeologist. The moai and the *ahu* (platforms on which some of the moai were erected) were even more incredible and awe inspiring than I had imagined from simply reading about them and viewing photographs. I have learned over the years that there is never any substitute for seeing the real thing—a lesson continually reinforced on every trip I take, be it to a new area (as Easter Island was for me at the time) or old familiar territory (as parts of Egypt feel for me now after so many trips there). But it was not just the moai that struck me, for they are only part of the landscape, the seemingly primeval complex of Easter Island. There are also the quarries from which the moai were carved, the numerous petroglyphs (rock carvings, many representing strange "birdmen"), the low and thick stone buildings ("houses" found at the stone village and ceremonial center of Orongo on the southwestern tip of the island), the spherical stone known as the navel of the world, the natural caves found across this volcanic island, the ancient volcanic calderas themselves, and of course the inexplicable rongorongo script. In many ways, it was too much to digest in three days, and so I simply took it all in, absorbing. I would try my best to make sense of it later.

Indeed, trying to make sense of the world is what drives me. I try not to readily accept simple pat answers uncritically. Studying so-called ancient mysteries, I have found that sometimes they are not quite so mysterious, as when data are misinterpreted (and, to put it bluntly, at times outright fraud is involved), while in other cases conventional and mainstream explanations serve to obscure and gloss over genuine mysteries. Actually, it seems to me, the latter is all too often the situation, as when those with vested interests feel they must preserve the status quo. (We will explore this topic further in the pages that follow.) In the case of Easter Island, it quickly became apparent to me that the standard archaeological explanations—that the island was first colonized by Polynesians about 1,500 years ago, who erected the moai, carved the petroglyphs, constructed the stone houses, and in the process brought ecological devastation to their tiny island such that it was a poor and impoverished people whom the Europeans encountered in 1722—were fundamentally flawed.

I am a trained geologist (Ph.D. in geology and geophysics from Yale University, 1983), and studying the varying levels of weathering and erosion and the degree of sediment built up around the moai (some that have been excavated were buried in up to six meters of sediment), I quickly became convinced that the standard story was improbable, to say the least. The high levels of sedimentation around certain moai suggested a much greater age than a mere 1,500 years. And what was the purpose of the low, thick, stone houses that oddly resemble modern bunkers or fallout shelters? Why did the indigenous people sometimes occupy the natural caves of the island? What about the stories of giants inhabiting the island in past times? And, perhaps most mysterious of all, what was the meaning of the rongorongo texts?

These are questions Katie and I pondered while we explored the island, but we had no ready answers. (I further discuss all of these topics later in this book.) One thing for certain, however, is that we did not find some of the conventional explanations very convincing. For instance, was the carving of the moai, perhaps ostensibly as part of an ancestor cult, really just "busywork" thought up by the chiefs and leaders as a way to keep the masses occupied and happy, so as to bond the elements of society together and avoid social turmoil? Was the rongorongo simply an indigenous eighteenth-century imitation of European writing? If this were indeed the case, then the rongorongo texts would be stripped of any antiquity, being a few centuries old at most, and would have little significance—a mere childish attempt by the "primitive" Easter Islanders to emulate the superior Westerners. What if, instead, the Easter Islanders were the guardians and keepers of ancient treasures? Conventional Western archaeologists, and their Western-trained Rapanui counterparts, are quick to dismiss such a notion (which, in my mind, elevates the status of the Rapanui) as mere fantasy.

Besides exploring the archaeological wonders of Easter Island, we also took in as much of the modern and traditional Rapanui ambiance as is possible in three days. I had the honor of meeting the current governor. We attended a "traditional" dance performance. (Honestly, I am not sure how traditional it was as much of the indigenous Easter Island culture was eradicated by European contact and has since been reconstructed based primarily on imported Polynesian models.) We dined on the local food. We hired a small outboard motorboat and cruised along the coast of the island. I even managed to make it briefly, after taking a dunk in the Pacific while trying to step from the boat as strong waves surged, to a little islet (tiny island) off the coast of the main island. I wanted to explore firsthand the pristine volcanic rocks and an ancient cave preserved on the islet.

On a very personal note, Katie and I were married on Easter Island—twice! During the afternoon of Monday, January 4, 2010, in the presence of an ambassador, two former governors, and a senior elder of the island, we were united during a civil ceremony at the appropriate Chilean government office on Easter Island. Then it was off to visit more moai and archaeological sites. That evening we were married again, this time in a traditional Rapanui ceremony presided over by the island elder who had attended our civil ceremony. We were lent traditional costumes adorned with feathers. Our skin and faces were decorated with paint, some made from the mud and minerals of the island, and we were crowned with feathered headdresses. I was allowed to borrow an antique bark-cloth cape, passed down through five generations, for the occasion. We were married barefoot, as we had always dreamed, in contact with the Earth, our Earth, and under the open sky, connecting with the cosmos. Not knowing the Rapanui language, we could not understand a word of the ceremony, but somehow the meaning came through. A feast in our honor followed the ceremony. It was a magical experience. We will be forever grateful for the hospitality and open hearts shown us. It was a unique honor to be the first couple married on Rapa Nui in the year 2010.

Tuesday morning, our last day on the island, we visited El Museo Antropológico Padre Sebastián Englert, where many fantastic, and I would add, somewhat inexplicable, artifacts from the island are housed, including a strange, alien-looking, small female moai carved of basalt. Then, our bags already packed, it was off to the airport to catch a 2:00 p.m. flight to Santiago. In Santiago, we transferred to a flight bound for New York City, and from there, caught our flight to Boston, Massachusetts, arriving home on the afternoon of January 6, 2010.

It was a dizzyingly exuberant trip; we were happy but exhausted. Flying back to the United States, there was no doubt in my mind that the trip had been worthwhile. Katie was right in urging we should go. But it was not until after we returned that I realized how worthwhile the trip really was. Not only had we been married in one of the most exotic locations on Earth, with a genuine indigenous ceremony; not only had we explored enduring archaeological mysteries firsthand, but for me the seventy-three hours on Easter Island helped crystallize and reignite two decades of contemplating the dawn and demise of ancient civilization. It all came into perspective about two weeks after we returned from Easter Island, with a simple yet profound observation made by Katie.

One evening, my mind still racing from all I had seen on Easter Island—and perplexed at the genuine enigmas and disgusted by the conventional explanations (or should I say nonexplanations)—Katie suggested that we rewatch a video titled *Symbols of an Alien Sky* (Talbott 2009; see also Talbott and Thornhill 2005). One portion of the video discusses the work of Anthony L. Peratt, a plasma physicist associated with Los Alamos National Laboratory in New Mexico, who became interested in ancient petroglyphs (Peratt 2003). I already knew of Peratt's work and indeed had met him at a conference many years earlier. In a nutshell (we will review his work in more detail later in this book), Peratt noticed that many petroglyphs found around the world appear to record the shapes that would have been seen in the sky if there had been a major solar outburst—a plasma discharge (ionized particles and associated electrical and magnetic phenomena)—in ancient times. If our Sun discharged a huge ball of plasma toward us, it would have dire consequences for Earth, including life and humanity, as the surface of the planet would be literally fried by the incoming electrical currents. Nothing like this has been seen in modern times, although small plasma discharges, known as coronal mass ejections (CMEs), are a regular feature of the modern Sun. However, as a geologist, I was aware that going back in time, the Sun has had periods of much higher activity, including at the end of the last ice age (circa 9700 BCE). Peratt and his colleagues postulated a major solar outburst in ancient times, but they did not specify a precise date or dates. They had also not considered one other very important thing.

Katie's simple but profound observation, while we watched the documentary, was that the rongorongo glyphs look remarkably similar to the petroglyphs that Peratt believes record plasma discharges and configurations, due to a major solar outburst, seen in the ancient skies. Could the rongorongo be a text, a scientific text if you will, that records in meticulous detail what was happening in the skies of long ago? Were the Easter Islanders in fact the keepers of an ancient, long forgotten, knowledge?

I was struck, as if by plasma itself. Many isolated threads, topics I had pursued for years and decades, suddenly began to fall into place. My work on redating the Great Sphinx of Egypt (discussed in chapter 2) indicates that civilization and sophisticated culture date back thousands of years earlier than mainstream archaeologists have generally accepted. The same story seems to hold true for the oldest Easter Island moai, which may be thousands of years older than conventionally believed. And within months of visiting Easter Island, Katie and I found ourselves in Turkey inspecting the incredibly sophisticated and also incredibly ancient—dating back twelve thousand years—site of Göbekli Tepe, confirming and reinforcing my work on the remote antiquity of early civilization. But the issue has always been, What could have happened to such an ancient, forgotten civilization? Why is there such a paucity of evidence for it?

Within weeks of our return, spurred by Katie's discovery, all that I had studied for so long came into sharp focus as the pieces began to fall into place, and a new story of a very ancient and long-forgotten civilization emerged. This is not another tale of lost continents and technologically advanced science-fiction-like beings loosely based on the overinterpretation of a few myths and legends. This is a story that combines the evidence of modern geology, geophysics, climatology, astrophysics, archaeology, comparative mythology, and many other disciplines. As we shall see, the catastrophes that occurred nearly twelve thousand years ago, eradicating this early, forgotten civilization, appear to be on the verge of occurring once again. Furthermore, those very ancient peoples may have known something about the world and the cosmos that has since been lost. But if we can break free from the shackles and blinders of conventional status quo paradigms and worldviews, we may be able to regain this essential knowledge.

In this book, we will explore these and related topics. Our story reaches back into the remote past and continues into the future. We need to understand multiple lines of evidence that together weave a new view of the origins of civilization, ancient history, our future, and the dynamics of the planet we live on. This is truly a grand puzzle with many parts. We will begin with a key piece, the Great Sphinx.

UPDATE: Katie's discovery that the rongorongo glyphs are very similar to the petroglyphs that Peratt and his group had been studying for years, and that both are ultimately representations of plasma discharges and configurations as would be seen in the sky during a major solar outburst, was confirmed by a member of Peratt's team in an email sent to us. It turns out that they had independently made this discovery some years earlier but had purposefully not published it.

Relative to the rongorongo depicting plasma configurations seen by ancient people, Changizi et al. (2006) have made the case that "The Structures of Letters and Symbols throughout Human History Are Selected to Match Those Found in Objects in Natural Scenes" (which is the title of their paper). Certainly, plasma configurations during a solar outburst would present exceptional "objects" and "scenes" to memorialize in a "script." Furthermore, other researchers have connected the rongorongo to the sky and stars (see, for instance, Dietrich 1999; Esen-Baur 2011), although not explicitly to solar outbursts and plasma configurations (other than Peratt and his team in their unpublished work).

2

THE GREAT SPHINX

I have to admit that the Mena House (named in honor of Menes, the legendary first dynastic pharaoh of a united Egypt) is my favorite hotel in the Greater Cairo area. I love the nineteenth-century ambiance and the history. In a land where the history overwhelms you, this is a hotel that boasts a story of its own; it is a place where kings, princes, presidents, Hollywood royalty, and celebrities from all spheres have stayed. But, more than anything else about the Mena House, I love the view. Book the right room and you can have a private balcony overlooking the Great Pyramid, the only surviving wonder of the ancient world.

The Mena House is located in Giza (a city unto itself that forms part of modern Greater Cairo), just a half kilometer north of the Great Pyramid. Making your way out of the gated entrance, you can stroll the ever-bustling streets to the pyramids. But be prepared for the army of venders who will quickly descend on you, plying their ancient trade of hawking trinkets and fake antiquities. If you don't feel like walking, there will be plenty of cabs for hire, as well as camels and horses.

Once situated far from any settlements, the Giza pyramids were built on the edge of the Sahara, the seemingly endless expanse of beautiful and forbidding dune-covered desert that stretches across the length of North Africa. Originally, the Mena House was a royal lodge used by Isma'il Pasha (1830–1895), who reigned as the Ottoman *khedive* (viceroy) of Egypt and Sudan from 1863 to 1879. Here the khedive and his guests rested and refreshed themselves when off on

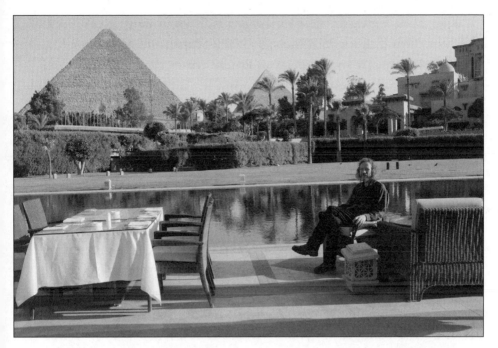

Figure 2.1. Robert Schoch relaxing at one of the restaurants at the Mena House, July 2016. In the background is the Great Pyramid (*left*), the Second Pyramid (*center back*), and the old section of the hotel (*far right*). (Photograph courtesy of R. Schoch and C. Ulissey.)

a hunting expedition in the desert or paying a visit to the pyramids. Of course, today the pyramids still sit on the edge of the Sahara (the desert has not moved), but roads crisscross and encircle the pyramids, which are quickly being walled in and surrounded by the ever-expanding modern neighborhoods necessitated by the burgeoning population of Greater Cairo.

The pyramids, and the Great Pyramid in particular, have justly earned their reputation as being among the most amazing marvels of the ancient world. Perfectly aligned to the cardinal points (the Great Pyramid is oriented to true north with a tolerance that could not be matched again until the late nineteenth and early twentieth centuries) and built of multi-ton stone blocks with a precision that defies easy explanation, the pyramids remain an enigma on many levels. Modern engineers and common folk alike wonder how they were built. I myself have taken a great interest in the pyramids, even writing two books about them (Schoch with McNally 2003; Schoch and McNally 2005). However, my first love on the Giza Plateau is something else, something very nearby: the Great Sphinx.

THE SPHINX AND I

The Great Sphinx of Egypt, perhaps the most famous statue in the world, has a very personal meaning to me. The Sphinx and I have a long history together. For over thirty years, the Sphinx has influenced and shaped my life, haunting me and speaking to me. I was first introduced to the problem of the age of the Sphinx in late 1989 by the "independent Egyptologist" John Anthony West (1932–2018), perhaps best known for his studies and popularization of the Egyptological work of the philosopher and mathematician R. A. Schwaller de Lubicz (1887–1961) and for his guidebook titled *The Traveler's Key to Ancient Egypt* (1985). Schwaller de Lubicz had suggested, in an almost offhand way, that the Great Sphinx was eroded by water, not wind and sand (see West 1993). West realized that if this were true, the implications would be profound. But who could confirm the nature of the weathering and erosion on the Sphinx? A geologist, of course! So West was on the lookout for an "open-minded" geologist who might critically and objectively take a look at the Great Sphinx.

A colleague of mine, Robert Eddy, an English and Rhetoric professor who just happened to be teaching in the same college as I in the late 1980s, had met West while teaching in Cairo. He knew that West was looking for a geologist, so he arranged for West to give a lecture at the university and then invited me to join him and West for dinner (West 2007). It only took one discussion and I was hooked.

The following summer, West and I traveled to Egypt. I first met the Great Sphinx face-to-face on June 17, 1990. Since then, I have been back many times, more times than I remember, not only to study the Great Sphinx but also to investigate other ancient mysteries in the land of the pharaohs as well.

It turned out that the issue of the weathering and erosion on the

Sphinx was fairly simple and straightforward from a geological point of view. After only a couple of trips to Egypt, intensively studying the statue and its surroundings and collecting underground seismic data with geophysicist Thomas Dobecki (discussed in this chapter in the section "Redating the Great Sphinx" and see Dobecki and Schoch 1992; see also chapter 2, "The Sands of Time," by R. Schoch in Schoch and Bauval 2017, 35–88), I felt confident enough to announce my results to the scientific community—and the world at large. At the October 1991 annual meeting of the Geological Society of America (GSA) I presented the evidence that the origins of the Great Sphinx must date back to at least the 7000 BCE to 5000 BCE range, or possibly earlier (this was allowed only after a formal abstract, submitted with West, was accepted based on positive professional peer review; see Schoch and West 1991). I made my case using scientific analyses, comparing erosion and weathering profiles around the Sphinx to the ancient climatic history of Egypt. I was immediately bombarded by the media and lambasted by establishment archaeologists and Egyptologists. My life has never been the same since that fateful conference. A 1993 NBC documentary titled *The Mystery of the Sphinx,* hosted by the late Charlton Heston and featuring me describing my research on-site in Egypt, was viewed by millions and received an Emmy Award (Sphinx Project 1993; the DVD version currently available has been reedited from the original show and most regrettably includes supplementary/extraneous material that detracts from the strong science initially presented).

Many people know me, or believe they know me (or more accurately, know of me), due to the controversy over the age of the Sphinx that my research has engendered. I was even told by one writer and filmmaker that she knew my work better than I knew it myself! Be that as it may, here I will share my story of the Great Sphinx—and my work with her (to me the Sphinx has always been feminine), as I know it. First, a little background information on this icon of antiquity (for further information and an update on the Great Sphinx, see chapter 15, page 309, as well as my various papers and books listed in the bibliography, particularly Schoch and Bauval 2017).

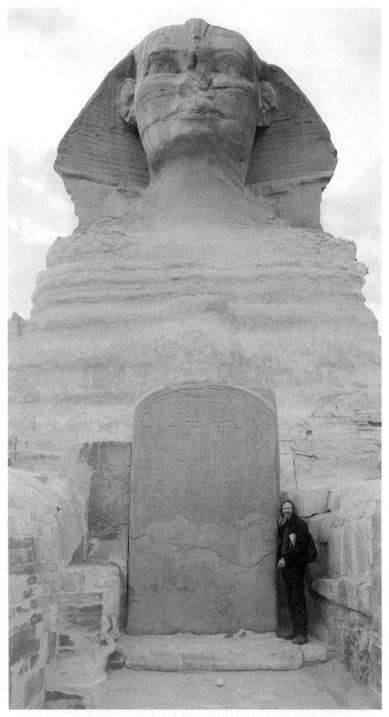

Figure 2.2. Robert Schoch next to the granite stela attributed to Thutmose IV between the paws of the Great Sphinx.

(Photograph courtesy of R. Schoch and C. Ulissey.)

HISTORY OF AN ENIGMA

Before we proceed further, it is important to understand the context of the Great Sphinx, in large part because conventional archaeologists heavily rely on this context to date the Sphinx. Their reasoning essentially comes down to this: the Sphinx is surrounded by structures that date to about 2500 BCE, therefore it too must belong to this period. Of course, if you give it a little thought, this is not necessarily true. Think of Rome. Here is a city that traces its history, according to tradition, back to the year 753 BCE. It contains magnificent architectural wonders, statues, and monuments spanning over two thousand years. Imagine if archaeologists thousands of years from now found both the Coliseum (first century CE) and the remains of the National Monument of Victor Emmanuel II (early twentieth century). Would they blithely conclude, since these structures are relatively close to each other, that they both fit into the same context and therefore are of the same age?

Returning to Egypt, the Great Sphinx is located on the eastern edge of the Giza Plateau, also known as the Pyramids Plateau, on the west bank of the Nile across from Cairo. The Sphinx sits southeast of the Great Pyramid, attributed to the Fourth Dynasty pharaoh Khufu (Cheops, circa 2550 BCE), and due east of the Second Pyramid, the pyramid generally attributed to the pharaoh Khafre (Khafra, Chephren, Khephren), possibly the son or brother of Khufu. The Second Pyramid is just slightly smaller than the Great Pyramid. A third major pyramid, though considerably smaller than the other two, is also located on the Giza Plateau; it is attributed to the pharaoh Menkaura (Menkaure, Mycerinus), possibly a grandson or son of Khufu. Thus, according to standard Egyptological thinking, the Giza pyramids all date to around the period of 2500 BCE. According to the same Egyptologists, the Sphinx is clearly "associated" with the pyramids, so it must be about the same age. They do not consider the possibility that the Sphinx could be much older than the pyramids—that the site could have been used and reused, new structures being added in the vicinity of much older structures. Or, even more heretical, could the pyramids themselves be misdated? Here it is important to point out that it is the three Giza pyramids that various researchers, most notably Robert Bauval (Bauval and Gilbert 1994; Bauval and Brophy 2011; Schoch and Bauval 2017), have correlated with the belt of the constellation Orion (representative of, in some guises, the Egyptian god Osiris). Furthermore, the precise correlation with Orion may not pertain to Egypt in 2500 BCE, but to a much earlier period—possibly going back to 12,000 BCE to 10,000 BCE (Bauval and Brophy 2011; Schoch and Bauval 2017). This is not to say that the pyramids themselves are necessarily physically this old, although portions of them, such as the bases and underground chambers, might well be extremely ancient. Even if the pyramids themselves were constructed around 2550–2450 BCE, they apparently mark or memorialize a very old period in time. This independent evidence of extreme antiquity on the Giza Plateau can only bolster my conclusion that the Sphinx is incredibly old.

The Great Sphinx is truly great in stature, being approximately twenty meters tall and seventy meters long. (The original length of the statue is difficult to determine because of the later repairs.) It is carved out of solid bedrock limestone and faces due east. On the vernal and autumnal equinoxes the Sphinx is precisely aligned with the rising Sun. On these mornings the first rays of daylight strike directly on her face. Only the head sits above the ground level; to carve the body, the ancients had to cut down into the rock, and thus the Great Sphinx actually sits in what is known as the Sphinx Enclosure, or Sphinx Ditch. Immediately in front of the Sphinx, at a lower level (lower elevation), sits the Sphinx Temple. While carving out the core body of the Sphinx, huge multi-ton blocks were removed from the Sphinx Enclosure and assembled as the Sphinx Temple, so the original Sphinx Temple is as old as the core body of the Great Sphinx.

The traditional academics of the late twentieth century attributed the Great Sphinx to the pharaoh Khafre, builder of the Second Pyramid, circa 2500 BCE. In contrast, some classical Egyptologists of the nineteenth and early twentieth centuries dated the Great Sphinx to an earlier predynastic period, foreshadowing my own work (see Schoch and Bauval 2017, 57). (For a discussion of how the Great Sphinx may have been referred to during the Old Kingdom, see Schoch and Bauval 2017;

regarding the form of the Sphinx prior to dynastic times, we now know that it was originally a statue of the goddess Mehit in her guise as a lioness; see this book, chapter 15, page 314.)

A granite stela (or stele) erected between the paws of the Sphinx by Thutmose IV, circa 1400 BCE, when excavated in the nineteenth century, was reported to include in its inscription the name, or at least part of the name, of Khafre. (This portion of the inscription has since flaked away.) This has been variously interpreted to indicate that either Khafre ordered the Sphinx carved or that Khafre ordered the Sphinx renovated, as Thutmose IV did over a millennium later. In reality, however, it is unclear if indeed it was the Fourth Dynasty pharaoh Khafre being named on the stela or what relationship the stela may have suggested that Khafre had to the Sphinx (Schoch and Bauval 2017). The bottom line is, the Thutmose IV stela provides no definitive evidence of when, or by whom, the Sphinx was constructed. Also possibly bearing on the origins of the Great Sphinx is the so-called Inventory Stela, alternatively known as the Stela of Cheops's (Khufu's) Daughter. Although the actual stela dates to the seventh or sixth century BCE, it purports to be a copy of an Old Kingdom text (Schoch and Bauval 2017, 118–23; Seyfzadeh and Schoch 2018). According to the Inventory Stela, the Great Sphinx was already in existence during the reign of Khufu. Indeed, Khufu is credited with repairing the Sphinx after it was struck by lightning (see further discussion in chapter 15). Modern Egyptologists generally dismiss the Inventory Stela as a Late Period fabrication.

In New Kingdom times (circa 1550 BCE to 1070 BCE or so), the Great Sphinx was sometimes referred to as Horemakhet (Hor-em-akhet, Harmakhet, Harmachis), which can be translated as "Horus of the Horizon" or "Horus in the Horizon," or as Ra-horakhty, translated as "Ra of the Two Horizons." In medieval Arabic times, one appellation given to the Great Sphinx was Abu el-Hol (Abu al-Hol, Abou el Hôl), "Father of Terror(s)" or "The Terrifying One." The name Sphinx is derived from the Greek language and referred originally to the Greek sphinx. Sphinx may come from a Greek word meaning "to strangle," as according to one legend, the Greek sphinx, often depicted as a winged lion with the head of a woman, had the habit of strangling and devouring those who could not answer her riddles. Another interpretation is that the word *sphinx* was derived, possibly through Greeks visiting Egypt, from the ancient Egyptian *Shesep-ankh,* sometimes translated as "living statue" or "living image," a term used to refer to royal statues during the Old Kingdom. The Sphinx is connected to the bedrock—"living rock."

REDATING THE GREAT SPHINX

I have studied extensively the nature and extent of the weathering and erosional features found on the statue directly, as well as the similar features found in the so-called Sphinx Enclosure (as already noted, the Sphinx sits in a hole or quarry, with its body below the level of the plateau behind it) and in the subsurface under and around the Sphinx. I have analyzed as well the numerous repairs to the Sphinx (some of which date back to Old Kingdom times). While my overall general conclusions have not changed since 1991, I have refined my thinking over the years.

Based on my geological analyses, I initially (and I now admit quite conservatively) calculated that the oldest portions of the Sphinx date back to the period of approximately 7000 BCE to 5000 BCE. I arrived at this conclusion through a variety of independent means, such as correlating the nature of the weathering with the climatic history of the area, calculating the amount of rock eroded away on the surface and estimating how long this may have taken, and calibrating the depth of subsurface weathering around and below the Sphinx.

Key to my redating of the Sphinx is the interpretation that the weathering and erosion observed on the body of the Sphinx and the walls of the Sphinx Enclosure is not due to the arid desert conditions found in the region during the last four thousand to five thousand years. Rather, the observed weathering and erosion resulted from rain, precipitation, and water runoff, and sufficient precipitation was available only during pre-Sahara conditions, prior to circa 3000 BCE (Schoch 1992b; Schoch and Bauval 2017, and references cited therein). Other geologists, such as Colin Reader and David Coxill (each working independently of me and also independently of each other; see Coxill 1998;

and Reader 1997/1999) have corroborated my analyses of the nature of the weathering and erosion, concluding that the causative agent was water and not wind and sand (see Schoch 2002; Schoch with McNally 2003; Schoch and Bauval 2017). I must note, however, that while Reader, Coxill, and I agree that the Sphinx was weathered by water and must date to an earlier period than the traditional attribution, we do not all agree on the same age estimate. In particular, Reader has argued that the Sphinx can still be accommodated into a very early dynastic time frame and thus is perhaps only a few hundred years older than the traditional date of circa 2500 BCE. However, I firmly believe that the extent of the erosion and weathering definitively push the core body of the Sphinx into a much more remote period. Furthermore, Reader does not take into adequate account the subsurface data that Dobecki and I collected (see discussion in this section, below, and Schoch and Bauval 2017), data that allow me to calibrate the rate of subsurface weathering and arrive at my age estimate for the Sphinx. My dating places the Sphinx well back into predynastic times, a period when many suppose that the technology and social organization did not exist to create such a monument.

Over the years, various Egyptologists and archaeologists have suggested to me that, yes, the Great Sphinx does show evidence of being weathered and eroded by rain, but this is because heavy rains in fact lasted well into the third millennium BCE. However, I believe this is incorrect, and there is evidence not far from Giza demonstrating just how early the hyperarid climatic conditions of the Sahara Desert set in. Mud-brick tombs called mastabas built on the Saqqara (Sakkara) Plateau, only about a dozen kilometers south of Giza and dated indisputably to circa 2800 BCE, show little if any rain weathering, even though they are built from a much softer and more vulnerable material than limestone and were subject to the same climatic conditions as the Great Sphinx. Mud-brick mastabas would be quickly destroyed by much lighter rainfall than would be required to weather and erode the Sphinx. It simply is not possible that the Sphinx could have been carved after 2800 BCE, the date of the mastabas, yet weathered so badly under the scant rainfall (as indicated must be the case based on the survival of the mud-brick mastabas) that it required extensive repair by Old Kingdom times (the date of the earliest repairs to the Sphinx and Sphinx Temple). It has been suggested to me that perhaps the Saqqara mud-brick mastabas survived in such good condition because they occur on higher ground than the Sphinx and Sphinx Enclosure, which would have been subjected to much more water runoff, even from scant rains. However, after taking this into account, I am still convinced that the mastabas in question are evidence of just how arid the area has been for the last five millennia. The archaeological evidence, in my assessment, does not support the assertion that there was enough rainfall around and after 2500 BCE to weather and erode the Sphinx to the state we observe on the statue.

Even though the Sphinx exhibits water erosion, this erosion was the result of precipitation and rain runoff, not from flooding or the rising of the Nile. Also, the Sphinx was not eroded from standing water sitting in the Sphinx Enclosure. (The idea that the Sphinx sat in a pool of water, or had a moat around it, does not stand up to geological scrutiny; see appendix 1, page 372.) Another important point I should make is that fossil shells, sea urchins, and so forth, can be found on the Giza Plateau, but these have nothing to do with the water erosion seen on the Sphinx. Rather, the fossil sea organisms are millions of years old and have weathered out of the limestone rocks from which the Sphinx, pyramids, and many other structures are built.

As I already mentioned, in the early 1990s I estimated that the oldest portions of the Great Sphinx date back to circa 5000 BCE or perhaps a bit earlier. (As I discuss later in this chapter, the head of the Sphinx is not the original head; it was evidently recarved in dynastic times.) Even as recently as 2007, I wrote, "Concerning my redating of the Sphinx, I emphasize that I am comfortable attributing it to the period of circa 5,000 B.C. or a bit earlier. Could it be considerably older? Based on the geological data, and depending on how one interprets the data, possibly. However, I have never claimed an age for the Great Sphinx prior to the 5,000 B.C. to 7,000 B.C. period" (Schoch 2007, 43).

Since 2007, I have come to modify my opinion on the possible antiquity of the Great Sphinx in the light of more recent data. My initial "conservative" dating of the Great Sphinx to circa 5000 BCE was based on an extreme view of both the surface and subsurface seismic data, attempting to squeeze the data into as short a time frame as possible. Much of this has to do with the seismic data, measuring subsurface weathering, which we collected around the base of the Sphinx (Dobecki and Schoch 1992). Subsurface weathering essentially consists of mineralogical and fabric changes of the rock that occur once the surface is exposed to the atmosphere; to the untrained eye, the rock may or may not look as if it is weathered. Over time, such weathering penetrates progressively farther (deeper) into the rock. This weathering can be detected using seismic wave velocity data.

The Sphinx itself faces east. The northern, southern, and eastern floors of the Sphinx Enclosure are weathered to a depth that varies between 1.8 and 2.5 meters below the surface. The western floor, however, is weathered less deeply, to a maximum of just 1.2 meters. This difference is not due to variations in the rock; the exposed floor of the enclosure on all sides belongs to the same stratum of limestone. Rather, the western floor has been weathering for a shorter period of time. Obviously, it must have been excavated at a considerably later date.

There are two excavated walls at the western end of the Sphinx Enclosure—two tiers, if you will. The higher wall, which lies farther west, is deeply coved and fissured by rain and water runoff. It must have been carved out when Egypt's climate was wet and rainy, well before the Old Kingdom. The second, lower wall, which is closer to the Sphinx's rump, shows much less precipitation weathering. It was along the base of this lower wall that the western seismic line, showing a depth of only 1.2 meters of weathering, was taken. The lower wall was excavated later than the higher wall, and certainly the western floor of the enclosure, where we took our seismic readings, was excavated later than the remainder of the enclosure—at a time when Egypt had already turned dry, during the Old Kingdom. Based on my analyses, I conclude that the Great Sphinx was carved and the Sphinx Temple was built well before the reign of Khafre, when heavy rain regularly washed across Egypt. Then Khafre claimed the site for himself, refurbishing the temple and Sphinx. Originally, I suspect, the sculpture's body emerged from the bedrock as if it were an integral part of the plateau. By carving the rump and digging out the western enclosure to a second, lower level (the wall of which is rather crudely carved), Khafre divided the monument from the rock and gave it its own separate aesthetic existence.

My analysis of the nature and depth of the subsurface weathering on the Giza Plateau indicates that it has taken 4,500 years for the subsurface weathering at the younger, western floor of the Sphinx Enclosure to reach a depth of 1.2 meters. Since the weathering on the other three sides is between 50 and 100 percent deeper, as a first estimate I believed it was reasonable to assume that this excavation is 50 to 100 percent— or approximately 2,200 to 4,500 years—older than the western end. If we accept Khafre's reign, circa 2500 BCE, as the date for the western enclosure, then this calculation pushes the date for the Great Sphinx's original construction back to the 7000 BCE to 4700 BCE range, or 6,700 to 9,000 years ago. Or, rounding, the origins of the Great Sphinx are pushed back to circa 7000 BCE to 5000 BCE.

However, there is the distinct possibility (actually, it is a certainty, as far as I am now concerned) that this analysis underestimates the age of the Sphinx. Subsurface weathering rates often proceed nonlinearly; that is, the deeper the weathering goes, the slower it progresses because of protection from the overlying material. If we assume this is the case, then the estimated date above is only a bare minimum. Nonlinear weathering suggests that the very earliest portion of the Sphinx could date to well before 7000 BCE; my best estimate is a date of circa 10,000 BCE (see further discussion in Schoch and Bauval 2017).

Sometimes people believe that my work confirms the age of the Sphinx as being on the order of 10,500 BCE, in line, for instance, with the prophecies of the late psychic Edgar Cayce (discussed in greater detail later in this chapter; see also Lehner 1974). This, however, is more a matter of opinion than fact. I do not deny a possible 10,500 BCE date, but my analysis has nothing to do with the prophecies of Cayce. However, Göbekli Tepe in Turkey (discussed in chapter 3) dates back to the end of the last ice age, circa 9700 BCE, and at this point I find it tenable and compelling, based on the evidence, that the oldest portions of the Great Sphinx may date back to this remote period as well.

It has been suggested that the leonine aspect of the Sphinx connects it to the constellation Leo. In terms of zodiacal precessional ages, the transition from the Age of Virgo to the Age of Leo occurred around 10,500 BCE. Is it just coincidence that, based on the geology, the Great Sphinx, with a lion's body symbolizing Leo, dates back to a very remote period? (Since I initially laid eyes on the Sphinx in 1990, I have hypothesized that originally the Sphinx may have had a lion's head, although I was at first thinking in terms of a male lion; now we have evidence that the statue originally had a female lion's head. The original statue represented the goddess Mehit in the form of a lioness; see chapter 15, page 314.) Could the Sphinx be a representation of the Age of Leo, or even date to the Age of Leo, circa 10,500 BCE to 8500 or 8000 BCE? (There is disagreement as to when this age begins and ends.) In the past, I have questioned this association, however, reasoning that it is not certain that the constellation of Leo as such was recognized some twelve thousand or more years ago, and even if the Great Sphinx does represent or commemorate, in some aspect, the Age of Leo, that does not necessarily imply that it was sculpted during that age. However, in my opinion at this point, the evidence indicates that the original Great Sphinx (that is, before the head was recarved to turn it into the Sphinx) actually dates to the Age of Leo. I feel we must be open to this possibility. Even more widely speculative is the idea that the Great Sphinx was carved not during the last Age of Leo, but during the preceding Age of Leo, some thirty-six thousand or so years ago. (This is something that John Anthony West liked to suggest.) Another widespread notion is to view the leonine-human hybrid aspect of the Sphinx as a representation of Leo and Virgo combined (the Age of Virgo is the age immediately preceding the Age of Leo)—the masculine and feminine, the animal or beastly vitality and the human intellect united. However, as I discuss below, the current human head of the Sphinx is not the original head. I have long favored the idea that originally the statue had a lion's head on a lion's body and that the leonine body (the lioness) was connected with, and emerged from, the bedrock of the plateau at the western end of the Sphinx Enclosure.

Even as my redating of the Great Sphinx has been attacked as impossible by some authorities, other serious researchers have suggested that I have underestimated the true age of the oldest portions of the Great Sphinx, perhaps by tens of thousands of years or more. In *The Neanderthal Legacy* (2008), the late Stan Gooch (1932–2010) asserts that the head of the Sphinx was carved deliberately to include both Neanderthal and Cro-Magnon features. Could this indicate that the Sphinx is tens of thousands of years old? According to Gooch, ancient Neanderthals and Cro-Magnons met and interbred about thirty-five thousand years ago, giving rise to modern humans. The idea of such interbreeding is intriguing, but I am not convinced that the Sphinx contributes to the evidence for such a claim. In my opinion, the head of the Sphinx is not the original head; furthermore, black, African, or Nubian features are found on the current Sphinx head (Schoch and Bauval 2017).

There are even more extreme interpretations as to the possible age of the Sphinx. Two members of the National Academy of Sciences of Ukraine, Vjacheslav I. Manichev and Alexander G. Parkhomenko (2008), citing my work, have reinterpreted the geological and erosional features on the Great Sphinx to mean that the core body of the statue could date back as far as eight hundred thousand years ago. And they are not referring to simply a natural outcropping that may have existed eight hundred thousand years ago that was later shaped into a statue.

The dating of Manichev and Parkhomenko could push the age of the Great Sphinx into a very remote time period, one that has been suggested for possible, but ambiguous, ancient structures, sculptures, or simulacra that are found in many parts of the world, such as Markawasi in Peru (Schoch 2006/2007), the Carpathian Sphinx (Welcome to Romania 2002; Schoch and Bauval 2017), or a possible stone circle dubbed Adam's Calendar in South Africa by researchers Johan Heine and Michael Tellinger with a claimed date of from 75,000 years ago (Heine and Tellinger 2008; Serrao 2008) to 160,000 through 200,000 years ago (Eden 2009). Personally, I am not convinced that the Great Sphinx is anywhere close to the age postulated by Manichev and Parkhomenko or that various claims of very ancient, very eroded statues are anything more than natural formations, but the prospects are intriguing (Schoch 2006/2007). Without going off on such limbs, as we will discuss further later in this book (see chapter 3), there is clear evidence for an early high culture at a remote period beyond just that of the Great Sphinx. (Since the first edition of this book was published, I have had a chance to visit and examine Adam's Calendar firsthand. I was not convinced that it is as old as claimed; indeed, from what I observed, it may be a predominantly or entirely natural feature. Likewise, I am convinced that the underwater structure off of the coast of Yonaguni, Japan, is also primarily or wholly a natural feature, although there is evidence of ancient human habitation on Yonaguni; see Schoch with McNally 1999.)

While most of the focus of, and controversy surrounding, my work has been on the Great Sphinx, to my mind the so-called Sphinx Temple, sitting directly in front of (east of) the Sphinx, is in many ways even more significant than the Sphinx itself from a construction and dating point of view (see fig. 2.3). The Sphinx Temple is built of megalithic limestone blocks, many weighing tens of tons, assembled in a tightly enclosed space. How these blocks were maneuvered is difficult to fathom. Pertinent to our current theme, however, is the fact that the Sphinx Temple (or at least the original parts of the temple, as it too, like the Sphinx, was reworked and repaired in dynastic times) was built contemporaneously with the oldest portions of the Great Sphinx. The blocks from which the temple was constructed were removed from around the body of the Sphinx as the statue was carved. The sculptors of the Sphinx did not simply chisel, pound, and shovel out the excess rock they needed to remove; rather, they meticulously quarried it as huge blocks used to construct the Sphinx Temple. Although it is in ruins today, I consider the building of the Sphinx Temple to be an engineering feat even more incredible than the carving of the Great Sphinx, and this occurred at the same time as when the original core body of the Sphinx was carved. That is, according to my current analyses, the Sphinx Temple dates back to circa 10,000 BCE.

THE CHANGING FACE OF THE SPHINX

I must stress that, in my assessment, the Great Sphinx of predynastic times did not look like the Sphinx we see today. It is only what I refer to as the core body (the torso or trunk) of the Sphinx that dates back

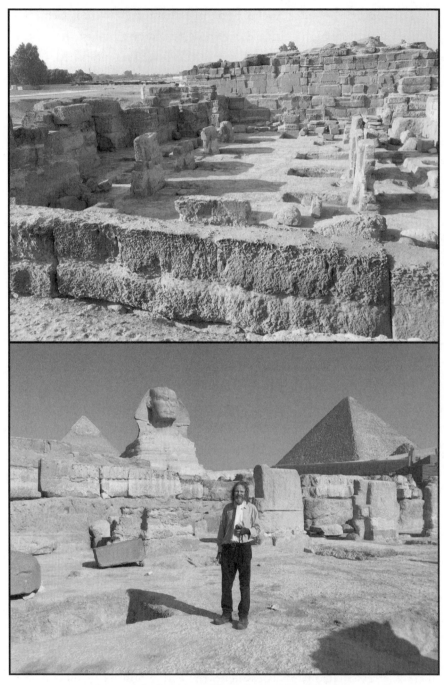

Figure 2.3. Overview of the Sphinx Temple (*top*).
Robert Schoch within the Sphinx Temple (*bottom*).
(Photographs courtesy of R. Schoch and C. Ulissey.)

to that much earlier period. The front paws have been heavily reworked and repaired (today they are mostly covered with modern blocks of limestone), and the head is surely not the original head. I have always contended that the head of the Great Sphinx is out of proportion relative to the size of the body. It is too small. In my opinion, the head was originally larger, but it was damaged by weathering and erosion, and to "repair" it the ancients recarved the head, resulting in its disproportionately small size today. Originally, the head may not have been that of a human. Indeed, we now have evidence, as I had long speculated, that the head was originally that of a lion to fit the leonine body. For decades I was thinking in terms of a male lion, but we now know that the statue was originally a lioness—the goddess Mehit (see chapter 15, page 314). As an aside, some years ago a noted Egyptologist refused to believe my observation that the current head of the Great Sphinx is too small for the body. He subsequently undertook an analysis of the proportions of many ancient Egyptian sphinxes, only to find that virtually all had similar head-to-body ratios, except for the Great Sphinx, in which case, the head was proportionally smaller.

In my opinion, based on analyses of the weathering and chisel marks as well as on stylistic considerations and the ethnicity of the head (evidently a "black African" or "Nubian" in my opinion; see Schoch and Bauval 2017), the current head of the Sphinx is a dynastic recarving, but probably older than the Fourth Dynasty. Some researchers have claimed that the current face of the Great Sphinx resembles the face found on statues of the pharaoh Khafre (builder of the Second Pyramid on the Giza Plateau) and have used this supposed evidence to support the attribution of the Sphinx to the period of Khafre, circa 2500 BCE. Personally, I never saw any similarity between Khafre and the Sphinx, but I am not formally trained in such analyses. In the early 1990s, forensic expert Frank Domingo (formerly with the New York City Police Department) undertook a detailed comparison of the face of the Sphinx and the face of Khafre, concluding that they certainly do not represent the same individual and, indeed, that they do not appear to represent people of the same race or ethnicity (Sphinx Project 1993; West 1993).

Some researchers have suggested that the face of the Sphinx represents that of Khufu (reputed builder of the Great Pyramid) and that either the Great Sphinx was ordered built by Khufu himself, or by his son Djedefre (Ra'djedef, who reigned for a short period between Khufu and Khafre), in the image of Khufu (see chapter 4, "A Case of Mistaken Identity," by Robert Bauval in Schoch and Bauval 2017, 135–73). Personally, I am not convinced that the current face of the Sphinx represents Khufu, in part because Khufu and his family members, if they were related by blood (rather than by adoption) to Khafre, might be expected to share the same ethnic and racial characteristics with Khafre. Based on the beautifully preserved statues of Khafre (unfortunately, only one tiny ivory statuette of Khufu remains today, and its authenticity has been questioned), Khafre was not of a strong black African or Nubian racial type, as is the current head of the Great Sphinx. However, it has been argued that Khufu himself had a more African face than Khafre (see Schoch and McNally 2005, 283).

I suspect the head of the Great Sphinx was recarved during the period of the First to Third Dynasties (ca. 2920 BCE–2575 BCE). Stylistically, to my eye, it might fit this early dynastic period. And the African or Nubian ethnicity of the Sphinx might fit an earlier period when the southern population of Egypt had greater sway than during certain later periods of Egyptian history. One must also remember that the head may have been further altered in later dynastic times. For instance, the entire Great Sphinx may have been modified, repaired, and brightly painted at various periods in its history, including during the New Kingdom. The current head as we view it today has been damaged, apparently both by weathering and by vandalism over the ages, and is possibly incomplete. It has been suggested that the Sphinx appears to be missing the uppermost part of its skull, the region of the crown chakra, or top of the head. Is this simply coincidental? Or was the crown purposefully removed for symbolic purposes? Also, to my eye, the current face of the Great Sphinx has always appeared to be either androgynous or female, and my personal intuition is that in fact it is a female face.

Admittedly, this is a subjective impression. Yes, parts of the Sphinx's "beard" (actually a ceremonial false beard) have been found and now reside in various museums (Schoch and Bauval 2017), but this proves nothing. The beard was added much later and subsequently removed or lost again. At any rate, a beard on the Sphinx would be a symbol, such as of royal power and authority, and not indicative of the gender of the statue. I have seen more than one living African woman whose face strongly resembled that of the Great Sphinx.

We now have hieroglyphic evidence from before the time of Khufu that the original statue was of the lioness Mehit and that she guarded an ancient archive. This new research is presented in the chapter I wrote for this revised edition: chapter 15.

A SECRET CHAMBER?

As part of our research on the Sphinx, geophysicist Thomas Dobecki and I undertook low-energy seismic studies around the Sphinx and elsewhere on the plateau. My primary concern with these studies was not to search for "buried treasure," but to gather good data on the nature, degree, and depth of subsurface weathering, both around the Sphinx and in areas containing confidently dated dynastic structures. Indeed, as discussed above, we acquired excellent data supporting my attribution of the Sphinx to 5000 BCE or earlier (and now interpreted, I believe more accurately, to indicate that the original statue dates back to circa 10,000 BCE). However, we also discovered evidence of a cavity or chamber under the left paw of the Sphinx. This chamber measures approximately twelve meters in an east-west direction, approximately nine meters in a north-south direction, and measured from the current level of the floor of the Sphinx Enclosure, it lies under approximately five meters of rock. Additionally, we found some lesser (and previously known) cavities under and around the Sphinx, and the data also indicate that there may be a tunnel-like structure running the length of the body under the Sphinx (see chapter 2 of Schoch and Bauval 2017).

A chamber in the vicinity of the paws of the Sphinx was certainly interesting to me, but I did not put that much emphasis on it. However, upon publication of our data (Dobecki and Schoch 1992), I soon found that a number of parties considered the chamber to be of extreme interest and importance. I still remember well the day, sitting in my office at Boston University between teaching classes, that I received a phone call from the Virginia Beach headquarters of the Association for Research and Enlightenment (ARE, informally known as the Edgar Cayce Foundation). Unbeknownst to me, the American psychic Edgar Cayce (1877–1945) had predicted that a "Hall of Records" would be found in the general area where we had discovered the chamber. According to Cayce, the ancient continent of Atlantis had been destroyed circa 10,500 BCE. The survivors dispersed to the far corners of Earth, founding new offshoot civilizations, including one that in time would come to be recognized as ancient Egypt. In several locations (Bimini in the Bahamas, the Yucatan, and Egypt; see Association for Research and Enlightenment 2011), including in the region of the Great Sphinx, they had secreted libraries recording their history, science, and accomplishments. Furthermore, the representative of the ARE informed me that my research on redating the Great Sphinx went a long way toward confirming the Cayce chronology of Atlantis and the building of structures on the Giza Plateau well before dynastic times. I found myself formally interviewed for the ARE's magazine, and I have spoken at their conferences in Virginia Beach. (To their credit, I would note that the ARE has a history of attracting top-notch researchers to speak at some of its conferences, researchers who in some cases are clearly antithetical to the main tenets and interests of the organization. I have always found the leaders and members of the ARE to be warm, friendly, open, and honest.)

Delving into the details of the Cayce readings, I found one that appears to pertain to the Atlantean Hall of Records in the vicinity of the Sphinx:

A record of Atlantis from the beginnings of those periods when the Spirit took form or began the encasements in that land, and the developments of the peoples throughout their sojourn, with the record of the first destruction and the changes that took place in the land. . . .

This in position lies, as the sun rises from the waters, the line of the shadow (or light) falls between the paws of the Sphinx, that was later set as the sentinel or guard, and which may not be entered from the connecting chambers from the Sphinx's paw (right paw) until the TIME has been fulfilled when the changes must be active in this sphere of man's experience.

Between, then, the Sphinx and the river. (Reading 378–16 [Association for Research and Enlightenment 2011]; listed as reading "10/29/33 [apparently the date] 0378–016/11" by Mandeville 1995–1999)

This prophecy is a bit confusing when trying to identify the actual location of the Hall of Records, but note that it mentions the "right paw" of the Sphinx. The chamber we found during our seismic studies is located below the left paw. Possibly the discrepancy can be explained this way: the Sphinx's left paw is the paw on the right side of a viewer standing face-to-face with the Sphinx.

It turns out that it is not only the members of the ARE who have a special interest in the discovery of chambers and tunnels under the Sphinx, but that members of many other groups do as well, such as various Rosicrucian and Freemason groups, who believe (with some good basis) that there is a complex network of tunnels and chambers below the surface of the Giza Plateau.

Questions I am often asked include: Where is the entrance to the chamber under the left paw of the Sphinx? And have the Egyptian authorities allowed you to explore the chamber, and if not, why not?

In answer to the first question, I have not located any entrance to the chamber on the surface. However, based on the seismic data and analyses, we found that just in front of (just east of) the Sphinx Temple, buried under the sand, there is a substantial drop in the bedrock (Schoch and Bauval 2017, 83). That is, if the sand and debris were removed from in front of the Sphinx Temple, it would be found that the temple sits atop a cliff with the Great Sphinx itself looming over the temple. This must have been a very dramatic sight. I speculate that the entrance to the chamber under the paw of the Sphinx may be found in the cliff face.

To this date, the Egyptian authorities have not allowed me to explore the chamber that we found. Certainly, they are well aware that

I would like to, and for the record, I have never been denied permission to do so outright; I have simply not been granted permission. I have some understanding of the complex intricacies and highly sensitive nature of exploring and excavating new archaeological finds in Egypt. I am not surprised that the authorities do not want to open more "cans of worms" at this time, and I am not an advocate of conspiracy theories. I am not aware of any credible evidence that the chamber has already been entered, as certain people have contended, but it is not impossible either. In recent years, there has been growing concern over the rising water table, due in large part to the exploding population in the vicinity of the Great Sphinx. Under this pretext, there has been drilling carried out by the Egyptian authorities around the Sphinx, including near the left paw. In a video posted on the internet (Hawass and Lehner 2009), the Egyptian authorities are shown drilling directly under the left paw, and they assert that there is no evidence of a chamber. Viewing the video, it is clear to me that they missed the chamber! They were drilling at the wrong angle (too sharp) to intersect the chamber that we located seismically. Also in recent years, I have observed that the Egyptians have begun, ever so slowly, to excavate the area in front of the Sphinx Temple. If they persist in their endeavors, at some point they should uncover the cliff we discovered three decades ago using geophysics, and I will not be surprised if a door or opening, leading to a passage under the Sphinx Temple and thus into the chamber under the Sphinx, is eventually found. Something I have learned while working in Egypt is patience. However, I would appreciate the opportunity to assist in the endeavor and continue my research.

SOME PERSONAL ANECDOTES CONCERNING THE SPHINX

Even before I first met John Anthony West in 1989, I had given some thought to the Great Sphinx. As a teenager, I loved ancient history, read profusely on the subject, and even acquired a few minor Egyptian antiquities from an aged fellow whose family had brought them out of Egypt when it was still legal to do so. But more directly applicable to my later research, I remember as a graduate student reading a couple of articles on the geology of the Great Sphinx.

In particular, a certain Egyptian researcher, later living and teaching in America, promulgated the notion that the Great Sphinx began as a *yardang;* that is, a natural hill or rock outcropping that had been weathered and shaped by the elements, primarily wind in the case of desert yardangs as found in Egypt. The ancient Egyptians, so his hypothesis went, saw in the yardang the crude shape of a sphinx (sort

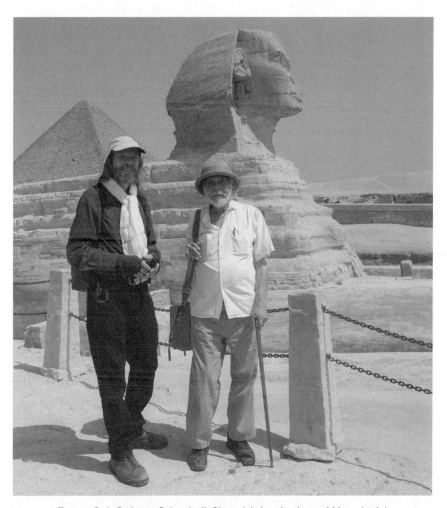

Figure 2.4. Robert Schoch (*left*) and John Anthony West (*right*)
at the Great Sphinx, July 2016.
(Photograph courtesy of R. Schoch and C. Ulissey.)

of like seeing the shapes of animals or people in clouds) and decided to start chiseling and carving the yardang to turn it into an actual sphinx. I recollect sitting in the geology department graduate student lounge at Yale University laughing over this crazy notion with my fellow geology graduate students. Remember, to free the body of the Sphinx from the bedrock, large blocks of limestone were quarried and removed. We thought it was hilarious that someone would think that wind could somehow carve out multi-ton blocks from around the body of the Sphinx and reassemble them as a temple in front of the statue.

Furthermore, the weathering and erosion features on the Sphinx (and mind you, we were basing this just on photos, as none of us had actually been to Egypt) did not appear to fit the yardang hypothesis. At most, perhaps the head of the Sphinx, which does sit above the level of the plateau, was once a yardang, but it has now been too heavily carved and recarved to tell for sure. We had our own theory: the author of the yardang hypothesis grew up in Egypt and as a small child visited the Great Sphinx. He was impressed by its size and majesty and also noted the heavy weathering to the statue, but did not at that time pay attention to the details of the geological and cultural context. Years later, without revisiting the Sphinx to check the geology and location, he based his theory on those formative impressions from childhood.

Once I had traveled to Egypt to study the Great Sphinx firsthand, I reinvestigated the yardang hypothesis. As we had discussed in graduate school, it made absolutely no sense (except, perhaps, for the head), but there was one important aspect to it. The author of the yardang theory observed, and acknowledged, the very ancient weathering features still preserved on the body of the Sphinx. Indeed, one way to view the yardang theory is that it provides a way to explain how such incredibly ancient weathering can be found on a dynastic structure. According to the yardang theory, the weathering came first, followed by the carving of the Sphinx. But given the context, this is patently impossible. The body of the Sphinx and the walls of the Sphinx Enclosure were weathered after being carved, and the weathering bears on the age of the Sphinx.

My earliest work researching the Sphinx was done on my own time without remuneration, and the travel expenses to Egypt were funded by a group, spearheaded by West, intent on producing a documentary on the subject. The immediate result was *The Mystery of the Sphinx,* hosted by Charlton Heston, also known as "Moses"; Heston played the role of Moses in the famous Cecil B. DeMille movie *The Ten Commandments* (Sphinx Project 1993; DeMille 1956). Contrary to some people's beliefs, I never earned any money from the documentary (despite various promises and agreements, and now the key persons involved have passed away). I make this point explicitly because, over the years, some of my critics have asserted that I became involved in the project for "fame and money." I never sought fame; indeed, the criticism from some quarters, even if unfounded, has hurt me. Regarding money, I am still waiting.

Not long after I became "notorious" for my work on the Sphinx, a senior faculty member at Boston University (I have taught there full-time since 1984), now deceased, told me that I had managed to immortalize myself by connecting my name to what is arguably the greatest and most recognizable sculpture on Earth. This was never my intention.

There are many personal anecdotes I can relate relative to my work with the Sphinx and the wide-ranging reaction to it. I will give a few here.

I first presented my analyses of the data on the Great Sphinx, coming to the conclusion that the core body dates well back to predynastic times, at the 1991 annual meeting of the Geological Society of America. Before the formal presentation I happened to run into a colleague of mine, a very talented geologist whose specialty was stratigraphy, the exact field that pertained to my data and analyses of the Great Sphinx. I showed him my data and explained my conclusions. His response: He began to laugh. My heart sank to the pit of my stomach. I was sure I must have made some fundamental mistake to induce such laughter from him, and in the next hour I was scheduled to present my work in the public forum. I asked hesitantly what was wrong. He answered (a paraphrase after all these years), "Nothing, nothing at all. It is just so obvious. Hasn't anyone ever looked at the Sphinx before? Where have all the Egyptologists been? Why didn't they see this long ago?"

Some weeks after the 1991 Geological Society of America presentation, I heard from one of my former undergraduate professors, a man I had always respected, though had never known well. He was scathing in his comments regarding my work on the Sphinx, vehemently contending that I was quite wrong in recasting the age as anything other than circa 2500 BCE. But his arguments against me made no logical or scientific sense, as far as I could determine. Then it came out that he was a devout, and apparently somewhat fundamentalist, Christian (although by no means a creationist or a proponent of a young Earth), and basically he somehow viewed the implications of my redating of the Sphinx as questioning his religious faith (how, I am not exactly sure). Scientists are humans too, and their deep beliefs and long-held assumptions can certainly cloud their ability to think clearly.

Concerning the bitterness of infighting among academics, I learned my lesson well many years ago at a Boston University faculty-staff Christmastime gathering. It was back in the early 1990s. During the holiday party, a faculty member with the Archaeology Department accosted me concerning my work on the Great Sphinx. I had never met her before, though she had attacked me in the local press. Suddenly, she appeared before me, face-to-face, as I was attempting to enjoy the hors d'oeuvres. She loudly spouted out a denunciation of my work and me, virtually spitting in my face, accused me of falsifying data and results, and called me a pseudoscientist. Then quickly, before I could respond, she disappeared back into the crowd. It was all quite disconcerting, and I even felt a bit threatened. Clearly, she had prepared her statement, ready to be delivered in a staccato voice if she happened to run into me. She did not want to open a dialogue on the subject. She did not care to learn about my evidence or analyses. I was the enemy as far as she was concerned, and that was that! I later learned that she and her colleagues in Archaeology were doing everything they could to make trouble for me behind the scenes, attempting to prevent me from any salary raises and spreading rumors in the Egyptian press (which I believe they thought I would never get wind of) that I was not a member of the Boston University faculty, though I had already received tenure, as they knew. These are classic tactics attempting to marginalize someone who dares to challenge the dominant paradigm. The goal is to generally make life miserable for the dissenter with the hope that the challenge to the status quo will quietly disappear (for more on such issues generally, see appendix 2, page 384).

At one Egyptological conference to which I was invited to speak, I gave a nice, stolid presentation on the evidence for an older Sphinx. I did not get many comments from the audience, but afterward I was approached by a very senior, elderly, and rather grandfatherly Egyptologist. His comment to me, and I can only paraphrase it now as it was many years ago, was to the effect that "I do not understand geology, and I cannot refute your evidence, but I know you are wrong. Now there are lots of rocks other than at Giza and in Egypt; I suggest you go study the rocks somewhere else." By his demeanor and the tone of his voice, I took this as more than just a friendly suggestion. It was clear that he did not want me studying the Sphinx, and he was not beyond gently threatening me, implying that there could be untold consequences if I persisted in my endeavors along such lines.

At another conference, to which I was invited to debate the age of the Great Sphinx, prior to the public discussions, I was sharing some of my data with a member of the "opposition." It was not that I was required to do so, but I shared my data of my own free will. I have never treated the controversy over the age of the Sphinx as a situation where I am determined to "win" and "prove" my hypothesis for an older Sphinx. Rather, my concern as a scientist and researcher is to gather the data, share the data, and honestly follow the data to wherever the data should lead. Anyway, I was showing this professional "geoarchaeologist" some of the seismic data that we had collected around and under the Sphinx. He was having a difficult time interpreting it; looking down at the table, I saw a potential problem. Gently, and trying not to embarrass him, I said, "You might want to look at it this way," and I turned the charts around, as he had been trying to read them upside down. Even when viewing them in their correct orientation, he seemed not to be able to follow them. I quickly realized that despite his position at a major university and a Ph.D. in a relevant field, this man had absolutely no clue as to what he was looking at or how to interpret the data, and he was too proud to ask for help. The rest of the so-called debate was not very illuminating from my point of view. I attempted to present and discuss real data, while my opponents at best skirted the issues and at worst lowered themselves to ad hominem attacks and insults against me personally.

At the same conference, I ran into one of my opponents, Mark Lehner, in a back hall; he has been hailed as one of the world's experts on the Great Sphinx, perhaps *the* world's expert. Many years earlier, he had been a follower of Edgar Cayce's teachings, even writing a book about them (Lehner 1974), but had since "seen the light" and become a conventional Egyptologist. We were alone and standing face-to-face, eye-to-eye. He said to me something like, "You can't really believe that the Sphinx is older than the Fourth Dynasty. You must know that is nonsense." Evidently, he was attempting to appeal to my academic, orthodox side. I almost felt like he was trying to "save" me from the unholy alternative theorists and the "New Age" camp, which he had once been so intimately associated with. He then asked me some question about my analyses of the Sphinx data. I honestly no longer remember the question, but I remember that the tone of his voice was rather bitter and sarcastic. I proceeded to answer in detail as he just stared at me with a blank look on his face, saying nothing. Then, as I was in midsentence, he simply turned around and walked away. I realized afterward that his "question" was meant as a rhetorical comment and that he had neither expected me to be able to answer it nor thought I would dare try to answer it. When I did answer him, he was caught off guard and apparently felt he had no other choice but to ignore me and walk away.

I have often felt that I am misunderstood when it comes to my work on the Sphinx. I am trained as a staid, traditional academic, with a Ph.D. from an Ivy League school (as mentioned, Ph.D. in geology and geophysics from Yale University, 1983) and a tenured teaching position. I think of myself as quite conventional, not as the radical alternative thinker that some have cast me. It is worth stressing that I believe in following the data to wherever they may lead, and my hypotheses and conclusions have not always gone over well with my traditional academic colleagues. In hindsight, I suppose I realize why I am thought of as a radical; it is not easy for people to accept that what they have always believed, what they may have staked their academic careers on, is not true after all. In my own way, I was threatening the established worldview.

I had pushed the Great Sphinx, arguably the grandest and most recognizable statue in the world, back into a period when humanity was supposedly just transitioning from a hunter-gatherer economy to a sedentary life. People seven thousand or more years ago were still brutish and unsavory, at least by modern civilized norms, or so the standard story went. Certainly, they were not carving giant statues out of solid limestone bedrock.

I have recounted some of my private experiences above, but I was really taken aback when my work became very public. Immediately after my announcement of an older Sphinx, I was under attack. Archaeologist Carol Redmount, of the University of California, Berkeley, was quoted in the media as saying, "There's just no way that could be true." The article continued, "'The people of that region would not have had the technology, the governing institutions or even the will to build such a structure thousands of years before Khafre's reign,' she said" (Dye 1991). As John Anthony West liked to point out sarcastically, Redmount— apparently a self-styled expert on ancient willpower—certainly speaks with authority when it comes to the subject of what people had "the will to build" thousands of years ago, so why should we doubt her pronouncements? Perhaps Redmount was directly channeling the ancients, West would jokingly suggest.

In other words, my data did not fit with the establishment archaeological paradigm of what our ancestors were like at that remote period long ago. I was challenging Redmount's worldview, and she was fighting back. This would be a scenario that would repeat itself, with different players, over and over. Thirty years later, I almost (almost, but not quite) feel like I am getting accustomed to it.

The initial hoopla peaked in February 1992 at a "debate" on the age of the Great Sphinx held at the Chicago meeting of the American Association for the Advancement of Science (Schoch 1992a). As the *New York Times* put it, "The exchange was to last an hour, but it spilled over to a news conference and then a hallway confrontation in which voices were raised and words skated on the icy edge of scientific politeness" (*New York Times* 1992).

Egyptologist Mark Lehner could not accept the notion of an older Sphinx, personally attacking me by labeling my research "pseudoscience."

He argued, "If the Sphinx was built by an earlier culture, where is the evidence of that civilization? Where are the pottery shards? People during that age were hunters and gatherers. They didn't build cities" (*New York Times* 1992).

At the time, I lacked any pottery shards. But I was sure of my science, and I persisted.

Decades later, we have something far better than pottery shards, and dated to an even earlier period than my initial, conservative Sphinx date of circa 7000 BCE to 5000 BCE. These new discoveries, found in southeastern Turkey, will prove critical to ushering in a new model concerning the how, when, and why of early civilization. To understand the clash of paradigms, we need to look at both the old thinking and how the new evidence not only confirms my initial work on the Great Sphinx but also changes our most basic assumptions about humanity twelve thousand years ago.

Figure 2.5. Two views of a small humanoid statue or "small man" from Göbekli Tepe, on display in the Şanliurfa Museum.
(Photographs courtesy of R. Schoch and C. Ulissey.)

3

GÖBEKLI TEPE AND THE ORIGINS OF CIVILIZATION

What were our ancestors like twelve thousand or more years ago? The most common image is one of small nomadic bands endlessly in pursuit of the next meal. Men hunted game while women and children gathered fruits, seeds, roots, shoots, insects, and other edibles. The height of technology was a finely worked stone knife blade or spear point; nets, baskets, and cordage ostensibly were also put to good use. Permanent structures were superfluous, for these nomadic groups never stayed in one place very long. Material goods were sparse, as possessions had to be limited to those easily carried. Jewelry (perhaps beads, animal teeth, or shells strung on a cord) and personal decoration (body paint, tattoos, and scarification) were prized. In colder climates appropriate clothing was fashioned from animal skins. Social institutions were minimal. Not until around ten thousand years ago did true agriculture and domestication appear, or so we have been taught (see, for example, Mithen 2007). This in turn allowed permanent settlement, leading to the specialization of labor, the development of crafts (including pottery and metalworking), the building of substantial structures, long-distance trade, and the slow and gradual evolution of complex societies.

None of this happened overnight, according to the standard chronology. It took thousands of years, and it was not until around 4000 BCE to 3000 BCE that true signs of high culture first appeared,

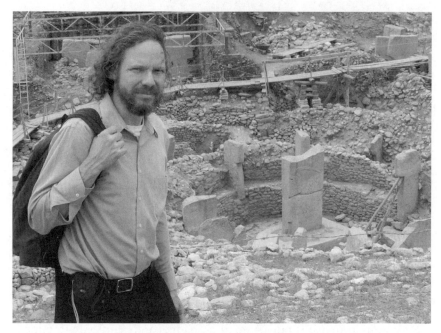

Figure 3.1. Robert Schoch at Göbekli Tepe, May 2010.
(Photograph by Catherine Ulissey.)

such as fine artistry in decorative crafts, written records, scientific observations of the heavens, complex political organizations, and megalithic building projects. This level of achievement was reached in Mesopotamia, the Nile Valley, and the Indus Valley by the end of the fourth millennium or the beginning of the third millennium BCE. A well-known example is the rise of dynastic Egypt about 3200 BCE to 3100 BCE and the building of the Djoser (Zoser) pyramid circa 2630 BCE. The major megalithic construction at Stonehenge in England is traditionally dated to this same period.

Although accepted as dogma by many, this nice neat scenario now appears to be completely wrong.

BETTER THAN POTTERY SHARDS

When I first publicized my redating of the Sphinx, I was challenged to name anything so old that was comparable to the Sphinx. Remember

Egyptologist Mark Lehner's very public rebuttal to me back in 1992 asking me to produce some pottery shards?

I duly noted that very ancient and sophisticated remains have been found at such sites as Jericho (in Palestine, with a stone wall and tower dating back to circa 9000 BCE; Science Daily 2011a; Schoch with McNally 1999) and Çatalhöyük (also spelled Çatal Hüyük, Çatal Höyük, or Çatalhüyük, a Neolithic settlement in southern Anatolia, Turkey, circa 7500 BCE to 5400 BCE; Schoch with McNally 1999), but admittedly these examples do not include megalithic constructions comparable to the Great Sphinx. The Sphinx seemed to sit in splendid isolation, with no cultural context. What I would have given for not merely some pottery shards but also a good example of megalithic structures securely dated to ten thousand or twelve thousand years ago. Now we have it!

A short drive from Urfa (alternatively Şanlıurfa), in southeastern Turkey just north of the border with Syria, atop a low mountain north of the Harran Plain, sits Göbekli Tepe (which has been translated as meaning "hill with a belly or navel" or "potbelly hill"). In 1995, the late Klaus Schmidt (1953–2014) of the German Archaeological Institute began excavating the site (Schmidt 2001, 2006/2008, 2007, 2010, 2012; Peters and Schmidt 2004; Birch 2008; Chandler 2009; Curry 2008a, 2008b; Mann 2011; Symmes 2010). In May 2010, Katie, John Anthony West, and I visited it for ourselves. We were amazed. (I have since returned to Göbekli Tepe a number of times, and always I am filled with awe upon viewing the accomplishments of these ancient people.)

Picture Stonehenge, multiply it by twenty, carve the pillars more ornately, place the circles next to one another, and intentionally bury them with a mountain of rock and dirt. This is Göbekli Tepe—so far! The portion excavated has yielded dozens of carved limestone megaliths, many of which date back to the extraordinarily early period of eleven thousand to twelve thousand years ago. Immense, finely carved, and decorated T-shaped limestone pillars, many in the range of two to five and one-half meters tall and weighing up to an estimated ten to fifteen or twenty tons, form circles. An unfinished megalith, left where it was being quarried, measures seven meters long. The workmanship

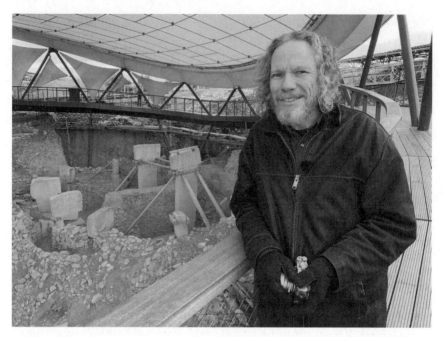

Figure 3.2. Robert Schoch at Göbekli Tepe on a cold January day, 2020.
(Photograph by Catherine Ulissey.)

is extraordinary, with clear, sharp edges that would do any modern mason proud. The major megaliths excavated thus far were originally erected in four distinct stone circles (labeled Enclosures A, B, C, and D by the archaeologists), ranging from ten to thirty meters in diameter. (The primary inner circles with the largest pillars are ten to twenty meters in diameter, and the surrounding stone walls are up to thirty meters in diameter.) Other stone megaliths have also been found. The hill of Göbekli Tepe covers some nine hectares (about twenty-two acres; Schmidt 2010) and, based on geophysical surveys, the entire site may cover three dozen hectares (about ninety acres) and contain another sixteen to twenty stone circles (Global Heritage Fund 2011a, 2011b; Chandler 2009). This is an immense complex!

Göbekli Tepe boggles the imagination. The date is incredibly early, even earlier than my "conservative" estimate for the date of the Great Sphinx. Göbekli Tepe dates back to the end of the last ice age. It may be a cliché, but pondering Göbekli Tepe, I cannot help but think of

Figure 3.3. Overview of Göbekli Tepe showing the modern covering, January 2020. (Panoramic photograph courtesy of R. Schoch and C. Ulissey.)

the opening scene of the classic 1968 movie *2001: A Space Odyssey*. In that film, a group of ape-like protohumans discovers a giant monolith; influenced by it, they learn to use tools, leading to civilization (Kubrick 1968).

Various pillars at Göbekli Tepe are decorated with bas-reliefs of animals, including foxes, boars, snakes, aurochs (wild cattle), Asiatic wild asses, wild sheep, birds (cranes, waterfowl, a vulture, and other forms of birds), a gazelle, and arthropods (a scorpion, ants, and/or spiders). The pillars may also carry symbols (Eilenstein 2011; Seyfzadeh and Schoch 2019a). In particular, the two central pillars of Enclosure D have arms, hands, belts, and loincloths, and on one of the belts are letter-like carvings (one resembles an *H,* and others resemble a *C* and a reversed *C*). Could the Göbekli Tepe people have had a form of now-lost writing? My answer is yes, as I discuss further in chapter 15, page 346. The carvings are refined, sophisticated, and beautifully executed. Not only are there bas-reliefs, but also carvings in the round, including a carnivorous beast, possibly a lion or other feline, working its way down a column, apparently in pursuit of a boar carved in relief below. In-the-round carvings of apparent carnivores, boars, humans, and other figures—including a strange sculpture that looks rather like a stone totem pole—have been uncovered; these are now housed in the Museum of Şanlıurfa, as is a life-sized statue of a man (seemingly lacking a mouth), which, though from Urfa, apparently dates to the Göbekli Tepe era. (This statue is generally known as Urfa Man; Batuman 2011, 76; a modern Turkish name for the statue is Balıklıgöl Heykeli, or the Statue / Man from the Fish Pools [of Abraham], as it was found near the Pools of Abraham in Urfa.) Also from Göbekli Tepe are beautiful stone beads with incredibly small holes drilled through their long axes, raising the issue of how this was accomplished with only "primitive" technology. Small stone plaques with engraved symbols on them have also been found at the site. And, according to Professor Schmidt, while some of the stone pillars were set directly into the local bedrock, others were set into a concrete- or terrazzo-like floor. Some of the pillars are very tall and thin, with what appear to be "weak" foundations. It has been speculated that this was purposeful, as originally the pillars may have been designed to hum in the wind, acoustically resonating like tuning forks (Batuman 2011, 74; see further discussion in the section on "The Power of Sound" in chapter 14, page 274). Looking only at style and quality of workmanship, one might easily suggest that Göbekli Tepe dates to between 3000 BCE and 1000 BCE. How wrong one would be. Based on radiocarbon analyses, the site goes back to the period of 10,000 BCE to 9000 BCE and was intentionally buried no later than circa 8000 BCE (and perhaps much earlier, or portions were buried earlier). That is, the site dates back an astounding ten thousand to twelve thousand years ago!

I have to admit that even I, the person who geologically redated the oldest portion of the Great Sphinx to an incredibly early date, was initially skeptical about the dating of Göbekli Tepe, despite the fact that this is a discovery made by mainstream academics. I do not take just any claim on face value. For instance, the contention that gigantic pyramids, dating back ten thousand to twelve thousand years ago or more, have been found on the outskirts of the

Figure 3.4. Front (*right*) and back (*left*) of an ancient statue ("Urfa Man") found in Urfa (Şanlıurfa), now on display in the Şanlıurfa Museum, that is believed to date back to the same time as Göbekli Tepe.
(Photographs courtesy of R. Schoch and C. Ulissey.)

Figure 3.5. Heads of two beasts found at Göbekli Tepe, now on display in the Şanlıurfa Museum.
(Photograph courtesy of R. Schoch and C. Ulissey.)

Figure 3.6. A bird figure found at Göbekli Tepe, now on display in
the Şanlıurfa Museum.
(Photograph courtesy of R. Schoch and C. Ulissey.)

Figure 3.7. Examples of small engraved bone (*top row*) and stone (*bottom row*)
plaques found at Göbekli Tepe, now on display in the Şanlıurfa Museum.
(Photographs courtesy of R. Schoch and C. Ulissey.)

Bosnian town of Visoko is simply false—something I discovered only after visiting and examining the so-called pyramids firsthand (on the Bosnian pyramids, see Archaeological Park 2011; Bohannon 2006; Fronza Videoproducties 2011; Markey 2006; Parzinger et al. 2006; Schoch 2006; and Woodard 2009). Therefore, it was important to me to both visit and examine Göbekli Tepe so as to fully understand the techniques and data used to determine the age of the complex located there.

I discussed the dating of Göbekli Tepe on-site with Professor Schmidt. It is based not only on calibrated radiocarbon dates of circa 9000 BCE or earlier taken on organic remains found in the material used to fill the site (these dates could be later than the actual occupation of the site), but also dates of circa 8000 BCE to 7500 BCE on pedogenic (formed with the soil) carbonate coatings and microstalactites

Figure 3.8. Professor Klaus Schmidt (*left*) and Robert Schoch (*right*) at Göbekli Tepe, discussing the site.
(Photograph courtesy of R. Schoch and C. Ulissey.)

on wall stones (see Peters and Schmidt 2004, 182). These carbonate coatings and microstalactites would have formed only after the burial of the site and after soil formation began, thus indicating that the site itself was buried by circa 8000 BCE (Batuman 2011, 72, cites a date of 8200 BCE for the burial). Taken together, I am convinced that the evidence indicates that the site was actively used in the tenth and ninth millennia BCE and was intentionally buried (as indicated by the systematic layers of the fill material and the material the fill contains, including flint and obsidian tools and waste, and animal and plant remains) prior to circa 8000 BCE. Why it was purposefully buried is a major mystery, one that we will return to. Arguably as much or more energy was expended burying the site as was used to originally carve and erect the stone pillars and walls.

The major, and older, stone circles (Enclosures A, B, C, and D) belong to Schmidt's Layer III. Overlying Layer III is the younger Layer II, which contains smaller pillars and structures and may date to the same period as the Neolithic site of Nevali Çori, an area northwest of Göbekli Tepe and similar in many respects to the Layer II period at Göbekli Tepe. Nevali Çori was excavated in the 1990s, but has since been flooded as a result of the Atatürk Dam built on the Euphrates River. Nevali Çori and Layer II of Göbekli Tepe may date to the second half of the ninth millennium BCE. In the catalog to accompany a 2007 exhibit at the Badisches Landesmuseum Karlsruhe, the earlier material at Göbekli Tepe, that of Layer III, is referred to as circa 9500 BCE to 8800 BCE, whereas the material from Layer II is referred to as circa 8800 to 8000 BCE, and material from Nevali Çori is dated as circa 8500 BCE to 7900 BCE.

In Enclosure D of Göbekli Tepe, there is a "wall plaster" composed of "loam, which also contains small amounts of organic material" (Dietrich et al. 2013, 36). A sample of this plaster was radiocarbon dated, yielding an age of 9745 to 9314 BCE ("calBC at the 95.4% confidence level"; see Dietrich et al. 2013, 36). Subsequent dated samples from Enclosure D are in "good agreement" with this date (Dietrich et al. 2013, 37). This is arguably the most accurate date to come from the earliest portions thus far excavated at Göbekli Tepe. However, it is not the date of the initial construction of this portion of Göbekli Tepe (that is, the erection of the pillars of Enclosure D). This radiocarbon date is from wall plaster on a wall that is secondary—a wall that was erected after the initial structure consisting of *T*-shaped pillars arranged in a Stonehenge-like fashion was built (see Sezen 2020, 47, who apparently independently came to the conclusion that the walls are a more recent construction than the erection of the pillars)—and furthermore, it is not inconceivable that this wall may have been plastered and subsequently replastered (perhaps more than once), as we commonly observe in ancient structures of later periods.

Based on the evidence, and incorporating archaeoastronomical analyses, I believe that the pillars of Enclosure D, including the two central anthropomorphic pillars, were erected by circa 10,000 BCE. This would date this stone circle and pillars to a time before the end of the last ice age (before 9700 BCE), thus placing them in the Younger Dryas (circa 10,900 BCE to 9700 BCE). Interestingly, in a 2003 paper, Pustovoytov and Taubald suggested, on the basis of reconstructed paleoenvironments using stable carbon and oxygen isotopes from pedogenic carbonates of Göbekli Tepe, that at least the oldest portions of Göbekli Tepe date back to the Younger Dryas. They wrote, ". . . of prime importance appears to be the fact that the early laminations of pedogenic carbonate at Göbekli Tepe recorded *in situ* isotopic signals distinctly different (relatively cool and dry environments) from those of most of the first half of the Holocene [the time since the end of the last ice age]. Considering that secondary carbonate started to accumulate once the PPNA [Pre-Pottery Neolithic A] stone enclosures were covered by fill, it is evident that the builder[s] of the enclosures should have experienced the harsh climatic conditions of the Younger Dryas" (29; italics in the original, comments in brackets by R. Schoch). In a later paper, however, Pustovoytov (2006) no longer mentions a possible Younger Dryas age for some of the Göbekli Tepe structures.

Enclosure D was subject to damage that resulted in some of the pillars being knocked over and broken in ancient times. This may have occurred during the turmoil at the end of the last ice age and shortly thereafter. Various pillars were reerected, and in some cases realigned and reworked. Relatively crude stone walls were built between, among, and around the pillars, forming circles or "spirals" of stone walls; in some cases, these secondary stone walls cover over older bas-reliefs (Schmidt 2012). Some of these walls were plastered; as noted, in the case of Enclosure D a radiocarbon date for some of this later plastering is 9745 to 9314 BCE (Dietrich et al. 2013), which places this secondary stone wall in a transitional period between the end of the last ice age and fully post–ice age times.

What do we make of Göbekli Tepe? Ten to twelve thousand and more years ago was supposedly the time of brutish, nomadic hunters and gatherers who, according to many academics, did not have the technology, governing institutions, or will to build structures such as those found at Göbekli Tepe. Clearly, there is a disconnect between what conventional historians and archaeologists have been teaching all these years and the physical evidence on the ground. Charles Mann wrote in *National Geographic,* "Discovering that hunter-gatherers had constructed Göbekli Tepe was like finding that someone had built a 747 [Boeing 747 commercial airliner] in a basement with an X-Acto knife [a small knife commonly used in model making]" (Mann 2011, 48; material in brackets added by R. Schoch).

Stanford University archaeologist Ian Hodder commented that Göbekli Tepe is "unbelievably big and amazing, at a ridiculously early date . . . huge great stones and fantastic, highly refined art. . . . Many people think that it changes everything. . . . It overturns the whole apple cart. All our theories were wrong" (Hodder, quoted in Symmes 2010).

Like my redating of the Great Sphinx, Göbekli Tepe forces us to reconsider our antiquity.

And as with my work on the Sphinx, the specialists are perplexed by Göbekli Tepe. Patrick Symmes wrote in *Newsweek,* "But the real reason the ruins at Göbekli remain almost unknown, not yet incorporated in textbooks, is that the evidence is too strong, not too weak. 'The problem with this discovery,' as [Glenn] Schwartz of Johns Hopkins puts it, 'is that it is unique.' No other monumental sites from the era have

Figure 3.9. Dioramas on display in the Şanlıurfa Museum showing supposed "hunters and gatherers" carving and moving the pillars of Göbekli Tepe (*left*) and pillars in Enclosure D at Göbekli Tepe (*right*). (Photographs courtesy of R. Schoch and C. Ulissey.)

been found. Before Göbekli, humans drew stick figures on cave walls, shaped clay into tiny dolls, and perhaps piled up small stones for shelter or worship. Even after Göbekli, there is little evidence of sophisticated building" (Symmes 2010).

Indeed, the Göbekli Tepe people appear to have reached a high level of sophisticated culture, flourished for a relatively short period of time (even if some thousands of years), and then suddenly disappeared. As Klaus Schmidt stated, "Even one thousand years later [after the purposeful burial of Göbekli Tepe and disappearance of the people], nothing is left of this world" (Schmidt, quoted in Batuman 2011, 80).

Göbekli Tepe poses a genuine mystery, one that I will attempt to unravel.

DEATH CULT CENTER OR THE
TRUE GARDEN OF EDEN?

Göbekli Tepe—in its immensity—exists. Despite the challenges it presents for mainstream archaeologists, it demands an explanation. Exactly what was Göbekli Tepe? Why was it constructed at the cost of enormous time and energy?

Following the theories of Schmidt (discussed further below), in the popular media, Göbekli Tepe has been hailed as the world's first temple (Curry 2008b; Mann 2011), the original Garden of Eden (Knox 2009a; see also Batuman 2011, 81, and Curry 2008a, 278, both citing a 2006 cover story in *Der Spiegel*), and even an ancient version of Disneyland (Mann 2011).

Based on the known evidence, it has generally been asserted that the site was not permanently inhabited, that no living areas have been found. Archaeologist Ted Banning of the University of Toronto has proposed a different view (Banning 2011; Stacey 2011). Despite their elaborate decoration and sophisticated artwork, Banning suggests that the structures at Göbekli Tepe may in fact have been houses, not temples or other religious buildings. Specifically, he suggests, the Göbekli Tepe constructions may represent large communal houses. He writes that they are "similar in some ways to the large plank houses [of the native peoples] of the Northwest Coast of North America with their impressive house posts and totem poles. . . . It is . . . likely that some of these buildings [at Göbekli Tepe] were the locus for a variety of rituals, probably including feasts, mortuary rites, magic, and initiations, . . . there is generally no reason to presume a priori, even when these are as impressive as the buildings at Göbekli Tepe, that they were not also people's houses" (Banning, quoted in Stacey 2011). Indeed, in October 2010, a stone sculpture resembling a totem pole was found at Göbekli Tepe (Schmidt 2010, 248).

The numerous animal bones found at Göbekli Tepe suggest feasting and/or animal sacrifices. It has been suggested that stone basins uncovered by Schmidt may have been used for alcoholic beverages, such as beer (Mann 2011, 57). Perhaps this was a meeting place, a site where different clans and tribes gathered to celebrate. Did each of the approximately two dozen stone circles belong to a different group? Some suggest that the *T*-shaped pillars represent stylized human figures.

The general consensus—not to say it is correct—is that Göbekli Tepe was a religious site, a very ancient temple, a holy and sacred spot, a series of shrines, a pilgrimage site. Studies of obsidian tools found at Göbekli Tepe reinforce the notion of this being a cosmopolitan gathering place. Several different sources for the obsidian have been identified, from as much as five hundred kilometers away. The style of some of the stone tools found at Göbekli Tepe suggests that people traveled to the site from as far as modern Iraq, Iran, along the middle portion of the Euphrates River, and various parts of the eastern Mediterranean (Jarus 2012).

Complementing and reinforcing the concept that Göbekli Tepe is a religious ritualistic center, Ian Hodder and Lynn Meskell (both professors at Stanford University) have argued that two of the major "symbolic themes" evident at Göbekli Tepe are: (1) phallocentrism (an emphasis on penises, both human and animal) and (2) a concern with wild, dangerous, and scary animals. Indeed, there are animals depicted at Göbekli Tepe that can be interpreted as fitting the latter category, such as boars with large canines (and wild boars are notably fierce beasts), lions and other felines, and apparent foxes, as well as snakes, scorpions, and carnivorous birds, such as vultures. Furthermore, some of these animals have prominent, and apparently erect, penises—such as certain animals generally interpreted as foxes. On one pillar, a headless human is depicted with a prominent erection, and an ithyphallic stone figure (30 cm tall) was found at Göbekli Tepe (Verit et al. 2005).

A naked woman lying on her back was crudely incised on a stone slab that was either part of a bench or the floor in one of the Göbekli Tepe structures (see Hodder and Meskell 2011; Verit et al. 2005). She has thin arms and her breasts dangle on each side of her body. Her misshapen legs are spread to either side, exposing her genital region. Something appears to be either protruding from or inserted into her vagina. Some have speculated that she represents a woman who has just given birth and that the umbilical cord is depicted protruding from her vagina. Others have suggested that intercourse is being depicted, but the male is represented only by a penis entering the vagina of the woman (and possibly the testes are crudely shown as well; it is difficult to interpret). Lines incised parallel to the presumed shaft of the penis may represent emissions from the vagina. The misshapen head of the woman has been interpreted as actually representing the glans penis (Verit et al. 2005, 209), in which case, she is effectively a penis, further supporting the concept of phallocentrism at Göbekli Tepe. Did this depiction on a stone slab mark a spot where intercourse actually took place, perhaps as some sacred ritual? Or, alternatively, simply for the sake of sex? Or it is a representation of an anthropomorphized plasma configuration as seen in the sky during a major solar outburst? (See chapter 6, page 118.)

Figure 3.10. Engraving on a stone slab found at Göbekli Tepe that resembles a woman, now on display in the Şanlıurfa Museum.
(Photograph courtesy of R. Schoch and C. Ulissey.)

Beyond these explicitly sexual depictions at Göbekli Tepe, Hodder and Meskell suggest that perhaps even the T-pillars "may themselves be evocations of the phallus, with an elongated shaft and a pronounced head" (2011, 237). Furthermore, these same authors view the pillars as possibly reinforcing their notion of a "scary animal" theme at Göbekli Tepe. "It is also possible that some of the pillars, with their long shaft and root, resemble teeth, and bared teeth and fangs are a recurrent motif at the site" (Hodder and Meskell 2011, 237).

While the phallic aspect, at least to some extent, may seem obvious—although my feeling is that Hodder and Meskell overemphasize it and I am not yet convinced that the T-pillars themselves are meant to represent erect penises—the scary animal motif is far from established in my opinion. My sense of many of the animals at Göbekli Tepe, with their bared teeth, is that they are happy or smiling in joy and mischief, rather like the Cheshire Cat. There is a luxuriant quality to the animals. In response to the scary animal theme proposed by Hodder and Meskell, Douglas Baird, of the University of Liverpool, has pointed out that the largest "figures" found at Göbekli Tepe are the central anthropomorphic T-pillars of one of the enclosures and that an animal (fox?)

Figure 3.11. Relief carving of a fox-like animal on one of the pillars at Göbekli Tepe; a small boar-like animal appears incised below the fox-like animal. (Photograph courtesy of R. Schoch and C. Ulissey.)

is nestled in under one arm (Baird 2011). That is, far from being "scary," the animals are dominated and subjugated by the humans (assuming the pillars represent humans rather than gods).

When I look at the carvings of animals, I think of shamans with their animal totems and guides. (Here I use *shaman* in the general colloquial sense, not the strict sense of Shirokogoroff 1935.) Images of birds are found at Göbekli Tepe, traditional symbols of the spirit or soul. Vultures in particular may represent birds that carried away the dead. On one of the pillars at Göbekli Tepe (Pillar 43), there is a vulture with a round object on its wing, and toward the bottom of the same pillar is a bas-relief of a headless man with a prominent erect penis. Could this somehow represent a mythos of life, death, and rebirth? Schmidt suggested that this scene might illustrate an ancient myth of vultures carrying away the heads of dead people (Batuman 2011, 80). Or might it be an early representation of the concept of a bird carrying the Sun across the sky (Batuman 2011, 78)? (And interestingly, on the edge of the pillar with the vulture is an animal that possibly resembles a lion: some people might even compare it to the original Sphinx in the form of a lioness.) Human bones found in association with Göbekli Tepe have been viewed as indications of a death cult (Vey 2011). Some of the human bones appear to have been unburied, perhaps left to be scavenged by wild animals, as was done in various later cultures (Tibet is an example; see David-Neel 1932). Could they even represent human sacrifices? Or was this a site of ancestor worship? In this connection, Brian Haughton writes, "Intriguingly, in recent excavations at Göbekli Tepe Schmidt's team have uncovered pieces of human bones in soils which came from the niches behind the stone pillars at the site. Schmidt believes the bones show that corpses were brought into the ritual areas demarcated by the engraved T-shaped stone[s], where they were then laid out and left to be stripped of their soft tissue by wild animals. Such activity would [suggest that] Göbekli Tepe [was] both a cemetery and a center of a regional death cult" (Haughton 2011; material in brackets added by R. Schoch). There have also been fragments of human skulls found at Göbekli Tepe that were artificially modified, which "could indicate a new, previously undocumented variation of skull cult in the Early Neolithic of Anatolia and the Levant" (Gresky et al. 2017, 1).

Figure 3.12. The "Vulture Pillar" (Pillar 43) of Enclosure D at
Göbekli Tepe. Overview of the carved side of the pillar (*bottom*).
Feline-like animal on the edge of the pillar (*top left*).
Overview of the uncarved side of the pillar (*top right*).
(Photographs courtesy of R. Schoch and C. Ulissey.)

Honestly, I find such speculations interesting, but until we have more evidence, they remain speculations. Certainly there are various reasons that human bone fragments might be found. There could have been a random death, a murder, or perhaps people died of natural catastrophes. Subsequently, wild animals scavenged the bodies because there was no one to attend to their immediate burial. Only later, perhaps, did survivors of the catastrophe return to collect and bury any remains that could be found. And we must consider the possibility that not all of the human remains found at Göbekli Tepe are due to the same cause. Regarding the artificially modified skulls, the evidence indicates that the modifications were made shortly after death (Gresky et al. 2017, 2), so in this case, the dead were being attended to by their fellows.

Göbekli Tepe has been hailed in some circles as figuratively, if not literally, the biblical Garden of Eden as described in the book of Genesis.

Yahweh God planted a garden in Eden which is in the east, and there he put the man he had fashioned.

Yahweh God caused to spring up from the soil every kind of tree, enticing to look at and good to eat, with the tree of life and the tree of the knowledge of good and evil in the middle of the garden.

A river flowed from Eden to water the garden, and from there it divided to make four streams.

The first is named the Pishon, and this encircles the whole land of Havilah where there is gold.

The gold of this land is pure; bdellium and onyx stone are found there.

The second river is named the Gihon, and this encircles the whole land of Cush.

The third river is named the Tigris, and this flows to the east of Ashur. The fourth river is the Euphrates.

Yahweh God took the man and settled him in the garden of Eden to cultivate and take care of it.

Then Yahweh God gave the man this admonition, "You may eat indeed of all the trees in the garden.

Nevertheless of the tree of the knowledge of good and evil you

are not to eat, for on the day you eat of it you shall most surely die."
(Jerusalem Bible, 1968, Genesis 2:8–17)

Like the fabled Eden, Göbekli Tepe lies between the northern portions of the Tigris and Euphrates Rivers. Although it is a bleak, bar-
ren desert landscape now, twelve thousand years ago Göbekli Tepe was
an area of abundant plant and animal life, a hunter-gatherer's paradise.
Göbekli Tepe is also an area where early domestication and agriculture
took place, more or less contemporaneously with the use of the structures, over several thousand years. The traditional view is that erecting a
complex on the order of Göbekli Tepe would have required a sedentary,
organized, labor force, and this would only be possible after domestication and agriculture were well established. But perhaps it was the other
way around. Did the gathering of large numbers of people at Göbekli
Tepe cause depletion of the local natural resources and essentially force
the development of agriculture? Early farming may have been disadvan-
tageous compared to gathering and hunting in a paradise. Farming was
time-consuming, backbreaking labor that yielded relatively poor nutri-
tion. As God said to Adam, after he ate the forbidden fruit that the
serpent convinced Eve to taste, "Accursed be the soil because of you.
With suffering shall you get your food from it every day of your life"
(Jerusalem Bible, 1968, Genesis 3:17). And there are snakes and serpents carved on some of the pillars of Göbekli Tepe.

WHAT ELSE DID THE BUILDERS OF GÖBEKLI TEPE HAVE?

On the face of it, the carved pillars that have been thus far excavated
at Göbekli Tepe indicate that their makers must have had an incredibly sophisticated material and social culture. Furthermore, remember
that at this point only a small proportion of the site has been excavated.
At least another sixteen to twenty stone enclosures are still under the
ground, and there may be many more structures and artifacts buried in
the surrounding hills and mountains. We do not know if the excavated
areas of Göbekli Tepe are even representative of the whole, or if entirely

different carvings, symbols, and types of structures will be found. In my opinion, it is premature to attempt to definitively "decode" or interpret the meaning and functions of the Göbekli Tepe carvings and structures. As I have already pointed out, some of the excavated pillars of Göbekli Tepe carry what may well be abstract symbols, even glimmerings of writing (see chapter 15, page 346). I will not be overly surprised if further excavations uncover more symbols or even what might be effectively a form of written language.

Göbekli Tepe is readily compared to Stonehenge in England, arguably one of the most famous archaeological sites in the world along with the Great Sphinx and Pyramids. But Stonehenge and the hundreds of other stone circles and related structures found throughout Europe and the British Isles (see, for instance, Burl 1976) are downright crude compared to Göbekli Tepe, yet these British and European stone megaliths are conventionally dated about five thousand to seven thousand or more years later than Göbekli Tepe! (This, of course, is assuming that the dates conventionally assigned to these structures are correct. Many of the dates are based on radiocarbon analysis of organic materials found in association with the stone circles, but it could well be that the stone circles are much older than the organic remains, being used and reused for many generations, indeed, for many millennia.)

What other material artifacts might the Göbekli Tepe people have had? It is difficult to know, especially since the majority of organic-based materials are extremely perishable and would not last for over ten thousand years. Certainly, I believe the Göbekli Tepe people had various implements of wood, leather, fur, and fiber. In particular, they surely would have had ropes, baskets, cords, nets, textiles, and other fiber-based artifacts. Beautifully woven textiles dating back to twelve thousand years ago—the end of the last ice age and Göbekli Tepe times—have been found in Peru (*Past Horizons* 2011; Maestri 2011). In addition to various stone beads, button-like artifacts carved from stone that could have been used with clothing are found at Göbekli Tepe (Badisches Landesmuseum Karlsruhe 2007a). In fact, evidence for full-fledged textiles, in the form of clay impressions of woven materials, date back twenty-five thousand years, and in a cave in the country of Georgia (north of eastern Turkey and the site of Göbekli Tepe) human-processed flax fibers (which traditionally are used to make linen) have been found that date back thirty thousand years or more (Harris 2009). No actual objects made from the fibers were found, as they may have degraded away or perhaps the fibers were only leftovers from mending or manufacturing objects. Archaeologist Ofer Bar-Yosef, of Harvard University, suggested the fibers were braided together to "make headgear, you can make baskets, you can make ropes and strings, and so on" (Bar-Yosef, quoted in Harris 2009). In my opinion, it is quite conceivable that they were making actual textiles that could have been used for clothing, to make bags, tents, and any number of other items. Interestingly, and tellingly, the thirty-thousand-year-old fibers from Georgia were purposefully dyed various shades of black, gray, pink, and turquoise. These ancient people had a sense of color and aesthetics.

Even in terms of stone or other nonperishable artifacts, it is naïve to assume that we have more than a vague inkling as to what the Göbekli Tepe people possessed. It is not as if they would casually leave their precious objects lying about willy-nilly for us to find over ten thousand years later. (Granted, they may have stored or buried, perhaps in a grave setting, certain objects, but then it is a matter of us locating them.) Certainly, based on such items as the stone beads and stone button-like objects found at Göbekli Tepe, it appears they had a fine aesthetic sense in terms of jewelry and personal ornamentation.

Other evidence from Turkey, suggestive of the material culture of the Göbekli Tepe people, further reinforces the contention that the level of technological and cultural sophistication in the region nine to twelve thousand or so years ago has been greatly underestimated. A fragment of an obsidian (volcanic glass) bracelet dated to 7500 BCE (just after Göbekli Tepe times) from the Neolithic site of Aşıklı Höyük in central Anatolia, Turkey, has been analyzed using modern high-tech methods (Thornhill 2011). The bracelet is described as having "a complex shape and a remarkable central annular ridge, and is 10 cm in diameter and 3.3 cm wide" (Physorg.com 2011a). Modern laboratory studies "revealed that the bracelet was made using highly specialized manufacturing techniques. The analyses carried out showed that the bracelet was almost perfectly regular. The symmetry of the central annular ridge is extremely precise, to the nearest degree and nearest hundred micrometers. This suggests that the artisans of the time used models to control its shape when it was being made. The surface finish of the bracelet (which is very regular, resembling a mirror) required the use of complex polishing techniques capable of obtaining a nanometer-scale surface quality worthy of today's telescope lenses" (Physorg.com 2011a). I would point out that the bracelet has been dated to circa 7500 BCE based on its context; it could actually be an artifact or heirloom from an earlier period that was passed down over the generations. A somewhat similar, and also incredibly sophisticated, stone bracelet was found in what is known as Denisova Cave, in the Altai Mountains, Siberia, and is believed to have been associated with the extinct species variously known as *Homo altaiensis* or the Denisovans, who are sometimes viewed as related to, or similar to, Neanderthals (Liesowska 2015; Zubova et al. 2017; Garau 2018). Initially dated to an astounding forty thousand years ago, more recent analysis of the stratum (geological layer) and context of the bracelet suggests that it may be sixty-five thousand to seventy thousand years old (*Siberian Times* 2017).

Besides their material culture, the Göbekli Tepe people surely had a rich oral and nonmaterial tradition that included mythology, history, religion, music, dance, and knowledge of the natural world, from the seasons and calendrical calculations and astronomy to the way to use plants, animals, herbs, and medicines. But I wonder if such knowledge was entirely oral and committed to memory, to be passed down from generation to generation. I do not think it inconceivable that the Göbekli Tepe people had some form of paper (be it paper as we think of it today or more a cloth or parchment substance) on which they made notations or even had what could be classified as actual writing.

Since I wrote the last paragraph in 2011–2012, there have been a number of developments regarding the possibility that the Göbekli Tepe people were literate, that they had actual writing. Various scholars have tentatively suggested that the Göbekli Tepe people had some form of wrting or "proto-writing," referring to both the images on the pillars of Göbekli Tepe (Cesarino 2012) and also images engraved on small stone plaques found at the site (see summary and references in Henley 2018). And more importantly, my colleague Manu Seyfzadeh identified connections between symbols on the pillars of Göbekli Tepe and later hieroglyphs found among ancient Anatolian scripts (see chapter 15, page 348, and Seyfzadeh and Schoch 2019a). And, perhaps even more astounding, some of the shapes and symbols apparently reflect solar plasma physics (see discussion in chapter 15).

If there is one thing that we should learn from the modern history of archaeology, it is that we have consistently underestimated the level of sophistication, and antiquity, of our forebears.

ANCIENT KNOWLEDGE
PURPOSEFULLY BURIED?

When I consider Göbekli Tepe, the first thing that comes to mind is that this was a center of knowledge, which of course is not incompatible with a religious site. Could the positions of the monoliths and the specific carvings on their surfaces encode information? Obvious suggestions are that the various stone circles were calendrical or astronomical. Might constellations be depicted or encoded in the carved reliefs or positions of the megaliths? Are there significant alignments among the stones? Did each circle refer to a different topic or branch of ancient knowledge?

Göbekli Tepe was built, used, and added to for a couple of thousand years. My interpretation is that there were three main phases. First, the beautiful *T*-shaped stone pillars were erected and carved. Typically, about a dozen such pillars were erected in a circle or oval, and two more stood in the center. Based on the roughened top surfaces that they bear, the pillars may also have supported some kind of roof or superstructure at some point in their history. Second, relatively crude stone walls were built between the outer pillars, forming circular enclosures. These walls abut, and in some cases appear to cover or hide, the carved reliefs on the pillars. It is also apparent that some of the *T*-shaped pillars had toppled over and were reerected when the secondary stone walls were built. I sense that the site was being converted into some kind of defensive structure. Finally, by no later than ten thousand years ago (perhaps much earlier), the entire complex was intentionally buried under tons of rock and earth. It has been suggested that portions of Göbekli Tepe may have been "buried" due to collapse of the structures and natural erosion from adjacent higher-lying areas and subsequent deposition at lower elevations (Gresky et al. 2017, 7). I agree that this is possible, and even likely to a certain extent, especially for certain younger portions of Göbekli Tepe, but it does not preclude intentional burial of the older portions, such as Enclosures C and D. Indeed, in Enclosures C and D we see evidence that pillars had fallen and were subsequently reerected before secondary stone walls were built, and then the entire enclosures were buried in debris. My observations of the debris on-site lead me to regard this initial or primary burial to have been artificial and not due to natural causes. (**UPDATE:** I want to point out that, as I discuss further below, I believe one plausible explanation for the burial of Göbekli Tepe was to protect and preserve the site—and the information, the message, it encodes—for posterity. Megalithic stones are quite durable; however, like many other materials on Earth, unprotected stone pillars would be vulnerable to the scorching temperatures of electrical plasma discharges produced during a solar outburst. The major solar outburst [or outbursts] at the end of the last ice age, and the attendant catastrophic events on Earth, explains, or provides a framework, for many of the enigmatic mysteries of the remote past.)

There is no doubt Göbekli Tepe was used and reused for a long time, by my estimate at least two thousand years, before being intentionally buried around 8000 BCE or earlier. Even long after its burial, Göbekli Tepe may have retained its importance for local peoples. Professor Schmidt suggested that some of the carved depressions and gouges, for instance on the tops of pillars (which may have been level with the surface of the ground at that time), may date to a time when the site was buried but still remembered as an important or holy site and people still came to partake of the energy of the site. As Veysí Yildiz, son of the local landowner, explained to us while we were visiting the site, even before the archaeological remains were discovered at Göbekli Tepe, the area was held in reverence. Stone-covered graves or memorial mounds

Figure 3.13. Burial or memorial mounds at the top of Göbekli Tepe by the mulberry tree. Seen in the summer (*left*) and the winter (*right*). (Photographs courtesy of R. Schoch and C. Ulissey.)

are found on the top of the site to this day by a mulberry tree, known as the "Wish Tree" (see World Heritage Nomination 2017, 18).

Why the different uses of the site? Why the eventual abandonment and burial? Had the temple, the sacred ground, come to the end of its life cycle? Was it ritually desanctified, decommissioned? Or did the people of Göbekli Tepe turn from hunting and gathering to agriculture, and in the process abandon their old ways, their old gods? Or did the people suffer natural catastrophes? Twelve thousand years ago (more precisely, circa 9700 BCE) the last glacial period came to an end, sea levels were rising, climates were fluctuating, and some people believe the poles were shifting and comets were bombarding our planet (more on this later; I am not a proponent of the "comet theory"), and as we shall see, there is strong evidence of a major solar outburst at this time. In the wake of calamity, did the people of Göbekli Tepe first attempt to fortify their structures and then, realizing that it was futile, bury them and flee? Did they hope to return again to uncover their monuments?

In a nutshell, we have evidence of high culture and civilization (and its aftermath) circa 10,000 BCE to perhaps as late as circa 8000 BCE, but then an apparent decline or hiatus for thousands of years, until the "rise" of civilization once again in Mesopotamia, Egypt, and elsewhere. What happened?

MISINTERPRETING GÖBEKLI TEPE

I believe it is evident that the remains we find today at Göbekli Tepe were not all built at the same time; they are not all of one piece. For some archaeologists, anthropologists, and prehistorians to interpret them as if they are is to misrepresent the data. Harvey Whitehouse of the University of Oxford published an extreme variation on the misconception. It is worth quoting him directly, so that I cannot be accused of misrepresenting his words:

> Göbekli Tepe comprises a series of Stonehenge-like circles of stone slabs, faintly resembling giant phalluses. In fact, these stones were quarried much, much earlier than Stonehenge—some 12,000 years ago. And each spectacular ring of towering monoliths was probably buried within days or weeks of its completion. The sheer effort of human labour involved is mind-boggling. Nobody knows how it was done without bulldozers, winches, cranes, or even steel hand tools. And nobody knows why. What inspired ancient foragers to push their stone-age technology to the very limits, cutting 20-tonne stones out of the hillside, dragging them up to the summit and placing them in painstakingly dug holes several metres deep? Why carve exquisitely realistic high reliefs of animals into their sides, only to hide these staggering creations from view under a pile of rubble? (Whitehouse 2012)

Based on his misinterpretation of the data, that the structures at Göbekli Tepe were built and then purposefully buried within days or weeks, Whitehouse interprets the site as representing essentially religious rituals that were, in their specifics, really rather pointless but that served to socially bond groups of individuals together, and sub-groups into larger groups. While certainly a site like Göbekli Tepe helped to solidify and bond people together, just as a great church, mosque, synagogue, or secular monument does today, to reduce Göbekli Tepe to nothing more than this is, I believe, downright mis-leading. It is one more academic ruse to try to force Göbekli Tepe into the standard paradigm and thus avoid acknowledging that the status quo has it all wrong.

Freestanding sculptures and other artwork found at Göbekli Tepe, placed on display in the museum in Şanlıurfa, reinforce in my opinion the sophistication of the people of this civilization. There are human figures, boars, feline-type beasts, and other animals, as well as a tall, enigmatic, intricately carved stone pillar that superficially resembles a totem pole of a later time and culture. What it actually represents eludes definitive interpretation at the present time, although my first instinct is that it may record the complexities of the psychical com-ponents of the human being, as expressed in a cycle of birth, death, and rebirth. I have no doubt that the carvings, both on the pillars and among the freestanding sculptures, have meaning and significance.

Figure 3.14. A carved stone sculpture (colloquially referred to by some as a "stone totem pole") found at Göbekli Tepe, now on display in the Şanlıurfa Museum. (Photographs courtesy of R. Schoch and C. Ulissey.)

Figure 3.15. An assortment of small stone sculptures found at
Göbekli Tepe, now on display in the Şanlıurfa Museum.
(Photographs courtesy of R. Schoch and C. Ulissey.)

These are not random creations or busywork undertaken as simple
bonding rituals to be immediately buried in debris. The beauty, sat-
isfaction, and joy of some of the Göbekli Tepe sculptures strike me.
These were a sophisticated people, a forgotten civilization, who had
an understanding, a comprehension, of themselves and the cosmos
that we would do well to rediscover.

A RECORD OF PRECESSION
AT GÖBEKLI TEPE

A hallmark of civilization is precise scientific observation. Astronomy is often considered the earliest yet most sophisticated of the sciences. A particularly subtle astronomical phenomenon, the discovery of which is generally credited to Hipparchus of Rhodes in the second century BCE (Magli 2004, 2009), is the slow movement of the stars relative to the equatorial coordinate system. This is commonly referred to as the precession of the equinoxes. The entire cycle, with stars returning to their "starting points," takes somewhat under twenty-six thousand years. Some researchers suggest that precession was known to the ancient Egyptians and other early civilizations and is reflected in myths worldwide (Lockyer 1894; de Santillana and von Dechend 1969). Others dispute such assertions. I found evidence of precession at Göbekli Tepe, adding another layer of sophistication to this remarkable site.

The major excavated portions (as of early 2020) of Göbekli Tepe lie on the southern slope of a hill looking out to the southern skies. Thus far, as mentioned above, the better part of four stone circles (enclosures) has been excavated in an area measuring about forty-by-forty meters. Additional younger and smaller pillars and structures have been partially uncovered, both twenty to thirty meters north and about eighty meters west of the major area of circles (the main, and older, portion of Göbekli Tepe under discussion here belongs to Schmidt's Layer III; the younger and smaller pillars and structures belong to Schmidt's Layer II), and approximately eighteen or more stone circles still under the earth have been identified. (Excavations are ongoing at Göbekli Tepe, and there are areas that have been apparently excavated or partially excavated that, as of early 2020, are covered over by a modern protective structure and not open to the public; my request to be allowed to see these excavations during my January 2020 visit was met with silence. I fully understand, however, that those in charge may not want to reveal what they have found until they have a chance to bring their excavations to a certain point and also analyze and publish their results.) Enclosure D is located the farthest north. To the southeast lies Enclosure C, and to the south of Enclosure D lie Enclosures B and finally A. The enclosures are very close to each other, almost abutting. Each enclosure possesses a pair of tall central pillars erected parallel to each other and ringed by a circle of shorter pillars with later stone walls between the pillars. If at some point the enclosures were covered over, they may have been entered from above; indeed, possible carved stone "portals" have been found that may have been set in a roof.

I believe that the pillars of Göbekli Tepe encode astronomical knowledge and also that the site itself was in part an astronomical observatory. Along these lines, Walter Cruttenden (2012) has suggested that a number of the relief carvings on the pillars may be representations of major constellations: the scorpion on one of the pillars may represent Scorpio, a vulture may represent Cygnus (possibly along with Lyra), the aurochs or bull may represent Taurus, snakes may relate to Ophiuchus and/or Hydra, the foxes may represent Vulpecula—to give just a few examples. The Egyptologist Ludwig D. Morenz, of the University of Leipzig, has suggested that the vulture (or eagle) depicted on one pillar with an outstretched wing carrying a "ball" may represent the sky bearing the solar disc or the Moon (Morenz 2012). Others have interpreted the "ball" as a human head, in part because lower on the same pillar appears a headless human body bearing an erect penis (Hodder and Meskell 2011).

Supporting the potential astronomical use of Göbekli Tepe, Donna Sutliff (an independent scholar working out of North Adams, Massachusetts) has suggested that the "T-shaped pillars . . . [may have] served an astronomical function, such as fixed points by which to discern the movement of the sun, moon, and stars similar to the way the Incas used pillars to note the sun's movements" (2012, 125). Along the same lines, retired computer professional Joe Plegge (2012) has analyzed Göbekli Tepe and come to the conclusion that the arrangements of the pillars and the holes found carved through some of them could have been used to track the equinoxes and solstices.

The central pairs of pillars in the enclosures at Göbekli Tepe are oriented generally toward the southeast, as if forming sighting tubes toward the sky. Remarkably, the central pillars of Enclosure D include arms and hands, with the hands positioned below the navel, framing the belly and navel area, and the anthropomorphic pillars are facing south. The Enclosure D central pillars are also wearing belts and loin-cloths (to my eye, the loincloths appear to be formed from fox pelts); overall, I have the impression that the pillars represent headless hunt-ers (equivalent, perhaps, to the "headless hunter" in the sky—namely Orion, whom the dynastic Egyptians equated with Osiris; see further discussion in chapter 15, page 358). The orientations of the central pillars vary from enclosure to enclosure, however. For Enclosure D the central pillars are oriented approximately 7° east of south. Those for Enclosures C, B, and A are approximately 13° east of south, 20° east of south, and 35° east of south, respectively. (These measurements are only approximate and are based on the plan of Göbekli Tepe pub-lished by Peters and Schmidt 2004, 186). These varying angles sug-gest the builders were observing stars and building new enclosures oriented progressively toward the east as they followed particular stars or star clusters over hundreds of years.

On the morning of the vernal equinox of circa 10,000 BCE, before the Sun rose due east at Göbekli Tepe, the Pleiades, Taurus, and the top of Orion were in view in the direction indicated by the central stones of Enclosure D (as noted above, these pillars face south; this is indicated by the positions of the hands and loincloths), with Orion's Belt not far above the horizon as dawn broke (as seen from the best vantage points in the area). (Alignments discussed in this sec-tion on Göbekli Tepe were determined using the 2003 version of the Starry Night Pro 4.5 computer program by Space Holding Company, Toronto.)

A similar scenario played out for the orientation of the central stones of Enclosure C in circa 9500 BCE and for Enclosure B in circa 9000 BCE. Enclosure A is oriented toward the Pleiades, Taurus, and Orion on the morning of the Vernal Equinox circa 8500 BCE, but due to precessional changes, the entire belt of Orion no longer rose above the horizon before dawn broke. By about 8150 BCE, the belt of Orion remained below the horizon at dawn on the morning of the vernal equinox. These dates fit well the time frame established for Göbekli Tepe on the basis of radiocarbon dating. Furthermore, Orion the constellation can be viewed as literally a torso in the sky with arms (but not legs), a headless hunter, similar to the iconography of the headless hunters represented by the central pillars of Enclosure D. Orion in the sky is most easily identified by its prominent "belt stars"—known simply as Orion's Belt.

The vernal equinox is easily observed and noted, and since the beginning of recorded history has been an important marker, celebrated with festivities. It marks the first day of the year in numerous calendars and is tied to cosmological creation stories. I suspect that these traditions go back to Göbekli Tepe times and even earlier. And, remember, the Great Sphinx, facing due east, faces precisely the location of the vernal equinox.

The Orion-Taurus region of the sky was a focus of ancient humans for tens of thousands of years in Europe and the Middle East. Here are located the asterisms of Orion's Belt and the Hyades, as well as the Pleiades. Orion and the Pleiades are explicitly mentioned in the Judeo-Christian Bible (see, for instance, Job 38:31 and Amos 5:8). Researchers such as Michael Rappenglueck, Frank Edge, and Luz Antequera Congregado have identified the constellation Taurus and the Pleiades among the paintings of Lascaux Cave in France, dating back 16,500 years ago (Seddon 2008; Thompson 2001–2007; Whitehouse 2000). Additionally, Rappenglueck asserts that a tiny tablet from Germany, carved of mammoth ivory and dating back at least 32,500 years, depicts the constellation Orion in the familiar guise of a narrow-waisted male figure with outstretched arms and legs (Whitehouse 2003). Given such evidence, it is reasonable that the Göbekli Tepe people recognized Orion as a human figure, even as a hunter. The animal remains found while excavating Göbekli Tepe (including leopards, a hyena, gazelles, aurochs or wild cattle, wild asses, foxes, red deer, Mesopotamian fallow deer, wild sheep and goat species, boars, chukar partridges, cranes, and vultures; see Batuman 2011, 78; Peters and Schmidt 2004; and Schmidt 2010), as well as the bas-reliefs

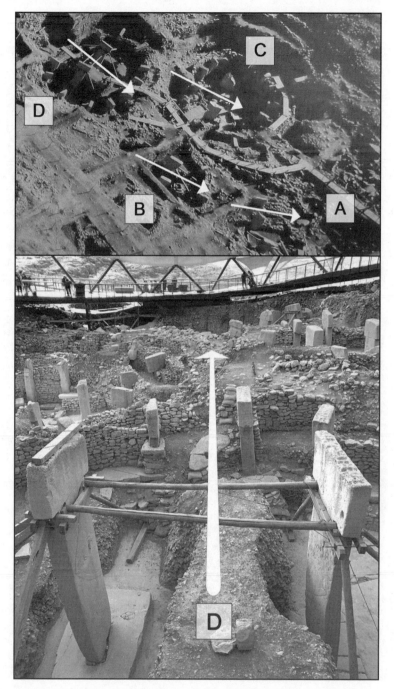

Figure 3.16a. Diagram showing the orientations of Enclosures A, B, C, and D
at Göbekli Tepe (*top*). View through the central pillars of Enclosure D
looking south and slightly east (*bottom*).

(Photograph of Göbekli Tepe courtesy of R. Schoch and C. Ulissey. Aerial view on display
in the Şanlıurfa Museum; photographed and arrows added by R. Schoch and C. Ulissey.)

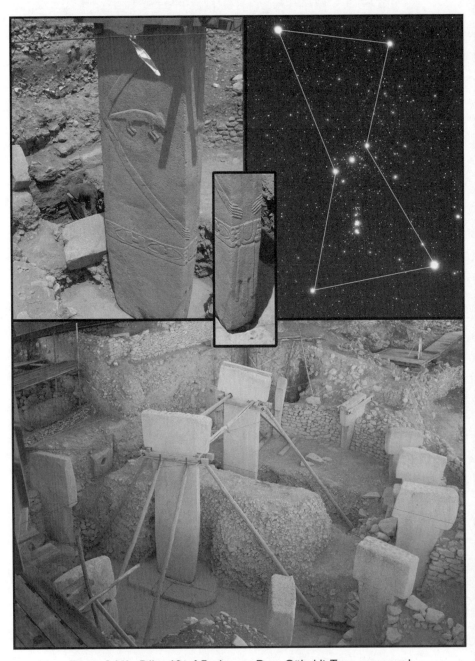

Figure 3.16b. Pillar 18 of Enclosure D at Göbekli Tepe compared
to the constellation of Orion (*top*). Overview of Enclosure D;
Pillar 18 is in the center back of this view (*bottom*).

(Photographs of Göbekli Tepe courtesy of R. Schoch and C. Ulissey.
Orion photo: modified from a public domain image.)

on the pillars, can be taken to indicate a hunting society—or possibly the zodiac that surrounds the constellation Orion. Studying the anthropomorphic pillars of Enclosure D, they may represent, in stylized form, Orion. Not only do they have arms (which could be interpreted as the arms of Orion brought down to the body), but also prominent belts (the belt stars of Orion) and fox pelt loincloths that may represent the Orion Nebula and associated features.

Interestingly, and I believe not merely coincidentally, Orion has been associated with other very ancient sites. In the Sahara Desert of southern Egypt, west of Aswan, is an area known as Nabta Playa. Here an ancient stone calendar circle, as well as many other megalithic erections and structures, has been identified by archaeologist Fred Wendorf, from Southern Methodist University, and his team and dated to circa 4000 BCE and earlier (Malville 1998).

Physicist Thomas Brophy (2002, 2012; see also Gaffney 2006) has carried out extensive analyses of Nabta. According to Brophy, three stones inside the Nabta calendar circle represent the belt of Orion (just as the three pyramids of Giza represent the belt of Orion according to the research of Robert Bauval; Bauval and Gilbert 1994; Schoch and Bauval 2017). The stones on the playa and the corresponding stars in the sky aligned on summer solstice nights between about 6400 BCE and 4900 BCE. Brophy found even more correlations, however. Three other stones in the Nabta calendar circle correspond to the configuration of Orion's upper portions/shoulders as they appeared in circa 16,500 BCE, nearly half a precessional cycle earlier than the previously mentioned alignment. Based on these and other analyses of monoliths in the area, Brophy concludes that the early inhabitants of Nabta Playa possessed incredibly sophisticated knowledge, the type of knowledge we associate with high culture and civilization. Furthermore, the dates of the Nabta structures are in line with my dating of the oldest portions of the Great Sphinx as well as the dating of Göbekli Tepe, and at Giza, Göbekli Tepe, and Nabta apparently the constellation of Orion (which for the ancient Egyptians represented the god Osiris during dynastic times) was of prime importance.

My suggestion that the Göbekli Tepe people were observing the Orion-Taurus-Pleiades region of the sky on the morning of the vernal equinox is simply a hypothesis. If they were observing stars (versus the Sun, for instance), then they needed to readjust their observations over the centuries due to precessional changes. And maybe they were observing something more than just the Sun, Moon, planets, and stars.

POSSIBLE DESCENDANTS
OF THE GÖBEKLI TEPE PEOPLE

Did the builders of Göbekli Tepe simply disappear, or did they perhaps pass on some of their heritage to later generations? Possibly, they buried their monuments, abandoned their homeland, and migrated to other parts of the world. Tantalizing evidence to support such a scenario has come from various fields. Egyptologist Ludwig D. Morenz (2012) has pointed out that the concept of a sky vulture, as interpreted on a pillar of Göbekli Tepe, is found thousands of years later in ancient Egypt. Similarly, Hodder and Meskell (2011, 238) note that ithyphallic statues from Göbekli Tepe and associated sites are similar to the ithyphallic Egyptian god Min, although they are quick to point out that they "do not wish to argue for direct cultural links." However, Joe Plegge (2012, 69) suggests explicitly that there may be direct links between the Göbekli Tepe people and the builders of Stonehenge of Wiltshire, Salisbury Plain, England. "My belief is that the builders of Göbekli Tepe created a megalithic structure used for celestial observations, and their descendants brought this knowledge with them when the[y] migrated to England and helped build Stonehenge," Plegge writes. According to conventional dating, the earliest stages of Stonehenge go back to about 3100 BCE, some five to six millennia or more after the demise of Göbekli Tepe. Furthermore, the two sites are separated by nearly four thousand kilometers and the English Channel. However, these conventional dates for Stonehenge may not be the entire story; activity at the site of Stonehenge, marked by very ancient postholes, goes back at least ten thousand years (Anonymous undated, "Stonehenge Post Holes"; Kinsley 2015).

So can we seriously suggest that the Göbekli Tepe people were the ancestors of the builders of Stonehenge? Plegge cites a paper published by geneticist Patricia Balaresque, of the University of Leicester, and colleagues that concludes, based on Y-chromosome data, that there was movement, migration, and expansion of lineages from Anatolia (the general area where Göbekli Tepe is located) into Western Europe over the last ten thousand years (Balaresque et al. 2010). Reinforcing this hypothesis is a linguistic study. Remco Bouckaert (Computer Science at the University of Auckland) and colleagues, after analyzing vocabulary data from 103 different Indo-European languages (ancient and contemporary), concluded that the Indo-European languages originated in Anatolia, the general region of modern Turkey that includes Göbekli Tepe, some eight thousand to ten thousand years ago (Bouckaert et al. 2012). Thus both the genetic data and linguistic analysis support the hypothesis that the Göbekli Tepe people and/or their descendants may have migrated out of Anatolia, ultimately to reestablish new societies, new cultures, and new civilizations elsewhere thousands of years later. In this sense, might we consider Göbekli Tepe the origin, the Garden of Eden, where civilization flourished some twelve thousand years ago, before the ice age ended?

NOT JUST A TEMPLE

Among the public and academics alike, Göbekli Tepe is most often referred to as a "temple," even the "World's First Temple"; however, I believe this is a matter of imposing our biases on these enigmatic structures. I suspect that, in modern terms, Göbekli Tepe served more as a university. Like many modern universities, it may have included ritualistic and religious aspects (many universities include theology in their curriculum, have chapels on their campuses, or are associated with a church or other religious organization), but Göbekli Tepe was also a center of that which we now refer to as "science," and like a modern library or museum (which today are often integral parts of a university), it preserved knowledge for future generations. Göbekli Tepe was used and reused for millennia, and then finally purposefully buried by those using the site in response to the catastrophes and cataclysms at the end of the last ice age (circa 9700 BCE). So, in the end, as they covered over their creation with earth and stone, did the Göbekli Tepe people believe they were leaving a "time capsule," a "message for the future"? I suspect so. They knew that eventually their creations would be found and uncovered. Now it is a matter of interpreting exactly what the "message" they left us is. This is a topic I am actively engaged in. By the way, I am not fully convinced by any of the numerous interpretations of the "Göbekli Tepe message" that have been offered so far. Most suffer, in my opinion, from the all too common weakness of interpreting an ancient site through the assumptions and biases of our modern society rather than attempting to understand the site in the terms and with the values of the people who actually built it. Furthermore, a very small percentage of Göbekli Tepe has been excavated thus far. To try to give a comprehensive and definitive interpretation of Göbekli Tepe based on a superficial analysis of only 5 or 10 percent, taken out of context, is simply untenable and irresponsible. The equivalent would be if an archaeologist of the future, twelve thousand years from now, interpreted an entire sprawling university complex based on the partial excavation of the remains of only one chemistry laboratory or only one alcove of the library that included a few books and murals illustrating comparative religion and theology.

We need to rid ourselves of our own biases and preconceived notions and let the people who erected Göbekli Tepe speak for themselves.

Standing at the northern end of the stone circles of Göbekli Tepe, looking toward the southern sky in the same direction as the anthropomorphic central pillars of Enclosure D, I wondered about the builders of this immense, and immensely sophisticated, site some twelve millennia ago. To my mind, these were an enormously talented, technologically adroit, knowledgeable people. These were not mere primitive savages or barbarians, but a civilized people. But what does it mean to be civilized? What is civilization? Had the builders of Göbekli Tepe genuinely crossed the line from savagery to civilization? To address this question, we need to turn to the issue of just what constitutes civilization. As we will see, opinions differ, but in the end, I am convinced that both the builders of Göbekli Tepe and the creators of the original Sphinx are representatives of a very early flowering of civilization, earlier than conventional archaeologists previously dreamed possible.

Figure 3.17. Various views and details of Pillar 18 of Enclosure D at Göbekli Tepe. Close up of the front of the pillar with the "belt buckle" and fox-pelt loincloth (*top left*). Overview of the pillar (*top right*). Carving of bird-like animals in the bedrock base of the pillar (*bottom*).
(Photographs courtesy of R. Schoch and C. Ulissey.)

4

DEFINING CIVILIZATION

As he stood on the Pont des Arts in Paris, looking at the Institute of France on one side and the Louvre on the other and toward the Cathedral of Notre Dame, British art historian Kenneth Clark commented, "What is civilisation? I don't know. I can't define it in abstract terms—yet. But I think I can recognise it when I see it; and I am looking at it now" (Clark 1969, 1).

If we are to understand how the evidence of Göbekli Tepe, the redating of the Great Sphinx, and other developing data overturn and rewrite the old paradigms of how, when, and why sophisticated culture and civilization began, we need to examine the views, assumptions, and hypotheses that have prevailed among historians, prehistorians, and archaeologists for the last century.

When and where did civilization begin? How far back in time does high culture go? Indeed, what do we mean by such terms as *civilization* or *sophisticated culture* and *high culture?*

When I was in college, more years ago than I perhaps care to remember, I learned the standard story that still holds sway in many circles: civilization and high culture date back to, at most, perhaps five or six thousand years ago. A handy marker for recognizing a true civilization was written language, and it was generally agreed that the earliest true writing could be dated to the late fourth millennium BCE (that is, circa 3500 BCE to 3000 BCE). The Sumerians are generally credited with developing writing about 3300 BCE to 3200 BCE, although the earliest Egyptian hieroglyphics may date back to the same period or even a century or so earlier, and there is also evidence of writing possibly from as far back as 3500 BCE found at Harappa, the Indus civilization, in what is now modern Pakistan (Whitehouse 1999; Wilford 1999). But then there are reports of much earlier possible writing from Henan Province in China, dated at 6600 BCE to 6200 BCE, inscribed on tortoise shells (Rincon 2003). I recollect a book I read while still an undergraduate, *The Roots of Civilization* by Alexander Marshack (1972; see also Elkins 1996), which argued that various lines, notches, and "scratchings" on ancient bone artifacts dating to 10,000 BCE and earlier, before the end of the last ice age, were in fact symbolic systems, including lunar calendar notations. Maybe our ancestors were not so primitive and stupid after all. (And see chapter 15, page 346, for the latest evidence of writing at Göbekli Tepe, around twelve thousand years ago.)

Kenneth Clark, in his book and television documentary series, attempted to clarify what he (and so many of his viewers and readers) thought of as civilization. Referring to the medieval Norsemen (a term Clark used interchangeably with Vikings), he wrote:

> Unlike the earlier wanderers, the Vikings had a rather splendid mythology, romanticised by Wagner. . . . When one considers the Icelandic sagas, which are among the great books of the world, one must admit that the Norsemen produced a culture. But was it civilisation? . . . Civilisation means something more than energy and will and creative power: something the early Norsemen hadn't got, but which, even in their time, was beginning to appear in Western Europe. How can I define it? Well, very shortly, a sense of permanence. The wanderers and the invaders were in a continual state of flux. They didn't feel the need to look forward beyond the next March or the next voyage or the next battle. And for that reason it didn't occur to them to build stone houses, or to write books. . . . [Clark says this despite his previous comments about the Icelandic sagas being "among the great books of the world."] . . . . Civilised man, or so it seems to me, must feel that he belongs somewhere in

space and time; that he consciously looks forward and looks back. And for this purpose it is a great convenience to be able to read and write. (Clark 1969, 14 and 17; comment in brackets by R. Schoch)

Maybe defining civilization and high culture in terms of a written language (or more accurately our knowledge of a recorded language, since we can easily miss things in the archaeological record) simply is not a fruitful approach. This is the conclusion I have come to while pursing my own research. But old ways of thinking die hard, and most archaeologists and historians still define civilization in terms of simple attributes such as having a written language. Why? In many respects the present mainstream paradigm, the paradigm that my work redating the Great Sphinx and the discovery of Göbekli Tepe threaten, can be traced back to the theories of one man, the great archaeological synthesizer V. Gordon Childe (1892–1957).

THE REVOLUTIONS OF PREHISTORY

Childe's primary goal was to establish an overarching theory of how and why civilization arose following a period of tens of thousands of years (or longer) when humans were biologically "modern" but still uncivilized. (We now have evidence of anatomically modern humans, *Homo sapiens,* from southern Ethiopia dating back to approximately 200,000 years ago [Hammond et al. 2017], and *H. sapiens* was in Western Asia by approximately 180,000 years ago [Stringer and Galaway-Witham 2018].) As part of his explanation, the Marxist Childe developed the key concepts of the Neolithic Revolution and the Urban Revolution (see Childe 1950; Bar-Yosef 1998), although in fairness to Childe, he was not a strict and dogmatic Marxist and the extent to which his politics influenced his science is open to debate (see Smith 2009, and references therein). Be that as it may, it is difficult to overstress the influence that Childe has had on subsequent scholars. In a review of Childe's contributions, Michael E. Smith wrote, "Often, this debt [to Childe's work] is acknowledged . . . but just as often scholars today go about their business without citing Childe. Nevertheless, the archaeological study of ancient complex societies is still dominated by the themes of urbanism, agricultural intensification and surplus, craft specialisation, social inequality, and the nature of power and the state, each of which was first applied to archaeological data in a systematic fashion by V. Gordon Childe and synthesised in his seminal paper in *Town Planning Review*" (Smith 2009, 22).

The paper Smith refers to is the 1950 article by Childe titled "The Urban Revolution," in which he outlined his basic concept of a "city" and thus the criteria to define and recognize "civilization." It is worth reviewing Childe's main points.

Building on the work of his predecessors, Childe distinguished three basic types of preindustrial societies, which he (and many others since) have referred to as savagery, barbarism, and civilization (these terms had already been applied as early as 1878 by Lewis Henry Morgan; see Smith 2009). Savages in this technical sense live off of wild foods that they obtain by hunting, fishing, gathering, foraging, and scavenging. Another, more acceptable modern term for such savages is hunter-gatherers (or gatherer-hunters, since in many such communities it may have been more the gathering, carried out primarily by women and children, perhaps, that really sustained the population).

Barbarians in the refined sense used by Childe might still hunt and gather to some extent, but they supplement their food supply by cultivating edible plants and/or by herding and breeding animals. Cultivation and herding began with a group of people, a community, initially protecting plots of wild plants or groups of wild animals. This slowly led to more and more interference with the wild stocks, such as weeding, watering, irrigation, feeding, and selective breeding—ultimately culminating in the domestication of plants and animals (see North and Thomas 1977, 240, for comments on this subject). Fully domesticated organisms are in some cases unable to survive without human interference, such as plants that cannot grow without watering, weeding, and harvesting (their seeds may not break open and sprout on their own), or animals that no longer can exist in the wild because they have been bred to be docile or their coats have been bred to grow to such a length that they must be shorn or else the animal will suffer (think of sheep).

The transition from savagery (a primarily hunter-gatherer society) to barbarism (a society using cultivation, agriculture, and domestication to a significant extent) Childe termed the Neolithic Revolution, after the Neolithic Period—the "New Stone Age" of Europe. Childe stated (1950, 3), "Barbarism began less than ten thousand years ago with the Neolithic Age of archaeologists" (in modern terms the Neolithic Period is often dated to circa 10,000 BCE to 4000 BCE). Childe's contemporary, George G. MacCurdy, explained the implications of barbarism in 1926, stating, "The control of food supply made village life possible, and this in turn, led to societal organization, without which discipline, important works such as fortification, megalithic monuments, lake villages, etc., could never have been consummated" (MacCurdy, quoted in Bar-Yosef 1998, 1).

The next stage beyond barbarism, according to Childe, is civilization. Civilization, he admitted, can be difficult to define. The word itself comes from the Latin *civilis* and is related to the concepts of *civis* (citizen) and *civitas* (city or city-state). So, civilization can be equated with the concept of city life. As Childe wrote:

> . . . and sure enough life in cities begins with this stage. But "city" is itself ambiguous so archaeologists like to use "writing" as a criterion for civilization; it should be easily recognizable and proves to be a reliable index to more profound characters. Note, however, that, because a people is said to be civilized or literate, it does not follow that all its members can read and write, nor that they all lived in cities. Now there is no recorded instance of a community of savages civilizing themselves, adopting urban life or inventing a script. Wherever cities have been built, villages of preliterate farmers existed previously (save perhaps where an already civilized people have colonized uninhabited tracts). So civilization, wherever and whenever it arose, succeeded barbarism. (Childe 1950, 3–4)

This transition from barbarism to civilization, from village life to the development of true cities, Childe defined as the Urban Revolution. In using the word *revolution* for both the Neolithic

Revolution and the Urban Revolution, Childe explicitly pointed out, "This must not of course be taken as denoting a sudden violent catastrophe; it is here used for the culmination of a progressive change in the economic structure and social organisation of communities that caused, or was accompanied by, a dramatic increase in the population affected" (Childe 1950, 3).

So for Childe (and so many other archaeologists, historians, prehistorians, sociologists, and anthropologists), the three fundamental evolutionary stages of humanity before the modern era (which might be dated to the Industrial Revolution, beginning in the eighteenth century) are:

1. Savagery (gatherers, hunters, and foragers)
2. Barbarism (cultivators, herders, agriculturalists, and husbandry practiced in village settings)
3. Civilization (urban living with literacy and other aspects of sophisticated, or high, culture, as we shall discuss further in the next section of this chapter).

Note that for Childe and like-minded thinkers, this series is both a hierarchy of stages from primitive (generally used to refer to savages and barbarians) to advanced (civilized peoples) and, for any particular people or geographic area, a progressive temporal sequence of development. Overall, humanity has progressed through these stages during the last twelve thousand years, but at any one time (including the present) there may exist simultaneously on the face of our planet different groups in different stages of development (see Coon 1954; Weyer 1959).

Given his emphasis on urban life, cities, and literacy as being fundamental to civilization, Childe dated the origins of civilization in the Old World to circa five thousand years ago (we would now probably say circa 4000 BCE to 3000 BCE) in three geographic areas: Egypt, Mesopotamia (the Tigris-Euphrates area, which includes the area where Göbekli Tepe is found), and the Indus River region of Asia (modern Pakistan and India). "It can be argued that all cities in the old world are offshoots of those of Egypt, Mesopotamia and the Indus basin," Childe wrote (1950, 9). Independently in the New World, cities and civilization arose thousands of years later.

THE ELEMENTS OF CIVILIZATION

Childe (1950; see also the review in Smith 2009) enumerated ten basic criteria that he considered distinctive of cities, urban life, complex society, and civilization compared to either savagery or barbarism.

1. Cities and early civilization represented an increase in size and population density over all previous forms of settlement (Childe 1950, 9).
2. Cities included "full-time specialist craftsmen, transport workers, merchants, officials and priests" who were not themselves primary food producers or procurers (Childe 1950, 11).
3. Those who were the primary food producers or procurers (fishing, hunting, and gathering could still occur along with agriculture) paid a "tithe or tax to an imaginary deity or a divine king who thus concentrated the surplus" (Childe 1950, 11).
4. "Truly monumental public buildings not only distinguish each known city from any village but also symbolise the concentration of the social surplus" (Childe 1950, 12). More recently, however, Smith points out, "Nearly all ancient complex societies built some form of monumental architecture, but so did much earlier societies, such as the Neolithic groups that built Stonehenge and other megalithic monuments. Nevertheless, Childe was correct to point out that monumental buildings served as deliberate symbols of the power and wealth of early rulers" (Smith 2009, 13).
5. "All those not engaged in food-production were of course supported in the first instance by the surplus accumulated in temple or royal granaries and were thus dependent on temple or court. But naturally priests, civil and military leaders and officials absorbed a major share of the concentrated surplus and thus formed a 'ruling class'" (Childe 1950, 12–13).

6. "They were in fact compelled to invent systems of recording and exact, but practically useful, sciences" (Childe 1950, 14). That is, scripts and forms of recording and writing were invented. Smith in his review of Childe's criteria notes, "Item 6, writing, is often dismissed as a universal criterion of complex societies based on the absence of writing in the Inka [Inca] and earlier Andean states. If we broaden Childe's concept to formal record-keeping [which the Inca and related societies had], however, then this was an important and universal characteristic of early states" (Smith 2009, 13; material in brackets added by R. Schoch).

7. "The invention of writing—or shall we say the invention of scripts—enabled the elaboration of exact and predictive sciences—arithmetic, geometry and astronomy" (Childe 1950, 14). This included calendars and sophisticated (at least for the times) mathematics. Smith, in contrast, states, "The development of practical sciences, is a trait not limited to states; calendars and mathematics originated long before the early states" (Smith 2009, 13).

8. Particularly important for our discussion is Childe's eighth distinguishing criterion, which I will quote in full. "Other specialists, supported by the concentrated social surplus, gave a new direction to artistic expression. Savages even in palaeolithic times had tried, sometimes with astonishing success, to depict animals and even men as they saw them—concretely and naturalistically. Neolithic peasants never did that; they hardly ever tried to represent natural objects, but preferred to symbolize them by abstract geometrical patterns which at most may suggest by a few traits a fantastical man or beast or plant. But Egyptian, Sumerian, Indus and Maya artist craftsmen—full-time sculptors, painters, or seal-engravers—began once more to carve, model or draw likenesses of persons or things, but no longer with the naïve naturalism of the hunter, but according to conceptualized and sophisticated styles which differ in each of the four urban centres" (Childe 1950, 15). Smith comments that this "is the least useful and relevant trait for understanding the early states. While all of the

early states had distinctive regional art styles, these were not necessarily any more sophisticated than the art of Neolithic groups. The social significance of visual art, however, underwent a major transformation in states, with most ancient rulers adopting an ideological (propagandistic) programme of visual representation that promoted their interests" (Smith 2009, 14). Indeed, the level of "sophistication" of artwork is arguably a subjective judgment, but to the art connoisseur not necessarily. Elements of style, composition, and technical ability are subject to more or less objective criteria by which art can be judged. I would contend that when such criteria are applied, the style and technical ability of the artwork seen at Göbekli Tepe are at the same level of sophistication as that seen among Egyptian, Sumerian, Indus, and Mayan artwork many thousands of years later.

9. "Regular 'foreign' trade over quite long distances was a feature of all early civilizations and, though common enough among barbarians later, is not certainly attested in the Old World before 3,000 B.C. nor in the New before the Maya 'empire'" (Childe 1950, 15). As Smith (2009) notes, trade dates back to well before civilization, probably to the earliest Paleolithic communities, but it expanded greatly with the founding of city-states.

10. "So in the city, specialist craftsmen were both provided with raw materials needed for the employment of their skill and also guaranteed security in a State organization based now on residence rather than kinship" (Childe 1950, 16).

CHALLENGING THE PARADIGM

The concepts of the Neolithic and Urban Revolutions have influenced thinking on the origins of agriculture and civilization ever since Childe codified them in the last century, and as with any highly influential paradigm, often these ideas have been taken as unquestioned assumptions by later researchers. But in fact new data and research have poked holes in the when, why, and how of these very assumptions and the mainstream understanding that goes along with them. The story of the origins of civilization must be rewritten.

First is the matter of dating. Childe, based on the dating of the sites known in his time, believed that the beginning of barbarism— the transition to cultivation, herding, agriculture, and husbandry, that is, the Neolithic Revolution—began within the last ten thousand years. And it was only with this transition that settled village life, more complex societal organization, megalithic monuments, and the like could occur. Now there is evidence that both village life and megalithic monuments occurred earlier than Childe and his contemporaries imagined, and at a stage when food was still procured by gathering and hunting. As a case in point, consider the settlements in the Levant (the region composing the modern area of Israel, the Palestinian territories, Jordan, Lebanon, and western Syria) that date back to circa 13,000 BCE to 10,000 BCE. Known to archaeologists as the Natufian culture, this culture apparently arose during the warming at the end of the last ice age, which brought a relatively wet climate to the Levant. There were abundant natural food supplies, from gazelles to hunt to wild barley, wheat, and rye to gather, which allowed the Natufians to settle down into permanent villages of up to several hundred people (Mann 2011, 56). Here we have villages not only earlier than Childe believed, but villages of savages—that is foragers, hunters, and gatherers—rather than cultivators or farmers.

Then the Natufians suffered setbacks with the abrupt cooling at the beginning of the Younger Dryas, circa 10,900 BCE to 10,800 BCE (the beginning of the end of the last ice age; see appendix 3, page 395), which also brought more arid conditions to the Levant. Local food supplies shrank and many Natufian villages collapsed, the people disbanding to wander in search of better regions. Some villages, however, may have tried to hang on, beginning to cultivate local plants such as rye, the first step toward true agriculture. This scenario for the origin of agriculture is diametrically opposed to Childe's ideas. For Childe, agriculture came first, and it was agriculture that allowed adequate foodstuffs to support a settled population and village life. Agriculture, according to Childe, came before the establishment of villages (and all that goes along with villages and larger settlements, such as an increase in the level of societal organization, monumental megalithic architecture, and so forth). But here is evidence to the contrary, that village life came first and agriculture (necessitated by climatic deterioration) was a way to maintain village life.

Another aspect of what we can refer to as the Childean paradigm involves the origin of organized religion. Magic, including that which is generally now referred to as shamanism (see, for instance, Shirokogoroff 1935), was suited to and used by savages, by hunter-gatherers. True organized religion with a complex social hierarchy, a priesthood, and strictly enforced rules and codes of conduct, according to the reigning paradigm, came later with the establishment of village life based on cultivation and domestication. Organized religion was essentially a way to control the populace, maintain order, promote cohesiveness, and keep the society together and functioning as a whole without the annoyance of dissidents. It also justified the social hierarchy; rulers received their privilege and power from the gods (later expressed as the divine right of kings). Childe, a Marxist atheist who was openly disdainful of organized religion, famously wrote, "Magic is a way of making people believe they are going to get what they want, whereas religion is a system for persuading them that they ought to want what they get" (Childe, quoted in McQueen 2011).

The bottom line is that formal organized religion was not necessary among savages, and true religion could not and did not develop until a stage of barbarism and sufficiently large permanent settlements based on cultivation and agriculture had been reached.

By Klaus Schmidt's thinking, Göbekli Tepe overturns the "village life and barbarism precedes organized religion scenario" (see Schmidt 2006/2008, 2007, and the popular review in Mann 2011). Schmidt viewed Göbekli Tepe as a massive temple complex, the world's oldest known temple, built of incredibly carved megalithic blocks by foragers, hunters, and gatherers at the very end of the last ice, with the oldest constructions at Göbekli Tepe dating back to circa 10,000 BCE to 9000 BCE and intentionally buried by circa 8000 BCE. According to Schmidt, a magnificent temple complex was built in stone prior to the development of agriculture, but at a time when village settlements of foragers and hunters were taking place. The building and maintenance of Göbekli Tepe (and any priesthood associated with it) would have required organization and planning among large groups of people, perhaps gathering from tens and hundreds of kilometers away at the site of Göbekli Tepe to both create the structures and carry out rituals and religious ceremonies. Schmidt suggested that the development of cultivation and agriculture may have occurred as a way to be able to maintain large populations at Göbekli Tepe. In other words, organized religion and the need and/or desire for a magnificent religious complex were the driving factors that necessitated the invention of agriculture, rather than agriculture ultimately leading to village life, which then required organized religion. Once again, the Childean paradigm is turned on its head. And if true writing is expressed at Göbekli Tepe, as I contend (see chapter 15, page 346), then in essence one can state that abstract ideas and symbols, mental constructs (be they religious in a modern sense or otherwise), were the driving force behind the rise of civilization, rather than materialistic needs and imperatives (such as simply maintaining and augmenting food supplies). This alternative view is decidedly nonmaterialistic, and I suspect it would not have sat well with the Marxist V. Gordon Childe who believed that material needs set the stage for ideology and belief systems, not vice versa.

Schmidt's specific hypothesis is based on the assumption that Göbekli Tepe is a temple or religious structure of some kind. However, if there is writing and symbolic notation expressing abstract ideas at Göbekli Tepe, then it may not matter whether or not it is literally a temple (versus, for instance, the ancient equivalent of a university or library or some combination of university-library-temple, or as Katie and I sometimes refer to it, "a university of the cosmos"), as arguably the mental ideas would be prior to and the motivating force behind the materialistic developments. Exactly what Göbekli Tepe represents—a temple or something else—is far from clear. The figures on the central pillars of one circle in particular at Göbekli Tepe, with their arms, hands, belts, and loincloths, are humanoid in form. Schmidt viewed these not as humans per se, but as supernatural beings, gods, resembling humans. Schmidt suggested the animals abundantly carved on the pillars were "guardians to the spirit world" (Mann 2011, 57). Do we have here the first clear representation of anthropomorphic gods, the form of gods that would be predominant in so many later religions, including the classic mythologies of the Greeks and Romans and the Judeo-Christian concept of God, in the likeness of whom humankind was created? Or is Schmidt's speculation here entirely off base? With the evidence at hand, it is difficult to know. More to the point, however, the distinction between the sacred and the profane, the spiritual world and the everyday world, the numinous and the ordinary, between religion and science as we now understand the concepts, may not have applied over ten thousand years ago. Indeed, arguably, these distinctions were much less relevant and were rarely made, even as recently as five hundred years ago. In my opinion, it is inappropriate to apply our values and beliefs to an ancient people whom we do not understand. But, still, when I visit Göbekli Tepe, I experience the ineffable.

THE FIRST ECONOMIC REVOLUTION

In the tradition of Childe's "revolutions," Douglass C. North (co-winner of the 1993 Sveriges Riksbank Prize in Economic Sciences in Memory of Alfred Nobel, generally referred to as the Nobel Prize in Economics) and Robert Paul Thomas suggested another prehistoric change, which they dubbed the First Economic Revolution. These authors assert that for prehistoric humans, still in the most basic hunter-gatherer stage of development, all "natural resources, whether the animals to be hunted or vegetation to be gathered, were initially held as common property. This type of property right implies free access by all to the resource" (North and Thomas 1977, 234). There was no incentive on the part of any single person or small group of people to protect or save resources, for what would be the point? If one person or group did not use them, then another person or group would. As long as the concept of common property rights, without any restrictions whatsoever, prevailed, the concepts of cultivation, agriculture, herding, and husbandry would be doomed to failure. Imagine attempting to tend a garden or herd, only to have anyone at any time come by and take whatever she or he desired. As North and Thomas write, "It is inconceivable that, from the very beginning, the first farmers did not exclude outsiders from sharing the fruits of their labours. Furthermore, the band was probably a small enough group to monitor easily the activities of its members to ensure that collective behaviour did not over-utilize the scarce protected land resource held in common by the group" (North and Thomas 1977, 235).

The concept of private property in a modern sense was not required, but the concept of communal property was—property held in common by the group or band for the benefit of the group or band collectively. North and Thomas assert, "The band in principle at least could have exploited its opportunities in agriculture by constraining its members with rules, taboos, and prohibitions, almost as effectively as if private property rights had been established" (North and Thomas 1977, 235).

Thus, the invention and enforcement of communal property rights, the First Economic Revolution, according to these authors, is key in explaining the development of agriculture, which in turn (following the reasoning of V. Gordon Childe) ultimately led to the Urban Revolution. They summarize their view as follows: "When common property rights over resources exist, there is little incentive for the acquisition of superior technology and learning. In contrast, exclusive property rights which reward the owners provide a direct incentive to improve efficiency and productivity, or, in more fundamental terms, to acquire more knowledge and new techniques. It is this change in incentive that explains the rapid progress made by mankind in the last 10,000 years in contrast to his slow development during the long era as a primitive hunter/gatherer" (North and Thomas 1977, 241).

One wonders how the Marxist, materialistic, atheistic V. Gordon Childe might have reacted to this hypothesis. Perhaps he would have nodded in approval at the concept of the First Economic Revolution. However, is the North and Thomas hypothesis compatible with the evidence of Göbekli Tepe? Perhaps, one could argue, rather than plots of land for agriculture, the first communal property took the form of structures like those erected at Göbekli Tepe.

MODERN BIASES

The Neolithic Revolution. The Urban Revolution. The First Economic Revolution. These are the components of the conventional, mainstream, status quo paradigm of how and when civilization arose. In many ways, the concept of revolutions as an explanation for the rise of civilization is both ethnocentric and anthropocentric. Let me explain what I mean.

Ethnocentric: That is, these theories are based primarily on the perceived way that humanity developed in Europe and Asia (and of course most of the theoreticians are Westerners) and particularly in the Middle East and Mesopotamia. Other cultures and peoples are then forced into the same theoretical categories. I do not believe that we should impose our values and preconceptions on other cultures, ancient or modern. What about the groups sometimes labeled as "complex hunter-gatherers," such as the native peoples of the northwest coast of North America (see Sassaman 2004) who developed a sophisticated culture, arguably a civilization, while remaining hunter-gatherers?

Anthropocentric: These theories are focused on human development, either largely independent of environmental changes on Earth or at best rather downplaying such environmental changes. The classic reasoning is along the following lines: climate change has occurred many times over the tens of thousands of years that humans have existed anatomically and physiologically in modern form, so even if climate change impacted or helped propel the development of agriculture and urban life, it did so only when humans were mentally and socially ready for such developments, such revolutions. Classic anthropocentrism, regarding humans as the central element in history and indeed the most significant entity in existence, the be all and end all of the universe, has a long and hoary history in the West. It dates back to the concept that our Earth is the center of the universe and that we humans are the epitome of God's creation. Of course, scientifically, we now realize that our Earth revolves around the Sun and that our Sun is just one of a virtual infinitude of stars in the universe. But I would venture to guess that many, perhaps most, people still consider humans somehow special and apart from nature. Even if they pay lip service to the concept that we are not quite so special, deep in their souls they are still primarily anthropocentric, and this is reflected in the way such people act in everyday life, not planning adequately (or at all) for "natural disasters" or other major environmental changes. One might go even further and argue that the ideological rigidity of some people (including some scientists) who insist even in the face of contradictory data that certain types of environmental change (global warming is an example) are solely due to human actions constitutes another form of anthropocentrism. (I discuss the issue of climate change later, in chapter 8.) Then there are those who openly proclaim, often on the basis of strong religious convictions, that humans are God's special creation. And in many cases, these same people go on to announce that they, their own ethnic or religious group, constitute God's chosen children in the divine scheme of history.

Ethnocentric and anthropocentric views (whether advocated explicitly or, perhaps worse, held unconsciously) can become mental straightjackets, hampering clear thinking on important issues, such as the how, when, and why of civilization—and what the future may hold for our modern civilization. As a geologist, I have long felt that there is a major disconnect between (1) the status quo archaeological paradigm explaining the rise of civilization, and (2) the geological evidence for major environmental turmoil and catastrophe at the end of the last ice age and immediately afterward, circa 10,000 BCE to 8000 BCE, the time of Göbekli Tepe and the original Great Sphinx. Furthermore, the Western World, and the Middle East in particular, is not necessarily the exemplar of the rise of civilization (despite the fact that many Westerners, with their ethnocentric beliefs, feel it is). Where might we find a culture, a civilization, isolated from the West for centuries and millennia? Even India and the Far East of China and Asia have had contact for millennia with the Middle East and Mediterranean region.

When the ambassador invited Katie and me to join him on the expedition to Easter Island, it crossed my mind that this might be just what I needed to help clear my mind and gain a different, non-Western, perspective on the origins of civilization. Not only does Easter Island exhibit the remains of a clearly advanced megalith-building culture, but it is also the home of an indigenous script, the rongorongo, and as we have seen, writing is often taken as the hallmark of civilization.

So let us now examine Easter Island more carefully.

Figure 4.1. Various images of Easter Island. Rano Kau volcanic crater (*top left*). View from the airplane approaching Easter Island (*top right*). A portion of the Tahai Ceremonial Complex (*bottom*). (Photograph courtesy of R. Schoch and C. Ulissey.)

5

TE PITO TE HENUA
(THE NAVEL OF THE WORLD),
EASTER ISLAND

Easter Island is emblematic of ancient mysteries. Located in the remote South Pacific just south of the Tropic of Capricorn—over 3,500 kilometers west of mainland Chile and over 2,000 kilometers from any other inhabited island—it is often considered the most remote populated location on Earth. It is also known as Rapa Nui, Isla de Pascua, and Te Pito Te Henua; the latter, sometimes written as Te Pito O Te Henua, has been translated as "the navel of the world," "navel and uterus," or "ends of the land," apparently referring to both the isolation of the island and the volcanic craters that compose it. The island is triangular in shape and so small that theoretically one can walk around its entire coast in two days.

The island remained bathed in secrecy, unknown to the Western world until its discovery by Dutch sailors under the command of Jacob Roggeveen on Easter Sunday 1722. The giant stone sculpted heads and torsos, known as moai, that are found in the hundreds on the island are megalithic mysteries that boggle the imagination. The average height and weight of the moai has been estimated at four meters and about twelve to thirteen tons, and the largest erected moai are up to ten meters tall and are estimated to weigh up to seventy-five tons. An unfinished moai still in the quarry is some twenty-one meters long with an estimated weight of perhaps 250 tons. How and why were they carved? By whom and when? These are still unanswered questions; to this day, the moai have eluded our best efforts to truly decipher their meaning.

The standard modern "solution" to the enigma of Easter Island is that the earliest of the hundreds of moai were constructed, beginning around 1,000 to 1,500 years ago, when the first Polynesian settlers arrived on Easter Island, and that moai carving continued until around the seventeenth century, ceasing shortly prior to European contact. The moai, according to this scenario, were essentially part of an ancestor and burial cult. The production of moai ceased as the Easter Islanders deforested their land and consequently brought environmental devastation to their tiny island, ultimately sparking tribal warfare, an impoverished society, and even cannibalism. But does this story, which in recent decades has gained wide circulation in both scientific and popular circles, really stand up to scrutiny? A clear analysis of the evidence does not convincingly support the "natives destroyed their environment" scenario (Peiser 2005). Rather, this may simply be a Western myth that both masks the destruction brought to the island and culture by European contact (which included notorious slave raids and effective genocide) and denies the true magnificence, antiquity, and high cultural and technological achievements of Easter Island civilization.

It was with such thoughts in mind that in January 2010 Katie and I, along with the ambassador, his family, and a few friends, undertook our short reconnaissance excursion to Easter Island to look into the mysteries for ourselves.

THE CHRONOLOGY AND DATING OF THE MOAI

The standard story of Easter Island does not detail the relative dating of the various moai and in fact relegates all of these statues to a fairly late time period, beginning on the order of approximately 1,000 to 1,500 years ago at the most.

Studying the moai with a geological eye, I was particularly impressed by the varying degrees of weathering and erosion seen on different moai, which could be telltale signs of major discrepancies in their ages. The levels of sedimentation around certain moai also impressed me. Some moai have been buried in up to an estimated six meters of sediment, or more, such that even though they are standing erect, only their chins and heads are above the current ground level. There are two basic explanations to account for such burial: (1) the moai were purposefully interred, perhaps to protect them or as part of some ceremonial ritual, or (2) the moai were buried by natural geological processes.

Examining the geology on-site, I saw no unequivocal evidence of intentional burial, although it is conceivable that some moai were partially buried purposely, perhaps as part of some ritual. Corroborating my observations along these lines, excavations of two moai by the Easter Island Statue Project have confirmed that "The dirt and detritus partially burying the statues was washed down from above and not deliberately placed there to bury, protect, or support the statues" (Easter Island Statue Project 2012).

High levels of sedimentation could occur quickly if there were catastrophic landslides, mudflows, or possibly tsunamis washing over the island, but I could not find any such evidence to support this hypothesis (and landslides or tsunamis would tend to shift and knock over the tall statues). Rather, to my eye, the sedimentation around certain moai suggests a much more extreme antiquity than most conventional archaeologists and historians believe to be the case—or believe to be possible. In contrast, I believe the evidence indicates that the first inhabitants of Rapa Nui may have reached the island prior to the end of the last ice age some twelve thousand years ago.

Not only does sedimentation around the statues suggest a longer and different chronology than conventionally accepted, but so too do weathering and erosion patterns and stylistic considerations. Although on one level most of the moai are stylistically similar and even stereotypic, at another level each is unique, and they could, I believe, be categorized according to stylistic types. The moai should, in addition, be sorted according to lithology (rock type) as well as weathering and erosion levels (taking orientation and relative exposure to the elements into account). Another key to solving the problem will be to compare weathering, erosion, and sedimentation rates in historical times. I have begun to gather photographs of various moai and landforms on Easter Island taken over the last 135 years so as to compare them geologically to their conditions today, and in this way attempt to get a quantitative handle on weathering, erosion, and sedimentation rates. So far, it seems that sedimentation over the last century has been on the whole relatively modest.

Even on our preliminary reconnaissance trip, I found evidence that the earliest moai may have differed materially from the later moai. The earliest moai appear to have been more finely worked from hard basalts as compared to the volcanic tuffs from which most moai, dated to later periods, were carved. The few surviving basalt moai have either been found at deeper stratigraphic levels, below other moai and the platforms on which later moai were erected, or the basalt moai were reused in later structures, thus indicating the basalt moai are among the earliest on the island. For instance, the famous basalt moai now in the British Museum was collected in 1868 from inside a stone structure at Orongo where it had been reused, and its back was partially recarved at a later period than the original statue (Van Tilburg 2007). Furthermore, at least one of the basalt moai (now housed in the museum on Easter Island) is, as previously mentioned, of a very strange form; with an elongated head and well-defined breasts, it is often considered a female while virtually all other moai are apparently males.

Another major puzzle, which is directly applicable to the chronology and dating of the moai, is the matter of where various moai were quarried. Quarries on the rim of the volcanic crater where large moai were carved from the volcanic tuffs are well exposed and still contain partially carved moai in place. I inspected these quarries carefully. However, the quarries where the few basalt moai were carved have never been definitively located, despite the small size of the island. Based on the geology of Easter Island, I expect that any suitable basalt deposits would occur lower in the stratigraphic section, so low in fact that they might currently be under sea level off the coast of the island. That is, the basalt quarries might be under water. How could this be? It is difficult to conceive that the ancient Easter Islanders were quarrying rock below sea level. Alternatively, the "lost basalt quarries" might be under sea level now because they are of extreme antiquity, and thus the basalt moai carved from them are extremely ancient. Sea levels have risen dramatically since the end of the last ice age, some twelve thousand years ago, and if the basalt moai were quarried along the coast of Easter Island from areas since inundated by the sea, this could help to date the basalt moai and is immediately suggestive that they are thousands of years older than conventionally believed to be the case.

The key to solving the puzzle of the basalt moai is to locate the quarries. If they are found under water along the coast, their depth and geological setting will shed light on their age and could lead to a major revolution in our thinking about the age, origin, importance, and sophistication of Easter Island culture. For one thing, while the later standard moai carved of volcanic tuffs could be relatively easily cut out of the rock using the primitive tools found in abundance on the island, the same cannot be said for the apparently earlier and more sophisticated basalt moai, which may have formed the model and set the standard for the later volcanic tuffs moai.

A fascinating Easter Island legend relates that one of the founders, King Hotu-Matua, came from a land called Hiva that was said to be slowly sinking below the sea (Mazière 1968). Similarly, the late ethnographer Thomas S. Barthel (1923–1997) records the following traditional legend:

> This island [Rapa Nui] was once a great land. The reason it became so small is because Uoke [a giant or god, also known as Uvoke] lifted the earth with a (mighty) pole and then let it sink (into the sea). It was because of the very bad people of Te Pito O Te Henua [i.e., Easter Island] that Uoke lifted the land (and let it crumble) until it became very small. (Barthel 1978, 3; material in brackets added by R. Schoch)

Are these legends suggestive of a people fleeing rising sea levels, perhaps thousands of years ago at the end of the last ice age when sea levels were rising worldwide? (In some places sea levels rose on the order of a hundred meters or more at the end of the last ice age; see Schoch with McNally 2003, 242.) Was the initial colonization of Easter Island prior to the final, highest, post–ice age rises in sea level, such that when first colonized it was a larger and more prominent island? Such a scenario would be compatible with the early carving of basalt moai from quarries along the coast that have since been submerged.

It is already more than pure speculation that the basalt moai may have been quarried from areas that are now under water. While on the island, we heard of reports that when the French marine explorer Jacques-Yves Cousteau (1910–1997) and his divers visited the island, they came across some very rectangular-looking holes or cavities in the basalt layers located off the coast. Could these indeed be ancient quarries? We began to track down leads as to divers, still on the island, who were with Cousteau's team and are willing and able to take us to these sites. It is our hope to dive and explore the possible quarries for ourselves on a return trip.

HOW WERE THE MOAI MOVED?

To this day, no one is absolutely certain how the moai were transported. Numerous theories involving brute manpower, ropes, wedges, levers, sledges, rollers, and so forth have been proposed. However, as Francis Mazière perceptively pointed out:

> One of the great problems that dominate Easter Island archeologically is the question of how the statues were moved to the ahu [ceremonial platforms on which they were erected], some of which are miles [kilometers] from the quarry. This problem has never been solved, and even the work of the Norwegian expedition of 1956 brought no answer, for [Thor] Heyerdahl's attempt at moving a moaï was in no way conclusive for . . . it was one of the smallest, and because it was dragged along by means of ropes over a very particular ground that exists nowhere on the island except at Anakena—sandy ground without any rocks sticking out of it. (Mazière 1968, 133; material in brackets added by R. Schoch)

Some traditional Easter Island legends state that the moai "walked" from the quarry to their final locations. This has been interpreted as indicating that the statues were raised upright, perhaps supported in slings hung from poles above, and then pivoted or rocked back and forth on their bases, thus moving them from one place to another; that is, they "walked." But was this really or always the case?

Another widespread Easter Island tradition is that the moai were transported by *mana,* that is, by supernatural forces or powers. As Katherine Routledge (1866–1935), who carried out an extended exploration of Easter Island in 1914–1915, wrote, "The natives are sometimes prepared to state that the statues were thrown down by human means, they never have any doubt that they were moved by supernatural power. We were once inspecting an ahu built on a natural eminence, one side was sheer cliff, the other was a slope of 29 feet [9 meters], as steep as a house roof, near the top a statue was lying. The most intelligent of our guides turned to me significantly. 'Do you mean to tell me,' he said, 'that that was not done by *mana?*'" (Routledge 1919, 198; italics in the original; material in brackets added by R. Schoch).

Alfred Métraux (1902–1963, a Swiss ethnologist who studied Easter Island extensively) wrote, "When the Easter Islanders of today are asked about the means by which the statues were transported, they only say: 'King Tiikoihu, the great magician, used to move them with the words of his mouth'" (Wolff 1948, 157, citing Métraux 1939, 771).

The concept of mana is not generally considered scientific and thus is simply dismissed by most Western archaeologists and historians, but does it mask something we do not know? Perhaps a profound mystery that has yet to be uncovered? I take a serious scientific interest in the paranormal, and based on my research, I have concluded that there is strong evidence in some cases for the reality of psychokinesis (that is, the movement of matter via mental means alone, sometimes referred to as telekinesis; see Burns 2003; de Martino 1972; Owen with Sparrow 1976; Roll 2003; Schoch and Yonavjak 2008, and references cited therein). Some of the best-documented cases of psychokinesis (once we have excluded fraud and delusion) are relatively spontaneous and unplanned, such as so-called poltergeist phenomena (in modern terminology often referred to as recurrent spontaneous psychokinesis, or RSPK).

Is it possible that the moai were moved paranormally? Did mana indeed have a role to play? I cannot say for certain, but I believe we should be open to the idea. In appendix 4 to this book (page 407), I speculate on the possibility that modern parapsychological insights into psychokinesis combined with a particular theory of gravity may provide a major clue to the mechanism underlying psychokinesis, and ultimately perhaps how the moai were moved. However, I would point out that even if psychokinesis is real, it has never been demonstrated to occur relative to anything other than small objects; moving moai would be much more challenging. Oddly, the psychotherapist Werner Wolff (1904–1957) seriously suggested that the moai had flown through the air, not via parapsychological mana, but by "natural mana," that is, by the explosions of the volcano where the moai were carved.

> Since great blocks of lava have been discharged by the volcanoes, why could such blocks not have been ejected after being shaped by sculptors in the workshop of the crater? This theory, in a way, would explain the so-called magic transportation, although imagining giant-statues flying through the air like ghosts seems a fantastic dream. Unconsciously, perhaps, each investigator has dismissed such a possibility; it does seem strange enough that this angle has never been discussed. . . .
>
> But the idea of flying statues did not seem strange to the natives— the concept was within the sphere of their imagination. C. E. Fox reports such a concept from San Christobal in the Solomons: "Levitation is described as common both in the case of sacred stones and of priests, some of whom were levitated large distances through the air." (Wolff 1948, 156, citing Fox 1924, 338)

As a geologist, I question whether moai were moved by volcanic power. Although carved of solid rock, I doubt that any moai would have survived intact after being shot like a missile from the volcano and then crash-landing on the ground. And I wonder how many human sculptors might have been killed, or how any could have survived, while working in a volcanic crater that was on the verge of erupting. And think of all the moai that may have shot out of the volcano only to land in the ocean surrounding the tiny island.

Interestingly, despite the emphasis on mana as the way the moai were moved, as recorded by Katherine Routledge, J. Macmillan Brown reported that the Easter Islanders did not even have a native word for mana. Brown resided on the island for five months in the early 1920s (some of the photos reproduced in his 1924 book are dated to 1922) and interviewed and worked with some of the same informants as did Routledge. Brown wrote, "[An] important *lacuna* [in the Easter Island vocabulary] is the word *mana,* which in Polynesian covered all that occult power which resides, not only in the supernatural and the ancestors, but in great living men and their deeds and their weapons and instruments. It was probably that there was no sense of this *aura* of the great and indeed no great individuality to embody it or ray it forth that the word dropped out of their Polynesian vocabulary" (Brown 1924, 279; italics in the original; material in brackets added by R. Schoch). Thus, Brown is not contending that the Easter Islanders of his time did not believe in mana, but simply that they did not have, or no longer had, a native word for the concept. Indeed, one might speculate, this was because the mana was no longer manifested on Easter Island after the population had been decimated and the indigenous culture all but eradicated in the wake of European contact beginning in 1722.

LEGENDS OF GIANTS

Sometimes it is suggested that the moai were huge simply because the peoples inhabiting an ancient Easter Island were huge. Indeed there is some, if at this point only very scanty, evidence that besides the giant moai, there may have been other giants on Easter Island. Literal living giants, that is. C. F. Behrens, who accompanied Roggeveen on the voyage that marks the generally accepted European discovery of Easter Island in 1722, reported, "With truth, I might say that these savages are all of more than gigantic size. The men are tall and broad in proportion, averaging 12 feet [3.65 meters] in height. Surprising as it may appear, the tallest men on board of our ship could pass between the legs of these children of Goliath without bending the head. The women can not compare in stature with the men, as they are commonly not above 10 feet high [3 meters]" (Quoted in Thomson 1891, 462).

What do we make of such a report? Could this be real?

Interestingly, traditional legends from the island of Flores, Indonesia, describe the existence of a race of diminutive people known as the Ebu Gogo (BBC 2004). A new species of fossil humans, *Homo floresiensis,* popularly referred to as hobbits, was discovered on Flores that may fit the description of the Ebu Gogo (Brown et al. 2004). The existence of *H. floresiensis* is based on subfossil remains from the end of the last ice age, as recent as twelve thousand years ago. However, some serious researchers have hypothesized that hobbits survived as a relict population until possibly as late as the nineteenth century (Sereno 2005, 9). Likewise, could the early reports of Easter Island be factual? Stories of giants are reported in sacred texts, myths, and legends around the world. Might these legends have a basis in fact? Might a relict population of giants have survived on Easter Island up until European contact? In this context it is worth pointing out that a study of skeletons from Greece and Turkey documented an average drop in height of about fifteen centimeters from the end of the last ice age (circa 10,000 BCE) to 3000 BCE, and modern people in this region are still not as tall on average as their ancestors of some twelve thousand years ago (Batuman 2011, 81). Certainly the vast majority of Easter Islanders at the time of European contact were of normal size, as reported by most of the accounts, but might Behrens have seen some members of a relict tall population? Or was he simply exaggerating, recounting a sailor's tale?

The discovery of solid physical evidence for giants on Easter Island would revolutionize our thinking about the ancient past, shedding new light on many myths and legends, and force us to rethink the development of humans through time. Along these lines, although it remains extremely controversial, there is evidence supporting the notion that

Neanderthals and/or other hominids or large primates may have survived into modern times in some remote regions (Shackley 1983; see also Ståhlberg and Svanberg 2017). One example may be the Almas (a Mongolian term that has been translated as "Wildman"), reported from the Caucasus, Pamirs, Tien Shan, and Altai Mountains. Could the Almas represent relict Neanderthal populations, or perhaps relict populations of *Homo altaiensis,* also known as the Denisovans? I believe this is a possibility.

The reports of giants on Easter Island tie in with another mystery: what was the origin or origins of the original peoples who inhabited the island? Most archaeologists and ethnologists concur that there are strong Polynesian influences in known Easter Island culture, but this may not be the entire story. There may have been more than one migration to the island, including settlers from both the west (Polynesia) and from the east (South America). The late Thor Heyerdahl (1914–2002) was a major advocate of a South American origin for the Rapanui (or at least one wave of settlers to the island, if not all the ancestors of the island's inhabitants; see the summary in his book *Easter Island: The Mystery Solved,* 1989). Among other evidence to support such a connection, Heyerdahl pointed out the similarity of the megalithic stonework of the ahu (a platform on which moai were erected) at Vinapu (southwestern Easter Island) to stonework seen in South America. He and his group also excavated a most unusual kneeling moai during their 1955–1956 expedition to the island. In its posture and physiognomy, this statue, it has been argued, compares favorably to similar statues found in South America (particularly at Tiahuanaco [Tiwanaku] in Bolivia). There is also genetic evidence that supports an ancient South American admixture to Easter Island as well as other regions of Polynesia (see Ioannidis et al. 2020 who, based on genetic data, make the case that South Americans, most likely from the area of modern Colombia, and Polynesians met and interbred as early as around 1100–1200 CE, possibly first in the Marquesas, and their descendants spread to other islands, including Easter Island).

Erik Thorsby, of the University of Oslo, summarized the results of his studies as follows:

Human molecular genetic data are obtained which strongly suggest that some Native Americans arrived early at Rapa Nui, probably as early as AD 1280–1495. Whether they sailed directly from South America to Rapa Nui on their own rafts or whether they came with Polynesians returning from visits to South America cannot be established by our studies, but the latter possibility may be the most likely given other evidence of early visits of Polynesians to South America. (Thorsby 2016, 1)

It is also worth noting that there is evidence for human habitation in terms of ecological disturbance and weeds long before the generally accepted date for the colonization of Easter Island. In a study by Núria Cañellas-Boltà and colleagues of vegetation and ecological changes on Easter Island as seen in lake sediments, the authors wrote:

The results show a long, gradual and stepped landscape shift from palm-dominated forests to grasslands. This change started c. 450 BC and lasted about two thousand years. The presence of *Verbena litoralis,* a common weed, which is associated with human activities in the pollen record, the significant correlation between shifts in charcoal influx, and the dominant pollen types suggest human disturbance of the vegetation. Therefore, human settlement on the island occurred c. 450 BC, some 1500 years earlier than is assumed. . . . Although the evidence is not conclusive, the American origin of *V. litoralis* re-opens the debate about the possible role of Amerindians in the human colonisation of Easter Island. (2013, 36)

Thus, there is evidence in both the vegetation data and the human molecular genetic data for a South American influence in pre-European contact times on Easter Island, and based on the vegetation data, this South American influence could go back thousands of years (for further discussion, see also Rull et al. 2016 and Rull and Giralt 2018).

A possibility that is rarely discussed but should be considered is that perhaps various cultural traits originated on Easter Island and spread both west, to Polynesia proper, and east, to South America. This hypothesis would be strengthened if it is demonstrated that the Easter Island civilization has an extreme antiquity and dates back to a time when sea levels were lower at the end of the last ice age (as discussed previously in this chapter) and the island was geographically larger and more prominent.

Adding to the enigma is the distinct possibility that Easter Island was "discovered" and colonized by two or more peoples or races in pre-European contact times, races who may not have always been at peace with each other. Persistent local legends recount that there were two groups on the island, referred to as the Hanau Eepe and the Hanau Momoko. These names have been translated into English as the "long-ears" (referring, apparently, to the artificially distended or elongated earlobes) and "short-ears," respectively, but the terms might also refer to being stout or big versus normal size. According to some traditions and interpretations, the Hanau Eepe were also characterized by lighter skin tones and sometimes-red hair, as opposed to the darker Hanau Momoko. Certain traditions relate that the Hanau Eepe brought moai carving and other civilized arts to Easter Island and that they generally dominated, and even enslaved, the Hanau Momoko. This situation ended when the Hanau Momoko rebelled against their masters, drove the Hanau Eepe to one corner of the island, and in an epic battle killed all or almost all (traditions vary) of the Hanau Eepe. Were the Hanau Eepe giants, of whom a few survived into the eighteenth century and were seen by Behrens?

Gordon White has proposed that prior to around the first millennium CE, Easter Island

> may have been a holy island that was not permanently occupied and used as a sacred or holy site. . . . Perhaps it was a combination of sacred site and sailing stop-off point, never occupied and visited at intervals determined by the stars and seasons, such as was the case with Göbekli Tepe.

White continues:

> It was a site that was used and known during a time when the sea levels were much lower, then it was abandoned or the original

inhabitants died out. Then it was recolonised by the descendants of these first occupiers in the first millennium CE and some of the remaining megalithic infrastructure, such as the basalt moai, were repurposed. (2016, 107)

White's hypothesis merits serious consideration. However, I suggest that Easter Island may have also been recolonized by a completely different group of people, rather than necessarily "the descendants of these first occupiers."

BIRDMEN PETROGLYPHS AND OTHER ANOMALIES

Easter Island is well-known not only for its gigantic moai but also for its carvings on stones and boulders, the petroglyphs (see Lee 1992). Many of these petroglyphs are of so-called birdmen and apparently relate to the birdman competitions. Associated with the ceremonial center of Orongo and persisting into the nineteenth century, these consisted of annual displays of skill and endurance as competitors swam to a small island (islet) off of the main island and vied to be the first of the season to acquire an egg from the migratory seabird, the sooty tern. (In long past times, it may have been the egg of a different bird, such as the frigate bird; Edwards and Edwards 2013, 378.) The winner and his clan were conferred with prestige and power for the following year. But was there something more underlying the birdman competition and its associated petroglyphs? Did the competition originate with some long forgotten event in the deep past, and did the final forms it took represent a degenerate version of a once more profound ceremony? I really have to wonder.

Exploring Easter Island firsthand, I quickly became convinced that the standard, and rather mundane, explanations for the island's remarkable indigenous civilization and its achievements do not necessarily hold up under detailed examination. On Easter Island are found low, thick-walled stone structures that appear to be constructed as if they were made to withstand a direct hit from a powerful aerial bomb.

And then there is perhaps the biggest Easter Island mystery of all: that of the enigmatic pieces of wood inscribed with mysterious glyphs—the rongorongo tablets. Before we can understand how the stone shelters and rongorongo fit into the bigger picture of the origin and demise of the earliest civilizations, we need to go back in time, to the end of the last ice age.

Figure 5.1. Birdmen petroglyphs associated with the birdman competition, Orongo, Easter Island.

(Photograph courtesy of R. Schoch and C. Ulissey.)

6

THE END OF
THE LAST ICE AGE

At the end of the last ice age, some twelve thousand years ago, Earth underwent dramatic, cataclysmic changes. It was not simply a matter of the climate gradually warming and the glaciers melting. No, something very sudden and very unusual took place, unlike anything, by orders of magnitude, that we have experienced since. The civilizations and high cultures of that remote time were either utterly destroyed or thrown for a mighty setback. Knowledge was lost, order devolved to chaos, and a dark age lasting thousands of years ensued. Yet, not all records were lost. Unrecognized until recently, consistently repeated petroglyph forms (engravings on rocks) around the globe reproduce what ancient peoples observed. Mirroring those petroglyphs are Easter Island's mysterious and barely known rongorongo texts, which may record in greater detail what happened when our world was thrown into turmoil.

THE YOUNGER DRYAS

Approximately fifteen thousand to eleven thousand years ago Earth experienced a series of climatic fluctuations. It had been extremely cold, with continental glaciers extending much farther than they do today, but the climate started to warm. Then there was a short cold spell, known as the Younger Dryas, before the final warming and the "official" end of the last ice age. Geologists have long argued over how quickly or gradually Earth's climate can change from very cold glacial conditions to modern-like conditions, and vice versa. The classical view is that such changes may happen very quickly from a geological perspective, perhaps over a few hundred to a thousand years or more, but relatively gradually from a human perspective. The latest research indicates otherwise.

Studying Greenland ice core data, from which temperature and climatic history can be extracted by analyzing changes in various isotopes and dust content at a virtually year-by-year scale, Jørgen P. Steffensen, of the Niels Bohr Institute at the University of Copenhagen, and his colleagues determined that such climatic transitions can in some cases occur in only a few years (Steffensen et al. 2008; for more details on this and related work, see appendix 5, page 416). They also pinpointed relatively precise dates for the climate changes. According to their study, the cooling that marks the beginning of the Younger Dryas dates to about 10,900 BCE. This cooling was very rapid from a geological perspective, but while some parameters show transitions over just a few years, other factors (for instance, changes in the dust record) are more gradual and seem to have responded much more slowly. The warming at the end of the Younger Dryas, which also heralds the end of the last ice age, began about 9700 BCE and may have occurred within an incredible three years—for all practical purposes instantaneously. More recent work has pinpointed the abrupt end of the last ice age to well within a year (Mayewski et al. 2014). Given our current inability to resolve the finest details of something that happened so long ago, it may have literally happened overnight.

How do we explain this pattern of abrupt climatic shifts? Being a geologist, I view Earth and our environment as unstable, full of unexpected surprises, at least over the long term. Climates change, sea levels rise and fall, volcanoes erupt, earthquakes rock the land and sea, and objects fall from the sky. In previous works, I have discussed how such natural cataclysms may have influenced the history of ancient civilizations (see Schoch with McNally 1999), and in particular I have pointed out strong evidence that Earth has experienced a series of encounters with comets or other similar natural phenomena (such as meteorites and asteroids) during historical and prehistoric times. There is evidence for impacts or close encounters with extraterrestrial objects around 7600 BCE, 4400 BCE, 3150 BCE, 2345 BCE, 1628 BCE, 1159 BCE, 207 BCE, 536 CE, and 1178 CE (Schoch with McNally 2003; undoubtedly this list is incomplete, especially for the period prior to 3150 BCE). Depending on the severity of the encounter (size of the comet, whether it actually touched the surface of Earth or perhaps resulted in a mid-atmosphere explosion, and so forth), dramatic climatic changes could be effected on Earth, which in turn could affect sea levels, and weather extremes can wreak havoc on animal and human populations, causing famines (see Than 2009 for a discussion of the effects of a sixth-century-CE cometary event). Bottom line, based on all the evidence, there is no doubt in my mind that these incidents, these cosmic catastrophes, had a profound influence on ancient civilizations. In some cases, migrations were sparked; in other cases, entire cultures may have been wiped out.

In 2003, I suggested that the end of the last ice age may have been brought about in part by comets bombarding Earth (Schoch with McNally 2003). A comet hitting the land or shallow ocean or exploding above the land's surface may have scattered dust and debris into the atmosphere, causing global cooling, which, although relatively sudden, would have taken some years to reach its full extent. This pattern fits well with the cooling at 10,900 BCE. Since I first hypothesized such an event, purported evidence of a comet exploding over North America circa 10,900 BCE has been presented (Firestone et al. 2007). Examining the evidence for a comet strike at this time, however, I do not find it fully convincing (see appendix 5, page 409). Instead, I suspect that it was a solar outburst that melted glacial dams and changed ocean circulation patterns, causing a cooling event (see chapter 15, page 323).

What about the warming event of circa 9700 BCE? Initially I hypothesized that comets hitting not the land or shallow water, but the deep oceans, may have brought about this warming. A comet, I speculated, might break the thin oceanic crust, releasing heat from the hot magma beneath. Vaporized and displaced water would rain down on Earth, and tsunamis would wash across coastal areas, all serving to warm the planet and bring the ice age to a final end. But even with a comet, or a series of comets, bombarding the oceans, could the warming happen as quickly and dramatically as the Greenland ice cores suggest? Should comets be implicated in a warming transition, or does the evidence rather suggest that comets will in most cases cause a cooling event? But if not comets, what?

THE FOURTH STATE OF MATTER

My attention turned to another outer space phenomenon: plasma, which is composed of ionized particles and associated intense electrical and magnetic phenomena that may originate from our Sun or possibly from the interactions of other extraterrestrial objects, such as a close flyby of an electrically charged asteroid or comet or maybe even a large object colliding with our Sun. The concept of a big chunk of rock or ice from outer space—a meteor, comet, or asteroid—colliding with Earth is easy to grasp. But plasma? Plasma is not necessarily readily familiar to the average person. Sometimes referred to as the fourth state of matter (in addition to solids, liquids, and gases), plasma consists of ions (electrically charged atoms or particles) and constitutes such familiar phenomena as lightning, fire, and the glowing material in a neon tube. The northern and southern polar lights—the auroras—are plasma phenomena, caused by the interaction between the solar wind (plasma emitted by the Sun) and Earth's magnetic field and magnetosphere.

Today lightning is a relatively minor weather phenomenon, and the auroras are little more than pretty lights in the sky, offering no threat to the inhabitants on Earth, but I do not believe this was always the case. In particular, our Sun is not as stable as most people generally believe. It undergoes relatively regular small-scale variations, such as the eleven-year sunspot cycle, as well as longer-term patterns (perhaps on the order of millennia and more). Presently unpredictable instabilities of the Sun can result in mass ejections of plasma (solar storms) that may reach Earth with far-ranging consequences. An 1859 solar storm, the Carrington Event, though relatively tame from a geological perspective, resulted in unusual auroras seen around the world. Additionally, tele-graph systems failed. If an equivalent solar storm hit today, possibly our modern electrical grids and communication systems would be devastated, with untold consequences.

Arguably, the Carrington Event was minor compared to other past events. In 1962 the astrophysicist and professor of astronomy at Cornell University Thomas Gold (1920–2004; recipient of the Gold Medal of the Royal Astronomical Society in 1985) wrote:

> The question I would like to tackle is whether solar outbursts of the present day [such as the 1859 event] are representative of all that has happened in geologic times or whether much greater outbursts have occurred from time to time. Our evidence that nothing very violent has taken place in historic times is concerned with such a short span of time only that it cannot answer the question. . . .
>
>   For one big outburst every ten thousand years, for example, . . . the earth's magnetic field could clearly not hold up the incoming gas, and it would indeed drive down to the atmospheric level. . . . This breakdown would be in the form of a series of sparks, burning for extended periods of time and carrying currents of hundreds of millions of amperes. One might search whether there is any geological record of surface fusing and vitrification of rock or sand which cannot be accounted for by volcanic or meteoritic events. (Gold 1963, 159, 161–163; quoted in Peratt et al. 2007, 778–779; and Peratt and Yao 2008, 2; material in brackets added by R. Schoch)

RECORDS ENGRAVED ON ROCKS

Four decades later, Anthony L. Peratt, a plasma physicist with Los Alamos National Laboratory, addressed the topic that Gold discussed (Peratt 2003). Powerful plasma discharges, much more powerful than the auroras observed in the present day, form structures known as plasma columns that can expand in some places and constrict or narrow in other places (due to "pinch instabilities"). In profile these plasma columns can form donut shapes and may look like intertwining snakes, a stack of circles, or even resemble human stick figures (the so-called stickman, squatting man, or squatter man figures, some of which include dots on their sides, apparently representing synchrotron radiation; van der Sluijs and Peratt 2010). In the modern day, powerful large-scale electrical discharges known as sprites occasionally occur in the upper atmosphere (about 80 to 140 kilometers above the surface of Earth). Some sprites take on stick figure forms and other shapes comparable to those of the plasma columns. Based on Peratt's models and experiments, in some cases the stick figure will have an upper cup shape (head) that has the appearance of a bird in profile. Peratt and his colleague W. F. Yao record that observers of the Carrington Event reported seeing "figures in the sky as if drawn with fire on a black background" (Peratt and Yao 2008, 3).

Peratt has studied ancient petroglyphs found around the world that are not only remarkably similar to one another but also apparently record with a high degree of accuracy the configurations that intense electrical and high-energy plasma phenomena would form in the skies. He and his colleagues (Peratt et al. 2007; see also van der Sluijs and Peratt 2010) have recorded and analyzed the orientations of innumerable petroglyphs spread over 139 countries, and not only do they share many similar morphologies, but they are also characterized by similar orientations. The petroglyph locations generally have a distinct southern field-of-view, and Peratt and Yao concluded that the associated plasma phenomenon showed "relativistic electron flow inward at Earth's south polar axis and hypervelocity proton impacts around the north polar axis" (Peratt and Yao 2008, 1). Intense radiation, including X rays and synchrotron radiation, would have been given off. (Synchrotron radiation is the result of charged particles moving at relativistic or ultra-relativistic velocities, that is, close to the speed of light, passing through magnetic fields that can cause them to have a radial acceleration, such as if they spiral or move in an arc or circular pattern.)

THE EASTER ISLAND CONNECTION

I was aware of Peratt's work, and through Peratt I knew of Gold's speculations, but I did not give them ample consideration—not until Katie and I returned from our brief excursion to Easter Island. Reiterating from chapter 1, one evening Katie suggested that we rewatch the video written and narrated by David Talbott, *Symbols of an Alien Sky* (Talbott 2009), which features Peratt's work connecting petroglyphs and plasma. As we watched, Katie suggested that the rongorongo script looks much like Peratt's petroglyphs and that it too might be a record of plasma phenomena in the ancient skies. It was a moment to give pause. Studying the rongorongo intensely, these enigmatic hieroglyphs, just like the petroglyphs, indeed appear to reproduce intense electrical and plasma phenomena. We see the same donut-like and intertwining shapes, the same odd humanoid figures, the same bird-like heads. The similarities are undeniable.

Although the Western discovery of Easter Island dates to Easter Sunday 1722, not until the 1860s did Europeans become aware of rongorongo. Unfortunately, between missionary zeal, attempts to separate new converts from old pagan ways, and internecine warfare, almost all of the rongorongo tablets and inscribed objects were burned or otherwise destroyed. Today just upward of two dozen remain (Fischer 1997b). Furthermore, natives literate in rongorongo were killed in fighting, succumbed to disease, or were carried off in slave raids. By the late nineteenth century, no one could genuinely read the rongorongo script.

Not only have the rongorongo tablets remained, until this point, undeciphered, but also there is no agreement among researchers concerning even the fundamentals of rongorongo. How far back in time it may go is a subject of debate. Some scholars have asserted it was invented on Easter Island during the late eighteenth century in imitation of European writing the natives had observed. A researcher in this camp is the linguist Steven Roger Fischer. After years of study, Fischer concluded it was a post-European contact invention. Furthermore, according to Fischer, the majority of the surviving rongorongo texts are cosmogonies or procreation chants that repeat, over and over, the generic formula of X copulates with Y to form Z. An example: "All the birds copulated with the fish: there issued forth the sun" (Fischer 1997b, 259). In other words, the rongorongo tablets are an Easter Island Kama Sutra! Fischer's "decipherment" has not received widespread acceptance.

Other researchers suggest the rongorongo script has an ancestry thousands of years old, though the surviving wooden tablets are at most a couple of hundred years old. The known tablets are copies of copies of copies . . . For many centuries scribes, not able to truly read the script, piously copied and recopied something they knew was important and held in reverence. Brother Joseph-Eugène Eyraud wrote in 1864, "But the little they [the Easter Islanders] make of these tablets persuades me to think that these characters, probably a script in origin, are for them now just simply a custom they preserve without attempting to account for it" (Fischer 1997b, 12; material in brackets added by R. Schoch).

Far from being an indigenous creation of the Easter Islanders, some researchers have suggested the rongorongo script originated in parts of Polynesia well west of Easter Island, or perhaps even in China. Others look to South America. Still others have seen similarities between rongorongo characters and the enigmatic ancient scripts of the Indus Valley civilization. One researcher seriously suggested that rongorongo is related to Egyptian hieroglyphics (for general discussions of these theories, see Fischer 1997b; Métraux 1957; and Wolff 1948). I have long advocated that there is good evidence supporting cultural contact across both the Pacific and Atlantic Oceans in remote ancient times (Schoch with McNally 2003), but looking carefully at such rongorongo analyses, I do not find them particularly convincing. A stylized fish, human figure, Sun, or vulva could conceivably look similar across unconnected cultures.

Perhaps treating rongorongo as a script, as a form of writing comparable to an alphabetical language, or even as a script based on pictographs, ideographs, or hieroglyphics is a wrong or incomplete approach. This brings us back to the plasma hypothesis. Like the petroglyphs that Peratt has studied (Peratt 2003), I believe the rongorongo tablets record plasma configurations in the very ancient skies. Each glyph may show one of the forms the plasma column took. In sequence, they record, like a scientific record, what was happening in the skies. Two things support this interpretation: First is the confirmation Katie and I received from a member of Dr. Peratt's research team that they had connected the rongorongo glyphs to plasma configurations modelled in their laboratory; when this book was first published, we did not have this confirmation. Second are Rapanui words and legends. Explorer Francis Mazière recorded an indigenous name for the island as Matakiterani, or "eyes gazing at the sky" (Mazière 1968, 9). He also recorded a legend of the sky falling (Mazière 1968, 57):

> In the days of Rokoroko He Tau the sky fell.
> Fell from above on to the earth.
> The people cried out, "The sky has fallen in the days of King Rokoroko He Tau."
> He took hold: he waited a given time. The sky returned; it went away and it stayed up there.

This legend could refer to strange plasma configurations, perhaps even manifested in part as tremendous bolts of lightning, seen in the sky and making contact with the land. Subsequently, the plasma "went away" and the sky returned to normal. The legendary king's name bears a striking similarity to *rongorongo,* and Tau is similar to *ta'u,* a category of inscriptions commemorating a series of deeds or events (Fischer 1997b, 288). When a staff covered with rongorongo texts was collected in 1870 by Chilean naval officers, the commander, Don Anacleto Goñi, reported that the natives could not decipher them, but "we, in asking explanations of the natives about said staff, were shown the sky and the hieroglyphs that [the staff] contained with such respect that I was inclined to believe that these hieroglyphs recalled something sacred" (Fischer 1997b, 26; material in brackets added by Fischer).

Curiously, the few surviving rongorongo tablets have many sequences of glyphs in common. This suggests they are based on a common source, they are recording the same phenomena, and they fit together to form a complete whole. It is similar to finding ancient manuscripts in the Middle East. Piecing together fragments of the book of Daniel, for instance, the entire work emerges.

Here is another enigma: Easter Island lies over 3,500 kilometers west of the coast of South America. On the mainland, in modern Peru, are found the Nazca lines and geoglyphs—huge drawings on the ground. Curiously, some of these drawings are hauntingly reminiscent of both

Peratt's petroglyphs and rongorongo glyphs. Are the Nazca geoglyphs part of the same story? Peratt and his colleagues (Peratt et al. 2007; Peratt and Yao 2008) mention the Nazca lines and Nazca pottery decoration as possible depictions of plasma phenomena. Katie speculates that the giant Nazca geoglyphs may mark the actual spots where certain incoming plasma configurations drove down to ground level and touched, or branded, the earth. Through time, the shapes were walked, chalked, venerated, and preserved. Although I have viewed the Nazca lines from both the air and at ground level (from an observation tower and looking beyond a fence), I have not had the opportunity to collect samples, but others have. Undertaking a petrographic and geochemical analysis of rock debris from the Nazca lines region, Andreas Weller and colleagues found glass fragments, which they classified as volcanic (Weller et al. 2013). I wonder if perhaps some of the glass fragments are the result of vitrification due to a solar outburst and associated electrical discharges. More significant and telling, however, are the findings of Tomasz Gorka and colleagues who, in carrying out geophysical magnetometry studies of the geoglyphs of the Palpa to Nazca region, found that "the total field measurements are dominated by remanent magnetization of lightning strikes" (Gorka et al. 2007, 178). This is an absolutely astounding discovery, in my assessment. What kind of conventional lightning strikes could cause widespread magnetization? Given the hyper-arid environment of the area for thousands of years, perhaps going back to the end of the last ice age (9700 BCE), what opportunity would there be for such massive lightning strikes to hit the area? Were there major electrostatic discharges unrelated to rainfall? I believe we should consider the concept of "lightning" from a solar outburst.

The connection (in ancient times) of our Sun to the divine is one direction my research with Katie has led; therefore, I refer you to the new chapter 15 for why these glyphs may have been venerated. I see similarities between Easter Island petroglyphs, rongorongo glyphs, Nazca geoglyphs, and plasma configurations. It is also perhaps worth noting that there seem to be similarities among some of the decorations on walls, pillars, and artifacts from the Neolithic sites of Nevali Çori and Çatalhöyük in Turkey, the petroglyphs that Peratt and his group have

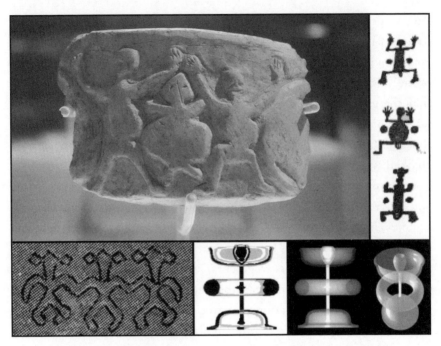

Figure 6.1. A fragment of a limestone bowl from Nevali Çori,
currently on display in the Şanlıurfa Museum (*top left*) compared to
rongorongo glyphs (*bottom left*), various petroglyphs (*top right*), and
plasma configurations (*bottom right*).

(Photograph of the Nevali Çori artifact courtesy of R. Schoch and C. Ulissey;
plasma and petroglyph illustrations courtesy of Dr. Anthony L. Peratt, reprinted with
permission from *IEEE Transactions on Plasma Science*, December 2003, vol. 31;
rongorongo glyphs from Thomson 1891.)

studied, the rongorongo glyphs, and the plasma configurations Peratt
has modeled (see Badisches Landesmuseum Karlsruhe 2007a, 2007b,
for information on Nevali Çori, Çatalhöyük, and related sites).

A PLASMA CATACLYSM

Returning to the end of the last ice age, although there have been climatic fluctuations since, the last major global warming event occurred
around 9700 BCE. I hypothesize a major plasma event occurred then,
one that had dramatic, catastrophic, cataclysmic effects globally.
Plasma hitting the surface of Earth could heat and fuse rock, incin-

erate flammable materials, melt ice caps, vaporize shallow bodies of water, and send the climate into a warming spell. The release of pressure that follows the melting of thousands-of-meters-thick ice sheets can induce earthquakes and even cause hot rock under pressure to melt and erupt to the surface as volcanoes. Interacting with the magnetic field and magnetosphere, this extreme plasma event may have even affected the rotation and axis of Earth. This plasma event, this solar outburst, is recorded by petroglyphs, geoglyphs, the rongorongo texts, and other artistic depictions around the world. (Admittedly, there may have been less dramatic plasma phenomena since 9700 BCE, which may have also been recorded. Some of our physical records may preserve oral traditions passed down over many generations or, like the rongorongo, may be copies of copies of copies . . . Peratt and his colleagues hypothesize three major episodes of auroral activity, each recorded in the rock art, between circa 10,000 BCE and 3000 BCE; see van der Sluijs and Peratt 2010, 42).

Many of the petroglyphs Peratt and colleagues have studied are undated, or doubtfully dated, but nonetheless clearly very ancient. While I was working on this book, a reader of my previous works alerted me to some particularly interesting petroglyphs located close to Adel in southern Oregon, near the borders with California and Nevada. Located on a basalt boulder near Greaser Canyon, the Greaser petroglyphs exhibit squiggles, rings, and odd lizard-like figures, all of which might represent super auroral displays and solar outbursts. Particularly interesting is the tentative date that has been suggested for these petroglyphs; they could possibly be up to twelve thousand years old (Volcanoguy 2007). That is, these petroglyphs could be contemporaneous with the plasma events that occurred during the end of the last ice age in circa 9700 BCE!

While attending a conference in Sedona, Arizona, in early October 2011 (at which I spoke about some of the subjects covered in this book), Katie and I had the opportunity to view some of the local ancient petroglyphs firsthand. As with the numerous petroglyph locations that Peratt and his group have studied, the petroglyph site we visited had a southern field-of-view and the petroglyphs themselves showed many forms that seem to record auroral displays and plasma configurations in the skies. In June 2014, John Anthony West, Katie, and I traveled to Sandane, Norway, to attend and speak at a conference. While in Norway, we had a chance to examine the very ancient petroglyphs (dating back to the end of the last ice age; see Lindgaard 2013) found at Ausevik, where we observed a number of diagnostic shapes that Peratt has determined refer to plasma configurations that would be seen in the sky during a major solar outburst. (Relative to the orientation of petroglyphs, interestingly, Richard P. Erwin [1930, 39] long ago noticed that in Idaho petroglyphs typically occur on southern exposures, but he attributed this to the relative lack of lichens on southern exposures, which Erwin contended grew more commonly on northern exposures. I find Erwin's hypothesis for the orientation of petroglyphs less than fully convincing; rather, his observations support the hypothesis that many petroglyphs record auroral and plasma displays.)

Figure 6.2. Examples of some of the diagnostic plasma configurations found among the petroglyphs at Ausevik, Norway.
(Photographs courtesy of R. Schoch and C. Ulissey.)

Solar activity over the last 11,450 years has been reconstructed in various manners, particularly using beryllium-10 (^{10}Be) and carbon-14 (^{14}C) isotope data from ice cores, sediment cores, and tree rings (Vonmoos et al. 2006). Among other factors, solar activity can be gauged based on sunspot numbers (higher numbers of sunspots correlate with higher solar activity), which in turn can be reconstructed for the past using isotope data (such as ^{14}C and ^{10}Be; see appendix 5, page 413). Such studies show a number of minima and maxima in solar activity. Maxima occur, for instance (looking at the two millennia just after the end of the last ice age) at circa 9375 BCE (as far back as the data go in the particular study), 8915 BCE, 8350 BCE, 8030 BCE, 7850 BCE, 7780 BCE, and 7660 BCE, while minima occur at 9165 BCE, 8215 BCE, and 7515 BCE (Usoskin et al. 2007). However, it is important to realize that a major plasma phenomenon, such as a large coronal mass ejection (CME) from the Sun, may not correlate with overall background solar activity. The 1859 Carrington Event occurred between the last solar minimum of circa 1680 and the modern solar maximum, which dates to about 1960 and the following decades. As plasma physicist Paul Kintner, of Cornell University, commented, "The Carrington event happened during a mediocre, ho-hum solar cycle. . . . It came out of nowhere, so we just don't know when something like that is going to happen again" (Kintner, quoted in Brooks 2009).

Plasma events apparently can occur over very short periods of time, probably measured in days, weeks, and months. Such short-term events may be extremely difficult to identify hundreds and thousands of years later using ^{14}C and ^{10}Be isotopes. Whereas even a large plasma event in the distant past might not be readily detected in the ^{14}C and ^{10}Be records, there is the possibility that it could be picked up as a distinct nitrate spike. According to current theory, energetic particles associated with solar outbursts and CMEs increase atmospheric nitrate production, which is subsequently captured in ice cores. Ice cores dating back to 1561 show a series of nitrate events that correlate with solar events; the 1859 Carrington Event corresponds to the largest spike in the series (McCracken et al. 2001a, 2001b). In the deeper geological record, nitrate spikes also occur, such as major nitrate spikes during and after the end of the last ice age, including nitrate spikes that seem to bracket the Younger Dryas cold spell (circa 10,900 BCE to 9700 BCE) that preceded the final end of the last ice age and another major nitrate spike that may date to the middle or late ninth millennium BCE (Carlson 2010; Grootes et al. 1993; Mayewski et al. 1997; Melott et al. 2010). Nitrate spikes do not unambiguously indicate major plasma events, however; nitrate spikes are also associated with bolides such as comets, meteorites, and asteroids. The Younger Dryas may have been initiated by a comet impact or explosion in the atmosphere, producing an increase in nitrates and brought to an end by a large plasma event that also produced nitrates. To distinguish bolide-associated nitrates from plasma-associated nitrates, one may have to look to other markers, perhaps such as an iridium spike, which would be more readily associated with bolides than plasma.

UPDATE: I left the previous paragraph unchanged from the first edition of the book; for my latest thoughts on what initiated the Younger Dryas, circa 10,900 BCE, see chapter 15, page 319. Regarding the use of nitrate spikes correlating with solar events, this is a highly contentious issue (Mekhaldi et al. 2017). In a 2016 paper titled "Nitrate Ion Spikes in Ice Cores Not Suitable as Proxies for Solar Proton Events" the authors (Duderstadt et al.) basically argue that comparing their examination of the historical record of solar proton events (SPEs) to the nitrate spikes that correlate with these known SPEs, they find that the large nitrate spikes seen in the geological record would require such large solar events, such large SPEs, that this is virtually inconceivable. To quote from their abstract:

> These hypothetically large events are compared with probability of occurrence estimates derived from measured events, sunspot records, and cosmogenic radionuclides archives. We conclude that the fluence and spectrum of solar proton events necessary to produce odd nitrogen enhancements equivalent to the spikes of nitrate ions in Greenland ice cores are unlikely to have occurred throughout the Holocene [the time period since the end of the last ice age,

circa 9700 BCE, to the present], confirming that nitrate ions in ice cores are not suitable proxies for historical individual solar proton events. (Duderstadt et al. 2016, 2294; comment in brackets by R. Schoch)

However, my contention is that in fact the solar events that ended the last ice age were indeed much, much greater than anything that has occurred since; that is, the large events apparently indicated by the large nitrate spikes were real.

Based on the data we currently have, I believe that both comet/bolide impacts/explosions and major plasma events have influenced human prehistory and history. The end of the last ice age was a time when I believe a major plasma event (or events) occurred on Earth, for which there is an increasing amount of evidence, including the nitrate data, the petroglyphs, rongorongo records, and the intentional burial of Göbekli Tepe.

Interestingly, Plato's chronology places the fall of Atlantis close to the end of the last ice age. In Plato's dialogue titled *Critias,* the lead character recounts:

Let me begin by observing first of all, that nine thousand was the sum of years which had elapsed since the war which was said to have taken place between those who dwelt outside the pillars of Heracles and all who dwelt within them; this war I am going to describe. Of the combatants on the one side, the city of Athens was reported to have been the leader and to have fought out the war; the combatants on the other side were commanded by the kings of Atlantis, which, as I was saying, was an island greater in extent than Libya and Asia, and when afterward sunk by an earthquake, became an impassable barrier of mud to voyagers sailing from hence to any part of the ocean. (Plato, *Critias;* translated by Benjamin Jowett [1817–1893])

Here *Critias* is actually reporting what was told to Solon of Athens by an Egyptian priest in circa 600 BCE, so nine thousand years elapsed would place the fall of Atlantis at 9600 BCE, which is tantalizingly close to the modern dating of the end of the last ice age. I am not suggesting that either Göbekli Tepe or the Great Sphinx is literally a vestige of Atlantis (although some people have claimed that the Sphinx and accompanying pyramids were constructed by survivors from Atlantis). However, could the 9700 BCE event have helped inspire the Atlantis legend?

The plasma event of 9700 BCE may have eradicated advanced civilizations and high cultures of the time (the mythic Garden of Eden and the very real builders of Göbekli Tepe come to mind), and radiation emanating from the plasma may have affected mental and psychical abilities. Perhaps this is the basis for a universal myth of a fall from a golden age, a time when humans lived in harmony and ease. Summarizing his survey of the concept of paradise and a golden age across cultures, Richard Heinberg (1989, 54–55) wrote that such a myth has been found "from Mesopotamia to Iran, Egypt, India, China, Australia, North and South America, and Africa. Everywhere, we have encountered essentially the same myth—the story of a primordial era when humanity and Nature enjoyed a condition of peace, happiness, and abundance."

In this context, I cannot help but think of the bicameral mind theory of the late psychologist Julian Jaynes (1920–1997). In summary, Jaynes proposed that prior to a few thousand years ago ancient humans did not possess consciousness (metaconsciousness or meta-awareness) on the same level or of the same nature as modern humans. Among other characteristics, such persons often experienced auditory hallucinations that they interpreted as the voices of their gods giving commands and directing their actions. Their societies were differently organized than later societies, without the same level of central authority that was required to organize and control "fully conscious" individuals.

According to Jaynes (and his theory remains quite controversial), this "bicameral mind" condition ended, and modern human consciousness began, with a catastrophe that he dated to the late second millennium BCE. This period marks the collapse of the Bronze Age, a time of wars, migrations, and natural disasters (see Schoch with

McNally 1999, 128–30). In particular, during this period the volcano on the island of Thera (Santorini) erupted in the Aegean north of Crete, not only sending out ash, vapors, and debris, but also setting off a huge tidal wave that may have destroyed Minoan civilization. Jaynes writes, "The collapse of the bicameral mind was certainly accelerated by the collapse under the ocean of a good part of the Aegean people's land" (1976/1990, 212). I wonder if the core of Jaynes's theory might be correct, but perhaps his timing for the change in human mentality might be wrong. Instead of this change occurring in the second millennium BCE, might it have happened with the catastrophes at the end of the last ice age, 8,500 to 9,000 years earlier?

With the coming of the plasma, everything changed. People cowered for their lives; they sought shelter in caves, under cliffs, in dwellings built of thick stone or carved into mountainsides. Was it because of plasma events that the Göbekli Tepe people buried their creation, arguably expending as much or more time and energy to carefully and purposefully cover over (and thus protect) the structures as they had to erect them in the first place? What is more, when Katie and I visited Göbekli Tepe we were surprised to see numerous iconographic similarities between it and Easter Island.

The outstanding feature of Easter Island is the moai, as I have described. In the case of Göbekli Tepe, stone pillars dominate the scene. Amazingly, both the moai and the anthropomorphic central pillars of Enclosure D at Göbekli Tepe have arms and hands positioned similarly against the body, with hands and fingers extended over the belly and framing or drawing attention to the navel region—as if pointing to or framing the belly button. The moai are looking up at the skies, and I believe the Göbekli Tepe pillars, which are anthropomorphic (humanoid in form), are also looking toward the skies. Are they looking to identical phenomena? And then there is Urfa Man (the life-sized statue of a man now housed in the Museum of Şanlıurfa). It has a similar iconography of the arms and hands, and noticeably absent is a well-defined mouth, a similarity it shares with the "female moai" carved of basalt and now housed in the museum on Easter Island. And what about the very names of Göbekli Tepe and a traditional name for Easter Island,

Te Pito Te Henua? Both refer to the navel and can be interpreted as meaning "navel," "birth," "origins," or "beginning"—perhaps the navel or beginning of the world, the beginning of time, or the beginning of civilization? I believe these similarities are real, but I might have missed them if I had not been to both sites in close succession.

Due to the plasma event, humankind was thrown into a dark age for thousands of years, only to reemerge, amidst megalithic monuments dating to a much earlier time, with nascent abilities and vague and scattered memories of what had happened. Some of those memories took physical shape in the megalithic architecture found around the world; what better way to attempt an escape from fierce skies than in a protective solid stone "fallout shelter"? On Easter Island, there are numerous low stone "houses" with massive walls, and also the people often used the natural volcanic caves found on the island. Is this why? While most memories were vague, becoming little more than forebodings and legends of the fury of the gods against the ancestors, the rongorongo may precisely detail exactly what happened in the skies 11,700 years ago.

The rongorongo tablets may constitute the oldest surviving texts, thousands of years older than the Judeo-Christian Bible. Isolated on their tiny island, the Easter Islanders can be compared to medieval monks closely copying and recopying their treasured written archives. Maybe this is why, of all places, the detailed record survives on this remote little Pacific island. The sequences of the rongorongo glyphs may record the plasma configurations seen in the skies as they writhed and twisted, morphing from one form to another. These extremely accurate observations, meticulously recorded, may store valuable scientific information. I believe an important future task will be to decipher the details of their message. This is not just an exercise in reconstructing the past but also could be crucial to the survival of modern civilization. The rongorongo tablets may record not just the plasma configurations but also information on the first signs to expect, perhaps instabilities on the Sun's surface or subtle changes in the atmosphere, before a cataclysmic plasma outburst. Perhaps, as my wife Katie suggests, the rongorongo records a chronology of differing plasma intensities and associated electromagnetic currents. Astrophysicist Thomas Gold, in an offhand way, guessed that major plasma events might impact Earth approximately every ten thousand years. It has been 11,700 years since the last one; the next one could arrive at any moment! Let us fully understand what the ancients had to say to us—the warning and instructions they may have left for us—before it is too late.

Before we go too far with such a wonderful or outrageous (depending on one's inclination) theory involving major solar outbursts causing severe climate change, resulting in the end of the last ice age and devastation to high civilizations in remote antiquity, maybe we need to step back. Maybe we need a reality check. Can it actually be the case that our Sun is not the eternal, unchanging ball of fire in the sky that on a day-to-day basis we tend to take for granted? Who really doubts that tomorrow the Sun will rise once again, just as it did yesterday and the day before and the day before that . . . ? For many people, the Sun is a stable fixture of their world. Well, looks can be deceiving. We need to explore the modern understanding of our Sun as well as the context of our Sun in the larger cosmos.

7

OUR NOT-SO-ETERNAL SUN

Despite popular misconceptions, the Sun is not a stable, unchanging, eternal ball of fire in the sky. Indeed, from an astrophysical and geological perspective, the Sun is quite the opposite. Fueled by nuclear fusion reactions, it is unstable, continually seething and churning, in disequilibrium, discharging not only visible light, but also a large energy array across the electromagnetic spectrum, and belting out charged particles as well. While the Sun may have little hiccups from time to time, it can also suffer from major bouts of coughing, spewing massive "solar storms" Earth's way. Such storms, thousands of times more powerful than anything recorded in modern times, have left their marks in prehistoric records. It is inevitable that major solar storms will hit us again, and although there is no consensus as to exactly when, the evidence taken as a whole suggests that we are in for something major very soon—we may be overdue! And while experts may disagree on the details, it is clear that a major solar storm would have catastrophic consequences for our modern technological society.

SUNSPOTS

Some aspects of the Sun's activities are more or less regular and therefore crudely predictable, whereas others still elude accurate prognostication. There are apparent cycles in the Sun's activity, with various cycles taking place on timescales of decades, centuries, millennia, tens of millennia, and perhaps longer. And the truth is that we really do not understand the internal and external dynamics that drive these cycles. The Sun remains to this day a great unknown.

Perhaps the best-known solar cycle is that of sunspot activity. Sunspots are dark spots on the surface of the Sun, the largest of which can be visible to the suitably protected naked eye (that is, without telescopic magnification). Chinese sunspot observations date back to the fourth century BCE, and there were isolated observations of sunspots in the West during medieval times, generally misinterpreted as planets transiting (crossing) in front of the Sun. It was not until the early seventeenth century that European astronomers systematically recorded sunspots; Galileo correctly understood that they are features on the surface of the Sun. Since the Sun rotates on its axis, sunspots appear to move across the face of the Sun. The Sun rotates once approximately every twenty-five days at the equator, but since the Sun is not solid, its rotation changes with latitude: at the solar poles it takes about thirty-six days for one rotation (Russell 2005).

Sunspots, which can be up to hundreds of thousands of kilometers in diameter and move across the surface of the Sun at hundreds of meters per second, are relatively cool spots (3,000–4,500°K) against the background surface temperature of the Sun (5,780°K). They are in large part a magnetic phenomenon, and there is intense magnetic activity surrounding sunspots. Although sunspots themselves are relatively cool features, the areas surrounding their margins are brighter and hotter than the average surface temperature, with the result that more sunspots correlate overall with a brighter and hotter Sun. During the period from about 1645 to 1715, known as the Maunder Minimum, few sunspots were observed, and this corresponds with the middle of the so-called Little Ice Age (late sixteenth century through early nineteenth century), a time of cooling on Earth.

Over a period of approximately eleven years the number of sunspots increases, reaches a maximum, and then diminishes again. This is apparently due to, or correlated with, the changing of the magnetic field of the Sun on a more or less twenty-two-year cycle, known as the Hale cycle (see Dooling 1998). The Sun's magnetic field reaches peak strength during a solar sunspot minimum and reverses or flips in conjunction with the solar maximum (at the midpoint of a sunspot cycle), then flips back during the next solar sunspot cycle. A 2019 study found a correlation between the eleven-year solar cycle and related solar activity (sunspots, solar flares, and coronal mass ejections) and the planetary alignments of Venus, Earth, and Jupiter (Stefani et al. 2019). The researchers concluded that the tidal forces of these planets (their gravitational pull on the Sun) influence solar activity (Rabie 2019). This study, in my assessment, lays the foundation for more work on the influence of all the planetary bodies on solar activity, including changes in the Sun's magnetic field at various scales (for early work on such ideas, see Nelson 1974).

Scientists have been keeping track of sunspot cycles since March 1755; Solar Cycle 24 began in December 2008 (as I revise this book during late 2020, Solar Cycle 25 has just begun). Over this time, sunspot cycles have ranged in length from 9.0 to 13.7 years, and the maximum smoothed sunspot number (monthly number of sunspots averaged over a twelve-month period) has ranged from 48.7 (in the early nineteenth century) to 201.3 (during Solar Cycle 19, April 1954–October 1964). Another way of measuring sunspot activity is to measure the number of sunspot groups rather than the number of sunspots per se (Hoyt et al. 1994; Hoyt and Schatten 1998; Balmaceda et al. 2007; Clette et al. 2007; Vaquero 2007).

Two and one-half centuries of solar cycles is a very small sample. Fortunately, an estimate of the number of sunspot groups, indicative of solar activity, can be reconstructed using fluctuations of isotopes ^{14}C and ^{10}Be recorded dendrochronologically (in tree rings) and in polar ice cores. (The amount of ^{10}Be and ^{14}C in the atmosphere correlates inversely with solar activity.) This has been done with considerable accuracy back to circa 9500 BCE (essentially the end of the last ice age; see Solanki et al. 2004; and Usoskin et al. 2007), and the results are rather startling; our Sun has been more active over the last few decades (since about the middle of the twentieth century) than it has been for thousands of years previously. Depending on how the data are interpreted (the translation of the isotope data related to solar activity is not straightforward, but requires various forms of analyses), the current overall level of solar activity is the highest it has been since about 9500 BCE to 9000 BCE, near the end of the last ice age!

In circa 9500 BCE the Sun was extremely active, with a record number of sunspots. Between 9500 BCE and about 8000 BCE the number of sunspots fluctuated widely, with record lows around 9200 BCE followed by extreme highs circa 9000 BCE to 8800 BCE. That is, solar activity showed wild fluctuations during this period and over the subsequent millennia, and until about 6000 BCE continued to exhibit wide discrepancies between high and low sunspot numbers, but the highs were less high. Relatively low highs continued until recent times, with the periods of circa 6000 BCE to 3500 BCE and circa 200 BCE to 1900 CE recording particularly low solar activity compared to the end of the last ice age. Then something happened in the twentieth century; the Sun started to become extremely active. Solanki et al. wrote, "According to our reconstruction, the level of solar activity during the past 70 years is exceptional, and the previous period of equally high activity occurred more than 8,000 years ago. We find that during the past 11,400 years the Sun spent only of the order of 10% of the time at a similarly high level of magnetic activity and almost all of the earlier high-activity periods were shorter than the present episode" (Solanki et al. 2004, 1084).

Indeed, based on the analysis of Ilya G. Usoskin et al. (2007, 303, fig. 3), the Sun's activity today is higher than any time in the past since the period of 9500 BCE to 9000 BCE, just after the end of the last ice age. And remember that their data do not go back further than circa 9500 BCE.

Comparing the record of solar activity with reconstructed records of climate change over the last twelve thousand years (and more), I believe there are definite correlations. The Younger Dryas ended with an abrupt warming spell at the end of the last ice age, roughly 11,400 to 11,700 years ago (depending on the calibration used; dated to circa 9700 BCE in Steffensen et al. 2008), and it is clear from the solar records that the Sun was extremely active around this time. Analyzing 11,700 years of ice core records from Kilimanjaro in eastern equatorial Africa, Thompson et al. (2002) report abrupt climate changes (involving in each case sharp drops in temperature, followed by sharp rises) at approximately 6300 BCE, 3200 BCE, and 2000 BCE. A prominent dust layer in the ice core, interpreted as signifying drought conditions, accompanies the 2000 BCE event; Thompson et al. (2002, 592) point out that a similar dust layer is found in approximately contemporaneous (dated to circa 2300 BCE) ice cores from Huascarán in the Andes of Northern Peru. These periods of abrupt and severe climate change occur in each case during periods of high solar activity, particularly the 3200 BCE and 2000 BCE events (see Usoskin et al. 2007, 303, figs. 3 and 4). The Kilimanjaro data also show an abrupt and dramatic warming, accompanied by a huge increase in dust, at the very beginning of the sequence, circa 9700 BCE; this corresponds to the end of the last ice age (Steffensen et al. 2008) and the dramatic events taking place then.

The solar activity data, the climatic data, the petroglyphs, the rongorongo texts, and the demise of the early civilizations at the end of the last ice age indicate that something mighty—something catastrophic—was happening. All of the evidence points to some sort of solar outburst or cosmic event wreaking terror on the surface of Earth. Today the Sun is starting to exhibit the same behavior as seen over ten thousand years ago, when catastrophe hit. Will we heed the warning signs? Will we take the lessons of the past seriously and prepare for the future?

Based on the data, James A. Marusek, a physicist and engineer who until his retirement worked for the U.S. Department of the Navy, argues that the Sun is currently undergoing a state change (Marusek 2010). That is, the inherently unstable Sun is readjusting and re-equilibrating, as it must do periodically through geological time. In an analogy, our own planet Earth has an internal dynamo and is constantly readjusting and re-equilibrating itself as heat is released from the interior. This gives rise to earthquakes and volcanoes. Returning to our Sun, we may already have had a precursor of what is to come in the very near future, namely the solar storms of 1859, which I've previously mentioned.

There have been reports that the Sun is showing signs of going into a period of low numbers of sunspots when just the opposite had been expected (see Space Ref 2011; and Southwest Research Institute

2011). It has been suggested that the Sun is potentially entering a sort of hibernation or calm period, and this may even impact Earth by cooling the climate, not unlike the 1645 to 1715 Maunder Minimum, which corresponded to the Little Ice Age. It is not clear if this is really the case, but even if it is, it does not preclude the possibility there could be some very unusual activity of the Sun on the other extreme; that is, during a period of relative dormancy or hibernation there could be an incredible solar outburst. At the end of the ice age some twelve thousand years ago there were wild fluctuations in sunspot activity, wide swings between highs and lows, and it seems that during periods of low sunspot activity the energy builds up and erupts as massive solar outbursts rather than being given off as more numerous and smaller flares and CMEs. The 1859 Carrington Event occurred during the overall "quiet" Solar Cycle 10, and the May 1921 massive solar storm occurred during the overall rather average Solar Cycle 15. Perhaps, being a geologist, I like the analogy of a major active tectonic/earthquake zone where stress is building up. The stress and energy can be relieved either by many smaller earthquakes in succession over time, or the stress and energy can build up and continue to build up until they are finally released as one or a few major earthquakes (and the accompanying foreshocks and aftershocks). (Smaller earthquakes can still be substantial from a human perspective; for example, it takes about thirty-two magnitude 6 earthquakes to equal the energy released by one magnitude 7 earthquake.) A short-term lull in sunspot activity says to me that energy is building up in the Sun and will be released, probably sooner rather than later, in one or a few massive outbursts. My conclusion is that we better be prepared!

Something else worth noting is a point made by Espen Gaarder Haug (2010), namely that most people are woefully unaware, unprepared, or simply willfully and purposefully ignorant of so-called low-probability, yet high-impact, events such as natural disasters like major hurricanes, tornadoes, tsunamis, volcanic eruptions, pandemics, or extreme solar outbursts. These are sometimes referred to as Black Swan events. Exacerbating the situation, many people, whether economists, politicians, or even scientists, use the wrong types of mathematical models in analyzing events and planning for the future. In particular, analysts use Gaussian models, fitting or modeling data to the theoretical bell curve or normal distribution. However, compared to Gaussian models, many real world phenomena have higher peaks and fatter tails than are seen on a theoretical normal distribution. This means that the models underestimate the probability of large changes, whether they are price swings in financial markets or variations in solar activity (which Haug has analyzed). With respect to the Sun specifically, Haug concluded, "Sudden expected large changes in solar activity are much more likely to happen than any type of Gaussian model would assume . . . the risk is somewhat similar to massive stock market crashes and recessions; most people including politicians tend to underestimate the probability for them to occur. In short, many people, including people deeply involved in planning and preparedness for disasters, seem to have a Gaussian type of thinking. They do not appreciate the Black Swan phenomenon" (Haug 2010, 10).

As Haug points out, the historical record of solar storms is incredibly short and not at all representative. He wrote, "However, as we know from our discussion of the shortcomings of the Gaussian, the concept that there probably have been and will continue to be more powerful solar storms than [the 1859 Carrington Event] . . . is exactly what we should expect. What is the likelihood that the written record of solar storms over a few hundred years would detect the maximum solar storms for a sun that has been shining for billions of years? Close to zero" (Haug 2010, 10; material in brackets added by R. Schoch).

It was the astronomer John A. Eddy who, in 1976 (see Brody 2002, 147–49, for a historical perspective), ultimately convinced the scientific community of the reality of the Maunder Minimum (the relative lack of solar activity, as seen by the anomalous absence of sunspots, from about 1645 to 1715). Historically there was a long tradition, going back to Aristotle and before, that the Sun is perfect, unchanging, and eternal. Old ideas are often difficult to overturn, no matter how wrong the ideas may be. People are resistant to changing their fundamental beliefs. Eddy ends his seminal paper on the Maunder Minimum with the following words: "The reality of the Maunder Minimum and its implications of basic solar change may be but one more defeat in our long and losing battle to keep the sun perfect, or, if not perfect, constant, and if inconstant, regular. Why we think the sun should be any of these when other stars are not is more a question for social than for physical science" (Eddy 1976, 1200).

That is, all the evidence indicates that over time our Sun, like any other star, is extremely irregular, varying in intensity and activity. During the last ten thousand years or so, and especially during the last few thousand years, the Sun has been relatively stable overall (despite some minor fluctuations), and this has been a time when civilization arose—or re-arose—and flourished. But if we look at the longer prehistoric record, we soon learn that the Sun has had tremendous mood swings, and there is every reason to believe that another such swing, resulting in cataclysmic solar storms, could be imminent.

EARTH'S MAGNETOSPHERE

The Earth's magnetosphere has been called "Our Shield in Space" (NASA 1981), and indeed it helps protect Earth from the constant incoming barrage of particles from outer space, generally referred to as cosmic rays, which include plasma (charged particles) originating from our Sun (the solar wind), incoming particles from elsewhere in our galaxy, and particles from the universe in general. The magnetosphere of Earth is formed by the interaction between charged particles, particularly those composing the solar wind, and the magnetic field of Earth, which originates deep in the planet's core. The charged particles are deflected and flow, generating electric and magnetic currents that determine the configuration of the magnetosphere. The dynamics of the magnetosphere are very complex and continually change with variations in Earth's magnetic field, the solar wind, the heliosphere, the interplanetary magnetic field, the intensity of incoming cosmic rays, and so forth.

There are various ways to define the magnetic poles of Earth. The magnetic dipole centered within Earth intersects the surface of our planet at two antipodal points, known as the geomagnetic poles. These geomagnetic poles of Earth do not correspond to the geographic poles, defined by the rotation axis of our planet. The dipole is currently (2020) inclined to Earth's rotation axis by about 9.41° and "the geomagnetic north pole is at 72.68°W longitude and 80.65°N latitude, and the geomagnetic south pole is at 107.32°E longitude and 80.65°S latitude" (NOAA 2020; see also BGR 2020).

Another important aspect of Earth's magnetic field are the dip poles, which are the positions on Earth's surface where the geomagnetic field is vertical (perpendicular) to the surface of Earth (the Earth is not a precise sphere, but an ellipsoid). The north and south dip poles do not need to be antipodal (on opposite sides of Earth), and in fact they are not currently antipodal. The "2020 location of the north magnetic [dip] pole is 86.50°N and 164.04°W [in the Arctic Ocean] and the south magnetic [dip] pole is 64.07°S and 135.88°E [off the coast of Antarctica in the Indian Ocean opposite Australia]" (NOAA 2020; material in brackets added by R. Schoch). The magnetic dip poles of Earth vary in their locations over time; in recent years, the north magnetic dip pole has been migrating north-northwest at a rate of about fifty-five kilometers per year, whereas at other times, it has stayed in approximately the same location for a number of years (Russell 2007; Geological Survey of Canada 2008; National Geophysical Data Center 2012; Witze 2019; Livermore et al. 2020; NOAA 2020). Furthermore, the path of the north magnetic dip pole, as well as that of the south magnetic dip pole to a lesser extent, has significantly altered its direction over the course of the last five centuries. For instance, the north magnetic dip pole was traveling in a southerly direction for at least a century, until about 1859, when it began its modern predominantly northern migration. As pointed out by Mikhail Kovalyov (2019, 5), "The 1859 turn in the path coincided with the Carrington solar storm of 1859." Whether this was simple coincidence, or a significant correlation, remains an open question.

Regarding geomagnetic poles and magnetic dip poles, the National Oceanic and Atmospheric Administration (United States) website notes:

Scientists, map makers and polar explorers have an interest in the locations of the dip and geomagnetic poles. Although geomagnetic pole positions cannot be observed [directly with ground instruments], they are arguably of greater significance than the dip poles because the auroral ovals (approximate 5° latitude bands where the spectacular aurora is likely visible) are closely centered on the geomagnetic poles. They are usually displaced slightly to the night-side of the geomagnetic poles and greatly vary in size: bands of greatest activity occur between 15° and 25° from the geomagnetic poles. (NOAA 2020; material in brackets added by R. Schoch)

Sometimes Earth's magnetosphere is simplistically visualized as symmetrically positioned lines of force emanating from magnetic pole to magnetic pole, similar to a huge bar magnet, but this is incorrect. Earth's magnetosphere is blown and distorted, primarily by the solar wind, into what has been variously described as a teardrop shape or a bullet shape (with a blunt nose and elongated cylinder-like structure extending out into space). Facing the Sun ("upwind" toward the Sun), the magnetosphere is compressed and typically extends out for about sixty-five thousand to ninety thousand kilometers from Earth's surface, whereas the magnetotail (extending away from the Sun) can extend well over one million kilometers. The overall "cylinder" shape of the tail is estimated at around 250,000 to 300,000 kilometers in diameter. (In comparison, the average diameter of Earth is 12,742 kilometers.)

Earth's magnetosphere includes the Van Allen radiation belts, discovered by James Van Allen and his colleagues based on data from the first American satellite mission in 1958. These consist of belts or layers of energetic charged particles (plasma) that are held in place by Earth's magnetic field. Two major belts have been distinguished: an inner belt extending from about two hundred to ten thousand kilometers above the Earth's surface and an outer belt extending about thirteen thousand to sixty thousand kilometers above the surface. Interestingly, a thin band of antimatter (specifically antiprotons) is trapped between the inner and outer Van Allen belts (Adriani et al. 2011).

The upper portion of our atmosphere, referred to as the iono-sphere because it contains ionized (electrically charged) particles, forms the inner boundary of the magnetosphere. Composed of various layers and distinguished by changes in ionization and electromagnetic properties, the ionosphere extends from about sixty kilometers to over five hundred kilometers (in some models and classifications, over one thousand kilometers) above Earth's surface. The ionosphere is of prac-tical importance in the modern world because, among other things, it exerts an influence on radio wave propagation over long distances. (High-frequency/short-wavelength radio waves can be bounced off of the ionosphere.) Schumann resonances are extremely low-frequency electromagnetic radiation global resonance phenomena that propa-gate through the cavity formed between the surface of Earth and the ionosphere.

The auroras, the northern and southern lights (aurora borealis and aurora australis), occur in the ionosphere when photons (light parti-cles) are given off by atoms going from an ionized or excited state to a ground state. Different types of atoms changing state, and how much energy is absorbed and subsequently released, cause different auroral colors. Thus, colors in the green range (including yellowish-greens), as well as some brownish-red colors, are attributed to emissions from oxygen atoms, while various blues and reds (and together they may form purples) are due to the emissions of nitrogen atoms. The atoms are excited by collisions as particles are trapped and funneled along the magnetosphere toward Earth's magnetic poles; they subsequently lose energy and give off the light observed as auroral lights. Auroras are primarily due to the solar wind, the stream of particles flowing in from the Sun. Under normal conditions, the auroras are seen along rings around the magnetic poles of Earth; these rings are typically located somewhere in the region of about 10° to 25° from the geomag-netic poles. During intense solar winds, solar outbursts, and coronal mass ejections (the corona is the outermost layer of the Sun, consisting of plasma, with a temperature measured in the millions of degrees; Mattson 2010) the auroras increase in intensity and are seen at lower latitudes as the aurora zone expands.

A SOLAR PROTON EVENT AT THE END OF THE LAST ICE AGE

Paul LaViolette (2011a) has marshaled evidence that a major solar flare accompanied by a super solar proton event (SPE), or events, at the end of the last ice age "fried the Earth" (to use the description of LaViolette's hypothesis put forth in the popular *Space Daily;* see *Space Daily* 2011). During an SPE, protons are accelerated to incredibly high energy levels and penetrate into our atmosphere. (Note: solar proton events are also commonly referred to as solar particle events, and in both cases the acronym SPE is used for such an event; indeed, whatever moniker is applied, most of the particles ejected by the Sun during such an event are protons.)

LaViolette bases his conclusions on meticulous analyses of radiocarbon concentrations in sediment cores from the Cariaco Basin (off the coast of Venezuela) correlated with acidity spikes, high nitrate ion concentrations, and changes in ^{10}Be deposition rates in the Greenland ice record, all of which he argues are indicators of a sudden cosmic ray influx, in turn correlating with solar activity as expressed specifically through solar flares and SPEs. Additionally, there would also have been accompanying CMEs on an enormous scale. LaViolette dates the event, which is the major focus of his 2011 paper published in the journal *Radiocarbon,* to "12,837 +/− 10 cal [calendar] years BP [before the present = approximately 10,887 BCE, as the "present" in BP dates is typically defined as the year 1950]" (LaViolette 2011a, 1) and equates it with major faunal extinctions in North America at this time. This is approximately (or possibly exactly; see appendix 3, page 395) the start of the Younger Dryas, for which I am adopting a date of circa 10,900 BCE. In a footnote to his paper, LaViolette (2011a, 17) notes that the same type of pattern is seen in the sediment and ice data at the end of the Younger Dryas (i.e., the very end of the last ice age). LaViolette dates this terminal ice age event to "11,571 cal yrs BP" (= approximately 9621 BCE), which corresponds closely to the approximately 9700 BCE date derived by Steffensen et al. (2008) for the end of the last ice age. To quote LaViolette directly relative to this event, "This suggests that an overly active Sun may have played a significant role also in causing abrupt climatic change at the end of the ice age" (LaViolette 2011a, 17, footnote).

In his paper, LaViolette discusses some of the effects of a massive SPE and the attendant solar activity for the Earth. The ozone layer, our protection from deadly ultraviolet (UV) rays, would have been greatly depleted, with major ozone holes forming in some areas, that is, if the ozone layer had not been destroyed completely! Increased doses of damaging, and potentially lethal, UV radiation could have posed a major hazard for organisms on Earth, especially in high and middle latitudes. Besides the increased UV radiation, high-energy cosmic rays that are part of a major SPE would penetrate the atmosphere and raise radiation levels on the ground. According to LaViolette's calculations, unprotected organisms at sea level during the event of "12,837 cal yrs BP," which is the focus of his paper, could have accumulated radiation doses of 3 to 6 Sieverts (a unit of radiation exposure, 1 Sievert = 100 rems [an older unit of radiation doses]) over a period of two or three days. Lethal radiation doses for humans are in the range of about 3.5 Sieverts, and for many large mammals in the 3- to 8-Sievert range. The best mode of protection at the time, both from the UV radiation and the cosmic ray radiation, would have been to seek safety in caves and other underground shelters (*Space Daily* 2011; LaViolette 2005).

Interestingly, the Austrian archaeologist and speleologist Heinrich Kusch and his wife, Ingrid Kusch, have documented hundreds upon hundreds of tunnel systems under Neolithic settlements found throughout Europe and Turkey, some dating back to around twelve thousand years ago (Kusch and Kusch 2011). According to Heinrich Kusch, based on the number of tunnels that have survived to the present day, the original extent of such tunnels must have been absolutely enormous! Furthermore, many of the tunnels "are not much larger than big wormholes—just 70 cm wide—just wide enough for a person to wriggle along but nothing else. They are interspersed with nooks, at some places it's larger and there is seating, or storage chambers and rooms. Taken together it is a massive underground network" (Heinrich Kusch, quoted in *Austrian Times* 2011; see also *Daily Mail* 2011).

An immediate question is, Why were these tunnels built? What was their use? An incredible amount of time and effort went into their construction, and so their purpose could not have been trivial. To quote Heinrich Kusch, "The precision with which they were built in prehistoric times is unbelievable. Miners and tunnel construction engineers I spoke with were stunned. . . . It would be hard to dig tunnels as these even with today's means. They are hewn very exactly in the hardest granite and people most probably didn't even have metal when the tunnels were built" (Heinrich Kusch, quoted in *Austrian Times* 2011).

It has been suggested that perhaps these tunnels were used by early humans to escape predators or enemies, or perhaps they served as underground passages from one place to another (*Austrian Times* 2011). I suggest that the tunnels were primarily built as safe havens and refuges from catastrophes occurring on the surface of Earth, providing shelter from major solar outbursts (including CMEs and SPEs). In my opinion, the fact that such events were occurring around twelve thousand years ago, the very time when many of the tunnels were carved, is not simple coincidence. Also, I speculate that many artificial caves and tunnels that have been dated to later periods (such as the Bronze Age, circa 3300 BCE to 1200 BCE) by archaeologists may have their origins much earlier, at the end of the last ice age some twelve thousand years ago.

Reinforcing the notion of caves being used in antiquity for protection, here is one more tantalizing piece of evidence. While on Easter Island in November 2012, Katie and I were walking back to our small bus after having just explored some of the natural lava tube caves, when our native Rapanui driver and guide offered a startling revelation. According to local tradition, he stated, at one time the people had lived in the caves for a thousand years due to the harsh conditions on the surface. He knew nothing about my theories concerning solar outbursts and the necessity, in the distant past, to seek shelter below ground, in thick rock shelters, or within megalithic structures. Indeed, although the caves on Easter Island are natural, it is evident that they were used during ancient times. Artifacts and even human skeletons have been found in the caves, ancient paintings are still to be seen on the ceiling of one cave, and many caves have been modified by the addition of interior stonework such as bench-like structures and masonry composed of local rock forming neat walls that narrow the entrances to just the width of a single person—all the better for protection from whatever was taking place on the surface.

THE UNDERGROUND
REFUGES OF CAPPADOCIA

Another place we find underground tunnels and indeed entire cities is in the Cappadocia region of Turkey. Over two hundred underground complexes are reported in Cappadocia; most have not been adequately explored, and it seems certain that many more wait to be discovered. Two of the best known are Kaymakli and Derinkuyu, portions of which are open to the public. To this day, nobody really knows the true extent of these or other underground cities of the area, but they were substantial. Kaymakli consists of at least eight floors or underground stories (only four of which are currently accessible), each extending in a labyrinthine manner over a vast area. The city may have supported a popu-

Figure 7.1. View of structures carved into the rock, Cappadocia, Turkey.
(Photograph courtesy of R. Schoch and C. Ulissey.)

lation of three thousand to four thousand people plus farm animals and supplies, all housed underground. Derinkuyu, with an estimated twenty floors and extending an estimated eighty-five meters below the surface, may have supported anywhere from a few thousand to ten thousand people plus their livestock and goods. And the underground cities may not have been entirely isolated from one another. Kaymakli and Derinkuyu are less than a dozen kilometers from each other, and there are reports of a tunnel that may connect them.

Each underground city included all of the necessities to support its inhabitants. In some cases, each level appears to have been able to function as an independent unit. There were living quarters for both humans and beasts, the barns and animal stalls being generally located near the entrances. There were storage areas, wineries, kitchens, dining rooms, bedrooms, schools, and churches complete with naves, altars, and seating platforms for the congregation. There were also specialty areas, such as a room at Kaymakli containing a huge round platform

Figure 7.2. Robert Schoch in the underground city of Kaymakli, Cappadocia, Turkey. (Photograph courtesy of R. Schoch and C. Ulissey.)

of igneous rock, with dozens of depressions carved into the top, which may have been used for melting, refining, and working copper. Air was provided to the cities by ingenious ventilation shafts that open to the surface but are often camouflaged. Water was supplied by deep wells tapping into underground aquifers and rivers. The underground cities were entered via narrow passageways, and similar narrow passageways, so tight that it can be difficult to squeeze through, connected different areas and levels. The passages could be blocked, thus protecting the inhabitants inside, with huge round stone "doors" (in the range of one or two meters in diameter, a half meter thick, and weighing around five hundred kilograms) that could be easily wheeled into place (or opened again) from the inside but not from the outside. Evidently these underground cities with their narrow passages and protective barriers served as some kind of fortifications or protective refuges, but from what? And why? And when?

The standard archaeological answers to these questions are fairly straightforward and make some sense, at least superficially. There is plenty of evidence that various underground cities were occupied during Greek and Roman times and into the early Christian and Byzantine period. In particular, Byzantine churches carved into the rocks abound, many dating to the tenth through thirteenth centuries, but this is late in the history of Cappadocia. Most historians concede that underground cities were used earlier, possibly during the period of the Hittite Empire, which controlled the region from about the eighteenth century BCE to the twelfth century BCE (with so-called Neo-Hittite peoples surviving until about 700 BCE.). Furthermore, the standard view is that people did not necessarily live underground continuously, but rather retreated underground when enemies invaded their lands. A question that remains unresolved, if this scenario is true, is how exactly the people underground could survive while their enemies were free to roam the surface, not only on foot but also by horseback. The underground cities are dependent on ventilation shafts that open to the surface. Would not an enemy easily figure out how to locate the ventilation shafts, even if they were initially camouflaged, and block them, resulting in the suffocation of everyone underground? The locations of the underground cities might be easily found due to smoke coming from ventilation shafts, for there is evidence that fires for cooking and other purposes were used in the underground cities. Additionally, piles of debris on the surface—removed from the subsurface when the cities were carved out—would identify where an enemy should search to locate underground cities. Significant piles of debris are no longer to be found. Apparently, they have eroded away and become dispersed; this suggests that the underground cites date back much earlier in time than is usually believed to be the case.

Studying the underground cites of Cappadocia firsthand, I believe that they would have provided an ideal shelter during a major solar outburst. The accompanying solar flares, CMEs, and SPEs would cause strong electrical discharges to hit Earth, burning and incinerating materials on the planet's surface and would also raise radiation levels on the surface of Earth. The best way to protect oneself? Go deep underground. This is not to deny that the underground networks of Cappadocia were used, reused, expanded, and built anew for thousands of years after the end of the major solar outbursts. A tradition was established and passed down from generation to generation, even perhaps as the origin of the tradition was lost to memory.

I need to point out here that a critic, when I once presented this interpretation of the origin of the underground constructions of Cappadocia, objected strenuously that the building of these structures would have taken a long time, time that he asserted was not available to the people as they would have all been killed quickly by increased radiation. However, he did not understand the nature of major solar outbursts, which come in waves with lulls between. A solar outburst would occur, with damaging consequences, at least in some areas, and incredible displays—warning signs—in other areas. People would seek shelter as they could, be it in natural caves or already built artificial structures. Then, given the warnings, I believe they would have made preparations for another solar outburst. The next solar outburst would come and go, reinforcing for the survivors the need to be prepared, and thus the underground complexes would be expanded. Eventually, the Sun decreased its outbursts, but for many generations, the people would still be concerned that the catastrophic events of the past could return. Slowly, over thousands of years, such memories might fade, even as the tradition of underground structures was carried on.

ÇATALHÖYÜK: CIVILIZATION IN DECLINE

As discussed in chapter 3, with the site of Göbekli Tepe we have evidence for advanced civilization at the end of the last ice age. The underground structures of Cappadocia give us a sense of how humans may have survived the terrifying solar events that brought about the end of the last ice age. Another site in Turkey that I have had the opportunity to visit, known as Çatalhöyük, postdates Göbekli Tepe by some two thousand years, and I believe it is representative of the state of human culture during the "dark age" that lasted for thousands of years before the reemergence of civilization during the fourth millennium BCE.

Figure 7.3. A view of Çatalhöyük.
(Photograph courtesy of R. Schoch and C. Ulissey.)

Located on the Anatolian plain southeast of the city of Konya (in south-central Turkey), Çatalhöyük was occupied for over two thousand years, from circa 7500 or 7400 BCE to circa 5400 or 5200 BCE, and may have been home to a population of 3,500 to 8,000 people at any one time. The site consists of numerous mud-brick and plastered houses or buildings constructed adjacent to each other with their walls abutting. There was little in the way of open areas or streets between the buildings, and there were few windows. The dense collection of buildings presented a solid wall around the perimeter, reminiscent of a later fortified castle, fort, or city. The houses had flat mud-brick roofs on which many daily activities were carried out: cooking, eating, and socializing. Indeed, the rooftops may have served as paths from one dwelling to another, and as streets connecting multiple dwellings. Entrances to the buildings consisted of small openings at the tops of the walls and through the roofs. (Ladders and steps were used to reach them from the ground.) The inhabitants were packed tightly into small homes, with an estimated five to ten people typically in each family unit. Each house had a large room for living, eating, and sleeping; side rooms were used for storage.

But this was not just a city for the living. Over four hundred skeletons have been found buried under the plaster floors, particularly under platforms used as sleeping areas. One house had over sixty skeletons buried beneath it! In 2004, a woman was found buried in a fetal position, cradling against her chest a human skull that had been plastered and painted with red pigments on at least three separate occasions before being interred with her. Was this some form of ancestor worship? Were the dead, in some cases, given status on a par with the living?

Çatalhöyük is a city of mud-brick and plaster, not monumental stone structures. It is a city with murals and paintings covering the interiors of many houses. Depicted are men hunting wild deer and cattle, vultures flying over headless people (perhaps a death ritual?), female figures, and many abstract designs. Also found are paintings and bas-reliefs of leopards sculpted into the plaster walls. There are sculpted clay figurines of animals, human heads, and possibly the "Mother Goddess" (this interpretation is subject to debate), and bull skulls (bucrania) with prominent horns plastered and mounted onto walls, benches, and pillars.

In my judgment, the site of Göbekli Tepe shows all the signs of being "more advanced" than Çatalhöyük. It is as if Çatalhöyük represents a decline from the higher civilization of Göbekli Tepe to a cultural dark age, relatively speaking, thousands of years later. And Çatalhöyük is not alone. There are very similar sites showing all of the same attributes. One example is the geographically close and slightly earlier to approximately contemporaneous Aşıklı Höyük. Interestingly, as mentioned in chapter 3, Aşıklı Höyük has yielded an incredible obsidian bracelet. Found within a context that dates to circa 7500 BCE, it presents a genuine enigma. According to modern laboratory analyses, the bracelet was made using highly specialized manufacturing techniques that seem to be out of place for this period. I wonder if this bracelet may be even older. Perhaps it was an antique, a remembrance of an earlier and more sophisticated time thousands of years before, handed down from generation to generation as a treasured legacy of the even more remote past for the people of that distant time long ago.

DISTURBING THE MAGNETIC FIELD OF EARTH

Returning to the subject of a solar proton event (SPE) at the end of the last ice age, LaViolette (2011a) also determined that an enormous SPE would significantly disturb the geomagnetic field of Earth and induce a partial (or possibly complete, at least for a short period of time) collapse of the magnetosphere. Earth is surrounded by a dust cloud composed of interplanetary debris plus particles that the solar wind blows off the surface of the Moon. These dust particles can acquire electrical charges by interaction with electrons in the interplanetary plasma, by photoionization due to the solar UV radiation, and by other means. The charged particles (including particles of antimatter, as we have seen) are trapped in the magnetosphere, held and essentially protected there. But with a partial or complete collapse of the magnetosphere, cosmic rays, SPEs, and CMEs could heat the particles up, causing them to melt, and subsequently they would resolidify, forming spherules. Furthermore, dust particles and spherules could be jettisoned into the atmosphere and eventually fall to the surface of Earth. Thus, according to the hypothesis regarding solar flares, SPEs, and CMEs at the end of the last ice age, a layer or layers of extraterrestrial debris should be found at some geological and archaeological sites dating to this period.

LaViolette points out that layers of extraterrestrial debris, including nanodiamonds (as have been reported in some layers dating to the end of the last ice age; see appendix 5, page 410), do not necessarily imply that a comet, meteorite, or asteroid either hit Earth or exploded in the atmosphere. Furthermore, by the SPE hypothesis, it is expected that the extraterrestrial dust layer would accumulate on some parts of Earth more than on others, and in some places there might be no accumulation of extraterrestrial debris at all. This is due to the fact that the solar proton flux and debris cloud, interacting with Earth's magnetosphere, would be irregular, with large spatial variations. Indeed, the data indicate that accumulations of extraterrestrial debris at the end of the last ice age show just this pattern, which has led some scientists to call foul and question the integrity and reliability of their colleagues' work when evidence for extraterrestrial debris at the end of the last ice age was reported by one group, but another group at a different location could not replicate the results. By the SPE scenario, a pattern of such debris in some places but not in other areas is what is to be expected!

I believe that LaViolette (2011a) puts together a very powerful and compelling argument that our Sun was much more active, by orders of magnitude, at the end of the last ice age. The core of LaViolette's meticulous work is that our Sun is not stable, but goes through periods of major instability and increased activity (whatever the cause of such instability and increased activity may be), and the last major (there have been ups and downs since then) occurrence of such increased solar activity was at the end of the last ice age; that is, unless we are willing to acknowledge that the Sun is ramping up right now and again going into a period of instability and increased activity after a lull of over ten thousand years.

UPDATE: I want to point out that I am well aware of the following theory:

The **Electric Sun theory** (also *Electric Star theory,* and *Electric Sun Model* and *Electric Sun Hypothesis*) is the idea that the Sun (and stars) derives the main sources of its power electrically from its surroundings, rather than from within by nuclear fusion (the mainstream view). (Quoted from ElectricUniverse.info; material in parentheses are part of the original quotation; bold and italics also occur in the original quotation.)

This theory is associated with the general "Electric Universe" paradigm and remains highly controversial and is generally dismissed by the mainstream. From my perspective, whatever the source of the power of the Sun may be, the overall essence of the work I have pursued remains intact. Our Sun goes through periods of instability and volatility.

8

COSMOCLIMATOLOGY

There has been increasing evidence for, and acknowledgment of, connections between climate, Earth's magnetic field, solar activity, and related extraterrestrial and other "subtle" factors (Courtillot et al. 2007; Mackey 2007). Much of this work goes against the reigning paradigm, the common consensus that has solidified around the topic of global climate change (more commonly referred to as global warming). The general consensus view, for instance, has been that increases in global temperatures seen in the twentieth and twenty-first centuries have been due primarily or totally to the actions of humans, most notably the increase of greenhouse gases (such as carbon dioxide) in the atmosphere due to the burning of fossil fuels and deforestation. Natural factors and cycles have been downplayed or ignored, despite the fact that changes in greenhouse gases have been correlated with global temperature changes for hundreds of thousands—even millions—of years, long before humans could conceivably have been causing such changes. Indeed, increases in carbon dioxide may in part be a consequence of global warming rather than a cause (Ferreyra 2011). Increases in temperature due to other factors (such as increases in solar activity) may warm the oceans, for instance, resulting in the release of carbon dioxide and an inability to absorb more carbon dioxide; once the carbon dioxide is in the atmosphere, it may further reinforce global warming. This of course does not necessarily totally negate the contribution that human-released greenhouse gases may make to global warming, but it may put such factors into perspective.

PROTECTING THE PARADIGM

Following the reigning paradigm that the major portion of global warming observed over the last century is due to human actions, the Intergovernmental Panel on Climate Change (IPCC; see discussion in Mackey 2007) and like-minded scientists (see, for instance, Pittock 2009) have taken the position that even if there might be a link between solar variability and climate, the effects would be so negligible (particularly as compared to human-induced climate change) as to be insignificant from a pragmatic point of view, and therefore any such link can be dismissed or ignored for all practical purposes. Indeed, the critics of solar variability as an explanation, partial or complete, of climatic change on Earth have charged that solar variability research may have political motivations. The well-known solar variability skeptic Barrie Pittock asserts, "Solar influences might be suggested as an alternative explanation of climatic change because that might undermine some unwelcome hypothesis such as that recent climate variations are due to human emissions of greenhouse gases" (Pittock 2009, 486).

Of course, the opposite may be readily the case also; solar (and other, for that matter) influences might be dismissed as too insignificant to be an alternative explanation for climate change, as that might inconveniently undermine the current politically correct notion that significant climate change is due to human causes. After all, former United States Vice President Al Gore and the IPCC were awarded the 2007 Nobel Peace Prize for their work establishing and publicizing the presumed link between human activities and climate change. As a case in point, at the CERN (European Organization for Nuclear Research, formerly called Conseil Européen pour la Recherche Nucléaire) labs in Geneva, the CLOUD (Cosmics Leaving Outdoor Droplets) experiment is examining the role particles from space, such as cosmic rays, may play in cloud formation, which in turn affects weather and climate. CERN Director General Rolf-Dieter Heuer told the scientists who are involved with the experiments not to draw conclusions from their results! Heuer is quoted as saying, "I have asked the colleagues to present the results clearly, but not to interpret them. That would go immediately into the highly political arena of the climate change debate. One has to make clear that cosmic radiation is only one of many parameters" (Heuer, quoted in Calder 2011; see also Orlowski 2011).

In this quotation, Heuer is apparently referring to the work and theories of Henrik Svensmark, director of the Center for Sun-Climate Research at the Danish National Space Center. Much of Svensmark's work has focused on how cosmic rays can affect the formation of clouds and thus in turn have a large impact on Earth's climate (see further discussion below).

In a review article of work along these lines, Svensmark writes, "During the past 10 years, considerations of the galactic and solar influence on climate have progressed so far, and have found such widespread applications, that one can begin to speak of a new paradigm of climate change. I call it cosmoclimatology and . . . I suggest that it is already at least as secure, scientifically speaking, as the prevailing paradigm of forcing by variable greenhouse gases. It has withstood many attempts to refute it and now has a grounding in experimental evidence for a mechanism by which cosmic rays can affect cloud cover" (Svensmark 2007, 1.18). In other words, cosmoclimatology challenges the status quo, politically correct, consensus view that global warming is due primarily or solely to modern human activities.

Science journalist and commentator Nigel Calder opines, "CERN has joined a long line of lesser institutions obliged to remain politically correct about the man-made global warming hypothesis. It's OK to enter 'the highly political arena of the climate change debate' provided your results endorse man-made warming, but not if they support Svensmark's heresy that the Sun alters the climate by influencing the cosmic ray influx and cloud formation. . . . The once illustrious CERN laboratory ceases to be a truly scientific institute when its Director General forbids its physicists and visiting experimenters to draw the obvious scientific conclusions from their results" (Calder 2011).

Unfortunately, the case of CERN and the unpopularity in some circles of Svensmark's research are not isolated incidents in science. Indeed, such attitudes have meant that antiparadigm analyses were, and are, often given short shrift or dismissed out of hand by many in the mainstream scientific community. (This community, of course, is composed predominantly of specialists in other fields. Just because someone is a scientist, that does not mean that he or she is in a position to properly judge conclusions outside of his or her area of expertise.) The social institutions of modern science reinforce these attitudes and actions. As pointed out decades ago by Thomas Kuhn (1962), scientists beholden to a reigning paradigm downplay, belittle, or simply ignore other theories, approaches, and points of view. To give a specific modern example, in cellular biology the theoretical model of a sodium-potassium pump (also known as the membrane pump theory) is almost universally accepted as the mechanism used by cells to maintain the proper levels of sodium and potassium in their interior environments. Yet, as reviewed by L. Edelmann (2005), a mass of experimental data and theoretical calculations indicate that the sodium-potassium pump theory is flawed and that, indeed, better models, models that fit the data more precisely, have been developed. (One model, developed by Gilbert Ling and summarized by Edelmann [2005], is known as the association-induction hypothesis. Martin Chaplin has developed another model, discussed by Bennett Daviss [2004]. The details of the competing models are not important to our present discussion.)

If there is a better model, one that fits the data more accurately, how can it not be accepted by "objective" scientists? The fact is that the objectivity of science, or at least of the practitioners—the scientists—is a myth. Scientists, individually and collectively, have vested interests, whether those interests involve personal prestige, monetary rewards (grants, salaries), defending their "intellectual turf" and pet theories, or other considerations (see appendix 2, page 384). The modern institutions of science serve primarily to reinforce the status quo, the mainstream thinking, the conventional wisdom of the time. Publication in high-status scientific journals is the way for the typical scientist to advance her or his career. Submissions to such journals are subjected to the peer review system. The reviewers act as censors, generally guarding the status quo and rejecting any work that differs too radically from their own work and ideas or that of their conventional colleagues.

There has been much discussion concerning the flaws of the peer review system (see Edelmann 2005), and in the United Kingdom the members of parliament have even taken an interest in these issues. As stated in a BBC News article concerning the report of the House of Commons Science and Technology Committee (2011) on peer review in scientific publications, "'Peer-reviewed' has become a byword for 'scientifically sound and approved,' but complaints have arisen in recent years that the process can sometimes work to suppress radical new ideas, and can fail to catch fraudulent research" (Boettcher 2011).

Not only is peer review commonly used to determine which articles are published, it is also used to determine who receives scientific grants, which projects are funded, if and when scientists are hired and promoted, and so on.

There are other powerful factors beyond the peer review system that reinforce the status quo. As honor and prestige are heaped on those advocating particular hypotheses, theories, and paradigms, competing theories are further marginalized. Returning to the case of the sodium-potassium pump, once Jens Christian Skou was awarded a portion of the 1997 Nobel Prize in Chemistry for the discovery of Na/K-ATPase (an enzyme equated with the sodium-potassium pump), it became virtually impossible to question the reigning dogma or present contradictory evidence and alternative theories. Likewise, the 2007 Nobel Peace Prize was awarded to the promoters of the human-induced global warming hypothesis. As L. Edelmann aptly states, "Awarding Nobel Prizes becomes an act of canonizing ideas and hypotheses into fully-fledged sacrosanct theories" (Edelmann 2005, 727).

The religious imagery and analogy here are quite fitting. The accepted paradigm, the scientific dogma, is not to be fundamentally questioned. Small additions and tweaking, elaborations and expansions, and building on the accepted paradigm are acceptable and even encouraged, but questioning the fundamental basis of the paradigm is not allowable. Radically dissenting views and any data that challenge the accepted paradigm must be suppressed. Heretics are persecuted or ignored. (In past centuries, this might mean torture or death. In modern times it might mean exclusion from the scientific community by being locked out of jobs, publication outlets, and grant funding.) Ultimately, such tactics constitute "cheating by concealment" and "discreet fraud," to apply the terms of Edelmann (2005).

Galileo Galilei (1564–1642) was prosecuted and convicted by the Inquisition for his heliocentric worldview (that the Sun is the center of the solar system and Earth orbits around the Sun). Of course, at the time, a geocentric worldview (Earth is at the center, with the Sun, Moon, planets, and stars all revolving around Earth) was the reigning paradigm. As an example of "cheating by concealment" and "discreet fraud," Edelmann points out that in Galileo's time, "All the reasons proving the earth is at the centre of the universe would be referenced in a [status quo, mainstream] review, epicycles of certain planets would not be mentioned at all, or, at the very best, as marginal problems. A heliocentric world-view—favoured by a (known) minority—which can easily explain these epicycles, would not show up in this review . . . this would constitute an obvious fraud" (Edelmann 2005, 727; material in brackets added by R. Schoch).

But that was the seventeenth century. Surely such scientific fraud would not take place today, four hundred years later! Using the example of the sodium-potassium pump, Edelmann points out that such fraud is very much with us to this day. "Extensive reviews about this pump have been released without mentioning published experiments that falsify the pump idea and without acknowledging that phenomena attributed to the pump cannot only be explained without the assumption of an energy consuming pump, but that they can be predicted directly within the framework of AIH [association-induction hypothesis]. Experimental results, which could foster doubts about the truthfulness of MPT [membrane pump theory], are not only left out of many reviews, but they are also left out of more detailed textbooks of cellular biology" (Edelmann 2005, 727; material in brackets added by R. Schoch).

This is a particularly insidious form of fraud, one that is self-perpetuating as a new generation of scientists, learning from reviews and textbooks, is never even exposed to the anomalous data, data that question the accepted paradigm, and alternative hypotheses and theories are ignored. In such a context, it is difficult to even be aware that another viewpoint is possible, and this is exactly as intended by the guardians of the status quo! One wonders how much material of high scientific merit, hidden in the obscure recesses of little-known and low-status publications or never published at all, is being covered up by status quo mainstream scientists promoting their own agendas and following their own deep subconscious beliefs and obsessions, which may effectively amount to a religion.

As Edelmann notes, "Obsessed with the overvalued idea that the solution to a scientific problem . . . is to be found within the framework of the accepted paradigm . . . , an alternative paradigm is *a priori* rejected" (Edelmann 2005, 728; italics in the original).

Nothing has changed, it seems, since Galileo's time.

Interestingly, however (and maybe there is some hope here), it does not take a majority to sway the masses, whether they make up the collective scientific body or the public at large. A study carried out at Rensselaer Polytechnic Institute (see Xie et al. 2011) indicates that when 10 percent of a population holds strongly and unshakably a certain belief, this belief will be adopted by the majority. Thus, to gain widespread acceptance for an idea actually only requires convincing 10 percent of the group under concern (such as the community of scientists). But of course this is a double-edged sword. The initial 10 percent (with the majority following in its wake) may be convinced of an idea independent of whether that idea is valid or not. Ultimately, science is not democratic; that is, the fact that a majority holds a certain belief (whether a majority of scientists or a majority of the general public) does not guarantee that the idea is valid or true. Indeed, one can argue that history says quite the opposite; the geocentric worldview, now discarded, is but one famous example.

A NEW PARADIGM: COSMOCLIMATOLOGY

Returning to the science of climate change on Earth, an important fact is that the Sun is not literally at the center of our solar system, with all of the other planets revolving around the Sun. Yes, in a general sense the Sun is in the center with everything else going around it, but the Sun itself is moving in an orbit around the center of mass of the solar system (known as the barycenter). The diameter of the Sun is about 1.4 million kilometers, and it moves around the barycenter within a circle that has a diameter of a little over two solar diameters. The orbital path of the Sun is not even close to a simple circle or ellipse (as are the planetary orbits), but due to the gravitational and tidal influences of the planets, the Sun's orbit takes the form of an epitrochoid (Mackey 2007, 956), that is, a larger circle that is connected to a small circle or ring nested within it on one side. Another way of describing this is that the Sun is, for most of any one orbit, following a large and nearly circular path, but then its orbit tightens into a smaller radius, goes backward relative to its previous direction (referred to as a kind of retrograde motion), completes a loop, and then heads forward again along the larger circular path. It is believed that no alignment of the Sun and all of the planets (plus asteroids, comets, and other objects in the solar system, for that matter) is ever exactly and precisely the same, and therefore no two epitrochoid-shaped orbits of the Sun are exactly the same.

There is an apparent periodicity in the orbit of the Sun along the epitrochoid path (Perryman and Schulze-Hartung 2010), corresponding to eight distinct patterns of such epitrochoid orbits, each of which takes about 179 years for the Sun to complete; this periodicity in turn apparently corresponds to periodicities in planetary positions around the Sun (Mackey 2007). The Sun's motion significantly affects its internal dynamics and activity. The Sun is not internally homogeneous nor is it truly spherical (it has an oblate spheroid shape); portions of the Sun are solid-like (the core), much is fluid-like, and the rest is gaseous. Furthermore, the internal aspects of each portion or layer of the Sun are "lumpy" rather than homogeneous. Its motions affect differentially its various portions, and the Sun on its orbit travels through its own electromagnetic fields to varying degrees at different times. It has been suggested that these motions may correlate with the Sun's eleven-year sunspot cycle, the twenty-two-year Hale cycle (during which the Sun's magnetic dipole undergoes an inversion cycle, back and forth), and longer-term periodicities and trends in solar activity (see review in

Perryman and Schulze-Hartung 2010). In particular, during the time when the Sun is following the path of the small retrograde loop-the-loop in its epitrochoid orbit it can be characterized as in a chaotic phase and as generally less active or relatively dormant, and when it is on the larger radius forming a nearly circular path it is in an ordered phase and relatively more active. The Maunder Minimum, a time of relatively few sunspots and cooler climates, has been correlated with a time when the Sun was on the small loop of its orbit (Mackey 2007, 958).

What this means is that there is interplay between the Sun and the planets, and indeed all of the components of the solar system. The Sun's activity affects the planets (including Earth), but the planets also affect the Sun. How much each planet contributes overall to affecting the Sun, however, remains an open question. On the one hand, the massive outer planets, Jupiter and Saturn, are important components of the collective gravitational effect the planets have on the Sun, but on the other hand, although much smaller and less massive, the closer inner planets (Mercury, Venus, Earth, and Mars) can have significant effects, too. In his book *Apocalypse 2012,* Lawrence E. Joseph (2008, 111) quotes independent researcher and author Richard Michael Pasichnyk as stating, "The Earth's magnetic field undergoes changes of intensity that reflect the magnitude of changes in solar activity *before* they take place on the Sun . . . magnetic data for the Earth at sunspot minimum indicates the 'depth' of the following maximum" (italics in the original statement by Pasichnyk). If this is true, it suggests that Earth's magnetic field influences the Sun, as well as vice versa. However, I have not been able to confirm that this is the case. At any rate, solar activity certainly influences, or at the least is correlated with, geomagnetic activity.

Vincent Courtillot and colleagues (Courtillot et al. 2007) analyzed solar irradiance (electromagnetic radiation from the Sun in all its forms), several different geomagnetic indices, and global temperatures over the twentieth century. They found a strong correlation among all of these factors; however, beginning in the middle 1980s, climate (global temperature) deviates from the tight correlation with all of the other factors. These authors write:

We view the fact that the long-term "overall magnetic trend" is essentially common to all these [magnetic] indices . . . as evidence that the entire system of ionospheric and magnetospheric currents, despite all their complexity, pulses in rough unison with the Sun on a decadal scale (and that this also applies to the main spectral components of total solar irradiance—i.e. photons—and also to the solar wind—i.e., particles). None of this was a priori obvious. Note that magnetic variations revealed by the new indices, which reflect precisely the changes in the UV-X [ultraviolet] component of the irradiance, are a far more sensitive indicator (by several orders of magnitude!) than the total solar irradiance which varies by only ~1‰ [approximately one part per thousand, or a tenth of one percent].

If solar activity is correlated to climate over much of historical times, it might be expected that the "overall magnetic trend" would correlate with the recent evolution of global temperature, and this is indeed the case up to the mid-1980s, but not since then. . . . Of course, the relation . . . [in] this case does not imply a causal link from Earth's magnetism toward climate, but from the Sun to both climate and magnetic changes. Clearly, 100 yr is not enough to ascertain that such a correlation is robust, but it is as impressive as many of the correlations of time series proposed over this time range. (Courtillot et al. 2007, 331–32; material in brackets added by R. Schoch)

After the middle 1980s the global temperature diverges, increasingly dramatically, from the indices for solar radiation and geomagnetic strength and variation. This anomalous climate change may be genuinely caused by human activities, such as the increase of greenhouse gases. Greenhouse gases have been increasing for over a century, and it may only be as of the middle 1980s that they have begun to overpower (perhaps only temporarily) other factors; the truth, however, is that we do not know for certain.

Those who argue against, or simply dismiss, a correlation between solar variations and climate claim that in order for such correlations "to be convincing a linking physical explanation or mechanism is needed" (Pittock 2009, 485). This is actually a bogus argument; if the correlations hold up to scrutiny, they should be taken at face value and possible mechanisms can be explored. This is the approach that Courtillot et al. (2007) take. They discuss three major mechanisms by which changes in solar activity could affect climate: (1) changes in the amount of radiation given off by the Sun, which ultimately change the heat input to the lower atmosphere, leading to climate change; (2) changes in solar UV radiation that can cause changes in the stratospheric ozone layer, affecting the temperature of the stratosphere; and (3) changes in the concentration of galactic cosmic rays (GCRs; cosmic rays from our galaxy, but from beyond our solar system) impacting the Earth. GCR input to the Earth is controlled or modulated by the Sun's magnetic activity and the Earth's magnetic field (which in turn is affected by solar magnetic activity). This third mechanism appears to be the most significant of the three.

Cosmic rays may act on Earth's climate by affecting cloud cover, creating cloud condensation nuclei and thus more clouds, which generally lower surface temperatures on the planet (Svensmark 2007). Cosmic rays may also affect the electrification of thunderstorms, which is related to lightning and the severity of the storms, and cosmic rays may affect ice formation in storms. The magnetic field of Earth acts as a shield against cosmic rays, with the shielding effects varying over time as the magnetic field fluctuates and also varying among geographic locations on the planet. (The magnetic field varies from place to place.) Earth's magnetic field is strongly influenced by the Sun's magnetic field in complex ways as the two fields interact, and the geomagnetic field also varies in orientation and intensity for reasons that are not fully understood. The Earth's magnetic field has declined in strength by about 5 percent per century since at least 1840 and it may have been declining since 1600 or earlier (Brown et al. 2018). Furthermore, there are credible scientific predictions that the geomagnetic field could disappear over the next millennium, then reappear in flipped form (reversed relative to the previous magnetic field; see McKie 2002, but see Brown et al. 2018 for a counter view). A weakened or nonexistent geomagnetic field will let in more cosmic rays and solar particles, subjecting Earth to abnormally large amounts of extraterrestrial radiation that could damage and destroy satellites and, depending on the intensity, ground-based electronics. The radiation may even pose a direct risk to life on the surface of Earth; perhaps the only way to escape would be via seeking shelter underground. Large increases in radiation could heat the atmosphere and cause major climate change. In a worst-case scenario, the ultimate consequences could be devastating. To quote Paul Murdin, of the Institute of Astronomy at the University of Cambridge, "These solar particles can have profound effects, . . . On Mars, when its magnetic field failed permanently billions of years ago, it led to its atmosphere being boiled off. On Earth, it will heat up the upper atmosphere and send ripples round the world with enormous, unpredictable effects on the climate" (Murdin, quoted in McKie 2002).

While the effects of a significantly weakened geomagnetic field may remain speculative, it now seems clear that there are correlations between variations in the Sun's magnetic field (which affects the geomagnetic field) and weather in the short term and climate in the long term. To cite one important study, based on data going back to 1876, Robert G. V. Baker, of the School of Environmental Studies, University of New England, Australia, concluded, "The interaction between the directionality in the Sun's and Earth's magnetic fields, the incidence of ultraviolet radiation over the tropical Pacific, and changes in sea surface temperatures with cloud cover—could all contribute to an explanation of substantial changes in the SOI [Southern Oscillation Index, a measure of changes in surface air pressure between the tropical western and eastern Pacific] from solar cycle fluctuations" (Baker, quoted in Science Daily 2008; material in brackets added by R. Schoch).

Based on such studies, it appears that solar cycles, which are in large part magnetic cycles, correlate with changes in rainfall as well as variations in ocean currents (which in turn have many other climatic impacts). New understandings clearly indicate that relatively "minor" changes in the Sun can be magnified through various physical processes (for instance, the formation of clouds), with the result that such small variations have very large impacts on Earth. Overall, based on studies of detailed data spanning 1,800 years, Ilya G. Usoskin et al. (2005, 9) found "that periods of higher solar activity and lower cosmic ray flux tend to be associated with warmer climate, and vice versa."

Il-Hyun Cho and colleagues have found additional evidence that solar activity can directly affect the weather and climate on Earth. Solar winds (consisting of charged particles) are accompanied by "magnetic clouds" that can interfere with Earth's magnetism, disrupting our magnetic shield that regulates incoming particles and energy. Cho et al. (2011), analyzing data going back to the 1980s, looked at twelve high-speed solar wind events, comparing them with changes in air pressure at sea level over South Korea. They discovered a correlation between these events and slight increases in air pressure occurring just after the events. Most of these events were also accompanied by what are known as Forbush decreases, which are decreases in GCR intensity that are believed to be caused by the magnetic field of the solar wind removing GCRs from the vicinity of Earth. A Forbush decrease may occur during a CME, for instance, and during such an event particles from the solar wind can be injected deep into Earth's atmosphere. These particles can heat the atmosphere, causing it to expand, therefore increasing surface pressures. The charged particles can also have other effects, such as ionizing atoms of the atmosphere, which in turn form nuclei promoting water droplet formation. The study of air pressure over South Korea is important because it demonstrates that such solar-induced effects take place not only at high magnetic latitudes, where Earth is more susceptible to such influences, but at relatively low latitudes as well.

Turning to the archaeological and geologically recent geomagnetic records, Yves Gallet et al. (2006) have suggested a correlation between geomagnetic events consisting of magnetic intensity increases (which they refer to as "archeomagnetic jerks"), cooling episodes in the North Atlantic region, enhanced aridity in the Middle East, and abrupt societal changes around 2600 BCE, 2000 BCE, and 1500 BCE to 1200 BCE. While one might expect a decrease in cosmic rays, resulting in a warming event and increased aridity due to an increase in the geomagnetic intensity, Gallet et al. found the opposite; however, it must be remembered that they were not necessarily looking at overall global climate changes (the climate in a certain region can cool even as the   .

global climate warms overall), and there may be many other factors that they did not account for (for instance, solar variability and the Sun's influence on the geomagnetic field may have come into play).

As mentioned previously, Henrik Svensmark (2007) has offered a comprehensive new paradigm of climate modulation on Earth, which he labels cosmoclimatology. The core of this paradigm is the observed correlation between low-level clouds (below about three kilometers in altitude) and cosmic rays; more cosmic rays correlate with more low-level cloud cover. The cosmic rays release electrons and act as catalysts for cloud condensation nuclei. Cosmic rays in the atmosphere are affected by a number of factors, among the foremost in the present day being the magnetic field of the Sun. Stronger solar magnetism (generally correlated with a more active Sun overall, at least in recent times) sweeps away or protects Earth from cosmic rays, lowering their count and thus decreasing low-level cloud cover. Since cloud tops generally scatter and reflect incoming sunlight back to space rather than allowing it to warm Earth's surface, a less active Sun magnetically, correlating with more incoming cosmic rays and thus resulting in more low-level cloud cover overall, results in a cooler Earth. Likewise, a more active Sun results in a warmer Earth. The data spanning a period of centuries and millennia on climate changes, solar activity, and cosmic ray fluctuations confirm these correlations.

Interestingly, and perhaps counterintuitively, the incoming cosmic ray flux affects primarily low-level clouds. Apparently there are always lots of cosmic rays available to induce cloud formation high in the atmosphere, but it is lower in the atmosphere that cosmic rays are in short supply (fewer of them make it down toward the surface), and thus changes in the quantity of cosmic rays are expressed primarily in changes in low-altitude clouds. Another aspect of Svensmark's work is "the Antarctic climate anomaly." While increased low-level cloud cover on Earth today generally decreases surface temperatures, over Antarctica the opposite is found to be the case. The explanation is that the bright snow and ice of Antarctica have a higher albedo, a higher reflective power, than even the low-level clouds. The result is that increased low-level cloud cover over Antarctica warms the surface locally, rather than cooling it. Data show that over the last few millennia when overall surface temperatures of Earth decreased, those of Antarctica increased, and vice versa.

Svensmark (2007) notes that in the present day about 60 percent of all incoming cosmic rays have high enough energies such that they are not appreciably affected by either the Sun's magnetic field or Earth's magnetic field. About 37 percent of incoming cosmic rays have intermediate energies and are affected by the Sun's magnetic field but not by the weaker magnetic field of Earth. And only about 3 percent of incoming cosmic rays are of low enough energy that they are affected by both the Sun's magnetic field and Earth's magnetic field. Thus, in the present day it is the Sun's magnetic field that primarily influences low-level cloud cover and climate, with Earth's magnetic field playing a more minor role (but not necessarily an insignificant role, as very slight changes in temperature may have major ramifications for organisms on the surface of Earth, including humans).

Moving back in time from the present, the cosmoclimatology paradigm has been applied to explain major alterations in Earth's climate spanning millions, hundreds of millions, and even billions of years (Svensmark 2007). On a broad scale, it is recorded in the geological record that Earth has undergone major alterations between "hothouse" conditions (for instance, around 500, 375, 250, and 100 million years ago) and "icehouse" conditions with periodic glaciations (for instance, around 450, 300, and 150 million years ago, along with the most recent ice age of the last few million years up to virtually the present, geologically speaking). These broad climatic changes appear to correlate with the movement of our solar system around the center of our Milky Way galaxy, with icehouse periods corresponding to encounters with spiral arms of the galaxy that have a concentration of explosive stars ejecting large numbers of cosmic rays, which in turn result in a cooling effect on Earth. Going back even further in time, there were widespread glaciations on Earth about 2.3 billion years ago and 700 million years ago. Based on astrophysical data, these were periods of high rates of star formation, which would have resulted in a significant increase of cosmic rays impacting our solar system and Earth.

While cosmoclimatology, as developed by Svensmark, helps to

cogently explain many aspects of Earth's changing climate, there is one area in which it so far fails: explaining the sudden onsets and, especially, the sudden terminations of ice ages. As Svensmark writes, "Large rises in temperature within the glacial periods, related to cosmic-ray decreases, do not melt the main ice sheets. Terminations leading to interglacial conditions seem to need an insolation trigger . . ." (Svensmark 2007, 1.24). I believe that the missing triggers, the missing pieces of the puzzle, are the quasi-periodic solar outbursts (CMEs, solar energetic particle events, and related phenomena) that can trigger interglacial and possibly also glacial periods as long as the "background" conditions are correct. (A less compelling argument, in my opinion, for the trigger to end an ice age is that as ice sheets and snow cover build up during an ice age, at some point their albedo will become higher than that of the clouds overhead and extra cloud cover will warm the surface, as presently seen in Antarctica, thus ending a glacial period. Such a mechanism cannot account for the extremely rapid increase in temperature at the end of the last ice age, circa 9700 BCE. The Greenland ice sheet, which is "dirty" and thus lacks the bright whiteness and high albedo of the Antarctic ice sheet, does not exhibit the "Antarctic warming mechanism." The continental glaciers of the last ice age were assuredly closer in their characteristics to the current Greenland ice sheet than the current Antarctic ice sheet.)

I believe we can agree with Svensmark when he remarks, "The physics of the Sun and the heliosphere runs through the story on all timescales from the early Earth to the present day" (Svensmark 2007, 1.24). As we have seen, Svensmark is certainly not the only researcher who is finding correlations between climatological factors on Earth and factors involving the Sun, our galaxy, and even stars and galaxies beyond the Milky Way.

Saumitra Mukherjee in an article titled "Cosmic Influence on the Sun-Earth Environment" (2008) reviews much of the literature on this subject, as well as contributing new observations. According to Mukherjee, not only can weather anomalies, such as droughts, storms, unusual hot and cold spells, and major rainfalls and snowfalls, be correlated with extraterrestrial factors (including starbursts; that is, exploding stars), but so can many earthquakes. Mukherjee writes,

". . . oscillations in the planet's magnetic field often occur right before quakes; these oscillations . . . often correlate strongly with astronomical and solar events. But geologists are afraid to say something ridiculous along the lines of 'sunspots cause earthquakes,' despite the fact that, in a certain sense, they do . . . [ellipses in the original] radio wave propagation (e.g., ionospheric 'whistlers'), which appears to play a role in earthquakes, and it can be studied by closely monitoring the impact of the solar wind on the ionosphere" (Mukherjee 2008, 7740).

Mukherjee then goes on to give examples, including the following:

A sudden rise in electron flux and planetary indices 36 hrs before 26th January 2001 earthquake of Kutch, (Gujarat, India) and its sudden fall before the occurrence of [the] earthquake was observed. Similar observations were made in several other cases also including the Andaman Islands. Coronal Mass Ejection, increase in Kp values [a standard measure of geomagnetic activity] . . . , sudden increase in Kp indices and electron flux can be forewarning of seismic disturbance in earthquake prone active fault areas and other environmental changes of earth. On 24th January 2001 an Earth directed coronal mass was ejected, which took two days to reach the earth's surface and may have triggered the active fault in the Katrol Formation of Kutch to produce a major earthquake of magnitude 7.9 in Gujarat, west coast of India. This area was reported as seismically active. In the entire world, a total of 65 earthquakes have been reported on the same day. (Mukherjee 2008, 7742; material in brackets inserted by R. Schoch)

Skeptics will say that these correlations are simple coincidences and not significant. But one certainly has to wonder (and see further discussion in chapter 15, page 366). As we shall see in the next chapter, the work on earthquake prediction carried out by the late Raffaele Bendandi was in some cases amazingly accurate, and Paul LaViolette suggests that the 9.0 magnitude earthquake of December 26, 2004, off the west coast of Sumatra had an extraterrestrial cause.

UPDATE: Something that Katie I ponder at times is whether, as our solar system journeys around the center of the galaxy, passing alternately above and below the galactic plane (following a wave pattern), we might encounter different space environments that could at times "agitate" or "destabilize" or "energize" our Sun: in an analogy, as Katie sometimes refers to it, we might hit cosmic "rip currents" that may be responsible for the periodic instabilities of our Sun, resulting in episodes of solar outbursts.

9

GALACTIC SUPERWAVES AND INTERSTELLAR DUST CLOUDS

According to the new paradigm of cosmoclimatology, solar and galactic influences can have major effects on the climate of Earth. If the work of certain cutting-edge scientists is correct (as a scientist myself, I believe their work has validity), the extraterrestrial influences go far beyond those that we have discussed so far.

GALACTIC SUPERWAVES

Paul LaViolette has long advocated the proposition that our Earth and solar system are subject to periodic, intense volleys of galactic cosmic rays (GCRs), which he terms galactic superwaves (see LaViolette 2005, 2009). This was the subject of his 1983 Ph.D. dissertation at Portland State University, and it is a topic that he has pursued and refined ever since.

The galactic center of our galaxy, the Milky Way, is viewed from Earth in the direction of Scorpius, Sagittarius, and Ophiuchus, seen visually as the brightest region of the Milky Way. At the core of our galaxy is a black hole, as indicated by a sixteen-year-long study published in 2008 (see Ghosh 2008). In the 1960s and 1970s it was discovered that the cores of galaxies can undergo explosive phases, releasing tremendous amounts of energy—as much energy as hundreds of thousands to billions of supernovae going off at the same time. (Supernovae are extremely energetic exploding stars; see LaViolette 2009.) Even though it was realized that our own galaxy might be subject to similar events, it was generally assumed that although there may have been some minor core activity perhaps as recently as fifteen thousand years ago, there has been no major core activity for millions of years and the core will remain relatively quiet and stable for millions of years to come. Furthermore, it was reasoned at the time, even if the galactic core did undergo a major explosion, our location on the outskirts of the galaxy, some twenty-seven thousand or so light years from the center, would ensure that we would suffer few if any consequences.

LaViolette's work totally revises the thinking on this subject. Based on many lines of evidence, including analyses of ice core data that record such information as temperature and climatic changes, solar activity levels, acid fallout from the atmosphere, cosmic ray bombardments, and cosmic dust accumulations, LaViolette has come to some startling conclusions. First, the galactic core is much more unstable than previously believed. Instead of undergoing a major explosion on the order of once every hundred million years, it does so approximately once every ten thousand years. Second, our position toward the edge of the galaxy will do little to protect us from the onslaught of cosmic rays. The cosmic rays traveling outward from the core (the galactic superwave) at nearly the speed of light would affect the entire galaxy. Third, the last galactic superwave hit Earth around 12,900 years ago, near the end of the last ice age, impacting the climate and helping to drive many ice age animals to extinction (including mastodons, mammoths, and many types of birds). As we saw in chapter 7, LaViolette has argued that a solar proton event (SPE) hit Earth at the end of the last ice age. The galactic superwave may have initiated solar instability, resulting in a solar outburst and accompanying SPE.

According to LaViolette (2009) a galactic superwave could appear literally overnight. A brilliant blue-white light, brighter than Venus, will appear in the direction of the galactic center. Then, within days, cosmic rays traveling close to the speed of light will hit. As they do, not only will we be showered with particles directly, but the cosmic rays (charged particles) moving at ultrarelativistic speeds (near the speed of light) through the magnetic fields of space also will emit electromagnetic radiation known as synchrotron radiation (due to the radial acceleration of the particles, for instance, as they move in an arc or spiral through magnetic fields). And cosmic rays hitting atoms in the atmosphere will release even more radiation. In all, Earth will be bombarded by a plethora of radiation taking various forms, including radio waves, visible light, UV light, X rays, and gamma rays. Amidst all of this, I believe extreme auroral phenomena will be seen in the skies all over the globe. I also believe that the bombardment of cosmic rays and energy from the galactic core will destabilize and energize the Sun, resulting in massive solar outbursts. Some of these will surely hit Earth, which in a weakened state (with the atmosphere damaged and the magnetosphere compromised) will be all the more vulnerable. Indeed, LaViolette notes (2009, 3) that even a minor galactic superwave event would have many of the same effects as a major solar outburst (such as a Carrington-level event or greater). In particular, as the galactic superwave hits it will bring with it a high-intensity electromagnetic shock, known as an electromagnetic pulse (EMP). This will cause surges in power grids, damaging transformers and resulting in blackouts around the world (see Maccoby 2010). Satellites, electronic communications systems, computer equipment, and other electronics will be damaged or destroyed. Earth's atmosphere could be ionized, the ozone layer will be thinned or lost completely, and UV light and radiation penetration to the surface will increase.

LaViolette also suggests that a large galactic superwave entering our solar system would vaporize frozen cometary debris and blow the resulting dust and gases into the solar system. The cosmic dust could enter Earth's atmosphere, scattering sunlight, trapping heat in the upper atmosphere, and possibly causing the lower atmosphere to become considerably cooler. Turbulence and imbalances in the atmosphere, as it adjusts to new conditions, would lead to severe storms with increased precipitation that, if conditions were cold enough, could accumulate as snow and ice. LaViolette believes he has found just such cosmic/cometary dust in the Greenland ice record.

Dust and other materials crashing into the Sun, according to

LaViolette, "would energize the Sun, increasing its luminosity and its cosmic ray output" (2009, 4). This could result in solar outbursts, including flares, SPEs, and CMEs, that could ultimately cause the climate of Earth to heat up (as well, of course, as wreak havoc on the surface). Ultimately, to quote LaViolette, "On some occasions the invading cosmic dust could produce a prolonged cold spell or even initiate an ice age if one was not already in progress; at other times it could produce a period of excessive warmth which could terminate an existing ice age or produce a brief interstadial [a relatively warm period during a glacial age]" (LaViolette 2009, 4; material in brackets added by R. Schoch).

LaViolette cites the work of Herbert A. Zook and colleagues (1977), who analyzed solar flare tracks preserved in the glassy surfaces of Moon rocks. (Ionized particles given off from the Sun and traveling through the glass damage the silicate structure, which is observable microscopically.) Based on their analyses, Zook et al. concluded that solar flare activity, which can be taken as an overall measure of solar activity, has varied by a factor of fifty over the last sixteen thousand to twenty thousand years, with a peak in activity around the end of the last ice age. They roughly estimate this peak activity at sixteen thousand years ago, but this estimate could be off by several thousand years, and I believe the peak activity may correlate with the very end of the last ice age, which for present purposes I am considering to be about twelve thousand years ago. In deriving their estimate, Zook et al. assumed that the meteoroid impact rates on the Moon have remained relatively constant over the time period they analyzed. LaViolette contends, "If the cratering rate was higher prior to 10,000 BP [before the present], as the Galactic Explosion Hypothesis suggests . . . then the solar flare activity change . . . would be underestimated. The peak at 16,000 BP would then be expected to increase and shift to a more recent date. Thus, this data would be compatible with the solar outburst date of 14,000 calendar years BP (12,000 C–14 years BP) . . ." (LaViolette 2011b). If the solar system, including the Moon, was being bombarded with dust and debris at the end of the last ice age, causing meteoroid impact rates to be higher than since that time, as would probably be the case if a galactic superwave hit, then the lunar data can be interpreted with even more confidence to indicate an extremely active Sun at the end of the last ice age.

Based on his interpretation of the prehistoric record, LaViolette believes that the next galactic superwave could hit at any time. According to his basic analysis, a galactic superwave should hit Earth about once every ten thousand years, and the last one occurred at or near the end of the last ice age, which is on the order of 11,700 years ago—so we may be overdue! Predicting the time of the next galactic superwave on the basis that they occur about every ten thousand years is very crude and approximate. In June 2009 LaViolette and his colleagues at the Starburst Foundation analyzed ^{10}Be deposition peaks in ice cores. Deposition rates of ^{10}Be are an important indicator of cosmic ray activity, which in turn is related to solar activity; typically, low solar activity (and colder temperatures) is followed by high solar activity (and warmer temperatures), as we saw in the case of the ice cores from Kilimanjaro (see discussion in chapter 7, page 137). LaViolette and his colleagues found recurrent patterns indicative of the following time periods: 28,500 +/− 2,200 years; 11,500 +/− 550 years; and 5,750 +/− 100 years (LaViolette 2009, 11). By my analysis, if the last major period of elevated solar activity was at the end of the last ice age, about 11,700 years ago, then we are just about due (or slightly overdue) for the next wave of high solar activity (whether it is caused by an incoming galactic superwave, which "energizes" the Sun, or some other factor). I would also note that there are signs of unusual solar activity, involving wide swings between high and low sunspot numbers, during the period of circa 4000 BCE to 3000 BCE (see Usoskin et al. 2007); this may correspond to the 5,750-year cycle detected by LaViolette and his group, and again suggests that we are on the verge of the next period of increased solar activity.

GRAVITATIONAL WAVES AND EARTHQUAKES

LaViolette (2009, 3–4) suggests that a galactic superwave electromagnetic pulse (EMP) could be accompanied by a gravitational wave (essentially a ripple in space-time, predicted by Einstein's theory of general relativity). The passing of a major gravitational wave could, LaViolette suggests, trigger earthquakes and volcanic eruptions on Earth. As evidence for such an effect, LaViolette points to the 9.0 magnitude earthquake of December 26, 2004, off the west coast of Sumatra, which caused a massive tsunami. On December 27, 2004, Earth was hit by a major gamma ray burst from a giant flare given off by an ultrahigh-magnetic neutron star located nearly fifty thousand light years away (Wanjek 2005; Kazan 2009). It has been estimated that more energy was released from this flare in one-tenth of a second than the Sun has given off in the last one hundred thousand years (Kazan 2009). Is there a connection between the two events—the earthquake and the onslaught of gamma rays? LaViolette believes so. According to LaViolette the gamma ray burst would be accompanied by a gravitational wave, but the gravitational wave would propagate very slightly faster than the gamma rays, and thus strike Earth slightly before the gamma rays, triggering the earthquake.

LaViolette is not the first person to suggest that increased earthquake activity or seismic activity (including volcanic activity) may be linked to extraterrestrial factors. In Iceland studies have linked global warming to increased volcanic activity (Brahic 2008). To put it simply, the melting of thick ice caps decreases the pressure on the rocks and magma below, increasing the rate at which the magma melts and migrates to the surface, which ultimately results in an increase in the number and/or intensity of volcanic eruptions. It is estimated that Vatnajökull, the largest glacier on Iceland, is currently melting at a rate of five cubic kilometers a year simply due to current global warming. Beyond increased local volcanic activity, the release of pressure in one area of the crust may propagate or transmit stress changes to other portions of the crust (and underlying layers), perhaps even tens, hundreds, or thousands of kilometers from the place where the ice is melting. This could result in increased earthquake and volcanic activity around the world. Likewise, increased pressure can cause stress, resulting in greater volcanic and earthquake activity; the pressure could be due to the buildup of ice (for instance, during an ice age) or, more applicable to the present day, to sea-level rises that redistribute large amounts of water, which are of considerable weight, over the surface of Earth. Volcanologist Bill McGuire, professor of geohazards at University College London, is quoted by *New Scientist* as stating, relative to the current level of global warming, "We are going to see a massive increase in volcanic activity globally. If we look back at previous warm periods, that is what happened" (McGuire, quoted in Brahic 2008).

By one analysis, using United States Geological Survey data, the annual earthquake energy of Earth rose by a factor of five times between 1973 and 2007 (Chalko 2008). I personally question whether some of this apparent rise may be due to better monitoring of earthquake activity over the decades, but even a rise of, say, 20 percent (rather than the 500 percent reported) would be significant in my opinion. The author of this earthquake study, Tom J. Chalko, has also suggested that global warming could cause the overheating of the interior of Earth to the point that it might suffer an internal meltdown and thence explode (Chalko 2004). Deep within Earth heat is generated by gravitational compression and radioactive decay, and this is what melts and keeps molten rock that spews from volcanoes, and it is the power source that drives tectonic activity. Chalko's basic argument is that if the surrounding atmosphere of Earth becomes too hot, then not enough heat will be able to escape quickly enough from the interior of Earth, and it may undergo a meltdown analogous to a meltdown in a nuclear reactor. This in turn, according to Chalko, could possibly lead to nuclear enrichment and ultimately a gigantic explosion. Ultimately, I do not find this scenario convincing because, if for no other reason, geologically Earth has gone through periods during which atmospheric temperatures were much warmer than today and the planet did not explode.

Increased volcanic and earthquake activity due to present-day global warming is, in my assessment, a very real possibility, and the data appear to support that it is happening now. Picture the last ice age, with huge masses of ice in the form of continental glaciers. Any factor, such as a major solar outburst that sends a CME and SPE hurtling our way, which could quickly melt the ice, might cause the crust to snap back and readjust after being pressed down for so long by such weight. Possibly this could cause sudden cataclysmic earthquakes and volcanic activity around the world at an order of magnitude or more greater than what we are experiencing today. It has been calculated that volcanic activity in Iceland was ten times more frequent ten thousand to twelve thousand years ago (Dacey 2010). Furthermore, torrential downpours would have simultaneously occurred as the heated atmosphere became laden with evaporated water, adding further to the havoc on Earth.

Here I believe it is worth mentioning the legendary Raffaele Bendandi (1893–1979), an Italian "self-taught seismologist" (he built his own seismographs that were sold worldwide) who was famous (or infamous, depending on one's point of view) for his earthquake predictions. Bendandi first came to public attention when an earthquake struck the Italian province of Le Marche on January 4, 1924. In November of the previous year, Bendandi had registered his prediction with a notary that an earthquake would strike on January 2, 1924. Although he was off by two days, his forecast was still incredible. He went on to successfully predict a number of other earthquakes, including a major earthquake on May 6, 1976, that left nearly one thousand people dead and forty-five thousand homeless. The dictator Benito Mussolini (1883–1945) took Bendandi very seriously, awarding him with membership as a knight of the Order of the Crown of Italy but also banning him from making further predictions publicly, apparently because it was not good for tourism or the morale of his countrymen (for information on Bendandi, see Fidani [2009?], 2011, and *Telegraph* 2011).

Is there anything to Bendandi's predictions? Cristiano Fidani, a physicist with the National Institute of Nuclear Physics, Perugia, has analyzed Bendandi's predictions in detail and found them to be remarkably accurate in many cases (Fidani [2009?], 2011). The question, therefore, is how did he make his predictions? Apparently, he based his predictions at least in part on tidal influences between the Sun, planets, Moon, and other celestial bodies. In this context, it is important to note that while the Sun contains over 99 percent of the mass of the solar system, the solar system has angular momentum as it rotates, and the planets account for about 98 percent of the solar system's angular momentum (Mackey 2007, 967, endnote viii). As we have seen in previous chapters, there is evidence that the planets affect the dynamics of the Sun and the resulting solar activity. Bendandi was interested in the issue of what causes the sunspot cycles and how the solar cycles and associated electromagnetic phenomena may be correlated with earthquakes. According to Fidani, "Additionally, he [Bendandi] repeatedly stressed that earthquakes are events that affect the entire globe. According to Bendandi, it was this lack of a global vision regarding the event that prevented others from successfully forecasting. Why he did not reveal the prediction method was due to the difficulty Bendandi had in identifying the location of events" (Fidani [2009?], 3; material in brackets inserted by R. Schoch).

Since Bendandi's death in 1979, an increasing number of scientists are taking seriously the idea that earthquakes and volcanic activity may have extraterrestrial causes. Richard Mackey summarizes some of this work:

According to Barkin and Ferrandiz (2004), the tidal forces of the sun and moon acting on the earth as a whole produce elastic energy that resides in the earth's core and crust that is significantly greater than the sum of the elastic energies of the separate pairs of bodies. Some of the elastic energy is dissipated as heat and contributes, as the periodicities of the tides determine, to the warming of the earth and the oceans. Most of the remainder is retained in the solid material of the earth, resulting in deformations, ultimately in the form of earthquakes and volcanoes. Some of the elastic energy is retained by the moon, resulting in moonquakes which correlate closely with earthquakes. Barkin and Ferrandiz (2004) found that the formation of elastic energy is non-linear. The moon and the sun periodically amplify each other's gravitational effect on the earth in a non-linear manner that closely correlates with major earthquakes. Major earthquakes and moonquakes coincide with extreme variations in tidal elastic energy. (Mackey 2007, 959–60)

The scientific community is slowly realizing that such factors, which are correlated with solar activity, which in turn affects the climate of

Earth, cannot be ignored if we are to truly understand the dynamics of our planet, the Sun, and our solar system as a whole. Bendandi's ideas may be vindicated.

See further discussion in chapter 15, page 366, on correlations between earthquakes and solar activity.

ARE WE ENTERING A COSMIC INTERSTELLAR CLOUD?

The popular concept of interstellar space—deep space, the seemingly infinite distances between our solar system and the next star or solar system—is one of blackness and nothingness, a vacuum. It turns out that this is a misconception. Although certainly a vacuum by everyday standards, the "interstellar medium" (as it is commonly called) contains in extremely rarified form mostly hydrogen (typically about 89 percent) and helium (about 9 percent) atoms, along with the atoms of various other elements, charged particles, and miscellaneous molecules and particulate matter that are perhaps best referred to as dust. Our solar system is in large part protected from the interstellar medium by the barrier set up by the heliosphere, effectively a bubble around our solar system created by the Sun. This bubble is a result of the solar wind, which is composed of charged particles and magnetic fields (a moving electrically charged particle creates a magnetic field) emanating from the Sun at speeds on the order of several hundred kilometers per second. At some point beyond the orbits of Neptune and Pluto the solar wind slows down and meets the interstellar medium.

A shock wave, or termination shock, forms at the outer edge of the heliosphere where the solar wind particles moving out meet the interstellar medium particles rushing in (moving on the order of hundreds of kilometers per second). Beyond the termination shock is the heliosheath, an area that seems to be filled with magnetic bubbles (each on the order of up to hundreds of millions of kilometers wide; Atkinson 2011) created by the interactions between the heliosphere and the interstellar medium. The theoretical boundary beyond which the solar winds do not seem to penetrate (at least not to any great extent) into the interstellar medium is known as the heliopause.

Adding to the complications of the heliosphere is the fact that the Sun rotates on its axis, carrying or moving the solar wind and associated magnetic fields. This creates a rotating wave or ripple structure that can be pictured as the twirling skirt of a spinning dancer. Furthermore, the entire solar system is moving relative to the interstellar medium. This creates a bow shock, not unlike the wake left by a ship as its bow cuts through the water. And the interstellar medium is not consistent throughout. It varies greatly, ranging from relatively dense and cold areas ("molecular clouds") containing about a million atoms or molecules per cubic centimeter (10^6 molecules per cm^3; for comparison, liquid water contains approximately [on the order of the magnitude of] 10^{22}, that is, ten thousand million million million molecules per cubic centimeter) to hot and rarefied regions containing but a single ion or atom per ten thousand cubic centimeters (10^{-4} per cm^3). As our solar system moves through the interstellar medium, it encounters, enters, and passes through clouds and other inhomogeneities (perhaps small accumulations of gas or clusters of interstellar debris, maybe the remnants of an exploded star) of varying densities. Key questions are, Where is our solar system now relative to local interstellar clouds and bubbles, and where is it headed in the future?

Why are such questions even important? Because they address phenomena that could—almost certainly will—have direct consequences for life on Earth. No one really knows what the consequences of entering a dense interstellar cloud will be, but there are various models and theories as to what might happen. The increased pressure of the dense cloud on the heliosphere could cause it to contract in size and also begin to leak as interstellar particles enter the inner solar system. Earth itself could be bombarded with energetic protons and cosmic rays (not truly rays at all, but moving charged subatomic particles), which in turn could deplete the oxygen in our atmosphere, damage the ozone layer (thus letting in more dangerous UV radiation), and as they smash into atoms in our atmosphere, create even more dangerous and high-speed subatomic particles, X rays, gamma rays, and the like (Winters 2008). That is, we would be showered with increased levels of radiation on the surface of

Earth. Some researchers believe that the shower of particles penetrating the atmosphere could cause more clouds to form, decreasing the amount of sunlight reaching the surface and increasing the amount of precipitation, ultimately cooling Earth and possibly sending our planet into an ice age. Interstellar dust, it has also been suggested, could "pollute" the interplanetary medium, the space between the Sun and Earth, thus blocking some of the sunlight from reaching Earth and causing our climate to cool.

Rather than the climate cooling, however, just the opposite may ultimately occur. The addition of cosmic particles (cosmic dust) to our solar system, if they reach all the way to the Sun (as could indeed occur if we meet a dense cloud), could potentially energize and destabilize the Sun, resulting in massive solar outbursts (such as CMEs and SPEs). This could be similar to the energizing effect on our Sun of a galactic superwave, as mentioned by LaViolette (2009, 1) and discussed previously in this chapter. It might be that meeting an interstellar cloud would initially, and over a very short period, cause increased radiation levels and climatic cooling on Earth, followed shortly thereafter by major global warming correlated with solar outbursts from the Sun.

But what does all this matter? The fact is that there is evidence that we, our solar system, are either on the verge of entering or in the process of entering an interstellar cloud. The time frame for this to occur, possibly measured in years rather than decades, is too close for comfort.

In 1978 Alfred Vidal-Madjar (2007 recipient of the Ampere Prize of the Academy of Sciences, France, among other awards) and his colleagues published a paper in the *Astrophysical Journal* with the provocative title "Is the Solar System Entering a Nearby Interstellar Cloud?" Their conclusion was yes. According to their calculations, based on the data then available, there is a nearby interstellar cloud in the direction of Scorpius-Ophiuchus (that is, close to the direction of the galactic center). Our solar system is approaching this cloud (or it is approaching us) at a velocity of fifteen to twenty kilometers a second, and it is currently 0.03 parsecs (about one-tenth of a light year) away. Doing a couple of quick conversions and calculations, assuming that we are approaching the cloud at twenty kilometers per second and it is indeed 0.03 parsecs away, then we should meet up with it in about 1,500 years. From an astronomical point of view, this is a mere blink of the eye and a time so close it might as well be tomorrow, or even yesterday for that matter!

Additional work has confirmed that there are many interstellar clouds in our immediate galactic neighborhood, including one we are approaching in the direction of the galactic center, as determined by Vidal-Madjar et al. (1978). In a 2008 paper, also published in the *Astrophysical Journal,* Seth Redfield and Jeffrey L. Linsky documented fifteen nearby (within fifty light years of us) interstellar clouds and determined that our solar system is currently between the Local Interstellar Cloud (so named because it was originally believed that we were within the boundaries of the cloud) and the G cloud (the closest cloud to us in the direction of the galactic center) and that we are moving at a rapid rate toward the G cloud. In a press release prepared by the University of Colorado, where Redfield and Linsky carried out their research, their conclusions are summarized as follows: "We're now on a collision course with the G cloud, which stands between us and the galactic center. Linsky says we'll enter the G cloud in less than 5,000 years—perhaps even tomorrow. Once that happens, there's a chance the G cloud will affect the Sun's solar wind and Earth's climate" (University of Colorado 2008).

This is in agreement with the work of three decades earlier. And note that Linsky estimates the date of entry could be anywhere from "less than 5,000 years" in the future to tomorrow. As I already stated, a few thousand years is a blink of the astronomical eye.

In more general terms, Saumitra Mukherjee, professor of geology and remote sensing at the School of Environmental Sciences, Jawaharlal Nehru University, New Delhi, India, suggests that our solar system has already entered some type of interstellar cloud. He writes:

> The Sun has entered the zodiac's 13th house. An interstellar wind hit our planet. It's a helium-rich breeze from the stars, flowing into the solar system from the direction of Ophiuchus. The Sun's gravity focuses the material into a cone and Earth passes through it

during the first week of December. Earth was inside the cone during 25th December 2004 and 23rd February 2005. Grains of stardust are very small, about one hundredth the diameter of a human hair, hence they do not directly influence the planets of the Solar System. However, the dust particles move very fast, and produce large numbers of fragments when they impact asteroids or comets. It is, therefore, conceivable that an increase in the amount of interstellar dust in the Solar System will create more cosmic dust by collisions with asteroids and comets. It is possible that the increase of stardust in the Solar System will influence the amount of extraterrestrial material that rains down to Earth. How the Earth's surface temperature adjusts to a given change in star-solar radiation depends on the processes by which the climate system responds to variations in the energy it receives. . . . Some of these factors amplify the effects of changes that are imposed; others reduce them. (Mukherjee 2008, 7748)

Regarding the specific dates mentioned in this quotation, Mukherjee states:

On 25th December 2004 and 23rd February 2005 hailstorms and snowstorms were reported in the Northern Hemisphere, while in the tropics a sudden drop in temperature led to foggy and smoggy conditions. An earthquake measuring 9.0 of Richter scale on 26th December followed the sudden changes in the environment. An earthquake measuring 6.4 on the Richter scale occurred on Tuesday 22 February in Zarand, Kerman Province (750 KM southeast of Tehran) at 05:55 local time. Weather conditions in the region were difficult as there was heavy snowfall, resulting in a number of road blockades. (Mukherjee 2008, 7745)

It has been noticed in December 2004 as well as in February 2005 in Los Alamos National Laboratory that there were unexpected star explosions halfway across the galaxy. This type of explosion produces high-energy γ [gamma] rays. This explosion packed so much power that it briefly altered Earth's upper atmosphere during December 2004 and February 2005. The blast originated about 50,000 light-years away and was detected on December 27. The blast was caused by magnetar. This star blast has influenced the geophysical variables of sun and sudden lowering in planetary indices Kp [a standard measure of geomagnetic activity] and E-flux [electron flux]. This might have been caused by repulsion of the magnetic field in Sun-Earth Environment and the magnetic field of star flare. Global warming in this century has corresponded with lowered cosmic ray intensities. Cosmic rays help the formation of dense clouds in the lower atmosphere while having a little negative effect on cloud cover in the upper atmosphere. (Mukherjee 2008, 7746; material in brackets inserted by R. Schoch)

Someone who is also adamant that we are entering an interstellar cloud sooner rather than later (indeed, he agrees that we may have already entered it at this point) and that it will have, and perhaps already is having, major ramifications for life on Earth is the Russian geophysicist Alexey N. Dmitriev. In a 1997 paper originally published in Russian and subsequently translated into English with the title "PlanetoPhysical State of the Earth and Life," he summarized his basic conclusions as follows:

Current PlanetoPhysical alterations of the Earth are becoming irreversible. Strong evidence exists that these transformations are being caused by highly charged material and energetic non-uniformity's in anisotropic interstellar space which have broken into the interplanetary area of our Solar System. This "donation" of energy is producing hybrid processes and excited energy states in all planets, as well as the Sun. Effects here on Earth are to be found in the acceleration of the magnetic pole shift, in the vertical and horizontal ozone content distribution, and in the increased frequency and magnitude of significant catastrophic climatic events. There is growing probability that we are moving into a rapid temperature instability period similar to the one that took place 10,000 years ago. The adaptive responses of the biosphere, and humanity, to these new conditions may lead to a total global revision of the range of species and life on Earth. It is only through a deep understanding of the fundamental changes taking place in the natural environment surrounding us that politicians, and citizens alike, will be able to achieve balance with the renewing flow of PlanetoPhysical states and processes. (Dmitriev 1997)

Dmitriev bases his conclusions on Russian analyses of geophysical and astrophysical data, including data from space probes to the outer edges of the solar system, such as Voyager 1 and Voyager 2 (both launched by NASA in 1977). Using the Voyager information as a baseline, Dmitriev and his colleagues have determined that changes have been taking place in the solar system as a whole in recent decades, changes that shortly will, or already are beginning to, directly impact the Sun and Earth. According to Dmitriev, "This development of events, as it has become clear in the last few years, *is being caused by material and energetic non-uniformity's* [sic] *in anisotropic interstellar space.* In its travel through interstellar space, the Heliosphere travels in the direction of the Solar Apex in the Hercules Constellation. On its way it has met (1960s) non-homogeneities of matter and energy containing ions of Hydrogen, Helium, and Hydroxyl in addition to other elements and combinations. This kind of interstellar space dispersed plasma is presented by magnetized strip structures and striations" (Dmitriev 1997; italics in the original).

Essentially, Dmitriev is stating that our solar system is entering an interstellar cloud, in agreement with other researchers, such as Vidal-Madjar and colleagues and Redfield and Linsky (discussed previously in this chapter). Also, Dmitriev estimated that the cloud is in the direction of the Hercules Constellation; Hercules is just north of Scorpio-Ophiuchus and the galactic center, so this is in agreement too with the work of other independent researchers.

As is apparent from his summary, quoted above, Dmitriev (1997) predicts that there will be major, even catastrophic, effects on Earth as we enter the interstellar cloud. Some of the things we should expect are:

1. A strengthening shock wave in front of the heliosphere, ultimately leading to the input of matter (at least partially in the form of plasma), radiation, and energy into the inner solar system.

2. New and unusual solar phenomena, including a general increase in the activity of the Sun. The magnetic properties of the Sun are changing, which in turn affects the heliosphere. Increased solar outbursts can be expected, including CMEs, with the result that geomagnetic storms on Earth will increase in frequency and magnitude. (*Geomagnetic storm,* also sometimes referred to as a geomagnetic disturbance, is a general name for a major disturbance in Earth's magnetosphere caused by factors external to Earth, such as a solar outburst.)

3. Transformations in the atmospheric envelope that encompasses Earth (including the ionosphere [ionized by solar radiation] at very high levels, the stratosphere, and the troposphere down to ground levels) could result in climatic disturbances and extremes, including an increase in major storms, such as cyclones, hurricanes, and typhoons. The ozone layer of the stratosphere will be affected, with less ozone in the stratosphere (where it protects us by absorbing harmful UV radiation) and more ozone at and near ground level (where it is a highly reactive and dangerous chemical that can threaten life). Reiterating, Dmitriev states, *"There is a growing probability that we are moving into a rapid temperature instability period similar to the one that took place 10,000 years ago"* (1997; italics in the original). Here he is referring to the climatic changes that took place at the end of the last ice age.

4. Increases in seismic activity, including major earthquakes and volcanoes, on Earth. Seismic/geological effects are correlated with, and possibly triggered or influenced by, solar activity, according to Dmitriev and his colleagues. Major underwater earthquakes can create enormous tsunamis, and volcanic activity spewing ash into the atmosphere can impact the climate.

5. Significant shifts, on the order of over one hundred kilometers per decade, in the magnetic poles of Earth, possibly accelerating

to two hundred kilometers per year. Since Dmitriev's paper was published in 1997, his predictions of accelerating shifts in Earth's magnetic poles seem to be coming true (see discussion in the section on "Earth's Magnetosphere" in chapter 7, page 142). Ultimately, the poles could invert or flip. Furthermore, magnetic anomalies in the Earth's crust are increasing in number. In addition, it should be pointed out that since the middle of the nineteenth century the magnetic field of Earth has been decreasing in strength (Barry 2006). Based on ships' logs and other data going back to about 1590, Earth's magnetic field was possibly stable (in terms of strength) until around 1840. After that, it began to decline in strength at a rate of about 5 percent per century, a decline that continues to this day. At the current rate, Earth's magnetic field will drop to zero within one thousand to two thousand years (McKie 2002) and then possibly "flip," building up strength in the opposite direction. However, if the decline in strength accelerates, as may be the case according to the work of Dmitriev and his colleagues, the magnetic field could disappear and/or flip much sooner. As Earth's magnetic field declines, the magnetosphere provides less protection from solar radiation and other incoming materials and energy, making us even more vulnerable to solar outbursts or other onslaughts.

Dmitriev is not the only scientist who is concerned about Earth's weakening magnetic field. Gauthier Hulot, of the Paris Geophysical Institute, has found that the magnetic field is weakening, particularly near the poles of Earth, and this is interpreted as a sign that the poles are getting ready to flip (McKie 2002). Alan Thomson, of the British Geological Survey, Edinburgh, was quoted in 2002 as saying, "Earth's magnetic field has disappeared many times before—as a prelude to our magnetic poles flipping over, when north becomes south and vice versa. . . . Reversals happen every 250,000 years or so, and as there has not been one for almost a million years, we are due one soon" (Thomson, quoted in McKie 2002).

There is disagreement as to how long a full reversal of Earth's magnetic field might take. The standard view is that, from a human perspective, it will occur slowly and incrementally, taking thousands of years or longer. However, evidence from ancient lava flows in Oregon record a 6° change per day, meaning that a complete reversal (180°) could occur in only a month. This study was widely dismissed as implausible, with the results due to some error. Then another study of lava flows in Nevada indicated a change of 53° in a year. If this rate were constant through a full 180°, it would mean a reversal, a full flip of Earth's magnetic poles, could occur in less than four years (Bogue and Glen 2010; Jarboe et al. 2011; Wilkins 2010). This is still amazingly fast. Another possibility is that it actually takes longer for a full pole shift and that the shift is not smooth and gradual. Perhaps it shifts in spurts and jerks of a few tens of degrees at a time and then settles down for several years or centuries before starting up again (Chou et al. 2018). The bottom line is that we just do not know, and thus we do not know what to expect in the future.

Ultimately, Dmitriev believes that a major transformation of life on Earth, including human life, will be necessary. Humanity will be faced with major challenges, and we must transform and adapt ourselves if we are to survive. Dmitriev wrote in 1997:

This high-energy atmospheric phenomena, which was rare in the past, is now becoming more frequent, intense, and changed in its nature. The material composition of the gas-plasma envelope is also being transformed. It is quite natural for the whole biota of the Earth to be subjected to these changing conditions of the electromagnetic field, and to the significant deep alterations of Earth's climatic machinery. These fundamental processes of change create a demand within all of Earth's life organisms for new forms of adaptation. *The natural development of these new forms may lead to a total global revision of the range of species, and life, on Earth.* New deeper qualities of life itself may come forth, bringing the new physical state of the Earth to an equilibrium with the new organismic possibilities of development, reproduction, and perfection. In this sense *it is evident that we are faced with a problem of the adaptation of humanity to this new state of the Earth;* new conditions on Earth whose biospheric qualities are varying, and non-uniformly distributed. Therefore, the current period of transformation is transient, and the transition of life's representatives to the future may take place only after a deep evaluation of what it will take to comply with these new Earthly biospheric conditions. Each living representative on Earth will be getting a thorough "examination," or "quality control inspection," to determine it's [sic] ability to comply with these new conditions. *These evolutionary challenges always require effort, or endurance, be it individual organisms, species, or communities.* Therefore, it is not only the climate that is becoming new, but we as human beings are experiencing a global change in the vital processes of living organisms, or life itself; which is yet another link in the total process. We cannot treat such things separately, or individually. (Dmitriev 1997; italics in the original)

But when will these dramatic changes occur? As he relates in his book *Apocalypse 2012,* journalist Lawrence E. Joseph traveled to Siberia and spoke with Dmitriev directly. When Joseph pushed Dmitriev on the time frame for major impacts on Earth from the interstellar energy cloud, Dmitriev had this to say: "The global catastrophe—hurricanes, earthquakes, volcanoes synchronizing and amplifying each other in a positive feedback loop that will spin out of control, threatening the very existence of our modern civilization—we have been talking about should probably happen in ones, not tens, of years" (Dmitriev, quoted in Joseph 2008, 142–43).

This is pretty scary stuff, coming from a well-respected scientist (according to Joseph, Dmitriev has published over three hundred articles in academic journals, written several scholarly books, and is the recipient of numerous awards and citations in his homeland; Joseph 2008, 120).

Dmitriev is certainly not the only physicist who believes major changes on Earth could happen sooner rather than later. While researching his book *Apocalypse 2012,* Joseph visited and interviewed physicist Pierre J. Cilliers of the Hermanus Magnetic Observatory in South Africa (the name of the observatory was changed to SANSA

[South African National Space Agency] Space Science on April 1, 2011; see SANSA 2010). Cilliers researches geomagnetic activity, including intense disturbances in the geomagnetic field and their ramifications, such as the risks posed by geomagnetically induced currents (see, for instance, the paper by Ngwira et al. 2011, on which Cilliers is a coauthor). He is also an avowed Christian. In his interview with Joseph, Cilliers stated, "The Lord said that a sign of the end of times would be an increase in storms, earthquakes, and other catastrophes. He is the author of the Bible and the author of Nature. When we see conflict, it is either because we don't understand his Revelation or because we confuse our observation" (Cilliers, quoted in Joseph 2008, 216).

When asked by Joseph about the possibility that the world could either end or profoundly change in 2012, Cilliers answered, "It is not unlikely that this will occur in our lifetime" (Cilliers, quoted in Joseph 2008, 217).

What about profound changes during previous lifetimes? A strong case can be made that the Judeo-Christian Bible, the Bible that Cilliers cites, contains accounts of solar outbursts and plasma events that occurred during ancient times.

10

EZEKIEL'S VISION

Let us turn to the ancient records once again. Further evidence supporting the theory that both the petroglyphs studied by Anthony Peratt and his team (Peratt 2003; Peratt et al. 2007; Peratt and Yao 2008; van der Sluijs and Peratt 2010) and the rongorongo glyphs represent powerful auroral forms and plasma configurations in the sky comes from the Judeo-Christian Bible.

In the first chapter of the book of Ezekiel it is written, "I looked; a stormy wind blew from the north, a great cloud with light around it, a fire from which flashes of lightning darted, and in the centre a sheen like bronze at the heart of the fire" (Jerusalem Bible, 1968, Ezekiel 1:4).

This is often regarded as the clearest description of an auroral display in the Bible (see Eather 1980, 35; Silverman 2006). Ezekiel was probably making his observations around 593 BCE from Nippur (approximate geographic latitude 32° north and geographic longitude 45° east), about one hundred kilometers south of Babylon (Siscoe et al. 2002). The fact that Ezekiel's "vision" originated in the north is in agreement with a major auroral display, and based on the graphs of sunspot and solar activity as reconstructed by Solanki et al. (2004) and Usoskin et al. (2007), this may have been a period of strong solar activity, with major fluctuations between high and low numbers of sunspots.

There are those who question whether Ezekiel was observing an auroral display. William Hutton and Jonathan Eagle (2004, 145, footnote 13) state, "Details of Ezekiel's vision following verse 4 do not comport with an auroral display." In fact, though, the very opposite may be true. The details of Ezekiel's vision, understood in the context of the imagery commonly used to describe major auroral displays in ancient, medieval, and Renaissance times, are very much in accord with a major, spectacular auroral and/or plasma display. This imagery in turn is very similar to that seen on the petroglyphs studied by Peratt and his team and in the rongorongo glyphs.

Ezekiel continues his description as follows:

In the centre I saw what seemed four animals. They looked like this. They were of human form.

Each had four faces, each had four wings.

Their legs were straight; they had hoofs like oxen, glittering like polished brass.

Human hands showed under their wings; the faces of all four were turned to the four quarters.

Their wings touched each other; they did not turn as they moved; each one went straight forward.

As to what they looked like, they had human faces, and all four had a lion's face to the right, and all four had a bull's face to the left, and all four had an eagle's face.

Their wings were spread upward; each had two wings that touched, and two wings that covered his body;

And they all went straight forward; they went where the spirit urged them; they did not turn as they moved.

Between these animals something could be seen like flaming brands or torches, darting between the animals; the fire flashed light, and lightning streaked from the fire.

And the creatures ran to and fro like thunderbolts.

I looked at the animals; there was a wheel on the ground by each of them, one beside each of the four.

The wheels glittered as if made of chrysolite. All four looked alike, and seemed to be made one inside the other.

They went forward four ways and kept their course unswervingly.

Their rims seemed enormous when I looked at them and all four rims had eyes all the way round.

When the animals went forward, the wheels went forward beside them; and when the animals left the ground, the wheels too left the ground.

Where the spirit urged them, there the wheels went, since the spirit of the animals was in the wheels.

When the animals moved on, they moved on; when the former halted, the latter halted; when the former left the ground, the wheels too left the ground, since the spirit of the animal was in the wheels.

Over the heads of the animals a sort of vault, gleaming like crystal, arched above their heads;

Under this vault their wings stretched out to one another, and each had two covering his body. (Jerusalem Bible, 1968, Ezekiel 1:5–23)

Describing or depicting powerful auroral displays in anthropomorphic and zoomorphic terms as living creatures moving through the sky surrounded by or in the midst of fire and with rings or wheels is an iconography found among many ancient classical (Greek and Roman) through Renaissance writers and authors (Eather 1980; Laine 2004; Guskova et al. 2010). Sometimes the imagery was described as warring armies or as strange mixed animal-human figures (as by Ezekiel) that often included bird-like features, such as bird's heads or wings. During the 1859 Carrington Event, the auroral display seen from La Unión, San Salvador, was described as including figures "painted with fire": "On the night of Sept. 2d, a most extraordinary phenomenon was witnessed . . . a dense black cloud arose in the east, and commenced to spread over the colored portion of the heavens, presenting a most curious spectacle; for in the parts where the cloud was not dense enough, the red light shone through, and formed a thousand fantastic figures, as if painted with fire on a black ground" (quoted in Loomis 1860, 265–66; see also Clark 2007, 20).

Here it is worth noting that these "fantastic figures" were particularly prominent through cloud cover. During major solar outbursts with their accompanying auroral and plasma configurations, unlike anything witnessed in historical times, but the likes of which occurred prehistorically, including at the end of the last ice age, incineration and the setting of fires on the ground could promote cloud formation. Furthermore, even if the clouds were extremely dense, the incredibly powerful (perhaps orders of magnitude greater than occurred during the Carrington Event) and bright plasma configurations would shine through, creating the "fantastic figures" recorded in petroglyphs around the world and in the rongorongo.

Wheels and rings in the skies are also commonly referenced in historical descriptions of auroral displays, and as Silverman (2006, 206) has pointed out, nineteenth-century descriptions of great auroras (including the ones associated with the Carrington Event) in some cases included descriptions of wheels in the sky. Independently, Peratt (2003, 2005) has predicted and modeled various anthropomorphic, bird-like, and wheel-like forms that would be seen in the skies during major solar outbursts and their associated plasma discharges. Furthermore, this same imagery is seen in the petroglyphs studied by Peratt and colleagues and in the rongorongo glyphs.

Ezekiel continues his detailed description, adding yet another element, that of sound.

I heard the noise of their wings as they moved; it sounded like rushing water, like the voice of Shaddai [God], a noise like a storm, like the noise of a camp; when they halted, they folded their wings, and there was a noise.

Above the vault over their heads was something that looked like a sapphire; it was shaped like a throne and high up on this throne was a being that looked like a man.

I saw him shine like bronze, and close to and all around him from what seemed his loins upward was what looked like fire; and from what seemed his loins downward I saw what looked like fire, and a light all around like a bow in the clouds on rainy days; that is how the surrounding light appeared. It was something that looked like the glory of Yahweh. I looked, and prostrated myself, and I heard a voice speaking. (Jerusalem Bible, 1968, Ezekiel 1:24–28)

Sound has often been associated with auroras in popular accounts, both ancient and modern. Additionally, trained researchers have on occasion described hearing sounds in conjunction with auroras. In different locations and across various cultures and peoples, the descriptions have generally been similar: hissing, crackling, rustling, or swishing sounds (Hautsalo 2005). Yet the scientific community has generally dismissed such auroral sounds as either other sounds only mistakenly considered to be emanating from auroral displays or as simple imagination and fantasy (Laine 2004). In large part, this was because of the modern perception that auroral displays seen to the eye are typically on the order of a hundred kilometers or so in altitude, and therefore it was believed that no audible sound could travel down to ground level and be heard. Now, it turns out, sounds created by or associated with major auroras do indeed appear to be real, even if not always heard or often faint when heard, and they can be of rather inconsistent quality (Laine 2004; Hautsalo 2005; Solensky 2007). The cause of these sounds is still uncertain. One suggestion is that the sounds are the result of the buildup and discharge of static electricity at or near ground level. Another suggestion is electrophonic transduction due to very-low-frequency (VLF) radio waves associated with the auroras. Some VLF radio waves have the same frequencies as audible sounds, and very thin, long conductors such as hair or blades of grass might act as antennae, picking up the VLF radio waves, vibrating and converting them into audible sound. Interestingly, VLF radio waves have been detected in conjunction with both auroral displays and meteors, and in both cases similar types of sounds have been reported. At any rate, the point here is that Ezekiel was not necessarily incorrect to associate sound with an auroral display, and to describe the sound as the "noise of their wings" is in agreement with the way that auroral sounds have often been described.

Of course, Ezekiel ultimately heard more than rustling, hissing, crackling, and swishing sounds from the auroral display; God spoke to him explicitly. This part of Ezekiel's vision is well beyond what one can expect from an auroral display directly, but Ezekiel was after all a priest, a prophet, and a visionary. He was subject to ecstatic and mystical states and probably trained in the interpretation of omens, and we should not be surprised that the genuine sight of a powerful auroral display would result for Ezekiel in a direct message from the Almighty. The auroral displays associated with the 1859 Carrington Event inspired religious forebodings and end-times fears. A specific example was given in the October 8, 1859, issue of *Harper's Weekly:* "In Columbus, Ohio, a sixteen-year-old girl described as 'of considerable intelligence and pre-possessing appearance' was taken into custody by a Sheriff after witnessing the auroral display. 'Her agitated state necessitated that she be moved to the lunatic asylum. The conclusion drawn from this, and no doubt her utterances, implied that she had become deranged from viewing the aurora borealis a short time ago. She was convinced that all of this spectacular auroral activity meant that the world was soon to come to an end'" (quoted by Green et al. 2006, 153).

RONGORONGO

Note to the reader: I have left this section on the rongorongo script essentially intact, as it was originally published in the first edition of this book (2012). At that time this discussion was, admittedly, highly speculative. Since it was published, a member of Dr. Peratt's team contacted us to say that they too had discovered the connection between the rongorongo forms, the petroglyphs, and the plasma configurations observed in the skies during a major solar outburst; however, they had not published their discovery. Please keep this in mind as you read this section.

The mysterious Easter Island rongorongo script appears to match both the petroglyphs that Peratt and his team have been studying and more generally the broad descriptions (such as Ezekiel's vision) ascribed to major auroral phenomena observed over the ages. I realize that this interpretation of rongorongo may not make certain linguists in particular happy, but so far there has been no compelling decipherment or interpretation of rongorongo otherwise. Yes, many hypotheses have been put forth, but none has been universally agreed on. Indeed, there has not even been agreement on whether rongorongo is truly a form of writing per se. Do the glyphs represent speech sounds or syllables? Are they effectively an alphabet? Or do the glyphs represent words or morphemes (small units that have meaning in a language, including morphemes that stand alone or can modify other morphemes, such as prefixes and suffixes or morphemes that denote plural)? Perhaps rongorongo is some type of mnemonic device or protowriting using some set of symbols representing ideas, concepts, and things (ideographs and pictograms)? Some people would even suggest that it was basically used for decorative purposes.

Given the traditions of how the rongorongo tablets were valued and held in reverence, it is difficult to believe that they did not record something regarded as extremely important. And what could be more important than strange shapes in the sky that were associated with the catastrophes of the end of the last ice age? The rongorongo inscriptions that still survive, inscribed on wooden tablets, are quite evidently modern (that is, at most a few centuries old), but that does not mean their message cannot be much more ancient. Even among the corpus of classical Western literature, the oldest surviving physical manuscripts often postdate their authors by a thousand years or more. For instance, the oldest surviving manuscript for about half of the dialogues of Plato (circa 429–423 BCE to 348–347 BCE), now housed in the collection of medieval manuscripts of the Bodleian Libraries at the University of Oxford, was produced in Constantinople and dates to circa 895 CE, over 1,200 years after its author died. Or, to give another example held by the Bodleian, the library system contains the oldest known copy of the *Discourses of Epictetus* (circa 55–135 CE, recorded by his student Arrian, circa 86–160 CE), and the copy dates from the twelfth century CE, a thousand years after it was originally written.

Based on the similarity of the rongorongo glyphs to the images seen in the skies during super auroral events and, as modeled by Peratt (2003, 2005), powerful solar outbursts and the resulting plasma configurations that would have been observed, I believe that the rongorongo glyphs were initially inspired by those events in the skies. The rongorongo was a record of what was seen—literally—and it was recorded in a way that made sense to the scribes and copyists of the time. In a like manner, Ezekiel's "vision" was indeed an accurate record, translated into the terminology and imagery of the day, of real events playing out in the skies. The rongorongo texts can be viewed as a sacred scripture, as a Rapanui "Bible," or more pertinent to this discussion, as a scientific text dating back thousands of years and recording in minute detail exactly what happened during that catastrophe of long ago. Apropos to such an interpretation of the rongorongo is the notion that many ancient myths, including those of the Greeks and Romans, were not simply fantasy stories but indeed were records and descriptions of real events playing out in the heavens. Pivotal in such studies is the work of Giorgio de Santillana and Hertha von Dechend, who in their 1969 book *Hamlet's Mill* argued persuasively that many classical ancient and European myths (such as those of the Norse) can be interpreted as recording movements and events in the heavens, including such subtle effects as precession.

Just as over time the deep astronomical meanings of classical Western myths were lost, both to the common folk and the educated elite (although one has to wonder if some still understood their full importance, but perhaps kept such knowledge secret), so too the original significance of the rongorongo may have been lost even as the characters and texts were faithfully copied and recopied. Even if some Rapanui still held the key to the rongorongo upon European contact in 1722, their knowledge may have died with them as the Easter Island population was devastated over the following centuries. Interestingly, of the approximately twenty-five original rongorongo texts that have survived (there is disagreement over the authenticity of some), several texts are partial repetitions or close copies of one another, suggesting that these were very important texts of which there were multiple copies. This overlap would not be readily expected if the texts recorded mundane events. It is also not at all clear that the various texts all date from the same period. There are variations in the "punctuation" (or lack of punctuation), the actual forms of the glyphs, and the style and manner in which they were inscribed on the wooden tablets. I would not be surprised if the rongorongo, originally inspired by plasma configurations in the skies millennia ago, was also later used as a form of writing to record more mundane or trivial matters. In analogy, in other cultures writing may have originated for one purpose and then later was applied to other purposes. If this is the case, then a first step in fully interpreting and understanding the rongorongo texts might be to figure out which ones harken back to auroral displays and plasma configurations directly and which texts are more derived and contain the same or similar glyphs put to other uses beyond recording plasma configurations.

Some of the work on attempting to decipher the rongorongo script may help support the plasma interpretation. One widely reported "decipherment" of the rongorongo is that good portions of the known texts are creation chants. A native Easter Islander informant named Ure Vaʻe Iko (Daniel Ure Vaeiko) in the late nineteenth century supposedly "read" some of the rongorongo inscriptions from the tablet known as Atua Matariri (most of the tablets have their own names) in the form of "X, Ki ai Kiroto Y, Kapu te Z," where X, Y, and Z are the names of gods, goddesses, objects, or things (see Thomson 1891, 520). This phrase has been translated along the lines of "X, by copulating with Y, produced Z" or "X, by mounting into Y, let Z come forth"; thus, as an example of some such "translated" verses, we have "Moon, by mounting into Darkness, let Sun come forth," "Killing, by mounting into Stingray, let Shark come forth," and "Stinging Fly, by mounting into Swarm [of insects], let Horsefly come forth" (Wikipedia 2011a; material in brackets added by R. Schoch).

Following up on this reading, Steven Roger Fischer proposed a decipherment of the rongorongo, the core of which is triads of glyphs along such procreation lines. To give one of Fischer's translations, a triad from the Santiago staff (a wooden staff collected in 1870 by Chilean naval officers and covered with rongorongo texts) reads, "All the birds copulated with the fish: there issued forth the sun" (Fischer 1997a, 200). Fischer applied this formula to other rongorongo texts, ultimately concluding, "Nearly all the surviving *rongorongo* inscriptions . . . are procreation chants. . . . In fact, only some 15 percent of the *rongorongo* corpus seems *not* to constitute procreation chants of this type" (Fischer 1997a, 207; italics in the original).

Honestly, at first I was dismissive of Fischer's supposed translation, and indeed his work has hardly received wide acceptance. Upon analysis, other researchers have not found that the triads stressed by Fischer are nearly as common as he states, and it has also been pointed out that following Fisher's translation scheme, virtually anything may be copulating with anything else, in all kinds of unlikely combinations (Wikipedia 2011a; see also Melka 2009 and Guy 2000).

Another line of criticism of Fischer's decipherment is that it is based on the "reading" of a nineteenth-century informant, but it is far from clear that Ure Va'e Iko could actually read the rongorongo texts. He was under duress from the Westerners pressing him, and he may have effectively made something up to please them—not fabricated anew, but rather based on things he had either learned or simply overheard in his childhood and youth. In particular, Jacques Guy (Tehaha 2011; de Laat 2009, 211) has suggested that Ure Va'e Iko vaguely remembered what might be termed "spelling lessons" that he overheard or learned while positioned as a servant to the then king of Easter Island. Or, more specifically and accurately, Ure Va'e Iko may have vaguely remembered formulaic instructions on how to form compound glyphs from other glyphs—even if Ure Va'e Iko was not substituting the correct glyphs into the formula, but simply feeding nonsense to the Westerners who were actively pressing him and plying him with alcohol.

Taking auroral displays and plasma configurations into account as the possible inspiration for and initial driving force behind the rongorongo, I do not think either the procreation chant hypothesis or the single-plus-single-to-compound-glyph hypothesis is totally ludicrous. In both cases, what do we have? One glyph combining with another to give rise to something else, or more generally one glyph or figure reacting, changing, morphing into another glyph or figure, which in turn may morph into another figure or figures, and so on and on. This is what would be seen in the skies during a major plasma outburst and what was recorded in the form of the rongorongo glyphs. Later, possibly, the glyphs were also applied to other types of writing and recording purposes, but initially I believe they referred to events in the skies.

There is one rongorongo tablet that many of those who have seriously studied the rongorongo corpus agree appears to include a lunar calendar; that is, it is based on explicit observations of the sky. This is the tablet called Mamari (Thomson 1891, plates 44–45; Fischer 1997b, 412–18). The calendar section seems to record twenty-eight to thirty days (it is open to interpretation), indicated by what appear to be repeated crescent moons, along with repeated sets (apparently pairs or triads) of glyphs interspersed among the days and nights recorded (Guy 2011). No one has definitively interpreted what the interspersed glyphs may mean. Again, I wonder if they are recording configurations in the sky repeated over a period of a month.

M. de Laat (2009) has offered a comprehensive decipherment and interpretation of rongorongo. In the book *Words Out of Wood,* de Laat presents translations and interpretations of three rongorongo tablets, all of which (according to de Laat) are stories in the form of dialogues. One involves a man who is accused of murdering a woman, probably his wife. Another involves three women who had a bad encounter with a man who threatened them with "magic eyes" that can cast a curse. The third text that de Laat discusses involves some people, actually corpses, who, having been buried, are resurrected, but once brought back to life complain that they were better off dead (in "another state of awareness," as de Laat puts it, 2009, 110) since their bodies are damaged and mutilated, and they are thus apparently reinterred.

If there is validity to de Laat's interpretation, I wonder if the stories could have been inspired by, or be a recounting of, auroral displays and plasma configurations in the sky, combined with theological themes, not unlike Ezekiel's vision, which led to a direct message from his God. De Laat's work, however, has come under heavy criticism on many levels, including phonetically and grammatically, in terms of the use of Tahitian words and phrases that would not be expected in an ancient (pre-European contact) language (Wikipedia 2011a, 2011b; see also Horley 2009). On a broader scale, an anonymous Wikipedia contributor wrote, "It would be remarkable for these rare pieces of wood to record such exchanges verbatim. Yet the ligature . . . , which de Laat identified as a man named Taea, is found in six of the surviving texts, fully *half* of the corpus that is indisputably authentic and in good condition, presenting this figure, who is supposed to have murdered his wife, as one of the most important protagonists in the Rapa Nui tradition. Yet there is no such Taea in the surviving Rapa Nui oral literature" (Wikipedia 2011a; italics in the original).

At this point, only time will tell how well de Laat's interpretation of the rongorongo will stand up to further scrutiny. For my part, I believe that the evidence points to the rongorongo as a record of plasma outbursts in the ancient skies at the end of the last ice age, about twelve thousand years ago.

MORE BIBLICAL, ANCIENT, AND EVEN STONE AGE DEPICTIONS OF AURORAL DISPLAYS?

Other than the petroglyphs and rongorongo script, Ezekiel's description of an auroral display is not the oldest. Silverman (2006) notes Assyrian and Babylonian descriptions of the seventh and sixth centuries BCE (around the time of Ezekiel) that probably refer to aurora. In the Bible itself, an account in the book of Genesis, which may originally date back some four thousand years, could refer to auroral displays (Eather 1980, 34). "When the sun set and darkness had fallen, there appeared a smoking furnace and a firebrand that went between the halves" (Jerusalem Bible, 1968, Genesis 15:17). The imagery symbolizes God walking between the two halves of a dead animal in an ancient ritual used to seal contracts, in this case a covenant between God and Abram (Abraham).

Likewise, in the book of Jeremiah (late seventh century BCE) it is written, "I see a cooking pot on the boil, . . . with its contents tilting from the North" (Jerusalem Bible, 1968, Jeremiah 1:13).

Although certainly not as conclusive as Ezekiel's description, this could be a reference to an auroral display. Here again it is important that the image, apparently seen in the sky, was from the north, as would be expected in this case for an auroral event, and auroras have been described many times throughout history as appearing to be like boiling pots (Eather 1980, 35).

The book of Zechariah (late sixth century BCE) records what may also be an auroral display. "I saw a vision during the night. It was this: a man was standing among the deep-rooted myrtles; behind him were horses, red and sorrel and black and white" (Jerusalem Bible, 1968, Zechariah 1:8).

In and of itself, it is questionable if this is based on an auroral event, but given the context of night, it is quite possible; the foliage, the man, and the horses and their colors all fit an auroral event.

In the second book of Maccabees (circa 170–168 BCE) another auroral display is apparently recorded (see *National Geographic* 1939). "It then happened that all over the city for nearly forty days there were apparitions of horsemen galloping through the air, in cloth of gold, troops of lancers fully armed, squadrons of cavalry in order of battle, attacks and charges this way and that, a flourish of shields, a forest of pikes, brandishing of swords, hurling of missiles, a glitter of golden accoutrements and armour of all kinds. So everyone prayed that this manifestation might prove a good omen" (Jerusalem Bible, 1968, 2 Maccabees, 5:2–4).

One other possible biblical reference to auroral displays is worthy of mention here, that of the book of Enoch. Enoch the man is mentioned in the book of Genesis as being a seventh generation descendant of Adam; that is, he was from a very early period. The book of Enoch in its present form dates to the second or first century BCE (R. A. Gilbert, in Charles 2003, vii), but it is quite possible that it records much older traditions and images, passed down through the centuries and millennia to us. Considered in many mainstream circles to be heretical, by the late fourth century CE the book of Enoch was generally condemned and survived only through some fragmentary Greek manuscripts (the original language was probably Hebrew and/or Aramaic) and an Ethiopian translation (the Ethiopian Christian church being much more accepting of the book). Whatever their origin, the texts of the book of Enoch contain some vivid passages that can be interpreted as amazing auroral and plasma displays. Here is a sampling from the book of Enoch 17:9–11: "And I saw a flaming fire. And beyond these mountains is a region, the end of the great earth: there the heavens were completed. And I saw a deep abyss, with columns of heavenly fire, and among them I saw columns of fire fall, which were beyond measure alike toward the height and toward the depth" (Charles 2003, 16).

Going even further back in time, dating to the period of up to twenty thousand years ago or more, we find human-created abstract, meandering patterns on cave walls, referred to by the French cave art researcher Henri Breuil (1877–1961) as macaronis. These have been interpreted as depictions of auroral displays (NASA 2006). In 1976 George Siscoe wrote, "The most dramatic example of this possibility is to be found on the ceiling of the cave of Rouffignac in France, where lines drawn in the red clay ceiling resemble the folded curtain patterns of the aurora" (Siscoe, quoted in van der Sluijs 2010).

Interestingly, the cave art of Rouffignac has been dated to circa 11,000 BCE (Milan 2003), or about the time of the end of the last ice age, a period that saw intense solar activity.

I wonder about other possible allusions to intense solar activity. Thinking back to the Great Sphinx, there is a record that Khufu repaired lightning damage to the statue (see chapter 15, page 339)—is this the remembrance of a major solar outburst? And then there is Göbekli Tepe, which Katie and I have visited on numerous occasions. We wonder if not only the "snakes" but also the *H* symbol that appears on various pillars could represent, in highly stylized form, a plasma configuration or "cosmic thunderbolt" with a pinch instability (compare the *H* to illustrations of plasma discharges and stylized "thunderbolts" in Talbott and Thornhill 2005; see additional discussion in chapter 15, page 350).

Further supporting the contention that such literary and artistic creations as discussed above really do record auroral events is another line of evidence, but this time it is an absence of allusions to auroras in Norse (Viking) literature (including literature from or referring to Greenland and Iceland) of the period circa 700 CE to 1300 CE. On the face of it, many people would expect that of all the world's literary creations, those of peoples living in the far north would most definitely include auroral descriptions; after all, it is the land of the aurora borealis, the northern lights. However, it turns out that there is a striking lack of such descriptions in the Norse literature from this period, with most references to the auroras being by people who had never actually seen them, but had only heard about auroras from others (Richman 1981). The explanation? At this time there was a lull in solar activity and the number of sunspots (Solanki et al. 2004; Usoskin et al. 2007), so auroral displays were much reduced in extent and number, and those that did occur were confined to exceptionally high latitudes, even farther north than the Norse lived. This helps confirm that when descriptions of auroras are found in the ancient and medieval literature, it means that such displays were real, genuinely observed phenomena. The descriptions do not occur when there were no such auroral displays to observe.

And there is another line of evidence supporting major auroral events and solar outbursts, evidence that comes from both European literary traditions and an archaeological enigma: vitrification.

Figure 10.1. Robert Schoch on site studying the walls of the
Mote of Mark, Scotland, which contain ancient vitrification.
(Photograph courtesy of R. Schoch.)

11

GLASS CASTLES, FIRE FROM THE SKY, AND THE SPOILS OF THE GODS

Ancient Celtic traditions and Arthurian romances abound with tales of "glass castles" and "glass cities." Ancient vitrified (that is, turned to glass) remains of stonework, buildings, and cities have been reported from around the globe (Brigantes Nation 2002; Condick 2009). Here I am using the term *vitrification* in the sense of rock melted and turned to glassy substances; I am not including the more general concept of supposedly "softened" and "molded" rock (as, for instance, discussed by Jan Peter de Jong 2007–2008; see Tributsch 2017 for possible evidence that the Inca of Peru used acidic mud to soften rock material, and see Heldal and Storemyr 2015 for a discussion of the possible use by the ancient Egyptians of fire and heat to quarry rock; see also Wootton et al. 2013). Admittedly, some of the reports of vitrification are more reliable than others. Among the best-documented examples of ancient vitrification are various hill forts of the United Kingdom, particularly Scotland (Christison 1898). Having studied ancient hill forts in Scotland and Wales, I can testify to the authenticity of vitrification there. But what is its origin and significance? Drawing from decades of fieldwork that has taken me from Egypt to Easter Island, the answer I propose ties in with plasma and the new way of thinking about our ancient past that I am advocating in this book.

VITRIFIED FORTS

Relatively few people are aware of vitrified stone forts, one of the great mysteries of antiquity. To the untrained eye, vitrified forts are not particularly impressive. They generally appear to be walls of stone rubble, lacking any true masonry work, built on the tops of hills. The majority of known vitrified forts are found in Scotland, with others reported from England, Ireland, Wales, and also France, Germany, and as far afield as Turkey and Iran. A typical example of a vitrified fort, one that I have examined firsthand, is the Mote of Mark in Scotland.

What distinguishes a vitrified fort? The stone walls and structures have been subject to intense heat, to the point where some of the rocks have melted and fused, forming masses of material that can resemble the slag produced when smelting and refining metals, similar to materials produced during some types of volcanic eruptions. It is referred to as vitrification (the Latin word *vitrum* means "glass") because the melted rock can solidify as a crude, generally dark, glass, which hundreds or thousands of years later may not look much like glass at all to the untrained eye. In order to melt and vitrify the rock, incredibly high temperatures are required—on the order of 1,000° Centigrade. The vitrification typically occurs on the tops and outer surfaces of the rock walls and not in their interiors. The big questions are, How could this occur, and why? Before we address these questions, we need to consider another thorny issue: the time frame of the vitrified forts, which in turn bears on the issue of how the forts may have been vitrified.

HOW FAR BACK DOES VITRIFICATION GO?

It is generally agreed among conventional historians and archaeologists that vitrified forts date back to at least the Iron Age (in the United Kingdom, about 800 BCE to the early centuries CE) and were used up through the early Dark Ages, circa 700 CE and later. The latter portion of this span, the late fifth and sixth centuries CE, corresponds to the time when the famous King Arthur supposedly lived and died. King Arthur and the Knights of the Round Table may have

gathered at a vitrified hill fort known as Camelot. A Welsh manuscript records a poem, titled "PREIDDEU ANNWN" ("The Spoils of
Annwn"; Annwn refers to the "otherworld" or the world of the gods;
see Higley 2010), attributed to the British bard Taliesin of the middle
and late sixth century CE. The poem tells of Arthur and a glass fortress
or castle (for general comments on vitrified forts and glass castles of the
Arthurian romances, see Comte 2002 and Squire 1905). Who would
think of making a fort of glass? Traditionally, the reference to glass has
been seen as a fanciful metaphoric analogy to the realm of the gods and
other beings. But could it have been rooted in reality? Could genuine
vitrified forts have been the basis for the concept of a glass fortress or
castle? I believe the answer is yes.

However, this is not to say the vitrified forts necessarily originated
at the time of the legendary chieftain. Vitrified forts may have been
an inheritance from a much more remote period. Arthur and his contemporaries may have reused already very ancient forts, structures that
had undergone vitrification centuries or millennia earlier. Indeed, the
vitrified forts and other megalithic stonework might very well have
been considered the "spoils of Annwn," that is the "spoils of the gods,"
the remnants of the world of the ancient gods. The Mote of Mark (the
Scottish vitrified fort, also known as Rockcliffe) illustrates this possibility. During excavations, artifacts from the Roman and early Christian
periods were found along with an abundance of material from the
sixth and seventh centuries CE and even a piece of Mediterranean glass
that could date to the ninth century CE. But, more remarkably, over a
hundred worked flints possibly dating to the Mesolithic Period—that
is, the period of circa 8000 BCE to 4000 BCE—were found (Royal
Commission 2010). Thus, the Mote of Mark may trace its origins to ten
thousand years ago (or more) and was intermittently used and reused
over the course of nine millennia!

THE HOW AND WHY BEHIND VITRIFICATION

How did the Mote of Mark and other forts come to be vitrified? A
number of explanations have been proposed (see Schoch 2010c). Some

believe that the builders of the forts did it purposefully, or alternatively, that it was the result of attackers attempting to destroy the forts. If purposeful, perhaps vitrification was a way to bond and strengthen the rock walls in lieu of mortar. Huge amounts of wood and other flammable substances were presumably piled against the walls and set ablaze, creating intense heat and melting the surface rocks. The problem is that virtually all studies conclude that vitrified walls are actually weaker and more brittle than nonvitrified walls. The vitrification occurs only on the upper surfaces and tops of walls, which are otherwise built on foundations of rubble and thus could easily collapse.

Another popular theory suggests the vitrification resulted from enemy attacks. The forts were originally built of stone and wood, with wooden superstructures and in some cases wooden logs inside the stone and rubble walls. The assaulting enemy might have purposefully set the fort on fire, and the ensuing conflagration may have caused the vitrification. But could setting fire to a fort really generate the extremely intense heat necessary to melt rock? And why would the defenders continue to build structures containing so much wood that they were vulnerable to such attacks when there was certainly plenty of stone available?

Or, did the attackers possess a fire-based weapon that we no longer understand? Did they have something similar to modern napalm? Had they discovered a toxic mixture of flammable chemicals (the recipe being a closely guarded secret that has since been lost) that could generate enormous temperatures and could not be extinguished? The classical ancients mention "Greek fire" that could be hurled and catapulted at the enemy and would even burn under water. But whatever Greek fire may have been, even if the accounts are not exaggerated, it is difficult to see how it could be used extensively enough to cause the amount and degree of vitrification seen on the forts.

Some researchers have suggested that vitrification along the tops of fort walls was the result of lighting beacon fires. But it is odd that beacon fires would be intense and hot enough to vitrify the rock. And those forts that are vitrified continuously around the perimeters, does that mean beacon fires were built in continuous lines along the tops of the walls? This too seems odd; it would perhaps make more sense to build beacon fires at designated spots best observed by those who were intended to see the fires. Or were the tops of the forts purposefully vitrified to make a sort of walking path?

At a loss to explain the reasons behind the vitrification of the forts, one researcher suggested vitrification was a purposeful ceremonial or religious rite, despite the fact that the vitrification weakens the structure! Perhaps, according to this theory, vitrification was used to dedicate or christen a fort, was an act of supplication to a deity, served to commemorate a victory or other significant event, or was done simply to inspire the masses. I cannot say that I find this theory particularly compelling.

More exotic theories have been proposed to explain the vitrification. One early idea suggested that the structures were built near ancient volcanoes and that the builders used naturally molten rock to construct their forts. In actuality the forts are not near active volcanoes, and how the builders would have transported and manipulated molten rock is a difficult question to answer. Another theory, popular to this day in some circles, is that the vitrification was the result of ancient atomic warfare. The vitrification occurs predominantly on the tops and outer edges of the walls, as if blasted by an incredibly intense heat from above. Furthermore, vitrified forts tend to be found on the tops of hills and other promontories. To some, it sounds like melted rock could have been produced by an atomic bomb exploding in the sky above, but did the ancients have nuclear weapons in the remote past?

FIRE FROM THE SKY

As appealing as ancient nuclear weapons may be to some sensibilities, I have my doubts, and as a geologist I tend to look for other, more naturalistic explanations first. However, the evidence does suggest that the causative factor originated from the skies above. A possible explanation, which I have heard more than a few times from various people over the years, is that perhaps the midair explosion of a meteor, comet, or asteroid was responsible (Unexplained-Mysteries.com 2005). Such an incoming space object (bolide) could create a tremendous blast in the atmosphere, generating intense heat and massive destruction over a widespread area, as was the case in Tunguska, Siberia, in 1908. The Tunguska object exploded with an estimated force of between five hundred and two thousand Hiroshima atomic bombs, scorching and leveling trees over a vast area, yet no major crater formed, perhaps because the explosion took place about five to eight kilometers above Earth's surface. As I have documented in my 2003 book *Voyages of the Pyramid Builders,* Earth has had close encounters with comet-like objects, including the Tunguska incident, a number of times in the last six thousand years, and certainly many times prior to recorded history. Indeed, there is good documentation for a comet intersecting with Earth's orbit in the middle of the sixth century CE, the traditional period of King Arthur. Might a comet have been responsible, at least in part, for initiating the beginning of the Dark Ages, a time of calamity and loss? I find the comet explanation for the vitrified forts plausible, but there are other phenomena that originate in the sky as well. Even if it can be demonstrated that some vitrification dates to the sixth century and correlates with a cometary impact, it may be an incorrect oversimplification to conclude that all episodes of vitrification were due to close encounters with comets.

Major lightning strikes can cause intense heat discharges that result in the melting, fusing, and vitrification of sand and rock. Lightning that strikes silica or quartz sand (or similar substances) can cause the sand to melt, fusing the sand grains together to form natural glass tubes and other structures, known as fulgurites. The forts sitting at high elevations could have served as lightning rods, attracting intense electrical currents that resulted in their vitrification. But is simple lightning, as we know it today, intense enough and extensive enough to explain the amount and degree of vitrification observed on the ancient forts? I believe something more is needed.

Lightning is actually a type of plasma phenomenon. Could at least some of the vitrification be due to plasma events? I believe so, and I believe that some of the forts date as far back as twelve thousand years ago or more—the spoils of a primordial civilization, the spoils of the "gods"—and were hit by solar/plasma outbursts. This is what caused the vitrification and created the glass castles.

PLASMA IMPACTS

Certain common themes of antiquity may reflect the historical impacts of plasma phenomena. Let us look at a few examples.

Deluge stories are found around the globe (Heinberg 1989; Witzel 2012). Perhaps the best known is that of Noah and the Great Flood, related in chapters 6 and 7 of the book of Genesis:

> God said to Noah, "The end has come for all things of flesh; I have decided this, because the earth is full of violence of man's making, and I will efface them from the earth.
>
> Make yourself an ark out of resinous wood. Make it with reeds and line it with pitch inside and out. . . .
>
> . . . For my part I mean to bring a flood, and send the waters over the earth, to destroy all flesh on it, every living creature under heaven; everything on earth shall perish.
>
> But I will establish my Covenant with you, and you must go on board the ark, yourself, your sons, your wife and your sons' wives along with you.
>
> From all living creatures, from all flesh, you must take two of each kind aboard the ark, to save their lives with yours; they must be a male and a female.
>
> Of every kind of bird, of every kind of animal and of every kind of reptile on the ground, two must go with you so that their lives may be saved.
>
> For your part provide yourself with eatables of all kinds, and lay in a store of them, to serve as food for yourself and them."
>
> Noah did all this; he did all that God had ordered him. . . .
>
> . . . In the six hundredth year of Noah's life, in the second month, and on the seventeenth day of that month, that very day all the springs of the great deep broke through, and the sluices of heaven opened.
>
> It rained on the earth for forty days and forty nights. . . .
>
> . . . The flood lasted forty days on the earth. The waters swelled, lifting the ark until it was raised above the earth.

The waters rose and swelled greatly on the earth, [and the ark sailed on the waters.

The waters rose more and more on] the earth so that all the highest mountains under the whole of heaven were submerged.

The waters rose fifteen cubits higher, submerging the mountains.

And so all things of flesh perished that moved on the earth, birds, cattle, wild beasts, everything that swarms on the earth, and every man.

Everything with the breath of life in its nostrils died, everything on dry land.

Yahweh destroyed every living thing on the face of the earth, man and animals, reptiles, and the birds of heaven. He rid the earth of them, so that only Noah was left, and those with him in the ark. (Jerusalem Bible, 1968, Genesis 6:13–14, 17–22; 7:11–12, 17–23)

The story of Noah and the ark has many versions in different cultures (see reviews in Heinberg 1989 and Witzel 2012). Examples include the deluge story of the Sumerian/Babylonian flood survivor Utnapishtim, recounted in the Epic of Gilgamesh (Foster 2001), and the Greek legend of Deucalion and his wife Pyrrha who survived a flood, but flood traditions are much more widespread than the Mediterranean region, the Middle East, and Mesopotamia. In the Hindu tradition the first man, Manu, is warned by a great fish of a coming deluge and is ordered to build a boat, which he stocks with seeds; the savior fish guides his boat to the highest peak of the Himalayas. In the mountains of Yunnan, in southwest China, the indigenous Lolos people tell the story of a great flood and the hero Du-mu, who survived with his sons (who were accompanied by otters, wild ducks, and lampreys) in a hollow log. The aborigines of central Australia pass on the tradition that a huge flood of long ago brought famine to the land and only a few people and animals survived on the mountain ridges. In the Americas there are numerous flood traditions, often featuring a hero and various accompanying animals who survive on a raft. In Hawaii, there is an indigenous tradition of a great flood.

The book of Genesis tells of forty days and forty nights of rain, or in other words it rained continuously for an incredibly long period of time. What might have caused this? A major plasma event could vaporize large amounts of water from lakes and oceans, which in turn would rain down continuously and cause widespread flooding. My research has determined that the Great Sphinx in Egypt dates back minimally to circa 10,000 BCE and was subject to intense rains. Could these rains be the rains that followed plasma bombardments? I believe so.

But flood stories are not the only catastrophes recorded by ancient traditions. As Richard Heinberg writes, "While the Deluge is the most widely and vividly remembered catastrophe of ancient times, most cultures retained traditions of other world-destructions as well" (Heinberg 1989, 107).

Heinberg then goes on to give a number of examples. The Greek poet Hesiod (circa 700 BCE) spoke of the end of an age in the following terms: "The life-giving Earth crashed around in burning . . . all the land seethed. . . . It seemed even if Earth and wide Heaven above came together; for such a mighty crash would have arisen if Earth were being hurled to ruin, and Heaven from on high were hurling her down" (Hesiod, quoted by Heinberg 1989, 107). I cannot help but think this describes the long-distant memory of a major solar outburst, a major plasma event, and the subsequent geological disturbances (as the Easter Island legend, recounted on page 103, may have also recorded).

The North American Hopi tribal traditions include accounts of the world being destroyed by fire from above and also the people seeking safety underground (Heinberg 1989, 108–9). Again, plasma comes to mind. And according to some Hopi elders, their ancestors emerged from below the ground. Could these ancestors have been survivors of a plasma event who had sought refuge from the surface onslaught?

Major plasma phenomena could cause not only vitrification, but if sufficiently intense could also literally incinerate the surface of Earth, including human structures and artifacts. Only massive stone structures or materials that were buried, hidden in caves, or otherwise protected from the aerial bombardment would have a chance of surviving. Is this why the ancients often built megalithic stone structures (even after the plasma was gone, remembering what had happened in the past)? Do some of these stone structures actually belong to another time—to the "world of the gods"? Is this why in some regions dwellings were not so much built, but rather carved into cliffs or deep underground in bedrock? The extensive rock-cut churches and dwellings of Cappadocia (Turkey), the solid stone buildings of Petra (Jordan), the rock-cut churches of Lalibela (Ethiopia), the Ajanta and Ellora caves and structures (India), and the cliff dwellings of the Anasazi (western United States) come to mind. Is some of this the handiwork of a more advanced people facing potential annihilation? Furthermore, a plasma event would significantly decrease the stratospheric ozone layer for years, or longer, subjecting all life to harmful UV light. One strategy to try to protect oneself would be to stay underground as much as possible during daylight hours (see Todericiu 2007). Perhaps this theory explains why we see no significant activity indicative of advanced civilization for thousands of years—until it kick-starts again in Egypt and elsewhere.

Plato (circa 429–423 to 348–347 BCE), in his *Timaeus* (this dialogue and the accompanying *Critias* recount the Atlantis legend), writes of a memory of recurring catastrophes and ancient civilizations that were destroyed. In the dialogue an Egyptian priest is speaking to Solon of Athens (circa 638 to 558 BCE).

One of the priests, who was of a very great age, said: O Solon, Solon, you Hellenes are never anything but children, and there is not an old man among you. Solon in return asked him what he meant. I mean to say, he replied, that in mind you are all young; there is no old opinion handed down among you by ancient tradition, nor any science which is hoary with age. And I will tell you why. There have been, and will be again, many destructions of mankind arising out of many causes; the greatest have been brought about by the agencies of fire and water, and other lesser ones by innumerable other causes. There is a story, which even you have preserved, that once upon a time Paethon [also spelled Phaethon or Phaeton or Phaëton], the son of Helios [the Sun], having yoked the steeds in his father's chariot, because he was not able to drive them in the path of his father, burnt up all that was upon the earth, and was himself destroyed by a thunderbolt. Now this has the form of a myth, but really signifies a declination of the bodies moving in the heavens around the earth, and a great conflagration of things upon the earth, which recurs after long intervals; at such times those who live upon the mountains and in dry and lofty places are more liable to destruction than those who dwell by rivers or on the seashore. . . .

. . . Just when you and other nations are beginning to be provided with letters and the other requisites of civilized life, after the usual interval, the stream from heaven, like a pestilence, comes pouring down, and leaves only those of you who are destitute of letters and education; and so you have to begin all over again like children, and know nothing of what happened in ancient times, either among us or among yourselves. (Plato, *Timaeus*; translated by Benjamin Jowett [1817–1893]; material in brackets added by R. Schoch)

These words from Plato are certainly subject to interpretation. Some would dismiss them as mere fantasy, while others might interpret them as referring to a comet hitting Earth (see for instance Allan and Delair 1997). However, I believe they describe quite precisely a major solar outburst and the accompanying plasma discharge and the aftermath of such an event—including the virtually total destruction of any civilization of the time and the attendant losses. All that remained is a vague memory of the past age, often seen as a golden age, and the memory of the destruction of that age. As Heinberg points out, "It is worth noting briefly the existence of physical signs—signs of ocean-level changes and of the simultaneous extinctions of large numbers of plant and animal species—that suggests that relatively recent, worldwide destructions have indeed taken place. Geologists and archaeologists are generally undecided about the interpretation of this evidence and often refer to it as 'mysterious.' But for the mythologist and the psychologist, there can be no question: the *memory* of catastrophe is universal, and the terror persists" (Heinberg 1989, 111; italics in the original).

Plasma discharges are electrical in nature. We do not know the full effects and ramifications of subjecting living organisms, including humans, to intense electrical fields. Those who survive might be altered genetically, mentally, and psychically. Laboratory studies demonstrate that plant seeds and fish eggs, subjected to strong electrical fields, can be altered genetically, giving rise to either previously unknown varieties of organisms or apparently ancestral organisms that were believed to have gone extinct. In one experiment, normal trout eggs, electrically stimulated, gave rise to a giant trout (Bürgin 2007; see also Burke and Halberg 2005 for related work on the electrical properties of ancient monuments and their effects on living organisms, such as enhancing seed growth). Mental functioning and psychic ability are affected by electromagnetic fields (Burns 2003; Wilkinson and Gauld 1993; Schoch and Yonavjak 2008). Van der Sluijs and Peratt (2010, 35) suggest that humans subjected to strong electrical fields during heightened auroral activity and plasma discharges may have been subject to induced hallucinations. Depictions of such hallucinations, they suggest, may be found among ancient rock art and, along with direct renditions of auroral activity (in the form of the petroglyphs), may record major ancient plasma discharges. I wonder if such strong electrical fields could have consequences well beyond simple and temporary hallucinations. Could occasional periods of intense plasma phenomena on Earth act to alternatively accelerate, or decelerate, organismal change, both physical and mental? Might powerful plasma phenomena act as a switching mechanism, causing biological and mental changes? Many cultures have a tradition of cyclical change, such as the Gold, Silver, Bronze, and Iron Ages; the Yuga Cycle; or the Precessional Cycle of the World Ages. We are currently transitioning from the Age of Pisces to the Age of Aquarius. Might plasma phenomena be involved in transitions from one age to another? Aquarius is generally depicted as the Water Bearer, but astrologically it is an Air Sign, so is the "water" that Aquarius pours forth the "cosmic waters" (Ulissey with Schoch 2020) or, in other words, electrical plasma streams? We suspect so.

We live in a plasma universe. A National Research Council report states, "Plasma is . . . ubiquitous in the universe. Plasmas pervade intergalactic space, interstellar space, interplanetary space, and the space environments of planets" (National Research Council 2004, 5). It is foolish to ignore the possibility that major plasma events have influenced our past—for they clearly have. And we can be certain the plasma will hit again.

In modern recorded history, the largest plasma event to ever hit Earth was the Carrington Event.

Figure 11.1. Rock-cut cave-like structures at Ajanta (*top*) and Ellora (*bottom*), India. (Photographs courtesy of R. Schoch and C. Ulissey.)

12

THE CARRINGTON EVENT

On Thursday, September 1, 1859, the British astronomer Richard C. Carrington was observing and sketching an unusually large and dark group of sunspots at his personal observatory at Redhill, about thirty-two kilometers south of central London (Cliver 2006). Carrington, although technically an amateur (his family was in the brewery business), was an expert on the Sun and had devoted his time and resources to unraveling its mysteries. Suddenly, on that fateful day, at 11:18 a.m. local time (Greenwich mean time), Carrington observed intense white flashes of light coming from two locations within the sunspot group he was drawing. He was so startled by this unusual phenomenon that he wanted a witness to corroborate his observations. In his own words, he "hastily ran to call some one to witness the exhibition . . . [but he could find no one nearby], and on returning within 60 seconds, was mortified to find that it was already much changed and enfeebled" (Carrington 1859, 14; also quoted in Stewart 1861, 427).

The flashes were now "vanishing as two rapidly fading dots of white light" (Carrington 1859, 14), and by 11:23 a.m. they had disappeared. Carrington had observed firsthand an incredibly intense but short-lived solar flare. As it turns out, there was another witness to the event. Richard Hodgson was observing the Sun at the same time from his house and observatory at Highgate (about eight kilometers north of central London), and he too saw the white flashes (Hodgson 1859). (As a side note, this is sometimes referred to as the first solar flare ever reported [see, for instance, Cliver 2006, 119], but according to Brody [2002, 130], the early sunspot observer and electrical experimenter Stephen Gray observed a solar flare in 1705, but no one paid much attention to his observation.)

At Kew Observatory, about sixteen kilometers east of central London, self-recording magnetographs, owned by the Royal Society, were in operation monitoring Earth's magnetic field. At the very time of Carrington's observation of the solar flare a relatively small but abrupt disturbance was detected in the tracings of the magnetographs (Stewart 1861). The magnetic field seemed to return to normal, but then about seventeen and one-half hours later all hell broke loose, and the magnetographs went off the scale. We now understand that this is what happens when a huge coronal mass ejection (CME)—a giant bubble of ionized gas ejected by the Sun—hits Earth's magnetosphere. The CME was not merely recorded on the magnetographs (now generally referred to as magnetometers), but it also was seen around the world as incredible auroral displays in the night skies over the next several days—and at unusually low latitudes. More importantly, and tellingly, the telegraph systems of the time were widely affected. The two hundred thousand kilometers of telegraph lines then in use (Green and Boardsen 2006, 130) suffered major disruptions and failures, becoming unusable as unwanted electrical currents flowed through the wires. In some cases the telegraph operators found that they could disconnect the batteries they normally used and send messages via the induced current. In other cases the induced currents sent "fantastical and unreadable messages" (quoted from National Research Council 2008, 6). There were instances where sparks flew from telegraph receiving instruments, some operators were nearly electrocuted, and several telegraph stations reportedly burned down (Odenwald and Green 2008).

The 1859 geomagnetic storm, and its associated phenomena, is now generally referred to as the Carrington Event. The Carrington Event is not just an historical oddity, but is also of extreme importance to both our understanding of the dynamics of solar outbursts and our ability to predict the ramifications of future solar events. For this reason it has been studied extensively, and it is worthwhile for us to look at it in a bit more detail.

The Carrington Event actually consisted of two parts, two CMEs, along with the accompanying geomagnetic storms and visible auroras, which occurred over the period of approximately August 28 through September 5, 1859. Around the world, as night fell, fantastical auroral displays were seen in the skies, beginning on the evening of August 28 Greenwich time. Simultaneously, magnetometers recorded violent magnetic disturbances, and telegraph systems were affected. By August 30 things had calmed down, and they remained so through August 31 and September 1 (the day Carrington made his remarkable observation), with the exception of the small blip picked up by the Kew Observatory magnetometers (mentioned above) that coincided with Carrington's observation of a solar flare preceding the arrival of the CME. But then on September 2 more brilliant auroras appeared throughout the world, there was a larger magnetic disturbance than the August 28 and 29 event, and telegraph lines went absolutely crazy. Things did not calm down again until September 3 and 4, and the effects, in much diminished intensity, lingered for up to several days afterward.

There was no clear understanding in 1859 of the relationship of sunspots, solar flares, auroral events, geomagnetic disturbances, and the effects on practical technology, such as the telegraph systems of the time. Ironically, given that the event is commonly named after him, Richard Carrington, good scientist that he was, cautioned against too quickly concluding that there was a causal connection between the solar flare he observed and the auroral displays and geomagnetic disturbances. It could all be simply a matter of coincidence, or so he suggested, stating, "One swallow does not make a summer" (Carrington 1859, 15). We now have a better understanding of these phenomena and their interrelationships, but the picture is far from complete!

Based on modern analyses of the data, we can now tentatively reconstruct the major aspects of the Carrington Event (see Odenwald and Green 2008; Smart et al. 2006). In late August of 1859 a major sunspot group appeared. On or around August 26 and 27 a solar flare (although unobserved) may have occurred, as well as a solar proton event (SPE) and a CME. The CME may have taken on the order of forty to sixty hours to cross the distance from the Sun to Earth, arriving on August 28 and creating the first wave of outstanding auroras and the accompanying geomagnetic storm. When it reached Earth, the CME compressed Earth's magnetosphere. Based on the magnetometer readings, the magnetic field of the CME was in the shape of a large, spiraling helix. Initially the orientation of the magnetic helix actually reinforced Earth's magnetic field, but as the plasma continued to flow around and past Earth, its magnetic field pivoted such that the CME's magnetic field was opposite to that of Earth's, and it was at this point that the two magnetic fields interacted (they were said to reconnect), releasing tremendous amounts of energy, resulting in the magnificent auroras and the disruptions in telegraph services. As noted above, things settled down after a day or so.

On September 1, Carrington and Hodgson observed the solar flare. Given how bright it was, modern estimates suggest the surface temperature of the Sun at the point of emission was close to 50 million degrees Celsius. An enormous amount of energy was released, not only as visible light but also as intense X rays and gamma rays that, traveling at the speed of light, hit Earth eight and one-half minutes later. A CME was also released from the Sun, but charged particles take considerably longer than electromagnetic radiation (which includes visible light, X rays, and gamma rays) to cross from the Sun to Earth. In this particular case, however, the CME traveled more quickly than is typical. The late-August CME had effectively formed a cavity in space that had not yet been filled in by plasma from the solar wind, and thus the early-September CME traveled at a speed of some 2,380 kilometers per second, hitting Earth a mere seventeen to seventeen and one-half hours after leaving the Sun. As this CME hit, its magnetic field was pointed opposite to that of Earth's, resulting in an immediate geomagnetic storm and brilliant auroras at low latitudes. Intense currents were induced on the surface of Earth and in the ground, resulting in the disruptions to telegraph systems. The magnetosphere of Earth was compressed to just seven thousand kilometers or less (it normally extends to about sixty-five thousand kilometers or more), and the Van Allen belts (which normally trap incoming particles, protecting Earth) were temporarily eliminated.

Protons were accelerated by the solar flare and the CME to incredibly high energy levels and penetrated into our atmosphere, creating a major solar proton event (SPE). According to one estimate, this reduced the stratospheric ozone layer by 5 percent, and it took years to fully recover. Furthermore, energetic protons hitting the nuclei of nitrogen and oxygen atoms created a shower of neutrons that rained down onto the surface of Earth. In 1859 there was no technology to detect the SPE or the shower of neutrons and their associated elevated levels of radiation. Today, among other effects, there would be widespread failure of computers and other electronics.

By September 4 the CME had passed, and any lingering effects remained only for a few more days. In 1859 civilization suffered little more than a bit of inconvenience and minor damage to the telegraph system. Such would not be the case if a Carrington-level event occurred today!

Historically, the Carrington Event is apparently the largest such event in the last 450+ years (based on nitrate concentrations in ice cores going back to 1561; see McCracken et al. 2001a, 2001b). However, based on the evidence of the petroglyphs and rongorongo texts, it seems evident that much larger solar outbursts have occurred in the past (see further discussion in chapter 15, page 319). And a truism of geology is that if something has happened in the past, it can happen again in the future—and all the indications are that a major solar outburst will occur sooner rather than later!

Another troubling aspect of such a major solar outburst is that, as we have already discussed to some extent, it may be incredibly difficult to impossible to predict significantly in advance. We may not be aware of its coming more than a few hours to a few days before it hits. It is worth quoting plasma physicist Paul Kintner, of Cornell University, once again: "The Carrington event happened during a mediocre, ho-hum solar cycle. . . . It came out of nowhere, so we just don't know when something like that is going to happen again" (Kintner, quoted in Brooks 2009).

An important consideration is that any incoming solar outburst has a magnetic field, which as we discussed earlier in this chapter relative to the CMEs of the Carrington Event, may take the shape of a spiraling helix. How this magnetic field aligns and interacts with Earth's magnetic field upon arrival of the solar outburst can be a major factor in determining how severe the effects of any particular geomagnetic storm will be (Vergano 2012). It can be very difficult or virtually impossible with current technology to determine the exact orientation of the magnetic field of an incoming solar outburst before it is detected by satellites, giving a very short lead time (measured in hours or minutes). Yet, even if we cannot predict the precise orientation of the incoming magnetic field, any large outburst will cause major disruptions to modern technological society. In the case of the Carrington Event, the spiraling magnetic field of the initial incoming CME changed its orientation as it passed by our planet, insuring (so it seemed) that the full effects of the outburst would be experienced on Earth.

RAMIFICATIONS OF A CARRINGTON-LEVEL (OR GREATER) EVENT

It is difficult to imagine the magnitude of the socioeconomic impact of a Carrington-level (or greater) event in the twenty-first century. I believe that the clock is counting down until the next such event, and the longer the Sun retains its pent-up energy, the larger the next major solar event could be. At the same time, we as a society, with our increased reliance on ever-more-sophisticated and fragile electronics, are becoming increasingly vulnerable to even relatively small-scale solar events. These two trends are placing us on a collision course with disaster. And here disaster will be in the literal sense of the word; the word *disaster* can be taken to mean an ill-fated star (where *star* is used in the astrological sense of a star, our Sun, or a planet).

To make matters worse, modern global systems have become incredibly interconnected and interdependent. This results in efficiency when everything is running smoothly, but comes at the price of extreme vulnerability relative to what would have been minor disruptions in the past. To give one example, in an article in the *Nation* magazine, Matt Stoller writes, "Barry Lynn of the New America Foundation has been studying industrial supply shocks since 1999, when he noticed that global computer chip production was concentrated in Taiwan. After a severe earthquake in that country, the global computer industry nearly shut down, crashing the stocks of large computer makers. This level of concentration of the production of key components in a globalized economy is a new phenomenon. Lynn's work points to the highly dangerous side of globalization, the flip side of a hyper-efficient global supply chain. When one link in that chain is broken, there is no fallback" (Stoller 2011).

Applying this to a solar outburst, such as a Carrington-level event or greater, imagine if during the catastrophe the only factory producing a particular critical part, vaccine, or medicine was put offline.

In 2009 the staid British journal *New Scientist* published an article with the provocative title "Space Storm Alert: 90 Seconds from Catastrophe," which opens with the following lines:

> It is midnight on 22 September 2012 and the skies above Manhattan are filled with a flickering curtain of colourful light. Few New Yorkers have seen the aurora this far south but their fascination is short-lived. Within a few seconds, electric bulbs dim and flicker, then become unusually bright for a fleeting moment. Then all the lights in the state go out. Within 90 seconds, the entire eastern half of the US is without power.
>
> A year later and millions of Americans are dead and the nation's infrastructure lies in tatters. The World Bank declares America a developing nation. Europe, Scandinavia, China and Japan are also struggling to recover from the same fateful event—a violent storm, 150 million kilometres away on the surface of the Sun.
>
> It sounds ridiculous. Surely the Sun couldn't create so profound a disaster on Earth. Yet an extraordinary report funded by NASA and issued by the US National Academy of Sciences (NAS) . . . claims it could do just that. (Brooks 2009; see also National Research Council 2008 for the NAS report that *New Scientist* is referring to)

In fact, this scenario is not so ridiculous at all, as the *New Scientist* article goes on to relate (see also *International Business Times* 2011b; Lovett 2011; National Research Council 2008). Indeed, if things do not change, it may be inevitable.

Our modern technological society is, without exaggeration, totally dependent on a constant supply of electricity. An immediate worry concerning a major solar outburst is the vulnerability of modern electricity grid systems—the wires that crisscross nations and, indeed, the entire world. The high-voltage systems will essentially act as huge antennae, picking up and channeling direct current (DC) as a result of a solar outburst. The power transmission lines are designed to carry alternating current (AC), and although the geomagnetically induced current may be relatively weak compared to the currents that normally flow through the transmission lines, since the geomagnetic current is a DC current it can saturate the transformers and system (Jaggard 2011).

Among other effects, the all-important transformers along grid lines could heat up and melt, causing massive blackouts. This famously happened in Canada's Quebec province, when on March 13, 1989, a solar storm disrupted Hydro-Quebec transmission lines and in less than two minutes a blackout occurred, affecting six million people for nine to twelve hours (Berge 2011). In this particular case a billion-ton cloud of gas and plasma was released from the Sun, with the energy of thousands of nuclear bombs exploding simultaneously, and headed toward Earth at a speed of approximately 1.6 million kilometers an hour (Odenwald 2009). Besides the Quebec blackout, due to the solar flare accompanying the March 1989 solar storm (which was nowhere near the size of the Carrington Event), short-wave radio signals were disrupted, including the jamming of Radio Free Europe, which was being broadcast into Russia; initially the Kremlin was suspected as the culprit. Such geomagnetic storms can affect the entire globe, especially the stronger storms (at the level of the Carrington Event and greater), but the immediate risk is most severe at higher magnetic latitudes due to the fact that the incoming electric currents are funneled or sucked into Earth's poles. Thus northern latitude Quebec was hard hit by the March 1989 solar storm, and during the solar storms that occurred around Halloween in 2003, there were blackouts in the city of Malmö,

Sweden, and transformers failed in South Africa (Jaggard 2011).

But, returning to the March 1989 storm, not only Quebec was affected. Spectacular auroras were seen as far south as Florida and Cuba, indicative of the strength of the storm. In the United States no blackouts occurred as a result of the March 13, 1989, storm, but this was perhaps simply a matter of good fortune. Over two hundred power grid problems were reported across the United States within minutes of when the solar storm hit (Odenwald 2009). And there were still more direct consequences, as reported by Sten Odenwald: "In space, some satellites actually tumbled out of control for several hours. NASA's TDRS-1 communication satellite recorded over 250 anomalies as high-energy particles invaded the satellite's sensitive electronics. Even the Space Shuttle Discovery was having its own mysterious problems. A sensor on one of the tanks supplying hydrogen to a fuel cell was showing unusually high pressure readings on March 13. The problem went away just as mysteriously after the solar storm subsided" (Odenwald 2009).

A May 1921 geomagnetic storm, caused by a solar outburst, was intermediate in size, between the 1859 Carrington Event and the March 1989 solar storm that affected Quebec. In 1921 electrical grid systems and associated technology were not nearly as extensive or as susceptible to geomagnetically induced currents as our systems are today. According to some studies, a 1921-level solar storm could cause 300 to 350 or more large extra-high-voltage (EHV) transformers to fail or be permanently damaged in the United States, resulting in major electrical grid collapses with resulting blackouts for 130 million people, and the blackouts could last for years (see National Research Council 2008). Likewise, transformers would fail around the world; according to one estimate, over 2,000 EHV transformers could be adversely impacted globally (Stein 2012). Large transformers, once damaged by overheating, burning, and melting, cannot be repaired but must be replaced. There are few crews trained to replace the transformers, and few spares of these large and expensive transformers on hand. Once the supply of spare transformers has been exhausted, new transformers will have to be manufactured. Even in normal times it can take a year or more to have a large transformer built and delivered. How will it even be possible to build transformers in areas without electricity to power manufacturing facilities?

The scenario described in the previous paragraph is based on the May 1921 geomagnetic storm. A Carrington-level event would be much worse. Plus, in either case, not only the United States would be hit, but also nations around the world. Globally electrical grids would be damaged, with attendant blackouts. And it would be the most developed, technologically sophisticated, modern, industrialized countries that would be most affected. Less developed countries and regions, less dependent on modern infrastructure, would experience fewer disruptions, but given the interconnectedness of the global economy, surely they would ultimately feel the impacts too. Loss of electrical power for any length of time, say more than a day or two, is not a minor nuisance in the developed world. Our entire modern societies run on, and are dependent on, a ready and reliable supply of electricity. Without electricity, such necessities as water and sewage treatment would be affected, and in short order water would stop flowing in our public water systems. Those living in high-rise apartment buildings, where water has to be pumped to reach their floors, would lose water straightaway. All electrical appliances would stop working, from computers, lights (imagine the dark nights!), refrigerators, microwaves, and televisions to just about everything else associated with our electronically based society. Battery-powered devices would last only as long as the batteries hold—and then what?

Office buildings, apartment complexes, factories, government buildings, certain small communities, and so forth have backup generators, but such generators will last only as long as there is fuel to power them. Depending on what measures may be in place, within days or weeks the fuel will run out. Even if more fuel is theoretically available, without electricity there may be no way to deliver it. Gas pumps at service stations will not work without electricity; transportation by petroleum-powered vehicles will come to a halt. Furthermore, without electricity traffic lights (so essential to keeping order in large modern cities) will stop functioning. Much public transportation in some cities, such as trolleys, subways, and electric bus lines, is directly dependent on electricity that will no longer be available. Underground tracks, such as for subways, may become flooded from penetrating rain and groundwater without electric pumps to keep them dry.

Buildings will lack air-conditioning, which is directly dependent on electricity. In hot areas, people may die from heat stroke, especially after the drinkable water runs out. In cold regions, buildings and people may freeze. Some heating systems use electricity directly. Others, which use oil or natural gas as the fuel, still depend on electricity to pump the fuel, to circulate water or air through the building, to ignite the fuel in the furnace, and to regulate the temperature through electric thermostats. No electricity, no heat!

Without refrigeration, many foodstuffs will quickly go bad. Even as people's food spoils, fresh supplies will be unavailable. With most or all transportation shut down, any food in supermarkets or food stockpiled elsewhere will quickly run out and not be replenished. The same holds true for other items, from toilet paper to prescription drugs, which many people simply take for granted. Likewise, medical supplies that need to be kept under controlled temperature conditions may be ruined, and as supplies are exhausted no more will be available. Indeed, any hospital, once the fuel supply for its emergency backup generators is exhausted, will be in very bad shape.

Ultimately, due to the devastation caused by a Carrington-level (or greater) event, hundreds of millions of lives could be lost.

Ironically, many of the very things that make our modern society so "efficient," such as lack of redundancy (why keep old-fashioned bulky paper copies of records when they can be stored electronically?), not wasting space warehousing materials and supplies locally, and the concept of just-in-time delivery that is so dependent on steady and reliable transportation networks, make us especially vulnerable and even helpless in the face of massive grid failures and blackouts.

Beyond the disruption of electricity grid systems, electronic communication and satellite systems could be significantly disrupted. With a major solar outburst, satellites could literally leave their designated orbits as the density of the atmosphere they travel through changes, causing them to change speed. High-frequency (HF) radio communications, such as those routinely used by aircraft, and HF navigation signals from Global Positioning System (GPS) satellites will be scrambled and disrupted. A major breakdown in communication systems could lead to literal anarchy. Even a government is dependent on reliable communications to govern and control the distribution of services and goods and maintain law and order.

During an extreme geomagnetic storm—that is, on the upper end of the geomagnetic storms actually experienced in modern times—induced currents in oil and natural gas pipelines can reach hundreds of amperes (National Research Council 2008, 40), leading to serious issues of rapid corrosion, the degradation and disintegration of the material of which the pipes are made. Rusting of iron is a form of corrosion. In pipelines corrosion can result in pitting, cracking, and ultimately leaking or full-scale failure of pipes. The exact effects of a Carrington-level event, much less a tremendous solar storm on the scale of those at the end of the last ice age, are unknown. It seems likely the induced currents could be strong enough to ignite the oil or natural gas in many pipelines. To make matters worse, during a major geomagnetic storm the flow meters can malfunction, and thus the magnitude of a leak, for instance, may not be readily measurable.

A very specific and serious worry involves the roughly 442 nuclear reactors worldwide (96 are located in the United States; the exact numbers change as various reactors are built or shut down; the numbers cited are from the International Atomic Energy Agency website, April 2020). As was demonstrated by the March 2011 Fukushima Daiichi nuclear power plant disaster, when electricity is lost and cooling pumps can no longer keep the reactor cool, the reactor can overheat, potentially melting down (or exploding), and radioactive materials will be released to the environment. And it is not just the actual reactors that are of serious concern. Highly radioactive spent fuel rods are typically stored at nuclear reactor sites in containment ponds. These ponds must be continually cooled. It is estimated that with loss of power to the cooling system, the typical containment pond will boil away, and the spent fuel rods will become superheated, burn, and/or cause explosions, releasing radioactive material into the environment (Stein 2012). In the face of a major solar outburst, we could have hundreds of Chernobyl-type situations around the planet simultaneously and, with massive blackouts to boot, no foreseeable way to even attempt to realistically deal with the situations. It is difficult enough to attempt to address a Chernobyl- or Fukushima-level nuclear disaster in isolation!

One of the major results of a Carrington-level event could be the collapse of electronic-based financial and monetary systems. In the twenty-first century more and more of our financial transactions are carried out in terms of electronic money, that is, in terms of simply numbers in computers. There is for the vast majority of "money" in modern industrialized countries actually nothing beyond the electronic accounting system. The money has no physical backing—certainly not gold or other valuables, and not even paper bills or token coins. Quantitative finance expert Espen Gaarder Haug (2010, 2) points out that in 1991 the United States Federal Reserve determined that 69 percent of all U.S. dollars were in purely electronic form. Three decades later this number has surely increased; Haug estimates that 90 percent of the U.S. money supply is purely electronic, and a similar situation occurs for many other countries.

In the case of a major solar outburst, one that would overload power grids, thus burning out transformers, causing widespread blackouts, disrupting communication systems, and damaging and destroying computers and all sorts of electronic systems, the basis for the global monetary system, as well as national monetary systems, could be destroyed. Not only would transactions be "temporarily" impossible (where *temporarily* could encompass not just days or weeks, but months or years), but also in many cases electronic financial records could be severely compromised or completely destroyed, such that it would be impossible to reconstruct the system as it was prior to the impact. The only saving grace might be if financial institutions and companies had their records securely backed up in safe havens well protected from the solar onslaught. Possibly the best bet would be storage in self-contained (certainly not connected to an external power grid) and secure caves and tunnels deep inside mountains with tens of meters of solid rock to provide shielding from radiation.

It seems that some governments are taking the threat of a major solar outburst seriously. During the summer of 2011 there were reports that "the British government has been warned that a massive surge of energy from the Sun could hit the Earth in the next 18 months. In a worst-case scenario, it could blow out the national grid and leave parts of the country without electricity for months" (Don and Aikman 2011).

Therefore, according to the same article, the British government is making plans to deal with such a scenario, including invoking emergency powers to shut down the electricity grid (purposefully causing massive, though hopefully temporary, blackouts) in an attempt to protect the infrastructure from the worst effects. On the other hand, it was reported that in Australia (which is at lower latitudes than Britain and arguably therefore less vulnerable to some types of solar outbursts), "... electricity experts are not convinced the solar flare will have anywhere near the catastrophic effects predicted in Britain and think any electromagnetic surge will go largely unnoticed" (Don and Aikman 2011). One wonders, however, if the attitude expressed by the Australian officials—and the same holds true for government leaders and spokespeople elsewhere around the world—is actually a cover so as to avoid concern and potential panic among an ignorant public, even as those in the know secretly make plans to protect themselves and their institutions.

In the United States proposals have been made before Congress to invest in safeguards to help protect our electric grid systems from a major solar outburst. By one estimate, for a few billion dollars various measures could be put into place, such as building special protective devices into the electrical grid system, stockpiling and storing spare transformers and other parts and equipment (including backup generators and fuel) in secure locations (hardened steel containers and underground caves and facilities are possibilities), and storing at least a year's worth of diesel fuel for backup generators at every U.S. nuclear facility (Stein 2012). Unfortunately, so far Congress has failed to act positively on such proposals, worrying about seemingly more immediate concerns. (As a side note, many of the proposed safeguards and backup plans that have been suggested to help mitigate the damage caused by a major solar outburst would also be applicable to an attack on the nation using a powerful electromagnetic pulse [EMP]. Such an EMP would have many similar effects to those of a major solar outburst, including massive electrical discharges with disruption and damage to electronic systems, telecommunication systems, and electrical grid systems. By detonating a powerful nuclear explosion in the atmosphere over us, an enemy could create a major EMP.)

In the Obama Whitehouse there was recognition of the seriousness of solar outbursts and other space weather events. On October 13, 2016, President Barack Obama signed an executive order titled "Coordinating Efforts to Prepare the Nation for Space Weather Events." The opening section of the order reads as follows:

> Space weather events, in the form of solar flares, solar energetic particles, and geomagnetic disturbances, occur regularly, some with measurable effects on critical infrastructure systems and technologies, such as the Global Positioning System (GPS), satellite operations and communication, aviation, and the electrical power grid. Extreme space weather events—those that could significantly degrade critical infrastructure—could disable large portions of the electrical power grid, resulting in cascading failures that would affect key services such as water supply, healthcare, and transportation. Space weather has the potential to simultaneously affect and disrupt health and safety across entire continents. Successfully preparing for space weather events is an all-of-nation endeavor that requires partnerships across governments, emergency managers, academia, the media, the insurance industry, non-profits, and the private sector.
>
> It is the policy of the United States to prepare for space weather events to minimize the extent of economic loss and human hardship. The Federal Government must have (1) the capability to predict and detect a space weather event, (2) the plans and programs necessary to alert the public and private sectors to enable mitigating actions for an impending space weather event, (3) the protection and mitigation plans, protocols, and standards required to reduce risks to critical infrastructure prior to and during a credible threat,

and (4) the ability to respond to and recover from the effects of space weather. Executive departments and agencies . . . must coordinate their efforts to prepare for the effects of space weather events. (Obama 2016)

Obama's presidency ended just a few months later, in January 2017, and the succeeding administration need not follow through on the policies and intentions of the preceding administration.

Since the first edition of this book was published in 2012, there has been growing recognition of the risks posed by extreme weather events, including significant solar activity (see, for instance, Abt Associates 2017; Boyle 2017; Gannon et al. 2019; Love et al. 2019; Worman et al. 2017). Indeed, in July 2012, the Sun ejected a powerful CME that, fortunately, was not directed precisely toward Earth. (As it was, it was too close for comfort.) This CME was more powerful than the Carrington Event and occurred "during a modest solar activity cycle" (Baker et al. 2013, 585; see also Ngwira et al. 2013). If our planet had been hit, the consequences would have been severe and virtually unfathomable. There has also been increased attention paid to the effects and impacts of solar activity, geomagnetic activity, and so forth on human health (see Novik et al. 2019, who discuss impacts on the brain and heart, and Vieira et al. 2019, who discuss cardiovascular issues enhanced by geomagnetic disturbances driven by solar activity; for a review of behavioral effects of space radiation on animals, see Kiffer et al. 2019; for a general discussion of the effects of solar and geomagnetic activity on biological organisms, see Davidson 2019, and references therein; see Krukowski et al. 2018 for a study comparing male and female mice, where the females did not display the same negative behavioral and cognitive effects as males when exposed to simulated galactic cosmic radiation; see Cucinotta and Cacao 2017 for a discussion of cancer risks due to exposure to galactic cosmic rays [GCRs]; see Qu et al. 2016 for a discussion of sunspot activity correlated with disease outbreaks; for a review of how geomagnetic field intensity, as related to solar activity, may correlate with and have played a role in the evolution and extinction of large mammals, including various human species, over the last seventy thousand years, see Channell and Vigliotti 2018; and see Wickramasinghe et al. 2020 for a discussion of the possibility that the origin of the 2019 coronavirus "was probably linked to the arrival of a pure culture of the virus contained in cometary debris" [Wickramasinghe et al. 2020, 1]).

When will another major solar event occur—another Carrington-level event or greater? How can we predict the next "big one"? One technique is to look at the rates of occurrence of past solar events and from such data attempt to estimate probabilities for future events. Using this approach, Pete Riley of Predictive Science in San Diego concluded that the probability of a Carrington-level event occurring within the next decade (that is, by 2022, as he published his study in 2012) is approximately 12 percent (Riley 2012). Another way of saying this is that there is a 1 in 8 chance of a Carrington-level event by 2022. (I would add that if such does not occur by 2022, then pragmatically—in terms of our thinking and planning—every year after that the chance of a Carrington-level event hitting Earth increases.) Riley's analysis indicates a much higher probability of a major solar event occurring than most scientists, including Riley, expected. However, it is only a probability over a given period of time, and it does not pinpoint when the next Carrington-level event will happen (see Moriña et al. 2019, who calculate a probability on the order of one-tenth that of Riley 2012).

While some may put their trust in modern science to predict the next event, others turn to ancient prophecies—and to perhaps the most famous prophecy of all, one associated with a specific date that is attributed to the Mayan calendar and commonly correlated with our calendar as the year 2012. This is the next topic we need to explore.

13

THE 2012 DATE OF
THE MAYA

Before entering into a chapter with "2012" in the title, let me be clear regarding one thing. I never believed that anything dramatic, catastrophic, or cataclysmic would necessarily happen during the year 2012. I originally wrote this book in late 2011 and early 2012 with the full expectation that it would be read in 2013, and hopefully for many years to come. I was never a supporter of the exact precision of the 2012 date. I always considered the 2012 date to be much more figurative than literal. Figurative, that is, in the sense that something might happen, but not necessarily in 2012 or precisely on December 21, 2012. Rather, I believe that at some point in the first quarter or half of the twenty-first century a major catastrophe could occur on our planet. We may "hit the wall," as Katie sometimes says. What the nature of this catastrophe might be, we cannot be absolutely certain; however, I believe that much of the evidence points to a major solar outburst and plasma event—and based on the hard science that we have discussed throughout this book, the catastrophe could be imminent. It could occur today, tomorrow, or twenty years from now. We just do not know when.

But people want to know when. Human nature is uncomfortable with uncertainty. Certainty (supposed certainty), even if based on ill-founded knowledge, is preferable to the human psyche compared to uncertainty. Some have found the certainty they seek in ancient prophecies, particularly those attributed to the Mayan culture of Central America.

The Maya were a highly advanced people living primarily in what is now southern Mexico, the Yucatan Peninsula, and the area of Guatemala, Belize, El Salvador, and Honduras, although their cultural influence spread much farther. The Maya possessed a sophisticated civilization that featured writing, incredible architectural achievements (including stone pyramids), and detailed astronomical knowledge. The "classic" Mayan period dates from about 250 CE to 900 CE, but Mayan origins can be traced back to at least the middle of the third millennium BCE, and the civilization lasted up until European contact in the early sixteenth century. Indeed, the Mayan peoples are still with us to this day.

The Maya (and Mesoamericans more generally) used different calendars to keep track of different types of events and different lengths of time. The Calendar Round, which had a cycle of fifty-two years (approximately the lifetime of an individual), was used for many everyday purposes. The Long Count calendar was applied to long periods of time and various historical and pseudohistorical or mythological events; this is the calendar that ties in with the 2012 date popularized in some Western circles as the potential end of Earth, or at least the end of life as we know it. Just as we have days, months, and years, the Maya used five basic units for their Long Count calendar (Jenkins 2006): *kin* = 1 day, *uinal* = 20 days, *tun* = 360 days, *katun* = 7,200 days, and *baktun* = 144,000 days. After each period of thirteen baktuns (also referred to as *b'ak'tuns;* each baktun is approximately 394.25 years), according to one interpretation of the tradition, the calendar reset to zero and began again. Thirteen baktuns composed a "world age," and at the reset point the Maya believed an old world age came to an end, and a new world age or creation began. According to Richard Heinberg, "The Mayans counted their world ages as consecutive Suns—Water Sun, Earthquake Sun, Hurricane Sun, and Fire Sun—according to the nature of the catastrophe that closed the epoch" (Heinberg 1989, 62). These are referred to as the Mayan Sun Cycles.

By one interpretation of the Mayan legends, we are currently coming to the end of the Fifth Sun or Age, and this Age will end with global destruction by fire and earthquakes. The previous Age, the Fourth Sun, ended in cataclysmic destruction caused by a worldwide flood, which was followed by a new creation inaugurating the Fifth Sun (Lehman 2008). The last creation took place on (according to standard accepted correlations between the Mayan calendar and the current Gregorian calendar) August 11, 3114 BCE (the so-called start date of the Mayan calendar), and the last day of the thirteenth baktun since then fell on December 21, 2012. Thus, the present world age, the Fifth Sun, having lasted just over 5,125 years, should have come to an end. What, if anything, was supposed to happen on that day or the next was the big question that was on many people's minds as we approached December 21, 2012. The day came and went, and apparently not much occurred. I happened to be in Egypt at the time; there was no better place to be, from my perspective, just in case the world had come to an end.

The date of December 21, 2012 (a Friday) corresponded to the winter solstice in the Northern Hemisphere. That the Maya picked this as the "end point" of their calendar may not be insignificant. On the winter solstice the Sun is at its lowest in the sky and the daylight time is the shortest of the year. This is in concert with the imagery of a catastrophe, but to me it did not necessarily mean that a catastrophe would hit precisely on December 21, 2012. In my opinion, the end point of the Mayan calendar could be a metaphor and warning for that which is imminent, but not a precise prediction of when the catastrophe will occur.

Paul LaViolette placed some credence in the possibility that the end date of the Mayan calendar, conventionally accepted as December 21, 2012 CE, in the Gregorian calendar (but this date has been questioned, as we will discuss later in this chapter), might well mark some type of cataclysmic and catastrophic event; in particular, according to LaViolette (2009), the arrival of a galactic superwave (as discussed in chapter 9). Tying the Mayan calendar to modern science, LaViolette pointed to a minor ^{10}Be spike in the ice core record from Vostok (East Antarctica) dated to circa 3300 +/− 200 BCE that may represent a "relatively minor" galactic superwave and may also correlate with the 3114 BCE date marking the beginning of the Mayan calendar.

I should also point out that there is evidence of abrupt climate change at approximately 3200 BCE in the ice core record of Kilimanjaro (eastern equatorial Africa; see Thompson et al. 2002). With the Vostok [10]Be spike in mind, LaViolette suggested, "The Maya may have designed their calendar not only to mark the date of arrival of this past superwave, but also to predict when the next one might come" (LaViolette 2009, 12).

LaViolette went on to compare the 5,125-year cycle of the Maya (LaViolette referred to it as a 5,124-year cycle) to the 5,750 +/− 100-year cycle he found in the [10]Be record or possibly a slightly shorter potential cycle of 5,400 years that he and his group detected with much less certainty. It goes without saying that if both the Maya and their modern interpreters are correct, the next catastrophe (whether the arrival of a galactic superwave and/or a major solar outburst) is just around the corner.

But were the Maya even intending to predict a coming catastrophe? Were they aware of, or taking particular note of, solar-related events and the like? The answers to these questions run the range from one extreme to another.

Many modern researchers predicted that the year 2012 would mark major changes on Earth. Catastrophic, apocalyptic, doomsday scenarios proliferated: volcanic and earthquake activity, a reversal of Earth's magnetic poles, or a change in the spin axis of Earth with devastating results as the ocean basins readjusted and the crust of Earth crumpled like a piece of paper wadded into a ball. As society collapsed under the stress, the fabled Armageddon would be upon us, as foretold by prophecies of the American Hopi Indians, the biblical book of Revelation, the sibylline books of ancient Rome, and the quatrains of Nostradamus.

Major catastrophic changes are part of Earth history. Sixty-five million years ago the world changed forever and the dinosaurs were wiped out when an asteroid crashed off the coast of the Yucatan Peninsula of Mexico (Alvarez et al. 1980; Yarris 2010). Closer to our time, Earth apparently had a close encounter with a comet in the sixth century CE, causing the major climate changes, crop failures, famines, plagues, and devastation that sparked the Dark Ages (Schoch with McNally 2003). Indeed, we can document a series of comet events and solar outbursts occurring over thousands of years, and one such major event is recorded at roughly 3150 BCE (whether it was a comet impact or a solar outburst is uncertain), which coincides closely with the start of the Mayan calendar in 3114 BCE. Could the end of the Mayan calendar in 2012 CE mark the catastrophe that will bring our destruction? Or so some asked. By my own calculations, based on the semiperiodicity of cometary bombardments in the past (see Schoch with McNally 2003), we might expect a major comet to intersect Earth's orbit around 2012 to 2035. However, as we now know, it is not just comets and asteroids that we should fear. The Sun itself could be the cause of a major catastrophe. Or perhaps a comet hitting the Sun could initiate a major solar outburst.

The Maya were dedicated and meticulous astronomers, and they developed (or possibly inherited) a sophisticated astronomy and calendrical system, the subtleties and nuances of which I suspect are still not fully understood or appreciated to this day. The Mayan astronomers would have certainly noted any unusual events in the skies, but unfortunately, few Mayan texts and records have survived. One Mayan book that has come down to us is the Popol Vuh, the sacred Mayan book of creation (sometimes translated as "The Book of the People"), which survived only because the original Mayan hieroglyphic version (see Saravia 1984), now lost, was transcribed using the Spanish alphabet in the sixteenth century. (The Popol Vuh was still in the native language even after transcription.) Members of the lineages that had once, before the Spanish incursion, ruled the region carried out this work in the town of Quiché, northwest of modern Guatemala City. Even their transcription survives only as a later copy. Between 1701 and 1703 the friar and priest Francisco Ximénez was able to study the manuscript. Fortunately, he took the time to copy it and also provided a Spanish translation (Tedlock 1986, 27–30).

In the Popol Vuh are references to past creations and catastrophes, and some of the language is strongly suggestive of solar outbursts and associated phenomena. Dennis Tedlock provides this translation:

Again there comes a humiliation, destruction, and demolition. The manikins, woodcarvings ["the first numerous people here on the face of earth"] were killed when the Heart of Sky devised a flood for them. A great flood was made; it came down on the heads of the manikins, woodcarvings [that is, the people of the time] . . . they were killed, done in by a flood: There came a rain of resin from the sky. . . . The earth was blackened because of this; the black rainstorm began, rain all day and rain all night. (Tedlock 1986, 84; material in brackets added by R. Schoch based on Tedlock's analysis)

LaViolette (2009, 11) speculates that the Heart of Sky (which he refers to as the Heart of Heaven) might be a reference to the galactic core. I wonder if the "rain of resin" falling from the sky might reference powerful auroral displays and plasma phenomena as well as the dust, debris, and conflagrations that would accompany them. In particular, could the rain of resin be a description of the extraterrestrial dust and spherules jettisoned from the collapsing magnetosphere raining down onto Earth? (See discussion in chapter 7, page 154.)

In another section of the Popol Vuh, we read:

And when the war befell the canyons and citadels, it was by means of their genius that the Lord Plumed Serpent and the Lord Cotuha blazed with power. Plumed Serpent became a true lord of genius:

On one occasion he would climb up to the sky; on another he would go down the road to Xilbalba [the underworld of Mayan mythology].

On another occasion he would be serpentine, becoming an actual serpent.

On yet another occasion he would make himself aquiline, and on another feline; he would become like an actual eagle or a jaguar in his appearance.

On another occasion it would be a pool of blood; he would become nothing but a pool of blood.

Truly his being was that of a lord of genius. All the other lords were fearful before him. The news spread; all the tribal lords heard about the existence of the lord of genius. (Tedlock 1986, 212–13; material in brackets added by R. Schoch)

This can be interpreted as auroral displays and plasma configurations, described as serpents, eagles, jaguars, and ultimately a pool of blood, morphing from one shape into another, as would actually be seen in the sky during a particularly powerful solar outburst. This description, although from a different cultural context (and by the time it was copied or recorded in final form it may have undergone some modifications, making it less purely descriptive of the natural phenomena it was originally based on), is remarkably similar to the descriptions of powerful auroral phenomena from the time of Ezekiel to modern times. It also fits the imagery of the ancient petroglyphs and the rongorongo script.

According to John Major Jenkins (1964–2017), who studied Mayan cosmology intensively and in particular the cosmology relative to Mayan beliefs about the end of one "world age" after a time period of thirteen baktuns, "Each period ending in the Long Count, including all the various place value levels, were seen to be like-in-kind replays of the great period-ending event that occurs at the end of the 13-Baktun period. As such, the next 13-Baktun period-ending (in 2012) should be a big replay of the events described for 3114 BCE. That scenario involves the rebirth of the Sun Lord from the sky-earth cleft" (Jenkins 2006).

Furthermore, according to Jenkins, "The texts associated with these Creation monuments state that 'Creation happens at the Black Hole,' at 'the Crossroads,' and 'the image' will appear in the sky. At that time, a new Solar Age begins and the Sun Lord gets reborn" (Jenkins 2006).

Jenkins did not believe, however, that these Mayan references to the Sun and its rebirth are indicative of a catastrophic event such as a major solar outburst. His interpretation was very different, and he backed it up with both modern astronomy and direct interpretation of the Mayan texts and monuments. Jenkins (2010) pointed out that on the solstice date of December 21, 2012 (the date when the path of the Sun reaches its lowest point below the celestial equator, marking the beginning of winter in the Northern Hemisphere), the Sun would be in alignment (as viewed from Earth) with the plane of our Milky Way galaxy, that is, the galactic equator (which in the sky is marked by a dark rift in the Milky Way). This point is essentially at the nuclear bulge of the galaxy, which in turn is very close to the galactic center or core. Thus, the 2012 galactic alignment can be thought of loosely as the alignment of our Sun with the galactic center. As Jenkins himself pointed out, it is difficult to pinpoint precisely when the December solstice Sun would be precisely aligned with the galactic equator, and there is more or less an "alignment zone" some years or even a decade or more on either side of 2012 CE. However, the December solstice Sun is certainly not always involved in such an alignment.

Due to the phenomenon known as precession, the background stars in the sky slowly shift relative to the equatorial coordinate system used to map their positions. But this slow drift, generally attributed to a long-term "wobble" in the spin axis of Earth (although there are other explanations, such as the idea that our Sun has a companion star; see Cruttenden 2006), is very slow indeed, taking nearly twenty-six thousand years to complete a full cycle. Another way of saying this is that the position of the Sun on the December solstice (as well as on the June solstice and the equinoxes in March and September) slowly moves through the sky relative to the background stars, including the Milky Way. Thousands of years ago the December solstice Sun was well away from the Milky Way on one side, and thousands of years from now it will be well away on the other side of the Milky Way—again viewed from the perspective of an observer on Earth. Jenkins contended that the Mayan calendar was engineered to complete the thirteenth baktun, counting from the 3114 BCE beginning of the cycle, at the exact date of the December 2012 solstice galactic alignment. This certainly suggests some very sophisticated and precise astronomical observations and calculations.

But what is the significance of the galactic alignment? According to Jenkins (2010), the Maya believed that the 2012 galactic alignment would correspond to a great transformation on Earth. But this transformation is not to be found in the outer physical world, but rather the inner world, the soul. Jenkins summarized this view by writing, *"2012 bodes a challenge and an opportunity for humanity to rebirth itself.* Such a transformational rebirth can only be accomplished through sacrifice, sacrificing the illusions that bind us to states of suffering and limitation. We can reconnect with the higher source, our true selves, the centre and source of the world. This invitation is reflected in the galactic alignment, our Sun's rare alignment with the cosmic heart and source (symbolised by the galactic centre)" (Jenkins 2010; italics in the original).

Jenkins is certainly not the only person to suggest that the 2012 date may signify mental awakening and spiritual transformation rather than doomsday, as we transition to a higher level of consciousness. To take an extreme (in my view incredulous) example, David Wilcock, who claims to be the reincarnation of the American psychic Edgar Cayce (1877–1945), long suggested that some kind of spiritual or psychic transformation would take place in 2012. To quote from his website (as posted prior to December 2012, and there one could also find the "evidence" to support the contention that Wilcock is the reincarnated Cayce):

After the full completion of the Solar/Precessional/Galactic Cycle in late 2012, the Earth will no longer remain as a third-density planet. . . .

Together, we will clean, repair and renew the Earth with our newfound telekinetic abilities. One sweep of a hand will purify an entire polluted lake or river, or transform a festering garbage dump into rich soil. The crumbling ruins of city skyscrapers will sprout up into bold and beautiful trees, and the oceans will burst with fish, dolphins and whales.

Everyone will be telepathic, and no one will be able to hide anything from each other. Flying and psychic teleportation from one spot to another will also be possible, although we might not try to develop these abilities at first, not realizing that we now have them. . . . We will also regain membership in the Confederation of Planets in Service of the One Infinite Creator, our own "local" group in the Galaxy. This will give us the ability to travel among the stars and meet with other planetary cultures. . . .

Our neurological and spiritual capabilities will be so dramatically enhanced that it is not quite possible for us to really comprehend what it is going to feel like until we actually arrive there. The euphoria and bliss of day-to-day existence will be nearly fathomless in its depth. (Wilcock 1999/2009)

For some, this foreseen shift in consciousness was to be associated with physical global cataclysmic changes on Earth as well (see Joseph 2008). Spiritual enlightenment and physical catastrophes are not mutually exclusive! Wilcock noted, "The Earth will already have been cleansed from its magnetic pole shift/crustal displacement as the Grid realigns itself with the instreaming fourth-dimensional vibrations. This 'pole shift' will remove much of the traces of modern civilization from the Earth's surface" (Wilcock 1999/2009).

For others, such as Jenkins, the shift was to be much more subtle and related to more subtle cosmic events. As we have seen, due to the precession of the equinoxes, on the winter solstice of 2012, the rising Sun was aligned with the galactic center of our galaxy. Scientific analysis has found that the relationship between the galactic center and Earth's horizon relative to a person's location on Earth affects cognitive performance and psychic abilities (see Bremseth 2008, as well as further discussion in chapter 14, page 269). Perhaps the 2012 galactic alignment, some suggested, could have influenced the general level of consciousness worldwide.

A shift in global consciousness could also be indicated by the changing world ages. According to my analyses, using the vernal equinox as viewed from Egypt specifically, the transition from the Age of Pisces (an age of belief) to that of Aquarius (an age of knowledge) occurred around the year 2012 (give or take a decade or so). ("Belief" and "Knowledge" are astrological keywords associated with Pisces and Aquarius, respectively.)

Or perhaps the 2012 shift in consciousness would be sparked by a message from another civilization, or so it was suggested in certain quarters. Some predicted that extraterrestrials or otherworldly beings would reveal advanced knowledge to us lowly humans (see Wilcock 1999/2009, for instance). Others suggested the civilization we need to learn from is one that existed very long ago.

HALLS OF RECORDS:
THE HAWARA LABYRINTH

How could an ancient civilization communicate with us today? They could have left messages in their myths and calendars (as the Maya may have done), they could have encoded them into the remains of temples and monuments (many a person has attempted to decode the Great Pyramid of Giza, Egypt, in a search for ancient knowledge; see Schoch and McNally 2005), or they could have left explicit records in a hidden and secure place.

Many writers have popularized the concept of a hall of records that stores the advanced knowledge of a long-lost civilization, be it that of Atlantis or some other ancient culture of high achievements. The still-unopened chamber under the paws of the Great Sphinx that my colleagues and I found using seismic techniques has been hailed as just such a hall of records. But this is not the only possible location for a hall of records in Egypt. Enter the mystery of Hawara and the labyrinth.

In Greek mythology, Daedalus (known for crafting wings with which to fly) built a maze-like structure known as the Labyrinth on Crete to contain the Minotaur (part man, part bull). But the Cretan labyrinth was not the only one, or even the original labyrinth. Herodotus (fifth century BCE) and other Greek and Roman writers described a magnificent labyrinth in Egypt, containing three thousand rooms on two levels. Pliny the Elder (first century CE) related that the Egyptian labyrinth was already 3,600 years old in his time.

Since the nineteenth century, the Egyptian labyrinth has been identified with an area on the southern side of the Middle Kingdom mud-brick (originally sheathed with limestone) pyramid of Amenemhet III (late nineteenth century BCE) at Hawara. It was here that I traveled with an NBC crew in March 2009 to help shoot a television documentary.

What I found at Hawara, besides the pyramid, was an area of approximately seventy-five thousand square meters littered with the remains of pottery, human bones, fragments of stone sculptures, pieces of limestone and granite columns, and blocks of carved quartzite. Here some mighty structure once stood, but little remains. Much of the ancient labyrinth was pillaged thousands of years ago, during Ptolemaic and Roman times, as a ready source of building stone. Still, there are signs that something more might remain deeply buried in the ground. Geophysical studies by the Egyptian National Research Institute of Astronomy and Geophysics have suggested there are structures remaining to be discovered under the sands of Hawara (Khalil et al. 2010).

To my dismay, there is now a canal running near the Hawara pyramid and right through the area of the labyrinth. I attempted to enter

Figure 13.1. The area of the reputed ancient labyrinth at Hawara (*top*); the base of a large stone column (set on its edge for display) in the foreground and the Hawara pyramid in the background (*bottom left*); and the entrance to the Hawara pyramid showing the megalithic stone structure under the mud-bricks (*bottom right*). (Photographs courtesy of R. Schoch and C. Ulissey.)

the pyramid, but before I could get very far, the passage was entirely blocked by mud and water. I fear that whatever remains of the labyrinth, buried deep below the surface, is now also flooded by the elevated water table.

And what exactly was the Hawara labyrinth? One interpretation is that it contained and protected, in its maze of courtyards, passageways, and chambers (which Herodotus relates as being covered with inscriptions), the most important and sacred knowledge possessed by the Egyptians—knowledge possibly acquired from a still earlier civilization, perhaps one that had experienced cataclysmic events.

Does the core of the labyrinth remain, waiting to be uncovered? Perhaps it contains the knowledge we need as we face the uncertainty of the future. I just do not know, but I believe the Hawara labyrinth merits further exploration, and time is of the essence, but it is not the only place that a reputed hall of records may be located.

HALLS OF RECORDS:
THE CHAMBER UNDER THE SPHINX

As I mentioned in chapter 2, back in the early 1990s geophysicist Thomas Dobecki and I carried out seismic surveys around and under the Sphinx to measure the depth of subsurface weathering (Dobecki and Schoch 1992; Schoch and Bauval 2017). The depth of subsurface weathering confirmed my dating of the Sphinx, but we found more besides. Under the Sphinx are two major cavities or chambers and a tunnel-like feature. There is a cavity under the left rear haunch. Under the left front paw there is a large rectangular chamber. This chamber has received much attention for, as I discussed in chapter 2, the late, great American psychic Edgar Cayce predicted that a hall of records containing information from the lost civilization of Atlantis would be found in this area. Dobecki and I also found a tunnel-like structure running under and along the length of the body of the Sphinx, from the rear of the statue to the chamber under the left paw.

For decades, I believed the original Great Sphinx may have been a male African lion; we now have evidence that it was a female lion, a lioness (see chapter 15, page 314). Previously, wildly speculating, I suggested (Schoch 2012b, 214) that "perhaps the tunnel under the body represents an erect phallus, universally a potent symbol. In mating, the male lion mounts the female from behind, and we can envision this in the Lion-Sphinx. The seed of the phallus is directed toward the chamber, the hall of records, under the left paw. So how might we interpret this symbolism?" However, given the evidence that the original Great Sphinx was a lioness, who would not have had a penis, I retract this speculation.

Imagine a highly advanced civilization, one that existed a very, very long time ago, but is now lost. Perhaps this primordial civilization seeded other civilizations, including the one that ultimately gave rise to us. But memories fade quickly, especially in the formative years. How much does the typical adult recollect from his or her earliest years? This is why parents sometimes preserve baby books for their children—scrapbooks or memory books of precious photographs and mementos, the history of a child and the child's family and ancestry. As an act of love, did the founding civilization put together a scrapbook for its children? For future civilizations to come? For us? Is this the prophesied hall of records, under the left paw of the Sphinx? And why the left paw? The heart is on the left. Perhaps there is a correlation here, one of love.

If the Lioness-Sphinx seeded our civilization and protects our memory book, it may also encode further secrets. The Lioness-Sphinx, carved of stone in times immemorial, is aligned with the cosmos and perhaps points to a location in the heavens. In the night sky the lion is Leo. Astrologically, the Sun is the ruler of Leo, and Leo rules the heart. Regulus, the most regal of the Royal Stars, the star of honor and dignity, is at the breast and heart of Leo. The Lioness-Sphinx faces due east, and on the vernal equinox in about 9000 BCE the Sun was in conjunction with Regulus and Venus (representing, among other things, love), and they all rose together that morning as the Lioness-Sphinx faced the rising Sun. What is the Lioness-Sphinx telling us? Should we look toward Regulus for answers? Does Regulus in the sky correspond to the chamber, the hall of records, our ancestry, humanity's inheritance?

Figure 13.2. Seismic velocity map beneath the Great Sphinx as
determined by refraction tomography. The outline of the Sphinx is shown
as a dashed line and the chamber under the left paw is labeled A.
(Illustration courtesy of R. Schoch and C. Ulissey.)

Perhaps I am venturing into dangerous territory. As an individual
with a curious mind, I can entertain outrageous scenarios. But as a scientist, I must stick with the data, and so I go no further.

HOW ACCURATE IS THE
MAYAN CALENDAR?

An issue that must be addressed is whether the Mayan calendar has
been accurately correlated with the modern Gregorian calendar. Does
the last day of the thirteenth baktun really correspond to December 21,
2012? The most commonly used correlation today, which is the one that
comes up with the December 21, 2012, end date, is known as the GMT
correlation, named after the initials of the three researchers involved:

Joseph Goodman, Juan Martinez-Hernandez, and John Eric Sydney Thompson. This standard correlation dates back to the first third of the twentieth century. The GMT correlation is linked to astronomical events recorded by the Maya, and when precisely these events occurred, as a way to synchronize the Mayan and modern Gregorian calendars. If the astronomical events are misdated or misidentified, then the correlation is called into question (O'Neill 2010).

Gerardo Aldana (University of California, Santa Barbara) had doubts about the GMT correlation; in particular, he questioned the accuracy of modern interpretations of some of the Mayan astronomical observations (Physorg.com 2011b; *Santa Barbara Independent* 2010; Heussner 2010). For instance, in one case a certain Mayan reference has generally been assumed to refer to the planet Venus (one aspect of the Mayan calendar relied heavily on the cycles of Venus), but it may in fact refer to a meteor. If such is the case, it throws the standard GMT correlation into doubt. Aldana points out a number of reasons why the GMT correlation may not be accurate, although he does not propose a new correlation. If the standard correlation is off (although it is not yet proven that this is the case; Jenkins [2011] presented strong evidence supporting the GMT correlation), then how much off might it be? How inaccurate might the December 21, 2012, date be? Possibly it is off only on the order of sixty days (O'Neill 2010), or possibly it is off by up to a century (Longo 2010). For some, this possible inaccuracy in the Mayan calendar correlation will serve as an excuse and rationale to dismiss the entire "2012 issue" as New Age nonsense. In my opinion it is a nonissue since I have never taken the precise date, or year, as definitive. Rather, as I explained at the beginning of this chapter, for me the significance of 2012 is that something will happen! Whether the catastrophe hits in 2025, 2037, or 2050, we would do well to be prepared.

2012 IN NEW ZEALAND AND ELSEWHERE

Lawrence E. Joseph (2008, 211) relates a Maori (New Zealand) legend that supposedly includes the date of 2012. Rangi (the Sky) and Papa (the

Earth) will in the future come back together, and in the process will hold each other so tight that their children (humanity) will be caught between them. The children, after struggling mightily to push Rangi and Papa apart, will quarrel and bicker among themselves. Ultimately the fighting will consume the children, and Rangi and Papa will reunite once again, destroying humanity and everything else that gets crushed between them. Just before this final destruction, however, a canoe will come down from the heavens to save those few people who are spiritually deserving.

And when will this coming together of the Sky and the Earth happen? Lo and behold, the Maori elders (who refused to go on record, but passed the knowledge on to Joseph) stated that it would begin in 2012. But, and it is a big but, it is not at all clear that this legend is really of an ancient and indigenous origin. According to Joseph, "A number of Maori myths and legends turn out to have been created in the early nineteenth century by Western anthropologists who visited New Zealand and either grossly misconstrued or outright invented ersatz tales that were gradually incorporated into Maori lore" (Joseph 2008, 211).

Generations later such stories have become interwoven with the pre-European contact cultural attributes, and it can be difficult or impossible to tease out what is original. This is a problem around the world when attempting to collect "ancient" traditions supposedly passed down from generation to generation verbally and now revealed to the too-often gullible Westerner by the eager-to-please "elder," "wisdom keeper," "shaman," or the like (who often expects, or even demands, some form of remuneration in exchange for imparting her or his knowledge). In the case of the Maori legend, I have a difficult time believing that they independently came up with the date of 2012, or anything even close to such a date.

The Hopis and Cherokees, being native North American peoples who could easily have been influenced by their brothers and sisters to the south in Mesoamerica, are another matter. However, I remain skeptical that their stories of either an end to the world as we know it or our emergence into a new world age in 2012 (and some say precisely on December 21, 2012) are anything more than modern New Age hubbub infiltrating the native lore, although there are apparently genuine indigenous legends of world ages—even if not necessarily mentioning 2012—among these groups (Heinberg 1989; Witzel 2012). My feeling is the same about the Q'ero Indians of Peru. Supposedly their lore stated that time itself would cease in 2012 (Joseph 2008, 210), but then perhaps they did share this notion, or at least the 2012 date, with the Maya in pre-Columbian times. At this point we just do not know, but I would not put a lot of stock in it.

What I do put a lot of stock in is that the ancients were neither stupid nor ignorant. They knew things that we no longer know. They had an understanding and awareness of the cosmos that we have either forgotten or lost. I believe there is something genuine in the concept of ancient wisdom, something that perhaps is just beginning to be rediscovered by a few scientists, philosophers, scholars, and visionaries of the modern world. Let us now turn our attention to some cutting-edge developments in science that may shed light on the ancient mysteries.

UPDATE: It has now been demonstrated that, as I have believed for a long time, some (but certainly not all—one must be careful and use discretion, critical analysis, and sound judgment) "myths" and "traditions" date back thousands of years, and even back to the end of the last ice age. For instance, summarizing their studies of indigenous Australian stories, Nicholas Reid et al. (2014) write:

> Can preliterate Indigenous languages tell us anything factual about the distant past, or does the transmission of historical facts become inevitably corrupted? Changes in sea levels around the Australian coast are now well established. Marine geographers can now point to specific parts of the Australian coast and know with some confidence what the sea levels were at a particular time before the present. This paper reports on a substantial body of Australian Aboriginal stories that appear to represent genuine and unique observations of post-glacial increases in sea level, at time depths that range from about 13,400–7,500 years BP. This paper makes the case that

endangered Indigenous languages can be repositories for factual knowledge across time depths far greater than previously imagined, forcing a rethink of the ways in which such traditions have been dismissed.

(For further details on these studies, see Reid 2015, Reid and Nunn 2015.)

14

ANCIENT WISDOM, NEW DISCOVERIES, AND NEW SCIENCE

According to ancient and traditional teachings—the perennial wisdom—we ("we" as individuals, "we" in terms of humanity, and "we" in the sense of life as a whole) are an intimate part of the universe. We are not isolated from each other or from Earth and the cosmos. We are connected; we are tethered to the cosmos. This simple yet profound notion, ultimately, is the essence of much ancient wisdom; it is the core message of the sages of old. The microcosm and the macrocosm are reflections of each other and united at the most fundamental level. The Hermetic teachings proclaim, "As is the Inner so is the Outer; as is the Great so is the Small; as it is Above, so it is Below: there is but one Life and Law" (Hermetic postulate, as quoted by Bowen [1936?], 31).

Another common ancient tradition, found across many cultures worldwide, is that of cycles of time, life, and humanity (Godwin 2010; Selbie and Steinmetz 2010; Witzel 2012). This is expressed in various ways: the concept of the Golden, Silver, Bronze, and Iron Ages; the Yuga Cycle of Hindu traditions; or the zodiacal precessional ages. Two key points of this ancient teaching must be emphasized:

1. These cycles materially, mentally, and spiritually impact humanity; that is, we are not immune to the larger influences of nature and the cosmos.

2. There have been other ages, and there will be more in the future, some better and some worse than the present age. Indeed, ancient traditions agree that we are currently far from a "golden age" (Heinberg 1989); rather, most such traditions would place us in an age of coarse materialism with diminished mental and psychic abilities and a lack of understanding of that which is genuinely important.

Modern science, and society at large, has often downplayed or outright dismissed such ancient traditions. The individual has been viewed as supreme, inviolate, and isolated from other individuals. Many "modern and educated" people believe that the thoughts in one's own head, if not acted on physically, stay in one's head. That is, psychic phenomena such as telepathy (direct mind-to-mind interactions without the use of the normal senses) do not and cannot occur, despite the overwhelming evidence to the contrary (see Bem 2011; Bremseth 2008; Burns 2003; de Martino 1972; de Vesme 1931a, 1931b; Laszlo 2003, 2004; Myers 1903; Owen with Sparrow 1976; Utts 1991; Schoch and Yonavjak 2008). Likewise, many members of society today consider these times, with our modern sophisticated technology, to be the height of civilization. For them it is nonsense to think that any society or people of antiquity could have been in any way more knowledgeable than we, at least collectively, are today (whether it be technological knowledge, philosophical insight, religious revelation, or mental and psychical abilities). Even more ridiculous, according to such thinking, is the notion that we are somehow linked to the cosmos and subject to cycles, ebbs, and flows beyond our control. It often seems to me that the hubris of modern society knows no bounds.

As we have seen already, Earth (and therefore all life on Earth) is very much subject to the vagaries of our Sun, and more generally our galaxy and universe. But it is not just on the macroscopic and materialistic scales that we are tied, tethered, to our Sun, solar system, galaxy, and cosmos. There is evidence that at an even deeper level the macrocosm impacts directly the microcosm. Unbeknownst to the average person, or even the average scientist, new discoveries are being made in both the physical and biological sciences, discoveries that stand to upend the very foundations of modern conventional ways of thinking. These new findings confirm the truth of both mystical revelations and the tenets of ancient wisdom, that we are inescapably linked to each other and to larger cycles that we as yet cannot fully comprehend. Let's take a look at some major discoveries.

BREAKING UP THE PARTY:
THE NONCONSTANCY OF RADIOACTIVE DECAY

Certain forms of atoms, known as radioactive isotopes, are inherently unstable and are said to undergo radioactive decay when they spontaneously break down into smaller constituent particles. The instability of a radioactive isotope is due to too many particles (protons and neutrons) being squeezed into the center of the atom (the nucleus) when it was originally formed, either at the time of the origin of the known material universe or subsequently, such as when elements are synthesized in the center of a star or form from colliding particles during a supernova explosion. Think of a holiday party in a small apartment with too many friends packed into a confined space. As much as everyone might initially enjoy the gathering, over time the situation becomes uncomfortable, with elbows poking into ribs, voices forming a cacophonous chorus that drowns out any individual conversation, and then even misunderstandings and hard feelings possibly arising. Eventually the party breaks up as individuals and small groups split off. The party disintegrates. Likewise, from the crowded center of a radioactive isotope, eventually individual particles and/or groups of particles are ejected (collectively known as the radiation given off by a radioactive isotope). How quickly the party ends, how quickly a given sample of a radioactive isotope breaks down, is commonly expressed in terms of the half-life (how long it takes for half of any sample to disintegrate) or decay rate (the longer the half-life, the lower the decay rate). For instance, radioactive plutonium-239 (^{239}Pu) has a half-life of approximately twenty-four thousand years, and radioactive carbon-14 (^{14}C) has a half-life of approximately 5,730 years.

Radioactive isotopes are more common, and thus of more profound importance, than many people realize. They are found not only in atomic bombs and nuclear power plants, but they also occur dispersed throughout the entire Earth and universe. Every living being and every material object contains some percentage of radioactive isotopes. A fundamental principle of modern nuclear physics is that the radioactive decay rate for any particular unstable isotope of an element is constant. This is the case whether the decay rate is based on a traditional experimental approach or calculated using the equations of quantum mechanics.

This constant decay rate is, according to establishment science, truly constant under all conditions and is independent of temperature, pressure, chemical environment, and so forth. (Established science does acknowledge a few exceptions to the general rule of constant decay rates, but they involve only certain types of radioactive decay when the atoms are subjected to, for instance, extremely strong electric fields, and these exceptions do not invalidate the general analysis discussed here.) Indeed, assuming the inviolate nature of decay rate constants, radioactive isotope decay has become a standard method of dating both geological specimens and archaeological artifacts. Carbon-14 (radiocarbon) dating, to give one example, is now one of the most commonly used methods to date everything from fragments of burned charcoal in a Late Stone Age fireplace to Egyptian mummies.

To question the presumed constancy of such constants as decay rates could not only suggest "that decades of established science is flawed" (Cartwright 2008), but could also call into question the absolute time frame, in terms of years into the past, of prehistory, and even of Earth and cosmic history. We might be forced to not only rethink our science, but to rethink our history as well.

In August 2008, physicists Jere Jenkins and Ephraim Fischbach, of Purdue University, burst on the scene with an incredible claim. Decay constants are not so constant! Through detailed analysis, they found that the decay rate of radioactive manganese-54 (^{54}Mn) fluctuates in correlation with solar flares (Jenkins and Fischbach 2008). And that was not all. It was also found that the decay rates of radioactive silicon-32 (^{32}Si) and radioactive radium-226 (^{226}Ra) vary over time and that the variations correlate with the changing distance between the Earth and the Sun (Jenkins et al. 2008). When the Earth is closest to the Sun (in January), the decay rate increases; when the Earth is farthest from the Sun (in July), the decay rate decreases.

These are incredible, absolutely astounding results with profound ramifications. Not only should decay rates be constant, according to conventional physics, but also if there is any inconstancy found, it should certainly not be due to solar flares or something as subtle as the changing distance between the Earth and the Sun. This would be the equivalent of suggesting that how quickly a holiday gathering in New York disperses is a function of how crowded the vegetable markets are in Shanghai.

Celestial mechanics influencing, or correlating with, fundamental physical processes on the surface of Earth! According to conventional wisdom, this is the stuff of medieval thinking, superstition, and astrology—wrongheaded and ignorant notions that were dismissed long ago. Either the data on varying decay rates are wrong or conventional establishment science is flawed. The stakes could not be higher. Thus, it is not surprising that the work of Jenkins, Fischbach, and colleagues found a cold reception among many mainstream physicists—primarily, it would seem, because the data and analysis threaten conventional thinking and worldviews. As physicsworld.com reporter Jon Cartwright wrote, "As more scientists hear about the claimed relation of decay constants to solar activity, reactions vary from disbelief to rejection. 'I don't understand this at all, what it could possibly be,' says John Barrow of Cambridge University. 'It's a gigantic effect. . . . It sounds as though it's related [to solar activity], but it really can't be'" (Cartwright 2008; material in brackets in the original article).

Why is it that "it really can't be"? Perhaps because it would overturn some of conventional scientists' most cherished notions about the world and universe and force them to rethink much of what they think they know.

Even more dismissive was David Wark of Imperial College London:

"If a student brought this to me I would advise them to understand their experiment before they start coming up with wild correlations of detector noise with natural phenomena picked at random" (Wark, quoted in Cartwright 2008).

The data used by Jenkins, Fischbach, and colleagues span some five years and fifteen years for silicon-32 and radium-226, respectively, and for these periods of time consistently, without exception, the data correlate with the orbit of Earth around the Sun. Jenkins, Fischbach, and colleagues even calculate formal probabilities that the correlations could be simply due to chance, with the result that the odds are astronomically low (6×10^{-18} and 1×10^{-29} for the respective data sets). Yet someone like Wark feels smug in publicly dismissing the data as "detector noise" that somehow just happens to appear to correlate with a fundamental natural phenomenon. In turn, Fischbach and colleagues (2009) have suggested that there may be natural mechanisms, such as the variations in the flux of neutrinos (or anti-neutrinos) from the Sun, that could have an effect on nuclear decay rates.

If correct, the work of Jenkins, Fischbach, and colleagues demonstrates a connection between one of the most fundamental processes known in physics, namely nuclear decay rates (which should, according to conventional science, be a result of quantum processes in the nucleus and unaffected by the external macroscopic world), and a very subtle cosmic influence, namely the orbit of the Earth around the Sun. Perhaps it is justifiable to question, and possibly even dismiss without more corroborative analysis, the radical implications of this work. Indeed, studies by other researchers have concluded that nuclear decay constants are indeed constant after all. Analyzing a large set of data at fourteen laboratories around the globe, S. Pommé (European Commission, Joint Research Centre, Belgium) and colleagues (2016, 5), concluded "The observed seasonal modulations can be ascribed to instrumental instability, since they vary from one instrument to another and show no communality in amplitude or phase among—or even within—the laboratories." But there are more data from a very different line of studies spanning over four decades that in fact support the findings of Jenkins, Fischbach, and colleagues.

TEETH ON THE BELL CURVE: FLUCTUATIONS
IN BASIC NATURAL PROCESSES

In 1998 the Russian biophysicist Simon E. Shnoll, of Moscow State University, and his colleagues published a groundbreaking paper (Shnoll et al. 1998; see also Shnoll 2006 and Tennenbaum 2000) summarizing forty years of detailed investigations into fundamental physical, chemical, and biological processes. Despite being published in a prominent Russian physics journal and also being translated into English, the work of Shnoll and colleagues has been largely ignored, perhaps because, if true, the implications are radical and far-reaching. Like the findings of Jenkins, Fischbach, and colleagues on varying radioactive decay rates, the work of Shnoll and his colleagues undermines the very foundations of much of modern science and has profound implications bearing on the nature of the universe, reality, and our place in the cosmos. Again, this is material that conventional scientists are, at first glance, inclined to dismiss as nonsense, but the data have been corroborated over and over again throughout many decades.

Shnoll and colleagues have studied the statistical distribution of the fluctuations in the decay rates of numerous radioactive isotopes as well as statistical variations in the rates of reaction of various different types of physical, chemical, and biological processes. These so-called fine structures of the decay rates and other processes, plotted as graphs, show a spread or scatter of data that by conventional established science is normally considered noise in the measurements, something to be eliminated or simply ignored rather than studied.

Think of a standard bell curve, then give it a jagged edge. By conventional thinking, as more and more measurements are taken of natural physical, chemical, and biological processes, the scatter or "roughness" (the jagged edge) of the data will decrease. When plotted using standard techniques, the data will fall on a smooth bell-shaped curve. However, putting conventional thinking to the test, Shnoll and colleagues have consistently found that more and better data of the natural processes they have studied do not smooth out the supposed noise, but rather definite patterns in the fine structure emerge. The curve that should, according to conventional science, be smooth is in fact rough. Picture the curve as having serrations or teeth on its surface, and furthermore, as more data are collected, the serrations become more distinct and pronounced. There is something going on here. There is a message in the fine structure, if only we can figure out what it says. Imagine a roulette wheel. Give it a spin, and any number on its face should have an equal chance of coming up. If certain numbers consistently appear more often than they should, we logically conclude it is not a fair wheel. Something is influencing it. Someone has tipped the roulette wheel toward certain numbers. Likewise, the work of Shnoll and his colleagues indicates that something unaccounted for by modern conventional science is influencing basic natural processes at the most fundamental level.

The implications of Shnoll's findings are profound. They call into question the entire concept of randomness in natural processes as currently understood by science and in particular as predicted by quantum physicists (see Tennenbaum 2000). The Shnoll findings indicate that modern conventional science does not fully understand the most basic natural processes and what subtle factors may influence them.

But the work of Shnoll and colleagues does not stop with simply finding consistent and repeatable patterns in the fine structures of various processes. Amazingly, the fine structures of very different and incredibly diverse processes have been found to correspond in their patterns when measured simultaneously, even at entirely different laboratories located at large geographic distances from one another. For instance, the beta activity of hydrogen-3 (^{3}H), the beta activity of carbon-14 (^{14}C), the alpha activity of plutonium-239 (^{239}Pu), the reaction rate of ascorbic acid and dichlorophenolindophenol, and the reaction time of water protons all showed similar fine structures (similar jagged edges) when measured simultaneously, yet the measurements were made in different contexts using different techniques. The last sentence may sound overwhelming to the uninitiated, but to put it into a more human context, ascorbic acid is commonly known as vitamin C, and how quickly it reacts is fundamental to human physiology (as well as that of many other organisms). Plutonium-239 atoms are highly radioactive, extremely deadly, and found in certain types of atomic bombs and nuclear power plants. Carbon-14 is found in all organisms, and it, like hydrogen-3 and protons in water, is scattered throughout Earth and indeed the known universe. Somehow, as amazing at it may appear, there are connections, or at least correlations, between the fundamental natural processes in us, plutonium-239 in a nuclear reactor, and protons in the water of the world's oceans.

Conventional establishment science has no cogent explanation for such connections, and indeed the standard way of dealing with such claims is to simply dismiss or ignore them out of hand. It is as if two identical roulette wheels, one in New York and another in Paris, were spun simultaneously and independently of each other, but each time they both came up with the same distribution of numbers. To make the analogy even more accurate, assume that the two roulette wheels are made out of different materials and are spun by different means (representing different processes), yet they still come up with the same results. The work of Shnoll and colleagues has been repeated and repeated over and over for many decades. It is robust and must no longer be ignored.

Perhaps the most important, puzzling, and profound aspect of the work of Shnoll and colleagues is that they have found that the fine structures of the processes they have studied vary consistently in correlation with astronomical cycles. This supports the work of Jenkins, Fischbach, and colleagues, but takes it even further. Shnoll and his colleagues have found periodicities in the fine structures that correspond to both the solar day (1,440 minutes) and the sidereal day (1,436 minutes; the time it takes Earth to make one full turn on its axis relative to the fixed stars rather than the Sun). They have also found periodicities of 27.3 days (corresponding to the sidereal month, the time it takes the Moon to return to the same position among the stars) and 365.25 days (the yearly cycle).

The reasons behind these correlations are obscure, but apparently they have something to do with more than just local effects. In this context, local can be defined as within our solar system. Correlations of fine structures with the sidereal day and the sidereal month indicate cosmological factors beyond our local solar system. This should not be the case according to conventional established science. As D. S. Chernavskii, editor of *Physics—Uspekhi,* in which the Shnoll et al. (1998) paper was published, commented, "It is demonstrated that the fine structures of histograms for quite diverse random processes (physical, chemical, biological, etc.) are similar and vary in sympathy. Moreover, these periodical changes correlate with the changes in our solar system, and possibly in our universe" (Chernavskii 1998, 1035).

Such findings appear to confirm, with new science, the ancient maxim, "As above, so below."

FLUCTUATING FIELDS: CONSCIOUSNESS AND THE COSMOS

It is not just physico-biological processes at the atomic and subatomic levels that are correlated with astronomical processes, but mental processes as well. The evidence is overwhelming that certain paranormal phenomena, such as spontaneous instances of telepathy, are real (see Bem 2011; Bremseth 2008; Burns 2003; de Vesme 1931a, 1931b; Laszlo 2003, 2004; Myers 1903; Owen with Sparrow 1976; Utts 1991; Schoch and Yonavjak 2008). Detailed analysis has demonstrated that spontaneous cases of such mental phenomena as telepathy and clairvoyance are correlated with geomagnetic fluctuations (Wilkinson and Gauld 1993). This is very interesting on numerous accounts. If telepathy and similar phenomena were not real, but rather a result of fraud and deception (including naïve self-deception), there is no reason to believe that reported incidences would correlate with the changing geomagnetic flux. Furthermore, the geomagnetic flux is affected by many parameters, not least of which are astronomical and cosmic factors (Mackey 2007).

Additionally, it has been found that paranormal mental phenomena are correlated with local sidereal time, which in turn is a function of one's relationship to the center of our galaxy (Bremseth 2008). These types of data demonstrate that mental activity and states of consciousness are correlated with cosmic factors. Again, the lesson is that we are connected in a most profound way with each other and the universe at large. This lesson applies whether one adopts a strict reductionism attitude (the belief that the mind is simply a function of the processes taking place in the material brain) or a dualism approach (the mind is, to at least some degree, independent of the material brain, but the brain may act as a filter for sensory and other input to the mind). Either way, the mind and consciousness, as well as the fundamental workings of physical, chemical, and biological processes in the material brain, are inextricably tethered to the larger world.

ELFS: TUNING IN TO THE EARTH

Another manner by which we are connected to each other and to the Earth at large is through extremely low-frequency (commonly referred to as ELF) electromagnetic waves. ELF waves are part of a continuum from very-high-frequency waves, such as gamma rays and X rays (with frequencies of over 10^{16} Hz [hertz; cycles or beats per second], that is a 1 followed by sixteen zeros!) through visible light (frequencies in the range of around 5×10^{14} Hz) to radio waves (frequencies below about 10^{11} Hz). ELF waves have frequencies on the order of only a few hundred Hz to less than 1 Hz (in some cases, ultra low-frequency [ULF] waves with frequencies below about 3 Hz are distinguished). Human brain wave activity falls within the ELF range, and it is now known that ELF waves can influence human electrophysiological signals (Cosic et al. 2006). The natural resonance of electromagnetic waves oscillating between the surface of Earth and the ionosphere peaks at various frequencies around 7.8, 14, 21, 26, 33, and 39 Hz (see Farmer and Hannan 2003; and Bliokh et al. 1980). These resonance frequencies, known as Schumann resonances, correlate with brain wave frequencies, and indeed humans can synchronize their own brains and consciousness with the Schumann frequencies (Hainsworth 1983; Miller and Miller 2003). On a personal note, I have found that sometimes I unconsciously shake my leg or tap my finger; crudely measuring the frequency of such movements, they are generally in the range of 3.8 to 4.0 Hz, that is, in harmony with Schumann resonances.

In deep meditation, slowing down the dominant brain wave frequency to synchronize and resonate with the dominant Schumann frequency of about 7.8 Hz allows the individual to tap into what might be referred to as the planetary frequency, or natural Earth frequency.

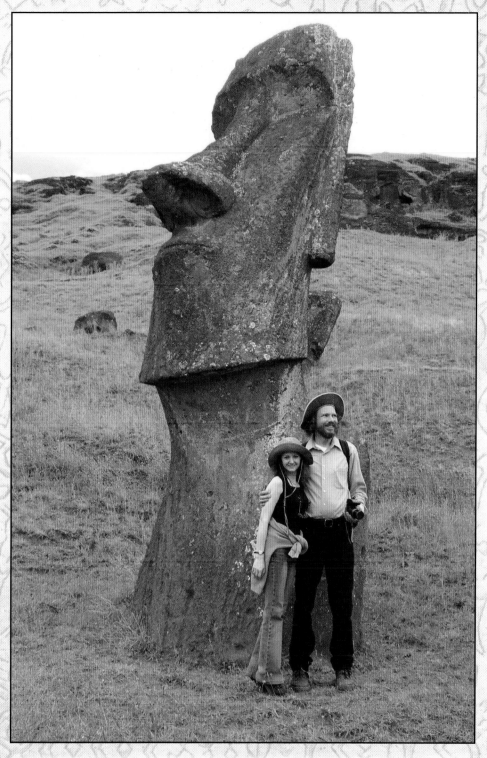

Plate 1. Catherine Ulissey and Robert Schoch standing
next to a moai at Rano Raraku, Easter Island, January 2010.
(Photograph courtesy of R. Schoch and C. Ulissey.)

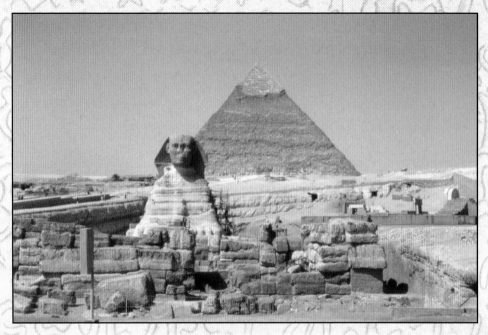

Plate 2. The Great Sphinx of Egypt, with the ruins of the Sphinx Temple in
the foreground and the Second Pyramid (attributed to Khafre) in the background.
Photograph taken by R. Schoch in the early 1990s.
(Photograph courtesy of R. Schoch.)

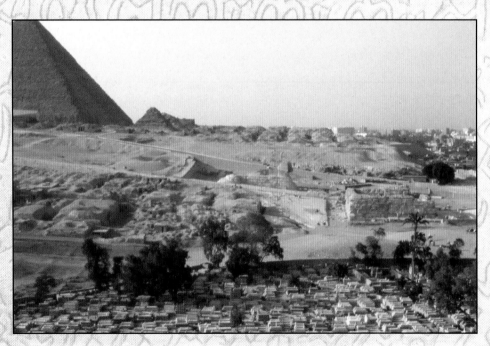

Plate 3. A side view of the east-facing Great Sphinx seen from the south,
with a portion of the Great Pyramid in the background.
Photograph taken by R. Schoch in the early 1990s.
(Photograph courtesy of R. Schoch.)

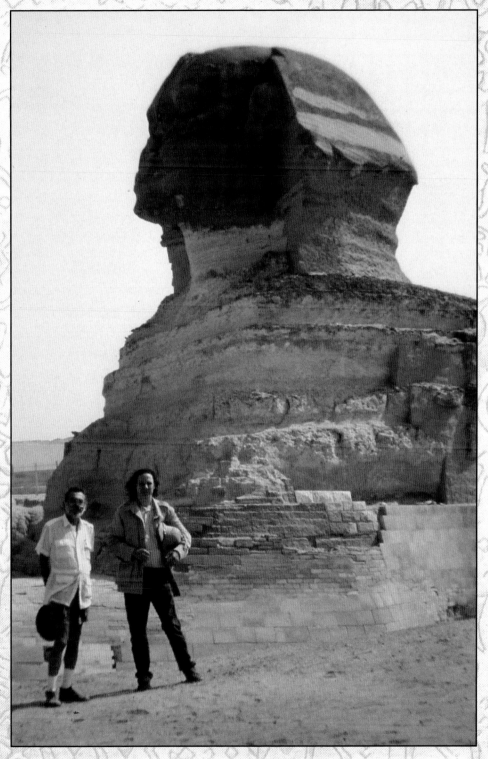
Plate 4. Early 1990s photograph of John Anthony West (*left*)
and Robert Schoch (*right*) standing in front of the Great Sphinx.
(Photograph courtesy of R. Schoch.)

Plate 5. Early dynastic mud-brick mastabas, circa 2800 BCE, on the Saqqara Plateau. In the background is the Step Pyramid (attributed to Djoser / Zoser). Photograph taken by R. Schoch in the early 1990s.
(Photograph courtesy of R. Schoch.)

Plate 6. View of the western end of the Sphinx Enclosure; the rear of the Sphinx is seen on the left and the two-tiered western wall on the right. Photograph taken by R. Schoch in the early 1990s.
(Photograph courtesy of R. Schoch.)

Plate 7. Precipitation-induced (rain) weathering and erosion on
the southern wall of the Sphinx Enclosure.
(Photograph courtesy of R. Schoch.)

Plate 8. Wind-induced weathering and erosion on Old Kingdom tombs,
Giza Plateau. Photograph taken by R. Schoch in the early 1990s.
(Photograph courtesy of R. Schoch.)

Plate 9. Overview of Göbekli Tepe, looking toward the south.
(Photograph courtesy of R. Schoch and C. Ulissey.)

Plate 10. View of Enclosure D at Göbekli Tepe, looking toward the southwest.
(Photograph courtesy of R. Schoch and C. Ulissey.)

Plate 11. Panoramic view (produced from a composite of several photos) of
Göbekli Tepe looking toward the northwest corner.
(Photograph courtesy of R. Schoch and C. Ulissey.)

Plate 12. Enclosure C at Göbekli Tepe, pillars and details.
(Photographs courtesy of R. Schoch and C. Ulissey.)

Plate 13. Various views of pillars at Göbekli Tepe.
(Photographs courtesy of R. Schoch and C. Ulissey.)

Plate 14. The statue of a man found in Urfa that is believed to
date back to the general time of Göbekli Tepe (*left*).
Robert Schoch beside the same exhibit at the Museum of Şanlıurfa (*right*).
(Photographs courtesy of R. Schoch and C. Ulissey.)

Plate 15. Details of pillars at Göbekli Tepe.
(Photographs courtesy of R. Schoch and C. Ulissey.)

Plate 16. Pillar 18 in Enclosure D of Göbekli Tepe.
(Photograph courtesy of R. Schoch and C. Ulissey.)

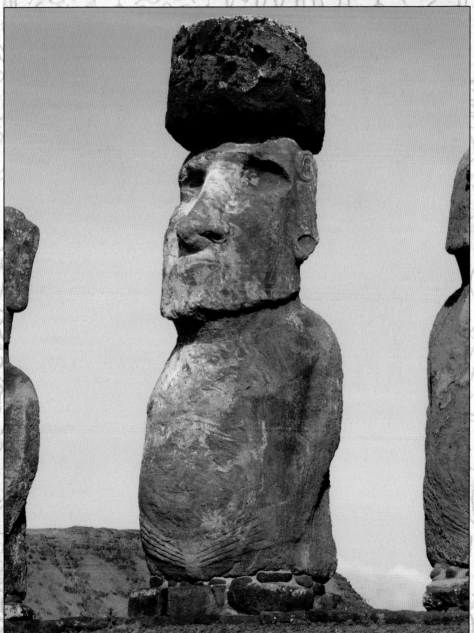

Plate 17. Close-up and distance view of moai on Ahu Tongariki, Easter Island.
(Photographs courtesy of R. Schoch and C. Ulissey.)

Plate 18. Stone structures at Orongo, Easter Island.
(Photograph courtesy of R. Schoch and C. Ulissey.)

Plate 19. Front and rear view of a basalt moai from Easter Island
now in the British Museum, London.
(Photographs from Routledge, 1919, figures 31 and 106.)

Plate 20. Rongorongo tablet.
(Photograph from Thomson, 1891, plate XL.)

Plate 21. Unfinished moai (horizontal) in the background in the quarry at
Rano Raraku, with various erected and buried moai (only the tops of
their heads and faces showing) in the foreground, Easter Island.
(Photograph courtesy of R. Schoch and C. Ulissey.)

Plate 22 (left). Partially excavated moai at Rano Raraku, Easter Island.
(Photograph from Routledge, 1919, figure 72.)

Plate 23 (right). Female moai carved of basalt and now
housed in the museum on Easter Island.
(Photograph courtesy of R. Schoch and C. Ulissey.)

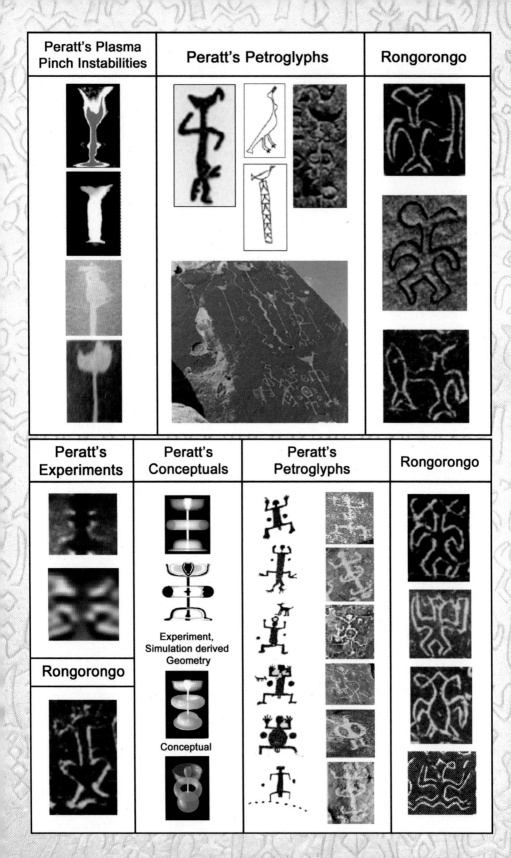

Peratt's Plasma Pinch Instabilities	Peratt's Petroglyphs	Rongorongo

Peratt's Experiments	Peratt's Conceptuals	Peratt's Petroglyphs	Rongorongo

Experiment, Simulation derived Geometry

Conceptual

Rongorongo

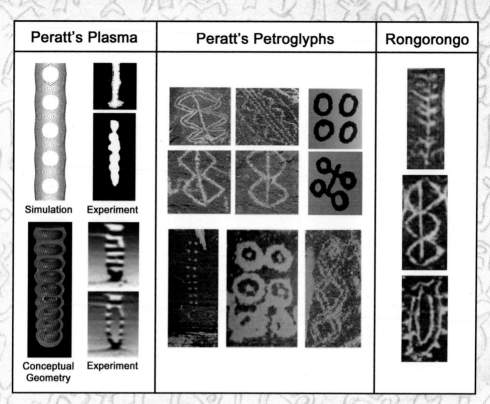

Plate 24 (*opposite* and *above*). Comparisons of plasma configurations, petroglyphs, and rongorongo glyphs.
(Plasma and petroglyph illustrations courtesy of Dr. Anthony L. Peratt, reprinted with permission from *IEEE Transactions on Plasma Science*, December 2003, vol. 31.)

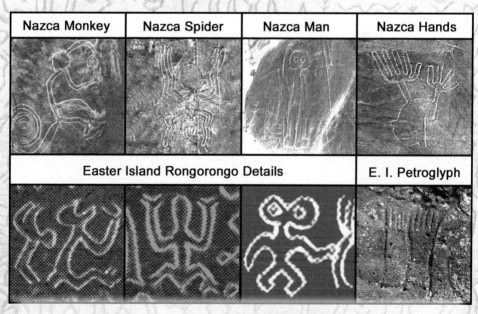

Plate 25. Nazca geoglyphs compared to rongorongo glyphs and an Easter Island petroglyph.
(Photographs courtesy of R. Schoch and C. Ulissey.)

Plate 26 (*right*). Composite image of a Coronal Mass Ejection (CME) from the Sun. (Courtesy of Solar and Heliospheric Observatory, European Space Agency and National Aeronautics and Space Administration.)

Plate 27 (*left*). Example of vitrified rock found in the walls of the Mote of Mark, Scotland. Specimen approximately 12 cm across. (Photograph courtesy of R. Schoch.)

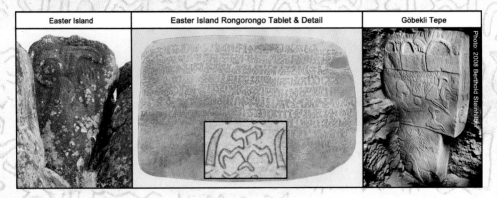

| Easter Island | Easter Island Rongorongo Tablet & Detail | Göbekli Tepe |

Plate 28. Comparison of an Easter Island petroglyph and an Easter Island rongorongo glyph (Thomson, 1891) to carvings at Göbekli Tepe. (Photograph of Göbekli Tepe pillar courtesy of Berthold Steinhilber, 2008; photograph of Easter Island petroglyph courtesy of R. Schoch and C. Ulissey.)

Plate 29. The Aurora Borealis, or Northern Lights, seen from Eielson Air Force Base, Alaska. (Photograph courtesy of U. S. Air Force, Joshua Strang, photographer.)

Thus we can harmonize with the inherent rhythm of both our physical world ("breathing with the Earth," as expressed in Becker and Selden 1985, 243) and the global biosphere, including other conscious beings (human and nonhuman). In such a state, synchronized with the natural 7.8 Hz Schumann resonance of Earth, all the phenomena associated with theta waves (brain waves around 4 to 8 Hz that occur during deep meditation), such as expanded consciousness and insight, are manifested—plus, types of extrasensory experiences (for instance, telepathy) are enhanced. Synchronizing thus with the planetary resonances, through such techniques as meditation, drumming, chanting, and trance dancing, has been practiced for thousands, and probably tens of thousands, of years or longer (see Miller and Miller 2003). We can learn to literally tune in to the Earth.

Why is it that synchronizing with Schumann resonances may enhance telepathy and other paranormal mental experiences? Could ELF waves be the carrier waves for telepathic information? Telepathy is known to penetrate Faraday cages (metal or wire enclosures that shield against most electromagnetic signals), and ELF waves can penetrate Faraday cages. Speaking of ELF waves in the range of Schumann resonances, Itzhak Bentov suggests, "Such a long wavelength knows no obstacles, and its strength does not attenuate much over large distances. Naturally, it will go through just about anything: metal, concrete, water, and the fields making up our bodies. It is the ideal medium for conveying a telepathic signal. Likewise, ELF can be used as a mode of radio communication; it is especially useful for communication with submarines" (Bentov 1981, 53; see also Bliokh et al. 1980, 153–55). Supporting both the reality of telepathy and the notion that some kind of physical wave is involved with direct mental communications, in his study of shamanism the Russian ethnographer Sergei Mikhailovich Shirokogoroff noted:

In the preceding chapters [of his massive monograph, *Psychomental Complex of the Tungus*] I have already given some facts observed among the Tungus and Manchus, which point to the existence of reading of thoughts. I have admitted the possibility of such a reading which is not based upon a system of inferences made from facts, but seemingly in direct communication, probably by a means of physical waves. For the time being the existence of these "waves" is a mere hypothesis, but this may be, at least temporarily, admitted, for the phenomena of "reading of thoughts" in a great number of cases cannot be understood as the result of mere "intuition" or coincidences [of] parallelism of thought in two individuals. This peculiarity is not characteristic of all shamans, some of whom may use it in a lesser degree, others in a greater one; but all of them make this attempt. Communication at a distance is apparently based upon the same physical condition. The shamans attain it by different methods, namely, they may do it in their dreams, during extasy [ecstasy], or in a "normal" state of concentration on a "desire" which they "think strongly". In all these cases the shamans say that they "send the soul" with a communication. It must be pointed out that this can be better done during the night, i.e. exactly during the period good for transmission of waves, undisturbed by sun rays. Another condition must not be forgotten, namely, the shamans attain extasy [ecstasy] much more easily in the dark. (Shirokogoroff 1935, 361; material in brackets added by R. Schoch)

Shirokogoroff's description could well fit the notion of an ELF wave being the carrier wave of telepathic thoughts, even to the point that telepathy works better at night. The fact that the shamans can better reach a state of ecstasy in the dark—that is, at night—may also be an indication that they are using ELF waves, probably in the Schumann frequencies, to reach altered states of consciousness. This may be an extremely ancient technique of gaining knowledge.

Thus, ELF waves in the Schumann frequency range may be a way that one human consciousness can connect with another and also tap into the larger collective consciousness and the Earth as a whole. ELF waves and Schumann frequencies are known to be affected by climate cycles and changes, which in turn are strongly affected by, and even regulated by, astronomical factors, including the relative positions of and resonances among the Sun and planets (see review in Mackey 2007).

Here again we discover correlations that according to the dogma of conventional established science are totally unexpected or even "impossible." According to the new science, there are meaningful relationships among fundamental physical phenomena (electromagnetic waves of extremely low frequency), astronomical phenomena (the relative positions of the Sun and planets, and even the stars and galactic center), and brain waves, which in turn affect states of consciousness. Using different terminology, mystics and certain scholars (often in the context of religion, esoteric studies, or occult studies) have accepted and explored such connections since ancient times.

Looking at a broader time frame, and in the context of our variable and unstable Sun, galaxy, and universe, the ionosphere and magnetosphere (as well as the general electromagnetic environment that envelopes us) are subject to changes and fluctuations that could significantly vary the frequency of Schumann resonances. During a major CME or other solar outburst, the ionosphere can change in its shape and properties, including increases in the electric currents and charges in the ionosphere and magnetosphere. Waves are distorted as they pass through a turbulent ionosphere (Rengaswamy 2008). Such factors materially affect various radio communications. Could they also affect mental and psychical processes and phenomena? The work demonstrating that spontaneous cases of telepathy and clairvoyance are correlated with geomagnetic fluctuations (Wilkinson and Gauld 1993) supports this hypothesis.

Major solar outbursts and plasma discharges, well beyond anything seen in the modern era, including the Carrington Event, have happened in the past—including at the end of the last ice age. Plasma discharges are electrical in nature. As discussed in chapter 11 (page 221), we do not know the full ramifications of subjecting living organisms, including humans, to intense electrical fields, but the effects could be profound, altering organisms genetically, mentally, and psychically.

Very disturbing to me personally is the ongoing High-frequency Active Auroral Research Program (HAARP). HAARP is an ionospheric research program jointly funded and carried out by the U.S. Navy, the U.S. Air Force, the U.S. Department of Defense, and the University of Alaska (see the HAARP website: www.haarp.alaska.edu). HAARP facilities include an array of radio transmitters and antennae that cover an area of over a dozen hectares north of Gakona, Alaska. This is used to send signals and energy into the ionosphere in order to see what will happen; that is, experiments are carried out directly on the ionosphere. This, of course, might raise alarms—and it has. Without getting into conspiracy theories—HAARP has been blamed for disruptions of the jet stream, changes in regional weather patterns (resulting in storms, droughts, floods, hurricanes, and so on), the initiation of earthquakes, major power outages, and the downing of airplanes, to name just a sampling—I seriously wonder what inadvertent (or intentional) effects the HAARP experiments might have, even if the energies used are ostensibly very low relative to natural events, such as the Sun's impact on the ionosphere.

Could ionospheric disruptions caused by HAARP, even if relatively "minor," have subtle but profound effects on life, including human mental states? Very small changes in collective mental states may lead to major material effects, such as whether aggression breaks out in the form of a major conflict, perhaps an all-out war, or which candidate is elected to high office. On another front, I am concerned that the constant modern bombardment of people by electromagnetic radiation, from cell phones to radio communications to power lines to circuits in walls, may have ill and unexpected consequences. There is increasing evidence that organisms, including humans, may be incredibly sensitive to ultraweak electromagnetic fields (see Ho 2011, and references cited therein).

THE POWER OF SOUND

Sound, a type of vibration, can have a very powerful and direct influence on the human mind. Researchers studying ancient megalithic stone structures around the world have discovered that in many cases the monuments may have been specifically designed to manipulate sound and produce specific sensory effects and induce particular mental phenomena. Acoustical studies have been carried out at such sites as the stone temples on the island of Malta (circa 3700 BCE to 2400 BCE according to conventional dating), at the ceremonial site of Chavín de Huántar in Peru (circa 1200 BCE to 400 BCE), at Newgrange (circa 3200 BCE) in Ireland, and at a site known as Wayland's Smithy in England (fourth millennium BCE). In a study of various ancient sites including Wayland's Smithy and Newgrange, Jahn et al. (1995) summarized their results as follows:

> Rudimentary acoustical measurements performed inside six diverse Neolithic and Iron Age structures revealed that each sustained a strong resonance at a frequency between 95 and 120 Hz (wavelength [approximately] 3 m[eters]). Despite major differences in chamber shapes and sizes, the resonant modal patterns all featured strong antinodes at the outer walls, with appropriately configured nodes and antinodes interspersed toward the central source. In some cases, interior and exterior rock drawings resembled these acoustical patterns. Since the resonant frequencies are well within the adult male voice range, one may speculate that some forms of human chanting, enhanced by the cavity resonance, were invoked for ritual purposes. (1995, 1; material in brackets added by R. Schoch)

Stone structures, pillars, and enclosed spaces could be used to magnify, conduct, and enhance certain sounds, producing resonances and standing waves, while filtering out other sounds (*Popular Archaeology* 2012). In particular, it has been found that certain enclosed chambers in monumental stone structures show strong resonances at sound frequencies of between about 95 Hz and 120 or 130 Hz (Eneix 2012). For instance, Linda Eneix, an expert on the ancient Malta temples, states that structures there resonate in the range of around 110 or 111 Hz (Eneix 2012).

According to Eneix,

> Regional brain activity in a number of healthy volunteers was monitored by EEG [electroencephalogram] through exposure to different sound vibration frequencies. . . . The findings indicated

that at 110 Hz the patterns of activity over the prefrontal cortex abruptly shifted, resulting in a relative deactivation of the language center and a temporary shifting from left to right-sided dominance related to emotional processing and creativity. This shifting did not occur at 90 Hz or 130 Hz. . . . In addition to stimulating their more creative sides, it appears that an atmosphere of resonant sound in the frequency of 110 or 111 Hz would have been "switching on" an area of the brain that bio-behavioral scientists believe relates to mood, empathy and social behavior. Deliberately or not, the people who spent time in such an environment under conditions that may have included a low male voice—in ritual chanting or even simple communication—were exposing themselves to vibrations that may have actually impacted their thinking. (Eneix, quoted in *Popular Archaeology* 2012; material in brackets added by R. Schoch)

If this is true (and I have no reason to doubt it), these ancient peoples were manipulating sound for some very subtle and sophisticated reasons. And they may have been doing so much earlier than the temples of Malta. Commenting on the site of Göbekli Tepe, which dates back nearly twelve thousand years (see discussion in chapter 3), Eneix has stated, "In the center of a circular shrine . . . a limestone pillar 'sings' when smacked with the flat of the hand. Obviously made to represent a human with a decorated belt and hands carved in relief at its waist, it bears unexplained symbols in the area of the throat" (Eneix, quoted in *Popular Archaeology* 2012).

Eneix goes on to wonder, "How curious that such varied ancient structures, separated by so much time and distance, should have common features which imply sophisticated knowledge. . . . Did the architects of the day each make and develop their own discoveries or did they inherit a concept from some older school of learning? Adding the time element to other fields of comparison suggests human trail-blazing of monumental proportion" (Eneix, quoted in *Popular Archaeology* 2012). I believe that the case can be made that the ancients as we know them did indeed inherit much of their knowledge from even more ancient peoples, from "some older school of learning." This may be one more example of lost knowledge that is only now being rediscovered.

Since the first edition of this book came out in 2012, an archaeo-acoustic analysis of Enclosure D (which includes the famous Pillar 18 that has the word for "God" inscribed on it; see chapter 15, page 349) has been published. The authors, Paolo Debertolis and colleagues, summarize their important and fascinating results:

> Thanks to the site's discoverer [Klaus Schmidt] we had the possibility to record the vibrations coming from the subsoil, magnetic fields and the sound produced by hitting with hand on central pillar n.18. The results are amazing and confirm that Göbekli Tepe has the same archaeoacoustic aspects of many other typical sacred sites we have studied in Europe and Minor Asia. However, the most interesting finding was understanding that the pillar we examined is probably at the centre of a sophisticated mechanism of vibrations and magnetic fields affecting the brain. This discovery is in contrast with our knowledge of the level of technology produced by the civilization who built these sacred temples. (Debertolis et al. 2017, 107; material in brackets added by R. Schoch)

Most unfortunately, however, the authors continue:

> Our results have to be considered as preliminary results, however due to the death of the person who discovered the site and the current geopolitical situation in Turkey we cannot continue the research. We hope other researchers will be able to confirm our results in [the] future.

All too often, politics and "external factors" can hamper scientific investigation (see appendix 2, "Politics, Money, and Science," page 384).

THE POWER OF WATER

Liquid water is essential to life as we know it. Without liquid water we could not exist. The chemical formula for water is H_2O, two hydrogen atoms joined to an oxygen atom: this simple molecular formula for water belies its incredible, and often subtle, complexity, a complexity that science is only beginning to discover. There is now strong evidence that liquid water, particularly in living systems, clusters into frameworks with the ability to store and transmit information and mediate chemical and biological functions. As Bennett Daviss wrote in a 2004 review article, "Evidence is mounting that water in living systems naturally gathers into frameworks of 14, 17, 21, 196, 280, or more molecules. Some say that the clusters' apparent existence necessitates redesigning simulation models of life processes. And support is growing behind the idea that these intricate structures play key roles in operations ranging from molecular binding to turning on and off basic cell processes" (Daviss 2004).

Since these words were written, it has become apparent that the subtlety and power of water (particularly the power to encode, preserve, and transmit information) is even greater than suspected.

The concept of water memory (that liquid water can encode, store, and transmit information), which is essentially the basis of homeopathy, has a long and tumultuous history. More often than not the mainstream scientific community has flatly rejected the notion of water memory—this despite the growing, if still controversial, evidence that water can carry information (see reviews by Chaplin 2007; Dunning-Davies 2011a, 2011b; Hutchinson 2008; Milgrom 2003; Pringle 2003; and Singh 2008). Discoveries discussed in the first paragraph of this section concerning the incredible complexity of liquid water under some circumstances provide a theoretical way that indeed water could store and transmit information.

Another twist to water, which may have wide-reaching implications, is that in addition to the classic three phases (states) of liquid, solid, and gas, water can also exist in a fourth phase known as "exclusion zone water" (or EZ water, for short). Work on this phase of water has been pioneered by Gerald Pollack, although there were forerunners who suggested that there might be a fourth phase of water. Apparently, this fourth phase occurs primarily at liquid water interfaces and consists of "a liquid crystalline phase" (Pollack 2013; see also Pollack 2017). EZ water has been demonstrated independently by various researchers; how extensively it occurs and how to explain it theoretically remain controversial (Elton 2019).

Extremely controversial experiments carried out by a group led by Luc Montagnier have shed light on the relationship between organisms, DNA, and water. (Montagnier was co-winner of the 2008 Nobel Prize in Medicine for his work on identifying HIV [human immunodeficiency virus] and its relationship to AIDS [acquired immunodeficiency syndrome]; however, see Papadopulos-Eleopulos et al. 2004 for an argument that HIV does not cause AIDS.) Central to Montagnier's work is his discovery (disputed by many mainstream scientists) that sequences of DNA (deoxyribonucleic acid, the basic genetic material of most life on Earth; some viruses use the related RNA [ribonucleic acid] as genetic material) dissolved in water at very high dilutions can emit weak electromagnetic signals or fields, specifically in the ELF range. Montagnier and his group then went on to demonstrate that, in their own words, "These [electromagnetic] fields can be induced by suitable procedures in water dilutions which become able to propagate the information contained in the DNA of the original organisms to other ones" (Montagnier et al. 2010, 1; see also the review by Ho 2011).

The experiments of Montagnier et al. were cogently summarized in *New Scientist* as follows:

> Two adjacent but physically separate test tubes were placed within a copper coil and subjected to a very weak extremely low frequency electromagnetic field of 7 hertz. The apparatus was isolated from Earth's natural magnetic field to stop it interfering with the experiment. One tube contained a fragment of DNA around 100 bases long; the second tube contained pure water.
>
> After 16 to 18 hours, both samples were independently subjected to the polymerase chain reaction (PCR), a method routinely used to amplify traces of DNA by using enzymes to make many copies of the original material. The gene fragment was apparently recovered from both tubes, even though one should have contained just water. . . .
>
> DNA was only recovered if the original solution of DNA—whose

concentration has not been revealed—had been subjected to several dilution cycles before being placed in the magnetic field. In each cycle it was diluted 10-fold, and "ghost" DNA was only recovered after between seven and 12 dilutions of the original. (Coghlan 2011)

In effect, if the experiment is correct (and I personally have no reason to doubt it), the DNA in the original solution appears to have transmitted information concerning its structure to the adjacent pure water, and then when the proper ingredients were added to the pure water a copy of the DNA could be produced! The information itself, Montagnier et al. suggest, is transmitted via ELF waves emitted by the DNA that in turn imprint the structure of the DNA on the water in the form of water nanostructures that can then be used by enzymes to create a copy of the DNA from raw ingredients (specifically nucleotides in this case). This the editors of *New Scientist* referred to as "teleported DNA" (Coghlan 2011, and accompanying editorial).

Reaction to this work has been strong. An editorial in *New Scientist* opined, "It's good to have an open mind but not so open that your brains fall out. This week we report claims about the way that DNA behaves that are so astonishing that many minds have already snapped shut" (editorial accompanying Coghlan 2011).

Jeff Reimers, a theoretical chemist at the University of Sydney, Australia, was quoted as saying, "If the results are correct, these would be the most significant experiments performed in the past 90 years, demanding re-evaluation of the whole conceptual framework of modern chemistry" (Reimers, quoted in Coghlan 2011).

Perhaps modern chemistry (as well as modern physics, modern biology, modern astronomy, modern climatology, modern anthropology, and modern archaeology) needs to be reevaluated!

Montagnier et al. discuss the implications of a "theory of liquid water based on Quantum Field Theory" wherein the "binding [of liquid water molecules into larger structures] is actually induced by the time-dependent radiative long range em [electromagnetic] field. Short range static bonds, such as H-bonds [hydrogen bonds between water molecules], then set in as a consequence of the molecule condensation induced by such long range radiative fields" (Montagnier et al. 2010, 5; material in brackets added by R. Schoch).

In other words, background electromagnetic fields play a crucial role in determining the structures, properties, and capabilities of water (H_2O) and thus the ability of water to store and transmit information, as demonstrated by the experiments of Montagnier et al.

Reading first the *New Scientist* article about their work and then beginning to read the original paper by Montagnier et al., I noticed that the 7 Hz electromagnetic frequency they used to "excite" the DNA is very close to the basic Schumann resonance of 7.8 Hz. Reading further the original Montagnier et al. paper, I saw that this had not escaped the notice of the authors! As Montagnier et al. explain, how certain ions in a cell respond to background electromagnetic fields of various frequencies is extremely important. Based on their analysis, these researchers conclude that life on Earth at a cellular level is finely tuned and adapted to the natural Schumann resonances, with the most basic resonance occurring at approximately 7.8 Hz. They note that their work may "provide a rationale for the observed impact of ELF fields on the physiological activity" (Montagnier et al. 2010, 8).

Montagnier et al. end their paper with the following perceptive remarks: "Our work is interdisciplinary, involving biologists, physicists, and medical doctors. There are of course many unresolved questions raised by our findings, which deserve more work and more interactions. DNA signalling is stimulated by 7 Hz naturally occurring waves on earth [the basic Schumann resonance]. Waves produced by the human brain are also in the range of 7 Hz. These are interesting questions to be asked and possibly answered" (Montagnier et al. 2010, 10; material in brackets added by R. Schoch).

Might this be a reason that calm meditation, generating brain waves in the Schumann frequencies, is so healthful and particularly useful in physiological healing?

Many people, including scientists and physicians, simply dismiss weak and/or ELF electromagnetic fields as being trivial and not capable of having any impact on living organisms (including humans). Such an attitude may be a huge mistake. Background electromagnetic fields, even if incredibly weak, may be all-important to the proper physiological and mental functioning of humans and all of life on Earth. Tampering with such background electromagnetic fields may have inadvertent and unexpected consequences. Yet, modern technology does just this; we are bathed and surrounded by "unnatural" electromagnetic fields. And when we look at the course of geological history over millennia to billions of years, we have to ask ourselves, How have electromagnetic fields on the surface of Earth changed, and what were the consequences? During major solar outbursts and plasma phenomena, such as at the end of the last ice age, what effect did changing electromagnetic fields have on the people of the time and on life more generally? Perhaps going underground and in caves would have served as protection from higher-frequency waves while allowing the benefits of Schumann low-frequency waves (which can penetrate much deeper and through much thicker rock) to be maintained, that is, assuming that Schumann resonances were not totally disrupted.

ENTANGLED DIAMONDS

In the mysterious world of quantum mechanics the concept of entanglement occurs when particles interact and are then separated, but they are still somehow correlated (or more accurately, anticorrelated) in terms of their characteristics. Acting on one particle will result in an effect or outcome on the other particle, even if a considerable distance physically separates the particles and there is no direct conventional physical or energetic link between them. To use a crude analogy, if two coins in the process of being tossed are entangled in a quantum mechanical sense, when one coin comes up heads the other coin will come up tails (remember, they are anticorrelated). Albert Einstein referred to quantum entanglement as *"spukhafte Fernwirkung"* (spooky action at a distance), but it has been demonstrated experimentally numerous times, and the effects of entanglement seem to propagate either instantaneously or at a speed thousands of times faster than the speed of light (which is highly perplexing). For a long time, quantum entanglement, as demonstrated experimentally, was generally considered limited to very small microscopic objects, such as subatomic particles, atoms, isolated molecules, and microscopic crystalline structures. In December 2011, a group of physicists from the University of Oxford, the National Research Council of Canada, and the National University of Singapore announced the successful quantum entanglement, using lasers, of oscillation patterns of atoms in two macroscopic (approximately three millimeters in size) diamonds at room temperature and separated by a distance of about fifteen centimeters (Lee et al. 2011; Duan 2011).

Leaving the details of the experiments aside, the quantum entanglement of the diamonds is not particularly controversial for the experimental results are clear and definitive. The entanglement of macroscopic diamonds at ordinary room temperature under ordinary conditions demonstrates, I believe, that it is wrong to assume that quantum entanglement (and other "mysterious" quantum effects as well) is limited to the microscopic world and can have no real consequences in our everyday lives. There has long been talk in some circles (though previously unconvincing) that certain psychic or paranormal phenomena such as telepathy could be due to quantum entanglement. Now the entangled diamonds appear to provide strong evidence that such entanglement and correlation of information is indeed possible. In my experience, telepathy tends to work best when one is in a mental state decoupled from the immediate surrounding environment, which allows the mind of the individual to couple or entangle with the mind of another individual (or individuals).

Like minds in telepathic rapport, diamonds best maintain their quantum entanglement when they can be decoupled from "distractions" or the entanglement is stronger than the distractions. (In the case of the diamonds, distractions might include such phenomena as being excited by environmental changes, like temperature or physical movement.) Of course, most hardcore physicists tend to dismiss telepathy as nonsense even as they will accept the quantum entanglement of diamonds. It also needs to be pointed out that phenomena generally regarded as telepathic may include a mixture of phenomena due to different causal mechanisms; thus, some forms of telepathy may be the result of quantum entanglement, and other forms of telepathy may be due to electromagnetic radiation, particularly in the extremely long wavelength and ELF range, as discussed in the "ELFs: Tuning In To the Earth" section earlier in this chapter (page 270).

UPDATE: Building on the work of Olivier Costa de Beauregard (1987), Price and Wharton (2016) have argued that entanglement can be explained "without action-at-a-distance, if the influence followed an indirect, zigzag path through space and time, via the point in the past where the two particles intersect." That is, at a quantum level the effect can precede (that is, "precede" from our temporal perspective) the cause. Or, in other words, at the quantum level, retrocausality is real (for a review of retrocausality in quantum mechanics, see Friederich and Evans 2019).

THE FINE STRUCTURE OF THE UNIVERSE

In modern physics the fine-structure constant, denoted by α (alpha), is generally considered a fundamental constant of the universe. It basically characterizes the strength of the electromagnetic force or interaction, it is dimensionless (that is, unitless), and its currently accepted value is approximately .007297 = 1/137.036. In turn, α can be expressed in terms of other physical constants such as Planck's constant, the elementary charge, the electric constant, the magnetic constant, the Coulomb constant, and the speed of light in a vacuum; thus, α can be viewed as summarizing a number of fundamental properties of the universe as we know it. Indeed, matter in a stable state, and therefore life as we know it, could not exist if the fine-structure constant differed very far, even by a small percentage, from its current value; carbon atoms, for instance, upon which life as we know it is based, would not form naturally. The great physicist Max Born (1882–1970; Nobel Prize in Physics, 1954) is quoted as saying, "If α [the fine-structure constant] were bigger than it really is, we should not be able to distinguish matter from ether [the vacuum, nothingness], and our task to disentangle the natural laws would be hopelessly difficult. The fact however that alpha has just its value 1/137 is certainly no chance but itself a law of nature. It is clear that the explanation of this number must be the central problem of natural philosophy" (Born, quoted in Miller 2009, 253; bracketed material in the original).

But the fine-structure constant, and consequently other related physical "constants," might not be so constant after all. An accumulating body of evidence suggests that there are changes in the fine-structure constant over space and time (see Webb et al. 2010; Berengut and Flambaum 2010; for differing views, see Carroll 2010, and Orzel 2010). As the staff of the popular *Space Daily* (2010) wrote, this "finding could mean rethinking the fundaments [the foundations] of our current knowledge of physics" (material in brackets added by R. Schoch). As we have summarized above, this is not the only evidence that suggests our current models in science need to be rethought.

The fine-tuning of the fine-structure constant (α) and other physical constants, such that they are "just right" for life, and humans in particular, to exist is sometimes referred to as the anthropic principle. Why α is just right has long perplexed some of the greatest of modern thinkers. (Admittedly, other people have simply dismissed it as a nonissue, arguing that we just happened to have evolved to fit our environmental conditions; the environment and physical constants were not designed to fit us.) The nonconstancy of the fine-structure constant may help solve this conundrum. As Julian C. Berengut and Victor V. Flambaum write:

> Discovery of a spatial variation in the fundamental constants of nature has massive implications for the "fine-tuning" problem. This is the question of why the constants of nature seem to be finely-tuned for life to exist. While the anthropic principle can be invoked to explain such tuning of the Universe, there remains the question of how it could come about. With the detection of spatial variation of constants we begin to have a natural explanation for fine-tuning: with many possibilities for combinations of constants all occurring within the (possibly infinite in extent) Universe, we simply appear in the part of the Universe that is consistent with our existence. (Berengut and Flambaum 2010, 1)

A MATTER OF TIME

In April 2012 a research team from the U.S. National Institute of Standards and Technology reported on an experiment involving the generation of light pulses traveling faster than the speed of light in a vacuum (Glasser et al. 2012). A wave peak on a pulse of light was forced to move from back to front along the light beam as the light itself was traveling at the standard speed of light, such that the pulse traveled faster than the speed of light in a vacuum. If refined, such a technique could possibly allow information to be sent faster than the speed of light. This work follows on the heels of a major brouhaha over another alleged instance of faster than light speeds—reports that neutrinos (electrically neutral and weakly interacting subatomic particles) had been measured traveling faster than the speed of light while passing through 732 kilometers of rock from the CERN particle physics laboratory in Geneva, Switzerland, to a particle detector in the Laboratori Nazionali del Gran Sasso in Italy (Adam et al. 2011). This raised a huge stir, as standard modern mainstream physics theories, many based in large part on Einstein's special theory of relativity (first proposed in 1905), have long assumed that the speed of light in a vacuum is the upper limit of how fast anything can travel; therefore, if such results were correct, some of the most basic assumptions in modern physics would need to be reevaluated. Ultimately, based on carrying out further experiments, including at other labs, it was announced, "the original . . . measurement can be attributed to a faulty element of the experiment's fibre optic timing system" (Bertolucci 2012).

A major objection to the possibility of superluminal (faster than the speed of light) travel is that it will upset cherished notions of time and temporal ordering (conventional thinking asserts that the past must occur before the present, which must occur before the future). From our perspective, particles traveling faster than light might be viewed as traveling backward in time (arriving one place before they depart from another place) or through other dimensions, and this would open the possibility of effects occurring before causes (although exactly what "before" means in this new notion of time is open to debate; see Moskowitz 2011; Palmer 2011a; Wolchover 2011). That is, the concept of retrocausality (the future influencing the present and the past), which many people (including many theoretical physicists) instinctively reject, would have to be taken seriously. Yet there is evidence of retrocausality. A group centered in Vienna, Austria, headed by Anton Zeilinger (Ma et al. 2012), has experimentally demonstrated that the decision as to whether or not two particles at a quantum level are entangled or in separate quantum states can be made after the particles have been measured (and may no longer exist). Furthermore, there is solid parapsychological support for retroactive influences on the human mind.

THE INFLUENCE OF THE FUTURE ON THE PAST

We live in a cause-and-effect world. Causes come before their effects, not vice versa. Time is unidirectional, moving from the past to the present to the future. We might regret or cherish the past, but we cannot go back in time. I teach. My students study and then take the exam. It would not make sense for them to first take the exam and do their studying afterward. Well, they might learn the material after the fact, but that is hardly going to help them on the exam that they already took!

In the last paragraph I have described the commonsense world that most people know and believe in. Few seriously question it, yet it just might be wrong. Take the example of studying for an exam after taking the exam. Daryl J. Bem of Cornell University reported on a series of "retroactive facilitation of recall" experiments (Bem 2011). Students were shown forty-eight words (nouns, such as names of animals or foods) and then asked to recall as many of the words as they could remember. After the recall test, the students were subjected to practice with half of the words (picked randomly by a computer). That is, the students "studied" half of the words after taking the test. By commonsense thinking this after-the-fact studying should have no bearing on how the students did on the test. However, such was not the case. The students did significantly better on the recall of the words that they practiced, even though the practice followed taking the test. To quote from Bem's paper directly, "The results show that practicing a set of words after the recall test does, in fact, reach back in time to facilitate the recall of those words" (Bem 2011, 419).

These are astounding results, but they corroborate a huge array of data that the skeptics and debunkers have consistently refused to acknowledge, data that support the idea that the future can influence the present and the past (Schoch and Yonavjak 2008).

Another one of Bem's experiments involved the precognitive detection of erotic stimuli. Subjects were able to determine, at a level significantly more frequent than random, behind which "curtain" on a computer screen an erotic image would appear, even though the position of the erotic image was not determined until after the subject made her or his choice. That is, the subjects seemed to be able to access information from the future. An argument against the precognition hypothesis is that perhaps the subjects could psychokinetically cause the computer to position the image behind the screen of choice. This hypothesis was considered by Bem, but was rejected as less likely than genuine precognition since he obtained significant results with these experiments using both true random number generators as well as pseudorandom number generators (which use a mathematical algorithm to generate a series of "random" numbers—a series that presumably is immune to change via psychokinesis) as ways to determine randomly the image placements. Furthermore, these Bem precognition studies in the laboratory form part of a continuum with numerous other examples of precognition, including the detailed precognition of specific future events by individuals, such as the dozens of people who "precognized" the 1966 Aberfan disaster. A huge pile of coal slag and debris came crashing down on Aberfan, Wales, killing 144 people (see discussion in Roy 1990). (As a side note, I recollect the following line from *The Stranger* by Albert Camus: "From the dark horizon of my future a sort of slow, persistent breeze had been blowing toward me, all my life long, from the years that were to come." [Camus 1946, 152])

THE SCIENCE OF THE FUTURE

Is there any scientific theory that can cogently account for the future influencing the past?

In physics the transactional interpretation of quantum mechanics, developed by John G. Cramer, of the University of Washington, Seattle, explicitly introduces the concept of the future influencing the present or past (the present is the past relative to the future) at the quantum (submicroscopic) level. Building on the work of such luminaries as famed physicist John Wheeler (1911–2008) and Nobel Prize–winning physicist Richard Feynman (1918–1988), the transactional interpretation uses both "retarded waves" (temporally "normal" waves propagating forward in time) and "advanced waves" (waves that propagate backward in time) sent out by an "emitter" and receivable by an "absorber." (The same entity may variously be an emitter or an absorber.) A quantum event consists of an exchange of such waves. As Cramer describes it, an "offer" wave is sent out in one time direction and a "confirmation" wave is sent back in the other time direction, thus completing the quantum event (Cramer 1986). According to Cramer, the collapse of the wave function, when quantum probabilities are manifested as realities, is accomplished through the exchange of the offer wave and confirmation wave; when summed together, the overall process is essentially nontemporal.

Elaborating on the transactional interpretation, Cramer writes:

In the quantum world, the plane of the present must be a fuzzy region with the past on one side in time and the future on the other, but with some uncertainty in the central region about which is the past and which is the future. Across this region there must occur the freezing of possibility into reality, but possibility and actuality are mixed and smeared by time indeterminacy. ... The transactional interpretation asserts that at the quantum level time is a two-way street, in which at some level the future determines the past as well as the past determining the future. (Cramer 2001, 3, 5)

If this is the case in the quantum world (I find the evidence convincing), then I believe it is not only conceivable but also highly likely that this two-way street is applicable not solely to the quantum level, but in some cases manifests at the macroscopic level. Indeed, the overwhelming evidence for precognition and retrocausality supports this conclusion (Schoch and Yonavjak 2008).

Let us return to Bem's recall research. A potentially significant point concerning Bem's "retroactive facilitation of recall" experiments is that those tested did not know the results of their tests (at least this appears to be the case based on Bem's description of the experiments) prior to the practice for the test. That is, each subject took the test and then immediately practiced without being aware of the results of the test just taken. This seems to tie in with the concept that the future can influence or affect the past, but it cannot change the past. Once a quantum transaction or a series of quantum transactions that we can observe macroscopically takes place (is completed), the event or events are fixed (although in some cases we may view an event as fixed that at a quantum level is not yet fully completed and thus is mutable). As the physicist Olivier Costa de Beauregard (1911–2007) put it, ". . . telegraphing backward in time does not mean 'reshaping' history, but shaping it from the future" (Costa de Beauregard 1987, 284).

In the case of the experiments by Bem, if the subject already knew what she or he had scored on the recall test, I hypothesize that the result would not be changed by further after-the-fact practice. So long as the result of the test remained indeterminate (at least from the perspective of the subject), future practice by the subject could exert an influence on the past (the result of the recall test), but this possibility (the influence of the future practice on the result of the past test) would end once the subject learned the result of the test. It does not matter if other people know the outcome of the test (or if the outcome has been recorded mechanically or electronically), as long as the subject does not know the outcome. In a similar context, using the example of paranormally influencing a lottery drawing via psychokinesis, Garret Moddel, of the College of Engineering and Applied Science, University of Colorado, has written, "It is not necessary to consider the knowledge that others have of yesterday's outcome if you have not been informed of their knowledge. The outcome that others knew of will simply be the one that exists in response to your intention" (Moddel 2006, 68).

We might regard such a situation as one where the past event exists; however, it was not brought about simply by past events but by future events as well.

But if future events exist, at least to the extent that they can influence the present and past, where does that leave us? Is the future already fully determined, in which case some might argue that free will is an illusion? Or is the future itself more like an influence, a tendency, neither totally absent nor fully existent, something that pulls on us, draws us toward it, but does not force us irrevocably into any particular fate or destiny? These are issues that I ponder as I continue to explore the nature of time.

ZEP TEPI

The point of this chapter is that new science—hardcore, no-nonsense, cutting-edge science—is demonstrating that fundamental physical, chemical, and biological processes, astronomical phenomena, life, Earth, consciousness, and the cosmos are all interrelated. This is not a metaphorical or literary allusion: the connections are real and inescapable. Recognizing these relationships entails a major revision of how we view the world and our place in it. Furthermore, these connections are not posited just in the present, but they also extend both back in time and into the future. That is, we are strongly influenced by the past and—given the strong evidence supporting the reality of precognition (Richet 1931; Saltmarsh 1938) and retrocausation (Bem 2011)—possibly even by the future to some extent. I believe that future science will acknowledge the ancient wisdom.

As I bring this book to a close, I cannot help but ponder the ancient Egyptian concept of Zep Tepi (Crystal 2011; Schoch and Bauval 2017; also referred to as Tep Zepi, see Heinberg 1989, 44). In ancient Egyptian, Zep Tepi means the "first time," the time of the creation, the beginning of civilization, a golden age when the "gods" lived among mankind, when the gods and humans walked hand in hand. The concept of Zep Tepi refers to the first or primordial civilization, but it also has a deeper cosmological meaning and implications as well: the creation of time itself.

Egyptologist Rundle Clark succinctly captured the essence of Zep Tepi, writing:

> This epoch—*zep tepi*—"the First Time"—stretched from the first stirring of the High God in the Primeval Waters. . . . All proper myths relate events or manifestations of this epoch. Anything whose existence or authority had to be justified or explained must be referred to the "First Time." This was true for natural phenomena, rituals, royal insignia, the plans of temples, magical or medical formulae, the hieroglyphic system of writing, the calendar—the whole paraphernalia of the civilization . . . all that was good or efficacious was established on the principles laid down in the "First Time"—which was, therefore, a golden age of absolute perfection . . . . (Clark 1978, 263; quoted by Bauval and Brophy 2011, 241; italics in the original)

Robert Bauval and Thomas Brophy (2011), in their book on the origins of ancient Egyptian civilization, date Zep Tepi to an era around 12,000 BCE based on the astronomy of the ancient Egyptians, especially as recorded at Giza (site of not only the Great Sphinx but also the Great Pyramid). Although their full analysis is much more extensive and involves a number of other lines of evidence, they summarize a central aspect of their reasoning as follows: "The southern shaft of the Queen's Chamber [of the Great Pyramid] invites us to consider two altitudes of the star Sirius, one at 39.5 degrees and the other at 0 degrees, thus determining two dates: 2500 BCE, which is probably the actual construction date of the pyramid, and 12,000 BCE, which represents a date in the remote past that has to do with the beginning or first time of the ancient Egyptians' history defined with calendrical computations of the Sothic cycle and precession cycle of the star Sirius" (Bauval and Brophy 2011, 246–47; material in brackets added by R. Schoch).

This date of circa 12,000 BCE falls near the end of the last ice age, and very roughly (within a couple of millennia) can be viewed as about the time of Göbekli Tepe and, quite possibly, the origins of the Great Sphinx (see Schoch and Bauval 2017). Does Zep Tepi refer to the first flowering of civilization, just prior to the end of the last ice age? As I have pointed out in previous chapters, the name Göbekli Tepe and a traditional name for Easter Island, Te Pito Te Henua, both refer to the navel, perhaps indicative of birth, origins, and beginnings, as in the beginning of civilization at the end of the last ice age. Was this the original golden age, the first time of civilization? Was it brought to an end by solar outbursts? Thousands of years later, was it an epoch primarily remembered in myth, and later were the myths relegated to the status of fairy stories, of no historical value, and ultimately dismissed by modern science?

Yet, at many levels this may be an injustice; even as history may be transformed into myth, it may retain value of a different nature, perhaps of a more fundamental nature, such as the true relationship of humanity to the cosmos—as is beginning to be rediscovered. I find truth in the following words of the great Romanian philosopher and historian of religion Mircea Eliade (1907–1986): "'Myth' and 'history' represent two different modes of existing in the World, two different approaches of the mind to the interpretation of the data of reality—modes of being and activities of the mind that, in any case, are not mutually exclusive. A people, as well as an individual, can be conscious of its responsibilities in history and courageously assume them, while at the same time continuing to enjoy the ancient myths and legends and to create new ones; for they account for other dimensions of human existence" (Eliade 1972, 131–32).

OUR PAST AND OUR FUTURE: A FEW FINAL REMARKS

Sometimes it can be difficult to bring a book to a close. There is so much more one could write, always another fact or reference one might add. I hesitate as I send this typescript to the publisher. Why? Because I fully realize that much of the material discussed in this book is highly controversial and will not be readily accepted by mainstream conventional thinkers. I ponder what the critics may say. Some will dismiss the scientific evidence I present out of hand, not giving it a sincere and objective look. Others will label me an alarmist, someone who is predicting that a major solar outburst (or other natural catastrophe) will soon bring about the "end of the world," or at a minimum the end of modern civilization and technological societies as we know them. To defend myself, I would assert that I am only pointing out what could happen given our current understanding of Earth, our solar system, and the universe at large. Whether or not such events will happen, when they may, and the specifics of such a catastrophe are not in my realm to predict. Yet I brace myself for the potential name-calling ("Schoch is an alarmist," "Schoch is a pseudoscientist," "Schoch just likes the publicity") for I have heard it all before. (I have even been referred to as a heretic.)

The controversy over the age of the Great Sphinx has hardened me against personal attacks. In truth, the staunchest critics—the defenders of the status quo—will probably never change their views, never give up their most cherished paradigms, and this is one of the primary messages that I would like to impart to my readers. If you have read this book carefully, I hope you realize that I am simply a person who looks at all of the evidence, following it to logical conclusions, even if those conclusions are not in agreement with mainstream views. But still, I wonder, have I said enough? Ultimately, however, if a book is to be published, eventually the author must let go. Yet, the story continues to develop. So let us, in closing, briefly summarize the main threads of the narrative.

As I have described in this book, geological data indicate that the last ice age ended extremely suddenly, catastrophically, around 9700 BCE. This is the time of Göbekli Tepe, the date of the earliest incarnation of the Great Sphinx (at that time taking the form of a lioness), and, I believe, the date of a major solar outburst that is recorded in petroglyphs and the rongorongo texts of Easter Island, further supported by studies of ice cores, sediment cores, and lunar data. Yes, there are many petroglyphs around the globe, and some have nothing to do with solar outbursts, but other petroglyphs (those studied intensely by Anthony Peratt and discussed in this book) do represent solar/plasma configurations and major auroral displays (and of these, some may represent major auroral displays since the end of the last ice age). Likewise, even if some of the surviving rongorongo glyphs and texts may ultimately prove to have been used for linguistic purposes, this will not negate the idea that the rongorongo glyphs were first inspired by plasma configurations in the skies and that the earliest rongorongo texts document a major solar outburst.

Our unstable Sun, erupting at the end of the last ice age, melted glaciers that covered much of the land, evaporated tremendous amounts of water, and warmed the climate. In places the surface of the planet was incinerated as a huge plasma ball hit, and tremendous electrical storms filled the atmosphere, touching down to set conflagrations. To escape the terror, the few survivors may have been forced to seek shelter underground and in caves. Only megalithic rock structures could withstand the onslaught. No doubt this is why there is such a scarcity of physical remains from this early period.

Bathed in steam, the atmosphere could only hold so much water before it would precipitate out as tremendous and protracted rains. This, combined with the melting of the glaciers, would have created huge floods. Deluges are a part of myth and legend among virtually every ancient culture around the world; the Judeo-Christian biblical Noachian flood is but one example. Recollections of cataclysmic events destroying an advanced civilization that flourished thousands of years before the civilizations of ancient Egypt, Sumeria, or Greece are also nearly universal. Tying in with my work on the Great Sphinx, a key consideration in my analysis is that the Sphinx was weathered and eroded by water, by precipitation, not simply by wind and sand. Yet the Sphinx sits on the edge of what is now the Sahara Desert. Could deep fissures and other water-induced erosional features on the body of the lioness—on the body of the Great Sphinx—be the scars of this cataclysmic epoch? I believe so.

Since those catastrophic times, for the past ten thousand years, our Sun has been relatively quiescent, but it is now entering an active period once again, the likes of which have not been seen since the end of the last ice age. This we need to understand in order to assess the future realistically. To point out the facts as described in this book is, in my opinion, simply prudent. Civilization was dealt a mighty setback around 9700 BCE, one that lasted thousands of years. We are just beginning to remember, to reconstruct, what happened in those ancient times. Should events of the past recur—indeed, the study of geology teaches they do—we would do well to collectively prepare.

I believe we are at the beginning of a new cycle; major changes are on the horizon. The ramifications and reverberations of the coming changes could be much more extensive than most people want to imagine. It is imperative to acknowledge that our planet and all of life on it, including humanity, are much more intimately connected to, and affected by, the cosmos than most people realize. We do not live in isolation. Consequently, the coming changes could hit hard, impacting our way of life and threatening our very existence. However, this need not be the case. As I have outlined in this chapter, many new discoveries (or some would say, many rediscoveries of ancient wisdom) are being made in diverse scientific disciplines at an accelerating pace. I see many cracks developing in conventional, mainstream, status quo thinking, and as these cracks widen to form chasms, a new paradigm is emerging. This is a paradigm of interconnectedness, a paradigm of cooperation, a paradigm that transcends mere materialism, a paradigm of complexity where consciousness and spirit play a vital role.

Now is the time for a realistic assessment, stripped of ideological blinders, of our past, our potential future, and our place in the grand scheme of things. It is my hope that this book will help contribute to the new paradigm, the new understanding, of our world. With knowledge and insight, I believe we can face the coming changes. Working together, we can address whatever the future may hold.

From Stars We Come and Thence We Return

Why should those points of light in the firmament . . . be less accessible than the dark ones on the map of France? We take a train to go to Tarascon or Rouen and we take death to reach a star.

VINCENT VAN GOGH (1853–1890)
QUOTED BY HAWKSLEY 2002, 15

Mythologist Ev Cochrane has written, "Although an aura of mystery surrounds the religious beliefs of the ancient Egyptians this much is certain: they were obsessed with the stars. The leading gods were identified with prominent stars; their most impressive and enduring monuments—the pyramids—were decorated with stars and patterned after a celestial prototype; and their single-minded goal, upon dying, was to return to a celestial Hereafter where they hoped to be reunited with the sun god and the Imperishable Stars [the circumpolar stars]" (Cochrane 2009, 1; material in brackets added by R. Schoch).

This idea of coming from the stars and returning to the Sun and stars inspired my wife, Katie, to develop a theory that she calls the G! theory ("G" stands for our concept of God, the grand architect of the universe). In a nutshell, her initial proposal was that stars are made of hydrogen, a major element in our physical makeup as well. (Our bodies contain a large component of water [H_2O], and hydrogen is an important component of organic carbon-based molecules that make up all organisms.) And, a large percentage of the matter within us can be traced back to stars—stardust. What if, Katie suggests, when we die, our hydrogen is released and, being light, it floats up to the heavens (to space), where it collects as clouds, collapses under gravitational attraction, is compressed, and we are literally reborn as stars? What if this is a grand (or the grandest) cycle of life?

Information and Consciousness

There is increasing scientific evidence that liquid water can form nanostructures with the ability to encode, store, and transmit information (see discussion in the section titled "The Power of Water," page 277). The case can be made that information is the most fundamental aspect of the universe, and one can cogently argue that information is ultimately equivalent to thought or consciousness (see further discussion in appendix 4, page 402). Max Planck, the founder of quantum theory and winner of the 1918 Nobel Prize in Physics, stated in a 1931 interview, "I regard consciousness as fundamental. I regard matter as derivative from consciousness. We cannot get behind consciousness. Everything that we talk about, everything that we regard as existing, postulates consciousness" (Planck, quoted in Fussell 1933, 199).

This is a very interesting, and powerful, statement.

If, as I believe, consciousness presupposes information, then there must be a way to record and manipulate information if consciousness is to exist (such consciousness we self-evidently seem to have, if in fact I am consciously writing this book and you are consciously reading this book). But what are the mechanisms to record information? In the everyday macroscopic world writing, symbols, artwork, digital encoding using numbers, analog recording using waves, and so forth immediately come to mind. In the biological world genetic information is encoded in the structure of DNA, with the nucleotides often compared to the letters of an alphabet. But how is the "information of consciousness," including emotions, recorded or imprinted? Is the human brain, or any biological brain, truly comparable to an electronic computer storing bits of information in a material medium? Can consciousness exist independent of gross material structures such as a brain or some other "machine"—be it a natural biological machine (perhaps as simple as a single cell, or simpler) or be it a human-made artificial machine? (Arguably some forms of computers and other "artificial intelligence" are on the verge of reaching true consciousness, or perhaps they already have done so, although we do not realize it.) Entities like crystals and rocks can also record information. Does this mean they possess consciousness at some level? What about plants and single-celled organisms? The work of Cleve Backster (2003) indicates that they do possess consciousness and that this consciousness can be detected using electronic equipment such as a polygraph (lie detector) connected to a plant or by electronically monitoring the behavior of cells. As unbelievable as it may sound to some, Backster's experiments demonstrate that plants, and even cultures of cells, can respond to thoughts, emotions, and intentions.

The "consciousness and information problem" is a real issue. The power of water to store and transmit information (see page 277) may provide a clue to the more general concept of consciousness in the universe. Water, on the face of it, is a very simple structure chemically; each molecule is composed of two hydrogen atoms and one oxygen atom. If such a simple structure can encode, store, and transmit information—a basic requirement of consciousness—could one of its simple components, namely hydrogen atoms, do the same? Might hydrogen atoms be able to store information and thus form the basis for consciousness?

Hydrogen is the simplest known element (although still composed of smaller subatomic particles). Hydrogen atoms are the most abundant atoms in the universe. (However, we still do not know what form most of the mass of the universe takes; it appears to be in the form of something other than elements, perhaps the mysterious and elusive "dark matter," "mirror matter," or some other exotic form.) Hydrogen, furthermore, is the most common element of our Sun and most stars, and hydrogen pervades our solar system. So could "simple hydrogen" be a carrier of information, and thus the seat of consciousness at some level? Could we, as biological organisms, essentially encode messages and information in the hydrogen of our bodies while we are alive, and then upon death, when our bodies decay and disintegrate away, release hydrogen and its encoded information to be recycled again? After bodily death does our hydrogen gather, regroup, and form new entities, new suns, that carry on our information and consciousness at a different level or in a different form? Katie sums it up this way: somewhere in the heart of the Sun, entropy (disorder) changes to information and a new cycle begins (see appendix 4, page 400, for a discussion of entropy).

For my part, I am not sure what to think. Perhaps Katie is on to something with her G! theory. If water, and possibly simple hydrogen, can store and transmit information, perhaps there is an even simpler level of matter that can store information—simpler than an atom of hydrogen or a single proton. (The simplest form of a neutral hydrogen atom consists of a proton and an electron; there are also ions [charged forms] and isotopes [containing neutrons] of hydrogen.) Perhaps some subatomic particle or entity, a hypothetical "informaton" (a fundamental information particle, the name derived from "informa-" and "-ton"), has the ability to code and transmit information and withstand disintegration and decay, allowing information and consciousness to persist.

From Star to Star

Consciousness remains a mystery at many levels, and as Planck expressed, consciousness appears to be fundamental to all else. This is an idea compatible with ancient wisdom. Summarizing the ancient concepts, P. G. Bowen expressed it in these words: "BEING (or any Being) in ultimate metaphysical analysis is a compound of three elements, neither of which has any independent manifestation, or is knowable otherwise than in interaction with the other two. They are CONSCIOUSNESS, ENERGY, and SUBSTANCE. All three exist in everything . . ." (Bowen [1936?], 28; capitalization in the original).

Figure 14.1. Ancient Egyptian depictions of our return to the Sun and Stars upon bodily death. Depiction of the deceased becoming a Star and joining the Sun in the sky, from a sarcophagus in the Egyptian Museum, Cairo (*left*). The deceased being prepared for the journey to the Stars and Sun; depiction from a tomb in the Valley of the Kings (*right*). Note that the departed is carried on a bed in the shape of a lion (representing the Sun) and includes various plasma depictions, as also seen in the so-called "Khafre statue" illustrated as Figure 15.11. Anubis is shown both attending the deceased and also seated in the lower vignette.
(Photographs courtesy of R. Schoch and C. Ulissey.)

Here, according to my interpretation of the ancient wisdom and beliefs, Bowen is referring to the material manifestation of the world as we currently experience it. Ultimately, I believe, consciousness is prior, and from it energy and substance manifest, but with our current sensory limitations, we cannot perceive consciousness independent of its manifestation via energy and substance.

Perhaps we will someday reach a level of elevated, greatly expanded consciousness compared to that of today. Might this occur during a future cycle or age? Was this the case deep in the past? Could this be the ultimate meaning of a golden age? Was this the ideal during the Egyptian first time, during Zep Tepi?

Contemplating the practice of mummification while working on the revision of this book, Katie suggests that this could have been a way to "hold the hydrogen together," to keep the information of the person "as complete as possible," on the journey to the afterlife. To bind the personality, if you will. After all, we have examined how water molecules like to bond; perhaps it is the hydrogen within that inspires this.

The Ancient Egyptians may have been right all along. We come from stars and thence we return.

15

THE SOLAR-INDUCED DARK AGE (SIDA) AND OTHER MATTERS ARISING

I composed the text for the first edition of *Forgotten Civilization* during the second half of 2011 and early 2012. (An Italian-language edition was published in June 2012; the first edition in English was published in August 2012.) At that time, in some circles, there was much discussion of the impending "2012 Event" ostensibly predicted by the Maya (see chapter 13), an event that now many Skeptics and Debunkers (here I capitalize these terms purposefully, to emphasize the ideological biases of those to whom I am referring) scoff at as having never happened. All the doomsayers and fearmongers were wrong, they proudly declare. The year 2012 came and went, and nothing happened. However, is this really so? Or was the timing a bit off? Or was something initiated in 2012 that is now rising to the surface and beginning to manifest? These thoughts are going through my head due to the fact that as I am writing this update the coronavirus (COVID-19) pandemic is sweeping across the planet, wreaking havoc on one nation after another, severely straining social institutions and the very fabric of society as people are ordered to stay at home as much as possible. Restaurants and other businesses, as well as many government offices, have been closed down. Students at schools, colleges, and universities have been sent home, and all teaching is being handled remotely online. Many cannot work at all, which is taking a formerly unimaginable toll on personal finances and the collective economy. Hospitals cannot handle the sick. Medical supplies and equipment are inadequate. Shelves are empty in the grocery stories. There is a general sense of chaos, panic, and desperation. The streets have never been so empty. When we need to go out for some essential reason, such as purchasing food, it is mandated that we wear a mask or other face covering and stay at least six feet (two meters) away from everyone else—the operative term is "social distancing"—in order to try to slow the spread of the virus. I am holed up in a tiny apartment with my wife, Katie, and we are attempting to make the best of things. Fortunately, we still have electricity and water continues to flow from the faucet. Such basic services remain intact.

On the one hand, I feel like the COVID-19 pandemic is giving humanity a small taste of what it will be like if Earth is hit by a major solar outburst. Of course, there have been major pandemics in the past: perhaps the two most famous are the Black Death of the middle fourteenth century and the H1N1 Influenza Pandemic of 1918 (regarding the Black Death, see Shipman 2014; this is often referred to as the Great Bubonic Plague, but whether it was actually an outbreak of bubonic plague or something else has been questioned [see Duncan and Scott 2005], although this in no way diminishes the consequences of the Black Death; regarding the 1918 Pandemic, see Jordan 2019). Another famous and often cited pandemic is the Justinian Plague of the middle sixth century, also attributed to an outbreak of bubonic plague. Recently, it has been suggested that the Justinian Plague (named after the Byzantine ruler at that time), although quite real, may not have been as consequential a pandemic in terms of numbers of deaths and societal impact as sometimes believed (Mordechai et al. 2019). In my opinion, the history of past pandemics indicates that they can be very serious and deadly, but they pass and thus far humanity has been resilient.

On the other hand, a pandemic is very different in many respects from the expected consequences of a major solar outburst. During a pandemic, people are sick and dying, and social distancing, sanitation, and other preventative measures must be observed to try to slow or stem the spread of a disease until vaccines are developed and circulated. (Of course, the exact measures taken must be adjusted to the specific type of disease involved.) Or, particularly in the past before the concept of artificial vaccines, as people caught the disease, some would survive, and at that point they would have natural antibodies to the disease (as is still the case today for those who recover from a disease). In the past, pandemics have eventually run their course, and humankind has continued. However, a major solar outburst could (or will) have very different, and more widespread, consequences than a pandemic.

As I have discussed in earlier chapters of this book, the consequences and ramifications of a major solar outburst to our modern technological society, which is so dependent on electronics and the flow of electricity, will, I believe, be extremely profound. If the electrical grid system collapses, if the flow of electricity ceases, our modern society will be sent into a disastrous tailspin. Without electricity, water will not flow from most of the faucets (how many people have their own private artesian well?), food and other necessities will not be distributed, communication beyond word of mouth will be virtually impossible, and mass panic and chaos—the likes of which has never been seen—will take hold. This will also be an ideal setting for disease to spread, exacerbating the situation; we could expect a pandemic under such conditions. We will have entered a modern Solar-Induced Dark Age (or SIDA).

I genuinely dislike being the messenger of such horrific news, but based on the evidence (and my guiding principle is to always follow the evidence, wherever it may lead), I am convinced that humanity has experienced Solar-Induced Dark Ages in the past, and given our active star (our Sun), we will be hit again by a major solar outburst—and the next one will not be in the distant future. Indeed, I am convinced it is imminent and will most likely be experienced by at least some of those alive today as I write these words.

SIDA: SOLAR-INDUCED DARK AGE

This brings me to various updates and developments since I initially wrote *Forgotten Civilization* back in 2011–2012. First, I will focus on the concept of SIDA. Katie and I would often discuss that period encompassing the span of some six thousand years since the solar outburst (or outbursts—more on this below) that ended the last ice age (circa 9700 BCE) and the reemergence of civilization during the fourth millennium BCE. It was awkward and cumbersome to always refer to this as the "period from the end of the last ice age to the reemergence of civilization six thousand years later"—or something to that effect—and in a flash of insight, Katie came up with the acronym SIDA for "Solar-Induced Dark Age." I immediately liked it, and it is a term that has now gained traction with the public. I began using it during interviews and lectures, and I placed it in print (for instance, Schoch 2015; Schoch and Bauval 2017, 460; Schoch 2020a). There is a certain irony, but truth, to the term. Our Sun is the giver of light and life on Earth, yet our Sun can also bring death and destruction—a Dark Age. The ancient Egyptians knew this well, and they immortalized the concept of the different aspects of our Sun in their myths and traditions.

For those who prefer a non-genetic acronym (that is, an acronym that does not refer to the origin of the Dark Age), SIDA can also stand for "Subsequent to the Ice Datum Age"; in this sense, it marks a period

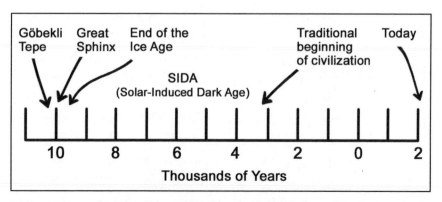

Figure 15.1. Timeline of civilization from the end of the last ice age to the present. (Illustration courtesy of R. Schoch and C. Ulissey.)

of time without referring to the presumed cause (our Sun) underlying the delineation of this segment of time or its consequences (namely a Dark Age for humanity). Rather, in this context, SIDA simply refers to a certain time period, the beginning of which is the point in the Greenland ice cores that marks the end of the last ice age (in geological terms, the "golden spike" that is the marker for the beginning of this time period) and the end of which is the establishment (or reestablishment) of civilization during the fourth millennium BCE. As a golden spike for the latter, I suggest the first occurrence of the earliest glyphs on clay seal impressions found at Abydos, Egypt (see Mitchell 1999), which date to the middle of the fourth millennium BCE. As a side note, I do realize that the acronym SIDA has other meanings in other contexts, as is typical of many acronyms. For instance, in some contexts SIDA stands for "Security Identification Display Area" or "Swedish International Development Cooperation Agency," and in several languages SIDA refers to AIDS (Acquired Immune Deficiency Syndrome). Unfortunately, in this day and age, it can be difficult to develop unique acronyms; however, the use of any particular acronym in context is generally clear. And, if one likes, SIDA (as Sida) can simply be treated as a proper name for a time period, without considering it an acronym, on a par with other geological time periods such as Triassic, Cretaceous, Holocene, and the proposed Anthropocene (discussed in appendix 5, page 432).

The concept of SIDA is conceptually of high importance. Recognition of this period in humanity's history has far-reaching implications. Our current cycle of civilization, the period since the end of SIDA with the reemergence of civilization during the period of the fourth millennium BCE, is not the first cycle of civilization. There was an earlier cycle of civilization, one that culminated at the end of the last ice age (evidenced by the origins of the Great Sphinx, taking the form of the lioness Mehit, as I discuss below, and the sophistication of Göbekli Tepe), before it was devastated and thrown back to a more primitive state by the natural calamities of circa 9700 BCE. How far back in time, prior to 9700 BCE, this earlier cycle of civilization originated, currently we do not know. What were its antecedents? Certainly, in my assessment, there must have been a considerable period of time leading up to the level of development recorded by the monuments and artifacts that have survived from that remote period (and what did these people have, and know, that has not survived?). And where would humanity be in the present day if this early flowering of civilization had not suffered a mighty setback nearly twelve thousand years ago? How advanced might our technology be? What types of societies would have developed? Or might humanity have brought about its own demise though hubris and lack of foresight?

We have solid evidence of two cycles of civilization, the Urianic Cycle of Civilization (UCC or simply "Urianic" or "Urian") and our New or Current Cycle of Civilization (NCC or CCC), which we can refer to as "Neocivilianic" ("Neociv" for short), or the time of the new (neo) civilization. I hope readers will allow me the opportunity to coin these terms in order to have handy labels for these periods of human history, just as we commonly refer to the Middle Ages and the Renaissance, for instance. (I have attempted to coin names/terms that do not have other meanings.) These terms refer to time periods during which these cycles of civilization flourished. The early cycle of civilization, the Urianic (UCC), included the people who built Göbekli Tepe as well as those who carved the original statue that was later transformed into the Great Sphinx. The term Urianic is based on the old German and ultimately Proto-Indo-European root word *ur*, which refers to "original," "early," "primitive," or "proto" (Neufeldt and Guralnik 1988). The Urianic refers to all civilized people living at that time, not only those in the vicinity of modern Urfa. Currently we do not know how far back in time the Urianic extends; this will be determined by future discoveries as Göbekli Tepe and other sites continue to be explored and excavated. The Urianic ended circa 9700 BCE, with the end of the last ice age. Our Current Cycle of Civilization (CCC), the Neocivilianic (Neociv), began approximately 5,500 years ago and is ongoing. Between these two cycles of civilization we have SIDA, which lasted approximately six millennia. But were there even earlier cycles of civilization, separated by earlier SIDAs? Given that modern humans have existed on planet Earth for nearly two hundred thousand years (Hammond et al. 2017), along with various other species of humans, such as *Homo neanderthalensis* (Neanderthals), *Homo altaiensis* (Denisovans), and *Homo floresiensis* (so-called "hobbits"), and given the evidence that our star (our Sun) is not as stable through time as was once assumed, I believe we have to be open to the concept that there were even earlier cycles of civilization and earlier SIDAs. Possibly, some of these are recorded in the common myths and proto-myths that have been passed down from tens of thousands of years before the end of the last ice age; some mythemes, including themes of destruction and the reemergence of humanity, may go back to well over fifty thousand years ago (see Witzel 2012). And might the Mayan Sun Cycles refer to this as well?

Looking to the future, as frightening as it may be to ponder, we have to face the possibility that humanity will experience future cycles of civilization punctuated by SIDAs. The story of a civilization developing and flourishing, only to be knocked down by a major solar event, and—following another SIDA—civilization reemerging once again, may well be what the future holds, as long as humanity is not exterminated completely. How long any particular SIDA lasts will be a function of the state of civilization prior to the decimating event and how serious and impactful the particular devastating event is.

This broad cyclicity of civilizations on Earth, which is well beyond the view of conventional historians who discuss the rise and fall of particular civilizations and societies in various regions of the planet during the last six thousand years, is one of the major themes of my current work. It provides a framework for looking at the "big picture" of civilizations, along with interspersed dark ages (SIDAs), over tens of thousands of years. Furthermore, it is in agreement with many ancient traditions (including Plato's recounting of the Atlantis story) that there have been many civilizations that came and went on this planet over many millennia. This is often expressed as the Four Ages (Golden, Silver, Bronze, and Iron, or the equivalent in various cultures). The concept of world ages (where each age lasts for some significant length of time) dates back to over twenty thousand years ago (Witzel 2012, 160).

RECENT DEVELOPMENTS REGARDING
THE GREAT SPHINX

Subsequent to the publication of the first edition of *Forgotten Civilization* in 2012, I coauthored with my colleague Robert Bauval the book titled *Origins of the Sphinx: Celestial Guardian of Pre-Pharaonic Civilization* (Schoch and Bauval 2017). In *Origins of the Sphinx,* we compiled all of the evidence thus far, including Bauval's work on the "Orion Correlation" (which contends that the three major pyramids on the Giza Plateau relative to the Nile River correlate with the belt stars of Orion and the Milky Way at circa 10,500 BCE), and we reinforced the case that the earliest incarnation of the statue we now know as the Great Sphinx was probably that of a lion and dates back to the circa 10,500 BCE period; that is, the origins of the Sphinx go back to before the end of the last ice age (as I had earlier contended in *Forgotten Civilization* and elsewhere). Furthermore, we presented evidence that (as I had previously suggested) not only do the proto-Sphinx and the so-called Sphinx Temple (which sits due east of the Sphinx) and the so-called Valley Temple (just to the south of the Sphinx Temple) date to this early period, but so too do the oldest portions (those constructed of megalithic blocks) of the so-called Mortuary Temple (on the eastern side of the Second Pyramid) and the original causeway running from the Mortuary Temple to the Valley Temple.

The original English-language edition of *Origins of the Sphinx* was in print by the end of March 2017. In May of 2017, Robert Bauval and I participated in back-to-back conferences in California and Arizona. One of the attendees at the conferences was our colleague and friend Dr. Manu Seyfzadeh (a dermatologist with a passion for ancient Egypt), who privately revealed to us an amazing discovery he had made: hieroglyphic evidence dating back to earliest dynastic times that apparently refers to the Great Sphinx and an archive under the Sphinx. At Seyfzadeh's invitation, Bauval and I joined him as coauthors on a scholarly paper describing this discovery (Seyfzadeh, Schoch, and Bauval 2017; see also Neyland 2019). This new discovery, summarized here, reinforces the conclusion that the origins of the Great Sphinx date back to a remote time prior to dynastic Egypt (as John Anthony West and I had espoused since the early 1990s; West 2007).

The pharaoh (king) Khufu (Fourth Dynasty, middle twenty-sixth century BCE) is the traditional builder of the Great Pyramid. Khufu's vizier (a high official) was a man named Hemiunu, a beautiful statue of whom was discovered on the Giza Plateau in 1912; this statue is now housed in the Roemer- und Pelizaeus-Museum, in Hildesheim, Germany. As Seyfzadeh pointed out to Bauval and me, on the base of the statue of Hemiunu there is a dual/tandem title that has eluded full translation by the Egyptological establishment. This tandem title is not an isolated instance; it is also found on a stunningly beautiful stela of the royal prince Wepemnefret, a son of Khufu who may have served as vizier following Hemiunu. Furthermore, this title goes back in time well before Khufu and the Fourth Dynasty, as it is also found on wooden panels of Hesy-Re (Hesy-Ra, or Hesire), a high official in the court of the pharaoh Djoser (middle or late 27th century BCE) of the Third Dynasty.

Before I proceed, I want to make the point that this dual title is found associated with individuals who preceded the date generally attributed to the Great Sphinx by conventional Egyptologists, namely circa 2500 BCE, during the reign of the Fourth Dynasty pharaoh Khafre. Possibly, Wepemnefret could have known Khafre during his lifetime, but without doubt Hesy-Re (Third Dynasty) lived a century or more prior to the time of Khafre and the supposed construction of the Great Sphinx.

This tandem title consists of seven distinct signs or symbols, as recognized by Egyptologists, written in the following order: (1) axe, (2) reed and inkwell, forming a single symbol, (3) sedge (a plant found in Egypt), (4) bread or bread loaf, (5) axe, (6) bent rod (this is a mysterious, previously undeciphered, sign), and (7) recumbent lioness. Even taking stylistic differences due to the different sculptors into account, analogous to different fonts that can be used for our alphabetic letters, these hieroglyphic signs are virtually identical. At the base of the Hemiunu statue and on the Wepemnefret stela, the last three signs (axe, bent rod, lioness) are placed very close together, or are even touching.

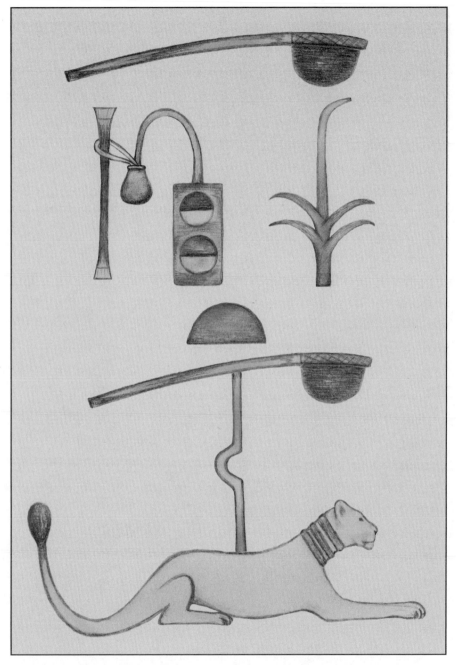

Figure 15.2. Rendition of the dual/tandem title found on the base of the statue of Hemiunu (in front of the left foot), on the stela of the prince Wepemnefret, and on the wooden panels of Hesy-Re.
(Illustration by and courtesy of Catherine Ulissey.)

Figure 15.3. A seal impression of the First Dynasty pharaoh Djer (*top*). The tandem title on a wooden panel from the tomb of Hesy-Re, Third Dynasty, Saqqara; artifact now located in the Egyptian Museum, Cairo (*bottom*).
(Djer seal impression from Petrie 1901, plate XVI;
photograph of Hesy-Re wooden panel courtesy of R. Schoch and C. Ulissey.)

In the inscription on the wooden panels of Hesy-Re, the vertical bent rod appears to touch the back of the lioness, as in the Hemiunu and Wepemnefret inscriptions, but the axe does not make actual contact with the bent rod. These slight differences are probably simply differences in artistic style and do not appear to be significant.

The axe symbol is standardly translated along the lines of overseer, master, architect, master builder, or carpenter; that is, it denotes some sort of high official or person in charge of something of major importance. The fact that there are two axes indicates that this is a dual title; in the three examples noted above, associated with three different individuals, the two titles occur together. The reed and inkwell, sedge, and bread loaf associated with the first portion of the dual title have generally been translated to mean that the official holding this title was the overseer of the royal scribes and/or architects. (The two are conceivably related, as architects would have to draw and record building plans and construction details.) This would be an extremely important position, for such a person would be responsible for royal records and accounts, which were essential in governing the vast territory held by the pharaoh.

But what could the second title represent? The axe of the second title is identical to that of the first, and thus presumably has the same meaning, that of an overseer or similar high official. But what is the apparent bent rod and what does the lioness represent? The lioness of this second title appears to be the same lioness represented elsewhere on the Wepemnefret stela, specifically in the name of the goddess Mehit (who could act as a protectress, taking the form of a female lion). Thus, the Egyptologist William Stevenson Smith (1907–1969) translated this title as "Craftsman of Mehit" (1963, 12). But what is the strange bent rod protruding from, or entering into, the back of the lioness? This is a symbol that has eluded Egyptologists, in part due to its extreme rarity. It was neither listed nor translated by either Alan H. Gardiner (1879–1963) or E. A. Wallis Budge (1857–1934). More recently, some Egyptologists have associated the bent rod with a mooring post used in the docking of a boat, but this appears to be based simply on a superficial visual similarity to mooring posts and neither seems convincing nor makes sense in the context under consideration.

I believe that Seyfzadeh solved the mystery of the bent rod by his suggestion that it represents a physical key that was used to open a lock. We know that by the Middle Kingdom (circa early second millennium BCE) the Egyptians had simple lock-and-key devices; now there is evidence that such devices go back to a much earlier period. Most likely, however, at such a very early date, locks and keys were familiar to only the elite nobility, and thus references to or depictions of such devices appeared very rarely.

Why would anyone stick a key in the back of a lioness? This makes no more sense than sticking a mooring post in her back, unless the lioness represents something else, such as a building or statue protecting a locked chamber or vault. Was the physical structure securing or protecting a locked vault in the shape of a lioness? Immediately, the Great Sphinx comes to mind. But the Sphinx as we see it today has a lion's body with a human head. However, the head was recarved in dynastic times. Since my earliest studies of the Great Sphinx, I have suggested that originally the statue was a recumbent lion. And the locked chamber or vault associated with a lioness, as apparently indicated by the dual title? During the seismic work that Thomas Dobecki and I carried out around the Great Sphinx in the early 1990s, we located a chamber under the Sphinx in the vicinity of the left paw (see chapter 2, page 29, and Schoch and Bauval 2017).

Now everything seemed to come together. The second portion of the dual title refers to an overseer, master, guardian, or possessor of a key that opened a vault that was, based on the first portion of the dual title (referring to scribes and records), an archive, a "Hall of Records," guarded by a lioness. Furthermore, based on the striking similarity between Mehit (as shown on the Wepemnefret stela) and the lioness in the dual title, this guardian lioness is Mehit.

In the real, physical, world, one might suspect that the actual archive was located in the chamber under the Great Sphinx and that, prior to the recarving of its head, the Sphinx was a representation of the lioness Mehit. The dual title can be translated concretely as "Overseer of the Scribes of the King and Master of the Key to the Lioness" or, more fluently, as "The King's Chief Librarian and

Guardian of the Royal Archives of Mehit." It is also a curious fact that the dual title occurs by the left foot of Hemiunu on his statue and the chamber that Thomas Dobecki and I found is under the left front paw of the Sphinx.

Were the "Royal Archives of Mehit" located on the Giza Plateau in a chamber under the Sphinx? The answer may lie in seal impressions of the First Dynasty pharaoh Djer (circa late thirty-first century BCE, some five hundred years prior to Khafre). One of the seals records a lioness with three bent rods inserted into her back (Petrie 1901, plate XVI); the later single bent rod and lioness symbol may be a simplification of this earlier sign. It should also be pointed out that on the Djer seal the vertical bent rods explicitly touch, or are connected to, the lioness, as seems to be the case in the second portion of the dual/tandem title associated with Hemiunu, Wepemnefret, and Hesy-Re. This suggests that the vertical bent rod and lioness may have been viewed as a "tandem hieroglyph," similar to a modern ligature where two or more letters may be joined together to form a single sign, such as *A* and *E* joined to form the ligature *Æ*.

Also on the Djer seal there appears to be a chambered edifice or structure depicted (possibly representing something underground?) on top of which sits an animal, protecting it. This is highly reminiscent of the way the Great Sphinx is shown sitting on or over an edifice more than a millennium and a half later on the granite stela erected by Thutmose IV (circa 1400 BCE) between the paws of the Sphinx. Furthermore, on the seal impression of Djer is found a symbol that may represent "ropes" or "stau," the latter being a fragment of the name Rostau, which is how the ancient Egyptians referred to the Giza Plateau where the Sphinx is located. (The plateau contains many underground caves and chambers, both artificial and natural, that could be accessed via ropes used to descend into them from ground level; hence the association of ropes and Rostau.)

Thus, there is a strong case to be made that as early as the First Dynasty (when some of the first written records in Egypt were kept), the Sphinx—which at that time was a lioness named Mehit—existed on the Giza Plateau and guarded a locked chamber where archives were stored. How far back in time the proto-Sphinx goes, so far the written records do not tell us; however, the various analyses carried out by Robert Bauval and me suggest a date going back to at least the eleventh millennium BCE. Such an extreme age is not contradicted by the hieroglyphic evidence that I have just discussed. Indeed, there is a hieroglyphic symbol that represents the forepart of a lion (sign F4 in the standardized sign list compiled by Alan Gardiner; see Seyfzadeh, Schoch, and Bauval 2017) that may have been inspired by the proto-Sphinx/lioness prior to the body being fully carved or, perhaps more likely, after a fully carved and very ancient lioness statue was split into two portions (see discussion below). This symbol may be the root of the ancient Egyptian word for "ancient" (that is, ancient to the Egyptians four thousand to five thousand or more years ago), which is in keeping with the proto-Sphinx (the original statue of the lioness Mehit) being extremely old indeed.

The name of Mehit as written on the Wepemnefret stela consists of three signs, which have been interpreted by some Egyptologists as: (1) coiled rope or whip, (2) bread or bread loaf, and (3) recumbent lioness. Intriguingly, according to E. A. Wallis Budge, the name of Mehit can mean "A Uraeus [the sacred serpent or snake] on the brow of Ra [Re, the Egyptian god of the Sun]" (Budge 1920; material in brackets added by R. Schoch). Thus, Mehit is associated with the Sun, and indeed throughout much of mythology around the world, the Sun is represented by, or associated with, a lion. (For instance, in classical Western astrology the Sun is associated with and rules the zodiacal sign of the lion, Leo.) Returning to Mehit, among other functions, in Egyptian mythology she was an enforcer of Ra's will on Earth. According to Budge, the name and word Mehit also has the meaning of "Rain" or "Flood"; that is, a flood or floods caused by torrential rains. Thus, Mehit connects the idea of a solar lioness and the Sun with prehistoric (ancient to the Ancient Egyptians) torrential rains and flooding.

Why would the Sun and a solar lioness be associated with torrential rains and flooding? Based on the evidence, I believe this harkens back to the end of the last ice age (circa 9700 BCE), when a major solar outburst (or outbursts) snapped Earth out of its last ice age, concurrently melting glaciers and evaporating massive amounts of water that subsequently fell as torrential rains, causing widespread flooding (which, in coastal areas, was exacerbated by the rise in sea levels). I am convinced, based on the overwhelming evidence, as presented in both this book and *Origins of the Sphinx,* that the original proto-Sphinx—which we can now demonstrate was the lioness Mehit—dates back to the eleventh millennium BCE or earlier. (Remember that the statue was not initially a Sphinx; the original head was recarved in early dynastic times.) And why does the current Sphinx show evidence of extreme weathering and deep erosion due to rainfall? Because it was subjected to the torrential rains caused by the solar outburst that ended the last ice age. In the name of Mehit the ancient dynastic Egyptians encoded and memorialized the solar outburst and accompanying torrential rains of circa 9700 BCE. Furthermore, this occurred during the Age of Leo, at which time the proto-Sphinx, the lioness Mehit, faced the Sun, located in the constellation of Leo, as together the Sun and Leo rose in the sky on the morning of the vernal equinox.

There is another provocative aspect of Mehit that I want to point out. In some of the depictions of the lioness, she is shown wearing three or four ornamental neck-rings. (These can be distinctly seen in the depictions of the lioness on Wepemnefret's stela and the wood panel of Hesy-Re, but are absent from the depictions on Hemiunu's statue and Djer's seal.) On the actual Great Sphinx, an apparent neck-ring was also present up until very recent times, as best seen in nineteenth- and early-twentieth-century photos, see figure 15.4. (It has since been obscured by modern repairs and reconstructions to the Sphinx.) Possibly the original proto-Sphinx was carved with neck-rings, or possibly the apparent neck-ring observed on the Great Sphinx is a feature that developed due to weathering and erosion of the rock, which was then interpreted as a neck-ring by the dynastic Egyptians. Either way, the appearance of a neck-ring feature on the actual Great Sphinx and the depiction of neck-rings on the lioness Mehit further corroborate the association of these two entities: at one time, the statue now known as the Great Sphinx took the form of the lioness Mehit. Although it may be viewed as wild

Figure 15.4. Photo taken before twentieth-century repairs to the
Great Sphinx showing a ridge in the neck region that may be a
possible counterpart to the neck-rings that appear on some images of
the lioness Mehit. Photo circa 1870s–1880s, from a glass lantern slide.
(Collection of R. Schoch.)

speculation, I also wonder if the neck rings of Mehit represent the torus
plasma shapes that could, according to Anthony Peratt, be seen in the
sky during a major solar outburst.

One final note: Seyfzadeh, Bauval, and I dedicated our Mehit article to John Anthony West (1932–2018), and we redesignated the tandem hieroglyph that we reinterpreted, composed of the bent rod and
the lioness, as the "J.A.W. Sign" in his honor (Seyfzadeh, Schoch, and
Bauval 2017).

OUR UNSTABLE SUN

One of the major themes of *Forgotten Civilization* is that our Sun is not as stable as has generally been assumed. Rather, it goes through periods of instability and disequilibrium; since I wrote the original text of this book, superflares have been documented on solar-type stars (Maehara et al. 2012).

I suspect that the instability of our Sun is cyclical, with significant periods of instability resulting in major solar outbursts occurring approximately every eleven thousand to thirteen thousand years. This may well tie in with the precessional cycle of approximately twenty-four thousand to twenty-six thousand years; that is, our Sun undergoes major instabilities every half of a precessional cycle. The precessional cycle may possibly be due to not just a simple "wobble" over time in Earth's spin axis, but rather it may be a result of our Sun (and thus our solar system) being a member of a binary star system (Cruttenden 2006, 2019). This may seem crazy to some, as we do not look up in the sky and see two Suns; however, the second Sun may be dark or hidden or so distant that we are not readily aware of it being our companion in a binary system (Cruttenden 2006, 2019). And as Walter Cruttenden has pointed out, many ancient traditions included the concept of a "Second Sun" or companion to our Sun (Cruttenden 2006). It may also be telling to note that binary star systems are quite common. In a survey of over 450 solar-type stars within twenty-five parsecs (about 81.5 light-years) of our Sun, it was found that approximately 56 percent of the stars did not have companion stars (or more accurately, did not have companion stars that had been found and confirmed), approximately 33 percent of the primary stars had a binary companion, approximately 8 percent belonged to triple-star systems, and approximately 3 percent belonged to systems with more than three stars (Raghavan et al. 2010; Boss and Keiser 2014). In terms of the total number of stars studied, both primary stars and companion stars, about two-thirds of the studied stars are members of either binary or multiple-star systems. Theoretical analyses suggest that there is a high probability that our Sun originally, when first formed, had a binary stellar companion (Siraj and Loeb 2020).

Recent work on stars in general has found that many are much more unstable than was previously believed. Pertinent to the possible periodicity of solar outbursts, there are stars that undergo recurring novae or nova-like phenomena. Many nova-type phenomena are associated with binary star systems, and while it was once thought that in most cases "typical" recurring novae might have a periodicity on the order of millions of years, a recent comprehensive study concluded that many stars exhibiting nova-type phenomena may erupt "at a rate of about once every 10,000 years rather than once every few million years" (quoted from American Museum of Natural History 2020; see Hillman et al. 2020 for the original study). This time frame fits well the periodicity that I have suggested for major solar outbursts from our Sun.

Related to this work on the periodicity of nova-like phenomena in stars is the concept that various stars, including our Sun, can undergo what are now being termed "micronova" (or "micro-nova" or "mininova") events. Ben Davidson has popularized the term and applied it to the major solar outbursts of our Sun, referring to a "Solar Micronova" that corresponds to the end of the last ice age, approximately twelve thousand years ago (see Davidson 2018). When a micronova occurs, the star involved (for instance, our Sun) may throw off a shell of material that is composed of not just photons and various ions but also actual chunks of matter (dust and debris). This may consist of material that congealed on the surface of the star and was then ejected, and/or material that congealed and coalesced as it traveled through space. Shells of such material have been documented for various recurrent novae and nova-like (nova-type) stellar phenomena, such as the stars T Pyxidis (Izzo et al. 2014) and V1315 Aql (Sahman et al. 2018). Here it should be noted that recurrent novae can occur with a periodicity on the order of decades to potentially millions of years (for instance, T Pyxidis was observed to erupt in 1890, 1902, 1920, 1944, 1966/1967, and 2011; AAVSO 2011; see Schaefer 2009 for a review of known galactic recurrent novae; see also Munari 2012; Mukai 2014). As already noted, it has now been concluded that some nova-like phenomena occur on the order of about ten thousand years. Furthermore, it has been estimated that a nova-like phase may last on the order of approximately 2,000 to 2,400 years (Sahman et al. 2018) for some stars. I am not contending that these stars are the same type of stars as is our Sun; however, in the not so distant past, no one even contemplated such time frames for nova-like phenomena for such stars. And in the past, a much more extreme stability was assumed for our Sun; so, even if the stars studied and cited above differ from our Sun, I believe it is useful to use them as a potential analogy for what may be the nature and behavior of our Sun.

Thinking about our star, the Sun, I wonder if it may well have a periodicity on the order of eleven thousand to thirteen thousand years (as previously mentioned) with nova-like phases lasting on the order of two thousand to three thousand years. As I hypothesize below, the end of the last ice age, marked by the Younger Dryas, may have experienced a period of significant and severe solar outbursts—which we may term a nova-like phase or micronova period for our Sun—that lasted a couple or few thousand years. The evidence suggests to me that the Younger Dryas cooling period was initiated circa 10,900 BCE (some people date it closer to 10,800 BCE) by a solar outburst, and the end of the Younger Dryas (which marks the end of the last ice age) was brought about by a major solar outburst at circa 9700 BCE, with additional (probably smaller) outbursts occurring for another one or two millennia following the end of the last ice age. This scenario fits well with some of the latest data on the timing and duration of nova-like phenomena (micronovae). And as Davidson (2018) has pointed out, if during a micronova of our Sun a shell of materials is thrown off, some of this material can (most likely will) hit Earth as physical impactors, so some of the data that various researchers have pointed to as evidence of a comet (or other impactor) hitting our planet at the beginning of the Younger Dryas may, even if they do indicate a physical impactor, be attributable to a solar micronova (or, in other words, a solar outburst or series of solar outbursts). As Davidson (2018) has stated, "A solar micronova satisfies all the catastrophe evidence, including the cyclical nature, . . . AND impactor-like evidence." (See further discussion in appendix 5, page 419.)

While the global climate was beginning to warm toward the end of the last ice age, the Younger Dryas, lasting for about 1,200 years (from about 10,900 BCE to 9700 BCE), was a cold spell before the final and sudden warming that occurred at 9700 BCE. In fairness to the "comet hypothesis," a physical impactor hitting Earth (or exploding in the atmosphere) could conceivably cause a sudden cooling spell due to the resulting dust and debris that would be injected into the atmosphere, literally blocking the Sun and causing increased cloud cover and so forth. However, having studied in detail the purported evidence that has been put forth to support the hypothesis of a comet hitting Earth (if not a comet, it might have been a meteor, asteroid, or other impactor or impactors, according to some), I remain unconvinced that it was necessarily a comet or a similar physical object. All of the evidence (which, as I write this, continues to be put forward by the comet proponents; see for instance Moore et al. 2020 and the references therein) is, in my assessment, also compatible with some sort of solar outburst or micronova (see discussion in appendix 5, page 428). This is even more the case if, as discussed already, a solar micronova included the Sun shedding and ejecting significant chunks of debris that might hit Earth as physical impactors. But how could a solar outburst (possibly representing the beginning of a micronova-like phase of solar activity) bring about a cold spell? This is an issue that long troubled me, until what I suspect is the answer was published during the summer of 2018.

In July 2018, Lloyd D. Keigwin (of the Woods Hole Oceanographic Institution) and his colleagues published a paper titled "Deglacial Floods in the Beaufort Sea Preceded Younger Dryas Cooling" in which they present evidence indicating that it was a massive glacial flood that changed ocean circulation patterns in the Atlantic, thus initiating the Younger Dryas cooling. This influx of fresh water apparently suddenly stalled, slowed, or shut down the ocean circulation pattern known as the Atlantic Meridional Overturning Circulation (AMOC; also referred to as the Gulf Stream System). This is a northward flow of warm upper layer water that is brought from the Southern Hemisphere and tropics up to the Northern Atlantic. By analyzing oxygen isotope ratios (^{18}O compared to ^{16}O) in the shells of planktonic foraminifera (single-celled amoeba-like organisms that live in tiny shells that can be preserved and collect in the sedimentological record; when alive, they live in the water column, and when they die, their shells can fall through the water column and collect on the bottom, becoming part of the geological record), Keigwin et al. (2018) found a significant depletion in ^{18}O and determined that there was a huge influx of glacial melt water, ice, and sediments at ~12.94 ± 0.15 ka (12,940 ± 150 years ago). This places the event quite precisely, taking geological uncertainty into account, at the start of the Younger Dryas.

As stated by Neal Driscoll (of the Scripps Institution of Oceanography and one of the authors on the Keigwin et al. 2018 paper), their work with oxygen isotopes "is the smoking gun for fingerprinting glacial lake out-bursts" (quoted in Mooney 2018). Just how sudden the "lake outbursts" may have been remains a point of contention. In their paper, Keigwin et al. (2018) state that the lowest drop in ^{18}O, based on their analysis of foraminifera shells, lasted about 130 years. However, this may be mis-leading as the initial flooding could have dumped massive amounts of fresh water into the ocean, thus reducing the salinity of the seawater to the point that the foraminifera could not survive. It is possible that the main flooding event happened incredibly quickly, perhaps when ice dams were melted (my suggestion) and water poured into the sea. All of this could have taken place over the course of a year or less, and as Keigwin et al. (2018) point out, if this had been the case, then the planktonic fora-minifera would initially have been unable to survive, and therefore they would not record the initial catastrophic flooding. The signal that does survive in the geological record is compatible with huge and very sudden "glacial lake outbursts" (referring back to the quote from Driscoll).

Immediately I asked myself, what would cause such sudden melting (such as the melting of ice dams resulting in the release of tremendous amounts of water)? The answer: a major solar outburst. Now all of the pieces seemed to fall into place. Unusual solar activity had initiated the beginning of the Younger Dryas, and a major solar outburst had also ended the Younger Dryas (thus ending the last ice age). Supporting this contention, remember that Paul LaViolette (2011a) has presented com-pelling evidence (primarily ^{14}C in sediment sequences correlated with data from ice cores) that there was a "super-sized solar proton event" (SPE; LaViolette 2011a, 303) at the beginning of the Younger Dryas (see discussion in chapter 7, page 145).

I believe that we may have now discovered the cause of the beginning of the Younger Dryas circa 10,900 BCE, which is a cooling event in the Northern Hemisphere, and the cause of the end of the Younger Dryas (end of the last ice age) at 9700 BCE, which was a dramatic warming event worldwide. In both cases, it was unusual solar activity, powerful outbursts from our own Sun. Furthermore, in my mind, all of the evidence and data pertaining to the catastrophes close to and precisely at the end of the last ice age, both those at the beginning of the Younger Dryas and at the end of the Younger Dryas, fall into place. If the solar outbursts included micronova-type phenomena, then actual chunks of matter (impactors) may indeed have hit Earth at this time in some regions, this in addition to massive electrical storms and plasma discharges—the "lightning and thunderbolts" discussed in previous chapters of this book.

I also want to point out that actual craters on the surface of our planet may be evidence of electrical storms and plasma (electrically charged particles) hitting Earth during a solar outburst rather than a comet or other physical impactor. Studies have now demonstrated that plasma outbursts can create electrical scarring and cratering (Talbott 2011). And I would point out that long ago, studying data collected by the Apollo missions to our Moon, Thomas Gold (1969, 1345) concluded that on the surface of the Moon "Some glazing ["glazing" refers to glassy surfaces and vitrification; note added by R. Schoch] is apparently due to radiation heating; it suggests a giant solar outburst in geologically recent times." To put this in modern terms over half a century later, Gold is saying that our Moon was hit by a major solar outburst "in geologically recent times" (which I believe corresponds to the end of the last ice age), and if the Moon was hit, then surely the Earth was hit as well. Cratering on the Moon may be due not only to impactors (meteors and so forth) but also to direct electrical discharges during solar outbursts as well (see "Craters and Platinum-Group Spikes" below on page 330).

I need to also mention that in November 2018 a paper was published titled "A Large Impact Crater beneath Hiawatha Glacier in Northwest Greenland" (Kjær et al. 2018). Many proponents of the comet theory for the end of the Younger Dryas quickly jumped on this as evidence for their argument. However, reading the actual journal article and looking at the details of the stratigraphy, the crater does not appear to me to necessarily date to the Younger Dryas. As the authors write, "The sum of these tentative age constraints suggests that the Hiawatha impact crater formed during the Pleistocene, as this age is most consistent with inferences from presently available data" (Kjær et al. 2018, 9). The Pleistocene dates from approximately 2.6 million years ago to 11,700 years ago. Impactors collide with Earth, no doubt, and the Hiawatha crater may (or may not) be evidence of such. But the Hiawatha crater has yet to be dated to the Younger Dryas, as so many comet theorists apparently wish it to be. And, if it turns out that it is dated to precisely the beginning of the Younger Dryas, it might possibly be the result of a major electrical discharge from our Sun rather than the result of a comet strike. Or possibly it was the result of a physical impactor thrown off by our Sun during a micronova type of event, or possibly a stream of comets, asteroids, or other objects both hit the Sun and intersected Earth's orbit. Comets and other material impacting the Sun could potentially destabilize our star and initiate a solar outburst, while some of the debris from the stream in outer space might actually hit some of the planets, including Earth. If this had been the case, and I am not convinced that it was (I mention it for heuristic purposes), then Earth may well have been hit by a comet or other impactor at this time, but the primary causative factor initiating the start of the Younger Dryas would have been unusual solar activity.

Returning to unusual solar activity, since the first edition of *Forgotten Civilization* was published in 2012, there has been a wealth of evidence discovered that indicates our Sun has not been as stable and consistent since the end of the last ice age as has often been believed, although the "unusual activity" ("abnormal activity" or "extreme activity") of our Sun since the end of the last ice age is not in any manner comparable to the incredible outbursts that occurred, I believe, at the end of the last ice age. Here is a brief list of incidents of unusual solar activity over the last eight millennia that have been discovered thus far. (Regarding the use of radionuclides to determine unusual solar activity, see the update to "A Note on the Reconstruction of Solar Activity through Geological Time" in appendix 5 on page 415.)

* * * * * * * * * *

5480 BCE: Miyake et al. (2017) analyzed the ^{14}C content of tree rings of bristle cone pines from the White Mountains of California, dated from 5490 BCE to 5411 BCE using dendrochronology. They found a large increase in ^{14}C during the period from 5481 BCE to 5471 BCE (which they labeled the "5480 BC event"). After careful analysis and comparisons to other solar events, these authors concluded that the 5480 BCE event was most likely the result of SPEs, which either occurred during the beginning of a grand solar minimum or occurred with or shortly before unusual solar magnetic activity. I want to point out that from our perspective today, an SPE or SPEs on the order of magnitude of those that were most likely responsible for the 5480 BCE event would be devastating for our modern electrical- and electronic-based technological society. And furthermore, if one of the scenarios suggested by Miyake et al. is correct, and looking at the data I believe it is, the SPE or SPEs of the 5480 BCE event occurred during a grand solar minimum, the time when some people might intuitively believe that the Sun would be least expected to produce such an outburst.

3372–3371 BCE: Wang et al. (2017) identified a rapid increase in ^{14}C in 3372–3371 BCE when analyzing the carbon isotope content of tree rings in an ancient sample of the Chinese wingnut tree that was dated through dendrochronology. Based on their detailed analysis of this event, Wang et al. concluded that it was most probably caused by a significant SPE. These authors point out that if an equivalent event occurred today, it would cause damage to electronics and power grids, deplete atmospheric ozone (which would allow more ultraviolet rays to reach ground level and could have severe repercussions on the surface of Earth, including most likely killing some sensitive organisms, such as plants and algae at the bases of food chains), and "possibly affect the weather" (Wang et al. 2017, 4).

814–813 BCE: Jull et al. (2018) identified an unusual increase (excursion) in ^{14}C around 814–813 BCE based on the analyses of tree rings of sequoia from California and cedar from Japan. These authors found a very similar pattern in the ^{14}C data for the 814–813 BCE event as found for the 5480 BCE event, and like the earlier event, the 814–813 BCE event may have been a major solar event (such as an SPE; Jull et al. [2018, 1245] also suggest it may have been, or included, a solar flare or a CME) associated with a solar minimum.

660 BCE: This event, dated to approximately 660 BCE (circa 2610 BP, or before the present, where the "present" is considered 1950 CE) was identified based on increases in ^{14}C in the tree rings of German oaks (Park et al. 2017) and in Greenland ice cores (O'Hare et al. 2019) based on increased concentrations of ^{10}Be and ^{36}Cl (a chlorine isotope) that correlate with raised levels of ^{14}C production (for instance, measured in tree rings) at this time. It was also apparently recorded in Assyrian astronomical/astrological records of the seventh century BCE (Hayakawa et al. 2019). After detailed analysis, O'Hare et al. concluded that the increase in cosmogenic radionuclides at 660 BCE was due to an extreme SPE or, as they also label it, "an enormous solar storm" (O'Hare et al. 2019, 5961). The 660 BCE event was comparable to the 774–775 CE event (see below), which is generally considered the largest SPE thus far identified during the last ten thousand years (that is, approximately since the end of the last ice age). Furthermore, based on the $^{36}Cl/^{10}Be$ ratio for the 660 BCE event, O'Hare et al. concluded that it was a "hard spectrum event"—in other words, many of the protons of the SPE or SPEs at that time had very high energies and, in terms of modern technology, would have been particularly damaging.

774–775 CE: This event, often referred to as the Charlemagne event because it occurred during the time of Charlemagne (742?–814), was first identified by Miyake et al. (2012) on the basis of ^{14}C concentrations in Japanese cedar trees. They also found that this correlated with a sharp increase in ^{10}Be recorded in the ice layers from Dome Fuji in Antarctica at around 775 CE. Based on their initial analyses, Miyake et al. concluded that the spike in ^{14}C production occurred in less than one year, and in their opinion, "Only two known phenomena [could be responsible for the 774–775 event] . . . a supernova explosion or a large solar proton event (SPE)" (Miyake et al. 2012, 241). In a 2013 paper announcing the discovery of the 993–994 event (see below), Miyake et al. (2013) hypothesized that "a solar origin is a plausible cause of ^{14}C increase events," referring to both the 774–775 event and the 993–994 event. In a paper published the same year, I. G. Usoskin et al. (2013) made the case that the 774–775 event is best explained as the result of an extreme SPE. Following the earlier work of Miyake et al. (2012) and Usoskin et al. (2013), further work by various researchers around the globe has corroborated the 774–775 event. Jull et al. (2014) found evidence of ^{14}C excursions in the tree rings of larch in northern Siberia and bristlecone pines in the White Mountains of California. Güttler et al. (2015) reported similar data from trees in New Zealand, and Liu et al. (2014) reported a ^{14}C excursion at this time in corals from the South China Sea. It seems there is little doubt that this was an event that was experienced worldwide.

993–994 CE: Based on the measurement of ^{14}C in tree rings from a Japanese cedar, the same tree that they used to identify the 774–775 CE event, Miyake et al. (2013; see also Miyake et al. 2014) found a rapid increase in 993–994 CE. They also found an increase in ^{10}Be in the Antarctic Dome Fuji ice core at about 774 CE and 994 CE, thus corroborating the ^{14}C data. Miyake et al. (2013, 4) suggest that the 993–994 event, while smaller than the 774–775 event, was still significant and much larger than anything witnessed in modern times.

1052 CE: Interestingly, looking at the data in figure 4 of the 2013 article by Miyake et al., there also appears to be an increase in ^{10}Be at around 1050 CE. Even though they did not find an increase in ^{14}C at this time, could the ^{10}Be data indicate a solar event? Possible supporting evidence that some sort of unusual solar event may have occurred around 1050 CE comes from the *Scottish Chronicles*, where it is recorded for the year 1052 CE that there was,

A tower of fire seen at Ross-Deala, on the festival of St. George, during the space of five hours, blackbirds innumerable going into and out of it, and one large bird in the middle of it. (Jeremiah 1870, 175)

This sounds like it could have been due to an unusual solar event that was accompanied by unusual plasma / electrical configurations (which might be termed aurorae or a "tower of fire") seen in the sky. What exactly the "blackbirds" are remains uncertain, but they sound reminiscent of the bird-like shapes that plasma physicist Anthony L. Peratt has modeled and identified in plasma configurations that may be observed in the sky during a major solar outburst (see discussion in chapter 6, page 118). Might there have been a distinct 1052 event, or might this have been an event related to the 993–994 event? To use a geological earthquake analogy, nearly sixty years later, could there have been a sort of "aftershock" (a solar "hiccup") following the 993–994 event?

* * * * * * * * * *

It needs to be emphasized that the record of "unusual" solar events listed above is most assuredly very far from complete. It is simply a list of those events that have been identified up to this time. The current isotope data are in many instances not well enough resolved to identify SPEs and other solar outbursts. In many cases, annual (year-by-year) data of ^{14}C concentrations, for instance, are necessary (rather than the five-year or greater resolution that is standardly available) in order to identify solar events. Many solar outbursts (SPEs, major solar flares, CMEs, and so forth) may be hidden in the lower-resolution data currently available (Wang et al. 2017). Indeed, once we have more detailed and reliable information available to us, we may well find—I believe we will find—that what are now considered unusual solar events are in fact not so unusual.

Modern technological society has generally been lulled into a false sense of complacency when it comes to solar activity, primarily because we have witnessed directly (with technological devices that are sensitive to solar activity, whether or not designed for such purposes) such a very short span of time in the life of our Sun. Interestingly, and a real warning to us from a practical point of view, the 1859 Carrington Event (see chapter 12, page 224), which if it had occurred today would have had grave consequences for our modern technological society, does not appear in the documented annual tree ring data (Jull et al. 2014). This may show how "small" the 1859 Carrington Event was relative to the events reviewed above. There may have been many Carrington-level events over the last twelve thousand years that we currently have no record of. I do not think it is inconceivable that they occur with a frequency of perhaps once every century or so. The Carrington Event occurred in 1859, over a century and a half ago, so we may in fact be overdue for the next major solar event.

CRATERS AND PLATINUM-GROUP SPIKES

Just because something is accepted as a truism today does not necessarily mean it is true. This applies to all aspects of life, but here I want to focus on two specific "truisms" that have become generally, if in some cases tacitly, accepted among many scholars and laypersons alike: First, most craters on the surfaces of various planets, including Earth and the Moon, are the result of impact events (meteors, asteroids, comets, or other debris from outer space). The scars of such impacts are sometimes referred to as astroblemes ("star wounds"), which can include any signs or remnants of an impact crater. Second, anomalously high geochemical traces of various platinum-group elements (PGEs, which include platinum, iridium, osmium, palladium, rhodium, and ruthenium), particularly platinum and/or iridium, are indicative of an extraterrestrial impact by a meteor or other space object, as such objects often carry much higher concentrations of PGEs such as platinum and/or iridium (in particular) than is typically found on the surface of our planet.

Before I continue this discussion, I want to point out explicitly that there are known—because they were directly observed—instances of lightning forming craters. Although certainly small by geological and astrophysical standards, an example is the case of a fifteen-foot (4.6-meter) crater in a Fort Worth, Texas, parking lot created by a lightning strike at the end of October 2019 (Brumfield 2019). Think of lightning, but orders of magnitude greater than anything seen on Earth in modern times, and the destruction that even atmospheric lightning can cause. Of course, a small 15-foot (4.6-meter) crater in a parking lot is virtually nothing compared to a crater that is ten kilometers in diameter (for instance), but it demonstrates that lightning—natural electrical discharges—can directly create craters on Earth's surface. Likewise, I would point out that the documented cases of meteorites being directly observed in modern times hitting Earth are a far cry from an asteroid with a diameter of ten kilometers hitting Earth (Branch and Newton 2007). The point I wish to make here is that whether it is electrical discharges / lightning strikes, or asteroid / comet / meteor impacts, we do not have direct experiences in modern times (where we can consider "modern" to be the last five hundred years) of any such type of events at large, massive scales. We must work from, extrapolate from, the evidence of the past.

Let us consider the issue of craters on the surfaces of various planets and moons, including Earth and our own Moon. Most people today, scientists and the general public alike, consider the majority of craters to be the result of impacting meteors, comets, asteroids, and other objects. Historically, however, this has not always been the case. Until about 1900, many geologists and other scientists considered many, even most, craters (whether on Earth, the Moon, or elsewhere) to be the result of volcanic activity or activity related to volcanism (for instance, steam due to the heating of water by hot molten rock deep underground collecting in a natural cavity, and then ultimately building up so much pressure that it exploded). Actually, volcanic activity and genuine impact craters may be related, if a major impact sets off volcanic activity, particularly in a situation where the crust of Earth is penetrated deeply enough. However, solar activity, plasma discharges hitting Earth, and/or a micronova-type event from the Sun could create craters and initiate volcanic and earthquake activity as well.

Studies of some large craters on Earth, such as Meteor Crater in Arizona (approximately three-quarters of a mile [1.2 kilometers] in diameter), that are with a high degree of certainty genuinely attributable to a meteor or other physical impactor—for instance, due to fragments of undoubted meteorites having been collected in and around the crater—have yielded some interesting results. In detailed studies of Meteor Crater specifically, it was concluded that it was not the physical object per se that was of prime importance in creating the actual crater, but rather the shock wave accompanying the high-velocity impactor (Shoemaker 1987). I suggest that a tremendous shock wave could hit in a localized region during a huge plasma strike (electrical discharge strike), such as a plasma strike that could hit Earth, the Moon, or other planetary bodies during a major solar outburst, and create a crater similar to the craters that result from physical impactors.

Here I need to point out that not all craters are the same; not all craters were formed by the same mechanism. Undoubtedly, given that we can observe such activity in the present day, some ancient craters are the remains of volcanic calderas or other igneous activity. And some craters, I do not doubt, are truly the result of physical impactors, such as meteors, comets, asteroids, and the like. And some craters are the result of electrical discharges and plasma strikes, as we shall now explore in more detail. To attribute all craters on Earth or other planetary bodies to a single cause is, in my opinion, a mistake.

To my knowledge, the first person to put forth an electrical discharge hypothesis for some craters was Brian J. Ford in his 1965 paper analyzing craters on the Moon. Ford discusses the hypotheses of the volcanic and impact origin of lunar craters, acknowledging that each of these theories may account for some of the craters on the lunar surface; indeed, he illustrates a crater that he attributes to an impact. However, in his assessment, the volcanic and impact hypotheses do not account for all of the observed craters on the Moon; there are craters that fall into a third category.

Ford (1965) compared actual craters on the Moon with craters formed experimentally in the laboratory by spark machining (also known as electrical discharge machining, during which material is removed [eroded] using strong electrical discharges [sparks]) and found many significant features between the two. Admittedly, the scale of the craters produced experimentally was many orders of magnitude smaller than those Ford studied from photographs of the lunar surface (on the order of tens of microns [tens of thousandths of a millimeter] for the experimental craters versus tens of kilometers for the larger lunar craters). However, in the Earth and Planetary Sciences, many phenomena can be scaled up and down by many orders of magnitude (as noted by Nobel laureate in physics Hannes Alfvén [1990], relative to plasma physics in particular, the phenomena of which hold from scales in the laboratory to interstellar and intergalactic space dimensions). That is, small experimental models in the laboratory (such as models of rock deformation or erosional processes, to give just two examples) have been demonstrated to reflect the processes that occur in nature at much larger scales, and in some cases over much longer time periods.

Ford pointed out many telling features on various lunar craters that would not be expected if they had either a volcanic or impact origin, but such features are compatible with an electrical discharge origin. A puzzling feature of many lunar craters is the presence of small secondary craters found on the rims of larger primary craters. If these are the result of impact events, how did the secondary impact events "know" to hit just the rim of a crater? Or if one reverts to a volcanic hypothesis, it seems unlikely that so many small volcanic calderas would form precisely on the rims of larger volcanic calderas. Likewise, there are strings or chains of craters that get successively smaller in size. Again, these are difficult to explain by either impacts or volcanic activity. However, as Ford noted, these types of features are found experimentally during crater formation due to electrical discharges.

Since the 1960s there have been some follow-up studies using the approach pioneered by Ford (1965). Tara Desai, of the University of Milano-Bicocca, and colleagues have done a number of experiments using laser beams to simulate naturally occurring craters on planetary bodies. In the laboratory they have produced both simple bowl-shaped craters without a central uplift and also complex craters that can include a central uplift that may rise well above the original surface of the substrate. The explicit intention of these authors is to model meteoritic craters. In the abstract of their 2008 paper they state, "We obtain simple and complex craters similar in contour that are formed due to large meteorite impacts on the terrestrial surface" (Desai et al. 2008, 1132). They do not address the issue that they are creating such craters with "nonmaterial" energetic sources (that is, laser beams), and they never consider the possibility that perhaps in nature, as in their laboratory simulations, craters with the morphologies they created and analyzed could be formed by "natural laser beam equivalents" or, in other words "plasma beams," electrical discharges, and the like. I do not fault them for this, as they are working within the standard modern status quo paradigm in which everyone "knows" that such planetary craters (with relatively few exceptions, such as volcanic calderas or structures due to collapsed sinkholes) are created by massive impacting objects. Unwittingly, perhaps, these authors demonstrate that it is not safe to assume that craters in nature are caused by meteorites or other physical impactors, as identical features are found in craters created by electrical discharges.

Desai et al. (2008) experimentally created and studied craters larger than those studied by Ford (1965), but their craters were still very small—on the order of hundreds of microns in diameter—but remember, such plasma phenomena can be scaled up to an incredible extent with the analogies and comparisons of morphologies remaining valid. Building on the work of Ford and Desai et al., C. J. Ransom (2011) used a plasma discharge apparatus that created craters in the laboratory that were over a centimeter in diameter, and he did not limit himself to creating craters in metals (as in the studies of Ford 1965 and Desai et al. 2008), but also used various other materials as a ground substrate, such as sandstone, that may represent more realistic analogues to the surfaces of planets, moons, asteroids, or other space objects. There was an amazingly strong correlation between Ransom's experimental results and the craters found on our Moon and other planetary bodies (including, in my opinion, on Earth).

As mentioned at the beginning of this section, one of the truisms that is currently widely accepted in both the academic community and among the general public is that anomalously high geochemical traces of various platinum-group elements (PGEs), particularly platinum and/or iridium, are indicative of an extraterrestrial impact by a meteor, asteroid, or other space object. These are commonly referred to as platinum or iridium (or some other metal, depending on the elements being analyzed) "spikes." However, if our Sun undergoes a micronova-type of event, it might conceivably spew out chunks of matter that contain high concentrations of PGEs. Furthermore, platinum and other PGEs can be concentrated by terrestrial processes, such as igneous and volcanic activity (see review by Zientek et al. 2017). In addition to the types of mineral deposits and concentration methods that occur naturally in and on Earth, I will here suggest another hypothesis that I believe has merit and needs to be seriously taken into account.

The basic concept that I am introducing here is founded on the principle that powerful electrical discharges can "boil off," ablate, and erode away various elements at differing rates. Experimentally, it has been found that PGE metals have a low erosion rate when subjected to intense electrical discharges. In an important paper on this subject, F. Llewellyn-Jones summarized his findings:

> This paper outlines the nature of the various classes of electrical discharges—the high voltage capacitative spark discharge, the normal arc discharge, and the low voltage arc that occurs at electrical contacts—and discusses the physical processes that determine the dependence of the rate of electrode erosion on the physical properties of the metal. It is concluded that the most important properties conducive to low erosion rates are high boiling point, high thermal conductivity and high density, so providing the physical reason for the low erosion rates observed for the platinum metals when used as electrode and electrical contacts. (Llewellyn-Jones 1963, 58)

In a more recent study, P. Lukes and colleagues (Lukes et al. 2006) found that among the materials they studied, platinum was the least eroded under various conditions of electrical discharge.

Building on and extrapolating from this experimental work on the erosion of platinum (as well as iridium) under electrical discharge conditions, I suggest that during a major plasma discharge hitting Earth (as part of a solar outburst, for instance), platinum and/or iridium will resist erosion relative to other elements and thus be concentrated. This, I believe, could be one reason that platinum or other PGE spikes are found associated with features (such as spherules, craters, and so forth) that, traditionally and conventionally, have been attributed to material impact events; however, as we are now learning, these features could also result from powerful electrical plasma discharge events.

As we explore electrical discharge phenomena in both the laboratory and in the field, it turns out that many of the indicators that conventional thinking held to be unique and definitively diagnostic of physical impactors (meteors, asteroids, comets, and so forth) can also be the result of powerful electrical discharges. No longer should we consider craters (whether on the Moon, on Earth, or on other planetary objects) to necessarily be the result of impact events or volcanic activity. Likewise, platinum and iridium spikes can, based on experimental evidence, occur due to powerful electrical discharges. All told, much of the evidence that has been used to support impact hypotheses in the past should be reconsidered in terms of electrical discharges, plasma events, and solar outbursts.

A PLASMA STRIKE ON THE GIZA PLATEAU

While in Egypt during the summer of 2016, Yousef Awyan and Mohamed Ibrahim, two Egyptian colleagues, pointed out to me a very curious phenomenon on the Giza Plateau. In places, particularly in the vicinity of the Second Pyramid and its Mortuary Temple, the limestone bedrock is blackened and has a charred or burnt appearance, as if it had been subjected to incredibly high temperatures. It looks like it may have been melted and recongealed, resembling slag, scoria, or low-grade vitrified rock. As Katie and I explored this phenomenon further during subsequent trips to Egypt, we found more and more evidence of apparent vitrification on the Giza Plateau, including on the south side of the Mortuary Temple, where apparent vitrification extends beneath some of the megalithic ground-level blocks, and along the causeway running from the Second Pyramid to the Great Sphinx. In places, the vitrification runs deep (many, many meters into the bedrock, which can be seen when one descends into various shafts on the Giza Plateau) and underlies various Old Kingdom (and older) structures. If indeed the rock in places has been subjected to high temperatures, what could be the source? Human-produced fires are highly unlikely, even impossible in many of the locations I witnessed, given that some of the "burnt" features extend deep into the rock and cover a broad area and that the temperatures to create such features would most likely be well in excess of those of a typical (or perhaps any possible) conventional surface fire. Another possibility is lightning strikes, and this I support. Indeed, it is recorded on the ancient dynastic Inventory Stela (discussed below) that the Great Sphinx was struck by lightning.

Ordinary atmospheric lightning can melt sediment and produce mineralogical changes, forming structures known as fulgurites (colloquially, "fossilized lightning"). Typical fulgurites, however, are very

Figure 15.5. Two views of Robert Schoch with evidence (vitrified rock) of intense lightning or plasma strikes on the Giza Plateau (*left*) and the Inventory Stela (*right*). (Photographs courtesy of R. Schoch and C. Ulissey.)

different than the features I inspected on the Giza Plateau. Fulgurites generally form long and narrow glassy tubes of fused sediment and sand grains that extend vertically into the soil, sand, or rock. In size, they can be on the order of centimeters to meters long. In contrast, the features on the Giza Plateau are massive areas of apparently burnt rock and, if the interpretation that they formed due to heat is correct, as I propose, then something other than conventional lightning must have created them. But what?

Two other sources of intense and extreme heat that geologists often consider when faced with burnt and fused rock are volcanic activity and extraterrestrial impacts (such as meteorites, comets, and asteroids). Neither of these applies to the Giza Plateau. Giza is composed of sedimentary limestone, not igneous or volcanic rocks, and there is no indication of the intrusion of hot molten rock into the area from deep below the surface. What about a possible meteorite, asteroid, or other extraterrestrial object impacting on, or exploding over, the Giza area? Theoretically, such an event could create intense heat on the surface that could burn and melt rock. However, this seems highly unlikely in the case of the features at Giza. One would expect to see evidence of either a crater or a widespread circular pattern of surface destruction, neither of which is found at Giza. Furthermore, if already in existence, the Pyramids, the Sphinx, and other monuments, would likely have been destroyed. Instead, the apparently burnt features appear at various spots as if a dense sheath of plasma hit, and the apparently vitrified rock penetrates deep below the surface in tendril-like patterns. But, as already pointed out, the evidence does not support conventional lightning strikes. We need to search for another explanation. My hypothesis is electrical discharges and plasma strikes during a solar outburst. The Giza Plateau had literally been touched by the Sun in remote ancient times, and perhaps this is why it was considered a sacred spot (see further comments on this possibility below).

The ancient Egyptian Inventory Stela (discussed and illustrated in Schoch and Bauval 2017, and Seyfzadeh and Schoch 2018) records that thunderbolts (or what we now would call plasma discharges from a solar outburst) hit the Giza Plateau in distant ancient times. Although the physical stela probably dates to the seventh or sixth century BCE, it purports to be a copy of a text that goes back to Old Kingdom times, some two thousand years earlier. Importantly, the stela states that the Great Sphinx was already in existence during the reign of Khufu (also known as Cheops, circa the twenty-sixth century BCE, reputed builder of the Great Pyramid) and that Khufu repaired the statue. These repairs were necessary because the Great Sphinx, according to the stela, had been hit by lightning. The great Egyptian Egyptologist Selim Hassan (1887–1961), who carried out excavations at the Great Sphinx in the 1930s, had this to say about the Inventory Stela:

> If we could believe its inscriptions, we should have to credit Khufu with having repaired the Sphinx, apparently after it had been damaged by a thunderbolt. As a matter of fact, there may be a grain of truth in this story, for the tail of the nemes head-dress is certainly missing, and it is not a part, which, by reason of its shape and position, could be easily broken off, except by a direct blow from some heavy object, delivered with terrific force. There is actually to be seen on the back of the Sphinx the scar of this breakage, and traces of the old mortar with which it was repaired. . . . Therefore, it is perhaps likely that the Sphinx was struck by lightning, but there is not a particle of evidence to show that this accident happened in the reign of Khufu. (Hassan 1949, 224–25)

The relevant portion of the inscription on the stela reads as follows:

> The plans of the Image of Hor-em-akhet ["Horus in the Horizon," a name for the Great Sphinx, or the god the statue was believed to represent in dynastic times; remember that it was originally the lioness Mehit] were brought in order to bring to revision the sayings of the disposition [that is, Khufu wanted to refurbish the statue] of the Image of the Very Redoubtable [the Great Sphinx]. He [Khufu] restored the statue all covered in painting, of the Guardian of the Atmosphere [the Great Sphinx], who guides the winds with his gaze. He [Khufu] made to quarry [he had new

blocks cut and put into position] the hind part of the nemes head-dress, which was lacking, from gilded stone, and which had a length of about 7 ells [about 12 feet or 3.7 meters]. He [Khufu] came to make a tour, in order to see the thunderbolt, which stands in the Place of the Sycamore, so named because of a great sycamore, whose branches were struck when the Lord of Heaven [the Lord of Heaven may refer to the Sun, or Re/Ra, the "Sun god"] descended upon the place of Hor-em-akhet [the god of the Great Sphinx], and also this image [the statue of the Sphinx], retracing the erasure [damage to the statue] according to the above-mentioned disposi-tion. (Translated by Selim Hassan 1949, 223; comments in brack-ets by R. Schoch)

Based on the information above, I believe we can piece together a reasonable scenario along the following lines. During Old Kingdom times the core of the statue we now know as the Great Sphinx was already extremely ancient and showed damage from the ages, includ-ing being struck by what was recollected as "lightning." But, given the severe damage this "lightning" caused, it seems probable that it was not atmospheric lightning, but rather a solar plasma strike when the "Lord of Heaven" (the Sun) descended to Earth and struck the statue and the Giza Plateau more generally. This, I suggest, occurred during the major solar outburst and associated catastrophe that ended the last ice age, circa 9700 BCE, and devastated the early civilizations of the time, including the civilization that had carved the proto-Sphinx. Corroborating this hypothesis, the current Great Sphinx has a major fissure (or "crack") running through it that separates the rump from the front of the statue. This fissure may have been initially caused, or exacerbated (if a natural weak zone in the rock already existed), by a plasma strike that directly hit the statue. This "split lion" iconography goes back to the earliest dynastic period, at which time the statue was already split into two and considered very ancient. Indeed, the concept of an ancient "split lion" entered into early Egyptian creation myths (see discussion in Seyfzadeh and Schoch 2019b).

When Khufu went to view the "thunderbolt," as described on the

Inventory Stela, what was he looking at? Real thunderbolts are ephemeral; they do not remain to be viewed. I believe that Khufu went to see the result of the "lightning" (plasma strike) that was recorded in stone (fossilized lightning) where a "thunderbolt" had hit directly and left its signature of burnt, charred, fused, and vitrified rock. That is, Khufu went to see the very same type of feature pointed out to me on the Giza Plateau. The Old Kingdom dynastic Egyptians recognized such features as the scars and marks of an ancient solar outburst.

On the ground in Egypt we have physical evidence, beyond that at Giza discussed above, that may pertain to past solar events and associated plasma strikes on the surface of Earth. Here I highlight two such occurrences (Reimold and Koeberl 2014): First, Libyan Desert Glass, which stretches across 2,500 square kilometers of sand dunes in the vast Libyan Desert (the Great Sand Sea) in western Egypt. Consisting of chunks and fragments of vitrified rock, the Libyan Desert Glass has been dated to 28 to 30 million years ago. Second, Dakhleh Glass, which consists of fragments of burnt, melted, and vitrified rock found over an area of four hundred square kilometers in the region of the Dakhleh Oasis, central-western Egypt. It has been dated from one hundred thousand to four hundred thousand years ago.

Traditionally, Libyan Desert Glass and Dakhleh Glass have been attributed to meteorite or asteroid surface impacts or atmospheric airbursts; however, there is no direct and definitive evidence that such is the case in either instance. Neither Libyan Desert Glass nor Dakhleh Glass is associated with an impact crater, and neither shows the classic mineralogical and textural characteristics that are found in rock samples associated directly with known impact craters or meteorite and asteroid explosions. It seems that these natural glasses have been attributed to extraterrestrial impacts by default, because no other mechanism to create them has been proposed and/or seriously considered. Interestingly, Michael L. Joseph, in his 2012 thesis (University of South Florida) on fulgurites, has pointed out that Dakhleh Glass in particular, as well as certain other glasses that have been traditionally attributed to meteorite or asteroid impacts, shows many characteristics found in fulgurites produced by lightning. As he states, "These data suggest that certain enigmatic natural glasses, such as . . . Dakhleh and other unknown desert glasses, may be lightning-produced, in contrast to the meteorite burst or impact related origins that have commonly been propounded" (Joseph 2012, vi). Other studies of fulgurites and lightning strikes have reinforced Joseph's studies that many phenomena, such as shock lamella and mineralogical changes down to the atomic level, can be produced by lightning (Gieré et al. 2015; Chen et al. 2017; Elmi et al. 2017). For instance, based on their studies, Chen et al. (2017, 1) state, "Our study on rock fulgurites . . . demonstrates that the presence of shock features in rocks cannot be taken as unequivocal evidence for impact events." And Reto Gieré, of the University of Pennsylvania, a leader in the field of studying the effects of lightning strikes on rocks, has been quoted as follows:

> "I think the most exciting thing about this study is just to see what lightning can do," Gieré said. "To see that lightning literally melts the surface of a rock and changes crystal structures, to me, is fascinating." Gieré said the finding serves as a reminder to geologists not to rush to interpret shock lamellae as indicators of a meteorite strike. (quoted in Baillie 2015)

But how can typical atmospheric lightning produce widespread burnt and vitrified rock (glass) spread over hundreds to thousands of square kilometers, as with the Libyan Desert Glass and Dakhleh Glass? I suggest we are not looking at the products of atmospheric lightning, but rather evidence of electrical plasma strikes associated with major solar events in the past. Based on the dates cited above (if indeed they are correct), Libyan Desert Glass and Dakhleh Glass are evidence of major solar outbursts and plasma strikes prior to the solar event of 9700 BCE that ended the last ice age and destroyed the early civilizations of that time. Our Earth has been hit by a series of solar outbursts over the eons.

If the Giza Plateau was struck by plasma during a solar event, if the Giza Plateau had literally been touched by the Sun in remote ancient times, then in the minds of the population that inhabited the area, it may have been considered a sacred site worthy of pilgrimage and veneration. Or if it was already considered a sacred spot (which included a huge statue of a lioness and other structures), as I suspect, the plasma strike would have reinforced this view. Giza may have been an area that was directly hit by solar plasma outbursts on multiple occasions. Furthermore, the strike or strikes may have literally magnetized and "charged" the local bedrock. (Such remnant magnetism can be detected with geophysical instrumentation and can be used to identify ancient lightning strikes; see, for instance, Bates et al. 2019, and Maki et al. 2015. To my knowledge, such techniques have not thus far been applied to the Giza Plateau.) And strong or anomalous remnant geomagnetic and electromagnetic fields can have effects on human mental and psychical phenomena (see chapter 14, page 269, and Schoch and Yonavjak 2008 and references therein).

Interestingly and tellingly, Giza is not the only ancient site that appears to have been hit by a major "lightning" strike or strikes. In studying a site containing standing stones in Calanais, Scotland, using geophysical techniques, Bates et al. found that an ancient Neolithic site had been built on, or in association with, an area that had been hit by a significant lightning strike or strikes at least six thousand years ago (before 5900 BP). According to the authors, "It is not possible to determine if the strikes occurred before or after the stone circle had been constructed but the presence of the strikes here is none the less intriguing" (Bates et al. 2019, 16). They go on to say:

> There is at least a possibility that the strikes were associated with a feature of the landscape, such as a tree, or large, natural rock, that no longer exists. If such features had some cultural significance to the people on the island, then the stone circle might memorialise such a feature or simply record a natural event that was noticed and judged significant by contemporary communities. A comparison could be made with studies mapping lightning strikes at the Buffalo Slough Mound Group in Dakota [the site is actually in Goodhue County, Minnesota, but was used by the Dakota people; note by R. Schoch] where historical evidence, supported by archaeological and geophysical data, suggest that lightning was an important aspect

of the Dakota world view [here the authors cite Maki et al. 2015]. (Bates et al. 2019, 16)

In ancient Scotland and among native peoples of North America, lightning strikes were of great cultural significance, and I suspect that it was certainly not just smaller atmospheric lightning strikes that were always under consideration, but strikes resulting from solar outbursts and accompanying plasma discharges from the Sun as well (dense balls of ionized gas driving down to atmospheric and ground levels, sheaths of plasma hitting Earth). This was the case at Giza too, and I believe we will find that it was the case at many other ancient sites around the globe once we seriously begin looking for the evidence of major lightning and plasma strikes.

SOLAR PLASMA SYMBOLISM AT GÖBEKLI TEPE

In the years following the initial publication of *Forgotten Civilization* in 2012, as Katie and I studied in greater detail plasma physics and the work of Anthony Peratt specifically (see, for instance, Peratt 2005), I came to the realization that various symbols on some of the pillars at Göbekli Tepe appear to reflect plasma configurations and other representations of unusual solar activity. For instance, Pillar 43 (the so-called Vulture pillar of Enclosure D, due to the large bird depicted on it; see fig. 3.12, page 59) illustrates what I interpret as possible plasma or magnetic arcing on the Sun, which might be seen during a major solar outburst, and other pillars bear symbols that are, in my assessment, abstract depictions of the plasma configurations and electrical discharges that would be seen in the sky during a major solar outburst. As I discuss further below, these same abstract depictions were associated with the concept of gods or God—gods in and from the sky—and associated with the Sun. The ancient people of that time intimately associated the concepts of God, the Sun, electromagnetic discharges from the Sun, and plasma physics—all of which would make sense if people of that time had witnessed a major solar outburst. Yet the dating of certain pillars at Göbekli Tepe showing such solar-based imagery would, as best as I can determine, place them temporally prior to the end of the last ice age. For instance, I am convinced that Enclosures C and D both show evidence of the catastrophe that occurred circa 9700 BCE; pillars were toppled over and then hastily reerected, and crude stone walls were constructed prior to the site being finally purposefully buried. Yet, we also find iconography inspired by plasma configurations that would have been observed during a solar outburst. This made little sense in terms of a solar outburst (or outbursts) occurring only at the end of the last ice age, circa 9700 BCE. Had the Göbekli Tepe people witnessed previous solar outbursts? Did they somehow realize that another one was imminent? These perplexing questions troubled me, and I even began to doubt the evidence (but I persisted, as my guiding principle is that one should always follow the evidence), as there seemed to be something "wrong" or "missing" in the narrative I had developed—namely, that true civilization developed before the end of the last ice age and that this earlier cycle of civilization was all but extinguished by the solar catastrophe of 9700 BCE. It was only following a six-thousand-year "dark age" (SIDA, discussed earlier in this chapter), that civilization reemerged.

Now, with the recognition that major solar outbursts occurred at both the beginning of the Younger Dryas circa 10,900 BCE, and the end of the Younger Dryas circa 9700 BCE, thus ending the last ice age, the evidence falls into place. The Göbekli Tepe people experienced a major solar outburst at the beginning of the Younger Dryas, so they were well aware of such phenomena and could incorporate such knowledge into their civilization and record plasma and solar symbolism on their pillars and sculptures, and then they experienced another solar outburst at the end of the Younger Dryas, the one that decimated their advanced civilization and initiated SIDA (Solar-Induced Dark Age). Given the widespread effects and ramifications of unusual solar activity for these ancient people, it would not be unexpected that they may have developed a deep understanding of that which in modern terminology can be referred to as solar plasma physics. They may have known the critical signs to look for in the Sun, the unusual behavior of our star, observed before a solar outburst. Perhaps, in this manner, they had some forewarning before the major solar outburst that ended the last ice age (circa 9700 BCE) occurred. Indeed, the Göbekli Tepe people may have been living during a time period of particularly unusual solar activity, if indeed our Sun was going through an active micronova-like phase during the Younger Dryas and the millennia immediately following the end of the last ice age. These people may have witnessed a number of more minor, but still significant, solar outbursts in addition to the large ones that I now hypothesize marked the beginning and ending of the Younger Dryas. (And, we might speculate, if these people were living during the time of a golden age of high knowledge, they may have possessed insights into the workings of the cosmos that have since been lost.)

EVIDENCE OF TRUE WRITING AT GÖBEKLI TEPE

Traditional historians and archaeologists have often pointed to three major distinguishing characteristics by which one can identify "true civilization": (1) monumental stone architecture, (2) settled urban (city) life, and (3) writing. "Prehistoric" is often equated with a society being "pre-literate"; if they do not have any written inscriptions or records, then they do not have a true recorded "history" and are both "pre-historic" and "pre-civilized."

Furthermore, according to conventional status quo thinking, writing was first "invented" just prior to around 3000 BCE in Sumer and Egypt; therefore, we can date the onset of true civilization to this time. However, over six thousand years earlier in northern Mesopotamia, we find the incredibly sophisticated site of Göbekli Tepe (see chapter 3, page 43, and the recent reviews in Fagan 2017; Cesarino 2012; Henley 2018; Dietrich et al. 2019; Schoch 2018, 2020b; Notroff and Dietrich 2019; Sepici 2019; David 2020; Haklay and Gopher 2020; Johnson 2020; Sezen 2020). Many mainstream historians are hesitant to apply the label of "true civilization" to the builders of Göbekli Tepe because these ancient people ostensibly do not exhibit all three "necessary" features of "true civilization" (as enumerated above). However, I disagree. The evidence of monumental stone architecture at Göbekli Tepe is undeniable (as discussed in previous chapters). To create such structures, we can hypothesize that some form of urban population must have existed in the area, but so far it has not been found. I would point out, however, that the structures the Göbekli Tepe people lived in may not have been stone; rather, they could have been constructed of wood, mud-brick, or other perishable materials. In analogy, the cities that accompanied the pyramids, temples, and other monumental stone structures of dynastic Egypt thousands of years later have left few traces. Or perhaps the city of the Göbekli Tepe people still exists and is now referred to as the city of Urfa (Şanlıurfa), but it is covered over by twelve thousand years of more recent habitation. The site of Göbekli Tepe is not far from modern Urfa, and during road work and other construction projects in Urfa, very ancient archaeological remains are often found, including remains going back to Göbekli Tepe times.

Despite monumental architecture and possible urban settlements, the best argument for those researchers who would deny the title of "true civilization" to the creators of Göbekli Tepe is (or was) that they apparently did not have any form of writing. However, the latest evidence has completely changed this notion and demands that even the skeptics must rethink the "when" and "where" of the origins of civilization.

Ever since I first visited and studied the site of Göbekli Tepe during the summer of 2010, I have speculated that its builders had some form of written notation and communication, if for no other reason than the practicality and feasibility of planning, organizing the labor and crafts specialists, and ultimately constructing such wondrous stone monuments. But the few apparent symbols carved on the stone pillars, in isolation, offer little solid evidence for true writing and literacy (see Felice Cesarino 2012; Cesarino independently suggested that various symbols at Göbekli Tepe represent writing; however, I was not aware of his work until July 2020). Admittedly, the majority of writing by the Göbekli Tepe people might well have been on perishable materials that have not survived twelve thousand years; however, the absence of such physical evidence was pointed to by the skeptics as evidence that writing did not exist (even though this was faulty logic on their part). Now, through the insight of my colleague, Dr. Manu Seyfzadeh, we do have a potential context and comparison for the symbolic notation found at Göbekli Tepe. As Seyfzadeh noted, some of the symbols at Göbekli Tepe are remarkably similar to the Anatolian hieroglyphs (also referred to as Luwian and/or Hittite hieroglyphs) used in the same general region (modern Turkey) millennia later. Is this purely coincidental? We think not. Indeed, we published a paper pointing out some major similarities between the Anatolian hieroglyphs and the symbols carved on some of the Göbekli Tepe pillars (Seyfzadeh and Schoch 2019a; for a review of early ideas regarding the possibility of "proto-writing" at Göbekli Tepe, see Henley 2018).

Although there has been much work since, the Anatolian hieroglyphs were intensely studied and documented by the linguist Emmanuel Laroche (1914–1991) in his classic book titled *Les Hiéroglyphes Hittites* (1960). The Anatolian hieroglyphic inscriptions generally date to the second and early first millennia BCE (with many from the period of circa 1300–900 BCE). This is eight thousand years or more after the construction of Göbekli Tepe, yet there are remarkable correlations suggesting that at least fragments of a writing system used by the Göbekli Tepe people survived and were incorporated into the system of Anatolian hieroglyphs, in some cases with various modifications: such modifications would be quite understandable, and even expected, over such a vast length of time.

Laroche assigned numbers to the Anatolian hieroglyphs he catalogued, and attempted translations and interpretations; here I refer to various Anatolian hieroglyphs by these "Laroche Numbers" (LN).

The first and perhaps most important comparison between the Anatolian hieroglyphs and the writing at Göbekli Tepe involves LN 360 and symbols found prominently on the belt of one of the largest and most magnificent pillars at Göbekli Tepe, that known as Pillar 18.

360	⊕	239 (1)	凹
411	☾	239 (2)	凵
184	◡	239 (3)	凵

Figure 15.6. Anatolian hieroglyph Laroche Numbers 360, 411, 184, and 239.

(Illustration courtesy of R. Schoch and C. Ulissey, based on Laroche 1960.)

LN 360 consists of a crescent or *C* shape open to the right, followed (*left to right*) by two vertical parallel lines followed by a "reversed-*C*" or crescent open to the left. The prominent inscription on the belt of Pillar 18 includes a *C* shape followed by an *H* shape followed by a reversed-*C* shape. On the front edge of Pillar 28 at Göbekli Tepe the same three symbols, the same word, is carved vertically. LN 360 can be translated as "god," and Seyfzadeh and I hypothesize that the *C, H,* reversed-*C* at Göbekli Tepe is likewise a word meaning "god." Even before this suggested translation, there was speculation that the anthropomorphic pillars (some of the pillars have arms, hands, belts, and loincloths) were meant to represent gods or a god.

A slight discrepancy between LN 360 and *C, H,* reversed-*C* at Göbekli Tepe is that in LN 360 the middle character consists of two parallel vertical lines rather than an *H* shape. The *H,* with either one or two crossbars (and both forms, interestingly, appear at Göbekli Tepe), appears in Laroche's catalog as Number 239. In Anatolian hieroglyphs, an *H* shape may have had the meaning of a "gate," "portal," or "passageway." This concept of a gate or passage was possibly associated with a god or with gods, because gods could control the passage from one realm to another and, in particular, control the passage from life to death and life again, in the case of a belief in rebirth. And gods would mediate between the earthly and heavenly realms, between the material and spiritual realms. Thus, the symbol for a gate, portal, or passage may have been

Figure 15.7. Three views of Pillar 18 at Göbekli Tepe: detail of the belt (*left*), close-up of the front neck region (*right*), and overview image of the entire pillar (*center*). (Photographs courtesy of R. Schoch and C. Ulissey.)

a simplified emblem referring to gods or spiritual beings, and *H* shapes are found multiple times on a number of pillars at Göbekli Tepe. In Anatolian hieroglyphs, the horizontal crossbar of the *H* appears to have been omitted when used in the word or hieroglyph meaning "god."

Further supporting the association of the *H* symbol with the word "god" at Göbekli Tepe, and also strengthening the link between the Göbekli Tepe writing and the Anatolian hieroglyphs, on the top front of Pillar 18 is another set of symbols consisting, from top to bottom, of an *H* (which in this case has two horizontal crossbars), a circle with a dot in the center, and a crescent that is open to the top. The circle with a center dot and crescent combination occurs as LN 184 and is considered a symbol of the divine. This may represent the Sun and the Moon, and more generally the cosmos or heavenly realm. Alternatively, one might suggest that the circle with a dot in the center represents all of Earth; if you stand in one spot and rotate through 360 degrees (a full circle), the horizon will appear as a circle around the place you are standing. Or the circle with dot may represent our Sun, as is the case with current astrological symbols, and the crescent may represent the expanding debris and plasma observed during a solar outburst. Also, laboratory experiments have demonstrated that electrical discharge phenomena can produce craters with a central uplift (as discussed earlier in this chapter, on page 333), which creates the impression of a circle with a dot in the middle; this might be viewed as further supporting the plasma and solar outburst correlation to the symbol of this shape found at Göbekli Tepe. One could also view this as the Sun creating its own symbol—leaving its own fingerprint, if you will. However, geology is not so simple. Physical impactors (meteors, asteroids, comets, etc.) can also create craters with a central uplift, and both electrical discharge phenomena and physical impactors can create craters without a central uplift (that is, without the "dot" in the center). As I view it, though, the preponderance of evidence (well beyond this one symbol) points to a connection with the Sun.

Returning to LN 184 specifically, and its appearance at Göbekli Tepe, I hypothesize that this symbol combined with the *H* at Göbekli Tepe is stating that the god in question rules the cosmos, both heaven and Earth. Furthermore, the *H* with LN 184 could symbolize the gate or portal, or the location of connection between the mundane and the divine, the material and the spiritual, the terrestrial and the celestial; or in other words, it might represent a place where gods, or God, touched Earth.

Regarding the writing on the belt on the right side (the side with the animal under the arm) of Pillar 18 at Göbekli Tepe, the full inscription on that side is actually *C, C, H, C, H,* reversed-*C.*" (The first two *C*s, reading left to right, are slightly different from each other, as are the *H*s, but whether these differences are significant or not remains an open question.) The isolated *C* shape, or crescent open to the right, is comparable to LN 411, which is interpreted as having a connection to "dieu" (god). Personally, I speculate that this full inscription may signify "god of gods" (and was read right to left in this case). This raises the issue of whether the Göbekli Tepe people believed in a supreme god presiding over lesser deities. Were they monotheistic at some level?

All in all, I feel confident that the Göbekli Tepe people used written language. Admittedly, we have only a limited amount of their "writing" preserved on the structures so far uncovered. However, I predict that this is just the tip of the proverbial iceberg. I hope that eventually substantial texts from Göbekli Tepe times will be found. Until then, I am continuing to study the symbols—the writing—from this early period that have been recovered so far. And to return to the issue of "true civilization," there is now no doubt in my mind that the Göbekli Tepe people not only built monumental stone structures and most likely had large settlements that we should classify as cities, but also that they had the third (and in the opinion of some scholars, the most critical) diagnostic feature of civilization, namely writing and literacy. The Göbekli Tepe people were incredibly knowledgeable, with a well-organized and sophisticated society. They possessed a true civilization at the end of the last ice age—six thousand years before most conventional historians believe that true civilization first arose.

GOD AND THE SUN

An immediate question that I have to ask myself is, Why symbolize a god, or the supreme God, as *C, H,* reversed-*C*? And why place God in the sky? (Nowadays, many people simply take it for granted that God, or gods, are located above, in the heavens, and heaven has an explicitly religious connotation, but this was not always necessarily the case.) I believe the answer, and the second message of the LN 360 symbol, lies in plasma physics. As I have discussed at length elsewhere in this book, at various times, our Sun "exploded" with a mighty outburst or series of outbursts. I now hypothesize that, based on the evidence, it was a solar outburst that initiated the Younger Dryas, circa 10,900 BCE, melting ice dams and glaciers, causing a massive glacial flood that changed ocean circulation patterns in the Atlantic, thus initiating the Younger Dryas cooling (see discussion earlier in this chapter, on page 322). Pillar 18 and its associated pillars at Göbekli Tepe date, in my assessment, to the period just before the end of the last ice age (circa 9700 BCE), but the Göbekli Tepe people retained a collective memory of previous solar outburst events—as shown on the pillars.

Ice and sediment core data record solar outburst events, as do data from our Moon; however, another interesting line of evidence of our Sun dramatically affecting life on this planet comes from the preeminent plasma physicist Anthony Peratt at Los Alamos National Laboratory (see chapter 6, page 118). In short, various diagnostic electrical plasma configurations were seen in the sky during those tumultuous times, as elucidated by Peratt. Ancient people the world over witnessed a massive solar event or events (perhaps separated by significant periods of time, such as at the beginning and end of the Younger Dryas, and possibly at other times as well). During these events, the charged particles interacted with our atmosphere (as we see today in the northern and southern lights, only so much more intense that the auroras took on distinctive shapes), and ancient people recorded the shapes they saw in the sky on rock as petroglyphs and in their art. Peratt's published papers offer examples from over 130 countries, and other independent scientists are also explicitly recognizing similar ancient petroglyphs (see, for example, Kolnegari et al. 2020 for an example from Iran). A few of the shapes Peratt describes are stick-figured men with bird heads, stick-figured men with two dots on their sides (the dots indicating synchrotron radiation), large-eyed owl-like faces, cascading cylindrical shapes, and more (see discussion in chapter 6, page 118). I believe it is a reasonable hypothesis to suggest that the people living during those times reasoned that these events were the acts of gods (or a God). The *H* shape and the *C, H,* reversed-*C* together are in fact simplified representations of what people saw in the sky during the solar outbursts.

Thus, this series of symbols, this word (*C, H,* reversed-*C*), not only names God but also equates God with the Sun. As I discuss further below, the Sun was from the point of view of these ancient people acting as a conscious entity (a god, or God), which I believe is not far off of the mark. Indeed, a strong argument can be made that the Sun and stars are indeed conscious at some level and that consciousness pervades the entire universe (see Goff 2017; Hoffman 2008; Hoffman and Prakash 2014; Matloff 2016; Schoch 2019; Brooks 2020; Kleiner and Tull 2020; Mind Matters News 2020). Furthermore, as Katie has pointed out, our Sun is composed primarily of hydrogen and other simple elements and particles (protons, electrons, and so forth) that have been demonstrated to contain the ability to encode information. Scientists such as Luc Montagnier and Cleve Backster have pioneered research in this field. The ancient Egyptians, for instance, believed we come from the Sun and stars, and thence we can return after physical death. And I hold that there is now evidence that simple particles (for instance, the protons and electrons that make up hydrogen) can encode information—ultimately the stuff of consciousness, with matter arising from, or derivative of, consciousness (see chapter 14, page 297).

Fundamentally, I suggest that God is consciousness and that consciousness exists in and is expressed through basic particles, which in the universe we inhabit take the form of protons and electrons—that is, hydrogen, and hydrogen composes a large portion of our Sun—and streams of charged particles (electrical plasma; and plasma and magnetic fields may be conscious at some level). Here in the earliest known written word, which means "God," we see these connections.

To some readers, this may all seem like wild speculation; however, I am a firm believer that speculation and hypothesis formation is heuristic and fundamental to modern scientific research; we test our speculations against the evidence. Continuing with the above line of reasoning, there is more to consider. When we look at Pillar 43 at Göbekli Tepe, not only do we find additional *H* symbols, one of which is flipped by 90 degrees (as is also the case on the front belt buckle area of Pillar 18), but also at the top of the pillar we find three odd images that look like rectangles with inverted *U* shapes on them. To the right of each inverted *U* are different animals (some type of bird, some type of mammalian animal, and possibly a frog-like animal) jumping down, or sliding down, the up-side-down *U* shapes. These carvings have been variously interpreted as representing buildings or other structures, or as baskets or handbags (comparable to a woman's purse). However, in the context of Göbekli Tepe and the discussion above, I prefer a different interpretation, one first suggested to me by Katie. The symbolism along the top of Pillar 43 may represent the electromagnetic and plasma arcing that occurs on a highly active Sun. Such arcing is observed on our Sun today, but is not seen without proper instrumentation (and one should never look at the Sun directly without the proper protective equipment). During the time of a much more active Sun, as would have been observed at the end of the last ice age, probably just before and during the solar outbursts, such arcing may well have been readily seen by many people on Earth (or understood by the scientists of the time, if we credit these people with the advanced knowledge that they very well may have had), and they depicted this activity on Pillar 43. Furthermore, the "jumping" animals represent the movement and "snapping" of the magnetic and plasma arcs as they form and connect with each other and the surface of the Sun and also give rise to the ejection of plasma during a solar outburst.

Pillar 43 is sometimes referred to as the "vulture" pillar, named after the prominent bird, generally identified as a vulture, that appears on the pillar. On one wing, the vulture balances a "ball" that may represent our Sun. In my research, I have found that birds and bird-headed humans ("birdmen" and "birdwomen") appear prominently in many mythologies. However, these shapes (which later inspired more ornate and detailed or "realistic" depictions), as cutting-edge plasma physics now teaches, are also diagnostic of extreme solar events and high intensity plasma columns. We see this on Pillar 43 as well as on faraway Easter Island, where Katie and I have discovered that the Island's previously unidentified script, rongorongo, is plasma-inspired in nature. (This discovery, first made by Katie as described in chapter 1, was subsequently confirmed by a member of Peratt's research team.) We hold that the written text (or fragments of it, and of course more recent copies of copies of copies . . .) both records and was inspired by the giant solar event that occurred circa 9700 BCE (as well as, possibly, other significant solar activity). Likewise, Easter Island is famous for its "birdman" cult and the associated birdman petroglyphs, all of which may trace back to and memorialize an ancient solar event or events (as well as also incorporating later memories and events). Myths and symbols can often incorporate multiple layers of meaning and history that have accreted over the centuries and millennia, with the original meaning sometimes completely forgotten. Indeed, I find many similarities between the iconography of Göbekli Tepe and Easter Island. And there are other apparent connections around the world. For instance, a variation on the Göbekli Tepe word for "god," very similar to the form it takes on Pillar 28, appears on the chest of an Australian aboriginal man in a photograph published a century ago (Churchward 1922, plate LIX; see fig. 15.8). On rock art from the Kimberly region of Australia, similar motifs are found (illustrated by Australia's Northwest 2019), and the rock art of this region has been dated to twelve thousand years ago (Finch et al. 2020), which corresponds to the end of the last ice age. A variation on this form, which Katie and I have observed on-site, is found engraved on an ancient megalith at Knowth, near Newgrange, Ireland (see fig. 15.9). Interestingly, the petroglyph at Knowth showing a spiral is scientifically accurate according to plasma physics for the way that the core of a plasma torus spins. And the prominent *H* found abundantly at Göbekli Tepe is reminiscent of the "H blocks" at Puma Punku, near Tiwanaku, Bolivia (see fig. 15.10). Were there direct connections between these areas in ancient times? Were these "portal areas" where the Sun (God to these ancient people) touched down? Are the similarities derived from a common source or common knowledge of our Sun, consciousness, and plasma that pervades the universe? I doubt it is all a matter of coincidence. Rather, I believe they reflect shared advanced knowledge, science our civilization is just beginning

Figure 15.8. Pillar 28 at Göbekli Tepe with carved symbols on its front (*left*).
Image of an Australian aboriginal man with similar symbols on his chest (*right*).
(Photograph of Göbekli Tepe pillar, courtesy of R. Schoch and C. Ulissey;
photograph of Australian aboriginal man from Churchward 1922.)

to understand. (In my 2003 book *Voyages of the Pyramid Builders,* I discuss evidence for transoceanic contacts in ancient times.)

In the word symbolism found at Göbekli Tepe and other ancient sites, particularly the *C, H,* reversed-*C* and its derivatives, we have two concepts that are combined and presented: the Sun and God. This is a theme that permeates the ancient world: the Sun was worshipped as a deity. On a journey to India, Katie and I learned firsthand that among the Hindu tenets is the belief that the Sun is the one and ultimate God and the physical manifestation of the supreme God. Is there a distinct consciousness possessed by the Sun, the planets, the stars, and even perhaps the constellations (possibly, a "collective consciousness")? God, I would suggest, is primarily consciousness. To the Greeks, Romans, and many other ancient peoples, the celestial bodies

Figure 15.9. Robert Schoch beside a large plasma petroglyph at Knowth, Ireland.
(Photograph courtesy of R. Schoch and C. Ulissey.)

Figure 15.10. Megalithic "H blocks" at Puma Punku, Bolivia.
(Photograph courtesy of R. Schoch and C. Ulissey.)

were recognized as gods (Jupiter = Zeus, Apollo = Sun, and so on). What then is the *C, H,* reversed-*C* symbolism trying to convey? Why is the *T*-shaped Pillar 18 at Göbekli Tepe wearing this message? Is it directing our gaze to Orion, with its prominent belt? Pillar 18 may be intended as a recreation of Orion, the headless hunter. (The constellation in the sky, depending on how one interprets it, is primarily an hourglass-shaped "torso.") And the hunter is accompanied by the "dog star," Sirius. (This star is actually Sirius A; "Sirius" consists of two or possibly three stars in a binary or trinary system; Benest and Duvent 1995; Bond et al. 2017.) The dog star is in the constellation Canis Major, the "greater dog," and interestingly, it has been suggested that Sirius, the brightest star in the sky, could possibly be a binary companion to our Sun (see Brown, undated article). On Pillar 18 the "dog" is tucked under the hunter's right arm. On Pillar 18, the arms (which are spread out in the actual constellation) are brought down to the sides and the hands frame the navel region (reminiscent of the moai on Easter Island). The belt of Pillar 18 corresponds to the belt stars of Orion, and the fox-pelt loincloth can be seen as equivalent to the Orion Nebula, which "hangs" from the belt in the constellation. (Sometimes this is referred to as the sword, or the sword's sheath, of Orion.) And Orion is surrounded by the zodiac, a series of constellations, many of which represent animal forms, just as Pillar 18 at Göbekli Tepe is surrounded by a ring of smaller pillars with varied carvings. This iconography suggests yet another message that we are meant to discern. Do we, or does our star, have an umbilical connection to Orion? The Orion Nebula is a birthplace of stars. The writing and symbolism at Göbekli Tepe is most certainly speaking to us, though its message may be unclear at this time. It is worth noting that in dynastic Egypt, Orion in the sky was equated with Osiris (Schoch and Bauval 2017), who presided over the judgment of the deceased, and symbolized "the divine in mortal form . . . [and was] . . . the personification of physical creation and its cycles of becoming and return, death and renewal" (West 1985/1995, 74).

At this point, we really do not know just how sophisticated the Göbekli Tepe people were when it comes to subjects such as philosophy, theology, science (including astronomy and astrophysics, which are, of course, modern terms that sound much too sophisticated to be applied to a people living twelve thousand years ago at the end of the last ice age), and other fields. The modern bias tends to be toward downplaying and minimizing the level of accomplishments and sophistication of ancient peoples, particularly a people such as those of Göbekli Tepe, who are often labeled as primitive "hunters and gatherers," but were they? This remains an open question, especially in light of the discovery of potential early cultivation of various grains at a site on the Sea of Galilee (modern Israel) dating back to circa twenty-three thousand years ago (Snir et al. 2015).

According to the standard paradigm:

> . . . sociality and social intelligence [played a specific role] in the key development of humankind, that which has made modern humans a particularly intelligent type of primate. This development has nothing to do with *Homo habilis* or handaxes, bipedalism or brain size. It is the origin of farming at, or soon after, 10000 years ago. It is only with the economic basis that farming provides that writing, mathematics and digital technology could be invented and it is these that effectively define the nature of our cognition today. (Mithen 2007, 705; material in brackets added by R. Schoch)

Yet, with the discovery of writing at Göbekli Tepe specifically (see above), as well as the evident social and economic organization that must have gone into building and maintaining the complex, I assert that this often-accepted "truism" must be rethought. I should also note that hunter-gatherer societies have, historically, not always been so primitive—witness the native populations with their sophisticated societies of the Pacific Northwest Coast of America. (Sometimes such societies are referred to as "complex hunter-gatherers"; see Sassaman 2004.) However, one needs to remember that we possess an incredibly small sampling of the material culture of the Göbekli Tepe people (see chapter 3, page 80). If in twelve thousand years future archaeologists were to judge our civilization by an equally small sample of our material culture, just a smattering of modern sculptures and the foundations of a few buildings, how would they judge us?

As I have made the case earlier in this chapter, there is strong evidence that the people of Göbekli Tepe had a written language, although currently we have only a small sampling of their writing. Numerous stone circles identified at the site via geophysical techniques remain unexcavated. Furthermore, if the Göbekli Tepe people had writing, then it is probable that other populations and groups at that time were literate as well. Perhaps one day we will uncover a "library" or "archive" from this remote period, such as the archive the lioness who became the Great Sphinx guarded; perhaps some of the remains are still there to be found. Until that day, I believe it is important to continue to analyze the fragments of writing that have been recovered thus far. Furthermore, I believe we can also extract some of the ancient knowledge and wisdom from the symbols and works of art that have been passed down to us over the generations. Profound symbols and great works of art can convey the ineffable and the numinous directly, bridging cultural boundaries and crossing immense spans of time.

THE KHAFRE STATUE AND THE SUN

Housed in the collections of the Egyptian Museum in Cairo is a magnificent life-sized statue that is ostensibly a representation of the Fourth Dynasty pharaoh Khafre (circa 2500 BCE), whom conventional Egyptologists associate with the Second Pyramid and Great Sphinx (see Schoch and Bauval 2017). This statue is replete with solar and plasma imagery. In its beautiful artistry, it poses the questions: Can we travel to the Sun and stars to unite with them? Can we join them in the celestial realm? Ultimately, given the proper circumstances, do we become the Sun? And, properly interpreted, I have no doubt that the statue answers with a definitive yes.

As Katie likes to refer to it, the Khafre Statue is an example of "science encoded in the language of art." (For the sake of convenience, I will adopt the conventional Egyptological point of view that it is a

Figure 15.11. The Khafre Statue, Egyptian Museum, Cairo.
(Photographs courtesy of R. Schoch and C. Ulissey.)

statue of Khafre, although it is possible that it is an image of someone else—or perhaps simply a representation of a generic human—that was then appropriated by Khafre. And who knows how old the original statue is? Is it a much more ancient statue that was reused in dynastic times? Or could it be that the statue that currently exists is an ancient copy of an even earlier statue, just as the Romans copied earlier Greek statues?) The figure of Khafre is seated on a high-backed armless chair that carries solar and plasma symbolism. The chair has the legs and feet of a lion, and there are lions' heads on the front tops of the front legs. The lion traditionally is associated with the Sun, and Khafre seated on a "lion chair" can be interpreted to mean that he is riding on, or going to, or being carried by, the Sun. Furthermore, under the paws of the lion-legs, in both the front and back, are stacked discs (cascading rings), which Katie and I interpret as toroid disc structures (the plasma torus) that Anthony Peratt has determined would be seen in the sky during a solar outburst (see chapter 6, page 118). This reinforces the general solar connections. Further developing the solar plasma theme, on the sides of the chair are carved the traditional symbol that Egyptologists state memorializes the uniting of Upper and Lower Egypt. However, as de Santillana and von Dechend (1969) have suggested, this interpretation may not be the only way to view this motif. They suggest that it might refer to the celestial or astronomical "churning"—that is, the precession of the equinoxes. Another interpretation is that it is a stylization of a plasma torus, the "stick figures" and related configurations that solar particles take on at high intensity and as had been seen in the sky during major solar outbursts. It may also connote the uniting of Heaven and Earth (which was important to the ancient Egyptians) and furthermore allude to our return to the stars and Sun after this physical existence on Earth.

The figure of Khafre can also be seen as a type of birdman (a human figure with the head of a bird), a motif also recognized by Peratt in his study of plasma configurations. Behind the head of Khafre is the falcon representing Horus, Re-Horakhty, who is associated with the Living (Conscious) Sun (Re). Here the connection to the Sun is explicit and obvious to those who understand the symbolism—and plasma physics is just beginning to understand this. Ultimately, in my view, this great work of art (a true masterpiece) is not simply (possibly not even) a mere representation of a dynastic pharaoh but also refers to something much more profound, which is both spiritual (God) and scientific (plasma and solar science). The statue refers to the Sun and the heavens, to the grand cycle of the ages, to our journey to the Sun and stars upon the end of our physical and material existence on this planet (death of the body), and to our ultimate union with the Celestial, with the Divine. It is also interesting that this statue was initially found in a pit in the so-called Valley Temple to the south of the Sphinx Temple; the Sphinx Temple sits directly east of the Great Sphinx and the chamber under the Sphinx's left paw. If that chamber is an ancient archive of an advanced civilization, the Khafre Statue, and all it conveys, may be a profound message left by that early civilization to its progeny, us: We become the Sun.

Also in the Egyptian Museum, Cairo, is an artifact labeled a "Cow

Palette" that was found in a tomb dating back to about 5,500 years ago (predynastic Egypt), see figure 15.12. Its official label reads, "The cow's head with stars is probably an early representation of the Celestial Cow. Identified later with the goddesses Bat and Hathor, she lived in the heavens and gave birth to the sun god each morning." (Bat and Hathor were two goddesses who were often depicted with human faces and the ears and horns of a cow.) However, I propose that the depiction on this palette carries, like the petroglyphs studied by Peratt and the Khafre Statue, a more profound message, one plasma physics is just beginning to teach us, yet one understood by a civilization that for millennia was all but forgotten. The image on the palette, with its diagnostic features, appears to be a different artistic rendering of the "stickman" or "squatter man" shapes evident in the global plasma petroglyphs identified by Peratt, with the large stars on either side of the palette corresponding to the "dots" on either side of the anthropomorphic "stick-figure" engravings—the dots representing synchrotron radiation. At the same time, to my eye, the depiction on the palette appears to be a person flanked by stars, with a star for a head and hands that are stars. Is this simultaneously a warning regarding what our Sun can unleash and also a promise that we may embrace and join the stars in our evolutionary journey? I wonder at the extent that these incredibly ancient artifacts encode and express knowledge and insights from both science and philosophy that we are only now rediscovering. I ponder just how far back the message encoded in the symbolism found on this artifact goes. The palette itself, according to conventional archaeological dating, is a product of the time pertaining to the earliest glimmerings of our cycle of civilization (the Neociv), but the message it contains appears to be much more ancient, reflecting an understanding of advanced science. I also wonder if the physical artifact might be an heirloom or a copy of something from an earlier period that was passed down over the generations, but this is purely speculation. Regardless of its physical age, an artist from long ago left this work of art to us—to compel us to question, study, and learn, and quite possibly to convey to us a message of what we might become.

صلاية بقرة السماء   COW PALETTE

نقادة الثانية، حوالي ٣٦٥٠ـ ٣٣٠٠ق.م
شست
جرزة، مقبرة رقم ٥٩
سجل عام: ٤٣١٠٣

Naqada II, ca. 3650-3300 BC
Schist
Girza, Tomb 59
JE 43103

تعد صلاية رأس البقرة والنجوم هي
أقدم تصوير للبقرة المقدسة والتي
عرفت في البداية باسم «بات» و
«حتحور» عاشت في السماء
وأعطت الميلاد لإله الشمس كل
صباح.

The cow's head with stars on this palette is probably an early representation of the Celestial Cow. Identified later with the goddesses Bat and Hathor, she lived in the heavens and gave birth to the sun god each morning.

Figure 15.12. The Cow Palette, Egyptian Museum, Cairo. For comparison, illustrations of a petroglyph (*left*) and a plasma configuration (*right*) are included. (Photograph courtesy of R. Schoch and C. Ulissey; plasma and petroglyph illustrations courtesy of Dr. Anthony L. Peratt, reprinted with permission from *IEEE Transactions on Plasma Science*, December 2003, vol. 31.)

GUNUNG PADANG

In December 2013, Katie and I visited the megalithic archaeological site of Gunung Padang in West Java, Indonesia. After studying it carefully, I am convinced that the site was artificially constructed by ancient people (Schoch 2014a, 2014b). How long ago is the big question, but some very early dates, based on radiocarbon analyses, that geologist Danny Hilman Natawidjaja (2013) and his team are finding, circa the end of the last ice age, about twelve thousand years ago, and even earlier, suggest we are looking at something very old. The site requires much further study, though; these are preliminary findings. The blocks themselves from which the site was constructed were formed by nature, by volcanic activity millions of years ago, long before human civilization. The blocks are igneous (specifically andesite) and were formed by natural volcanic processes. However, and this

Figure 15.13. Various views of Gunung Padang, West Java, Indonesia.
(Photographs courtesy of R. Schoch and C. Ulissey.)

is very important, they form vertically in nature and are called by geologists "columnar joints" or "columnar jointing." The issue at Gunung Padang is that the stone columns have evidently been taken from their natural vertical positions and laid down (arranged by humans) horizontally to create the structures at this site. It is similar to the concept of building a house out of wooden logs. There are definite and distinct comparisons to be made between Gunung Padang and Nan Madol in Micronesia. At Gunung Padang, it is my conclusion that the blocks were not quarried a long distance away and then transported, but rather they probably occurred naturally right there on-site in this tectonically active region and were simply repositioned to form the ancient structures. It is also interesting that cavities or chambers have been found, using geophysical techniques, below the surface at Gunung Padang; they have yet to be explored. To my knowledge (as of 2020), no definitive artifacts have been found in association with the site (no sculptures, no stone or pottery utensils, no beads, no small art objects, etc.). Perhaps more detailed excavations might reveal something along these lines. However, just as there is a push by some scientists for broader exploration and excavation of Gunung Padang, so too is there opposition to such studies. It is a sacred site to many who do not want it tampered with.

EARTHQUAKES AND SOLAR ACTIVITY

A very controversial topic that I introduced in the original text of *Forgotten Civilization* is the matter of whether or not our Sun could in some manner cause or promote earthquakes (and thus potentially other geological activity) on Earth (see chapter 8, page 173). In the years since, there has been a steady interest in this topic (Davidson et al. 2015; Novik et al. 2019; Marchitelli et al. 2020) and continuing controversy as to whether, and if so to what extent, solar activity might modulate earthquake activity (and tectonic activity more generally, which would include deep magma activity, volcanic activity, and so forth). Based on a statistical analysis of earthquake activity versus such factors as sunspots and solar wind velocity, Jeffrey

Love and Jeremy Thomas concluded, "We cannot reject the null hypothesis of no solar-terrestrial triggering of earthquakes" (Love and Thomas 2013, 1165). That is, they found no compelling evidence to support solar activity having an influence on earthquake activity. However, I suggest that these authors were looking at the problem from too "coarse" a viewpoint, lumping various types of earthquakes together (those found on strike-slip [transform] faults versus normal and reverse [thrust] faults, or transform faults versus divergent plate boundaries, for instance) and then finding that earthquakes are not significantly correlated (from a statistical point of view) with crude overall aspects of solar activity. Taking a more nuanced approach, Tavares and Azevedo (2011) found a statistically significant influence of solar cycles on earthquakes. Further work by various groups of researchers has reinforced the view that solar activity can trigger and modulate earthquake activity on our planet (see Davidson et al. 2015; Davidson 2015, 2016; Sorokin et al. 2019).

Based on the data, I am convinced that there is a solar-terrestrial connection when it comes to earthquake and related activity, but exactly how solar activity might influence earthquake activity remains a stimulating topic of research. Despite their skepticism regarding the Sun influencing earthquake activity, Love and Thomas succinctly summarized some of the possible means by which solar activity might trigger earthquakes:

> In the search for reliable methods for predicting earthquakes, geophysicists have sometimes investigated natural phenomena that might affect their occurrence likelihood. In the context of critical-point accumulation of stress on a fault, a small "nudge" might be all that is needed to trigger an earthquake. The list of unconventional phenomena that might provide such a triggering nudge is long, and their relative importance has historically been controversial. . . . The great solar astronomer [Rudolf] Wolf [1816–1893] suggested that sunspots could influence the occurrence of earthquakes. Qualitatively, a solar-terrestrial effect on seismicity, if one exists, would almost certainly require some sort of coupling between the

Sun, solar wind, magnetosphere, and lithosphere. This coupling might, for example, cause small changes in the Earth's rotation rate, and these could result in more earthquakes. . . . Alternatively, magnetic storms might induce eddy electric currents in rocks along faults, heating them and reducing their shear resistance . . . , or induced currents might cause a piezoelectric increase in fault stress. (Love and Thomas 2013, 1165; references removed from the quotation and material in brackets added by R. Schoch)

Davidson et al., based on their statistical analysis, suggested that "the extremes in magnetism of the [solar] polar fields, and their polarity reversals, may be modulating the largest earthquakes on the planet" (Davidson et al. 2015, 310; material in brackets added by R. Schoch). Based on careful theoretical and mathematical analyses, combined with experimental data in the field, Sorokin et al. concluded that solar flares can stimulate seismic (earthquake) activity. They summarize their conclusions as follows:

We demonstrated by numerical calculations and subsequent comparison of their results with data of field observations that the absorption of ionizing radiation of solar flares may result in variations of telluric current densities in the seismogenic faults comparable with the current density generated in the Earth crust by artificial pulsed power sources used for active electromagnetic monitoring (MHD [magneto-hydrodynamic] generators and electric pulsed power systems of ERGU-600 type [a type of electrical generator facility]). Therefore, triggering of seismic events is possible by not only artificial sources of electric current injected into the Earth crust, but also the solar flares. (Sorokin et al. 2019, 32; material in brackets added by R. Schoch)

Note that solar flares can occur independently or semi-independently of other solar activity (such as CMEs), but any major solar outburst will almost certainly have associated solar flares that, according to the work of Sorokin et al. (2019), can trigger earthquakes.

In a significant and thorough study titled "On the Correlation Between Solar Activity and Large Earthquakes Worldwide," Vito Marchitelli and colleagues found "strongly statistically significant, evidence for a high correlation between large worldwide earthquakes and the proton density near the magnetosphere, due to the solar wind" (2020, 9). In their paper these authors define large earthquakes as those with a magnitude of greater than 5.6, and "demonstrate that it [the correlation of large earthquakes with solar activity] can likely be due to the effect of solar wind, modulating the proton density and hence the electrical potential between the ionosphere and the Earth" (2020, 9; material in brackets added by R. Schoch). There is a higher probability of a large earthquake occurring during the 24 hours following an increased period of proton density due to solar activity. Marchitelli and colleagues suggest that the

> . . . observed correlation implies that a high electric potential sometimes occurs between the ionosphere, charged by the high proton density generated at higher distances, and the Earth. Such a high potential could generate, both in a direct way or determining, by electrical induction, alterations of the normal underground potential, an electrical discharge, channeled at depth by large faults, which represent preferential, highly conductive channels. Such electrical current, passing through the fault, would generate, by reverse piezoelectric effect, a strain/stress pulse, which . . . could destabilize the fault favoring its rupture. The reverse piezoelectric effect would be due, in rocks, by the quartz minerals abundant in them. (Marchitelli et al. 2020, 8)

Marchitelli et al. (2020, 8) point out that the mechanism they propose for a correlation between solar activity and major earthquakes would "represent only a small destabilizing effect over an already critically loaded fault. So, the earthquake cycle would be anyway dominated by tectonic phenomena, but this small external triggering effect could generate the observed slight correlation among worldwide earthquakes." Importantly, this same mechanism would predict various phenomena that have been reported as accompanying major earthquakes. As the authors suggest,

> These kinds of effects, induced by high electrical potential between the ionosphere and the Earth, should likely be accompanied by electrical discharges in atmosphere, which would cause luminescence phenomena. Actually, there are numerous observations of macroscopic luminescence phenomena (named Earthquake Lights) before and accompanying large earthquakes. Moreover, these phenomena could also cause strong electromagnetic effects, which would be recorded as radio-waves; even such phenomena have been largely reported as accompanying, and generally preceding, large earthquakes. More in general, a lot of electro-magnetic anomalies, often well evident, are more and more frequently reported associated to moderate to large earthquakes. (Marchitelli et al. 2020, 8; see their original paper for references to the phenomena mentioned)

In future years, I suspect that much more progress will be made regarding correlations and mechanisms linking solar and terrestrial activity, including earthquake activity.

A BRIEF SUMMATION

As I hope that you (the reader) will appreciate, in my assessment there have been a number of lines of evidence that have been developed since 2011–2012 that support, verify, and enhance the major themes of the original text of *Forgotten Civilization*. I have reviewed briefly some of this evidence above, but there is much more that I (with Katie) and others continue to develop. In a nutshell, I stand by the overall message of the original edition of *Forgotten Civilization*. Today there is even more confirmation that our Sun is much more unstable, and potentially destructive, than has generally been assumed.

In 2011–2012 I was rather ambivalent regarding the cause of the beginning of the Younger Dryas (circa 10,900 BCE). Even though I had earlier been a proponent of meteors, asteroids, comets, and other physical impactors having a profound influence on both Earth and human history (see discussion in my 1999 book *Voices of the Rocks*), I was not convinced by the comet hypothesis as the initiator of the beginning of the Younger Dryas in particular. As I have elaborated in this chapter, I now find that there is a strong case to be made that unusual solar activity was the cause of both the beginning and the ending of the Younger Dryas (the end of the last ice age). In my assessment, all of the data put forward to support the comet hypothesis are compatible with the solar outburst hypothesis, and indeed much of the data better fit the solar hypothesis.

From a personal point of view, I feel a direct link to the people of the last cycle of civilization (those who carved the original lioness, later transformed into the Great Sphinx, and those who built and those who buried Göbekli Tepe) and also the brave souls who survived the six millennia of SIDA (the Solar-Induced Dark Age) that separates the last cycle of civilization from our own. At the end of the last ice age, circa 9700 BCE, the Sun underwent a mighty outburst and electrical plasma discharges hit Earth, including a direct strike on the lioness (later to become the Great Sphinx) of the Giza Plateau, creating a fissure that split her into two. Then the rains poured from the sky, causing the precipitation-induced weathering and erosion that Schwaller de Lubicz (see chapter 2, page 12) noticed on the body of the Sphinx and that John Anthony West brought to my attention in the late 1980s. That simple, but profound, observation set me on a path that I continue to follow over three decades later.

Ancient peoples around the world, our ancestors, accomplished amazing feats and also suffered mighty setbacks. The Ancestors are always with me, and I draw inspiration and strength from them. Especially in these unsettled times, we should not squander the past but rather learn from and build on the legacy that has been passed down to us.

To the Ancestors: Thank you.

WAS THE GREAT SPHINX SURROUNDED BY A MOAT?

The notion that the Great Sphinx of Egypt has its origins in extreme antiquity, dating back to circa 10,000 BCE, is an argument that I have developed over three decades based on painstaking analyses of the geology of the Giza Plateau (where the Great Sphinx and Great Pyramid are located). Conventional Egyptological thinking dates the Sphinx to circa 2500 BCE, during the Fourth Dynasty of the Old Kingdom. My dating places its origins long before the rise of dynastic Egypt, back to a time when, according to the traditional paradigm, high culture and civilization did not exist.

My work on the Great Sphinx has come under fire from a self-described antiestablishmentarian. Given the number of people who have been asking me about this "Sphinx theory," I feel it is imperative that I briefly address it here. While I eschew personal attacks and try to let unwarranted criticism of my work (typically by people lacking geological expertise but with personal agendas to defend) roll off my back, in some situations the unfounded attacks need to be addressed. This is particularly the case when the attacks are part of a weighty volume that purports to offer a new interpretation of the Great Sphinx, one that supposedly overthrows my decades of analyses. I refer specifically to *The Sphinx Mystery: The Forgotten Origins of the Sanctuary of Anubis* by Robert Temple with Olivia Temple (2009).

Here I will first summarize Robert Temple's theory and list six major points that disprove it. I will then briefly comment on his book specifically. This discussion will not only serve to rebut Temple's ill-founded hypothesis, but also to elaborate and clarify some of the details on which my analyses of the Great Sphinx are based.

ROBERT TEMPLE'S MOAT THEORY

Robert Temple (Temple 2009; Temple with Temple 2009) has proposed a moat theory (that is, the Sphinx Enclosure was purposefully filled with water such that the body of the Sphinx was submerged and sat as a statue in a small artificial lake) to explain the evidence of water weathering and erosion on the body of the Great Sphinx and on the walls of the Sphinx Enclosure. Temple contends that the moat theory explains the data adequately without hypothesizing that the Great Sphinx dates back to a much earlier period during which there was more rainfall than at present.

The body of the Sphinx, carved from the bedrock, sits largely below ground level, and various moat, pool, or artificial fountain hypotheses have been suggested for the Sphinx from time to time. I considered such notions carefully as far back as my early analyses of the geology of the Sphinx, starting in 1990. In summary, such moat theories and related theories do not hold water (to use a bad pun) and are not compatible with the features of the actual Great Sphinx, the Sphinx Enclosure, and the general geology and paleohydrology of the Giza Plateau.

SCRUTINIZING THE SPHINX

During a March 2009 trip to Egypt, just after becoming aware of Temple's hypothesis, I made it a point to look at the Great Sphinx and Sphinx Enclosure with fresh eyes to see if there could be anything to the moat class of theories. I will summarize briefly a half dozen points (for more details pertaining to some of these points, as well as various comments on the criticisms of K. Lal Gauri and his colleagues of my work, as cited by Temple with Temple [2009], see Schoch 2002 and the extensive discussions I included in Schoch and Bauval 2017).

1. Based on my observations and analyses, the Sphinx Temple (built out of blocks removed from the Sphinx Enclosure when the body of the Sphinx was initially carved) and the so-called Valley Temple to the south of the Sphinx Temple show signs of heavy precipitation-induced weathering and erosion on the limestone core blocks. These limestone temples were subsequently refurbished with Aswan granite ashlars during the Old Kingdom (as evidenced by an Old Kingdom inscription still found on a block located at the Valley Temple; possibly the inscription was added to a still older, prior to the Old Kingdom, granite block). The moat theory cannot explain the nature of the very ancient weathering seen under the Old Kingdom granite veneer.

2. There is much heavier surface erosion on the western end of the Sphinx Enclosure, and the surface erosion tapers off dramatically toward the eastern end of the enclosure. This is exactly what is to be expected based on the paleohydrology of the Giza Plateau and is incompatible with a moat theory where it is hypothesized that water was brought in from the Nile, which is located to the east. Furthermore, the nature of the surface erosion throughout the enclosure and on the body of the Sphinx is as expected if there were water running over or raining down on the rock layers. The erosion actually observed is not compatible with pooled water in the enclosure.

3. The highest levels of the middle member strata, as seen in the Sphinx Enclosure on the western end, are most severely eroded, which is compatible with the agency of precipitation. If the moat theory were true, then the lower strata on the eastern end of the Sphinx Enclosure would be most heavily eroded (caused by water being brought in via canals from the Nile), but the opposite is seen in reality. Indeed, the evidence is clear that the water erosion is due to precipitation and runoff, not from water and flooding of any type coming from lower elevations, such as the rising of the Nile.

4. The subsurface seismic data demonstrating the depth of weathering below the floor of the Sphinx Enclosure, based on my analyses (using areas excavated during the Old Kingdom for comparison), even when calibrated very conservatively, give an age of initial carving for the core body of the Great Sphinx of at least 5000 BCE. More than one geological colleague has suggested to me that a more realistic calibration gives a date thousands of years earlier. (My best estimate is circa 10,000 BCE.) And no, it is not the case that standing water in the Sphinx Enclosure would accelerate the depth of weathering below the floor of the enclosure.

5. The vertical fissures observed in the walls of the Sphinx Enclosure show diagnostic signs of having been formed by precipitation and water runoff. In my opinion, they do not show any characteristics that are diagnostic or even suggestive of having been formed by artificial dredging of the Sphinx Enclosure, as some have suggested.

6. If the Great Sphinx actually had sat in an artificial pool or lake, either the water level around the Sphinx would have had to have been the same as that of the surrounding water table or the walls and floor of the pool in which the Sphinx sat would have had to have been sealed up and watertight (and any artificial walls, such as on the eastern end, would have had to have been strong enough to withstand the pressure of the water). Evidently, the ancient water table was well below the level of the floor of the Sphinx Enclosure (or else the Sphinx Temple, for instance, would have been flooded). Due to the nature of the local geology (discussed under the heading "Geological Details" below), the Sphinx Enclosure could not have held a deep pool of standing water.

ANCIENT RAINS OR A MOAT?

Temple cites John Anthony West (who was responsible for my initial involvement with the Sphinx over three decades ago) and Robert Bauval as among the "popular writers who have campaigned for the idea that the Sphinx is of immense antiquity" (Temple with Temple 2009, 242). Temple recounts the gist of the argument: the Sphinx shows "water erosion" (Temple's term), Egypt is known today for its desert environment, and heavy rainfall occurred in Egypt in earlier times, therefore the Sphinx must date back to those earlier times ("about 10,000 BC" is the date Temple attributes to West and Bauval).

Temple states his own position as such: "I was never convinced by this argument from the very beginning for the simple reason that there is just no archaeological record at all for any important civilization during approximately seven thousand years of the time postulated between the 'ancient rain' and the apparent beginnings of high civilization in Egypt" (Temple with Temple 2009, 243).

Temple's argument might have carried some weight in 1990, but since the late 1990s, we have had the amazing megalithic site of Göbekli Tepe in Turkey, just north of the Syrian border (admittedly not in Egypt, but certainly close enough geographically to pertain to the argument; see discussion in chapter 3). Independent of the Great Sphinx, this well-dated site provides definitive evidence that high culture dates back to circa twelve thousand years ago! Why did Temple, whose book was published in 2009, completely ignore the evidence of Göbekli Tepe?

Temple accepts that "the apparent evidence of water erosion [in the area of the Sphinx] is so blatantly obvious to anyone that for someone supposedly knowledgeable wholly to deny it looks disingenuous" (Temple with Temple 2009, 243; material in brackets added by R. Schoch). Temple's denial of Göbekli Tepe, by ignoring the evidence the site supplies, "looks disingenuous."

Temple proposes an alternative theory to explain the evidence: *"that the Sphinx Pit* [Sphinx Enclosure] *was once a moat filled with water, and that the Sphinx was an island"* (Temple with Temple 2009, 244; italics in the original; material in brackets added by R. Schoch).

Having studied the evidence for the last thirty years (I, like Temple, have had access to the interior of the Sphinx Temple, the Sphinx Enclosure, and other areas that are off limits to the general public), I feel confident in repeating my statement that Temple's moat theory simply does not hold water. I will now further elaborate on only a few salient points that counter Temple's argument.

GEOLOGICAL DETAILS

An important fact is that the current top of the westernmost end of the southern wall of the Sphinx Enclosure is at least 6 to 7.5 meters higher in elevation than the current top of the eastern end of the same wall (as can be seen on the contour map reprinted on page 534 of Temple's book, and is also evident when examining the view shown in Plate 3 of the color insert of this book). The eastern end of the enclosure includes the western wall of the Sphinx Temple, which Robert Temple believes formed the eastern wall of the moat. The actual difference between the tops of the walls is perhaps nearly twice as much when comparing the highest point at the northwest corner of the Sphinx Enclosure to the lowest point at the top of the wall in the southeast corner. Water seeks its own level, thus since we find clear and prominent evidence of water erosion at the top of the far western end of the enclosure, if the moat theory were correct, the eastern end of the Sphinx Enclosure, as well as the walls along the southern and northern sides, would have had to have reached a comparable height as the western end, up to 6 to 7.5 meters or more higher (and perhaps nearly twice that in the far southeast corner) than the walls that currently remain. These would have been substantial structures indeed to hold back the pressure of such a large body of standing water, and in sum there is no definitive evidence for such structures, although Temple argues that various constructions to the east of the Sphinx Enclosure were removed. Furthermore, such a deep pool of water would not leave any portion of the current body of the Sphinx as an island, but would submerge it completely.

Another key point is that the Sphinx Enclosure is highly faulted and jointed. Additionally, the limestone bedrock is characterized by karst topography, with numerous openings and cavities through which water can drain. Indeed, it would leak like a sieve (another bad analogy, perhaps). To put it simply, I do not believe that the Sphinx Enclosure, even with massive walls built around it as described above, would hold a large standing body of water. The water would leak out into the numerous cavities and tunnels below the Sphinx and into the Giza Plateau more generally. In order to hold water without leaking, the bedrock and sides of the enclosure would have to be sealed up. This could conceivably have been done with some sort of mortar, cement, brick, or tile combination, but there is no evidence that this was the case. In fact, there is evidence that the rock forming the sides of the enclosure was left bare. If the rock had been covered, sealed, and protected, then it would not show the well-developed water erosion features that we observe to this day and that even Temple puts so much stock in. Furthermore, if the enclosure had been sealed in such a manner, this would not be compatible with the dredging theory, advocated by Temple, to account for the vertical fissures. These features and their distribution are the signs of rain and water runoff from higher up on the plateau to the west and north; they are incompatible with a moat theory.

In his book, Temple misrepresents various geological details, convoluting the facts to prop up his moat theory. For instance, he includes a photograph of what he refers to as "the swirling pattern in the rock where the water entered from the channel and then passed to the right into the open Sphinx Moat" (Temple with Temple 2009, 271). The features shown in the photo are actually nothing of the sort. They were formed millions of years ago due to mineralogical and chemical migration as the layers of limestone, which originally formed at the bottom of an ocean, were gradually uplifted and the water table receded. K. Lal Gauri and J. K. Bandyopadhyay explain this point in their book *Carbonate Stone* (1999), a work that Temple cites but perhaps did not read carefully.

SUBSURFACE WEATHERING

Temple purposefully misrepresents my work when he writes, "There is one other major point in Schoch's book with Robert Aquinas

McNally [*Voices of the Rocks* (1999)] that should be mentioned. He says that he determined through his geological investigations of the Sphinx Pit that there was deeper erosion to the north, south, and east of the Sphinx in the floor of the moat than there is to the west. This discovery substantiates the hypothesis of a moat fed from the east by the Nile" (Temple with Temple 2009, 289; material in brackets added by R. Schoch).

To put it simply, this is a complete fabrication on the part of Temple. What I wrote, which is also explained in detail in the academic paper that Thomas Dobecki and I (Dobecki and Schoch 1992) published but Temple never cites, although I list the reference in *Voices,* is this: "The north, south, and east floors of the trench surrounding the east-facing Sphinx are weathered to a depth of six to eight feet [approximately 1.8 to 2.5 meters] below the level of the enclosure's currently exposed surface. On the monument's western end, the Sphinx's rump, the weathering extends to only four feet [1.2 meters]" (Schoch with McNally 1999, 40; material in brackets added by R. Schoch).

Self-styled expert on geological erosion and weathering that he is, Temple must clearly know the difference between surface erosion (the breakdown and removal of material) and subsurface weathering (mineralogical changes without substantial removal of material). While the surface erosion is more pronounced on the western end of the Sphinx Enclosure, where the rocks are topographically higher and caught the brunt of rainwater runoff from the plateau in the period prior to dynastic times, the subsurface weathering below the floor of the Sphinx Enclosure is shallower on the western end. This does not support Temple's moat theory at all, but in fact contradicts it.

If the moat theory is correct, with water flowing in from the east, then the surface erosion, and not the depth of subsurface weathering, should be greatest on the eastern end. Since the floor of the Sphinx Enclosure is more or less at the same elevation across its surface, water entering from the east would quickly reach the western end (again, water seeks its own level), and once a meter or so depth of water was in the enclosure, the entire floor would be covered with water. Furthermore, the depth of the subsurface weathering is not dependent on the surface being covered with water. The depth of subsurface weathering is a function of how long ago the rock floor was exposed, not how much water has flowed over it.

The reason the subsurface weathering is less deep on the western end is that originally the rump of the Great Sphinx was carved down only to the depth of the ledge or terrace directly behind the Sphinx. Originally the Sphinx emerged from the bedrock. The sides and eastern portion show deeper subsurface weathering because they were totally carved down to the current floor of the Sphinx Enclosure thousands of years earlier than the rump, which, based on my analyses, was fully carved down to the current floor as part of the refurbishing of the statue during Old Kingdom times, circa 2500 BCE.

SPHINX OR JACKAL? LION OR DOG?

A major thesis of Temple's book is that the Great Sphinx was not originally a sphinx, but a jackal (wild dog) representing the god Anubis. My gut reaction is that if the Great Sphinx was initially meant to represent Anubis, then it should be facing west and not east. Anubis was associated with the west and the "land of the dead," which was considered to be in the west. Be that as it may, let us look further at the jackal versus lion controversy. Traditionally the body of the Sphinx has been viewed as that of a lion, and I (among others) have suggested that originally it was a statue of a lion (or more accurately, a lioness; see chapter 15, page 314). Temple argues that the body of the Sphinx cannot represent a lion because its back is flat and straight, whereas a lion has a massive chest and the back rises to the front. Temple contests that the straight back of the Sphinx matches that of Anubis as a jackal in its characteristic crouched pose with its forelimbs stretched before it. This may be so, but for me it is a moot point.

The body of the Sphinx is highly weathered and eroded, and I believe that the current flat state of its back is primarily a function of a flat geological bedding plane level, down to which the rock has eroded. (I have had the opportunity to walk on the back of the Sphinx and inspect it closely.) The flat back is not how it was originally carved.

Indeed, no significant original carved surfaces on the body of the Sphinx remain exposed for inspection. The body's surface is entirely weathered and eroded, in many places by a meter or more, and we just do not know what the exact original outlines of the body looked like. However, the curving tail on the right side of the body of the Sphinx, reconstructed in limestone blocks that have been used to fill in and repair the erosion, is much more leonine than jackal-like. (In ancient Egypt, Anubis as a jackal generally had a straight tail, often hanging down, very unlike the current curved tail of the Sphinx.) I do not believe that we can definitively say what the original body of the Great Sphinx looked like, but it certainly is compatible with that of a lion or lioness. (Here I will briefly note that I disagree with the details of the reconstruction of the Sphinx in the form of the lioness Mehit, as proposed by Robert Neyland [2019]; this does not negate my opinion that the Sphinx was originally a statue of the lioness, but I question the specifics of his reconstruction. In my assessment, Neyland has not sufficiently taken into account the severe weathering on the back and body of the statue. The weathering may simply give the superficial form and appearance of what Neyland interprets as an artifact of a former sculpture. I long ago observed the features that Neyland focused on; as a geologist, given the particular strata and the nature and degree of weathering and erosion, I attributed the features to natural processes. As already stated, I have been on the back of the current Sphinx, and it is in my assessment a weathering and erosional plane following the natural strata. Material removed from the back should probably be measured in meters, not centimeters, and I sincerely doubt that anything remains from the original phase of carving on the back. When we did some crude reconstructions of the former statue back in 1993 for *The Mystery of the Sphinx* [Sphinx Project 1993], we were clear to point out that the back is heavily weathered and eroded and that the current back is not the original back of the statue.)

The current head of the Great Sphinx is that of a human, and the modern, conventional Egyptological view is that the face represents either the Old Kingdom pharaoh Khafre, reputed builder of the Great Sphinx in circa 2500 BCE, or some other pharaoh (see discussion in

Schoch and Bauval 2017). I have made it very clear in my work that I do not believe the current head of the Great Sphinx is the original head. It is proportionally too small for the body and has been recarved. Furthermore, I have been explicit in suggesting that the current head of the Great Sphinx is not that of Khafre, and I discuss this at length (citing the work of the forensic expert Frank Domingo) in *Voices of the Rocks* (Schoch with McNally 1999), yet Temple (Temple with Temple 2009, 288) suggests that I believe the face of the Sphinx is that of Khafre. The truth is that I have suggested that the current pharaonic head is a recarving, perhaps dating to early dynastic times, prior to the time of Khafre. (Temple dates the current head to the Middle Kingdom, asserting that the face seen on the Sphinx is that of the Middle Kingdom pharaoh Amenemhet II, nineteenth century BCE.) Since Temple ostensibly read my book, either he suffered from a lapse of memory or he is purposefully misstating my position.

Temple suggests that originally the head on the Great Sphinx was that of a jackal, with elongated snout and upright pointed ears. The current head, according to Temple, was recarved from the neck portion of the original jackal head. Studying the original statue, there is really no way to confirm Temple's hypothesis of a jackal head, but from my perspective as a geologist, it seems highly unlikely. According to Temple's hypothetical reconstruction, the missing jackal ears situated above the level of the current head were over nine meters tall, and the face and snout of the jackal extended out from the current face by over nine meters. While the dolomitic limestone from which the head is carved might have been able to support a pair of nine-meter-tall vertical ears, I question whether the rock would have been strong enough to support a nine-meter projecting face and snout without anything propping it up from underneath. At best, positing a jackal face on the statue is wild speculation and highly questionable.

THE GRANDEUR OF THE GREAT SPHINX

All in all, after poring through Temple's book, my conviction that the Great Sphinx has its origins thousands of years before dynastic times remains as strong as ever. Furthermore, unless better evidence than that which Temple presents comes along, I will continue to think of the Great Sphinx as a sphinx or as a lion/lioness that was later recarved with a human head. The nobility, the grandeur, and the mystery of the Great Sphinx remain intact.

Figure AI.I. The Great Sphinx with the Great Pyramid in the background, along with tourists, camels, and a native Egyptian, circa early 1900s. (Collection of R. Schoch.)

APPENDIX 2

POLITICS, MONEY, AND SCIENCE

Despite the myth of the "objectivity" of "pure science," there is nothing fully objective about the way practicing scientists actually pursue their business. Scientists, like everyone else, are influenced either subtly or explicitly by combinations of social, political, and religious pressures (even when reacting against such factors) and by deeply ingrained assumptions and worldviews that are virtually inescapable. The status quo rewards "good" scientists, those who toe the party line, with prestige, honor, promotions, grant money, personal gain, and even wealth. But those who step out of line may be severely punished.

As science historians Juan Miguel Campanario and Brian Martin (2008) have pointed out, there are different strategies one can pursue as a scientist (or academic scholar more generally). Most scientists build their careers by accepting, and working within, the existing paradigm of the time, adding to the overall picture with carefully sifted bits of data and perhaps elaborating and slightly tweaking existing theories. The work they do is neither highly original nor spectacular, but in terms of peer acceptance and likelihood of success (whether measured in terms of contributions to the paradigm or, more honestly, promotion and upward mobility in terms of jobs and salaries), it is a good, conservative approach. Such a path, herding with the scientific pack, generally results in a stable career, moderate prestige, and the material benefits that go with being a well-paid industrial or academic scientist.

On the other hand, we can consider the "scientific risk-takers," those who pursue speculative or unusual ideas, do not dismiss anomalous data, and end up questioning the reigning paradigm. The stakes are high. If the dissident succeeds in having a new idea or theory accepted by the mainstream, the rewards in terms of prestige (which may result in funding, jobs, or other material benefits) can be enormous. However, the odds are stacked against the true innovator, and such a path is difficult, to say the least. Not only, one can argue, is there a high probability that the theories or ideas espoused by the innovator are false in an absolute sense, but even if there is something to them, there is also an incredible prejudice against new ideas among status quo scientists. As the Nobel Prize–winning physicist Max Planck (1858–1947), one of the founders of quantum mechanics, famously asserted, "A new scientific truth does not triumph by convincing its opponents and making them see the light, but rather because its opponents eventually die, and a new generation grows up that is familiar with it" (Planck, quoted in Kuhn 1962, 150).

POLITICS AND SCIENCE

Politicians often have the ability to halt the serious pursuit of certain scientific endeavors. This has been the case for thousands of years. Hero of Alexandria (first century CE) was well on his way to developing an effective steam engine. However, the politicians and administrators wanted nothing to do with such a device. The Roman Empire widely employed slave labor. If mechanical engines were used to irrigate fields or for other aspects of production, what would all those slaves do? Idleness could lead to rebellion. The first practical steam engine would have to wait another 1,600 years. Imagine what the world might be like today if the politicians had not squelched the invention of the steam engine two thousand years ago.

The patron of science, or of a particular scientist or field, can be all-important. A classic example is the Soviet agronomist Trofim Lysenko

(1898–1976), who gained the personal support of the dictator Joseph Stalin (1878–1953). Lysenko rose to prominence in the 1920s, garnering the attention of the Soviet leaders as someone ideologically compatible with the politics of the time. Lysenko had peasant roots; he despised classic academic theory and mere laboratory work, emphasizing practical techniques to increase crop yields. Lysenko was given the helm of the Academy of Agricultural Sciences of the Soviet Union and named director of the Institute of Genetics of the USSR Academy of Science. His anti-Mendelian, neo-Lamarckian (inheritance of environmentally acquired characteristics) views received high-handed official approval. Statutes outlawed dissenting opinions. In the end, Lysenko's "science" proved ineffective; many of his supposed results were either greatly exaggerated or simply fraudulent. Lysenko may be an extreme case, but it illustrates the abuses possible when those with power and money decide to support an agenda using science as the means.

On a different scale, I have seen the corrupting effects of money in Bosnia and Herzegovina. I am referring to the so-called Bosnian Pyramids located in the region of Visoko. Initially, I was excited about the prospect of very ancient pyramids. (Claims circulated that they were ten thousand or more years old.) Upon visiting the site, I discovered a massive hoax fueled by money, power, influence, and patronage. The major player is Semir Osmanagich, a Bosnian-American who continues to promote several natural hills as human-made ancient pyramids. He has solicited private, corporate, and government backing and funds to continue "excavations" there, excavations that only perpetuate the fraud by actually shaping the hills into what appear superficially to be step-pyramid structures. Osmanagich brings high-level politicians to the site, touting the great "discoveries" being made, and organizes "conferences" about the "pyramids."

While in Visoko exploring the site firsthand in 2006, I briefly met a former head of state of Yugoslavia, there to support the "pyramids" (Bosnia and Herzegovina is one of the countries that resulted from the breakup of Yugoslavia during the 1991–1995 wars), and I attended one of Osmanagich's conferences. The conference was a farce, with no hard evidence corroborating the reality of the "pyramids," but rather a lot of mumbo-jumbo and ambiguous comments generated by people claiming to be scientists (archaeologists, geophysicists, chemists, geologists— you name it), who were present simply because they were being paid and jobs were difficult to come by in the ravaged Bosnian economy. The politicians apparently knew nothing about science and cared even less. All they were concerned about was bringing in money, and the so-called pyramids formed a major tourist attraction, with small businesses, restaurants, and hotels sprouting up to serve the needs of the pilgrims to the site. And pilgrims they were, for they were coming to a virtually sacred spot, one that engendered national loyalty and pride in the antiquity and sophistication of Bosnia's origins—supposedly older than Egypt or perhaps any other civilization. To question the authenticity of the Bosnian pyramids was to insult the Bosnian people and their heritage. Nationalism can trump scientific evidence and reason. The paradigm, the accepted dogma, in the case of the so-called Bosnian pyramids was that they are authentic. Evidence to the contrary was ignored, or worse yet, those advocating a different view were vilified and persecuted. I was reminded of the Inquisition.

This brings us to a major problem with science today: the dominance of certain ruling paradigms. Those who control the money, jobs, prestige, technical publication outlets, and popular media (whether directly or subtlety) have a low tolerance for ideas that may challenge the desired result or accepted status quo. It seems that in the modern world if one wants to be sure to fit in, one does not question certain sacred cows. Among these are human-induced global warming, Darwinian evolution, gradualism, global plate tectonics, big bang cosmology, various aspects of materialism, and historical progressionism (the general concept that history is a one-way street going from dumb old "them" to modern, enlightened, technologically sophisticated "us"). Various other topics are anathema and shunned by any "serious" scientist who expects to receive grant funding; desires a decent university, government, or corporate position; and entertains the prospect of publishing in the most prestigious scientific journals, which in turn are taken by the popular media as presenting dogmatic truth worthy of reporting. Shunned subjects include nontraditional medicine, crop circles, UFOs, intelligent design, alternative archaeology (including the concept that some ancient peoples were much more sophisticated than traditionally believed), and paranormal (parapsychological) studies.

Parapsychology is an interesting case. Telepathy (direct mind-to-mind communication), psychokinesis (mind-over-matter), and precognition (reception of information about future events) have been studied extensively for more than a century by some of the best minds, including Ph.D.-level scientists and even Nobel laureates (for example, Charles Richet, Nobel Prize in Physiology/Medicine, 1913, and Brian Josephson, Nobel Prize in Physics, 1973). The basic phenomena have been demonstrated over and over again, and even been put to practical use (see Bem 2011; Bremseth 2008; Burns 2003; de Martino 1972; de Vesme 1931a, 1931b; Laszlo 2003, 2004; Myers 1903; Owen with Sparrow 1976; Utts 1991; and articles in Schoch and Yonavjak 2008).

There is a vast body of scientific literature on parapsychology, with specialized journals and societies. Yet, despite these facts, the "average scientist" does not consider parapsychology a science and, knowing nothing about the subject and its evidence, feels free to make disparaging statements about the field and any of its practitioners. If anything concerning parapsychology makes it to the popular media, the press is sure to interview some mainstream "acknowledged authority" and will be fed a bunch of rubbish supposedly debunking parapsychology. To belittle parapsychology even more, the media may include comments about crystal balls, fortune-tellers, false séances, or quack astrologers (versus true astrologers), thus further condemning parapsychology by association.

This attitude toward parapsychology is not new. Discussing telepathy, the great Russian ethnographer Sergei Mikhailovich Shirokogoroff (1889–1939), who studied at length the culture of the indigenous people of the Siberian region (whom he labeled the Tungus) during the early twentieth century, wrote:

> Transmission of thought at a distance was observed by several authors and interpreted in different manners. . . . Some time [a]go any one who dared to discuss these questions or to publish the facts met with criticism from the "scientists" who said that these were

"superstitions," "folklore," "immaterial approach," "lack of criticism," etc., while they themselves were merely impressed by the existing theories and hypotheses accepted as "truth". As a matter of fact such a behavior of scientists is as much ethnocentric as that of the Tungus and it is as much "folklore" as that designated as such by the scientists. (Shirokogoroff 1935, 118, footnote)

That is, to uncritically dismiss evidence (in this case, evidence supporting the reality of telepathy) as impossible—therefore it must be superstition or folklore—is in fact just a modern form of bias that supports the preconceptions of the modern scientists.

People who consider it their duty to maintain the status quo often attempt to dismiss ideas and data that counter their limited worldview with overly simplistic, patronizing remarks. One of their favorite mantras is along the lines that "extraordinary claims require extraordinary evidence" (Tressoldi 2011). This is an assertion that may sound superficially profound, but it does not hold up under careful and logical scrutiny as, when typically applied by the debunkers, it presupposes what is extraordinary in terms of claims and then sets an evidential standard that precludes the possibility of the claims being validated, no matter what the evidence. To give an extreme example, the nineteenth-century physicist and physician Hermann von Helmholtz (1821–1894) declared that no amount of evidence, not even the evidence of his own senses, could ever convince him that telepathy is real since he knew that it was impossible (see Schoch and Yonavjak 2008, 331). Talk about close-minded!

Given its low status, parapsychology has never been the recipient of adequate funding. In the early 1990s, it was estimated that the total expenditures devoted to parapsychological studies worldwide since 1882 (the year when the Society for Psychical Research was established, thus beginning systematic scientific studies of the paranormal) were at most equal to two months of psychology funding in the United States. In the last thirty years the situation has only become more dire as the Princeton Engineering Anomalies Research (PEAR) laboratory has shut down and the United States government and military are no longer (at least not publicly) funding parapsychological research or applications.

Between 1972 and 1995 the CIA (Central Intelligence Agency), the DIA (Defense Intelligence Agency), INSCOM (U.S. Army Intelligence Support Command), the NSC (National Security Council), and other federal departments funded, studied, and applied parapsychological techniques to military and intelligence objectives (Bremseth 2008). During the Iran hostage crisis (1979–1981), under the Carter administration, remote viewing was successfully used to identify American hostages and their locations as well as potential escape routes. In his book *White House Diary* (2010), Jimmy Carter mentions the successful use of parapsychology-based intelligence, stating, "The proven results of these exchanges between our intelligence services and parapsychologists raise some of the most intriguing and unanswerable questions of my presidency. . . . They defy logic, but the facts are undeniable" (see Carter 2010; quoted by Gavin 2010).

If there is scientific evidence supporting the reality of parapsychological phenomena and, more importantly, they actually work, as testified to by a former U.S. President, why did the government stop funding such studies? Why is parapsychology held in such low regard by the scientific community and the public at large? Why is there so much disinformation about the subject? Why are we not investing substantial funds in such a paradigm-breaking subject?

THREATENING THE PARADIGM

I believe the "problem" with parapsychology is indeed its paradigm-breaking aspect. The data of parapsychology suggest the possibility that mind can exist and operate independent of matter, that consciousness is a force or entity unto itself that can interact with other consciousnesses and also directly affect the material world. These concepts strike at the very foundations of a materialistic worldview, where everything can be explained by a combination of physical forces mixed with random accidents. The status quo "scientific" worldview typically leaves no room for a dualism between spirit and matter, nor even acknowledges the concept of spirit or soul as having an objective reality. To make matters worse, parapsychology takes seriously such issues as the possibility of an afterlife, discarnate spirits, and the idea of consciousness (at some level) pervading all of life and the universe.

It would seem that everything parapsychologists study and find evidence for threatens the status quo currently benefiting those in charge. Modern society is built on materialism and consumerism; those with the most money have the most influence (be it in politics, business, or otherwise) and reap the material benefits of society. They want to keep it that way. Superficially, it might appear that the relationship of parapsychology to religion would be more amicable, but such is not the case when it comes to many mainstream churches. Based on subservience to a god, with the intermediaries between the god and the everyday public being the officials of the church, there is little room for freedom of thought when it comes to the nature of spiritual beings, consciousness, and our souls. The dogma of the church (whichever church) should prevail and be accepted on blind faith without scrutiny.

While parapsychology is an example of a field shunned and disparaged by the mainstream, an example of a paradigm and dogma currently favored by the establishment scientific community is anthropogenic global climate change. The consensus view is that Earth is warming, with potentially disastrous consequences, and the primary culprit is human activity. In many scientific circles, to even suggest that this may not be the entire story is to face harsh consequences—loss of grant funding, diminished prestige, being passed over for promotion, inability to publish one's data and views.

The American Physical Society (APS), like many other scientific societies, has gone on record as supporting the reality of global warming, stating (language adopted by the APS Council on November 18, 2007):

Emissions of greenhouse gases from human activities are changing the atmosphere in ways that affect the Earth's climate. . . .

The evidence is incontrovertible: Global warming is occurring.

If no mitigating actions are taken, significant disruptions in the Earth's physical and ecological systems, social systems, security and human health are likely to occur. We must reduce emissions of greenhouse gases beginning now.

Because the complexity of the climate makes accurate prediction difficult, the APS urges an enhanced effort to understand the effects of human activity on the Earth's climate, and to provide the technological options for meeting the climate challenge in the near and longer terms. . . . (American Physical Society 2011)

Of course, such statements issued by mainstream scientific organizations become dogma virtually equivalent to papal encyclicals. They form the basis and rationale for investing major financial resources in the topic—in this case, global warming.

Charges of academic misconduct on the part of climate change proponents made the news with the scandal dubbed "ClimateGate." In November 2009 more than a thousand emails and several thousand documents were released by a hacker, acquired from a server used by the Climate Research Unit of the University of East Anglia. Allegations included the withholding of data, manipulation of data to support global warming scenarios, exaggeration of the certainty of the data supporting global warming, suppression of dissenting opinions, and plotting to remove from influential positions people (such as journal editors) who disagreed with climate change dogma. Subsequent investigations into these charges have neither fully supported the allegations nor totally exonerated the individuals involved, but they have engendered strong feelings and exposed just how vested the interests are and how much money can be at stake.

On October 6, 2010, Harold Lewis, emeritus professor of physics, University of California, Santa Barbara, sent a letter to the president of the APS, resigning in disgust from the society he had first joined sixty-seven years earlier. Professor Lewis asserts that the APS (and by extension, much of mainstream science) has been corrupted by money. To quote him:

The money flood has become the raison d'être of much physics research, the vital sustenance of much more, and it provides the support for untold numbers of professional jobs. . . . It is of course, the global warming scam, with the (literally) trillions of dollars driving it, that has corrupted so many scientists, and has carried APS before it like a rogue wave. It is the greatest and most successful pseudo-scientific fraud I have seen in my long life as a physicist. Anyone who has the faintest doubt that this is so should force himself to read the ClimateGate documents, which lay it bare. (Lewis 2010)

Even if one disagrees with Professor Lewis that global warming is the "most successful pseudoscientific fraud," his point that money drives much of modern science must be acknowledged. Those who control the money influence the science, both in terms of which topics are researched and, it would appear in at least some instances, the conclusions that are reached.

Here I am not judging the sides in the global warming debate. Personally, I am convinced that the bulk of the evidence indicates that Earth is warming. However, it appears to me that both natural and artificial factors are involved, and it is difficult to disentangle the two. Nature is not as simple as some people's thinking may be. This is true when it comes to global climate change, the interplay between matter and consciousness, evolution (evolution occurs, but is both more subtle and more complex than some simplistic formulations), or any of a myriad of other scientific issues. Even such subtleties, however, seem to threaten the status quo. Unfortunately, all too often dogmatism prevails and any freedom of thinking is confined to very narrow limits, at least if one wants to gain prestige, influence, and money while pursuing science.

A NOTE ON THE POLITICS OF GÖBEKLI TEPE

Göbekli Tepe is located in the southeastern portion of modern Turkey (see chapter 3). Historically, this area has been under the rule of many different regimes and nations, including the ancient Kingdom of Armenia. Some modern Armenians, referring to Göbekli Tepe by the name Portasar (in Armenian the name means "the centre of the Earth and life, navel, mountain" [Sezen 2020, 48] or "the navel of a mountain" [Tchalian 2019]), have claimed the site as part of their Armenian heritage and argued that it can only be properly interpreted in the light of Armenian culture and language. However, the Kingdom of Armenia reached its greatest extent around the first century BCE, a time many thousands of years after Göbekli Tepe. I am not convinced that there is any good evidence demonstrating that Göbekli Tepe exerted a particularly stronger influence on Armenian culture than it did on other later cultures also found in this area. In my opinion, to say that Göbekli Tepe needs to be interpreted primarily and specifically in terms of Armenian culture is sort of like saying that the native peoples of North America need to be interpreted in terms of English culture since the English language is now widely spoken in America and the current United States owes a heavy debt to British culture.

I also want to point out that Göbekli Tepe is often spelled as one word, "Göbeklitepe," especially in Turkey, and according to Başak Sezen (2020, 117), the name for the site of Göbekli Tepe in Kurdish is "Gira Miraza," which "means a place where you look for remedy for the problems." Sezen (2020, 117) adds, "It seems it was always a sacred place for the people."

A NOTE ON THE NAMING AND DATING OF THE END OF THE LAST ICE AGE

The final period of the last ice age is referred to as the Younger Dryas (circa 10,900 BCE to circa 9700 BCE). To place this into context, during its 4.5- to 4.6-billion-year history the Earth has undergone various periods when there were ice ages, extremely cold conditions, on the surface of our planet. The last such period (most recent period of ice ages) is known as the Pleistocene Epoch and dates from about 2.6 million years ago to the end of the Younger Dryas, about 9700 BCE. The period since the end of the Pleistocene, the period that we currently live in, is known as the Holocene Epoch. During the Pleistocene there were major fluctuations in climate and temperature, glaciers came and went, and there were glacial periods and interglacial periods (all of which have been given various technical names that we need not go into here). Arguably, the comings and goings of glacial and interglacial periods have not ended, and the current Holocene Epoch might better be considered merely the latest interglacial period. Only time will tell.

Why is the very end of the last ice age called the Younger Dryas? This period is named after the plant *Dryas octopetala,* whose remains are commonly found in sediments (typically as pollen grains) dating from this period. *Dryas octopetala,* which is still with us today, is an arctic-alpine member of the rose family that thrives under cold conditions at high altitudes and latitudes throughout the Northern Hemisphere (Ladyman 2011). During the last ice age, when times were colder and forests contracted, the range of *Dryas octopetala* expanded. Today it grows as a low evergreen shrub with leaves that resemble those of oak trees, hence it was named *Dryas* after the mythical Greek oak-nymphs, the dryads. The flowers are white (or very rarely, slightly yellowish) and typically have eight petals (thus the name *Dryas octopetala,* referring to eight petals). Common names for the species include mountain avens, white dryas, white dryad, alpine dryad, and white mountain avens.

If there is a Younger Dryas, is there also an Older Dryas? Yes. And indeed there is even an older period than the Older Dryas, known as the Oldest Dryas. The Oldest Dryas may date back to 17,000 BCE or 16,000 BCE, and the Older Dryas is intermediate in age between the Oldest Dryas and the Younger Dryas. The details of the dating of the Oldest and Older Dryas are contentious.

In this work I have generally referred to the end of the last ice age, or more specifically the end of the Younger Dryas, as dated to circa 9700 BCE and the beginning of the Younger Dryas as circa 10,900 BCE, following the chronology of Steffensen et al. (2008; see further discussion in the update to appendix 5, page 418). Others use different dates for these events, dates that may appear to be disparate by centuries. So, for instance, LaViolette (2011a) adopts a chronology that dates the end of the Younger Dryas to 11,543 BP (that is, either 9593 BCE or 9543 BCE, depending on whether "before the present" is considered before 1950 CE or 2000 CE, as both are used by various researchers) based on data from a sediment varve core (varves are thin layers of silt and clay deposited in lakes, often on an annual basis) from the Cariaco Basin (off the coast of Venezuela), which LaViolette equates to a date of 11,610 BP in certain Greenland ice core chronologies. That is, the 11,543 BP date is the same as the 11,610 BP date. This may seem like an error, but in fact it is very difficult to place precise calendar year dates on prehistoric and geological events. To give another example, in an October 2009 online update to his work, in a footnote LaViolette writes, "As of the time of this update (10/09), LaViolette has adopted the date 12,887 calendar years b2k. [before the year 2000 CE] (~11,000 C-14 years B.P. [before the present]) as the climax of this megafaunal extinction. PAL [Paul A. LaViolette]" (LaViolette 2011b; material in brackets added by R. Schoch). Here he is referring to the major extinction of many large mammals and other animals during the Younger Dryas and equating a "classic" date of eleven thousand years ago (which some would translate as 11,000 − 1950 = 9050 BCE) based on radiocarbon dating with 10,887 BCE (that is, 12,887 years before 2000 CE).

Of course, sometimes errors do occur. To give an example also taken from LaViolette (and I note that this is not LaViolette's error), in 1985 he published a major study of cosmic dust concentrations in an ice core that had been dated to the latter portion of the last ice age, circa 14,000 to 20,000 years BP. After LaViolette's work, however, the ice core he analyzed was redated to circa 38,650 to 78,500 years BP. Thus LaViolette's careful analysis referred to an entirely different period during the last ice age (see LaViolette 1985).

Years based on sediment layers such as varves or based on what is assumed to be the annual layering of snow or ice deposits may not always be exact. (There can be loss or misinterpretation in the record.) Likewise, isotopic techniques have errors of various kinds, including how to calibrate the dates. This has been a particular problem with the popular radiocarbon dating (based on the radioactive isotope ^{14}C). Uncalibrated radiocarbon dates can differ dramatically from calibrated radiocarbon dates, and various calibrations can result in different apparent absolute dates. (Absolute dates are dates in the past based on modern calendar years.) Also, in some cases there have been anomalously young, by thousands of years, radiocarbon dates reported for some apparent ice age (Pleistocene) animals, such as a date of about 4000 BCE for a mastodon tusk from Michigan (Skeels 1962, 123). Generally, it is believed that mastodons were long extinct at that time. To account for some such anomalous dates, LaViolette has suggested, "If a super SPE [solar proton event] had occurred as proposed and caused the ground level cosmic ray intensity to reach very high levels in certain geographic locations, this could explain why some megafaunal remains have anomalously young radiocarbon dates uncharacteristic of the strata age they are found in. That is, incident solar cosmic ray protons could have generated thermal neutrons within animal tissues which upon colliding with organic nitrogen could produce radiocarbon in situ in the animal remains" (LaViolette 2011a, 11, footnote; material in brackets added by R. Schoch).

Another possibility, in some cases at least, is that anomalously young dates could be due to simple intrusion of contamination containing younger carbon, or in the case of the mastodons, there may have been relict populations living much later than is generally assumed. Or in the case of the young mastodon cited above (which is an example cited in LaViolette 2011a), note that the date of the original paper is 1962; techniques have been refined since then. The bottom line is that such dating is fraught with many difficulties, and it is often unrealistic (and unreasonable) to expect (or demand!) precise and accurate dates in calendar years.

Not long after publishing a paper in which I referred to the end of the last ice age as around 9700 BCE, I received an email from a well-meaning "fan" politely informing me that I was mistaken, the ice age ended in 9550 BCE. I could only smile to myself as I thought about the writer's naïveté when it comes to geological dating. The truth is that we cannot necessarily pinpoint the exact age in years of the end of the last ice age (either 9700 BCE or 9550 BCE, or some other date around the two) or any other event that long ago, but we can determine approximately when events occurred and, more important, we can attempt to determine chronologies and sequences of what came earlier, what came later, and what occurred simultaneously. Thus, geologists do not commonly speak in terms of years, but in terms of events. The "end of the Younger Dryas" (which is the same as the end of the last ice age) is an event in time, whatever years are associated with it by one researcher or another (for a further discussion of chronologies and dating in geology, see Schoch 1989).

So the bottom line I would like to impress on readers regarding dates from long ago is this: take all calendar year dates with a large grain of salt, but when I speak of the end of the last ice age (the end of the Younger Dryas), for instance, I am referring to an event and time in history or prehistory that is, hopefully (as mistakes do occur), more or less equivalent from one author or researcher to another regardless of the calendar years they ascribe to it.

MOVING THE MOAI
Easter Island and Psychokinesis

Here I will explore the possibility that parapsychological insights into modern psychokinesis combined with a particular theory of gravity may provide a major clue to the mechanism underlying psychokinesis and ultimately perhaps to how the moai were moved. Admittedly, this discussion is nonconventional, even radical and outrageous to some, but I believe it is at least heuristic to consider.

GRAVITY AS AN ENTROPIC FORCE AND A THEORY OF PSYCHOKINESIS

In a 2010 paper, Erik Verlinde, of the Institute for Theoretical Physics, University of Amsterdam, developed the idea that gravity is not a fundamental force, but rather "an entropic force caused by changes in the information associated with the positions of material bodies" (Verlinde 2010, 1). Verlinde developed this theory in the context of a holographic concept of the universe, where the commonly understood structure of space-time is in fact an emergent property of information that can be visualized as stored on a surface or screen that wraps around the universe. In this conception, mass emerges from information on the holographic screen surrounding a region (even if we conceptualize that region as the entire known universe). Note: entropy is the degree of disorder within a system.

In the last paragraph I have tried to do justice, in quite abbreviated form, to Verlinde's thinking. Now I will develop it a bit further, and I will first state that my thoughts are an outgrowth of reading Verlinde's paper, but second, he may well not agree with my analyses, interpretations, and speculations.

To say that gravity is an entropic force is fundamentally saying that gravity as we observe it arises from the tendency of a system (which could be the entire universe) to statistically increase in entropy. Again, entropy is basically disorder within a system, and by the second law of thermodynamics, the entropy of an isolated nonequilibrium system will increase over time (that is, its order decays). A common everyday example of an entropic force is the pressure of a gas as the particles (atoms and molecules) spread out; a cellular example is the pressure of an osmotic gradient. If gravity is an entropic force, essentially the gravitational force is the tendency of objects (whatever objects are, as they may be epiphenomena) to move to positions of maximum disorder. Disorderly systems carry less information and orderly systems carry more information. Gravity can be equated with the tendency toward increasing entropy, which is increasing disorder, which in turn can be equated with minimizing informational content. Ultimately to "overcome" gravity, to act against the force of gravity, entails a change in the information content of a local system. In the everyday common "real world" we might change the information content of an object, say a stone, by physically lifting it up and placing it on a shelf. If it should be disturbed and fall down off the shelf, the local information content (ultimately encoded and stored on a holographic surface) would change once again.

In an ultimate sense, in a system completely lacking in information (no data encoded on the holographic screen), there would be no gravitational force as there could be no entropic force since minimal information and thus maximal disorder (entropy) would be the state of the system. One could visualize such a system as completely collapsed down to a single dimensionless point, but since there is no information in the system, there would be no mass (since mass emerges from information) or space-time. If information were to be inserted into the system, mass and space-time would emerge, and also gravity as an entropic force countering the information (statistically driving the system back to maximum entropy and minimum information). Information would create the universe as we know it, and inserting increasing amounts of information into the system would cause the universe to expand outward even as gravity countered the information tendency.

The most fundamental aspect of the universe, by this conception, is information (see also the discussion "From Stars We Come and Thence We Return," page 296). Information may be equated with thought or mind or consciousness or mental constructs independent of any material everyday conception. (Certain aspects of parapsychological studies strongly support the notion of the independence of thought or mind or consciousness from any kind of material object, like a physical brain.) The universe of mass and energy and forces, as we experience it on an everyday practical level, may have had its origin in a thought that inserted information into an otherwise blank (data-free) holographic system. (I will leave the question unanswered as to where the initial thought came from, although I cannot help but think of the famous lines from the Christian scriptures, "In the beginning was the Word [thought, information]: the Word was with God and the Word was God" (Jerusalem Bible, 1968, John 1:1; material in brackets added by R. Schoch). Inserting more thoughts, more information, expands and changes the system, allowing it to develop or evolve. Furthermore, thoughts at a certain level are self-perpetuating (here the memory of thoughts, the encoding and preserving of information, may play a key role) and self-expanding as they build, grow, and elaborate on themselves, and in this scenario they are all the while building and developing the "material world" and universe as we know it. Thinking entities who accept the epiphenomena of the everyday world as they experience it on a mundane level will put out more thoughts (habits of thinking), which indeed reinforce not just their status quo conception of the world but also literally their experiential world. Once thinking entities accept a particular worldview (including a conception of the world at the most fundamental level, such as the basic laws of physics), it will be self-perpetuating until or unless different information (thoughts) is inserted into the system at the most fundamental level.

So, by this hypothesis, inserting or changing information by mental means, by thoughts alone, can change (add to, rearrange, and integrate) the data on the holographic screen that "creates" the universe as we know it, and thus we can change the universe or some localized region or sector of the universe. In particular, changing information may allow gravity to be overcome, and this is precisely what we see in genuine cases of anti-gravitational psychokinesis. However, the key (or "trick") is actually changing the information. It seems clear that it is not enough (at least for the vast majority!) to simply "think" on a conscious level about producing a psychokinetic event, but a very deep unconscious or subliminal "belief" (for lack of a better term at the moment) must be present for information to be changed such that manifestations occur in the everyday "real" world. Furthermore, successfully injecting or modifying information so as to manifest observable changes may also require a collective level of belief, or at the least overcoming the collective disbelief (perhaps by the force of the "belief" of a single or few individuals), in a local system.

Among the best-documented cases of mind over matter (the movement of objects by nonphysical means) are so-called poltergeist instances (Roll 2003). In many such cases it appears that objects are moved paranormally (items thrown through the air or falling off of shelves when nobody is close enough to reach them and no physical means are apparent to account for the movement of the objects) due to the unconscious emanations of an emotionally or psychologically disturbed individual. In these instances, the person who is the source or focus of the poltergeist manifestations may have, at a deep unconscious level, broken ties with everyday reality, and as a result he or she is able to successfully change information in the holographic system, which results in manifestations in the "real world" that defy normal gravitational constraints. Other cases of genuine levitation, movements of objects, and other gravity-defying and psychokinetic phenomena (even to move an object horizontally, without perceptively lifting it vertically, can involve overcoming the force of gravity to some extent) have been documented in séance-type settings where a critical mass of the participants (it is not clear if 100 percent is always necessary) have apparently either allowed themselves at a deep level to "believe" that such things can occur or at least have gotten to an open attitude of suspension of disbelief (so as not to unduly hinder the process).

As a case in point along these lines, in 1869 and 1870 a committee of the London Dialectical Society investigated so-called spiritualistic phenomena, including experimenting with séances. Some of the investigators were apparently skeptical but open-minded, and on numerous occasions a heavy table, for instance, was witnessed to move in various directions without any human contact or other mechanical or physical explanation (London Dialectical Society 1873). Many other cases of levitations, movements of objects, and other physical phenomena are recorded in the serious literature (Owen with Sparrow 1976; Braude 2008; de Martino 1972).

Another context where psychokinesis appears to be well documented is on the microscopic or atomic level, for instance, influencing the rolling of dice or the actions of random event generators (Rhine and Rhine 1943; Jahn 1996; Burns 2003; Schoch and Yonavjak 2008, and references cited therein). In such cases, I hypothesize, it may be that it is easier to "believe" that psychokinesis can occur on a microscopic or atomic level, and therefore it is easier to insert or change information in the system, overcome entropy, and effect real changes manifested in the observable world.

Here it may be appropriate to mention the highly controversial work of Masaru Emoto (1943–2014). Quoting from the inside front cover of his 2004 book:

Dr. Masaru Emoto discovered that crystals formed in frozen water reveal changes when specific, concentrated thoughts are directed toward them. He found that water from clear springs and water that has been exposed to loving words shows brilliant, complex, and colorful snowflake patterns. In contrast, polluted water, or water exposed to negative thoughts, forms incomplete, asymmetrical patterns with dull colors.

The conclusions of Emoto, as well as his credentials (he had the title of "Doctor of Alternative Medicine" from the Indian Board of Alternative Medicine; Reville 2011), have been questioned, and he has been labeled a pseudoscientist. What really counts, however, is whether or not there is any genuine evidence to support Emoto's "discovery." In a controlled study, very weak and at best only marginally significant results were found to support Emoto's claims; the authors (and Emoto was one of the four authors) described their results in support of Emoto's work as "modestly significant" and "confirmed, weakly" (Radin et al. 2008, 489), and from their discussion, the conclusion that I draw is that more studies need to be done in order to adequately evaluate Emoto's claims.

In some cases, it has been claimed that individuals can manifest macroscopic psychokinetic effects by conscious will or volition. An example of such an individual was the Russian Nina S. Kulagina (Kulagin 1971; Vilenskaya 1995). I have to admit that I remain highly skeptical of reports of individuals who it is claimed can perform macroscopic psychokinetic feats on command, and I cannot vouch for the authenticity of Kulagina's phenomena, but it is instructive to consider her case. Typical for Kulagina was the movement of small and light objects, such as earrings, rings, envelopes, and such, across a tabletop; a 1971 report stated that the largest object moved was a glass vase weighing 380 grams. In order to effect positive results, Kulagina had to be in a suitable psychological state.

It was discovered that even the psychological state of the persons witnessing the experiment was of importance too. Interest, open mutual trust and friendly feelings are very helpful for the experiments. In cases when the initiative for the experiments did not come from the subject, when the circumstances were unfamiliar and the experiment organised in a different way, e.g., new apparatus, new objects, strangers present, then it is difficult to get good results. In

such cases, the subject has to exert more energy, takes longer to prepare the test, and her strain during the experiment is greater. . . .
The circumstances grow more complicated if some of the people
present do not believe in the success of the experiment or are scepti-
cal of the results. Sometimes, although conditions seem favourable
and the subject tried hard to carry out the experiment, the necessary
psychological state could not be produced in the subject. In some
cases the subject could identify those present who were hindering
this by concealed doubts and scepticism. Provided that they then
left the room, an atmosphere of confidence could be created and the
experiment completed successfully. If after this initial success, witnessed by all present, the sceptics were readmitted, their presence no
longer impeded results. (Kulagin 1971, 57–58)

The correct psychological state of not only Kulagina but also everyone present was very important to the success of the psychokinetic
endeavors. According to the theory I am developing here, it is essential
to adequately diminish or eliminate the individual and collective skepticism about whether such things as psychokinesis are possible before
information can be adequately manipulated to effect a "real-world"
psychokinetic event. Once success has been achieved in certain contexts, the "beliefs" of those who observed the success might be enough
to overcome the "doubts" of the skeptics. The limiting of successful
psychokinesis to relatively light objects in the case of Kulagina may be
both a function of what it was "believed" could be accomplished (it is
perhaps easier to believe, at the deepest levels of the unconscious, that
smaller and lighter objects can be affected) and the issue that perhaps it
requires a higher degree of information manipulation to psychokinetically move a heavier object (weight being a measure of the entropy that
needs to be overcome).

As a side note to the concept of gravity as an entropic force in a
holographic system, essentially gravity would be equivalent to information decay. To maintain records in the form of data encoded on the
holographic screen, the data would have to be continually reinforced
(perhaps by thought). But not only could it be reinforced, it could also

be changed (either purposefully or inadvertently), and anyone accessing the record may receive varying degrees of veridical information depending on the context. (In terms of an equivalence principle, if information can be added, then it can also be accessed and/or extracted or removed.) This may explain aspects of psychical or mental paranormal phenomena (such as telepathy, retrocognition, and precognition) and also suggests that both the past and the future from a human perspective may be malleable as the information encoded on the holographic screen can be manipulated. For thought-producing and thought-receiving entities like us, the most easily accessible and manipulated information is that of the immediate local environment (local from our perspective, that is, close in time and space from an everyday perspective).

EASTER ISLAND AND PSYCHOKINESIS

Returning to the moai of Easter Island, is there any truth to the legends of mana? Were the moai moved paranormally, by a form of psychokinesis, at least in part? Observing the moai on the island, especially around the major quarry, I could not help but get the impression that they had at least in some cases been popped out or tossed out of their resting places, as if by some semichaotic force. It is almost as if parts of the island had been subject to a poltergeist-style phenomenon, with moai strewn about. Perhaps, and of course this is wild speculation, once a moai was partially carved (more or less roughed out), it was moved out of its quarry spot paranormally or with paranormal assistance to some degree. The final positioning and raising of the moai on an ahu (ceremonial stand) may have been accomplished by more normal means.

Easter Island was literally a world unto itself, isolated in space by thousands of kilometers and isolated in time by many centuries and millennia. (This is succinctly expressed in the title of the book about Easter Island by Edmundo Edwards and Alexandra Edwards: *When the Universe Was an Island* [2013].) Easter Island may have formed the perfect psychokinesis laboratory. The inhabitants developed their own collective psyche and worldview, one that was perfectly "believable" to them and that included the ability to manipulate data on the local holographic screen and thus accomplish psychokinetic feats on moai weighing tens of tons. (To be clear, I do not imagine moai floating through the air: however, paranormal or psychokinetic beliefs may have helped to relieve the burden, decrease the "gravitational force" to a certain extent, making it easier to move and manipulate the huge statues.) The Easter Islanders may have had 100 percent, or nearly 100 percent, investment in the belief system of the island. We can think of the entire island being involved in a giant séance where everyone is a true believer. The resulting phenomena may have been well beyond the possibilities that most people can even entertain in our modern, Western-based, twenty-first-century culture.

Pursuing further research concerning the island and its "mysteries" (an admittedly overused term, but one that seems genuinely applicable here), we have much to learn from this small, isolated spot in the Pacific. Easter Island and its world prior to European contact may have been very different, at a deep level, from that which most people today perceive as reality. Indeed, it may have been so different that it is extremely difficult, if not virtually impossible, to fully grasp. However, in trying to comprehend the lost world of Easter Island, we open up new possibilities and begin to expose the assumptions, beliefs, and biases that prevent us from truly understanding the ultimate nature of reality. I can think of nothing that is more profound and worthwhile.

DID A COMET HIT EARTH AT THE BEGINNING OF THE YOUNGER DRYAS, CIRCA 10,900 BCE?

Note to the reader: This appendix was originally written for the first edition of this book (2012). For the sake of integrity and completeness, I have left it substantially as it was originally published, recognizing that, now following the new chapter 15, readers will find some repetition. If desired, the reader may skip immediately to the update of this appendix (page 416).

In 2007 an article was published in the prestigious *Proceedings of the National Academy of Sciences of the United States of America* titled "Evidence for an Extraterrestrial Impact 12,900 Years Ago That Contributed to the Megafaunal Extinctions and the Younger Dryas Cooling" (Firestone et al. 2007). In this paper, Richard Firestone, a physicist at Lawrence Berkeley National Laboratory in California, and his twenty-five coauthors suggested that circa 10,900 BCE a comet exploded over North America, killing off the mammoths and other animals and bringing the culture of the Paleo-Indian people who inhabited the region (known as the Clovis culture) to an end. Furthermore, they suggested that the dust and debris scattered into the atmosphere had a strong cooling effect, setting off the Younger Dryas cold snap that would last for the next dozen centuries. The evidence they offered in support of this hypothesis included a carbon-rich black layer, sometimes referred to as the black mat, found in many areas at the Younger Dryas lower boundary (that is, it dates to circa 10,900 BCE). This black mat, according to the authors, contains "(*i*) magnetic grains with iridium, (*ii*) magnetic microspherules, (*iii*) charcoal, (*iv*) soot, (*v*) carbon spherules, (*vi*) glass-like carbon containing nanodiamonds, and (*vii*) fullerenes [hollow molecules formed from carbon that can be spherical, tubular, or ellipsoid] with ET [extraterrestrial] helium, all of which are evidence for an ET impact and associated biomass burning at [approximately] 12.9 ka [12,900 years ago]" (Firestone et al. 2007, 16016; material in brackets added by R. Schoch).

Taken together, the evidence (if true and correctly interpreted) cumulatively is potentially suggestive of the debris and aftereffects of a comet explosion.

Yet, not everyone was convinced. Archaeologists Vance T. Holliday, of the University of Arizona, and David J. Meltzer, of Southern Methodist University, studying over forty Paleo-Indian sites, argued that the evidence for an extraterrestrial impact was, at best, nondefinitive. Holliday stated, "Whether or not the proposed extraterrestrial impact occurred is a matter for empirical testing in the geological record. Insofar as concerns the archaeological record, an extraterrestrial impact is an unnecessary solution for an archaeological problem that does not exist" (Holliday, quoted in Harrison 2010).

Mark Boslough, a physicist at Sandia National Laboratories in Albuquerque, New Mexico, has been quoted as saying, "It is an impossible scenario" (Boslough, quoted in Dalton 2011).

Interestingly, even oddly, the argument over what happened on Earth nearly thirteen thousand years ago may involve modern politics. There are indications that part of the issue is the fact that the comet scenario, wherein an extraterrestrial event causes major climate change, is seen by some as a possible rationale to dismiss the consensus view that current global warming is due to human activity. As Wallace Broecker, a geochemist at Columbia University who is internationally known for his contributions to climate research, stated, "Those who don't believe in human-produced global warming grab onto it [the comet theory]" (Broecker, quoted in Dalton 2011; material in brackets added by R. Schoch).

But the issues go deeper in this case, with allegations of nonreplicability, misrepresentation, and what essentially might be considered fraud.

Other researchers have attempted to replicate parts of the work carried out by Firestone et al. (2007), such as collecting and analyzing samples from the lower boundary of the Younger Dryas, and in some cases they have not found the same telltale markers (as described above) that the Firestone group reported. This has resulted in charges that the Firestone team's work cannot be replicated (Dalton 2011). Replication is often seen as the hallmark of modern science. In fact, this may be a somewhat misleading contention, as when it comes to certain types of phenomena, the results may not always be easily replicated. Assuming that a comet did explode over North America circa 10,900 BCE, chunks of debris would not necessarily scatter evenly over all areas. Large chunks might be thrown in particular directions, and smaller dust and debris would be carried by the winds (and possibly the magnetic field of Earth in the case of very small metallic particles) and be deposited preferentially in certain locations. Therefore, one site may contain an abundance of evidence interpreted as diagnostic of a comet explosion, whereas another site may lack such evidence. It should be noted that other groups of researchers have been able to find evidence similar to that first reported by Firestone et al. (2007), thus supporting and supplementing the comet hypothesis (Mahaney et al. 2010; Kurbatov et al. 2010; Boyle 2012; Israde-Alcántara et al. 2012). However, as I discuss in chapter 15, much or all of the evidence put forward as support for the comet hypothesis can also be viewed as supporting a solar outburst hypothesis. The evidence is not necessarily truly diagnostic of one scenario or the other.

But the allegations against the Firestone group go deeper still, and much of the controversy is focused specifically on one of the major authors, Allen West, who was given the second spot in the authorship list on the 2007 paper. Apparently much of the primary fieldwork for the paper, collecting sediment samples from over two dozen archaeological sites, was carried out by West, and the integrity of that work has been called into question. For instance, a carbon spherule, provided by West and independently dated using radiocarbon methods, that was claimed to be from the lower Younger Dryas boundary layer and should have been 12,900 years old turned out to be only two hundred years old (Dalton 2011). It is also alleged that the Firestone group misidentified supposed nanodiamonds and that their carbon spherules may represent fungus residue or insect excrement rather than evidence for a comet explosion.

Returning to Allen West, his background does not help the cause of the Firestone comet hypothesis in the eyes of the critics. Prior to changing his name to Allen West in 2006, he was Allen Whitt, who in 2002 was convicted in California for his part "in a scheme with two other men, with court records saying they collected fees up to $39,500 for questionable groundwater reports. He originally was charged with two felonies for falsely representing himself as a state-licensed geologist but agreed to a no contest plea to a single misdemeanor of false advertising as part of [a] plea bargain in which state records say he was fined $4,500" (Dalton 2011; word in brackets added by R. Schoch).

Such a past history of criminal activity does not necessarily mean that West cannot do good science today or that the comet hypothesis with which he is linked is wrong, but West's background certainly does not help his cause either. It only adds fuel to the controversy and allows the critics to launch personal ad hominem attacks, whether justified or not.

Ultimately, at this point I believe that, looking at all of the evidence, there is a very strong argument that catastrophic events of an extraterrestrial nature occurred at both the beginning (circa 10,900 BCE) and end (circa 9700 BCE) of the Younger Dryas. The evidence strongly suggests a major solar outburst and plasma event at 9700 BCE. Whether the 10,900 BCE event was due to a comet exploding, a solar outburst and plasma event, a galactic superwave, or some other catastrophic event is perhaps yet to be definitively determined; however, as I elaborate in chapter 15, I currently favor the solar outburst hypothesis. Possibly, it was due to a solar outburst, one that was either of a different nature than, or not as powerful as, the solar outburst of 9700 BCE, such that rather than warming the atmosphere and Earth with a tremendous blast of energy, it (while greatly exceeding any solar outburst seen in modern times, including the Carrington Event) strongly ionized the atmosphere and thus caused increased cloud cover, which in turn initiated a major cooling spell, and the solar outburst also melted ice dams that released fresh water into the Atlantic, changing circulation patterns that initiated a cooling event (see chapter 15, page 322). It is also conceivable, in my opinion, that in some cases comet impacts on Earth and solar outbursts could be correlated, for instance, in a situation where "space debris" enters the solar system, some of which hits the Sun, resulting in solar destabilization and increased solar activity, and some of the debris also hits Earth directly as a comet or meteorite.

In June 2012 further evidence was put forward in support of a cosmic impact at the beginning of the Younger Dryas. Richard Firestone, Allen West, and other coauthors published evidence of vitrified rock (melt-glass material and siliceous scoria-like objects) from Pennsylvania, South Carolina, and Syria, which they suggested could be the result of a comet or meteor (Bunch et al. 2012; Science Daily 2012). Alternatively, I suggest a solar outburst/plasma discharge as a possibility for the vitrified rock. In some cases the error ranges for the dating of the samples these authors analyze is on the order of 1,200 to 1,600 years, so it is possible that some of their samples pertain not to the beginning of the Younger Dryas but to its end.

A NOTE ON THE RECONSTRUCTION OF SOLAR ACTIVITY THROUGH GEOLOGICAL TIME

Solar activity can be reconstructed in various manners, such as by using ^{10}Be and ^{14}C data from ice cores, sediment cores, and dendrochronological sequences (Vonmoos et al. 2006). In essence the principle is that incoming cosmic rays in our atmosphere produce ^{10}Be, ^{14}C, and other radionuclides (see Nikitin et al. 2005), but when the Sun is active it sweeps away cosmic rays, and thus lower counts of these isotopes correlate with a more active Sun.

In private communication to me (see Schoch 2010c), a critic of Peratt's work (Peratt 2003; Peratt et al. 2007; Peratt and Yao 2008; van der Sluijs and Peratt 2010) has argued against the concept of power-ful plasma phenomena affecting Earth during the last twelve thousand years based on the ^{10}Be and ^{14}C data. This critic assumes that a powerful plasma event would last a century or more and would therefore signifi-cantly interfere with the production of ^{10}Be and ^{14}C in the atmosphere, meaning that these isotopes should show a perceptible decrease in ice cores and other stratigraphic sequences (relative to the "background" levels of the time) whenever such major plasma events occurred. This critic cites a study (Vonmoos et al. 2006) that, according to him, failed to record significant drops in ^{10}Be and ^{14}C during the last twelve thou-sand years. He therefore concluded that major plasma events, as sug-gested by Peratt and his colleagues, did not occur. However, I believe he has made incorrect assumptions and misinterpreted the data.

As noted in the last paragraph, this critic assumes that a powerful plasma event would last a century or more and therefore would have a significant effect on the production of ^{10}Be and ^{14}C. In my hypothesis, a major plasma event might only last on the order of days to months. The Carrington Event of 1859 lasted only a few days and would prob-ably not be picked up in the type of records of isotope production this critic cites. (The paper he cites does not include pertinent details for the nineteenth century.) In my assessment, even a plasma event orders of magnitude larger than the Carrington Event, if it was of very short temporal duration, may not be easily resolved (if at all) in the isotope records that we currently have; isotope production would be relatively high before and after the event, and the lack of production for a few days (or even months or possibly years) in a record from thousands of years ago would be very difficult to impossible to detect. Finding such a short-term dip in the isotopes is much more difficult than finding a spike, such as the iridium and associated spikes that can be indicative of major meteor, comet, and asteroid impacts—and also possibly solar events, as discussed in chapter 15.

Furthermore, the particular study the critic cites (Vonmoos et al. 2006) does not appear to me to support his assertions. The study goes back slightly over nine thousand years for ^{10}Be and it goes back 11,450 years for ^{14}C, and it shows spikes in solar activity at about 9400 BCE, 8900 BCE, 8300 BCE, and 8000 BCE (as well as spikes since then), all well above current solar activity.

UPDATE: Since the discussion above was written in 2011–2012, there have been advances in the use of various isotopes to measure solar activity through time. As O'Hare et al. write,

> Our Sun sometimes produces highly energetic particles, which are accelerated either by magnetic reconnection in solar flares or by shock waves associated with coronal mass ejections. Such energetic particles then follow trajectories along the interplanetary magnetic field lines, which together with the location of the event on the Sun, determine whether these particles hit the Earth's atmosphere. These phenomena are referred to as solar proton events (SPEs). . . . an extended record of the fluence, frequency, and energy distribution of SPEs can be obtained through the analysis of cosmogenic radionuclides, such as beryllium-10 (^{10}Be), carbon-14 (^{14}C), and chlorine-36 (^{36}Cl). These radionuclides are mainly produced via a nuclear cascade triggered by galactic cosmic rays reaching the Earth's atmosphere on average with much higher kinetic energy than the solar protons. Incoming galactic cosmic rays are modulated by the heliomagnetic and geomagnetic fields, with the strength of this modulation changing from decadal to millennial timescales. However, strong SPEs can lead to large fluxes of solar protons, causing a short-term rapid increase in the atmospheric production of radionuclides, which are subsequently stored in environmental archives, such as tree rings (^{14}C) and ice cores (^{10}Be and ^{36}Cl). (O'Hare et al. 2019, 5961; references removed from the quotation; material in parentheses in the original)

(For further discussion of these and related topics, see chapter 15, page 325.)

UPDATE TO APPENDIX 5:
FURTHER CONTROVERSIES CONCERNING THE
END OF THE LAST ICE AGE

The end of the last ice age, nearly twelve thousand years ago, was a pivotal time not only in the history of our planet but also for early cultures and civilizations during those tumultuous times. There were rapid climatic and environmental changes, as well as catastrophic geologic changes. Massive ice sheets (on the order of kilometers thick) quickly melted at high latitudes in the Northern Hemisphere, and pressure was released from the crust, setting off a cascading effect of earthquake and volcanic activity (Hoek 2008, 227, and references cited therein). Massive amounts of moisture in the atmosphere fell to the surface of Earth as torrential rains, causing widespread deluges and flooding. Huge quantities of fresh water that were dumped into the oceans upset and changed ocean circulation patterns, which in turn had further effects on the climate, as well as raising sea levels around the globe on the order of 120 meters or more, inundating low-lying coastal areas (Carlson 2013; see discussion in Schoch with McNally 2003). The triggering mechanism for the climatic changes may have been a major solar outburst (or series of solar outbursts or major solar eruptions), which, driving plasma (electrically charged particles moving at high speeds) down to the surface of Earth, would have set widespread fires and in selected areas literally incinerated the surface of our planet.

Dating the End of the Last Ice Age

The exact dating of the end of the last ice age has been subject to increasing refinements over the last few decades. Geologists divide time into named units similar to the method used by historians of civilization when they distinguish, for instance, the Medieval, Renaissance, or Victorian periods. The Pleistocene, which began approximately 2.58 million years ago (Gibbard et al. 2010), was the epoch prior to the end of the last ice age and the beginning of the Holocene (which we currently live in). The Pleistocene was characterized by alternating glacial periods (ice ages) and interglacial periods. Within glacial periods, stades (secondarily cold periods with further glacial advance) and interstades (when glaciers were either at a standstill or receded slightly) are also distinguished (Schoch 1989, 357, quoting the American Commission on Stratigraphic Nomenclature 1970). Realistically, the Holocene is thus far so short in duration that it should probably be considered simply another interglacial period. Classically, for instance, when I was a graduate student at Yale University in the early 1980s, the Pleistocene-Holocene boundary (sometimes referred to as the Last Glacial-Interglacial Transition) was typically dated to around ten thousand years before the present (Palmer 1983). Back then, we considered the last ice age to have ended very quickly and abruptly, but we were thinking in terms of geological time, and abrupt in such a context seemed to mean that the transition occurred over some decades or perhaps even centuries.

Based on ice core data from Greenland and other detailed evidence, the end of the last ice age (Pleistocene-Holocene boundary) has been dated to "11700 calendar yr b2k (before AD 2000) . . . with a maximum counting error of 99 yr" (Walker et al. 2009, 3, material in parentheses in the original; see also Walker et al. 2008, 264; and Head and Gibbard 2015). That is, it is dated in real years within a century of 9700 BCE (or more precisely, within 99 years of 9703 BCE with more than 95 percent probability; Walker et al. 2009, 14, note 1). Here I should make it clear that even in the literature other dates are often cited for the end of the last ice age, and part of the confusion arises from different dating systems that remain in common use (see Hoek 2008, and Fiedel 2011, for further discussion). For instance, uncalibrated radiocarbon (^{14}C) dates, often encountered in the older literature, can vary widely from calibrated radiocarbon dates and true "calendar year" dates. The commonly used "cal BP" (calibrated ^{14}C dates before the present, where "present" equals AD 1950 / 1950 CE) are numerically fifty years different from "b2k" and "BC" or "BCE" dates; thus 11,700 b2k = 11,650 cal BP = 9700 BCE, and in colloquial terms all of these equal "11,700 years ago" or "11.7 ka" where 2000 CE is used as the easily remembered baseline for the "present" (see, for instance, the usage in Steffensen et al. 2008).

There has been incredible refinement in locating the exact position of the Pleistocene-Holocene boundary. Analyzing a Greenland ice core, Mayewski et al. (2014) pinpointed the last three years of the Pleistocene and the first year of the Holocene in a five-centimeter-long section of the ice core. With their ultra-high-resolution laser sampling techniques involving hundreds of samples per centimeter and year of ice-time (measuring such markers as calcium, sodium, and iron concentrations), these researchers have pinpointed the abrupt end of the last ice age and the onset of the Holocene to well within a year, and inspecting their published data (see, for instance, Mayewski et al. 2014, 102, their figure 3), it is evident that they have refined data documenting the end of the last ice age down to the level of months, weeks, and possibly even days. The ice age ended quite suddenly indeed.

The Younger Dryas

Interestingly, the last ice age did not just "warm" and end. Rather, in the Northern Hemisphere, there was a warming period toward the end of the last ice age (the Allerød warming) followed by a cold spell (cold even relative to those glacial times), known as the Younger Dryas (lasting approximately 1,200 years), before the final sudden warming. The onset of the cooling event that initiated the Younger Dryas was also quite abrupt, although perhaps not quite as abrupt as the dramatic warming that ended the Younger Dryas (thus ending the last ice age and the Pleistocene). Based on Greenland ice core data, this cooling event is dated to approximately 10,900 BCE (Steffensen et al. 2008; Hoek 2008, 227, cites a date of 12,896 b2k [= 10,896 BCE] with a maximum counting error of 138 years).

Thus, the story of the end of the last ice age consists of glacial times, which suddenly (at least from a geological perspective) became even colder circa 10,900 BCE (the start of the Younger Dryas). The cold spell lasted for 1,200 years before Earth was abruptly snapped out of the last ice age (the end of the Younger Dryas) circa 9700 BCE. What are the explanations for the beginning and end of the Younger Dryas? These are topics that have baffled geologists for decades, which I will comment on further here (and see also the discussion in chapter 15).

Impact Hypothesis

Perhaps one of the best known and most controversial theories to explain the onset of the Younger Dryas is that a comet, meteor, asteroid, or other extraterrestrial object (a bolide) either hit Earth or exploded in the atmosphere 12,900 years ago, thus inducing the abrupt cooling event that marks the onset of the Younger Dryas. Although there were earlier theories along these lines, this idea gained widespread attention with the 2007 publication of an article by Firestone et al. that reputedly reported evidence for such an impact event. These authors proposed, "that one or more large, low-density ET [extraterrestrial] objects exploded over northern North America, partially destabilizing the Laurentide Ice Sheet and triggering YD [Younger Dryas] cooling. The shock wave, thermal pulse, and event-related environmental effects (e.g., extensive biomass burning and food limitations) contributed to end-Pleistocene megafaunal extinctions and adaptive shifts among PaleoAmericans in North America" (Firestone et al. 2007, 16016; material in brackets added by R. Schoch).

Here I want to make it clear that the end of the last ice age does not correspond to the potential strike by a comet or meteorite hypothesized by Firestone et al., even if such did occur, as has sometimes been incorrectly reported in the popular media; for instance, a 2007 headline from *Science News* reads: "Ice Age Ends Smashingly: Did a Comet Blow Up over Eastern Canada?" (Perkins 2007). Rather, this was the onset of the Younger Dryas, circa 10,900 BCE.

The impact hypothesis has spurred heated controversy, with arguments and counterarguments flying back and forth in the scientific literature as well as in the popular press. Personally, I am not averse to an impact hypothesis per se (see Schoch with McNally 2003), and initially, I found the arguments for such an impact at the beginning of the Younger Dryas quite intriguing. However, as more researchers have studied the issue, much of the data supporting the impact hypothesis has been questioned. For instance, Kennett et al. (2009, 12623) published an article supposedly documenting the presence of "shock-synthesized hexagonal nanodiamonds (lonsdaleite)" from the base of the Younger Dryas on Santa Rosa Island, California. This, if true, could support that an impact event occurred as lonsdaleite is known on Earth from meteorites and impact craters (although I believe we should remain open to the possibly that it could be produced under other rare circumstances as well). However, as pointed out by Boslough et al. (2012, 22) and Daulton et al. (2016), it has since been determined that the supposed lonsdaleite is not lonsdaleite at all, but a misidentification of other material, and the same holds true of other supposed reported occurrences of lonsdaleite in sediments dating to approximately 12,900 years ago. With the invalidation of the supposed lonsdaleite finds, one of the strongest lines of evidence supporting the Younger Dryas impact hypothesis had evaporated. Furthermore, it needs to be pointed out that various studies have demonstrated that nanodiamonds per se (as opposed to lonsdaleite) "do not provide unique evidence for a Younger Dryas impact" event (Tian et al. 2011, 40; see also Daulton et al. 2010; van Hoesel et al. 2012).

Other evidence put forth to support the Younger Dryas impact hypothesis has not fared any better, as discussed by Boslough et al. (2012; see also Pinter et al. 2011, and Holliday et al. 2014). Here I mention a few pertinent points. Much has been made of "black mat" layers in the geological and archaeological record that, it is claimed, mark precisely the start of the Younger Dryas and contain evidence of an extraterrestrial impact (such as magnetic grains containing iridium, glass-like carbon containing nanodiamonds, carbon spherules, and so forth) and its associated effects, such as widespread wildfires (Firestone et al. 2007; Haynes 2008). However, it has been demonstrated that many of these black mats are time-transgressive (that is, they do not all belong to a single point in time; Boslough et al. 2012, 20) and that black mats are commonly found in ancient wetland deposits of various ages, not just those marking the beginning of the Younger Dryas. In a study of black mats that ranged from six thousand years old to forty thousand years old, various supposed impact markers were found, "suggesting that elevated concentrations of these markers arise from processes common to wetland systems, and not a catastrophic extraterrestrial impact event" (Pigati et al. 2012, 7208; see also van der Hammen and van Geel 2008). Furthermore, certain carbonaceous spherules were found to be the result of fungus, not a comet or other impactor (Scott et al. 2010). Interestingly, and again arguing against the impact hypothesis, a carbon microspherule collected by Allen West (the second author on the Firestone et al. 2007 paper) from one of the supposed Younger Dryas lower boundary sites was independently radiocarbon dated to just 207 +/− 87 years BP, rather than the circa 12,900 years ago, as should have been the case if it really was from the base of the Younger Dryas (Boslough et al. 2012, 23). This just points up the problematic issues with the chronology and dating of the sites used to support the Younger Dryas impact hypothesis (see also van Hoesel et al. 2014, and Holliday et al. 2016).

The evidence from the geological and archaeological sites on which the comet/asteroid proponents rely was put to the test by David Meltzer et al. (2014, E2162; material in brackets added by R. Schoch), who concluded, "Only 3 of the 29 sites fall within the temporal window of the YD [Younger Dryas] onset as defined by YDIH [Younger Dryas Impact Hypothesis] proponents. The YDIH fails the critical chronological test of an isochronous event at the YD onset, which, coupled with the many published concerns about the extraterrestrial origin of the purported impact markers, renders the YDIH unsupported. There is no reason or compelling evidence to accept the claim that a cosmic impact occurred . . . and caused the Younger Dryas."

In yet another article, titled "Bayesian Chronological Analyses Consistent with Synchronous Age of 12,835–12,735 Cal B.P. for Younger Dryas Boundary on Four Continents" (Kennett et al. 2015), the authors claim to provide evidence supporting the impact hypothesis, but this is extremely problematic. For the sites analyzed, supposed evidence of an extraterrestrial object has been questioned or discredited. Even the purported synchrony is questionable as one can take issue with the appropriateness of applying Bayesian analyses to the data set. (Bayesian analysis is a particular type of statistical analysis that can be misapplied, leading to incorrect conclusions; see Boslough et al. 2015.) The authors attempt to link the start of the Younger Dryas to a platinum anomaly in a Greenland ice core that might indicate an extraterrestrial object. The platinum anomaly could have resulted from volcanic activity; the Laacher See supervolcano (Germany) exploded around 12,900 years ago

(Petaev et al. 2013; Baldini et al. 2018; Sun et al. 2020). If the platinum anomaly does indicate an extraterrestrial object, it may have been localized (e.g., a relatively small meteorite), noncataclysmic, and unconnected to the Younger Dryas triggering event (Boslough 2013).

James Wittke et al. (2013) argued that "10 million tonnes" of "impact spherules" were scattered across four continents by a fragmented comet or asteroid at the beginning of the Younger Dryas; however, it was subsequently demonstrated that many of these supposed "impact spherules" were of ancient human origin (for instance, siliceous scoria droplets produced when buildings were destroyed in fires) and furthermore do not all date to the start of the Younger Dryas (Thy et al. 2015). Indeed, dating is absolutely critical to an impact hypothesis: all of the evidence should date to the same point in time. It should be "isochronous."

Another argument against the impact hypothesis is that no crater (or craters) has yet been definitively identified as dating to circa 12,900 years ago. Such a crater would be very recent geologically and arguably should therefore remain relatively fresh and evident. It has been suggested that the impactor may have exploded in the atmosphere, breaking up into numerous fragments that cratered ice sheets, which subsequently melted (thus destroying the crater evidence). Possibly there is evidence of craters under the Great Lakes or Hudson Bay. Or perhaps the elliptical depressions known as the Carolina Bays found on the Atlantic Coastal Plain of the United States were created by the impacts (Firestone et al. 2007), but the dating of the Carolina Bays is questionable and not firmly linked to the beginning of the Younger Dryas. Indeed, based on the best evidence, the majority of the Carolina Bays landforms are much older than the supposed impact of circa 12,900 years ago (Holliday et al. 2014). The 1908 Tunguska explosion of an incoming extraterrestrial object over Siberia flattened a widespread area of forest without leaving a crater (see Schoch with McNally 2003). Could a much larger explosion and fragmentation of an incoming object, an explosion that was a million or more times larger than the Tunguska event (this is what is theoretically involved, according to Firestone et al. 2007), have occurred at the beginning of the Younger Dryas? Boslough et al. (2012) analyzed this possibility and found it highly unlikely, concluding that "consideration of basic laws of physics indicate that such a fragmentation or high-altitude airburst event would not conserve momentum or energy, would lie outside any realistic range of probability, and therefore did not occur during the YD [Younger Dryas] as described by Firestone et al. [2007]" (Boslough et al. 2012, 24; material in brackets added by R. Schoch; see also Boslough et al. 2013; for comments on the Hiawatha Crater in Greenland, see chapter 15, page 324).

Also countering the impact hypothesis is a detailed study of sediments deposited during the time spanning the beginning of the Younger Dryas at a site known as Hall's Cave in Texas (U.S.A.). Nan Sun and colleagues (2020) concluded that volcanic eruptions (such as from the Laacher See [Germany] super-volcanic eruption which occurred at about this time; Baldini et al. 2018), at least in part, contributed to the initiation of the Younger Dryas cooling. These authors based their conclusions primarily on the analyses of ratios of osmium (Os) isotopes found in the sediments that, they concluded, were most likely the result of a series of volcanic eruptions.

In a press release that accompanied their technical article (Randall 2020), Nan Sun was quoted,

"The isotope analysis and the relative proportion of the elements matched those that were found in previous volcanic gases," said Sun, lead author of the report.

Steven Forman (a co-author on the Sun et al. 2020 article) stated,

The Younger Dryas cooling lasted about 1,200 years, "so a sole volcanic eruptive cause is an important initiating factor, but other Earth system changes, such as cooling of the oceans and more snow cover were needed to sustain this colder period," Forman said.

Michael Waters, another co-author,

. . . added that the bottom line is that "the chemical anomalies found in sediments dating to the beginning of the Younger Dryas

are the result of volcanism and not an extraterrestrial impact."
(Randall 2020)

In their published paper these authors noted,

> Previously found YD [Younger Dryas] markers, such as nano-
> diamonds and other wildfire products, are not necessarily solely
> impact-induced. Instead, these could originate from high-
> temperature, large-scale volcanic eruptions whose explosive condi-
> tions are capable of producing molten silica and carbon spherules
> and possibly nanodiamonds (Lonsdaleite). (Sun et al. 2020, 7;
> material in parentheses is in the original article; material in brack-
> ets added by R. Schoch)

Thus, the evidence continues to mount that the so-called indicators
of an impactor at the beginning of the Younger Dryas may not be
definitive of a physical impact. (See Sweatman 2020 for an alternative
interpretation of the Hall's Cave data, suggesting that it is compatible with a physical impactor at the beginning of the Younger Dryas.
Ultimately, I consider this particular data set ambiguous, and it can be
interpreted in more than one manner. Such ambiguity appears to be
the case for much of the putative evidence relative to the issue of the
causative factors for the beginning and ending of the Younger Dryas.)
I suggest that volcanism could have been induced by solar activity, just
as it has now been demonstrated that earthquakes can be triggered by
solar activity (see chapter 15), or earthquakes triggered by solar activity
could have triggered volcanic activity. Furthermore, some or all of the
supposed evidence used to support the impact hypothesis could have
been the result of direct plasma strikes during a major solar outburst
(see further discussion in chapter 15).

After a thorough review of the Younger Dryas Impact Hypothesis
(YDIH), Holliday et al. summarize their conclusions as follows:

> In summary, the data and the hypotheses generated by YDIH pro-
> ponents contain errors of fact and errors of omission, and are contra-

dictory, inconsistent and incoherent. Much of the evidence used to support the idea is unfounded assertion and the corollary hypotheses are demonstrably false. Further, the published assertions are based on a lack of understanding of basic principals [*sic,* principles] of Quaternary geology, of the well-established geochronologic records at sites and locality, of the records of North American Paleoindian archaeology and late Pleistocene extinction, and of the physics of hypervelocity impact processes. The YDIH is poorly supported on the basis of data published by those on both sides of the debate and proponents rarely consider alternative hypotheses in interpreting those data. (Holliday et al. 2014, 527; material in brackets added by R. Schoch)

I heartily agree that we need to consider alternative hypotheses to explain the data.

If Not an Impact, Then What?

At this point, in my assessment, the evidence collectively points away from an extraterrestrial impact for the start of the Younger Dryas, but the issue of what exactly did trigger the onset of the Younger Dryas is unresolved. There remains evidence put forth of an unusual event at this time. For instance, Michail I. Petaev et al. (2013) report a platinum anomaly in a Greenland ice core that spans the beginning of the Younger Dryas. However, they offer no definitive conclusions as to what could have caused such an anomaly—whether extraterrestrial or terrestrial (such as a volcanic eruption).

The onset of the Younger Dryas remains somewhat of a mystery. As seen in the ice cores and sediment profiles, it was abrupt (Steffensen et al. 2008). But the changes that mark the beginning of the Younger Dryas "were not everywhere of the same severity, or in the same direction" (Fiedel 2011, 262). The Younger Dryas as a cooling event was primarily a Northern Hemisphere phenomenon. In some places, due apparently to shifts in atmospheric and oceanic circulation patterns, the Younger Dryas was wet rather than dry (cold and dry being the predominant condition in the Northern Hemisphere).

In the Southern Hemisphere, such as the southeast Atlantic, New Zealand, parts of South America, and Antarctica, the Younger Dryas was a period of warming, sometimes referred to as the "bipolar seesaw response" (Carlson 2013, 129; Carlson 2010). Still, there was greater cooling in high northern latitudes (by up to 10°C in Greenland relative to the previous period, or about 15°C colder than modern temperatures; Fiedel 2011, 262) than the warming in the southern latitudes, resulting in an overall net global cooling during the Younger Dryas of approximately 0.6°C (Shakun and Carlson 2010; Carlson 2013, 129).

Suggestions as to the cause and/or triggering mechanism behind the onset of the Younger Dryas have generally fallen into several broad categories, including: (1) changes in oceanic circulation; (2) changes in atmospheric circulation; (3) changes in atmospheric carbon dioxide concentrations; (4) changes in surface albedo; (5) volcanic activity (Baldini et al. 2018; Sun et al. 2020); (6) external "forcing events" such as an extraterrestrial impactor (discussed above), a supernova that could generate an interstellar shock wave and a wave of debris, causing perturbations to the atmosphere-Earth system (Firestone et al. 2006; Brakenridge 2011; see comments in Boslough et al. 2012, 15), or various other forms of cosmic radiation or cosmic dust; and (7) changes in solar radiation (Fiedel 2011; Renssen et al. 2000). Of course, these various factors are not necessarily mutually exclusive, and indeed one triggering mechanism may have caused other events to take place, the combined results of which initiated the Younger Dryas.

During the last couple of decades, among geologists and paleoclimatologists, it appears that the most widely accepted explanations have involved changes in oceanic circulation patterns, particularly involving changes in thermohaline circulation in the North Atlantic (Renssen et al. 2000) and slowing of the Atlantic Meridional Overturning Circulation (Carlson 2010) associated with concomitant atmospheric and climatic changes. Key to most such theories is an influx of cold fresh water into the North Atlantic that prevented the uprising or upwelling of warm salty water from the southern oceans, thus shutting down the overturning of ocean water with the result that the atmosphere over the ocean would remain cool rather than being warmed as it previously had been due to the upwelling of warm water (Fiedel 2011). What caused the influx of fresh water, according to such scenarios? The major suggestions are the melting of the Laurentide ice sheet of eastern Canada and the release of fresh water from Lake Agassiz (a huge ancient lake that formed due to the retreating ice sheet; it covered portions of Saskatchewan, Manitoba, and Ontario) that spilled massive amounts of water into the North Atlantic. Various methods used to date the timing of a massive discharge of water from Lake Agassiz have not always matched the onset of the Younger Dryas (Carlson 2010); some data have indicated that the discharge may have been a thousand years too late (Fiedel 2011, 263). However, Keigwin et al. (2018) presented evidence for a massive glacial flood that changed ocean circulation patterns in the Atlantic at the correct time to have initiated the Younger Dryas cooling (see discussion in chapter 15, page 322).

Solar Activity

At the onset of the Younger Dryas, a sudden increase in ^{14}C concentrations is observed. It has been suggested, although I believe unconvincingly, that this could be due to CO_2 changes in the atmosphere due to changing surface ocean temperatures modulating the amount of CO_2 absorbed by the oceans (Fiedel 2011). Another explanation is that the Sun (and possibly also Earth's magnetic field) weakened, allowing the greater penetration of cosmic radiation into our atmosphere, thus creating more ^{14}C (Fiedel 2011; Renssen et al. 2000; cosmic rays can transform ^{14}N to ^{14}C). Renssen et al. have argued the case that reduced solar activity could have initiated the onset of the Younger Dryas. They propose two mechanisms by which this could possibly occur. First, a reduction in solar UV radiation would entail a reduction in stratospheric ozone production and attendant changes in atmospheric circulation patterns, ultimately resulting in a cooling effect on the surface of our planet in middle to high latitudes. Second, reduced solar activity allowed more cosmic rays to penetrate our atmosphere, promoted aerosol formation and cloud nucleation, and resulted in more cloud cover globally with increased reflection of incoming solar radiation, thus cooling Earth.

While there may have been overall reduced solar activity during the Younger Dryas, LaViolette (2011a; see discussion in chapter 7, page 154) has suggested that there may have been a solar proton event (SPE; this acronym is also used to refer to a "solar particle event," which is basically the same thing as a solar proton event), during which protons were accelerated by the Sun to incredibly high energy levels and penetrated our atmosphere at the start of the Younger Dryas. A major SPE may account for the sudden increase in ^{14}C concentrations observed at this time (see the update to "A Note on the Reconstruction of Solar Activity through Geological Time" in this appendix, above on page 415).

It is now understood that even when the background activity of the Sun is relatively low, major solar outbursts can occur (for instance, the Carrington Event of 1859 occurred during an overall relatively quiet solar cycle; see chapter 12, page 228; likewise, a major solar outburst occurred from a quiet Sun in 1903; see Hayakawa et al. 2020). LaViolette (2011a) dates the Younger Dryas event that is the focus of his paper to 12,837 +/− 10 calendar years BP, which places it at just about 12,900 years ago, that is, at the beginning of the Younger Dryas (indeed, converting it to a b2k date of 12,887 +/− 10 years ago, it is virtually identical to the date for the beginning of the Younger Dryas, 12,896 b2k, cited by Hoek 2008). A possible SPE at the start of the Younger Dryas provides further evidence, in my opinion, that our Sun was going through a volatile, erratic, phase. An SPE may have ionized the atmosphere, increasing cloud cover and initiating a cooling spell; furthermore, as I discuss in chapter 15 (page 323), a major solar event at this time may have melted ice dams, releasing fresh water into the North Atlantic and changing ocean circulation patterns, which caused a dramatic cooling in the Northern Hemisphere. Then, I suspect, the Sun went into a period of reduced activity, essentially a partial shutdown, for 1,200 years.

Subsequently, as I have argued, our Sun "woke up" and erupted with a mighty outburst—or perhaps a series of closely spaced outbursts— circa 9700 BCE, thus terminating the Younger Dryas cold spell and literally snapping us out of the last ice age. Stars go through cycles of activity and inactivity, and after all our Sun is simply another star (see Pugh et al. 2015). As we have discussed previously, the end of the last ice age can be located in the Greenland ice record within not just a year, but virtually to the month, week, and perhaps even day. What could conceivably cause such a major and abrupt warming and climatic reorganization? In my assessment, the isotope and geochemical data, sediment data, and archaeological evidence (such as ancient petroglyphs; see Peratt 2003) all converge to corroborate the theory that a major solar outburst ended the last ice age. (I should point out that some researchers might suggest that an extraterrestrial object could have caused the warming of circa 9700 BCE. I do not believe the evidence is compatible with a comet, meteor, asteroid, or other bolide hitting Earth or exploding in our atmosphere at the end of the Younger Dryas. Furthermore, an impact or atmospheric explosion would most likely inject dust and debris into the atmosphere, which would have a cooling effect on the climate rather than a dramatic, virtually overnight, warming effect.)

In summary, I am convinced that, based on the current evidence, a very strong case can be made that the last stages of the last ice age, the onset and termination of the Younger Dryas, are linked to solar activity. An SPE or some type of solar outburst, circa 10,900 BCE, changed ocean circulation patterns and initiated a significant cooling of the Northern Hemisphere that was followed by overall reduced solar activity for 1,200 years. A major solar outburst ended the Younger Dryas, bringing the last ice age to a final close, circa 9700 BCE.

Göbekli Tepe and an Early Cycle of Civilization

The climatic changes and solar activity of the last millennium and a half of the last ice age had profound effects on the human populations of the time. I have made the case that an early cycle of advanced civilization arose before the end of the last ice age—thousands of years prior to the conventional date for the origins of civilization of circa 4000 BCE to 3000 BCE. Dramatic proof of this earlier period of civilization is the incomparable archaeological complex of Göbekli Tepe in southeastern Turkey (Schmidt 2011, 2012), the earliest portions of which, as I will argue below, predate the end of the last ice age. Göbekli Tepe exhibits

signs of destruction and rebuilding, and what appear to be fortifications (the building of crude stone walls around and between the earlier
erected and magnificently carved pillars), immediately postdating the
end of the last ice age.

As already mentioned in chapter 3 (page 50), but worth repeating
here (to a certain extent, each appendix of this book is designed to be
able to stand alone), in Enclosure D of Göbekli Tepe there is a "wall
plaster" comprised of "loam, which also contains small amounts of
organic material" (Dietrich et al. 2013, 36). A sample of this plaster was
radiocarbon dated, yielding an age of 9745 BCE to 9314 BCE ("calBC
at the 95.4% confidence level"; see Dietrich et al. 2013, 36). Subsequent
dated samples from Enclosure D are in "good agreement" with this date
(Dietrich et al. 2013, 37). This is arguably the most accurate date to
come from the earliest portions thus far excavated at Göbekli Tepe.
However, it is not the date of initial construction of this portion of
Göbekli Tepe (that is, the erection of the pillars of Enclosure D). This
radiocarbon date is from wall plaster on a wall that is secondary—a wall
that was erected after the initial structure consisting of *T*-shaped pillars
arranged in a Stonehenge-like fashion was built—and furthermore, it
is not inconceivable that this wall may have been plastered and subsequently replastered (perhaps more than once), as we commonly observe
in ancient structures of later periods.

Based on the evidence, and incorporating archaeoastronomical
analyses, I believe that the pillars of Enclosure D, including the two
central anthropomorphic pillars, were erected by circa 10,000 BCE
(see chapter 3, page 51). This would date this stone circle and pillars
to a time before the end of the last ice age (before 9700 BCE), thus
placing them in the Younger Dryas. Interestingly, in a 2003 paper,
Pustovoytov and Taubald suggested, on the basis of reconstructed
paleoenvironments using stable carbon and oxygen isotopes from
pedogenic carbonates of Göbekli Tepe, that at least the oldest portions of Göbekli Tepe date back to the Younger Dryas. They wrote,
". . . of prime importance appears to be the fact that the early laminations of pedogenic carbonate at Göbekli Tepe recorded *in situ* isotopic signals distinctly different (relatively cool and dry environments)

from those of most of the first half of the Holocene [the time since the end of the last ice age]. Considering that secondary carbonate started to accumulate once the PPNA [Pre-Pottery Neolithic A] stone enclosures were covered by fill, it is evident that the builder[s] of the enclosures should have experienced the harsh climatic conditions of the Younger Dryas" (Pustovoytov and Taubald 2003, 29; italics in the original, comments in brackets by R. Schoch). In a later paper, however, Pustovoytov (2006) no longer mentions a possible Younger Dryas age for some of the Göbekli Tepe structures.

Enclosure D was subject to damage that resulted in some of the pillars being knocked over and broken in ancient times. This may have occurred during the turmoil at the end of the last ice age and shortly thereafter. Various pillars were reerected, and in some cases realigned and reworked. Relatively crude stone walls were built between, among, and around the pillars, forming circles or "spirals" of stone walls; in some cases, these secondary stone walls cover over older bas-reliefs (Schmidt 2012). Some of these walls were plastered; as noted, in the case of Enclosure D, a radiocarbon date for some of this later plastering is 9745 to 9314 BCE (Dietrich et al. 2013), which places this secondary stone wall in a transitional period between the end of the last ice age and fully post–ice age times.

Thus at Göbekli Tepe we have direct evidence of an earlier cycle of civilization, one before the traditional "origin" of civilization some six thousand years or so later in Mesopotamia, Egypt, and the Indus Valley. Other evidence for this early cycle of civilization comes from Egypt (for example, the redating of the core body of the Great Sphinx—the head is a dynastic recarving—to the end of the last ice age). Likewise, in 2010 at the archaeological site of Wadi Faynan in southern Jordan, a twenty-two-meter by nineteen-meter amphitheater-like structure was found dating to circa 9700 BCE (Simmons 2014). Returning to Göbekli Tepe, here we see direct evidence, in the form of toppled and reerected pillars followed by hastily built secondary walls, of the cataclysmic events that accompanied the end of the last ice age. Ultimately, the early ice age civilizations suffered mighty setbacks and collapsed.

It should also be pointed out that the synchronicity of the major extinction of various Pleistocene mammals in North America has been demonstrated (the best analyses of the data indicate that the extinctions most likely all occurred at the same time geologically; Faith and Surovell 2009) and that they all occurred at the very end of the last ice age—that is, at the end of the Younger Dryas, circa 9700 BCE. Analyzing the work of Faith and Surovell, and in particular their figure 1, it is evident that the major cluster of extinctions occurs at circa 9700 BCE (which they label as "10,000" radiocarbon years BP) and not at the start of the Younger Dryas (circa 10,900 BCE).

The events that ended the last ice age and devastated this early cycle of civilization were triggered by a major solar outburst. The subsequent Solar-Induced Dark Age (or SIDA for short; see chapter 15, page 305) lasted from about 9700 BCE until the full reemergence of civilization during the period of circa 4000 BCE to 3000 BCE. By acknowledging this early cycle of civilization, dating back to the end of the last ice age (currently best exemplified by the earliest portions of Göbekli Tepe), we add an entirely new chapter to the history of humanity.

The Anthropocene

Due to both my training as a geologist and my interest in ancient civilizations, I cannot help but think about the future as well as the past. And when I ponder the future, I often think about not just a century from now, but millennia or tens of millennia, or more, into the future. Indeed, I often think about the end of humanity. Although it may seem pessimistic, I am of a mind that humanity will not last forever. Someday, humans will go extinct; there will be a future without us. Yet I suspect that there will be other advanced beings on Earth in the future, whether they are outer space extraterrestrials visiting our planet or some other intelligent and technological species that develops on our planet long after humans are gone. And what will they think of us, *Homo sapiens* (what name will they give to us?), and the indelible marks that we have left on Earth?

This brings me to the question: What will survive of humanity after we no longer exist as a living species? I have heard some people assert that nothing from us, none of our creations, will survive after a few thousand years or a few tens of thousands of years; however, as a geologist, I realize this is a nonsensical opinion (and, after all, the remains of Göbekli Tepe have survived for twelve thousand years). In fact, humanity will leave an indelible mark on our planet, one that will be evident even hundreds of millions or billions of years from now—of this I am certain. Why? As a geologist, I can find fossils of organisms, such as trilobites that lived and died hundreds of millions of years ago or the dinosaurs that went extinct about 65 million years ago, and without doubt these organisms had less of an impact on Earth than we humans are having today. There will not only be rare fossils of modern human remains preserved (indeed, some people go to great lengths to embalm or mummify the dead, so as to preserve and "fossilize" the body), but there will also be abundant "techno-fossils" surviving from our species and ancestors; these will include everything from stone tools (some of which are already hundreds of thousands to several million years old) to the remains of buildings and highways, trash disposed of in landfills, debris dropped into the oceans, remains of satellites and various "space junk" that will continue to orbit Earth, and so forth. Beyond Earth itself, there will even be materials that have been purposefully sent off of our planet, including remains left on our Moon, spacecraft orbiting the Sun, and probes penetrating interstellar space.

More insidious, and more pervasively, on Earth there will be preserved in the geological record traces of humanity's impact, traces composed of radioactive isotopes from nuclear weapons use and testing, microplastic particles, various artificial chemicals and reagents, ash fallout from coal-fired power plants, radioactive waste, and so forth. And concurrent with these markers will be the extinction of many other species in nature and the modification or destruction of many natural ecosystems. Millions of years from now, a future geologist of an unknown intelligent species will be able to analyze the rock record and find the layers that correspond to the rise and domination of Earth, for a short period of time, by *Homo sapiens* before our species went extinct. This period of human domination of the planet may even merit being recognized as a distinct geologic epoch, which many geologists and other scientists (as well as members of the general public) have begun referring to as the Anthropocene (for an introduction to this issue, see Malhi 2017; Waters et al. 2016; Waters et al. 2018; Wright et al. 2018; Zalasiewicz et al. 2019).

The name Anthropocene is derived from the Greek *anthropos,* meaning "human," and *–cene,* meaning "new" or "recent"; that is, recent from our current perspective, so it is the Recent Human Geologic Epoch. Just how "recent" it is—that is, when should we consider the Anthropocene to have begun (and thus the Holocene to have ended)— is a matter of debate. Many, including myself, would place the start of the Anthropocene in the middle of the twentieth century, marked by the beginning of nuclear bomb testing and its use in war, the devastation of the Second World War, and the acceleration of technology. A specific date that has been suggested for the exact initiation of the Anthropocene is July 16, 1945, the day that the first nuclear (atomic) bomb was detonated at Alamogordo, New Mexico, USA (Waters et al. 2015; see also Head and Gibbard 2015). Unfortunately, the "message" humanity leaves for the future, in terms of the remains and traces in the stratigraphic and geologic record, may be primarily one of destruction and wide-scale damage to the planet.

The Ancestors would not be happy with us.

BIBLIOGRAPHY

Here I list not only the references I cite directly, but also various other sources that I have found to be particularly useful pertaining to the subjects discussed in this book. The interested reader may find these sources helpful in pursuing these topics further.

AAVSO [American Association of Variable Star Observers]. 2011. "Outburst of the Recurrent Nova T Pyx." http://www.aavso.org/aavso-alert-notice-436 (article dated April 14, 2011; accessed July 28, 2020).

Abt Associates. 2017. *Social and Economic Impacts of Space Weather in the United States*. Bethesda, Md.: Abt Associates (written under contract for the NOAA National Weather Service).

Adam, T., N. Agafonova, A. Aleksandrov, O. Altinok, P. Alvarez Sanchez, A. Anokhina, S. Aoki, A. Ariga, T. Ariga, D. Autiero, A. Badertscher, A. Ben Dhahbi, A. Bertolin, C. Bozza, T. Brugière, R. Brugnera, F. Brunet, G. Brunetti, S. Buontempo, B. Carlus, F. Cavanna, A. Cazes, L. Chaussard, M. Chernyavsky, V. Chiarella, A. Chukanov, G. Colosimo, M. Crespi, N. D'Ambrosio, G. De Lellis, M. De Serio, Y. Déclais, P. del Amo Sanchez, F. Di Capua, A. Di Crescenzo, D. Di Ferdinando, N. Di Marco, S. Dmitrievsky, M. Dracos, D. Duchesneau, S. Dusini, J. Ebert, I. Efthymiopoulos, O. Egorov, A. Ereditato, L. S. Esposito, J. Favier, T. Ferber, R. A. Fini, T. Fukuda, A. Garfagnini, G. Giacomelli, M. Giorgini, M. Giovannozzi, C. Girerd, J. Goldberg, C. Göllnitz, D. Golubkov, L. Goncharova, Y. Gornushkin, G. Grella, F. Grianti, E. Gschwendtner, C. Guerin, A. M. Guler, C. Gustavino, C. Hagner, K. Hamada, T. Hara, M. Hierholzer, A. Hollnagel, M. Ieva, H. Ishida, K. Ishiguro, K. Jakovcic, C. Jollet, M. Jones, F. Juget,

M. Kamiscioglu, J. Kawada, S. H. Kim, M. Kimura, E. Kiritsis, N. Kitagawa, B. Klicek, J. Knuesel, K. Kodama, M. Komatsu, U. Kose, I. Kreslo, C. Lazzaro, J. Lenkeit, A. Ljubicic, A. Longhin, A. Malgin, G. Mandrioli, J. Marteau, T. Matsuo, N. Mauri, A. Mazzoni, E. Medinaceli, F. Meisel, A. Meregaglia, P. Migliozzi, S. Mikado, D. Missiaen, K. Morishima, U. Moser, M. T. Muciaccia, N. Naganawa, T. Naka, M. Nakamura, T. Nakano, Y. Nakatsuka, V. Nikitina, F. Nitti, S. Ogawa, N. Okateva, A. Olchevsky, O. Palamara, A. Paoloni, B. D. Park, I. G. Park, A. Pastore, L. Patrizii, E. Pennacchio, H. Pessard, C. Pistillo, N. Polukhina, M. Pozzato, K. Pretzl, F. Pupilli, R. Rescigno, F. Riguzzi, T. Roganova, H. Rokujo, G. Rosa, I. Rostovtseva, A. Rubbia, A. Russo, O. Sato, Y. Sato, J. Schuler, L. Scott. Lavina, J. Serrano, A. Sheshukov, H. Shibuya, G. Shoziyoev, S. Simone, M. Sioli, C. Sirignano, G. Sirri, J. S. Song, M. Spinetti, L. Stanco, N. Starkov, S. Stellacci, M. Stipcevic, T. Strauss, S. Takahashi, M. Tenti, F. Terranova, I. Tezuka, V. Tioukov, P. Tolun, N. T. Tran, S. Tufanli, P. Vilain, M. Vladimirov, L. Votano, J.-L. Vuilleumier, G. Wilquet, B. Wonsak, J. Wurtz, C. S. Yoon, J. Yoshida, Y. Zaitsev, S. Zemskova, and A. Zghiche. 2011. "Measurement of the Neutrino Velocity with the OPERA Detector in the CNGS Beam." http://arxiv.org/abs/1109.4897 and http://arxiv.org/ftp /arxiv/papers/1109/1109.4897.pdf (article dated November 17, 2011; accessed November 18, 2011).

Adriani, O., G. C. Barbarino, G. A. Bazilevskaya, R. Bellotti, M. Boezio, E. A. Bogomolov, M. Bongi, V. Bonvicini, S. Borisov, S. Bottai, A. Bruno, F. Cafagna, D. Campana, R. Carbone, P. Carlson, M. Casolino, G. Castellini, L. Consiglio, M. P. De Pascale, C. De Santis, N. De Simone, V. Di Felice, A. M. Galper, W. Gillard, L. Grishantseva, G. Jerse, A. V. Karelin, M. D. Kheymits, S. V. Koldashov, S. Y. Krutkov, A. N. Kvashnin, A. Leonov, V. Malakhov, L. Marcelli, A. G. Mayorov, W. Menn, V. V. Mikhailov, E. Mocchiutti, A. Monaco, N. Mori, N. Nikonov, G. Osteria, F. Palma, P. Papini, M. Pearce, P. Picozza, C. Pizzolotto, M. Ricci, S. B. Ricciarini, L. Rossetto, R. Sarkar, M. Simon, R. Sparvoli, P. Spillantini, Y. I. Stozhkov, A. Vacchi, E. Vannuccini, G. Vasilyev, S. A. Voronov, Y. T. Yurkin, J. Wu, G. Zampa, N. Zampa, and V. G. Zverev. 2011. "The Discovery of Geomagnetically Trapped Cosmic Ray Antiprotons." http://arxiv.org /PS_cache/arxiv/pdf/1107/1107.4882v1.pdf (article dated July 25, 2011; accessed August 7, 2011). See also: BBC News. "Antimatter Belt around Earth Discovered by Pamela Craft." www.bbc.co.uk/news/science-environment

-14405122 (article dated August 7, 2011; accessed August 7, 2011).

Alfvén, Hannes. 1990. "Cosmology in the Plasma Universe: An Introductory Exposition." *Institute of Electrical and Electronics Engineers Transactions in Plasma Science* 18, no. 1: 5–10.

Allan, Derek S., and J. Bernard Delair. 1997. *Cataclysm!: Compelling Evidence of a Cosmic Catastrophe in 9500 B.C.* Rochester, Vt.: Bear & Company.

Alvarez, Luis W., Walter Alvarez, Frank Asaro, and Helen V. Michel. 1980. "Extraterrestrial Cause for the Cretaceous-Tertiary Extinction." *Science* 208, no. 4448: 1095–108.

American Commission on Stratigraphic Nomenclature. 1970. *Code of Stratigraphic Nomenclature.* Tulsa, Oklahoma: American Association of Petroleum Geologists.

American Museum of Natural History. 2020. "Study Supports Contested 35-Year-Old Predictions, Shows That Observable Novae Are Just 'Tip of the Iceberg.'" Phys.org. https://phys.org/news/2020-03-contested-year-old-novae-iceberg.html (article dated March 24, 2020; accessed March 27, 2020).

American Physical Society. 2011. "National Policy 07.1 CLIMATE CHANGE (*Adopted by Council on November 18, 2007*)." www.aps.org/policy/statements/07_1.cfm (article dated 2011; accessed August 20, 2011).

Anonymous. Undated. "Stonehenge Post Holes." www.stone-circles.org.uk /stone/stonehengepostholes.htm (article undated; accessed April 12, 2020).

Archaeological Park. 2011. "Archaeological Park: Bosnian Pyramid of the Sun Foundation." www.piramidasunca.ba/en (general website for the Archaeological Park and the Bosnian Pyramid of the Sun Foundation; accessed July 7, 2011).

Association for Research and Enlightenment. 2011. "Seven Prophecies Yet to Come." www.edgarcayce.org/are/ancient_mysteries.aspx?id=1915 (undated page, but apparently 2011; accessed August 15, 2011).

Atkinson, Nancy. 2011. "Voyagers Find Giant Jacuzzi-like Bubbles at Edge of Solar System." www.universetoday.com/86446/voyagers-find-giant-jacuzzi -like-bubbles-at-edge-of-solar-system (article dated June 10, 2011; accessed March 29, 2012).

Australian News. 2011. "Scientists Change Tack on Sun Cycle." www.theaustralian .com.au/news/health-science/scientists-change-tack-on-sun-cycle/story -e6frg8y6-1226076023422 (article dated June 16, 2011; accessed July 5, 2011).

Australia's Northwest. 2019. "Kimberly Rock Art." www.australiasnorthwest .com/page/kimberley-rock-art (article dated 2019; accessed March 31, 2020).

Austrian Times. 2011. "Tunnel Vision." http://austriantimes.at/news/Around
_the_World/2011-08-03/35344/Tunnel_vision (article dated August 3, 2011;
accessed August 6, 2011).

Backster, Cleve. 2003. *Primary Perception: Biocommunication with Plants, Living
Foods, and Human Cells.* Anza, Calif.: White Rose Millennium Press.

Badisches Landesmuseum Karlsruhe. 2007a. *Die ältesten Monumente der Menschheit.
Vor 12.000 Jahren in Anatolien.* Stuttgart, Germany: Konrad Theiss.

———. 2007b. *Die ältesten Monumente der Menschheit. Vor 12.000 Jahren
in Anatolien. Als die Jäger sesshaft wurden.* DVD-ROM. Brühl, Baden-
Württemberg, Germany: Media Cultura/Theiss.

Bahn, Paul, and John Flenley. 1992. *Easter Island, Earth Island.* London:
Thames and Hudson.

Baigent, Michael, Nicholas Campion, and Charles Harvey. 1984. *Mundane
Astrology.* Wellingborough, Northamptonshire, England: Aquarian Press.
Second impression 1985.

Baillie, Katherine Unger. 2015. "Lightning Reshapes Rocks at the Atomic Level,
Penn Study Finds." https://penntoday.upenn.edu/news/lightning-reshapes
-rocks-atomic-level-penn-study-finds (article dated August 5, 2015; accessed
March 30, 2020).

Baird, Douglas. 2011. "[Comment on Hodder and Meskell.]" *Current
Anthropology* 52, no. 2 (April): 251.

Baker, D. N., X. Li, A. Pulkkinen, C. M. Ngwira, M. L. Mays, A. B. Galvin,
and K. D. C. Simunac. 2013. "A Major Solar Eruptive Event in July 2012:
Defining Extreme Space Weather Scenarios." *Space Weather* 11: 585–91.

Baker, Robert G. V. 2008. "Exploratory Analysis of Similarities in Solar Cycle
Magnetic Phases with Southern Oscillation Index Fluctuations in Eastern
Australia." *Geographical Research* 46, no. 4: 380–98. http://onlinelibrary
.wiley.com/doi/10.1111/j.1745-5871.2008.00537.x/abstract;jsessionid=1A
B19F01F0AA2841568C9ED8474E3A2C (article dated December 2008;
accessed July 16, 2011).

Balaresque, Patricia, Georgina R. Bowden, Susan M. Adams, Ho-Yee Leung,
Turi E. King, Zoë H. Rosser, Jane Goodwin, Jean-Paul Moisan, Christelle
Richard, Ann Millward, Andrew G. Demaine, Guido Barbujani, Carlo
Previderè, Ian J. Wilson, Chris Tyler-Smith, and Mark A. Jobling. 2010.
"A Predominantly Neolithic Origin for European Paternal Lineages." *PLOS*
[Public Library of Science] *Biology* 8, no. 1 (January): 9 pages.

Baldini, James U. L., Richard J. Brown, and Natasha Mawdsley. 2018. "Evaluating the Link between the Sulfur-Rich Laacher See Volcanic Eruption and the Younger Dryas Climate Anomaly." *Climate of the Past* 14: 969–90.

Balmaceda, L., N. A. Krivova, and S. K. Solanki. 2007. "Reconstruction of Solar Irradiance Using the Group Sunspot Number." *Advances in Space Research* 40: 986–89. www.mps.mpg.de/dokumente/publikationen/solanki /j245.pdf (article dated 2007; accessed September 9, 2011).

Banning, E. B. 2011. "So Fair a House: Göbekli Tepe and the Identification of Temples in the Pre-Pottery Neolithic of the Near East." *Current Anthropology* 52, no. 5: 619–60. www.jstor.org/pss/10.1086/661207 (article dated October 2011; accessed December 22, 2011).

Barkin, Yu V., and J. M. Ferrandiz. 2004. "Tidal Elastic Energy in Planetary Systems and Its Dynamic Role." *Astronomical and Astrophysical Transactions* 23, no. 4: 369–84.

Barry, Patrick. 2006. "Ships' Logs Give Clues to Earth's Magnetic Decline." www .newscientist.com/article/dn9148-ships-logs-give-clues-to-earths-magnetic -decline.html (article dated May 11, 2006; accessed June 29, 2011).

Barthel, Thomas S. 1978. *The Eighth Land: The Polynesian Discovery and Settlement of Easter Island.* Honolulu: University Press of Hawaii.

Bar-Yosef, Ofer. 1998. "Introduction: Some Comments on the History of Research." *Review of Archaeology* 19, no. 2: 1–5. http://reviewofarchaeology .org/images/Intro192.pdf (article dated 1998; accessed July 9, 2011).

Bates, C. Richard, Martin Bates, Chris Gaffney, Vincent Gaffney, and Timothy D. Rau. 2019. "Geophysical Investigation of the Neolithic Calanais Landscape." *Remote Sensing* 11, no 24: 18 pages.

Batuman, Elif. 2011. "The Sanctuary: The World's Oldest Temple and the Dawn of Civilization." *New Yorker,* December 19, 2011, 72, 74, 76, 78, 80–83.

Bauval, Robert, and Thomas Brophy. 2011. *Black Genesis: The Prehistoric Origins of Ancient Egypt.* Rochester, Vt.: Bear & Company.

Bauval, Robert, and Adrian Gilbert. 1994. *The Orion Mystery: Unlocking the Secrets of the Pyramids.* New York: Crown Trade Paperbacks.

BBC News. 2004. "'Hobbit' Joins Human Family Tree." http://news.bbc.co.uk/2 /hi/science/nature/3948165.stm (article last updated October 27, 2004; accessed July 29, 2010).

———. 2011. "Antimatter Belt around Earth Discovered by Pamela Craft." www .bbc.co.uk/news/science-environment-14405122 (article dated August 7, 2011; accessed August 7, 2011).

Becker, Robert O., and Gary Selden. 1985. *The Body Electric: Electromagnetism and the Foundation of Life*. New York: William Morrow.

Bem, Daryl J. 2011. "Feeling the Future: Experimental Evidence for Anomalous Retroactive Influences on Cognition and Affect." *Journal of Personality and Social Psychology* 100, no. 3: 407–25. http://psycnet.apa.org/journals /psp/100/3/407 (abstract; article dated March 2011; accessed August 20, 2011) and http://dbem.ws/FeelingFuture.pdf (author's typescript version; article dated March 2011; accessed August 20, 2011).

Benest, D., and J. L. Duvent. 1995. "Is Sirius a Triple Star?" *Astronomy and Astrophysics* 299: 621–28.

Bentov, Itzhak. 1981. *Stalking the Wild Pendulum: On the Mechanics of Consciousness*. New York: Bantam Books. First published 1977.

Berengut, J. C., and V. V. Flambaum. 2010. "Manifestations of a Spatial Variation of Fundamental Constants on Atomic Clocks, Oklo, Meteorites, and Cosmological Phenomena." http://arxiv.org/PS_cache/arxiv /pdf/1008/1008.3957v1.pdf (article dated August 24, 2010; accessed September 8, 2010).

Berge, Elizabeth. 2011. "Solar Issues Send Up Flares." *Facultative Matters,* April 2011, 1–4. www.genre.com/sharedfile/pdf/FacMatters201104-en.pdf (article dated April 2011; accessed July 11, 2011).

Berry, Janice. 1999. *Aurora Borealis: A Photo Memory*. Includes photos by Dennis C. Anderson, Larry Anderson, Wayne Johnson, Hugh Rose, Nori Sakamoto, and Todd Salat. Anchorage, Alaska: Todd Communications.

Bertolucci, Sergio. 2012. "Neutrinos Sent from CERN to Gran Sasso Respect the Cosmic Speed Limit." http://press.web.cern.ch/Press/PressReleases /Releases2011/PR19.11E.html (article dated June 8, 2012; accessed June 19, 2012).

Bettocchi, Lorena. 2009. "Rongorongo: Les Écritures de L'Ísle de Pâques." *Kadath: Chroniques des Civilisations Disparues* 105: 4–79.

BGR [British Geological Survey]. 2020. "Magnetic Poles." http://www.geomag .bgs.ac.uk/education/poles.html (article dated 2020; accessed 30 July 2020).

Biblical Archaeology Society Staff. 2011. "Göbekli 'Temple' May Have Also Been a House." www.biblicalarchaeology.org/daily/news/gobekli-"temple" -may-have-also-been-a-house (article dated October 10, 2011; accessed December 22, 2011).

Birch, Nicholas. 2008. "7,000 Years Older Than Stonehenge: The Site That Stunned Archaeologists." *Guardian,* April 23, 2008. www.guardian.co.uk

/science/2008/apr/23/archaeology.turkey (article dated April 23, 2008; accessed April 23, 2009).

Bliokh, Pavel Viktorovich, Aleksandr Pavlovich Nicholaenko, and Yu. F. Fillippov. 1980. *Schumann Resonances in the Earth-Ionosphere Cavity.* Translated by Seweryn Chomet. Edited by David Llanwyn Jones. Stevenage, England: Peter Peregrinus Ltd.

Bodleian Philosophy Faculty Library, University of Oxford. 2011. "Manuscripts and Rare Books: Medieval Manuscript Sources and Incunabula." www bodleian.ox.ac.uk/philosophy/collections/manuscripts (undated article; accessed June 28, 2011).

Boettcher, Daniel. 2011. "Peer-Review in Science 'Can Be Improved,' MPs Report." www.bbc.co.uk/news/science-environment-14314501 (article dated July 28, 2011; accessed August 7, 2011).

Bogue, Scott W., and Jonathan M. G. Glen. 2010. "Very Rapid Geomagnetic Field Change Recorded by the Partial Remagnetization of a Lava Flow." *Geophysical Research Letters* 37, L21308, 5 pages.

Bohannon, John. 2006. "Mad about Pyramids." *Science* 313: 1718–20. www .johnbohannon.org/NewFiles/bosnia.pdf (article dated September 22, 2006; accessed July 7, 2011).

Bond, Howard E., Gail H. Schaefer, Ronald L. Gilliland, Jay B. Holberg, Brian D. Mason, Irving W. Lindenblad, Miranda Seitz-McLeese, W. David Arnett, Pierre Demarque, Federico Spada, Patrick A. Young, Martin A. Barstow, Matthew R. Burleigh, and Donald Gudehus. 2017. "The Sirius System and Its Astrophysical Puzzles: Hubble Space Telescope and Ground-Based Astrometry." https://arxiv.org/pdf/1703.10625.pdf (article dated March 30, 2017; accessed April 5, 2020).

Boslough, M., K. Nicoll, V. Holliday, T. L. Daulton, D. Meltzer, N. Pinter, A. C. Scott, T. Surovell, P. Claeys, J. Gill, F. Paquay, J. Marlon, P. Bartlein, C. Whitlock, D. Grayson, and A. J. T. Jull. 2012. "Arguments and Evidence against a Younger Dryas Impact Event." In *Climates, Landscapes, and Civilizations.* Geophysical Monograph Series 198: 13–26.

Boslough, Mark. 2013. "Greenland Pt Anomaly May Point to Noncataclysmic Cape York Meteorite Entry." *Proceedings of the National Academy of Sciences of the United States of America* 110, no. 52: E5035.

Boslough, Mark, Alan W. Harris, Clark Chapman, and David Morrison. 2013. "Younger Dryas Impact Model Confuses Comet Facts, Airburst Physics."

Proceedings of the National Academy of Sciences of the United States of America 110, no. 44: E4170.

Boslough, Mark, Kathleen Nicoll, Tyrone L. Daulton, Andrew C. Scott, Philippe Claeys, Jacquelyn L. Gill, Jennifer R. Marlon, and Patrick J. Bartlein. 2015. "Incomplete Bayesian Model Rejects Contradictory Radiocarbon Data for Being Contradictory." *Proceedings of the National Academy of Sciences of the United States of America* 112, no. 49: E6722.

Boss, Alan P., and Sandra A. Keiser. 2014. "Collapse and Fragmentation of Magnetic Molecular Cloud Cores with the Enzo AMR MHD Code. II. Prolate and Oblate Cores." *Astrophysical Journal* 794, no. 44: 14 pages.

Bouckaert, Remco, Philippe Lemey, Michael Dunn, Simon J. Greenhill, Alexander V. Alekseyenko, Alexei J. Drummond, Russell D. Gray, Marc A. Suchard, and Quentin D. Atkinson. 2012. "Mapping the Origins and Expansion of the Indo-European Language Family." *Science* 337 (August 24): 957–60.

Bowen, Patrick Gillman. [1936?] *The Occult Way.* London: Rider and Company. [Book undated, but apparently published circa 1936; advertisements at the end of the book refer to books that "will appear early in 1937".]

Boyle, Rebecca. 2012. "Massive Extraterrestrial Rock Hit Earth 13 Millennia Ago, According to Nano-Evidence." www.popsci.com/science/article /2012-03/space-rock-impact-could-have-caused-ancient-cooldown-new -evidence-says (article dated March 5, 2012; accessed March 24, 2012).

———. 2017. "How We'll Safeguard Earth from a Solar Storm Catastrophe." www.nbcnews.com/mach/space/how-we-ll-safeguard-earth-solar-storm -catastrophe-n760021 (article dated June 14, 2017; accessed April 22, 2020).

Brahic, Catherine. 2008. "Melting Ice Caps May Trigger More Volcanic Eruptions." www.newscientist.com/article/dn13583-melting-ice-caps-may -trigger-more-volcanic-eruptions.html (article dated April 3, 2008; accessed July 5, 2011).

Brakenridge, G. Robert. 2011. "Core-Collapse Supernovae and the Younger Dryas/Terminal Rancholabrean Extinctions." *Icarus* 215: 101–6.

Branch, Walter, and Ken Newton. 2007. "Chronological Listing of Meteorites That Have Struck Humans, Animals, and Man-Made Objects (HAMs)." https://web.archive.org/web/20090831183851/http://imca.repetti.net /metinfo/metstruck.html (article dated July 29, 2007; accessed March 30, 2020).

Braude, Stephen E. 2008. "The Fear of Psi: It's the Thought That Counts." In

Darklore, vol. 2, edited by Greg Taylor, 99–111. Brisbane, Australia: Daily Grail Publishing.

Bremseth, L. R. 2008. "Unconventional Human Intelligence Support: Transcendent and Asymmetric Warfare Implications of Remote Viewing." In *The Parapsychology Revolution: A Concise Anthology of Paranormal and Psychical Research*, compilation and commentary by Robert M. Schoch and Logan Yonavjak, 233–51. New York: Jeremy P. Tarcher/Penguin. Bremseth article originally written in 2001.

Brigantes Nation. 2002. "Vitrification of Hill Forts: Gazeteer [Gazetteer] and Research Guide." www.brigantesnation.com/VitrifiedForts/VitrifieedForts. (article dated 2002, but possibly updated more recently; accessed July 7, 2010); see also https://brigantesnation.com/members/founder/activity/1581/ (undated; accessed July 20, 2020).

Briggs, Kevin, and National Communications System. 2008. "The Solar Superstorm (SS) Threat to Infrastructure." www.txarmymars.org/downloads/Solar-Superstorms.pdf (PowerPoint presentation dated July 28, 2008; accessed July 4, 2011).

Brody, Judit. 2002. *The Enigma of Sunspots: A Story of Discovery and Scientific Revolution*. Edinburgh, Scotland: Floris Books.

Brooks, Michael. 2009. "Space Storm Alert: 90 Seconds from Catastrophe." *New Scientist*, no. 2700: 31–35. www.newscientist.com/article/mg20127001.300-space-storm-alert-90-seconds-from-catastrophe.html (preview, article dated March 23, 2009; accessed July 11, 2011); copy of article available at: www.cc.gatech.edu/classes/AY2009/cs4001c_spring/documents/Space_storm_alert__90_seconds_from_catastrophe-_New_Scientist.pdf (accessed July 11, 2011).

———. 2020. "Is the Universe Conscious? It seems impossible until you do the maths [sic]. The question of how the brain gives rise to subjective experience is the hardest of all. Mathematicians think they can help, but their first attempts have thrown up some eye-popping conclusions." https://www.newscientist.com/article/mg24632800-900-is-the-universe-conscious-it-seems-impossible-until-you-do-the-maths/ (article dated April 29, 2020; accessed May 18, 2020).

Brophy, Thomas G. 2002. *The Origin Map: Discovery of a Prehistoric, Megalithic, Astrophysical Map and Sculpture of the Universe*. Foreword by Robert M. Schoch and Afterword by John Anthony West. New York: Writers Club Press (iUniverse).

———. 2012. "Nabta Playa's Prehistoric Astronomers." *Atlantis Rising*, no. 91: 45, 70–71.

Brown, John Macmillian. 1924. *The Riddle of the Pacific*. London: T. Fisher Unwin.

Brown, Maxwell, Monika Korte, Richard Holme, Ingo Wardinski, and Sydney Gunnarson. 2018. "Earth's Magnetic Field Is Probably Not Reversing." *Proceedings of the National Academy of Sciences of the United States of America* 115, no. 20: 5111–16.

Brown, P., T. Sutikna, M. J. Morwood, R. P. Soejono, Jatmiko, E. Wayhu Saptomo, and Rokus Awe Due. 2004. "A New Small-Bodied Hominin from the Late Pleistocene of Flores, Indonesia." *Nature* 431: 1055–61. www .nature.com/nature/journal/v431/n7012/full/nature02999.html (article dated October 28, 2004; accessed July 29, 2010).

Brown, William. Undated. "The Sun's Astral Companion: A Model for the Sun-Sirius System." www.viewzone.com/sirius.html (undated article; accessed April 4, 2020).

Brumfield, Loyd. 2019. "Lightning Strike Creates Crater in Fort Worth Parking Lot." www.dallasnews.com/news/2019/10/30/crater-erupts-after-lightning -strike-in-fort-worth-parking-lot/ (article dated October 30, 2019; accessed March 30, 2020).

Buchanan, Mark. 2008. "Why Nature Can't Be Reduced to Mathematical Laws." *New Scientist*, no. 2676: 12.

Budge, E. A. W. 1920. *An Egyptian Hieroglyphic Dictionary in Two Volumes*. London: John Murray.

Bunch, Ted E., Robert E. Hermes, Andrew M. T. Moore, Douglas J. Kennett, James C. Weaver, James H. Wittke, Paul S. DeCarli, James L. Bischoff, Gordon C. Hillman, George A. Howard, David R. Kimbel, Gunther Kletetschka, Carl P. Lipo, Sachiko Sakai, Zsolt Revay, Allen West, Richard B. Firestone, and James P. Kennett. 2012. "Very High-Temperature Impact Melt Products as Evidence for Cosmic Airbursts and Impacts 12,900 Years Ago." *Proceedings of the National Academy of Sciences of the United States of America* 109, no. 28. https://doi.org/10.1073 /pnas.1204453109 (early edition, 10 pages). www.pnas.org/content /early/2012/06/14/1204453109.abstract (article dated June 18, 2012; accessed June 29, 2012).

Bürgin, Luc. 2007. *Der Urzeit-Code*. Munich, Germany: F. A. Herbig.

Burke, John, and Kaj Halberg. 2005. *Seed of Knowledge, Stone of Plenty:*

Understanding the Lost Knowledge of the Ancient Megalith-Builders. Tulsa, Okla.: Council Oak Books.

Burl, Aubrey. 1976. *The Stone Circles of the British Isles.* New Haven, Conn.: Yale University Press.

Burns, Jean E. 2003. "What Is Beyond the Edge of the Known World?" *Journal of Consciousness Studies* 10, nos. 6–7: 7–28. Reprinted in *The Parapsychology Revolution: A Concise Anthology of Paranormal and Psychical Research,* compilation and commentary by Robert M. Schoch and Logan Yonavjak, 266–300. New York: Jeremy P. Tarcher/Penguin, 2008.

Calder, Nigel. 2011. "Climate Change: News and Comments: CERN Chief Forbids 'Interpretation' of CLOUD Results." https://calderup.wordpress. com/2011/07/17/"no-you-mustnt-say-what-it-means" (article dated July 17, 2011; accessed July 20, 2011).

Campanario, Juan Miguel, and Brian Martin. 2008. "Challenging Dominant Physics Paradigms." In *Against the Tide: A Critical Review by Scientists of How Physics and Astronomy Get Done,* edited by Martín López Corredoira and Carlos Castro Perelman, 9–26. Boca Raton, Fla.: Universal Publishers. www.bibliotecapleyades.net/archivos_pdf/against_thetide.pdf (book dated 2008; accessed August 26, 2011).

Camus, Albert. 1946. *The Stranger.* Translated from the French by Stuart Gilbert. New York: Vintage Books / Alfred A. Knopf / Random House.

Cañellas-Boltà, Núria, Valentí Rull, Alberto Sáez, Olga Margalef, Roberto Bao, Sergi Pla-Rabes, Maarten Blaauw, Blas Valero-Garcés, and Santiago Giralt. 2013. "Vegetation Changes and Human Settlement of Easter Island during the Last Millennia: A Multiproxy Study of the Lake Raraku Sediments." *Quaternary Science Reviews* 72: 36–48.

Carlson, Anders E. 2010. "What Caused the Younger Dryas Cold Event?" *Geology* 38, no. 4: 383–84.

———. 2013. "The Younger Dryas Climate Event." In *The Encyclopedia of Quaternary Science,* vol. 3, edited by S. A. Elias, 126–34. Amsterdam: Elsevier.

Carrington, R. C. 1859. "Description of a Singular Appearance Seen in the Sun on September 1, 1859." *Monthly Notices of the Royal Astronomical Society* 20: 13–15. http://articles.adsabs.harvard.edu/full/seri/MNRAS/0020//0000013.000 .html (article dated 1859; accessed July 11, 2011).

Carroll, Sean. 2010. "The Fine Structure Constant Is Probably Constant." http://blogs.discovermagazine.com/cosmicvariance/2010/10/18/the-fine

-structure-constant-is-probably-constant/ (article dated October 18, 2010; accessed August 11, 2011).

Carter, Jimmy. 2010. *White House Diary*. New York: Farrar, Straus and Giroux.

Cartwright, Jon. 2008. "The Mystery of the Varying Nuclear Decay." http://physicsworld.com/cws/article/news/36108;jsessionid=B130DA52EBB8E98 916171ACC78E97862 (article dated October 2, 2008; accessed October 11, 2008).

Çatalhöyük Research Project. Various Dates. [Archive Reports of excavations and research at Çatalhöyük from 1993 through 2017.] http://www.catalhoyuk .com/research/archive_reports (undated site; accessed August 3, 2020).

Cauwe, Nicolas. 2011. *Easter Island: The Great Taboo*. Louvain-la-Neuve, Belgium: Versant Sud.

Cesarino, Felice. 2012. "A Göbekli Tepe la più antica scrittura della storia dell'umanità?". *L'Editoriale* (December, 2012). Reprinted as a chapter in Cesarino, Felice. 2017. *La Scimmia ambiziosa* (2nd ed.), 171–96. Rome: Arbor Sapientiae.

Chalko, Tom J. 2004. "No Second Chance? Can Earth Explode as a Result of Global Warming?" *NU Journal of Discovery* 3: 3.1–3.9. http://nujournal. net/core.pdf (article revised October 30, 2004; originally published May 2001; accessed July 4, 2011).

———. 2008. "Earthquake Energy Rise on Earth." *NU Journal of Discovery*. 2 pages. http://nujournal.net/EarthquakeEnergyRise.pdf (article dated May 2008; accessed July 4, 2011).

Chandler, Graham. 2009. "The Beginning of the End for Hunter-Gatherers." *Saudi ARAMCO World* 60, no. 2: 2–9. www.saudiaramcoworld.com/issue/200902 /the.beginning.of.the.end.for.hunter-gatherers.htm (article dated March/April 2009; accessed August 28, 2011; photographs by Ergun Çağatay).

Changizi, Mark A., Qiong Zhang, Hao Ye, and Shinsuke Shimojo. 2006. "The Structures of Letters and Symbols throughout Human History Are Selected to Match Those Found in Objects in Natural Scenes." *American Naturalist* 167, no. 5: E117–E139 (e-article).

Channell, J. E. T., and L. Vigliotti. 2018. "The Role of Geomagnetic Field Intensity in Late Quaternary Evolution of Humans and Large Mammals." *Reviews of Geophysics* 57: 709–38.

Chaplin, Martin F. 2007. "The Memory of Water: An Overview." *Homeopathy* 96: 143–50. www.badscience.net/files/MW2.pdf (article dated 2007; accessed August 22, 2011).

Charles, Robert Henry, trans. 2003. *The Book of Enoch the Prophet.* Introduction by R. A. Gilbert. San Francisco: Weiser Books. Originally published 1912 by Oxford University Press.

Chauvet, Stephen. 1946. *La Isla de Pascua y Sus Misterios.* Santiago, Chile: Zig-Zag.

Chen, Jiangzhi, Chiara Elmi, David Goldsby, and Reto Gieré. 2017. "Generation of Shock Lamellae and Melting in Rocks by Lightning-Induced Shock Waves and Electrical Heating." *Geophysical Research Letters* 44: 12 pages.

Chernavskii, D. S. 1998. "Postscript." *Physics—Uspekhi* [Uspekhi Fizicheskikh Nauk; Russian Academy of Sciences] 41, no. 10: 1034–35. Postscript to article by Shnoll et al. 1998.

Childe, V. Gordon. 1950. "The Urban Revolution." *Town Planning Review* 21, no. 1: 3–17.

Cho, Adrian. 2011. "Where Does the Time Go? One Experiment Sees Neutrinos Traveling Faster Than Light. If the Result Can't Be Replicated, It May Never Be Explained Away." *Science* 334: 1200–1201.

Cho, Il-Hyun, Young-Sil Kwak, Katsuhide Marubashi, Yeon-Han Kim, Young-Deuk Park, and Heon-Young Chang. 2011. "Changes in Sea-Level Pressure over South Korea Associated with High-Speed Solar Wind Events." http://arxiv .org/PS_cache/arxiv/pdf/1107/1107.1841v1.pdf (article dated July 12, 2011; accessed July 17, 2011).

Chou, Yu-Min, Xiuyang Jiang, Qingsong Liu, Hsun-Ming Hu, Chung-Che Wu, Jianxing Liu, Zhaoxia Jiang, Teh-Quei Lee, Chun-Chieh Wang, Yen-Fang Song, Cheng-Cheng Chiang, Liangcheng Tan, Mahjoor A. Lone, Yongxin Pan, Rixiang Zhu, Yaoqi He, Yu-Chen Chou, An-Hung Tan, Andrew P. Roberts, Xiang Zhao, and Chuan-Chou Shena. 2018. "Multidecadally Resolved Polarity Oscillations During a Geomagnetic Excursion." *Proceedings of the National Academy of Sciences of the United States of America* 115, no. 36: 8913–18.

Christison, David. 1898. *Early Fortifications in Scotland: Motes, Camps, and Forts.* Edinburgh, Scotland: William Blackwood and Sons. See especially chapter 4, "Vitrified Forts."

Churchward, Albert. 1922. *Origin and Evolution of the Human Race.* New York and London: Macmillan Company and George Allen & Unwin.

Clark, Kenneth. 1969. *Civilisation: A Personal View.* New York: Harper and Row.

Clark, Rundle. 1978. *Myth and Symbol in Ancient Egypt.* London: Thames and Hudson.

Clark, Stuart. 2007. *The Sun Kings: The Unexpected Tragedy of Richard Carrington and the Tale of How Modern Astronomy Began.* Princeton, N.J.: Princeton University Press.

Clette, Frédéric, David Berghmans, Petra Vanlommel, Ronald A. M. Van der Linden, André Koeckelenbergh, and Laurence Wauters. 2007. "From the Wolf Number to the International Sunspot Index: 25 Years of SIDC [Solar Influences Data Analysis Center]." *Advances in Space Research* 40: 919–28. www.leif.org/EOS/Clette_JASR8745.pdf (article dated 2007; accessed September 9, 2011).

Cliver, E. W. 2006. "The 1859 Space Weather Event: Then and Now." *Advances in Space Research* 38: 119–29.

Cochrane, Ev. 2009. "Stars, Gods, and Religion in Ancient Egypt." www .maverickscience.com/horus.pdf (document dated 2009; accessed August 26, 2011); see also https://www.scribd.com/doc/250881758/Stars -and-Gods (document undated; accessed July 27, 2020).

Coghlan, Andy. 2011. "Scorn over Claim of Teleported DNA." *New Scientist,* no. 2795: 8–9. www.newscientist.com/article/mg20927952.900-scorn-over -claim-of-teleported-dna.html (preview; article dated January 12, 2011; accessed January 26, 2011).

Collin, Rodney. 1980. *The Theory of Celestial Influence: Man, the Universe, and Cosmic Mystery.* Somerset, England: Watkins. Reprint of 1954 edition.

Comte, Roland. 2002. "The Mystery of Vitrified Hillforts." www.brigantesnation .com/VitrifiedForts/TheMysteryofVitrifiedHillforts.htm (article circa 2002 [date of posted copyright]; accessed June 30, 2010).

Condick, Jeremy. 2009. "The Vitrified Forts of Scotland." http://logos_endless _summer.tripod.com/id139.html (undated article; accessed April 20, 2009).

Coon, Carleton S. 1954. *The Story of Man: From the First Human to Primitive Culture and Beyond.* New York: Alfred A. Knopf.

Copeland, Kyle, and William Atwell. 2000. "Flight Safety Implications of the Extreme Solar Proton Event of 23 February 1956." *Advances in Space Research* 63: 665–71.

Corredoira, Martín López, and Carlos Castro Perelman, eds. 2008. *Against the Tide: A Critical Review by Scientists of How Physics and Astronomy Get Done.* Boca Raton, Fla.: Universal Publishers. www.bibliotecapleyades.net /archivos_pdf/against_thetide.pdf (book dated 2008; accessed August 26, 2011).

Cosic, Irena, Dean Cvetkovic, Qiang Fang, Emil Jovanov, and Harry Lazoura.

2006. "Human Electrophysiological Signal Responses to ELF Schumann Resonance and Artificial Electromagnetic Fields." *FME* [Faculty of Mechanical Engineering, Belgrade] *Transactions* 34: 93–103.

Costa de Beauregard, Olivier. 1987. *Time, the Physical Magnitude.* Vol. 99, *Boston Studies in the Philosophy of Science.* Dordrecht, The Netherlands: D. Reidel Publishing.

Courtillot, Vincent, Yves Gallet, Jean-Louis Le Mouël, Frédéric Fluteau, and Agnès Genevey. 2007. "Are There Connections between the Earth's Magnetic Field and Climate?" *Earth and Planetary Science Letters* 253: 328–39. http://sd-1.archive-host.com/membres/up/1085636264/courtillot.pdf (article dated 2007; accessed July 8, 2011).

Coxill, D. 1998. "The Riddle of the Sphinx." *InScription: Journal of Ancient Egypt,* no. 2: 13–19.

Cramer, John G. 1986. "The Transactional Interpretation of Quantum Mechanics." *Reviews of Modern Physics* 58: 647–87. http://faculty.washington.edu/jcramer/TI/tiqm_1986.pdf (article dated July 1986; accessed August 20, 2011).

———. 2001. "The Plane of the Present and the New Transactional Paradigm of Time." In *Time and the Instant,* edited by Robin Drurie, chapter 9. Manchester, England: Clinamen Press. Available from http://arxiv.org/ftp/quant-ph/papers/0507/0507089.pdf (chapter dated 2001; accessed August 20, 2011).

Cruttenden, Walter. 2006. *Lost Star of Myth and Time.* Pittsburgh, Pa.: St. Lynn's Press.

———. 2012. Personal communication. (See Binary Research Institute; www.binaryresearchinstitute.org/.)

———. 2019. "Chapter 10. NASA Says Planet Nine Evidence Is Mounting." An additional chapter to *Lost Star of Myth and Time* (see Cruttenden 2006). 12 pages. Privately printed and distributed by Walter Cruttenden; undated, copy purchased October 5, 2019.

Crystal, Ellie. 2011. "Zep Tepi." www.crystalinks.com/zeptepi.html (undated article, website dated 1995–2011; accessed August 20, 2011).

Cucinotta, Francis A., and Eliedonna Cacao. 2017. "Non-Targeted Effects Models Predict Significantly Higher Mars Mission Cancer Risk Than Targeted Effects Models." *Scientific Reports / Nature* 7, no. 1832: 11 pages.

Curry, Andrew. 2008a. "Seeking the Roots of Ritual. In the Hills of Turkey, Researchers Are Slowly Uncovering the World's Oldest Monumental

Structures, Strange Monoliths Built by Hunter-Gatherers Perhaps 11,000 Years Ago." *Science* 319: 278–80.

———. 2008b. "The World's First Temple? Predating Stonehenge by 6,000 Years, Turkey's Stunning Gobekli Tepe Upends the Conventional View of the Rise of Civilization." *Smithsonian* 39, no. 8: 54–58, 60. www.smithsonianmag .com/history-archaeology/gobekli-tepe.html (article date November 2008; accessed August 28, 2011; photographs by Berthold Steinhilber).

Dacey, James. 2010. "Volcanic Hazards Could Become Fiercer and More Frequent." http://physicsworld.com/cws/article/news/42452 (article dated April 23, 2010; accessed July 5, 2011).

Daily Mail. 2011. "Going Underground: The Massive European Network of Stone Age Tunnels That Weaves from Scotland to Turkey." www.dailymail. co.uk/sciencetech/article-2022322/The-massive-European-network-Stone -Age-tunnels-weaves-Scotland-Turkey.html (article dated August 4, 2011; accessed August 5, 2011).

Dalton, Rex. 2011. "Comet Theory Comes Crashing to Earth: An Elegant Archaeological Hypothesis, under Fire for Results That Can't Be Replicated, May Ultimately Come Undone." www.miller-mccune.com/science/comet -claim-comes-crashing-to-earth-31180/ (article dated May 11, 2011; accessed May 22, 2011).

Daulton, Tyrone L., Nicholas Pinter, and Andrew C. Scott. 2010. "No Evidence of Nanodiamonds in Younger-Dryas Sediments to Support an Impact Event." *Proceedings of the National Academy of Sciences of the United States of America* 107, no. 37: 16043–47.

Daulton, Tyrone L., Sachiko Amari, Andrew C. Scott, Mark Hardiman, Nicholas Pinter, and R. Scott Anderson. 2016. "Comprehensive Analysis of Nanodiamond Evidence Relating to the Younger Dryas Impact Hypothesis." *Journal of Quaternary Science* (December 19). http://onlinelibrary.wiley.com /doi/10.1002/jqs.2892/epdf. 28 pages (accessed December 28, 2016).

David, Ariel. 2020. "Israeli Archaeologists Find Hidden Pattern at 'World's Oldest Temple' Göbekli Tepe. Neolithic Hunter-Gatherers Who Erected Massive Monoliths in Central Turkey 11,500 Years Ago Had Command of Geometry and a Much More Complex Society Than Previously Thought, Archaeologists Say." www.haaretz.com/archaeology/.premium-israeli -archaeologists-find-hidden-pattern-at-gobekli-tepe-1.8799837?fbclid=IwA R0RIO8YPOdRb4e54mJx2m3GChZht7uwUtF7yqDxRlxs4vbM0ZsQhi 5HfD8 (article dated April 28, 2020; accessed April 28, 2020).

David-Neel, Alexandra. 1932. *Magic and Mystery in Tibet*. Introduction by Dr. Arsène d'Arsonval. New York: Crown Publishers. Originally published in 1929 as *Mystiques et Magiciens du Thibet* and in 1931 in English as *With Mystics and Magicians in Tibet*. Reprinted in 1937.

Davidson, Ben. 2015. "A Surge and Short-Term Peak in Northern Solar Polar Field Magnetism Prior to the M8.3 Earthquake near Chile on September 16, 2015." *New Concepts in Global Tectonics Journal* 3, no. 3: 391–93.

———. 2016. "Research Update on Solar Polar Fields/Coronal Hole IMF and Large Earthquakes, and a Proposed Method for Quantifying Coronal Hole Geoeffectiveness." http://suspicious0bservers.org/wp-content /uploads/2016/04/NewPaper-4.pdf (paper posted 2016; accessed April 1, 2020).

———. 2018. "Earth Catastrophe Cycle: SOLAR MICRONOVA." Video posted on YouTube by Suspicious0bservers. www.youtube.com /watch?v=jTUJ7GtEx0Y (posted December 28, 2018; accessed December 28, 2018).

———. 2019. "Comment on 'Revisiting the Biological Ramifications of Variations in Earth's Magnetic Field.'" https://docs.google.com/document /d/1Y3hYBGMBsB_daHeRJXNXIsuwun5cvyfevHWnwTxwwVI/edit (undated, but written in 2019; accessed April 9, 2020).

Davidson, Ben, Kongpop U-Yen, and Christopher Holloman. 2015. "Relationship Between M8+ Earthquake Occurrences and the Solar Polar Magnetic Fields." *New Concepts in Global Tectonics Journal* 3, no. 3: 310–22.

Daviss, Bennett. 2004. "Structured Water Is Changing Models: Large Water-Molecule Clusters May Be Crucial to Cellular Processes." *Scientist* 18, no. 21: 14. Available from http://classic.the-scientist.com/2004/11/08/14/1 (article dated November 8, 2004; accessed March 16, 2012).

Debertolis, Paolo, Daniele Gullà, and Heikki Savolainen. 2017. "Archaeoacoustic Analysis in Enclosure D at Göbekli Tepe in South Anatolia, Turkey." The 5th Human and Social Sciences at the Common Conference, September, 25–29, 2017. *History and Archaeology*, 2017:107–14.

DeMille, Cecil B. 1956. *The Ten Commandments*. Film. Hollywood, Calif.: Paramount Pictures.

Desai, Tara, Dimitri Batani, Marco Bussoli, Anna Maria Villa, Riccardo Dezulian, and Eduard Krousky. 2008. "Laboratory Craters: Modeling Experiments for Meteorite Impact Craters?" *Institute of Electrical and Electronics Engineers Transactions in Plasma Physics* 36, no. 4: 1132–33.

de Jong, Jan Peter. 2007–2008. "Ancient Mysteries: Vitrified and Moulded Rocks." www.ancient-mysteries-explained.com/vitrified-rocks.html (article dated 2007–2008; accessed July 5, 2010).

de Laat, M. 2009. *Words Out of Wood: Proposals for the Decipherment of the Easter Island Script.* Delft, The Netherlands: Eburon.

———. 2011. "Proposals for the Decipherment of the Easter Island Script." http://easterislandscript.nl/index.html (website dated 2011; accessed July 6, 2011).

de Martino, Ernesto. 1972. *Primitive Magic: The Psychic Powers of Shamans and Sorcerers.* Bridport, Dorset, England: Prism. Also reprinted 1988 and 1999. Originally published 1948 as *Il Mondo Magico: Prolegomeni a una Storia del Magismo,* Torino, Italy: Giulio Einaudi.

de Santillana, Giorgio, and Hertha von Dechend. 1969. *Hamlet's Mill: An Essay on Myth and the Frame of Time.* Boston: Gambit.

de Vesme, Caesar. 1931a. *A History of Experimental Spiritualism.* Vol. I, *Primitive Man.* Translated from the French by Stanley de Brath. London: Rider and Company.

———. 1931b. *A History of Experimental Spiritualism.* Vol. II, *Peoples of Antiquity.* Translated from the French by Fred Rothwell. London: Rider and Company.

Dietrich, Laura, Julia Meister, Oliver Dietrich, Jens Notroff, Janika Kiep, Julia Heeb, André Beuger, and Brigitta Schütt. 2019. "Cereal Processing at Early Neolithic Göbekli Tepe, Southeastern Turkey." *PLOS* [Public Library of Science] *One* 14, no. 5: 34 pages.

Dietrich, M. H. 1999. "'Little Eyes'—on a Big Trip: Star Navigation as *Rongorongo* Inscriptions (Part III)." *Asian and African Studies* [Bratislava] 8, no. 2: 164–90.

Dietrich, Oliver, Çiğdem Köksal-Schmidt, Jens Notroff, and Klaus Schmidt. 2013. "Establishing a Radiocarbon Sequence for Göbekli Tepe. State of Research and New Data." *Neo-Lithics 1/13: The Newsletter of Southwest Asian Neolithic Research,* 36–41.

Dmitriev, Alexey N. 1997. "PlanetoPhysical State of the Earth and Life." *IICA Transactions* 4 [no pages on document]. Originally published in Russian; Russian-to-English translation and editing by A. N. Dmitriev, Andrew Tetenov, and Earl L. Crockett. www.tmgnow.com/repository/global/planetophysical.html (article dated January 8, 1998; accessed June 28, 2011); also available from https://www.mohr-mohr-and-more.org/downloads/dmitriev.pdf (article dated January 8, 1998; accessed July 18, 2020).

Dobecki, Thomas L., and Robert M. Schoch. 1992. "Seismic Investigations in the Vicinity of the Great Sphinx of Giza, Egypt." *Geoarchaeology* 7, no. 6: 527–44.

Don, Sallie, and Amos Aikman. 2011. "Brits to Shut Grid for Solar Flare." www.theaustralian.com.au/news/nation/brits-to-shut-grid-for-solar-flare /story-e6frg6nf-1226078128738 (article dated June 20, 2011; accessed July 11, 2011).

Dooling, Dave. 1998. "New Sunspot Cycle to Be Bigger Than Average." http:// science.nasa.gov/science-news/science-at-nasa/1998/ast13apr98_1 (article dated April 13, 1998; accessed July 11, 2011).

Duan, L.-M. 2011. "Quantum Correlation between Distant Diamonds." *Science* 334, no. 6060: 1213–14.

Duderstadt, Katharine A., Jack E. Dibb, Nathan A. Schwadron, Harlan E. Spence, Stanley C. Solomon, Valery A. Yudin, Charles H. Jackman, and Cora E. Randall. 2016. "Nitrate Ion Spikes in Ice Cores Not Suitable as Proxies for Solar Proton Events." *Journal of Geophysical Research: Atmospheres* 121: 2994–3016.

Duncan, C. J., and S. Scott. 2005. "What Caused the Black Death?" *Postgraduate Medical Journal* 81: 315–20. https://pmj.bmj.com/content/postgradmedj /81/955/315.full.pdf (article dated 2005; accessed March 22, 2020).

Dunning-Davies, J. 2011a. "Structure and Memory in Water." http://vixra.org /pdf/1101.0081v1.pdf (article submitted January 24, 2011; accessed August 12, 2011).

———. 2011b. "Structure and Memory in Water II." http://vixra.org /pdf/1101.0094v1.pdf (article dated 2011; accessed August 12, 2011).

Dye, Lee. 1991. "Sphinx's New Riddle—Is It Older Than Experts Say?: Archaeology: Geologists Cite Study of Weathering Patterns. But Egyptologists Say Findings Can't Be Right." *Los Angeles Times,* October 23, 1991. http://articles.latimes.com/1991-10-23/news/mn-183_1_great-sphinx (article dated October 23, 1991; accessed June 14, 2010).

Easter Island Statue Project. 2012. "Easter Island's Statues Reveal Bodies Covered With Unknown Ancient Petroglyphs." www.messagetoeagle.com /easterislandbodies.php (article dated June 7, 2012; accessed July 10, 2012); see also https://www.messagetoeagle.com/easter-islands-statues-reveal-bodies -covered-with-unknown-ancient-petroglyphs/ (article updated 23 March 2019, accessed August 2, 2020).

Eather, Robert H. 1980. *Majestic Lights: The Aurora in Science, History, and the Arts.* Washington, D.C.: American Geophysical Union.

Eddy, John A. 1976. "The Maunder Minimum." *Science,* n.s., 192, no. 4245: 1189–1202.

Edelmann, L. 2005. "Doubts about the Sodium-Potassium Pump Are Not Permissible in Modern Bioscience." *Cellular and Molecular Biology* 51: 725–29.

Eden, Dan. 2009. "Ancient '200,000 BC' Human Metropolis Found in Africa." www.newsrescue.com/2009/11/ancient-200000bc-human-metropolis -found-in-africa/ (article dated 2009; accessed August 18, 2011).

Edwards, Edmundo, and Alexandra Edwards. 2013. *When the Universe Was an Island: Exploring the Cultural and Spiritual Cosmos of Ancient Rapa Nui.* Hangaroa, Easter Island: Hangaroa Press.

Eilenstein, Harry. [2011]. *Göbekli Tepe: Die Bilderwelt des Tempels der Menschen.* Norderstedt, Germany: Books on Demand GmbH. [Copyright listed as "2009," but the copy I purchased in early 2013 was clearly updated since 2009 as it includes photographs that Katie and I took during our trip to Göbekli Tepe in May 2010 and that Eilenstein somehow acquired and used in his book without our permission and without acknowledging us. As of March 2, 2013, Amazon.com listed this book with a publication date of October 6, 2011.]

ElectricUniverse.info. Undated. "Electric Sun Theory." www.electricuniverse .info/electric-sun-theory/ (undated article; accessed April 14, 2020).

Eliade, Mircea. 1972. *Zalmoxis: The Vanishing God. Comparative Studies in the Religions and Folklore of Dacia and Eastern Europe.* Translated by Willard R. Trask. Chicago: University of Chicago Press.

Elkins, James. 1996. "On the Impossibility of Close Reading: The Case of Alexander Marshack." *Current Anthropology* 37, no. 2: 185–226. (The actual article ends on page 201; it is followed by comments from numerous scholars, including Alexander Marshack, and the response of Elkins to the comments.)

Elmi, Chiara, Jiangzhi Chen, David Goldsby, and Reto Gieré. 2017. "Mineralogical and Compositional Features of Rock Fulgurites: A Record of Lightning Effects on Granite." *American Mineralogist* 102: 1470–81.

Elton, Daniel C. 2019. "Compelling Alternative Theories for Exclusion Zone Phenomena in Water and Other Liquids." https://arxiv.org/pdf/1909.06822 .pdf (article dated September 15, 2019; accessed April 16, 2020).

Emoto, Masaru. 2004. *The Hidden Messages in Water.* Translated from the Japanese by David A. Thayne. Hillsboro, Ore.: Beyond Words Publishing.

Eneix, Linda. 2012. [Untitled article on the importance of sound in the design of ancient structures, particularly on Malta.] www.otsf.org/Archaeoacoustics. htm (undated article; accessed March 24, 2012).

Erwin, Richard P. 1930. "Indian Rock Writing in Idaho." *Twelfth Biennial Report of the Board of Trustees of the State Historical Society of Idaho,* December 31, 35–111.

Esen-Baur, Heide-Margaret. 2011. "Towards an Understanding of *Rongorongo.*" *Anthropos* 106: 439–61.

European Nuclear Society. 2012. "Nuclear Power Plants, World-wide." www .euronuclear.org/info/encyclopedia/n/nuclear-power-plant-world-wide.htm (article dated February 2, 2012; accessed March 24, 2012).

Fagan, Anna. 2017. "Hungry Architecture: Spaces of Consumption and Predation at Göbekli Tepe." *World Archaeology* 49, no. 3: 318–37.

Faith, J. Tyler, and Todd A. Surovell. 2009. "Synchronous Extinction of North America's Pleistocene Mammals." *Proceedings of the National Academy of Sciences of the United States of America* 106, no. 49: 20641–45.

Farmer, Brian W., and Robert C. Hannan. 2003. "Investigations of Relatively Easy to Construct Antennas with Efficiency in Receiving Schumann Resonances: Preparations for a Miniaturized Reconfigurable ELF Receiver." NASA/TM [Technical Memorandum]-2003-212647, October.

Ferreyra, Eduardo. 2011. "Correlation between Temperatures and CO_2 (A Shot in the Foot by the IPCC and UNEP)." www.mitosyfraudes.org/Calen /correlaEng.html (undated article; accessed July 13, 2011).

Fidani, Cristiano. [2009?]. "The Raffaele Bendandi Forecastings Inspired by the Great Earthquake." www.itacomm.net/EQL/engbent1908.pdf (article dated circa 2009; accessed July 5, 2011). www.itacomm.net/EQL/absbent1908 .pdf (article in Italian; accessed July 5, 2011).

———. 2011. "Alcune Conferme alle Previsioni dei Terremoti di Raffaele Bendandi." www.itacomm.net/EQL/2011_Fidani.pdf (article dated 2011; accessed July 5, 2011).

Fiedel, S. J. 2011. "The Mysterious Onset of the Younger Dryas." *Quaternary International* 242: 262–66.

Finch, Damien, Andrew Gleadow, Janet Hergt, Vladimir A. Levchenko, Pauline Heaney, Peter Veth, Sam Harper, Sven Ouzman, Cecilia Myers, and Helen Green. 2020. "12,000-Year-old Aboriginal Rock Art from the Kimberley Region, Western Australia." *Science Advances, Research Article*, AAAS [American Association for the Advancement of Science], 5 (February): 9 pages.

Firestone, R. B., A. West, and S. Warwick-Smith. 2006. *The Cycle of Cosmic Catastrophes: Flood, Fire, and Famine in the History of Civilization.* Rochester, Vt.: Bear and Company.

Firestone, R. B., A. West, J. P. Kennett, L. Becker, T. E. Bunch, Z. S. Revay, P. H. Schultz, T. Belgya, D. J. Kennett, J. M. Erlandson, O. J. Dickenson, A. C. Goodyear, R. S. Harris, G. A. Howard, J. B. Kloosterman, P. Lechler, P. A. Mayewski, J. Montgomery, R. Poreda, T. Darrah, S. S. Que Hee, A. R. Smith, A. Stich, W. Topping, J. H. Wittke, and W. S. Wolbach. 2007. "Evidence for an Extraterrestrial Impact 12,900 Years Ago That Contributed to the Megafaunal Extinctions and the Younger Dryas Cooling." *Proceedings of the National Academy of Sciences of the United States of America* 104, no. 41: 16016–21. www.pnas.org/content/104/41/16016 .full.pdf+html (article dated October 9, 2007; accessed August 8, 2011).

Fischbach, E., J. B. Buncher, J. T. Gruenwald, J. H. Jenkins, D. E. Krause, J. J. Mattes, and J. R. Newport. 2009. "Time-Dependent Nuclear Decay Parameters: New Evidence for New Forces?" *Space Science Reviews* 145: 285–335.

Fischer, Steven Roger. 1997a. *Glyphbreaker.* New York: Copernicus, an imprint of Springer-Verlag.

———. 1997b. *Rongorongo: The Easter Island Script.* Oxford, UK: Clarendon Press.

———. 2005. *Island at the End of the World: The Turbulent History of Easter Island.* London: Reaktion Books.

Flenley, John, and Paul Bahn. 2002/2003. *The Enigmas of Easter Island: Island on the Edge.* Oxford and New York: Oxford University Press.

Ford, Brian J. 1965. "Origin of the Lunar Craters." *SpaceFlight* [*Journal of the British Interplanetary Society*] 7, no. 1: 13–17.

Foster, Benjamin R., trans. and ed. 2001. *The Epic of Gilgamesh.* New York: W. W. Norton.

Fox, Charles Elliot. 1924. *The Threshold of the Pacific.* London: Kegan Paul, Trench, Trubner and Co; also published in the United States: New York: Alfred A. Knopf, 1925.

Friederich, Simon, and Peter W. Evans. 2019. "Retrocausality in Quantum Mechanics." https://plato.stanford.edu/entries/qm-retrocausality/ (article dated June 3, 2019; accessed August 1, 2020).

Fronza Videoproducties. 2011. "The Biggest Hoax in History?" www.thebiggest hoaxinhistory.com/en (documentary film dated 2011; accessed July 7, 2011).

Fussell, Joseph H. 1933. "Review and Comment." Review of *Where Is Science Going?* by Max Planck. *Theosophical Path* 43, no. 2: 198–213.

Gaffney, Mark H. 2006. "The Astronomers of Nabta Playa: New Discoveries Reveal Astonishing Pre-Historic Knowledge." *Atlantis Rising,* no. 56: 42–43, 68–70.

Gallet, Yves, Agnès Genevey, Maxime Le Goff, Frédéric Fluteau, and Safar Ali Eshraghi. 2006. "Possible Impact of the Earth's Magnetic Field on the History of Ancient Civilizations." *Earth and Planetary Science Letters* 246, nos. 1–2: 17–26. www.sciencedirect.com/science/article/pii /S0012821X06002792 (abstract; article dated June 15, 2006; accessed March 18, 2012).

Gannon, Jennifer L., Andrei Swidinsky, and Zhonghua Xu, eds. 2019. *Geomagnetically Induced Currents from the Sun to the Power Grid.* Hoboken, N. J., and Washington, D. C.: John Wiley and Sons, and the American Geophysical Union.

Garau, Annie. 2018. "Researchers Find Oldest-Ever Bracelet alongside Extinct Human Species." https://allthatsinteresting.com/oldest-jewelry-ever-found (original article dated May 16, 2017, and updated July 6, 2018; accessed April 12, 2020).

Gardiner, Alan. 1957. *Egyptian Grammar* (third edition, revised). Oxford, UK: Griffith Institute, Ashmolean Museum.

Gate Production and Maker Arts. 2010. *GobekliTepe: The World's First Temple.* DVD. Produced and directed by Ahmet Turgut Yazman, executive production by Kerem Akalin, script by Mehmet Yazman. Istanbul, Turkey: Maker Arts. See www.worldsfirsttemple.com.

Gauguin, Paul. 1961. *Noa Noa: Voyage to Tahiti.* Translated by Jonathan Griffin; postscript by Jean Loize. New York: Reynal and Company.

Gauquelin, Michel. 1973. *Cosmic Influences on Human Behavior.* New York: Stein and Day.

Gauri, K. Lal, and J. K. Bandyopadhyay. 1999. *Carbonate Stone.* New York: John Wiley and Sons.

Gavin, Patrick. 2010. "Carter's Weird Science." http://mobile.politico.com /storyclick.cfm?id=4931 (article dated October 20, 2010; accessed October 20, 2010).

Geological Survey of Canada. 2008. "Geomagnetism: North Magnetic Pole." http://gsc.nrcan.gc.ca/geomag/nmp/northpole_e.php (article dated January 16, 2008; accessed August 10, 2011. [Note: On July 20, 2020, this URL was not active, but the data was available from the United. States National Geophysical Data Center of the National Oceanic and Atmospheric Administration; go to www.ngdc.noaa.gov/geomag/faqgeom .shtml and click on "Where are the magnetic poles?".]

Ghosh, Pallab. 2008. "Black Hole Confirmed in Milky Way." http://news.bbc. co.uk/2/hi/science/nature/7774287.stm (article dated December 9, 2008; accessed June 29, 2011).

Gibbard, Philip L., Martin J. Head, Michael J. Walker, and the Subcommission on Quaternary Stratigraphy. 2010. "Formal Ratification of the Quaternary System/Period and the Pleistocene Series/Epoch with a Base at 2.58 Ma." *Journal of Quaternary Science* 25, no. 2: 96–102.

Gieré, R., W. Wimmenauer, H. Muller-Sigmund, R. Wirth, G. R. Lumpkin, and K. L. Smith. 2015. "Lightning Induced Shock Lamellae in Quartz." *American Mineralogist* 100, no. 7: 1645–48.

Glasser, Ryan T., Ulrich Vogl, and Paul D. Lett. 2012. "Stimulated Generation of Superluminal Light Pulses via Four-Wave Mixing." *Physical Review Letters,* April 26, 5 pages.

Global Heritage Fund. 2011a. "Göbekli Tepe, Turkey: Unique Early Neolithic Ceremonial Center." http://globalheritagefund.org/what_we_do/overview /current_projects/gobekli_tepe_turkey (undated article; accessed August 28, 2011).

———. 2011b. "Göbekli Tepe, Turkey: Unique Early Neolithic Ceremonial Center." http://globalheritagefund.org/images/uploads/projects /GHFGobekliTepeTurkey.pdf (undated article; accessed August 28, 2011).

Godwin, Joscelyn. 2010. *Atlantis and the Cycles of Time: Prophecies, Traditions, and Occult Revelations.* Rochester, Vt.: Inner Traditions.

Goff, Philip. 2017. "The Case for Panpsychism." *Philosophy Now,* no. 121: 6–8.

Gold, Thomas. 1963. "Large Solar Outbursts in the Past." *Pontificiae Academiae Scientiarum Scripta Varia* 25: 159–66; discussion, 167–74. Paper presented at Semaine D'Etude sur Le Probleme du Rayonnement Cosmique dans L'Espace Interplanetaire, Conference at the Vatican Academy of Sciences, October 1–6, 1962.

———. 1969. "Apollo 11 Observations of a Remarkable Glazing Phenomenon on the Lunar Surface." *Science* 165: 1345–49.

Gooch, Stan. 2008. *The Neanderthal Legacy: Reawakening Our Genetic and Cultural Origins.* Rochester, Vt.: Inner Traditions.

Gorka, Tomasz, Jörg W. E. Fassbinder, and Karsten Lambers. 2007.

"Magnetometry on the Geoglyphs of Palpa and Nasca (Peru)." *Studijné zvesti Archeologického Ustavu Slovenskej Akadémie Vied* 41: 176–79.

Green, James L., and Scott Boardsen. 2006. "Duration and Extent of the Great Auroral Storm of 1859." *Advances in Space Research* 38: 130–35.

Green, James L., Scott Boardsen, Sten Odenwald, John Humble, and Katherine A. Pazamickas. 2006. "Eyewitness Reports of the Great Auroral Storm of 1859." *Advances in Space Research* 38: 145–54.

Gresky, Julia, Juliane Haelm, and Lee Clare. 2017. "Modified Human Crania from Göbekli Tepe Provide Evidence for a New Form of Neolithic Skull Cult." *Science Advances, Research Article* (journal of the American Association for the Advancement of Science), June 28, 10 pages.

Grootes, P. M., M. Stulver, J. W. C. White, S. Johnsen, and J. Jouzel. 1993. "Comparison of Oxygen Isotope Records from the GISP2 and GRIP Greenland Ice Cores." *Nature* 366: 552–54.

Gu, Mile, Christian Weedbrook, Alvaro Perales, and Michael A. Nielsen. 2008. "More Really Is Different." Cornell University Library, e-prints, astrophysics. http://arxiv.org/abs/0809.0151 and http://arxiv.org/PS_cache /arxiv/pdf/0809/0809.0151v1.pdf (article dated August 31, 2008; accessed October 12, 2008).

Guhathakurta, Madhulika (Lika). 2011. "Space Weather Super-Storm: Not IF but WHEN and Extreme Solar Minimum." Presentation to UNCOPUOS [United Nations Committee on the Peaceful Uses of Outer Space] Meeting, Vienna, Austria, February 10, 2011. www.oosa.unvienna.org/pdf/pres /stsc2011/tech-14.pdf (article dated February 10, 2011; accessed July 11, 2011).

Guskova, E. G., O. M. Raspopov, and V. A. Dergachev. 2010. "Visual Evidence of Geomagnetic Excursion?" http://geo.phys.spbu.ru/materials_of_a _conference_2010/P2010/Guskova_et_al_2010.pdf (article dated 2010; accessed June 26, 2011).

Güttler, D., F. Adolphi, J. Beer, N. Bleicher, G. Boswijk, M. Christl, A. Hogg, J. Palmer, C. Vockenhuber, L. Wacker, and J. Wunder. 2015. "Rapid Increase in Cosmogenic ^{14}C in AD 775 Measured in New Zealand Kauri Trees Indicates Short-Lived Increase in ^{14}C Production Spanning Both Hemispheres." *Earth and Planetary Science Letters* 411: 290–97.

Guy, Jacques. 2000. Review of *Rongorongo: The Easter Island Script: History, Traditions, Texts* by Steven Roger Fischer. *Anthropos* 95, no. 1: 262–63.

———. 2011. "The Lunar Calendar of Tablet Mamari." www.netaxs

.com/~trance/mamari.html (undated article; accessed June 28, 2011).

Hainsworth, L. B. 1983. "The Effect of Geophysical Phenomena on Human Health." *Speculations in Science and Technology* 6, no. 5: 439–44.

Haklay, Gil, and Avi Gopher. 2020. "Geometry and Architectural Planning at Göbekli Tepe, Turkey." *Cambridge Archaeological Journal* 30, no. 2: 343–57.

Hammond, Ashley S., Danielle F. Royer, and John G. Fleagle. 2017. "The Omo-Kibish I Pelvis." *Journal of Human Evolution* 108: 199–219.

Harris, Richard. 2009. "These Vintage Threads Are 30,000 Years Old." www .npr.org/templates/story/story.php?storyId=112726804 (article dated September 10, 2009; accessed August 10, 2011).

Harrison, Jeff. 2010. "UA [University of Arizona] Archaeologist, Colleagues Find No Evidence of Catastrophic Impact." http://uanews.org/node/34499 (article dated September 30, 2010; accessed August 8, 2011).

Hassan, Selim. 1949. *The Sphinx: Its History in the Light of Recent Excavations.* Cairo: Government Press.

Haug, Espen Gaarder. 2010. "When Will God Destroy Our Money?" http:// papers.ssrn.com/sol3/papers.cfm?abstract_id=1591768 (article dated April 18, 2010; accessed July 3, 2011).

Haughton, Brian. 2011. "Göbekli Tepe—The World's First Temple?" www .ancient.eu.com/article/234 (article dated May 4, 2011; accessed August 28, 2011).

Haun, Beverley. 2008. *Inventing "Easter Island."* Toronto: University of Toronto Press.

Hautsalo, Janne. 2005. "Study of Aurora Related Sound and Electric Field Effects." Master's thesis, Helsinki University of Technology, Department of Electrical and Communications Engineering, Laboratory of Acoustics and Audio Signal Processing. www.acoustics.hut.fi/projects/aurora /ASoundsNews.html and http://lib.tkk.fi/Dipl/2005/urn007898.pdf (thesis dated June 9, 2005; accessed June 26, 2011).

Hawass, Zahi, and Mark Lehner. 2009. "Drilling under the Sphinx (Featuring Zahi Hawass and Mark Lehner)." www.youtube.com/watch?v=3qGzf ZHWbZE&feature=related (video posted October 15, 2009; accessed August 14, 2011).

Hawksley, Lucinda. 2002. "Introduction." In *Essential Van Gogh* by Josephine Cutts and James Smith, 6–15. Bath, United Kingdom: Parragon Publishing.

Hayakawa, Hisashi, Yasuyuki Mitsuma, Yusuke Ebihara, and Fusa Miyake. 2019. "The Earliest Candidates of Auroral Observations in Assyrian Astrological

Reports: Insights on Solar Activity around 660 BCE." *Astrophysical Journal Letters*, 884, no. 1 (October 7, 2019).

Hayakawa, Hisashi, Paulo Ribeiro, José M. Vaquero, María Cruz Gallego, Delores J. Knipp, Florian Mekhaldi, Ankush Bhaskar, Denny M. Oliveira, Yuta Notsu, Víctor M. S. Carrasco, Ana Caccavari, Bhaskara Veenadhari, Shyamoli Mukherjee, and Yusuke Ebihara. 2020. "The Extreme Space Weather Event in 1903 October/November: An Outburst from the Quiet Sun." *Astrophysical Journal Letters* 897, no. 1. https://iopscience.iop.org /article/10.3847/2041-8213/ab6a18 (article dated June 30, 2020; accessed July 31, 2020).

Haynes, C. Vance, Jr. 2008. "Younger Dryas 'Black Mats' and the Rancholabrean Termination in North America." *Proceedings of the National Academy of Sciences of the United States of America* 105, no. 18: 6520–25.

Head, Martin J., and Philip L. Gibbard. 2015. "Formal Subdivision of the Quaternary System/Period: Past, Present, and Future." *Quaternary International* 383: 4–35.

Heinberg, Richard. 1989. *Memories and Visions of Paradise: Exploring the Universal Myth of a Lost Golden Age*. Foreword by Roger Williams Wescott. Los Angeles: Jeremy P. Tarcher.

Heine, Johan, and Michael Tellinger. 2008. "Adams Calendar: Discovering the Oldest Man-Made Structure on Earth. 75,000 Years Ago." www.zuluplanet. com/intro/adamscalendar.pdf (article dated 2008; accessed September 11, 2011).

Heldal, Tom, and Per Storemyr. 2015. "Fire on the Rocks: Heat as an Agent in Ancient Egyptian Hard Stone Quarrying." *Engineering Geology for Society and Territory* 5: 291–95.

Henley, Tracy B. 2018. "Introducing Göbekli Tepe to Psychology." *Review of General Psychology* 22, no. 4: 477–84.

Heussner, Ki Mae. 2010. "Phew! 2012 Doomsday Date May Be Wrong." http:// abcnews.go.com/Technology/mayan-calendars-2012-doomsday-prophecy -wrong/story?id=11926347 (article dated October 20, 2010; accessed June 8, 2011).

Heyerdahl, Thor. 1989. *Easter Island: The Mystery Solved*. New York: Random House.

Heyerdahl, Thor, and Edwin N. Ferdon Jr., eds. 1961. *Reports of the Norwegian Archaeological Expedition to Easter Island and the East Pacific*. Vol. 1, *Archaeology of Easter Island*. Chicago: Rand McNally.

————. 1965. *Reports of the Norwegian Archaeological Expedition to Easter Island and the East Pacific*. Vol. 2, *Miscellaneous Papers*. Chicago: Rand McNally.

High-frequency Active Auroral Research Program [HAARP]. 2011. www .haarp.alaska.edu (website dated 2011; accessed August 12, 2011).

Higley, Sarah, text and trans. 2010. *"PREIDDEU ANNWN:* 'The Spoils of Annwn.'" www.lib.rochester.edu/camelot/annwn.htm (undated article; accessed April 25, 2010).

Hillman, Yael, Michael M. Shara, Dina Prialnik, and Array Kovetz. 2020. "A Unified Theory of Cataclysmic Variable Evolution from Feedback-Dominated Numerical Simulations." *Nature Astronomy*, March 23. www .nature.com/articles/s41550-020-1062-y (article dated March 23, 2020; accessed March 27, 2020).

Hilman Natawidjaja, Danny. 2013. *Plato Never Lied: Atlantis Is in Indonesia*. Jakarta: Booknesia.

Ho, Mae-Wan. 2011. "DNA Sequence Reconstituted from Water Memory?" www.i-sis.org.uk/DNA_sequence_reconstituted_from_Water_Memory .php (article dated July 20, 2011; accessed August 11, 2011).

Hodder, Ian, and Lynn Meskell. 2011. "A 'Curious and Sometimes a Trifle Macabre Artistry': Some Aspects of Symbolism in Neolithic Turkey." *Current Anthropology* 52, no. 2 (April): 235–63; including comments by outside readers, 251–58.

Hodgson, Richard. 1859. "On a Curious Appearance Seen in the Sun." *Monthly Notices of the Royal Astronomical Society* 20: 15–16. http://articles.adsabs. harvard.edu/full/seri/MNRAS/0020//0000015.000.html (article dated 1859; accessed July 11, 2011).

Hoek, Wim Z. 2008. "The Last Glacial-Interglacial Transition." *Episodes* 31, no. 2: 226–29.

Hoffman, Donald D. 2008. "Conscious Realism and the Mind-Body Problem." *Mind & Matter* 6, no. 1: 87–121.

Hoffman, Donald D., and Chetan Prakash. 2014. "Objects of Consciousness." *Frontiers in Psychology* 5, article 577: 22 pages.

Holliday, Vance T., Todd Surovell, David J. Meltzer, Donald K. Grayson, and Mark Boslough. 2014. "The Younger Dryas Impact Hypothesis: A Cosmic Catastrophe." *Journal of Quaternary Science* 29, no. 6: 515–30.

Holliday, Vance T., Todd Surovell, and Eileen Johnson. 2016. "A Blind Test of the Younger Dryas Impact Hypothesis." *PLOS One* [Public Library of Science], July 8, 1–13. http://journals.plos.org/plosone

/article?id=10.1371%2Fjournal.pone.0155470. (Accessed October 5, 2016)

Horley, Paul. 2009. Review of *Words Out of Wood: Proposals for the Decipherment of the Easter Island Script* by M. de Laat. *Rapa Nui Journal* 23, no. 2: 165–68.

House of Commons Science and Technology Committee. 2011. "Eighth Report—Peer Review in Scientific Publications." www.publications.parliament.uk/pa/cm201012/cmselect/cmsctech/856/85602.htm (report dated July 18, 2011; accessed August 7, 2011).

Hoyt, Douglas V., and Kenneth H. Schatten. 1998. "Group Sunspot Number: A New Solar Activity Reconstruction." *Solar Physics* 179, no. 1: 189–219.

Hoyt, Douglas V., Kenneth H. Schatten, and Elizabeth Nesmes-Ribes. 1994. "The One Hundredth Year of Rudolf Wolf's Death: Do We Have the Correct Reconstruction of Solar Activity?" *Geophysical Research Letters* 21, no. 18: 2067–70. www.leif.org/EOS/94GL01698.pdf (article dated September 1, 1994; accessed September 9, 2011).

Hua, Quan, Mike Barbetti, and Andrzej Z. Rakowski. 2013. "Atmospheric Radiocarbon for the Period 1950–2010." *Radiocarbon* 55, no. 4: 2059–72.

Hutchinson, Sarah Lyn. 2008. "The Memory of Water: A Critical Analysis of the Science behind a Homeopathic Theory." www.homeopathycanada.com /sites/default/files/research-papers/irp-sarah-hutchinson.pdf (article dated April 25, 2008; accessed August 12, 2011).

Hutton, William [pseudonym?], and Jonathan Eagle [pseudonym?]. 2004. *Earth's Catastrophic Past and Future: A Scientific Analysis of Information Channeled by Edgar Cayce.* Boca Raton, Fla.: Universal Publishers.

International Atomic Energy Agency [IAEA]. 2020. "Operational and Long-Term Shutdown Reactors." https://pris.iaea.org/PRIS/WorldStatistics /OperationalReactorsByCountry.aspx (article dated 2020; accessed April 9, 2020).

International Business Times. 2011a. "Solar Event That May Have Caused Last Ice Age Happening Again?" http://losangeles.ibtimes.com/articles /162919/20110614/solar-flare-ice-age-global-warming-sun.htm (article dated June 14, 2011; accessed July 5, 2011).

———. 2011b. "Solar Storms Could Cause Power Outages, Scrambled GPS, Communications Failure." www.ibtimes.com/articles/194172/20110808 /solar-storm-flare-electricity-risk-grid-caution-danger-magnetosphere-earth -electricity-space-geomagn.htm (article dated August 8, 2011; accessed August 8, 2011).

Ioannidis, Alexander G., Javier Blanco-Portillo, Karla Sandova, Erika Hagelberg, Juan Francisco Miquel-Poblete, J. Víctor Moreno-Mayar, Juan Esteban Rodríguez-Rodríguez, Consuelo D. Quinto-Cortés, Kathryn Auckland, Tom Parks, Kathryn Robson, Adrian V. S. Hill, María C. Avila-Arcos, Alexandra Sockell, Julian R. Homburger, Genevieve L. Wojcik, Kathleen C. Barnes, Luisa Herrera, Soledad Berríos, Mónica Acuña, Elena Llop, Celeste Eng, Scott Huntsman, Esteban G. Burchard, Christopher R. Gignoux, Lucía Cifuentes, Ricardo A. Verdugo, Mauricio Moraga, Alexander J. Mentzer, Carlos D. Bustamante, and Andrés Moreno-Estrada. 2020. "Native American Gene Flow into Polynesia Predating Easter Island Settlement." *Nature* 583 (July): 572–77, 6 pages.

Israde-Alcántara, Isabel, James L. Bischoff, Gabriela Domínguez-Vázquez, Hong-Chun Li, Paul S. DeCarli, Ted E. Bunch, James H. Wittke, James C. Weaver, Richard B. Firestone, Allen West, James P. Kennett, Chris Mercer, Sujing Xie, Eric K. Richman, Charles R. Kinzie, and Wendy S. Wolbach. 2012. "Evidence from Central Mexico Supporting the Younger Dryas Extraterrestrial Impact Hypothesis." *Proceedings of the National Academy of Sciences of the United States of America,* online publication prior to print version. www.pnas.org/content/early/2012/03/01/1110614109 .abstract (article dated March 5, 2012; accessed March 24, 2012).

Izzo, Luca, Massimo della Valle, Alessandro Ederoclite, and Martin Henze. 2014. "On the 2011 Outburst of the Recurrent Nova T Pyxidis." https:// arxiv.org/pdf/1407.7076.pdf (dated July 26, 2014; accessed March 27, 2020).

Jaggard, Victoria. 2011. "As Sun Storms Ramp Up, Electric Grid Braces for Impact." http://news.nationalgeographic.com/news/energy/2011/08/110803 -solar-flare-storm-electricity-grid-risk/ (article dated August 3, 2011; accessed August 8, 2011).

Jahn, Robert G. 1996. "Information, Consciousness, and Health." *Alternative Therapies* 2, no. 3: 32–38. Excerpts reprinted in *The Parapsychology Revolution: A Concise Anthology of Paranormal and Psychical Research,* compilation and commentary by Robert M. Schoch and Logan Yonavjak, 147–63. New York: Jeremy P. Tarcher/Penguin, 2008.

Jahn, Robert G., Paul Devereux, and Michael Ibison. 1995. "Acoustical Resonances of Assorted Ancient Structures." International Consciousness Research Laboratories, ICRL Report #95.1: 58 pages.

Jarboe, Nicholas A., Robert S. Coe, and Jonathan M. G. Glen. 2011. "Evidence from Lava Flows for Complex Polarity Transitions: The New Composite Steens Mountain Reversal Record." *Geophysical Journal International* 186: 580–602.

Jarry, Alfred. 1965. *Selected Works of Alfred Jarry.* Edited by Roger Shattuck and Simon Watson Taylor. New York: Grove Press. (On page 99 appears the following line, from a poem by Alfred Jarry [1873–1907] titled "Through the Door . . . " [This is the entire title of the poem]: "In the air hover hieroglyphs, darkly enthralling"; translated from the original French by S. W. Taylor. This reminds us of the plasma configurations seen during a solar outburst, as recorded by petroglyphs around the globe and the rongo-rongo script on Easter Island. Although he never pointed out this particular quotation to me, I mention it in honor of John Anthony West, who took a very serious interest in the works of Jarry.)

Jarus, Owen. 2012. "'World's Oldest Temple' May Have Been Cosmopolitan Center." www.livescience.com/19085-world-oldest-temple-tools-pilgrimage.html (article dated March 15, 2012; accessed March 24, 2012).

Jaynes, Julian. 1976/1990. *The Origin of Consciousness in the Breakdown of the Bicameral Mind.* Boston: Houghton Mifflin. Originally published in 1976; edition with afterword, 1990.

Jenkins, Jere H., and Ephraim Fischbach. 2008. "Perturbation of Nuclear Decay Rates during the Solar Flare of 13 December 2006." Cornell University Library, e-prints, astrophysics. http://arxiv.org/abs/0808.3156 and http://arxiv.org/ftp/arxiv/papers/0808/0808.3156.pdf (article submitted August 22, 2008; accessed October 11, 2008).

Jenkins, Jere H., Ephraim Fischbach, John B. Buncher, John T. Gruenwald, Dennis E. Krause, and Joshua J. Mattes. 2008. "Evidence for Correlations between Nuclear Decay Rates and Earth-Sun Distance." Cornell University Library, e-prints, astrophysics. Available from http://arxiv.org/abs/0808.3283 and http://arxiv.org/PS_cache/arxiv/pdf/0808/0808.3283v1.pdf (article submitted August 25, 2008; accessed October 11, 2008).

Jenkins, John Major. 2003. "Mayan Mysteries: Galactic Alignments in Ancient Traditions and the Future of Humanity." *New Dawn*, no. 76. www.newdawnmagazine.com/articles/Galactic%20Alignments.html (article dated January–February 2003; accessed July 2, 2011).

———. 2006. "The Mayan Lord of Creation and 2012." *New Dawn*, no. 97. www.newdawnmagazine.com/articles/the-mayan-lord-of-creation-and-2012 (article dated July–August 2006; accessed July 2, 2011).

———. 2010. "The Mayan Calendar and 2012: Why Should We Care?" *New Dawn,* special issue 4. www.newdawnmagazine.com/articles/the-mayan -calendar-and-2012-why-should-we-care (article dated 2010; accessed July 2, 2011).

———. 2011. "Steps in Understanding Calendar Continuity and in Verifying the Correct Correlation." *The Center for 2012 Studies,* Note 18, 1–18. www.thecenterfor2012studies.com/2012center-note18.pdf (article dated July 31, 2011; accessed May 5, 2012).

Jeremiah, John. 1870. "Early Mention of the Aurora Borealis." *Nature 3* (December): 174–75.

Jerusalem Bible. 1968. *The Jerusalem Bible,* with abridged introductions and notes; Alexander Jones, general editor. London: Darton, Longman and Todd.

Johnson, Lauren M. 2020. "A Temple That Predates Stonehenge Reveals Architectural Planning May Be Older Than We Think." https://www.cnn .com/2020/05/16/world/gobekli-tepe-building-discovery-trnd-scn/index .html (article dated May 16, 2020; accessed May 16, 2020).

Jordan, Douglas, with contributions from Terrence Tumpey and Barbara Jester. 2019. "The Deadliest Flu: The Complete Story of the Discovery and Reconstruction of the 1918 Pandemic Virus." *Centers for Disease Control and Prevention.* www.cdc.gov/flu/pandemic-resources/reconstruction -1918-virus.html (article last revised December 17, 2019; accessed March 22, 2020).

Joseph, Lawrence E. 2008. *Apocalypse 2012: An Investigation into Civilization's End.* New York: Broadway Books. Originally published 2007; 2008 edition with new epilogue.

Joseph, Michael L. 2012. "A Geochemical Analysis of Fulgurites: From the Inner Glass to the Outer Crust." Master's thesis, University of South Florida, College of Arts and Sciences, Department of Geology, i–vi + 1–102 pages.

Jull, A. J. Timothy, Irina P. Panyushkina, Todd E. Lange, Vladimir V. Kukarskih, Vladimir S. Myglan, Kelley J. Clark, Matthew W. Salzer, George S. Burr, and Steven W. Leavitt. 2014. "Excursions in the ^{14}C Record at A.D. 774–775 in Tree Rings from Russia and America." *Geophysical Research Letters* 41: 3004–10.

Jull, A. J. Timothy, Irina Panyushkina, Fusa Miyake, Kimiaki Masuda, Toshio Nakamura, Takumi Mitsutani, Todd E. Lange, Richard J. Cruz, Chris Baisan, Robert Janovics, Tamas Varga, and Mihály Molnár. 2018. "More Rapid 14C Excursions in the Tree-Ring Record: A Record of Different

Kind of Solar Activity at about 800 BC?" *Radiocarbon* 60, no. 4: 1237–48; Selected Papers from the 2nd Radiocarbon in the Environment Conference, Debrecen, Hungary, July 3–7, 2017.

Kantharia, N. G., Prasun Dutta, Nirupam Roy, G. C. Anupama, C. H. Ishwara-Chandra, A. Chitale, T. P. Prabhu, D. P. K. Banerjee, and N. M. Ashok. 2016. "Insights into the Evolution of Symbiotic Recurrent Novae from Radio Synchrotron Emission: V745 Scorpii and RS Ophiuchi." *Monthly Notices of the Royal Astronomical Society* 456: L49–L53.

Kazan, Casey. 2009. "December 27, 2004—The Most Powerful Space Blast Ever Measured Hit Earth." www.dailygalaxy.com/my_weblog/2009/12 /december-27-2004-the-most-powerful-space-blast-ever-to-hit-earth-.html (article dated December 26, 2009; accessed June 29, 2011).

Keigwin, L., S. Klotsko, N. Zhao, B. Reilly, L. Giosan, and N. W. Driscoll. 2018. "Deglacial Floods in the Beaufort Sea Preceded Younger Dryas Cooling." *Nature Geoscience* 11: 599–604. www.nature.com/articles/s41561-018 -0169-6 (article dated July 9, 2018; accessed March 27, 2020).

Kennett, Douglas J., James P. Kennett, Allen West, G. James West, Ted E. Bunch, Brendan J. Culleton, Jon M. Erlandson, Shane S. Que Hee, John R. Johnson, Chris Mercer, Feng Shen, Marilee Sellers, Thomas W. Stafford Jr., Adrienne Stich, James C. Weaver, James H. Wittke, and Wendy S. Wolbach. 2009. "Shock-Synthesized Hexagonal Diamonds in Younger Dryas Boundary Sediments." *Proceedings of the National Academy of Sciences of the United States of America* 106, no. 31: 12623–28; *PNAS Early Edition*, www.pnas.org/cgi/doi/10.1073/pnas.0906374106 (accessed June 22, 2020).

Kennett, James P., Douglas J. Kennett, Brendan J. Culleton, J. Emili Aura Tortosa, James L. Bischoff, Ted E. Bunch, I. Randolph Daniel Jr., Jon M. Erlandson, David Ferraro, Richard B. Firestone, Albert C. Goodyear, Isabel Israde-Alcántara, John R. Johnson, Jesús F. Jordá Pardo, David R. Kimbel, Malcolm A. LeCompte, Neal H. Lopinot, William C. Mahaney, Andrew M. T. Moore, Christopher R. Moore, Jack H. Ray, Thomas W. Stafford Jr., Kenneth Barnett Tankersley, James H. Wittke, Wendy S. Wolbach, and Allen West. 2015. "Bayesian Chronological Analyses Consistent with Synchronous Age of 12,835–12,735 Cal B.P. for Younger Dryas Boundary on Four Continents." *Proceedings of the National Academy of Sciences of the United States of America,* 10 pages. *PNAS Early Edition,* www.pnas.org/cgi /doi/10.1073/pnas.1507146112 (accessed 31 July 2015).

Khalil, Mohamed Ahmed, Abbas Mohamed Abbas, Fernando A. Monteiro Santos, Hany S. A. Mesbah, and Usama Massoud. 2010. "VLF-EM Study for Archaeological Investigation of the Labyrinth Mortuary Temple Complex at Hawara Area, Egypt." *Near Surface Geophysics* 8: 203–12.

Kiffer, Frederico, Marjan Boerma, and Antiño Allen. 2019. "Behavioral Effects of Space Radiation: A Comprehensive Review of Animal Studies." *Life Sciences in Space Research* 21: 1–21.

Kinsley, Austin. 2015. "10,000 Year Old Stonehenge Monument." www .silentearth.org/10000-year-old-stonehenge-monument/ (article dated February 20, 2015; accessed April 12, 2020).

Kjær, Kurt H., Nicolaj K. Larsen, Tobias Binder, Anders A. Bjørk, Olaf Eisen, Mark A. Fahnestock, Svend Funder, Adam A. Garde, Henning Haack, Veit Helm, Michael Houmark-Nielsen, Kristian K. Kjeldsen, Shfaqat A. Khan, Horst Machguth, Iain McDonald, Mathieu Morlighem, Jérémie Mouginot, John D. Paden, Tod E. Waight, Christian Weikusat, Eske Willerslev, and Joseph A. MacGregor. 2018. "A Large Impact Crater beneath Hiawatha Glacier in Northwest Greenland." *Science Advances, Research Article,* AAAS [American Association for the Advancement of Science], November 14, 11 pages.

Kjellgren, Eric, ed. 2001. *Splendid Isolation*: *Art of Easter Island*. With contributions by J. A. Van Tilburg and A. L. Kaeppler. New York: The Metropolitan Museum of Art/New Haven-London: Yale University Press.

Kleiner, Johannes, and Sean Tull. 2020. "The Mathematical Structure of the Intergrated Information Theory." https://arxiv.org/pdf/2002.07655.pdf (article dated February 18, 2020; accessed May 18, 2020).

Knox, Tom [Sean Thomas]. 2009a. "Do These Mysterious Stones Mark the Site of the Garden of Eden?" www.dailymail.co.uk/sciencetech/article-1157784 /Do-mysterious-stones-mark-site-Garden-Eden.html (article dated March 5, 2009; accessed April 23, 2009).

———. 2009b. *The Genesis Secret*. New York: Viking. (Novel that includes Göbekli Tepe as part of the setting and plot.)

Kolnegari, Mahmood, Mohammad Naserifard, Mandana Hazrati, and Matan Shelomi. 2020. "Squatting (Squatter) Mantis Man: A Prehistoric Praying Mantis Petroglyph in Iran." *Journal of Orthoptera Research* 29, no. 1: 41–44.

Kovalyov, Mikhail. 2019. "On the Correlation of Seismic Activity to Syzygies." *Russian Journal of Earth Sciences* 19, ES1005 (14 February 2019): 20 pages.

Krukowski, Karen, Katherine Grue, Elma S. Frias, John Pietrykowski, Tamako

Jones, Gregory Nelson, and Susanna Rosia. 2018. "Female Mice Are Protected from Space Radiation-Induced Maladaptive Responses." *Brain, Behavior, and Immunity* 74: 106–20.

Kubrick, Stanley, and Arthur C. Clarke. 1968. *2001: A Space Odyssey*. Film. Directed by Stanley Kubrick. Beverly Hills, Calif.: Metro-Goldwyn-Mayer [MGM] Inc.

Kuhn, Thomas S. 1962. *The Structure of Scientific Revolutions*. Chicago: University of Chicago Press. Fourth impression printed 1965.

Kulagin, Ing. V. V. [husband of N. S. Kulagina]. 1971. "Nina S. Kulagina." Paper presented at the Symposium of Psychotronics, Prague, Czechoslovakia, September 25, 1970. *Journal of Paraphysics* [published by Paraphysical Laboratory, Downton, Wiltshire, England] 5, nos. 1–2: 54–62.

Kurbatov, Andrei V., Paul A. Mayewski, Jørgen P. Steffensen, Allen West, Douglas J. Kennett, James P. Kennett, Ted E. Bunch, Mike Handley, Douglas S. Introne, Shane S. Que Hee, Christopher Mercer, Marilee Sellers, Feng Shen, Sharon B. Sneed, James C. Weaver, James H. Wittke, Thomas W. Stafford Jr., John J. Donovan, Sujing Xie, Joshua J. Razink, Adrienne Stich, Charles R. Kinzie, and Wendy S. Wolbach. 2010. "Discovery of a Nanodiamond-Rich Layer in the Greenland Ice Sheet." *Journal of Glaciology* 56, no. 199: 749–59.

Kusch, Heinrich, and Ingrid Kusch. 2011. *Tore zur Unterwelt: Das Geheimnis der unterirdischen Gänge aus uralter Zeit*. Graz, Austria: V. F. Sammler. First edition published 2009.

Ladyman, Juanita A. R. 2011. "*Dryas octopetala* L. White Mountain Avens." www.fs.fed.us/global/iitf/pdf/shrubs/Dryas%20octopetala.pdf (undated article; accessed August 8, 2011).

Laine, Unto K. 2004. "Denoising and Analysis of Audio Recordings Made during the April 6–7 2000 Geomagnetic Storm by Using a Non-Professional *Ad Hoc* Setup." Presented at the Joint Baltic-Nordic Acoustics Meeting 2004, Mariehamn, Åland. www.acoustics.hut.fi/projects/aurora/BNAM-ukl.pdf (article dated June 8–10, 2004; accessed 26 June 2011).

Laroche, Emmanuel. 1960. *Les Hiéroglyphes Hittites, Première Partie, L'écriture*. Paris: Éditions du Centre National de la Recherche Scientifque.

Laszlo, Ervin. 2003. *The Connectivity Hypothesis: Foundations of an Integral Science of Quantum, Cosmos, Life, and Consciousness*. New York: State University of New York Press.

———. 2004. *Science and the Akashic Field: An Integral Theory of Everything*. Rochester, Vt.: Inner Traditions.

LaViolette, Paul A. 1985. "Evidence of High Cosmic Dust Concentrations in Late Pleistocene Polar Ice (20,000–14,000 Years BP)." *Meteoritics* 20: 545–58. www.starburstfound.org/downloads/superwave/Meteoritics.pdf (article dated September 30, 1985; accessed August 26, 2011). Revised chronology available at www.starburstfound.org/downloads/superwave /Meteoritics.html (accessed August 26, 2011).

———. 1995. *Beyond the Big Bang: Ancient Myth and the Science of Continuous Creation.* Rochester, Vt.: Park Street Press.

———. 2005. *Earth Under Fire: Humanity's Survival of the Ice Age.* Rochester, Vt.: Bear & Company.

———. 2006. *Decoding the Message of the Pulsars: Intelligent Communication from the Galaxy.* Rochester, Vt.: Bear & Company.

———. 2009. "A Galactic Superwave Hazard Alert Update." www.starburstfound .org/downloads/superwave/Nexus2009.pdf and http://starburstfound.org /paper-archive (manuscript version consulted; article dated August 2009; accessed June 6, 2011).

———. 2011a. "Evidence for a Solar Flare Cause of the Pleistocene Mass Extinction." *Radiocarbon* 53, no. 2: 303–23. http://starburstfound.org /downloads/superwave/SPE.html and www.starburstfound.org/downloads /superwave/SPE.pdf (manuscript version consulted; article dated June 1, 2011; accessed June 6, 2011).

———. 2011b. "Lunar Evidence of Past Solar Activity." http://starburstfound. org/2011/02 (article dated February 2011; accessed July 5, 2011). Article excerpted from LaViolette's 1983 Ph.D. dissertation, "Galactic Explosions, Cosmic Dust Invasions, and Climatic Change."

Lee, Georgia. 1992. *The Rock Art of Easter Island: Symbols of Power, Prayers to the Gods.* Vol. 17 of *Monumenta Archaeologica,* I–XIV, 1–226. Los Angeles: University of California, Los Angeles, the Institute of Archaeology.

Lee, K. C., M. R. Sprague, B. J. Sussman, J. Nunn, N. K. Langford, X.-M. Jin, T. Champion, P. Michelberger, K. F. Reim, D. England, D. Jaksch, and I. A. Walmsley. 2011. "Entangling Macroscopic Diamonds at Room Temperature." *Science* 334, no. 6060: 1253–56.

Lehman, Helena. 2008. *The Language of God in Prophecy.* 10th ed. Elmwood Park, Ill.: Pillar of Enoch Ministry.

Lehner, Mark. 1974. *The Egyptian Heritage, Based on the Edgar Cayce Readings.* Virginia Beach, Va.: A.R.E. Press.

Lewis, Hal. 2010. "Professor Emeritus Hal Lewis Resigns from American

Physical Society." http://my.telegraph.co.uk/reasonmclucus/reasonmclucus /15835660/professor-emiritus-hal-lewis-resigns-from-american-physical -society (letter dated October 9, 2010; accessed August 20, 2011).

Lewis-Williams, David, and David Pearce. 2005. *Inside the Neolithic Mind: Consciousness, Cosmos, and the Realm of the Gods.* London: Thames & Hudson.

Liesowska, Anna. 2015. "Stone Bracelet Is Oldest Ever Found in the World." http://siberiantimes.com/science/casestudy/features/f0100-stone-bracelet -is-oldest-ever-found-in-the-world/ (article dated May 7, 2015; accessed April 12, 2020).

Lindgaard, Eva. 2013. "Style: A Strait Jacket on Hunters' Rock Art Research?" *Adoranten* 2013: 57–68.

Liu, Yi, Zhao-feng Zhang, Zi-cheng Peng, Ming-xing Ling, Chuan-Chou Shen, Wei-guo Liu, Xiao-chun Sun, Cheng-de Shen, Ke-xin Liu, and Weidong Sun. 2014. "Mysterious Abrupt Carbon-14 Increase in Coral Contributed by a Comet." *Scientific Reports / Nature*, January 16, 4 pages.

Livermore, Philip W., Christopher C. Finlay, and Matthew Bayliff. 2020. "Recent North Magnetic Pole Acceleration Towards Siberia Caused by Flux Lobe Elongation." *Nature Geoscience* 13: 387–91.

Llewellyn-Jones, F. 1963. "The Mechanism of Electrode Erosion in Electrical Discharges, Physical Basis of the Low Erosion Rate of the Platinum Metals." *Platinum Metals Review* 7, no. 2: 58–65.

Lockyer, Norman. 1894. *The Dawn of Astronomy.* New York: Macmillan. Reprinted, with a preface by Giorgio de Santillana, Cambridge, Mass.: MIT Press, 1964.

London Dialectical Society. 1873. *Report on Spiritualism, of the Committee of the London Dialectical Society, Together with the Evidence, Oral and Written, and a Selection from the Correspondence.* London: J. Burns.

Longo, Michelle. 2010. "Scientist of the Week: Gerardo Aldana." www.laboratory equipment.com/news-sow-aldana-101410.aspx?xmlmenuid=51 (article dated October 14, 2010; accessed October 20, 2010).

Loomis, Elias. 1860. "The Great Auroral Exhibition of August 28th to September 4th, 1859–3rd Article." *American Journal of Science and Arts,* 2nd ser., 39: 249–66.

Love, Jeffrey J., and Jeremy N. Thomas. 2013. "Insignificant Solar-Terrestrial Triggering of Earthquakes." *Geophysical Research Letters* 40: 1165–70.

Love, Jeffrey J., Hisashi Hayakawa, and Edward W. Cliver. 2019. "Intensity and Impact of the New York Railroad Superstorm of May 1921." *Space Weather* 17: 1281–92.

Lovett, Richard A. 2011. "What If the Biggest Solar Storm on Record Happened Today? Repeat of 1859 Carrington Event Would Devastate Modern World, Experts Say." http://news.nationalgeographic.com/news/2011/03/110302 -solar-flares-sun-storms-earth-danger-carrington-event-science/ (article dated March 2, 2011; accessed August 8, 2011).

Lukes, P., M. Clupek, V. Babicky, P. Sunka, J. D. Skalny, M. Stefecka, J. Novak, and Z. Malkova. 2006. "Erosion of Needle Electrodes in Pulsed Corona Discharge in Water." *Czechoslovak Journal of Physics* 56, suppl. B: B916–B924.

Ma, Xiao-song, Stefan Zotter, Johannes Kofler, Rupert Ursin, Thomas Jennewein, Časlav Bruknerl, and Anton Zeilinger. 2012. "Experimental Delayed-Choice Entanglement Swapping." *Nature Physics* (published online, www.nature.com/naturephysics, April 22; accessed June 19, 2012), 6 pages.

Maccoby, Nora. 2010. "Electromagnetic Pulses Could Destroy Power Grids and Redefine 'Modern' Life." www.thewip.net/contributors/2010/06/electro magnetic_pulses_could_d.html (article dated June 15, 2010; accessed June 24, 2011).

Mackey, Richard. 2007. "Rhodes Fairbridge and the Idea that the Solar System Regulates the Earth's Climate." *Journal of Coastal Research,* special issue 50: 955–68. www.griffith.edu.au/conference/ics2007/pdf/ICS176.pdf (article dated 2007; accessed July 10, 2011).

Maehara, Hiroyuki, Takuya Shibayama, Shota Notsu, Yuta Notsu, Takashi Nagao, Satoshi Kusaba, Satoshi Honda, Daisaku Nogami, and Kazunari Shibata. 2012. "Superflares on Solar-Type Stars." *Nature* 485: 478–81.

Maestri, Nicoletta. 2011. "Textiles from Guitarrero Cave: Earliest Examples of Agave Fiber Textiles." http://archaeology.about.com/od/textiles/a /Guitarrero-Textiles.htm (article dated 2011; accessed August 10, 2011).

Magli, Giulio. 2004. "On the Possible Discovery of Precessional Effects in Ancient Astronomy." http://arxiv.org/ftp/physics/papers/0407/0407108 .pdf (article dated 2004; accessed June 17, 2010).

———. 2009. *Mysteries and Discoveries of Archaeoastronomy: From Giza to Easter Island.* New York: Copernicus Books.

Mahaney, W. C., V. Kalm, D. H. Krinsley, P. Tricart, S. Schwartz, J. Dohm, K. J. Kim, B. Karpran, M. W. Milner, R. Beukens, S. Boccia, G. V. Hancock, K. M. Hart, and B. Kelleher. 2010. "Evidence from the Northwestern

Venezuelan Andes for Extraterrestrial Impact: The Black Mat Enigma."
Geomorphology 116, nos. 1–2: 48–57. http://cat.inist.fr/?aModele=afficheN
&cpsidt=22525087 (abstract; article dated 2010; accessed August 8, 2011).

Maki, David L, Sigrid Arnott, and Mike Bergervoet. 2015. "Lightning Induced
Remanent Magnetization at the Buffalo Slough Burial Mound Complex."
Minnesota Archaeologist 74: 30–47.

Malhi, Yadvinder. 2017. "The Concept of the Anthropocene." *Annual Review of
Environment and Resources* 42, no. 1: 77–104.

Malville, J. McKim. 1998. "Oldest Astronomical Megalith Alignment
Discovered in Southern Egypt by Science Team." www.colorado.edu/news
/releases/1998/03/31/oldest-astronomical-megalith-alignment-discovered-
southern-egypt-science (press release, dated March 31, 1998; accessed
March 16, 2012).

Mandeville, Michael Wells. 1995–1999. "The Hall of Records." www.michael
mandeville.com/phoenix/hallofrecords/hallrecordsfront.htm#horprophecy
(website dated 1995–1999; accessed August 15, 2011).

Manichev, Vjacheslav I., and Alexander G. Parkhomenko. 2008. "Geological
Aspect of the Problem of Dating the Great Egyptian Sphinx Construction."
In *Geoarchaeology and Archaeomineralogy, Proceedings of the International
Conference, 29–30 October 2008,* edited by R. I. Kostov, B. Gaydarska, and
M. Gurova, 308–11. Sofia, Bulgaria: St. Ivan Rilski.

Mann, Charles C. 2011. "The Birth of Religion." National Geographic 219,
no. 6: 34–59. http://ngm.nationalgeographic.com/2011/06/gobekli-tepe
/mann-text (article dated June 2011; accessed August 29, 2011). Photographs
by Vincent J. Musi.

Marchitelli, Vito, Paolo Harabaglia, Claudia Troise, and Giuseppe De Natale.
2020. "On the Correlation between Solar Activity and Large Earthquakes
Worldwide." *Scientific Reports / Nature,* July 13, 2020, 10 pages. (As this
book was going to press in late September 2020, a related paper by Vito
Marchitelli, Claudia Troise, Paolo Harabaglia, Barbara Valenzano, and
Giuseppe De Natale, titled "On the Long Range Clustering of Global
Seismicity and its Correlation with Solar Activity: A New Perspective for
Earthquake Forecasting," was announced as scheduled for publication in
Frontiers of Earth Science.)

Markey, Sean. 2006. "Pyramid in Bosnia—Huge Hoax or Colossal Find?"
http://news.nationalgeographic.com/news/2006/05/pyramidbosnia-1.html
(article dated May 12, 2006; accessed July 7, 2011).

Marshack, Alexander. 1972. *The Roots of Civilization*. New York: McGraw-Hill.

Marusek, James A. 2010. "The Sun Is Undergoing a State Change." www
.breadandbutterscience.com/StateChange.pdf (article dated March–
April 2010; accessed July 4, 2011). Also published as "El Sol y el Cambio
Climático" [The sun and the climate change]. *Athanor,* March–April 2010.
www.athanor.es.

Matloff, Gregory L. 2016. "Can Panpsychism Become an Observational
Science?" *Journal of Consciousness Exploration & Research* 7, no. 7: 524–43.

Mattson, Barbara. 2010. "The Sun's Corona." http://imagine.gsfc.nasa.gov/docs
/science/mysteries_l1/corona.html (article dated January 28, 2010; accessed
August 12, 2011).

Mayewski, P. A., S. B. Sneed, S. D. Birkel, A. V. Kurbatov, and K. A. Maasch.
2014. "Holocene Warming Marked by Abrupt Onset of Longer Summers
and Reduced Storm Frequency around Greenland." *Journal of Quaternary
Science* 29, no. 1: 99–104.

Mayewski, Paul A., Loren D. Meeker, Mark S. Twickler, Sallie Whitlow,
Qinzhao Yang, W. Berry Lyons, and Michael Prentice. 1997. "Major
Features and Forcing of High-Latitude Northern Hemisphere Atmospheric
Circulation Using a 110,000-Year-Long Glaciochemical Series." *Journal of
Geophysical Research* 102, no. C12: 26, 345–26, 366 (November 30, 1997).

Mazière, Francis. 1968. *Mysteries of Easter Island*. New York: W. W. Norton.
French edition, *Fantastique Île de Pâques,* Paris: Robert Laffont, 1965.

McCracken, K. G., G. A. M. Dreschhoff, D. F. Smart, and M. A. Shea. 2001a.
"Solar Cosmic Ray Events for the Period 1561–1994. 2. The Gleissberg
Periodicity." *Journal of Geophysical Research* 106, no. A10: 21,599–609.

McCracken, K. G., G. A. M. Dreschhoff, E. J. Zeller, D. F. Smart, and
M. A. Shea. 2001b. "Solar Cosmic Ray Events for the Period 1561–1994.
1. Identification in Polar Ice, 1561–1950." *Journal of Geophysical Research*
106, no. A10: 21,585–98.

McKie, Robin. 2002. "Sun's Rays to Roast Earth as Poles Flip." www.guardian
.co.uk/world/2002/nov/10/science.research (article dated November 10,
2002; accessed July 16, 2011).

McLaughlin, Shawn. 2007. *The Complete Guide to Easter Island*. 2nd ed. Los
Osos, Calif.: Easter Island Foundation.

McQueen, Humphrey. 2011. "Historians—V. Gordon Childe." http://home
.alphalink.com.au/~loge27/hist_ns/historian_v_gordon.htm (undated article; accessed July 10, 2011).

Mekhaldi, F., J. R. McConnell, F. Adolphi, M. M. Arienzo, N. J. Chellman, O. J. Maselli, A. D. Moy, C. T. Plummer, M. Sigl, and R. Muscheler. 2017. "No Coincident Nitrate Enhancement Events in Polar Ice Cores Following the Largest Known Solar Storms." *Journal of Geophysical Research: Atmospheres* 122: 11,900–11,913.

Melka, Tomi S. 2009. "Some Considerations about the *Kohau Rongorongo* Script in the Light of a Statistical Analysis of the 'Santiago Staff.'" *Cryptologia* 33: 24–73.

Melott, Adrian L., Brian C. Thomas, Gisela Dreschhoff, and Carey K. Johnson. 2010. "Cometary Airbursts and Atmospheric Chemistry: Tunguska and a Candidate Younger Dryas Event." *Geology* 38, no. 4: 355–58.

Meltzer, David J., Vance T. Holliday, Michael D. Cannon, and D. Shane Miller. 2014. "Chronological Evidence Fails to Support Claim of an Isochronous Widespread Layer of Cosmic Impact Indicators Dated to 12,800 Years Ago." *Proceedings of the National Academy of Sciences of the United States of America* 111, no. 21 (May 27): E2162–E2171.

Métraux, Alfred. 1939. "Mysteries of Easter Island." *Yale Review* 28: 758–79.

———. 1940. *Ethnology of Easter Island.* Bernice P. Bishop Museum Bulletin 160. Honolulu, Hawaii: Bernice P. Bishop Museum Press.

———. 1945. "Easter Island." *Annual Report of the Board of Regents of the Smithsonian Institution Showing the Operations, Expenditures, and Condition of the Institution for the Year Ended June 30, 1944.* Washington, D.C.: U.S. Government Printing Office, 435–51, plus four plates.

———. 1957. *Easter Island: A Stone-Age Civilization in the Pacific.* New York: Oxford University Press.

Michell, John. 1989. *Secrets of the Stones: New Revelations of Astro-archaeology and the Mystical Sciences of Antiquity.* Rochester, Vt.: Inner Traditions International.

Milan, Patricia. 2003. "The Cave of Rouffignac: Homage to the Mammoth." www.prehistoirepassion.com/grotte%20rouffignac.htm (article dated May 2003; accessed July 5, 2011).

Milgrom, L. R. 2003. "The Memory of Water Regained?" *Homeopathy* 92: 223–24. http://altcancerweb.com/homeopathy/science/memory-water -regained.pdf (article dated 2003; accessed August 12, 2011).

Miller, Arthur I. 2009. *Deciphering the Cosmic Number: The Strange Friendship of Wolfgang Pauli and Carl Jung.* New York: W. W. Norton.

Miller, Richard Alan, and Iona Miller. 2003. "Schumann's Resonances and

Human Psychobiology." Organization for the Advancement of Knowledge [O.A.K., Grants Pass, Ore.] www.nwbotanicals.org/oak/newphysics /schumann/schumann.htm (article dated 2003; accessed March 16, 2012).

Mind Matters News. 2020. "Why Is Science Growing Comfortable with Panpsychism ('Everything Is Conscious')?" https://mindmatters.ai/2020/05 /why-is-science-growing-comfortable-with-panpsychism-everything -is-conscious/ (article dated May 3, 2020; accessed May 18, 2020).

Mitchell, Larkin. 1999. "Earliest Egyptian Glyphs." *Archaeology* 52, no. 2 (March/April). https://archive.archaeology.org/9903/newsbriefs/egypt .html (article dated March/April 1999; accessed March 22, 2020).

Mithen, Steven. 2007. "Did Farming Arise from a Misapplication of Social Intelligence?" *Philosophical Transactions of the Royal Society B* 362, no. 1480: 705–18.

Miyake, Fusa, Kentaro Nagaya, Kimiaki Masuda, and Toshio Nakamura. 2012. "A Signature of Cosmic-Ray Increase in AD 774–775 from Tree Rings in Japan." *Nature* 486: 240–42.

Miyake, Fusa, Kimiaki Masuda, and Toshio Nakamura. 2013. "Another Rapid Event in the Carbon-14 Content of Tree Rings." *Nature Communications* 4, no. 1748: 6 pages.

Miyake, Fusa, Kimiaki Masuda, Masataka Hakozaki, Toshio Nakamura, Fuyuki Tokanai, Kazuhiro Kato, Katsuhiko Kimura, and Takumi Mitsutani. 2014. "Verification of the Cosmic-Ray Event in AD 993–994 by Using a Japanese Hinoki Tree." *Radiocarbon* 56, no. 3: 1189–94.

Miyake, Fusa, A. J. Timothy Jull, Irina P. Panyushkina, Lukas Wacker, Matthew Salzer, Christopher H. Baisan, Todd Lange, Richard Cruz, Kimiaki Masuda, and Toshio Nakamura. 2017. "Large ^{14}C Excursion in 5480 BC Indicates an Abnormal Sun in the Mid-Holocene." *Proceedings of the National Academy of Sciences of the United States of America* 114, no. 5: 881–84.

Moddel, Garret. 2006. "Entropy and Information Transmission in Causation and Retrocausation." In *Frontiers of Time: Retrocausation—Experiment and Theory,* edited by Daniel P. Sheehan, 62–74. Melville, N.Y.: American Institute of Physics. http://psiphen.colorado.edu/Pubs/Moddel06.pdf (article dated 2006; accessed August 20, 2011).

Montagnier, L., J. Aissa, E. Del Giudice, C. Lavallee, A. Tedeschi, and G. Vitiello. 2010. "DNA Waves and Water." http://arxiv.org/PS_cache /arxiv/pdf/1012/1012.5166v1.pdf (article dated December 23, 2010; accessed January 26, 2011).

Mooney, C. 2018. "Scientists May Have Solved a Huge Riddle in Earth's Climate Past. It Doesn't Bode Well for the Future." *Washington Post.* www.washingtonpost.com/energy-environment/2018/07/11/scientists -may-have-solved-huge-riddle-earths-climate-past-it-doesnt-bode-well -future/?noredirect=on (article dated July 11, 2018; accessed March 28, 2020).

Moore, Andrew M. T., James P. Kennett, William M. Napier, Ted E. Bunch, James C. Weaver, Malcolm LeCompte, A. Victor Adedeji, Paul Hackley, Gunther Kletetschka, Robert E. Hermes, James H. Wittke, Joshua J. Razink, Michael W. Gaultois, and Allen West. 2020. "Evidence of Cosmic Impact at Abu Hureyra, Syria at the Younger Dryas Onset (~12.8 ka): High-Temperature melting at >2200 °C." *Scientific Reports, Nature Research* 10: 22 pages.

Mordechai, Lee, Merle Eisenberg, Timothy P. Newfield, Adam Izdebski, Janet E. Kay, and Hendrik Poinar. 2019. "The Justinianic Plague: An Inconsequential Pandemic?" *Proceedings of the National Academy of Sciences of the United States of America* 116, no. 51 (December 17): 25546–54.

Morenz, Ludwig D. 2012. "Vom Himmel hoch . . . —Zu Bild-Zeichen geronnene Himmelsmetaphorik." *Göttinger Miszellen, Seminar für Ägyptologie und Koptologie, Georg-August-Universität (GM)* 232, 97–101.

Moriña, David, Isabel Serra, Pedro Puig, and Álvaro Corral. 2019. "Probability Estimation of a Carrington-like Geomagnetic Storm." *Scientific Reports/Nature* 9, 2393: 8 pages.

Moskowitz, Clara. 2011. "Warped Physics: 10 Effects of Faster-Than-Light Discovery." www.livescience.com/16214-implications-faster-light-neutrinos .html (article dated September 24, 2011; accessed November 20, 2011).

Mukai, Koji. 2014. "Recurrent Novae – A Review." https://arxiv.org /pdf/1407.4526.pdf (article dated July 14, 2014; accessed May 6, 2020).

Mukherjee, Saumitra. 2008. "Cosmic Influence on the Sun-Earth Environment." *Sensors* 8: 7736–52. www.mdpi.com/1424-8220/8/12/7736/pdf (article dated December 3, 2008; accessed August 12, 2011).

Munari, Ulisse. 2012. "Classical and Recurrent Novae." *Journal of the American Association of Variable Star Observers* [JAAVSO] 40: 582–97.

Myers, Frederic W. H. 1903. *Human Personality and Its Survival of Bodily Death.* 2 vols. London: Longmans, Green.

NASA [National Aeronautics and Space Administration]. 1981. "The Magnetosphere: Our Shield in Space," chapters 3–4 of *A Meeting with the*

Universe. http://history.nasa.gov/EP-177/ch3-4.html (chapter dated 1981; accessed August 9, 2011).

———. 2006. "The History of Auroras." www.nasa.gov/mission_pages/themis /auroras/aurora_history.html (article dated April 25, 2006; accessed June 27, 2011).

National Geographic. 1939. "The Mystery of Auroras." *National Geographic* 85, no. 5: 689–90.

National Geophysical Data Center [of the National Oceanic and Atmospheric Administration]. 2012. "Wandering of the Geomagnetic Poles." www .ngdc.noaa.gov/geomag/GeomagneticPoles.shtml (undated article; accessed March 18, 2012).

National Research Council of the National Academies, Committee on the Societal and Economic Impacts of Severe Space Weather Events. 2008. *Severe Space Weather Events—Understanding Societal and Economic Impacts, A Workshop Report.* Washington, D.C.: National Academies Press. www.nap.edu/catalog.php?record_id=12507 (book dated 2008; accessed July 4, 2011).

National Research Council of the National Academies, Committee on Solar and Space Physics. 2004. *Plasma Physics of the Local Cosmos.* Washington, D.C.: National Academies Press.

Nelson, John H. 1974. *Cosmic Patterns: Their Influence on Man and His Communication.* Washington, D.C.: American Federation of Astrologers.

Neufeldt, Victoria, and David B. Guralnik. 1988. *Webster's New World Dictionary.* 3rd College Edition. Cleveland and New York: Simon and Schuster.

New Scientist. 2011. "Why We Have to Teleport Disbelief." *New Scientist,* no. 2795: 5. www.newscientist.com/article/mg20927951.900-why-we-have-to -teleport-disbelief.html (editorial dated January 12, 2011; accessed January 26, 2011).

New York Times. 1992. "Scholars Dispute Claim That Sphinx Is Much Older." www.nytimes.com/1992/02/09/us/scholars-dispute-claim-that-sphinx-is -much-older.html (article dated February 9, 1992; accessed June 14, 2010).

Neyland, Robert S. 2019. "Mehit's Stump: Unmasking the Great Sphinx of Giza." *Archaeological Discovery* 8: 1–25.

Ngwira, Chigomezyo M., Lee-Anne McKinnell, and Pierre J. Cilliers. 2011. "Geomagnetic Activity Indicators for Geomagnetically Induced Current Studies in South Africa." *Advances in Space Research* 48, no. 3: 529–34.

Ngwira, Chigomezyo M., Antti Pulkkinen, M. Leila Mays, Maria M. Kuznetsova, A. B. Galvin, Kristin Simunac, Daniel N. Baker, Xinlin Li, Yihua Zheng, and Alex Glocer. 2013. "Simulation of the 23 July 2012 Extreme Space Weather Event: What If This Extremely Rare CME Was Earth Directed?" *Space Weather* 11: 671–79.

Nikitin, I., Yu. Stozhkov, V. Okhlopkov, and N. Svirzhevsky. 2005. "Do Be-10 and C-14 Give Us the Information about Cosmic Rays in the Past?" www .ast.leeds.ac.uk/~jh/ICRC/PAPERS/SH34/rus-nikitin-I-abs1-sh34-oral .pdf (article dated 2005; accessed November 26, 2011). Paper from the 29th International Cosmic Ray Conference, Pune, India.

NOAA [National Oceanic and Atmospheric Administration]. 2020. "Wandering of the Geomagnetic Poles." https://www.ngdc.noaa.gov /geomag/GeomagneticPoles.shtml (undated, but apparently posted or updated in 2020; accessed 30 July 2020).

Nobel Prize. 2011. "The Sveriges Riksbank Prize in Economic Sciences in Memory of Alfred Nobel 1993: Robert W. Fogel, Douglass C. North." http://nobelprize.org/nobel_prizes/economics/laureates/1993/index.html (undated article; accessed July 10, 2011).

North, Douglass C. 1993. "[Nobel] Prize Lecture." http://nobelprize.org /nobel_prizes/economics/laureates/1993/north-lecture.html (lecture given on December 9, 1993; accessed July 13, 2011).

———. 1999. "Dealing with a Non-Ergodic World: Institutional Economics, Property Rights, and the Global Environment." *Duke Environmental Law & Policy Forum* 10, no. 1: 1–12. www.law.duke.edu/shell/cite.pl?10+Duke +Envtl.+L.+&+Pol'y+F.+1 (article dated Fall 1999; accessed July 13, 2011).

North, Douglass C., and Robert Paul Thomas. 1977. "The First Economic Revolution." *Economic History Review,* n.s., 30, no. 2: 229–41.

Notroff, Jens, and Oliver Dietrich. 2019. "But What Is It Good For?— Experiences in Public Outreach of the Göbekli Tepe Project (DAI)." *Archäologische Information* 42 (early view, July 9): 14 pages.

Novak, G., D. T. Chuss, T. Renbarger, G. S. Griffin, M. G. Newcomb, J. B. Peterson, R. F. Loewenstein, D. Pernic, and J. L. Dotson. 2003. "First Results from the Submillimeter Polarimeter for Antarctic Remote Observations: Evidence of Large-Scale Toroidal Magnetic Fields in the Galactic Center." *Astrophysical Journal Letters* 583: L83–L86. http://iopscience.iop.org/1538-4357/583/2/L83/pdf/1538-4357_583_2 _L83.pdf (article dated February 1, 2003; accessed March 16, 2012).

Novik, Oleg, Feodor Smirnov, and Maxim Volgin. 2019. *Electromagnetic Geophysical Fields: Precursors to Earthquakes and Tsunamis; Impacts on the Brain and Heart.* Cham, Switzerland: Springer Nature.

Obama, Barack. 2016. "Executive Order—Coordinating Efforts to Prepare the Nation for Space Weather Events." https://obamawhitehouse.archives.gov /the-press-office/2016/10/13/executive-order-coordinating-efforts-prepare-nation -space-weather-events (order dated October 13, 2016; accessed April 9, 2020).

Odenwald, Sten. 2009. "The Day the Sun Brought Darkness." www.nasa.gov /topics/earth/features/sun_darkness.html (article dated March 13, 2009; accessed August 9, 2011).

Odenwald, Sten F., and James L. Green. 2008. "Bracing for a Solar Superstorm." *Scientific American* 299, no. 2: 80–87.

O'Hare, Paschal, Florian Mekhaldi, Florian Adolphi, Grant Raisbeck, Ala Aldahan, Emma Anderberg, Jürg Beer, Marcus Christl, Simon Fahrni, Hans-Arno Synal, Junghun Park, Göran Possnert, John Southon, Edouard Bard, ASTER Team, and Raimund Muscheler. 2019. "Multiradionuclide Evidence for an Extreme Solar Proton Event around 2,610 B.P. (~660 BC)." *Proceedings of the National Academy of Sciences of the United States of America* 116, no. 3: 5961–66.

O'Neill, Ian. 2010. "2012 Mayan Calendar 'Doomsday' Date Might Be Wrong." http://news.discovery.com/space/the-2012-mayan-calendar-doomsday-date -might-be-wrong.html (article dated October 18, 2010; accessed October 20, 2010).

Orlowski, Andrew. 2011. "CERN 'Gags' Physicists in Cosmic Ray Climate Experiment." www.theregister.co.uk/2011/07/18/cern_cosmic_ray_gag (article dated July 18, 2011; accessed July 20, 2011).

Orzel, Chad. 2010. "Why I'm Skeptical about the Changing Fine-Structure Constant." http://scienceblogs.com/principles/2010/09/_httpksjtracker mitedu20100907e.php (article dated September 14, 2010; accessed August 11, 2011).

Owen, Iris M., with Margaret Sparrow. 1976. *Conjuring Up Philip: An Adventure in Psychokinesis.* Toronto: Fitzhenry and Whiteside.

Palmer, Allison R. 1983. "The Decade of North American Geology: Geologic Time Scale [for the Earth]." *Geology* 11: 503–4.

Palmer, Jason. 2011a. "Light Speed: Flying into Fantasy." www.bbc.co.uk/news /science-environment-15034414 (article dated September 23, 2011; accessed November 18, 2011).

———. 2011b. "Neutrino Experiment Repeat at Cern Finds Same Result." www
.bbc.co.uk/news/science-environment-15791236 (article dated November 18,
2011; accessed November 18, 2011).

———. 2011c. "Speed-of-Light Results under Scrutiny at Cern." www.bbc
.co.uk/news/science-environment-15017484 (article dated September 23,
2011; accessed November 18, 2011).

Papadopulos-Eleopulos, E., V. F. Turner, J. Papadimitriou, Barry Page, David
Causer, Helman Alfonso, Sam Mhlongo, Todd Miller, Andrew Maniotis,
and Christian Fiala. 2004. "A Critique of the Montagnier Evidence for the
HIV/AIDS Hypothesis." *Medical Hypotheses* 63, no. 4: 597–601. http://
theperthgroup.com/SCIPAPERS/MHMONT.pdf (article dated 2004;
accessed August 13, 2011).

Park, Junghun, John Southon, Simon Fahrni, Pearce Paul Creasman, and
Richard Mewaldt. 2017. "Relationship between Solar Activity and $\Delta^{14}C$
Peaks in AD 775, AD 994, and 660 BC." *Radiocarbon* 59, no. 4: 1147–56.

Parzinger, Hermann, Willem Willems, Jean-Paul Demoule, Romuald Schild, Vassil
Nikolov, Anthony Harding, and Mike Heyworth. 2006. "DECLARATION
[Concerning the So-Called Bosnian Pyramids]." www.e-a-a.org/statement
.pdf (document dated December 11, 2006; accessed July 7, 2011).

Past Horizons. 2011. "12,000 Year Old Textiles Found in Peruvian Cave." www
.pasthorizons.com/index.php/archives/04/2011/12000-year-old-textiles
-found-in-peruvian-cave (article dated April 17, 2011; accessed August 10,
2011).

Peiser, Benny. 2005. "From Genocide to Ecocide: The Rape of Rapa Nui."
Energy and Environment 16, nos. 3–4: 513–39. www.uri.edu/artsci/ecn
/starkey/ECN398%20-Ecology,%20Economy,%20Society/RAPANUI.pdf
(article dated 2005; accessed August 31, 2011).

Peratt, Anthony L. 2003. "Characteristics for the Occurrence of a High-Current,
Z-Pinch Aurora as Recorded in Antiquity." *Institute of Electrical and
Electronics Engineers Transactions on Plasma Science* 31, no. 6: 1192–214.

———. 2005. "On the Origins of Icons from Antiquity." Presentation by
Dr. Anthony (Tony) L. Peratt given on May 5, 2005. www.youtube.com
/watch?v=6meaU1QcSdA&t= (posted on YouTube, March 28, 2018,
under the title "Peratt and Petroglyphs"; accessed March 29, 2020).

Peratt, Anthony L., John McGovern, Alfred H. Qöyawayma, Marinus Anthony
van der Sluijs, and Mathias G. Peratt. 2007. "Characteristics for the
Occurrence of a High-Current Z-Pinch Aurora as Recorded in Antiquity

Part II: Directionality and Source." *Institute of Electrical and Electronics Engineers Transactions on Plasma Science* 35, no. 4: 778–807.

Peratt, A. L., and W. F. Yao. 2008. "Evidence for an Intense Solar Outburst in Prehistory." *Physica Scripta* [The Royal Swedish Academy of Sciences] 130: 1–13.

Perkins, Sid. 2007. "Ice Age Ends Smashingly: Did a Comet Blow Up over Eastern Canada?" *Science News,* June 3, 2007. www.sott.net/article/133568 -Ice-Age-Ends-Smashingly-Did-a-comet-blow-up-over-eastern-Canada (accessed December 11, 2014).

Perryman, M. A. C., and T. Schulze-Hartung. 2010. "The Barycentric Motion of Exoplanet Host Stars: Tests of Solar Spin-Orbit Coupling." http:// arxiv.org/PS_cache/arxiv/pdf/1010/1010.0966v1.pdf and http://arxiv.org /abs/1010.0966 (article dated October 5, 2010; accessed July 13, 2011).

Petaev, Michail I., Shichun Huang, Stein B. Jacobsen, and Alan Zindler. 2013. "Large Platinum Anomaly in the GISP2 Ice Core: Evidence for a Cataclysm at the Bølling-Allerød/Younger Dryas Boundary?" 44th Lunar and Planetary Science Conference, 2 pages.

Peters, Joris, and Klaus Schmidt. 2004. "Animals in the Symbolic World of Pre-Pottery Neolithic Göbekli Tepe, South-Eastern Turkey: A Preliminary Assessment." *Anthropozoologica* 39, no. 1: 179–218.

Petrie, W. M. Flinders. 1901. *The Royal Tombs of the Earliest Dynasties.* Part II. London and Boston: Egypt Exploration Fund.

Physorg.com. 2011a. "Oldest Obsidian Bracelet Reveals Amazing Craftsmen's Skills in the Eighth Millennium BC." www.physorg.com/news/2011 -12-oldest-obsidian-bracelet-reveals-amazing.html (article dated December 21, 2011; accessed December 23, 2011).

———. 2011b. "UCSB Scholar's Reading of Hieroglyphic Verb Alters Understanding of Mayan Ritual Texts." www.physorg.com/news/2011 -11-ucsb-scholar-hieroglyphic-verb-mayan.html (article dated November 21, 2011; accessed November 22, 2011).

Pigati, Jeffrey S., Claudio Latorre, Jason A. Rech, Julio L. Betancourt, Katherine E. Martínez, and James R. Budahn. 2012. "Accumulation of Impact Markers in Desert Wetlands and Implications for the Younger Dryas Impact Hypothesis." *Proceedings of the National Academy of Sciences of the United States of America* 109, no. 19: 7208–12; *PNAS Early Edition,* www.pnas.org/cgi/doi/10.1073/pnas.1200296109 (accessed June 22, 2020).

Pinter, Nicholas, Andrew C. Scott, Tyrone L. Daulton Andrew Podoll, Christian

Koeberl, R. Scott Anderson, and Scott E. Ishman. 2011. "The Younger Dryas Impact Hypothesis: A Requiem." *Earth-Science Reviews* 106: 247–64.

Pittock, Barrie. 2009. "Can Solar Variations Explain Variations in the Earth's Climate? An Editorial Comment." *Climate Change* 96: 483–87. www .springerlink.com/content/0767x23205168108/fulltext.pdf (article dated 2009; accessed July 13, 2011).

Plato. 1998. *Critias*. Translated by Benjamin Jowett. www.gutenberg.org/cache /epub/1571/pg1571.txt (undated article, release date for text file is 1998; accessed August 22, 2011).

———. 2011. *Timaeus*. Translated by Benjamin Jowett. http://classics.mit.edu /Plato/timaeus.1b.txt (undated article; accessed August 22, 2011).

Plegge, Joe. 2012. *Turkish Stonehenge: Göbekli Tepe*. Dickinson, N. Dak.: Plegge Enterprises.

Pollack, Gerald H. 2013. "The Fourth State of Water: Beyond Solid, Liquid, and Vapor." *Edgescience*, no. 16: 14–18.

———. 2017. "Why Hydrogels Don't Dribble Water." *Gels* 3, no. 4: 7 pages.

Pommé, S., H. Stroh, J. Paepen, R. Van Ammel, M. Marouli, T. Altzitzoglou, M. Hult, K. Kossert, O. Nähle, H. Schrader, F. Juget, C. Bailat, Y. Nedjadi, F. Bochud, T. Buchillier, C. Michotte, S. Courte, M.W. van Rooy, M.J. van Staden, J. Lubbe, B.R.S. Simpson, A. Fazio, P. De Felice, T.W. Jackson, W.M. Van Wyngaardt, M.I. Reinhard, J. Golya, S. Bourke, T. Roy, R. Galea, J.D. Keightley, K.M. Ferreira, S.M. Collins, A. Ceccatelli, M. Unterweger, R. Fitzgerald, D.E. Bergeron, L. Pibida, L. Verheyen, M. Bruggeman, B. Vodenik, M. Korun, V. Chisté, and M.-N. Amiot. 2016. "Evidence Against Solar Influence on Nuclear Decay Constants." https://www.ncbi .nlm.nih.gov/pmc/articles/PMC5207040/pdf/nihms835317.pdf (article dated October 2016; accessed July 27, 2020).

Popular Archaeology. 2012. "Ancient Builders Created Monumental Structures That Altered Sound and Mind, Say Researchers." http://popular-archaeology .com/issue/march-2012/article/ancient-builders-created-monumental -structures-that-altered-sound-and-mind-say-researchers (article dated March 5, 2012; accessed March 24, 2012).

Price, Huw, and Ken Wharton. 2015. "Disentangling the Quantum World." *Entropy* 17, no. 12: 7752–67.

Price, Huw, and Ken Wharton. 2016. "Taming the Quantum Spooks: Reconciling Einstein with Quantum Mechanics May Require Abandoning the Notion That Cause Always Precedes Effect." https://aeon.co/essays

/can-retrocausality-solve-the-puzzle-of-action-at-a-distance (article dated September 14, 2016; accessed August 1, 2020).

Pringle, Lucy. 2003. "Is There Evidence for Memory of Water?" www.lucypringle.co.uk/articles/memory/ (article dated 2003; accessed August 12, 2011).

Pugh, C. E., V. M. Nakariakov, and A.-M. Broomhall. 2015. "A Multi-Oscillation in a Stellar Superflare." *Astrophysical Journal Letters* 813 (November 1): L5, 5 pages.

Pustovoytov, Konstantin. 2006. "Soils and Sediments at Göbekli Tepe, Southeastern Turkey: A Preliminary Report." *Geoarchaeology* 21, no. 7: 699–719.

Pustovoytov, Konstantin, and Heinrich Taubald. 2003. "Stable Carbon and Oxygen Isotope Composition of Pedogenic Carbonate at Göbekli Tepe (Southeastern Turkey) and Its Potential for Reconstructing Late Quaternary Paleoenvironments in Upper Mesopotamia." *Neo-Lithics 2/03, the Newsletter of Southwest Asian Neolithic Research*, 25–32.

Putigny, Bob. 1976. *Easter Island.* Photos by O. de Kersauson, M. Folco, and J. P. Duchêne. Foreword by Paul-Emile Victor. New York: Two Continents Publishing Group.

Qu, Jiangwen, Zhigang Gao, Ying Zhang, Milton Wainwright, Chandra Wickramasinghe, and Tareq Omairi. 2016. "Sunspot Activity, Influenza and Ebola Outbreak Connection." *Journal of Astrobiology and Outreach* 4, no. 2: 7 pages.

Rabie, Passant. 2019. "Planetary Orbits May Explain Mystery of Sun's 11-Year Cycle." https://www.space.com/planets-affect-solar-cycle.html (article dated June 18, 2019; accessed July 15, 2020).

Radin, Dean, Nancy Lund, Masaru Emoto, and Takashige Kizu. 2008. "Effects of Distant Intention on Water Crystal Formation: A Triple-Blind Replication." *Journal of Scientific Exploration* 22, no. 4: 481–93.

Raghavan, Deepak, Harold A. McAlister, Todd J. Henry, David W. Latham, Geoffrey W. Marcy, Brian D. Mason, Douglas R. Gies, Russel J. White, and Theo A. ten Brummelaaar. 2010. "A Survey of Stellar Families: Multiplicity of Solar-Type Stars." *Astrophysical Journal Supplement Series* 190: 1–42.

Raman, K. Sundara. 2011. "Space Weather—Sun Earth Relations." *International Journal of Astronomy and Astrophysics* 1: 10–14. www.scirp.org/Journal/PaperInformation.aspx?paperID=4374 (article dated March 2011; accessed November 25, 2011).

Randall, Keith. 2020. "Texas A&M Study: Cooling of Earth Caused By

Eruptions, Not Meteors: Analysis of sediment found in Hall's Cave shows volcanic eruptions are responsible for the cooling of Earth around 13,000 years ago." https://today.tamu.edu/2020/07/31/texas-am-study -cooling-of-earth-caused-by-eruptions-not-meteors/ (article dated July 31, 2020; accessed August 4, 2020).

Ransom, C. J. 2011. "Laboratory Modeling of Meteorite Impact Craters by Z-Pinch Plasma." *Open Astronomy Journal* 4, suppl. 2-M4: 185–90.

Reader, Colin D. 1997/1999. "Khufu Knew the Sphinx: A Reconciliation of the Geological and Archaeological Evidence for the Age of the Sphinx and a Revised Sequence of Development for the Giza Necropolis." www .ianlawton.com/as1.htm (article dated October 1997; revised August 1999; accessed August 30, 2011).

Redfield, Seth, and Jeffrey L. Linsky. 2008. "The Structure of the Local Interstellar Medium. IV. Dynamics, Morphology, Physical Properties, and Implications of Cloud-Cloud Interactions." *Astrophysical Journal* 673: 283–314.

Reich, Eugenie Samuel. 2012. "Flaws Found in Faster-Than-Light Neutrino Measurement: Two Possible Sources of Error Uncovered." www.nature .com/news/flaws-found-in-faster-than-light-neutrino-measurement-1.10099 (article dated February 22, 2012; accessed March 24, 2012).

Reid, N., Patrick Nunn, and M. Sharpe. 2014. "Indigenous Australian Stories and Sea-Level Change." http://research.usc.edu.au/vital/access/manager /Repository/usc:14264?queryType=vitalDismax&query=indigenous +australian+stories (article dated 2014, accessed April 15, 2020).

Reid, Nicholas. 2015. "Aboriginal Memories of Inundation of the Australian Coast Dating from More Than 7000 Years Ago." www.cdu.edu.au/sites /default/files/the-northern-institute/aboriginaltradsealevelscdu.pdf (article dated 2015; accessed April 15, 2020).

Reid, Nick, and Patrick D. Nunn. 2015. "Ancient Aboriginal Stories Preserve History of a Rise in Sea Level." https://theconversation.com/ancient -aboriginal-stories-preserve-history-of-a-rise-in-sea-level-36010 (article dated January 12, 2015; accessed April 15, 2020).

Reimold, Wolf Uwe, and Chrisitan Koeberl. 2014. "Impact Structures in Africa: A Review." *Journal of African Earth Sciences* 93: 57–175.

Rengaswamy, Sridharan. 2008. "Statistics of Ionospheric Fluctuations." http://lofar .strw.leidenuniv.nl/wiki/lib/exe/fetch.php?media=lions:sridhar_22may08 .pdf (PowerPoint presentation dated May 22, 2008; accessed August 12, 2011).

Renssen, Hans, Bas van Geel, Johannes van der Plicht, and Michel Magny. 2000. "Reduced Solar Activity as a Trigger for the Start of the Younger Dryas?" *Quaternary International* 68–71: 373–83.

Reville, William. 2011. "The Pseudoscience of Creating Beautiful (or Ugly) Water." www.irishtimes.com/news/science/the-pseudoscience-of-creating -beautiful-or-ugly-water-1.574583 (article dated February 17, 2011; accessed April 8, 2020).

Rhine, Louisa E., and J. B. Rhine. 1943. "The Psychokinetic Effect: I. The First Experiment." *Journal of Parapsychology* 7: 20–43. Excerpts reprinted in *The Parapsychology Revolution: A Concise Anthology of Paranormal and Psychical Research,* compilation and commentary by Robert M. Schoch and Logan Yonavjak, 138–44. New York: Jeremy P. Tarcher/Penguin, 2008.

Richet, Charles. 1931. *L'Avenir et la Prémonition.* Paris: Editions Montaigne.

Richman, Barbara T. 1981. "Shedding Light on the Aurora." *Eos, Transactions, American Geophysical Union* 62, no. 37: 665–66. (Summary of work by A. Brekke and A. Egeland.)

Riley, Pete. 2012. "On the Probability of Occurrence of Extreme Space Weather Events." *Space Weather* 10, no. S02012: 1–12.

Rincon, Paul. 2003. "'Earliest Writing' Found in China." http://news.bbc .co.uk/2/hi/science/nature/2956925.stm (article dated April 17, 2003; accessed April 4, 2009).

Roll, William G. 2003. "Poltergeists, Electromagnetism, and Consciousness." *Journal of Scientific Exploration* 17, no. 1: 75–86. Reprinted in *The Parapsychology Revolution: A Concise Anthology of Paranormal and Psychical Research,* compilation and commentary by Robert M. Schoch and Logan Yonavjak, 106–22. New York: Jeremy P. Tarcher/Penguin, 2008.

Rousseau, Steve. 2012. "The Faster-Than-Light Neutrinos Debate Rages On at New York's American Museum of Natural History on Tuesday Night [March 20, 2012], the 2012 Isaac Asimov Memorial Debate—Called 'Einstein on Trial: Testing Relativity' and Hosted by Neil deGrasse." www .popularmechanics.com/technology/engineering/extreme-machines /the-faster-than-light-neutrinos-debate-rages-on-7529427?click=pm_latest (article dated March 22, 2012; accessed March 24, 2012).

Routledge, Mrs. Scoresby [Katherine Pease Routledge]. 1919. *The Mystery of Easter Island: The Story of an Expedition.* London: Hazell, Watson and Viney.

Roy, Archie E. 1990. *A Sense of Something Strange: Investigations into the Paranormal.* Glasgow: Dog and Bone Press.

Royal Commission on the Ancient and Historical Monuments of Scotland. 2010. "Mote of Mark: Archaeological Notes." http://canmore.rcahms.gov .uk/en/site/64911/details/mote+of+mark (undated article; apparently continuously updated; accessed July 5, 2010).

Rull, Valentí, Núria Cañellas-Boltà, Olga Margalef, Sergi Pla-Rabes, Alberto Sáez, and Santiago Giralt. 2016. "Three Millennia of Climatic, Ecological, and Cultural Change on Easter Island: An Integrative Overview." *Frontiers in Ecology and Evolution* 4, article 29 (March): 4 pages.

Rull, Valentí, and Santiago Giralt, eds. 2018. *Paleoecology of Easter Island: Natural and Anthropogenic Drivers of Ecological Change.* A compilation of papers from *Frontiers in Ecology and Evolution.* Lausanne, Switzerland: Frontiers Media SA.

Russell, Randy. 2005. "Rotation of the Sun." www.windows2universe.org/sun /Solar_interior/Sun_layers/differential_rotation.html (article dated August 16, 2005; accessed March 25, 2012).

———. 2007. "Earth's Magnetic Poles." www.windows2universe.org/earth /Magnetosphere/earth_magnetic_poles.html (article dated August 22, 2007; accessed August 10, 2011).

Sahman, D. I., V. S. Dhillon, S. P. Littlefair, and G. Hallinan. 2018. "Discovery of an Old Nova Shell Surrounding the Cataclysmic Variable V1315 Aql." https://arxiv.org/pdf/1804.05596.pdf (article dated April 16, 2018; accessed March 27, 2020).

Saltmarsh, Herbert Francis. 1938. *Foreknowledge.* London: G. Bell and Sons.

SANSA [South African National Space Agency]. 2010. www.space-sci.sansa.org .za (website dated 2010, but updated periodically; accessed March 16, 2012).

Santa Barbara Independent. 2010. "2012 Prophecy, Mayan Calendar Correlation Questioned: Historical Data Brought to Bear by UCSB [University of California, Santa Barbara] Scholar Gerardo Aldana." www.independent .com/news/2010/oct/05/2012-prophecy-mayan-calendar-correlation -questione (article dated October 5, 2010; accessed June 8, 2011).

Saravia E., Albertina. 1984. *Popol Wuj: Antiguas Historias de los Indios Quiches de Guatemala, Illustradas con Dibjuos de los Codices Mayas. Advertencia, Version y Vocabulario de Albertina Saravia E.* Mexico City, Mexico: Editorial Porrúa, S. A.

Sassaman, Kenneth E. 2004. "Complex Hunter–Gatherers in Evolution and History: A North American Perspective." *Journal of Archaeological Research* 12, no. 3: 227–80.

Schaefer, Bradley E. 2009. "Comprehensive Photometric Histories of All Known Galactic Recurrent Novae." https://arxiv.org/pdf/0912.4426.pdf (article dated December 22, 2009; accessed March 27, 2010).

Schmidt, Klaus. 2001. "Göbekli Tepe, Southeastern Turkey: A Preliminary Report on the 1995–1999 Excavations." *Paléorient* 26, no. 1: 45–54.

———. 2006/2008. *Sie bauten die ersten Tempel: Das rätselhafte Heiligtum der Steinzeitjäger, Die archäologische Entdeckung am Göbekli Tepe.* Munich, Germany: Deutscher Taschenbuch Verlag.

———. 2007. *Taş Çaği Avcılarının Gizemli Kutsal Alanı Göbekli Tepe En Eski Tapınağı Yapanlar.* Istanbul, Turkey: Arkeolojí ve Sanat Yayınları.

———. 2010. "Göbekli Tepe—The Stone Sanctuaries. New Results of Ongoing Excavations with a Special Focus on Sculptures and High Reliefs." *Documenta Praehistorica* XXXVII: 239–56.

———. 2011. "Göbekli Tepe: A Neolithic Site in Southeastern Anatolia." In *The Oxford Handbook of Ancient Anatolia,* edited by Sharon R. Steadman and Gregory McMahon, chapter 42, 917–33. Oxford, UK: Oxford University Press.

———. 2012. *Göbekli Tepe: A Stone Age Sanctuary in South-Eastern Anatolia.* ArchaeNova/ex oriente e.V. Berlin [special edition produced by ArchaeNova and printed in Turkey by Kurtuluş Matbaası, Şanlıurfa, Turkey].

Schoch, Robert M. 1989. *Stratigraphy: Principles and Methods.* New York: Van Nostrand Reinhold.

———. 1992a. "How Old Is the Sphinx?" *Abstracts for the 1992 Annual Meeting of the American Association for the Advancement of Science,* Chicago, February 1992, 202.

———. 1992b. "Redating the Great Sphinx of Giza." *KMT, A Modern Journal of Ancient Egypt* 3, no. 2: 52–59, 66–70. (Reprinted with updates in Schoch and Bauval 2017, 337–70.)

———. 2002. "Geological Evidence Pertaining to the Age of the Great Sphinx." In *New Scenarios on the Evolution of the Solar System and Consequences on History of Earth and Man,* edited by Emilio Spedicato and Adalberto Notarpietro. Proceedings of the Conference, Milano and Bergamo, Italy, June 7–9, 1999, Università degli Studi di Bergamo, Quaderni del Dipartmento di Matematica, Statistica, Informatica ed Applicazion, Serie Miscellanea, Anno 2002, no. 3: 171–203. (Reprinted with updates in Schoch and Bauval 2017, 371–432.)

———. 2006. "The Dangers of Pyramid-Mania [letter debunking the supposed Bosnian 'pyramids']." *Science* 314: 925.

———. 2006/2007. "Introduction." In *Markawasi: Peru's Inexplicable Stone Forest*, edited and written by Kathy Doore, with a foreword by Peter E. Schneider, 14–20. Surprise, Ariz.: Kathy Doore. Copyright issued in 2006, but book not actually published until June 2007.

———. 2007. "Life with the Great Sphinx, Some Personal Reflections." In *Darklore*, vol. 1, edited by Greg Taylor, 38–55, 291 [endnotes]. Brisbane, Australia: Daily Grail Publishing.

———. 2008. "The Human and Cosmic Psyche." In *CPAK 2008* [Conference on Precession and Ancient Knowledge; published program with articles to accompany the conference, October 4–5, 2008], 31–32. Newport Beach, Calif.: Binary Research Institute.

———. 2009a. "Robert Schoch Replies: In an *Atlantis Rising* Exclusive, the Geologist Who Redated the Great Sphinx Takes on One of His Most Outspoken Critics Robert Temple." *Atlantis Rising*, no. 78: 41, 67–68.

———. 2009b. "Searching for the Dawn and Demise of Ancient Civilization." *New Dawn*, special issue no. 8: 17–24.

———. 2009c. "12,000 Years Old? Could Paradigm-Busting Evidence from Turkey Take the Sphinx-Age Debate to a Brand New Level?" *Atlantis Rising*, no. 76: 42–43, 69–70.

———. 2010a. "An Ancient Warning, a Global Message, From the End of the Last Ice Age." *New Dawn*, July–August 2010, 15–22.

———. 2010b. "Easter Island's Mystery Script: Is This the Fearful Story of a Planetary Catastrophe?" *Atlantis Rising*, no. 82: 42–43, 68–70.

———. 2010c. "Glass Castles and Fire from the Sky: A New Theory of Ancient Vitrification." *New Dawn*, special issue no. 13, 51–59.

———. 2010d. "Moving the Moai: Easter Island as a Possible Psychokinetic Laboratory." In *Darklore*, vol. 5, edited by Greg Taylor, 134–55, 268–70 [endnotes]. Brisbane, Australia: Daily Grail Publishing.

———. 2010e. "The Mystery of Göbekli Tepe and Its Message to Us." *New Dawn*, September–October 2010, 53–60.

———. 2010f. "Thoughts on Parapsychology and Paranormal Phenomena: Has Conventional Science Missed Something Profound?" In *Lost Knowledge of the Ancients*, edited by Glenn Kreisberg, 7–18, 229–30 [references]. Rochester, Vt.: Bear & Company.

———. 2011. "Easter Island and the Afterlife." *New Dawn*, January–February 2011, 59–66.

———. 2012a. *La Civiltà Perduta e la Catastrofi dal Sole: Il Passato e il Futuro dell'Umanità.* Rome: XPublishing [published June 2012].

———. 2012b. *Forgotten Civilization: The Role of Solar Outbursts in Our Past and Future.* Rochester, Vt.: Inner Traditions [published August 2012].

———. 2014a. "Journey to Gunung Padang: The Case for Lost Ice Age Civilization in Indonesia." *Atlantis Rising,* no. 104 (March–April): 41, 67–68.

———. 2014b. "Sundaland Rising, Gunung Padang: Indonesia's Mysterious Lost Civilization?" *New Dawn* 8, no. 1 (special issue, February): 3–10.

———. 2014c. *Die vergessene Zivilisation: Die Bedeutung der Sonneneruptionen in Vergangenheit und Zukunft.* Groß-Gerau, Germany: Ancient Mail Verlag [published July 2014].

———. 2015. "A Solar-Induced Dark Age? Disturbing Evidence from Bulgaria." *Atlantis Rising,* no. 110 (March–April): 28, 30, 63.

———. 2016. *Civilizatia uitata: Rolul exploziilor solare in trecutul si viitorul nostru.* Bucharest: Trebuie Sastii.

———. 2017. *Zapomniana Cywilizacja.* Warsaw: Amber.

———. 2018. "The Joe Rogan Experience #1124—Robert Schoch." www.youtube.com/watch?v=Vka2ZgzZTvo (interview occurred and video posted on YouTube, May 31, 2018; accessed March 31, 2020).

———. 2019. "Reality: Fundamentally Speaking—What Is It Anyway?" *Atlantis Rising,* no. 135 (May–June): 46–47, 71–72.

———. 2020a. "Rising from the Ashes of SIDA (Solar-Induced Dark Age)." Published by ORACUL [Organization for the Research of Ancient Cultures], March 7, 2020, 15-page stand-alone paper/booklet.

———. 2020b. "Trailer for *Civilization Before Civilization.*" Trailer for a proposed documentary; the approximately three-minute trailer features Robert Schoch onsite in Turkey (Cappadocia and Göbekli Tepe). www.youtube.com/watch?v=q_6-cceI8CE&feature=youtu.be (video posted on YouTube, March 7, 2020; accessed March 31, 2020).

Schoch, Robert M., and Robert Bauval. 2017. *Origins of the Sphinx: Celestial Guardian of Pre-Pharaonic Civilization.* Rochester, Vt.: Inner Traditions.

Schoch, Robert M., with Robert Aquinas McNally. 1999. *Voices of the Rocks: A Scientist Looks at Catastrophes and Ancient Civilizations.* New York: Harmony Books. For discussion of the Great Sphinx, see especially chapter 2, "A Shape with Lion Body and the Head of a Man," 33–51.

———. 2003. *Voyages of the Pyramid Builders: The True Origins of the Pyramids from Lost Egypt to Ancient America.* New York: Tarcher/Penguin. For discussion of the Great Sphinx, see especially the appendix, "Redating the Great Sphinx of Egypt," 278–98.

Schoch, Robert M., and Robert Aquinas McNally. 2005. *Pyramid Quest: Secrets of the Great Pyramid and the Dawn of Civilization.* New York: Jeremy P. Tarcher/Penguin.

Schoch, Robert M., and John Anthony West. 1991. "Redating the Great Sphinx of Giza, Egypt." Abstracts with programs. *Geological Society of America* 23, no. 5: A253.

———. 2000. "Further Evidence Supporting a Pre-2500 B.C. Date for the Great Sphinx of Giza, Egypt." Abstracts with programs. *Geological Society of America* 32, no. 7: A276.

Schoch, Robert M., and Logan Yonavjak, compilation and commentary. 2008. *The Parapsychology Revolution: A Concise Anthology of Paranormal and Psychical Research.* New York: Jeremy P. Tarcher/Penguin.

Science Daily. 2008. "Sun's Magnetic Field May Impact Weather and Climate: Sun Cycle Can Predict Rainfall Fluctuations." www.sciencedaily.com /releases/2008/12/081202081449.htm (article dated December 3, 2008; accessed July 16, 2011).

———. 2010. "Nanodiamonds Discovered in Greenland Ice Sheet, Contribute to Evidence for Cosmic Impact." www.sciencedaily.com/releases/2010/09 /100914143626.htm (article dated September 15, 2010; accessed May 24, 2011).

———. 2011a. "First Skyscraper Was a Monument to Intimidation: How Jericho's 11,000-Year-Old 'Cosmic' Tower Came into Being." www.sciencedaily .com/releases/2011/02/110217125205.htm (article dated February 17, 2011; accessed March 3, 2011).

———. 2011b. "Minority Rules: Scientists Discover Tipping Point for the Spread of Ideas." www.sciencedaily.com/releases/2011/07/110725190044 .htm (article dated July 25, 2011; accessed August 1, 2011).

———. 2012. "New Evidence Supports Theory of Extraterrestrial Impact." www.sciencedaily.com/releases/2012/06/120611193657.htm (article dated June 11, 2012; accessed June 25, 2012).

Scott, Andrew C., Nicholas Pinter, Margaret E. Collinson, Mark Hardiman, R. Scott Anderson, Anthony P. R. Brain, Selena Y. Smith, Federica Marone, and Marco Stampanoni. 2010. "Fungus, Not Comet or Catastrophe, Accounts for Carbonaceous Spherules in the Younger Dryas 'Impact Layer.'" *Geophysical Research Letters* 37: L14302, 5 pages.

Seddon, Christopher. 2008. "Ice Age Star Maps?" www.christopherseddon. com/2008/01/ice-age-star-maps.html (article dated January 1, 2008; accessed June 5, 2010).

Selbie, Joseph, and David Steinmetz. 2010. *The Yugas: Keys to Understanding Our Hidden Past, Emerging Energy Age, and Enlightened Future: From the Teachings of Sri Yukteswar and Paramhansa Yogananda.* Foreword by Swami Kriyananda. Nevada City, Calif.: Crystal Clarity Publishers.

Seo, S. Niggol. 2019. *Natural and Man-Made Catastrophes—Theories, Economics, and Policy Designs.* Hoboken, N.J.: Wiley/Blackwell/John Wiley & Sons.

Sepici, Levent. 2019. *The Enigma of Göbekli Tepe.* Istanbul, Turkey: My Matbaacılık Sanayi ve Ticaret Limited. (On page 95 of this book, Sepici used a photograph of ours, published as plate 16 in Schoch 2012b, without our permission and without crediting Katie, who took the photo, or me.)

Sereno, Martin I. 2005. "Language Origins without the Semantic Urge." *Cognitive Science Online* 3, no. 1: 1–12. http://cogsci-online.ucsd.edu/3/3-1.pdf (article dated 2005; accessed July 29, 2010).

Serrao, Angelique. 2008. "'Oldest Man-Made Structure' Unearthed." www.iol .co.za/news/south-africa/oldest-man-made-structure-unearthed-1.408210 (article dated July 14, 2008; accessed March 16, 2012).

Seyfzadeh, Manu, Robert M. Schoch, and Robert Bauval. 2017. "A New Interpretation of a Rare Old Kingdom Dual Title: The King's Chief Librarian and Guardian of the Royal Archives of *Mehit.*" *Archaeological Discovery* 5 (July): 163–77.

Seyfzadeh, Manu, and Robert M. Schoch. 2018. "The Inventory Stele: More Fact Than Fiction." *Archaeological Discovery* 6 (April): 103–61.

———. 2019a. "World's First Known Written Word at Göbekli Tepe on T-Shaped Pillar 18 Means God." *Archaeological Discovery* 7 (February): 31–53.

———. 2019b. "Major Geological Fissure through Prehistoric Lion Monument at Giza Inspired Split Lion Hieroglyphs and Ancient Egypt's Creation Myth." *Archaeological Discovery* 7 (September): 211–56.

Seymour, Percy. 1992. *The Paranormal: Beyond Sensory Science.* London: Arkana/Penguin Books.

Sezen, Başak. 2020. *Our Own "Aliens": Was Göbeklitepe a Colony of Civilization X?* E-book available through Amazon Media EU. [The copy consulted was sent as a Word.doc file by Sezen directly to R. Schoch.]

Shaar, Ron, Erez Ben-Yosef, Hagai Ron, Lisa Tauxe, Amotz Agnon, and Ronit

Kessel. 2011. "Geomagnetic Field Intensity: How High Can It Get? How Fast Can It Change? Constraints from Iron Age Copper Slag." *Earth and Planetary Science Letters* 301: 297–306. http://dss.ucsd.edu/~ebenyose /ShaarETAL10_Timna30_EPSL.pdf (article dated 2011; accessed July 16, 2011).

Shackley, Myra. 1983. *Still Living? Yeti, Sasquatch, and the Neanderthal Enigma.* New York: Thames and Hudson. Paperback edition published in 1986.

Shakun, Jeremy D., and Anders E. Carlson. 2010. "A Global Perspective on Last Glacial Maximum to Holocene Climate Change." *Quaternary Science Reviews* 29: 1801–16.

Shipman, Pat. 2014. "The Bright Side of the Black Death." *American Scientist* 102: 410–13.

Shirokogoroff, Sergei Mikhailovich. 1935. *Psychomental Complex of the Tungus.* London: Kegan Paul, Trench, Trubner. Reprint, Berlin: Reinhold Schletzer Verlag, 1999.

Shnoll, Simon E. 2006. "Changes in the Fine Structure of Stochastic Distributions as a Consequence of Space-Time Fluctuations." *Progress in Physics* 2: 39–45. www.ptep-online.com/index_files/2006/PP-05-08.PDF (article dated April 2006; accessed October 11, 2008).

Shnoll, S. E., V. A. Kolombet, E. V. Pozharskii, T. A. Zenchenko, I. M. Zvereva, and A. A. Konradov. 1998. "Realization of Discrete States during Fluctuations in Macroscopic Processes." *Physics—Uspekhi* [Uspekhi Fizicheskikh Nauk, Russian Academy of Sciences] 41, no. 10: 1025–34.

Shoemaker, Eugene M. 1987. "Meteor Crater, Arizona." In *Geological Society of America Centennial Field Guide—Rocky Mountain Section* (ed. Stanley S. Beus), 399–404. http://arrowsmith410-598.asu.edu/Lectures/Lecture20 /i0-8137-5402-X-2-0-399Shoemaker.pdf (article dated 1987; accessed July 20, 2020).

Siberian Times. 2017. "Is This Stunning Bracelet Made by Paleolithic Man for His Favourite Woman Really 70,000 Years Old?" https://siberiantimes .com/science/casestudy/features/could-this-stunning-bracelet-be-65000-to -70000-years-old/ (article dated August 2, 2017; accessed April 12, 2020).

Silverman, S. M. 2006. "Low Latitude Auroras Prior to 1200 C.E. and Ezekiel's Vision." *Advances in Space Research* 38: 200–208.

Simmons, Gail. 2014. "Jordan Long before Petra." www.saudiaramcoworld.com /issue/201406/jordan.long.before.petra.htm (article dated 2014; accessed November 13, 2014).

Simpson, John A. 2000. "The Cosmic Ray Nucleonic Component: The Invention and Scientific Uses of the Neutron Monitor." *Space Science Reviews* 93: 11–32.

Singh, Simon. 2008. "Could Water Really Have a Memory?" http://news.bbc .co.uk/2/hi/health/7505286.stm (article dated July 25, 2008; accessed August 12, 2011).

Siraj, Amir, and Abraham Loeb. 2020. "The Case for an Early Solar Binary Companion." https://arxiv.org/pdf/2007.10339.pdf (article dated July 22, 2020; accessed July 25, 2020).

Siscoe, George L., Samuel M. Silverman, and Keith D. Siebert. 2002. "Ezekiel and the Northern Lights: Biblical Aurora Seems Plausible." *Eos, Transactions, American Geophysical Union* 83, no. 16: 173–79. http://adsabs.harvard.edu /abs/2002EOSTr..83..173S (abstract; article dated 2002; accessed June 26, 2011).

Skeels, Margaret Anne. 1962. "The Mastodons and Mammoths of Michigan." *Papers of the Michigan Academy of Science, Arts, and Letters* 47: 101–33 .http://othello.alma.edu/~lopez_isnard/mastodon/site/High%20School /Documents/mastodons%20and%20mammoths%20of%20michigan.pdf (article dated 1962; accessed August 29, 2011).

Smart, D. F., M. A. Shea, and K. G. McCracken. 2006. "The Carrington Event: Possible Solar Proton Intensity-Time Profile." *Advances in Space Research* 38: 215–25.

Smith, Michael E. 2009. "V. Gordon Childe and the Urban Revolution: A Historical Perspective on a Revolution in Urban Studies." *Town Planning Review* 80, no 1: 3–29. www.public.asu.edu/~mesmith9/1-CompleteSet /MES-09-Childe-TPR.pdf (article dated 2009; accessed July 9, 2011). Also, www.mendeley.com/research/v-gordon-childe-and-the-urban-revolution -a-historical-perspective-on-a-revolution-in-urban-studies, which gives the page range as 1–20 (accessed July 9, 2011).

Smith, William Stevenson. 1963. "The Stela of Prince Wepemnofret." *Archaeology* 16: 2–13.

Snir, Ainit, Dani Nadel, Iris Groman-Yaroslavski, Yoel Melamed, Marcelo Sternberg, Ofer Bar-Yosef, and Ehud Weiss. 2015. "The Origin of Cultivation and Proto-Weeds, Long before Neolithic Farming." *PLOS* [Public Library of Science] *ONE* 10, no. 7: 12 pages.

Solanki, S. K., I. G. Usoskin, B. Kromer, M. Schüssler, and J. Beer. 2004. "Unusual Activity of the Sun during Recent Decades Compared to the

Previous 11,000 Years." *Nature* 431: 1084–87. www.nature.com/nature /journal/v431/n7012/abs/nature02995.html (article dated October 28, 2004; accessed August 21, 2011).

Solensky, Richard. 2007. "The Sound of the Aurora." www.damninteresting. com/the-sound-of-the-aurora/ (article dated November 16, 2007; accessed June 26, 2011).

Sorokin, Valery M., Alexey K. Yashchenko, and Victor A. Novikov. 2019. "A Possible Mechanism of Stimulation of Seismic Activity by Ionizing Radiation of Solar Flares." *Earthquake Science* [The Seismological Society of China and Institute of Geophysics, China Earthquake Administration] 32: 26–34.

Southwest Research Institute. 2011. "What's Down with the Sun? Major Drop in Solar Activity Predicted." www.boulder.swri.edu/~deforest/SPD-sunspot -release/SPD_solar_cycle_release.txt (press release dated June 14, 2011; accessed June 20, 2011).

Soza, Felipe L. 2007. *Easter Island, Rapa Nui.* Santiago, Chile: Editorial S&E S.A.

Space Daily. 2010. "Fundamental Constant Might Change across Space." www .spacedaily.com/reports/Fundamental_Constant_Might_Change_Across _Space_999.html (article dated September 7, 2010; accessed August 11, 2011).

———. 2011. "Did a Massive Solar Event Fry the Earth?" www.spacedaily.com /reports/Did_A_Massive_Solar_Proton_Event_Fry_The_Earth_999. html (article dated June 6, 2011; accessed June 6, 2011).

Space Ref. 2011. "Major Drop in Solar Activity Predicted." www.spaceref.com /news/viewpr.html?pid=33826&utm_content=api&utm_medium=srs.gs -twitter&utm_source=direct-srs.gs (article dated June 14, 2011; accessed June 20, 2011).

SpaceSecurity.org/Project Ploughshares. 2008. *Space Security 2008.* www .spacesecurity.org/SSI2008.pdf (report dated August 2008; accessed July 11, 2011).

Space Weather Enterprise Forum. 2011. "Solar Maximum: Can We Weather the Storm? Program, Sponsored by the National Space Weather Program Council, The National Press Club Ballroom, Washington, DC. June 21, 2011." www.ofcm.gov/swef/2011/SWEF%20Booklet.pdf (program dated June 21, 2011; accessed July 11, 2011).

Sphinx Project. 1993. *The Mystery of the Sphinx.* DVD of the NBC-TV special hosted by Charlton Heston, featuring John Anthony West and

Robert M. Schoch and originally aired on November 10, 1993. (Note that the DVD currently being sold has been altered from the original show seen on NBC [National Broadcasting Company] through reediting and the addition of supplementary material, some of which I am very unhappy with and do not endorse whatsoever; I was never consulted and had no control over the reedited version of the production. In fact, I did not see the final version of the show until it was aired.) Livonia, Mich.: The Sphinx Project. See www.bcvideo.com/bmom7_broadcast_.html (website dated 2009; accessed November 25, 2011).

Squire, Charles. 1905. "The Mythological 'Coming of Arthur.'" Chap. 21 in *Celtic Myth and Legend.* www.sacred-texts.com/neu/celt/cml/cml25.htm (book dated 1905; accessed July 7, 2010).

Stacey, Kevin. 2011. "Archaeologist Argues World's Oldest Temples Were Not Temples at All." www.eurekalert.org/pub_releases/2011-10/uocp -aaw100611.php (press release dated October 6, 2011; accessed December 22, 2011).

Ståhlberg, Sabira, and Ingvar Svanberg. 2017. "Wildmen in Central Asia." *Anthropos* 112: 1–11.

Stefani, F., A. Giesecke, and T. Weier. 2019. "A Model of a Tidally Synchronized Solar Dynamo." *Solar Physics* 294, no. 60: 27 pages.

Steffensen, Jørgen Peder, Katrine K. Andersen, Matthias Bigler, Henrik B. Clausen, Dorthe Dahl-Jensen, Hubertus Fischer, Kumiko Goto-Azuma, Margareta Hansson, Sigfús J. Johnsen, Jean Jouzel, Valérie Masson-Delmotte, Trevor Popp, Sune O. Rasmussen, Regine Röthlisberger, Urs Ruth, Bernhard Stauffer, Marie-Louise Siggaard-Andersen, Árn E. Sveinbjörnsdóttir, Anders Svensson, and James W. C. White. 2008. "High-Resolution Greenland Ice Core Data Show Abrupt Climate Change Happens in Few Years." *Science* 321: 680–84.

Stein, Matthew. 2012. "400 Chernobyls: Solar Flares, Electromagnetic Pulses and Nuclear Armageddon." http://truth-out.org/news/item/7301-400 -chernobyls-solar-flares-electromagnetic-pulses-and-nuclear-armageddon (article dated March 24, 2012; accessed March 24, 2012).

Stewart, Balfour. 1861. "On the Great Magnetic Disturbance which Extended from August 28 to September 7, 1859, as Recorded by Photography at the Kew Observatory." *Philosophical Transactions of the Royal Society of London* 151: 423–30.

Stoller, Matt. 2011. "How America Could Collapse." www.thenation.com

/article/162317/how-america-could-collapse (article dated July 27, 2011; accessed July 27, 2011).

Stringer, Chirs, and Julia Galaway-Witham. 2018. "When Did Modern Humans Leave Africa? A ~180,000-Year-Old Fossil from Israel Provides Evidence for Early Forays of *Homo sapiens* into Western Asia." *Science* 359, no. 6374 (January 26): 389–90.

Sukhodolov, Timofei, Ilya Usoskin, Eugene Rozanov, Eleanna Asvestari, William T. Ball, Mark A. J. Curran, Hubertus Fischer, Gennady Kovaltsov, Fusa Miyake, Thomas Peter, Christopher Plummer, Werner Schmutz, Mirko Severi, and Rita Traversi. 2017. "Atmospheric Impacts of the Strongest Known Solar Particle Storm of 775 AD." *Scientific Reports / Nature*, March 5, 9 pages.

Sun, N., A. D. Brandon, S. L. Forman, M. R. Waters, and K. S. Befus. 2020. "Volcanic Origin for Younger Dryas Geochemical Anomalies ca. 12,900 cal B.P." *Science Advances, Research Article*, AAAS [American Association for the Advancement of Science], 31 July 2020, 9 pages.

Sutliff, Donna. 2012. "The Sky's the Topic: A Reply to Hodder and Meskell." *Current Anthropology* 53, no. 1 (February): 125.

Svensmark, Henrik. 2007. "Cosmoclimatology: A New Theory Emerges." *Astronomy & Geophysics* 48, no. 1: 1.18–1.24. http://onlinelibrary.wiley .com/doi/10.1111/j.1468-4004.2007.48118.x/abstract (article dated January 25, 2007; accessed July 21, 2011).

Swan, James A. 1990. *Sacred Places: How the Living Earth Seeks Our Friendship.* Santa Fe, N. Mex.: Bear & Company.

Sweatman, Martin. 2020. "Volcanic or Cosmic Impact Origin of the YD Mini Ice-Age? New Evidence from Hall's Cave, Texas." https://cosmictusk.com /younger-dryas-volcanoes-or-comet-sun-befus-sweatman/ (article dated August 6, 2020; accessed 11 August 2020).

Symmes, Patrick. 2010. "History in the Remaking: A Temple Complex in Turkey That Predates Even the Pyramids Is Rewriting the Story of Human Evolution." *Newsweek,* March 1. www.newsweek.com/id/233844 (article dated online February 19, 2010; accessed April 29, 2010).

Talbott, David. 2009. *Symbols of an Alien Sky, Episode One.* Video. Portland, Ore.: Mikamar Publishing.

———. 2011. *Symbols of an Alien Sky, Episode Two: The Lightning-Scarred Planet Mars.* Video. Portland, Ore.: Mikamar Publishing.

Talbott, David, and Wallace Thornhill. 2005. *Thunderbolts of the Gods.* Portland, Ore.: Mikamar Publishing.

Tart, Charles. 1990. "Who Survives? Implications of Modern Consciousness Research." In *What Survives? Contemporary Explorations of Life after Death,* edited by Gary Doore, 138–51. Los Angeles: Jeremy P. Tarcher.

Tavares, Marilia, and Anibal Azevedo. 2011. "Influences of Solar Cycles on Earthquakes." *Natural Science* 3, no. 6: 436–43.

Tchalian, Adriana. 2019. "Reclaiming Our Ancient Heritage: Portasar (Göbekli Tepe)." *Armenian Mirror-Spector* 90, no. 11, issue 4604 (September 28): 14. https://mirrorspectator.com/2019/09/26/reclaiming-our-ancient-heritage-portasar-gobekli-tepe/ (article posted on internet dated September 26, 2019; accessed April 7, 2020).

Technology Review. 2011. "Solar Wind Changes Atmospheric Pressure over South Korea: Evidence Is Growing That Interplanetary Magnetic Fields Can Have a Significant Influence on Our Weather." www.technologyreview.com/blog/arxiv/26989 (article dated July 13, 2011; accessed July 17, 2011).

Tedlock, Dennis (translator). 1986. *Popol Vuh: The Mayan Book of the Dawn of Life.* New York: Simon and Schuster, A Touchstone Book.

Tehaha. 2011. "The Rongorongo of Easter Island: Is Recitation Atua-Matariri a Spelling Bee?" http://homepage.mac.com/spaelti/rongorongo_org/theories/spelling.html (undated article; accessed June 28, 2011).

Telegraph. 2011. "Rome Earthquake: Who Was Raffaele Bendandi?" www.telegraph.co.uk/news/worldnews/europe/italy/8505256/Rome-earthquake-Who-was-Raffaele-Bendandi.html (article dated May 10, 2011; accessed July 5, 2011).

Temple, Robert. 2009. "What Was the Sphinx?" *New Dawn,* no. 112: 47–52.

Temple, Robert, with Olivia Temple. 2009. *The Sphinx Mystery: The Forgotten Origins of the Sanctuary of Anubis.* Rochester, Vt.: Inner Traditions.

Tennenbaum, Jonathan. 2000. "Russian Discovery Challenges Existence of 'Absolute Time.'" *21st Century Science and Technology Magazine,* Summer. www.21stcenturysciencetech.com/articles/time.html (article dated Summer 2000; accessed September 4, 2008).

Than, Ker. 2009. "Comet Smashes Triggered Ancient Famine." *New Scientist,* no. 2689: 9. www.newscientist.com/article/mg20126882.900-comet-smashes-triggered-ancient-famine.html?DCMP=OTC-rss&nsref=online-news (preview; article dated January 7, 2009; accessed January 12, 2009).

Thompson, Gary D. 2001–2007. "Paleolithic European Constellations—Star Maps in Lascaux Cave in France 16,500–13,000 B.C." www.mazzaroth

.com/ChapterOne/LascauxCave.htm (article dated 2001–2007; accessed June 5, 2010).

Thompson, Lonnie G., Ellen Mosley-Thompson, Mary E. Davis, Keith A. Henderson, Henry H. Brecher, Victor S. Zagorodnov, Tracy A. Mashiotta, Ping-Nan Lin, Vladimir N. Mikhalenko, Douglas R. Hardy, and Jürg Beer. 2002. "Kilimanjaro Ice Core Records: Evidence of Holocene Climate Change in Tropical Africa." *Science* 298: 589–93. http://bprc.osu.edu/Icecore/589.pdf (article dated October 18, 2002; accessed July 14, 2011).

Thomson, William J. 1891. "Te Pito Te Henua, or Easter Island." In *Report of the U. S. National Museum, under the Direction of the Smithsonian Institution, for the Year Ending June 30, 1889, 447–552.* Washington, D.C.: U.S. Government Printing Office.

Thornhill, Ted. 2011. "Bracelet Reveals Amazing Craftsman's Skill from 7500BC (So Good It Couldn't Be Bettered Today)." www.dailymail. co.uk/sciencetech/article-2077525/Bracelet-reveals-amazing-craftsmans -skill-7500BC-good-bettered-today.html (article dated December 23, 2011; accessed December 26, 2011).

Thorpe, Nick. 2002. *Eight Men and a Duck: An Improbable Voyage by Reed Boat to Easter Island.* New York: Free Press.

Thorsby, Erik. 2016. "Genetic Evidence for a Contribution of Native Americans to the Early Settlement of Rapa Nui (Easter Island)." *Frontiers in Ecology and Evolution* 4, article 118 (October): 6 pages.

Thy, P., G. Willcox, G. H. Barford, and D. Q. Fuller. 2015. "Anthropogenic Origin of Siliceous Scoria Droplets from Pleistocene and Holocene Archaeological Sites in Northern Syria." *Journal of Archaeological Science* 54: 193–209.

Tian, H., D. Schryvers, and Ph. Claeys. 2011. "Nanodiamonds Do Not Provide Unique Evidence for a Younger Dryas Impact." *Proceedings of the National Academy of Sciences of the United States of America* 108, no. 1: 40–44.

Todericiu, Doru [also known by the pseudonym Pierre Carnac]. 2007. "Géomagnétisme des Abris Rocheux et Hominisation." *Kadath: Chroniques des Civilisations Disparues,* no. 103: 4–14.

Tressoldi, Patrizio E. 2011. "Extraordinary Claims Require Extraordinary Evidence: The Case of Non-Local Perception, a Classical and Bayesian Review of Evidences." *Frontiers in Psychology* 2, article 117, 5 pages.

Tributsch, Helmut. 2017. "On the Reddish, Glittery Mud the Inca Used for Perfecting Their Stone Masonry." *SDRP Journal of Earth Sciences & Environmental Studies* 3, no. 1: 309–24.

Ulissey, Catherine, with Robert M. Schoch. 2020. "Does the Water Bearer Bring Forth a River of Fire?" *eNews from NCGR* [National Council for Geocosmic Research], no. 337 (April 14).

Unexplained-Mysteries.com. 2005. "Atomic Blasts in Ages Past." www .unexplained-mysteries.com/forum/index.php?showtopic=48335&st=60 (website forum discussion of meteor, asteroid, and comet explanations for vitrification, dated November 30, 2005; accessed March 16, 2012).

University of Colorado. 2008. "Cloud Tripping through the Milky Way." http:// jila.colorado.edu/content/cloud-tripping-through-milky-way (press release dated Summer 2008; accessed August 25, 2011).

Urzeit-code.com. 2007. "The 'Primeval Code'—The Ecological Alternative to Controversial Genetic Engineering!" www.urzeit-code.com/index .php?id=23 (article dated 2007; accessed June 11, 2010).

Usoskin, I. G., M. Schüssler, S. K. Solanki, and K. Mursula. 2005. "Solar Activity, Cosmic Rays, and Earth's Temperature: A Millennium-Scale Comparison." *Journal of Geophysical Research* 110, no. A10102, 1–10. http://spaceweb.oulu.fi/~kalevi/publications/Usoskin_etal_JGR_2005 .pdf (article dated 2005; accessed July 16, 2011).

Usoskin, I. G., S. K. Solanki, and G. A. Kovaltsov. 2007. "Grand Minima and Maxima of Solar Activity: New Observational Constraints." *Astronomy and Astrophysics* 471: 301–9.

Usoskin, I. G., B. Kromer, F. Ludlow, J. Beer, M. Friedrich, G. A. Kovaltsov, S. K. Solanki, and L. Wacker. 2013. "The AD775 Cosmic Event Revisited: the Sun Is to Blame." *Astronomy and Astrophysics* 552, L3: 4 pages.

Utts, Jessica. 1991. "Replication and Meta-Analysis in Parapsychology." *Statistical Science* 6, no. 4: 363–403. Reprinted in *The Parapsychology Revolution: A Concise Anthology of Paranormal and Psychical Research*, compilation and commentary by Robert M. Schoch and Logan Yonavjak, 164–203. New York: Jeremy P. Tarcher/Penguin, 2008.

van der Hammen, T., and B. van Geel. 2008. "Charcoal in Soils of the Allerød-Younger Dryas Transition Were the Result of Natural Fires and Not Necessarily the Effect of an Extra-terrestrial Impact." *Netherlands Journal of Geosciences* 87, no. 4: 359–61.

van der Sluijs, Marinus Anthony [Rens, pseud.]. 2010. "Go Figure!" www .thunderbolts.info/tpod/2010/arch10/101217figure.htm (article dated Dec 17, 2010; accessed July 4, 2011).

van der Sluijs, Marinus Anthony, and Anthony L. Peratt. 2010. "Searching for

Rock Art Evidence of an Ancient Super Aurora." *Expedition* [University of Pennsylvania Museum of Archaeology and Anthropology] 52, no. 2: 33–42. http://penn.museum/documents/publications/expedition/PDFs/52-2/van%20der%20sluijs%20peratt.pdf (article dated Summer 2010; accessed December 23, 2011; see also www.penn.museum/expedition-back-issues/89-volumes-51-present/838-expedition-volume-52-number-2-summer-2010.html).

van Hoesel, Annelies, Wim Z. Hoek, Freek Braadbaart, Johannes van der Plicht, Gillian M. Pennock, and Martyn R. Drury. 2012. "Nanodiamonds and Wildfire Evidence in the Usselo Horizon Postdate the Allerød-Younger Dryas Boundary." *Proceedings of the National Academy of Sciences of the United States of America.* PNAS Early Edition, www.pnas.org/cgi/doi/10.1073/pnas.1120950109 (article dated May 15, 2012; accessed June 23, 2020), 6 pages.

van Hoesel, Annelies, Wim Z. Hoek, Gillian M. Pennock, and Martyn R. Drury. 2014. "The Younger Dryas Impact Hypothesis: A Critical Review." *Quaternary Science Reviews* 83: 95–114.

Van Tilburg, Jo Anne. 1994. *Easter Island: Archaeology, Ecology, and Culture.* Washington, D.C.: Smithsonian Institution Press.

———. 2007. "Hoa Hakananai'a Laser Scan Project." www.eisp.org/10/#more-10 (article dated September 2007; accessed March 26, 2012).

Vaquero, J. M. 2007. "Historical Sunspot Observations: A Review." *Advances in Space Research* 40: 929–41. Available from http://arxiv.org/ftp/astro-ph/papers/0702/0702068.pdf (article dated 2007; accessed September 9, 2011).

Vergano, Dan. 2012. "Solar Storm Delivers 'Pretty Good Shock' to Earth." www.sci-tech-today.com/news/Solar-Storm-Brings-Pretty-Good-Shock/story.xhtml?story_id=0210016EDON3&full_skip=1 (article dated March 6, 2012; accessed March 6, 2012).

Verit, Ayhan, Cihat Kurkcuoglu, Fatma Ferda Verit, Hasan Kafali, and Ercan Yeni. 2005. "Paleoandrologic Genital and Reproductive Depictions in Earliest Religious Architecture: Ninth to Tenth Millennium BC." *Urology* 65: 208–10.

Verlinde, Erik. 2010. "On the Origin of Gravity and the Laws of Newton." http://arxiv.org/PS_cache/arxiv/pdf/1001/1001.0785v1.pdf (article dated January 6, 2010; accessed July 28, 2010).

Vey, Gary. 2011. "Gobekli Tepe (Belly Hill), Turkey: Built 11,000 Years Ago!"

http://viewzone2.com/turkeyx.html (undated article; accessed August 28, 2011).

Vidal-Madjar, Alfred, Claudine Laurent, Paul Bruston, and Jean Audouze. 1978. "Is the Solar System Entering a Nearby Interstellar Cloud?" *Astrophysical Journal* 223: 589–600.

Vieira, Carolina Leticia Zilli, Danilo Alvares, Annelise Blomberg, Joel Schwartz, Brent Coull, Shaodan Huang, and Petros Koutrakis. 2019. "Geomagnetic Disturbances Driven by Solar Activity Enhance Total and Cardiovascular Mortality Risk in 263 U.S. Cities." *Environmental Health* 18: 10 pages.

Vilenskaya, Larissa. 1995. "Physical Mediumship in Russia." In *Incredible Tales of the Paranormal,* edited by Alexander Imich, 159–87. New York: Bramble Books.

Volcanoguy. 2007. "Greaser Petroglyph, OR [Oregon]." www.waymarking.com /waymarks/WM2DJ3 (photograph dated October 16, 2007; accessed July 17, 2011).

Vonmoos, Maura, Jürg Beer, and Raimund Muscheler. 2006. "Large Variations in Holocene Solar Activity: Constraints from ^{10}Be in the Greenland Ice Core Project Ice Core." *Journal of Geophysical Research* 111, no. A10105: 1–14. www.agu.org/pubs/crossref/2006/2005JA011500.shtml (article dated 2006; accessed July 7, 2010; this paper discusses both ^{10}Be and ^{14}C data).

Walker, Mike, Sigfus Johnsen, Sune Olander Rasmussen, Jørgen-Peder Steffensen, Trevor Popp, Philip Gibbard, Wim Hoek, John Lowe, John Andrews, Svante Björck, Les Cwynar, Konrad Hughen, Peter Kershaw, Bernd Kromer, Thomas Litt, David J. Lowe, Takeshi Nakagawa, Rewi Newnham, and Jakob Schwander. 2008. "The Global Stratotype Section and Point (GSSP) for the Base of the Holocene Series/Epoch (Quaternary System/Period) in the NGRIP Ice Core." *Episodes* 31, no. 2: 264–67.

Walker, Mike, Sigfus Johnsen, Sune Olander Rasmussen, Trevor Popp, Jørgen-Peder Steffensen, Philip Gibbard, Wim Hoek, John Lowe, John Andrews, Svante Björck, Les C. Cwynar, Konrad Hughen, Peter Kershaw, Bernd Kromer, Thomas Litt, David J. Lowe, Takeshi Nakagawa, Rewi Newnham, and Jakob Schwander. 2009. "Formal Definition and Dating of the GSSP (Global Stratotype Section and Point) for the Base of the Holocene Using the Greenland NGRIP Ice Core, and Selected Auxiliary Records." *Journal of Quaternary Science* 24, no. 1: 3–17.

Wandrei, Donald. 1948. *The Web of Easter Island.* Sauk City, Wisc.: Arkham House.

Wang, F. Y., H. Yu, Y. C. Zou, Z. G. Dai, and K. S. Cheng. 2017. "A Rapid Cosmic-Ray Increase in BC 3372–3371 from Ancient Buried Tree Rings in China." *Nature Communications*, November 14, 5 pages.

Wanjek, Christopher. 2005. "Cosmic Explosion among the Brightest in Recorded History." www.nasa.gov/vision/universe/watchtheskies/swift _nsu_0205.html (article dated February 18, 2005; accessed June 29, 2011).

Waters, Colin N., James P. M. Syvitski, Agnieszka Gałuszka, Gary J. Hancock, Jan Zalasiewicz, Alejandro Cearreta, Jacques Grinevald, Catherine Jeandel, J. R. McNeill, Colin Summerhayes, and Anthony Barnosky. 2015. "Can Nuclear Weapons Fallout Mark the Beginning of the Anthropocene Epoch?" *Bulletin of the Atomic Scientists* 71, no. 3: 46–57.

Waters, Colin N., Jan Zalasiewicz, Colin Summerhayes, Anthony D. Barnosky, Clément Poirier, Agnieszka Gałuszka, Alejandro Cearreta, Matt Edgeworth, Erle C. Ellis, Michael Ellis, Catherine Jeandel, Reinhold Leinfelder, J. R. McNeill, Daniel deB. Richter, Will Steffen, James Syvitski, Davor Vidas, Michael Wagreich, Mark Williams, An Zhisheng, Jacques Grinevald, Eric Odada, Naomi Oreskes, and Alexander P. Wolfe. 2016. "The Anthropocene Is Functionally and Stratigraphically Distinct from the Holocene." *Science* 351, no. 6269 (January 8): 137 and aad2622-1–aad2622-10.

Waters, Colin N., Jan Zalasiewicz, Colin Summerhayes, Ian J. Fairchild, Neil L. Rose, Neil J. Loader, William Shotyk, Alejandro Cearreta, Martin J. Head, James P. M. Syvitski, Mark Williams, Michael Wagreich, Anthony D. Barnosky, An Zhisheng, Reinhold Leinfelder, Catherine Jeandel, Agnieszka Gałuszka, Juliana A. Ivar do Sul, Felix Gradstein, Will Steffen, John R. McNeill, Scott Wing, Clément Poirier, and Matt Edgeworth. 2018. "Global Boundary Stratotype Section and Point (GSSP) for the Anthropocene Series: Where and How to Look for Potential Candidates." *Earth-Science Reviews* 178: 379–429.

Webb, J. K., J. A. King, M. T. Murphy, V. V. Flambaum, R. F. Carswell, and M. B. Bainbridge. 2010. "Evidence for Spatial Variation of the Fine Structure Constant." http://arxiv.org/PS_cache/arxiv/pdf/1008/1008.3907v1.pdf (article dated August 23, 2010; accessed September 8, 2010).

Welcome to Romania. 2002. "Sphinx." http://romania.ici.ro/en/alfabet/pagina. php?id=147 (article dated October 10, 2002; accessed March 16, 2012).

Weller, Andreas, Silvia Rosas, Michael Eidner, and Kerstin Hartsch. 2013. "Geophysical, Petrographic and Geochemical Survey on the Nazca Lines." *Journal of Earth Science and Engineering* 3: 159–67.

West, John Anthony. 1985. *The Traveler's Key to Ancient Egypt: A Guide to the Sacred Places of Ancient Egypt.* New York: Alfred A. Knopf. 2nd edition, 1995: Wheaton, Ill.: Quest Books. (The 1995 edition of this book includes a "Sphinx and Pyramid Update," 448–57, which contains a discussion of the early work by Robert Schoch on the redating of the Great Sphinx.)

———. 1993. *Serpent in the Sky: The High Wisdom of Ancient Egypt.* Wheaton, Ill.: Quest Books. Original edition published 1979 by Harper and Row (New York). (The 1993 edition includes a "Sphinx Update," 225–32, discussing the early work of Robert Schoch and others regarding the true age of the Great Sphinx.)

———. 2007. John Anthony West introduces Robert Schoch at the Conference for Precession and Ancient Knowledge (CPAK), San Diego, California, October 2007. www.youtube.com/watch?v=e4cll_-Y214 (posted on YouTube, March 25, 2020; accessed March 31, 2020).

Weyer, Edward, Jr. 1959. *Primitive Peoples Today.* Garden City, N.Y.: Doubleday and Company.

White, Gordon. 2016. *Star.Ships: A Prehistory of the Spirits.* Bucknell, UK: Scarlet Imprint.

Whitehouse, David. 1999. "'Earliest Writing' Found." http://news.bbc.co.uk/2/hi /science/nature/334517.stm (article dated May 4, 1999; accessed April 4, 2009).

———. 2000. "Ice Age Star Map Discovered." http://news.bbc.co.uk/2 /hi/871930.stm (article dated August 9, 2000; accessed June 5, 2010).

———. 2003. "'Oldest Star Chart' Found." http://news.bbc.co.uk/2/hi/science /nature/2679675.stm (article dated January 21, 2003; accessed June 5, 2010).

Whitehouse, Harvey. 2012. "Human Rites." www.aeonmagazine.com/being -human/harvey-whitehouse-ritual/ (article dated December 12, 2012, accessed December 15, 2012).

Wickramasinghe, N. Chandra, Edward J. Steele, Reginald M. Gorczynski, Robert Temple, Gensuke Tokoro, Jiangwen Qu, Daryl H. Wallis, and Brig Klyce. 2020. "Comments on the Origin and Spread of the 2019 Coronavirus." *Virology: Current Research* 4, no. 1 (March 6): 4 pages.

Wikipedia. 2011a. "Decipherment of Rongorongo." http://en.wikipedia.org /wiki/Decipherment_of_rongorongo (article modified at various times; accessed July 6, 2011).

———. 2011b. "Talk: Decipherment of Rongorongo." http://en.wikipedia.org

/wiki?title=Talk:Decipherment_of_rongorongo (article modified at various times; accessed June 25, 2011).

Wilcock, David. 1999/2009. "Introduction to the Wilcock/Cayce/Ra Connection." www.divinecosmos.com/component/content/36?task=view (article dated February 1999 and updated March 15, 2009; accessed August 14, 2011).

Wilford, John Nobel. 1999. "Who Began Writing? Many Theories, Few Answers." www.nytimes.com/library/national/science/040699sci-early -writing.html (article dated April 6, 1999; accessed April 4, 2009).

Wilkins, Alasdair. 2010. "Earth's Magnetic Field Could Reverse Itself in Just Four Years . . . and Maybe It Once Did." http://io9.com/5630707/earths -magnetic-field-could-reverse-itself-in-just-four-yearsand-maybe-it-once-did (article dated September 5, 2010; accessed July 17, 2011).

Wilkinson, H. P., and Alan Gauld. 1993. "Geomagnetism and Anomalous Experiences, 1868–1980." *Society for Psychical Research, Proceedings* 57: 275–310.

Winters, Jeffrey. 2008. "How a Cloud of Space Dust Could Wipe Out Life on Earth." http://discovermagazine.com/2008/whole-universe/30-how -a-cloud-of-dust-could-wipe-out-life-on-earth (article dated December 30, 2008; accessed June 25, 2011).

Wittke, James H., James C. Weaver, Ted E. Bunch, James P. Kennett, Douglas J. Kennett, Andrew M. T. Moore, Gordon C. Hillman, Kenneth B. Tankersley, Albert C. Goodyear, Christopher R. Moore, I. Randolph Daniel Jr., Jack H. Ray, Neal H. Lopinot, David Ferraro, Isabel Israde-Alcántara, James L. Bischoff, Paul S. DeCarli, Robert E. Hermes, Johan B. Kloosterman, Zsolt Revay, George A. Howard, David R. Kimbel, Gunther Kletetschka, Ladislav Nabelek, Carl P. Lipo, Sachiko Sakai, Allen West, and Richard B. Firestone. 2013. "Evidence for Deposition of 10 Million Tonnes of Impact Spherules across Four Continents 12,800 y Ago." *Proceedings of the National Academy of Sciences of the United States of America,* published online May 20: E2088–E2097.

Witze, Alexandra. 2019. "Earth's Magnetic Field Is Acting Up: Erratic Motion of North Magnetic Pole Forces Update to Model that Aids Global Navigation." *Nature* 565: 143–44.

Witzel, E. J. Michael. 2012. *The Origins of the World's Mythologies.* Oxford, UK: Oxford University Press.

Wolchover, Natalie. 2011. "What Would It Be Like to Travel Faster Than the

Speed of Light?" www.lifeslittlemysteries.com/neutrinos-faster-speed -light-2044 (article dated September 23, 2011; accessed November 20, 2011).

Wolff, Werner. 1948. *Island of Death: A New Key to Easter Island's Culture through an Ethno-Psychological Study.* New York: J. J. Augustin.

Woodard, Colin. 2009. "The Mystery of Bosnia's Ancient Pyramids: An Amateur Archaeologist Says He's Discovered the World's Oldest Pyramids in the Balkans. But Many Experts Remain Dubious." www.smithsonianmag .com/history-archaeology/The-Mystery-of-Bosnias-Ancient-Pyramids .html (article dated December 2009; accessed July 7, 2011).

Wootton, W., B. Russell, and P. Rockwell. 2013. "Stoneworking Techniques and Processes (Version 1.0), the Art of Making in Antiquity: Stoneworking in the Roman World." www.artofmaking.ac.uk/content/essays /3-stoneworking-techniques-and-processes-w-wootton-b-russell-p-rockwell (article dated 2013; accessed on January 23, 2018).

World Heritage Nomination. 2017. *Göbekli Tepe: Nomination for Inclusion on the World Heritage List.* Nomination Document. Ankara, Turkey: Turkish Ministry of Culture and Tourism, i–iv + 1–126 pages.

Worman, Stacey, Susan Taylor, Terrance Onsager, Jeffery Adkins, Daniel N. Baker, and Kevin F. Forbes. 2017. "Chapter 29—The Social and Economic Impacts of Moderate and Severe Space Weather." In *Extreme Events in Geospace: Origins, Predictability, and Consequences,* edited by Natalia Buzulukova, 701–10. Amsterdam: Elsevier.

Wright, Christopher, Daniel Nyberg, Lauren Rickards, and James Freund. 2018. "Organizing in the Anthropocene." *Organization* 24, no. 4: 455–71.

Xie, J., S. Sreenivasan, G. Korniss, W. Zhang, C. Lim, and B. K. Szymanski. 2011. "Social Consensus through the Influence of Committed Minorities." *Physics Review E* 84, no. 1, item no. 011130: 1–8. http://pre.aps.org /abstract/PRE/v84/i1/e011130 (abstract; article dated July 22, 2011; accessed August 1, 2011.

Yarris, Lynn. 2010. "Alvarez Theory on Dinosaur Die-Out Upheld: Experts Find Asteroid Guilty of Killing the Dinosaurs." http://newscenter.lbl.gov /feature-stories/2010/03/09/alvarez-theory-on-dinosaur (article dated March 9, 2010; accessed August 25, 2011).

Zalasiewicz, Jan, Colin N. Waters, Martin J. Head, Clément Poirier, Colin P. Summerhayes, Reinhold Leinfelder, Jacques Grinevald, Will Steffen, Jaia Syvitski, Peter Haff, John R. McNeill, Michael Wagreich, Ian J. Fairchild, Daniel D. Richter, Davor Vidas, Mark Williams, Anthony D. Barnosky, and

Alejandro Cearreta. 2019. "A Formal Anthropocene Is Compatible with but Distinct from Its Diachronous Anthropogenic Counterparts: A Response to W. F. Ruddiman's 'Three Flaws in Defining a Formal Anthropocene.'" *Progress in Physical Geography* 43, no. 3: 319–33.

Zientek, Michael L., Patricia J. Loferski, Heather L. Parks, Ruth F. Schulte, and Robert R. Seal II. 2017. "Platinum-Group Elements," *U.S. Geological Survey Professional Paper 1802-N, chapter N of Critical Mineral Resources of the United States—Economic and Environmental Geology and Prospects for Future Supply,* i–x + 1–94 pages.

Zook, Herbert A., Jack B. Hartung, and Dieter Storzer. 1977. "Solar Flare Activity: Evidence for Large-Scale Changes in the Past." *Icarus* 32: 106–26.

Zubova, A. V., T. A. Chikisheva, and M. V. Shunkov. 2017. "The Morphology of Permanent Molars from the Paleolithic Layers of Denisova Cave." *Archaeology, Ethnology and Anthropology of Eurasia* 45, no. 1: 121–34.

Shall I manage to recover any trace of the past, so remote and so mysterious? . . . the present had nothing worthwhile to say to me. To get back to the ancient hearth, revive the fire in the midst of all these ashes.

PAUL GAUGUIN (1848–1903)
QUOTED FROM GAUGUIN 1961, 6

ABOUT THE AUTHORS

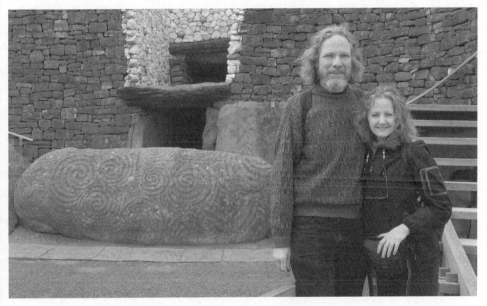

Robert Schoch with his wife, Catherine Ulissey, at Newgrange, Ireland.
(Photograph courtesy of R. Schoch and C. Ulissey.)

Robert M. Schoch has been a full-time faculty member at the College of General Studies at Boston University since 1984, where he is also director of the College's Institute for the Study of the Origins of Civilization (ISOC). Schoch earned his Ph.D. in geology and geophysics at Yale University. He also earned an M.S. and an M.Phil. in geology and geophysics from Yale as well as a B.S. in geology and a B.A. in anthropology from George Washington University.

In the early 1990s, Schoch stunned the world with his geological analysis of the Great Sphinx of Egypt, demonstrating that the monument and the walls of its enclosure bear the scars of extreme water weathering and erosion. As Egypt has known hyperarid climatic conditions for the past five millennia, Schoch concluded that the monument traces its origins to an earlier (pre-Sahara) epoch and a previously unidentified civilization, thus throwing a major monkey wrench into the orthodox view of the rise of civilization. Schoch's courageous assertions of decades ago have been confirmed with the discovery of the astoundingly sophisticated twelve-thousand-year-old megalithic complex of Göbekli Tepe in southeastern Turkey. Although he initially placed the origins of the Great Sphinx (it was originally a lioness; the head has since been recarved) in the period of circa 7000–5000 BCE, thousands of years earlier than its standard attribution of circa 2500 BCE, new data and discoveries have led Schoch to now push the monument back to the end of Earth's last ice age, a glacial period brought to a close by massive solar events, circa 9700 BCE.

Schoch's interests extend well beyond strict geology and geophysics to anthropology, environmental science (he is a coauthor of the university textbook, *Environmental Science: Systems and Solutions*), and biology/paleontology (a genus of fossil mammals was named after him in honor of his graduate research). Schoch has contributed to magazines, journals, and reviews. He is the author, coauthor, and/or editor of a number of books, both technical and popular, that have been translated into multiple languages; these books include *Phylogeny Reconstruction in Paleontology; Stratigraphy: Principles and Methods; The Evolution of Perissodactyls; Horns, Tusks, and Flippers: The Evolution of Hoofed Mammals; Voices of the Rocks; Voyages of the Pyramid Builders; Pyramid Quest; The Parapsychology Revolution;* and *Origins of the Sphinx.*

Schoch's work has been instrumental in spurring renewed attention to the interrelationships between geological and astronomical phenomena, natural catastrophes, and the early history of civilization. He has been a featured speaker at international conferences and symposia, and he has appeared on many podcasts, radio programs, and television shows; the Emmy-winning documentary *The Mystery of the Sphinx*, which first aired on NBC, remains a favorite among audiences.

Schoch has been quoted extensively for his revolutionary research on ancient cultures and monuments around the world. In acknowledgment of his scientific contributions to the study of ancient civilizations, in 2014 Schoch was awarded the title of Honorary Professor of the Nikola Vaptsarov Naval Academy in Varna, Bulgaria. Schoch and his wife, Catherine Ulissey, travel the world in their pursuit of a deeper understanding of humanity's past.

Robert Schoch's website is

www.robertschoch.com

Catherine Ulissey was a twenty-year professional ballet and Broadway dancer, beginning her career at the age of sixteen and performing with the Maryland Ballet, the Feld Ballet (where she also served the company as Ballet Mistress), and the original Broadway cast of *The Phantom of the Opera* (she later went on to help supervise one of its world touring productions). Ulissey also performed in the Broadway casts of *The Mystery of Edwin Drood* and the original productions of *The Red Shoes* and *Rags*. In 2002, she graduated from Emerson College with a B.A. in visual and media arts (summa cum laude) and has subsequently enjoyed a teaching career (of dance) for close to two decades, contributing to the education of students at the Boston Ballet School, Harvard University's Dance Program, American Repertory Theater, and Wellesley College. Inspired by her husband's research from the moment she learned of it, she is enormously proud to now contribute to it.

INDEX

Numbers in *italics* indicate illustrations.
Numbers in *italics* preceded by *pl.* indicate color insert plate numbers.

BOOKS OF RELATED INTEREST

Origins of the Sphinx
Celestial Guardian of Pre-Pharaonic Civilization
by Robert M. Schoch, Ph.D., and Robert Bauval

Atlantis and the Cycles of Time
Prophecies, Traditions, and Occult Revelations
by Joscelyn Godwin

Black Genesis
The Prehistoric Origins of Ancient Egypt
by Robert Bauval and Thomas Brophy, Ph.D.

Earth Under Fire
Humanity's Survival of the Ice Age
by Paul A. La Violette, Ph.D.

The Neanderthal Legacy
Reawakening Our Genetic and Cultural Origins
by Stan Gooch

Science and the Akashic Field
An Integral Theory of Everything
by Ervin Laszlo

Secrets of the Stones
New Revelations of Astro-archaeology and
the Mystical Sciences of Antiquity
by John Michell

INNER TRADITIONS • BEAR & COMPANY
P.O. Box 388
Rochester, VT 05767
1-800-246-8648
www.InnerTraditions.com

Or contact your local bookseller